SOLOMON ZEITLIN'S
Studies in the Early History of Judaism

SOLOMON ZEITLIN'S

Studies in the Early History of Judaism
History of Early Talmudic Law

Selected with an introduction

by the author

VOLUME IV

KTAV PUBLISHING HOUSE, INC.

NEW YORK

1978

Library of Congress Cataloging in Publication Data (Revised)

Zeitlin, Solomon, 1886–1976.
Solomon Zeitlin's Studies in the early history of Judaism.

Vol. 3 also has special title: Judaism and Christianity; v. 4: History of early Talmudic law.
Includes bibliographical references.
1. Judaism—History—Addresses, essays, lectures. 2. Jews. Liturgy and ritual—Addresses, essays, lectures. 3. Jews—Identity—Addresses, essays, lectures. 4. Jesus Christ—Passion—Role of Jews—Addresses, essays, lectures. 5. Talmud—Criticism, interpretation, etc.—Addresses, essays, lectures.
I. Title: Studies in the early history of Judaism. II. Title: Judaism and Christianity. III. Title: History of early Talmudic law.
BM45.Z44   296'.09'01   72–5816
ISBN 0-87068-208-3 (v. 1)

MANUFACTURED IN THE UNITED STATES OF AMERICA

TABLE OF CONTENTS

Note: Tables of Contents for Volume I, II, and III can be found at the back of this book.

FOREWORD

On Tuesday, December 28, 1976 (7 Tevet 5737), Professor Solomon Zeitlin (born May 28, 1886), after a short illness, passed away at the age of ninety years. Till only a few days before his demise he worked feverishly to complete much of his life-work, even to the last moments contemplating other projections. In his Introduction to this fourth volume of his collected studies, printed here without alteration, he wrote: "This volume contains *thirty* essays that have appeared in various publications during a period of over sixty years in which I deal with the development of the *halaka* (law) during the Second Commonwealth and the Tannaitic period." He added: "I also include here two essays in French: 'Les Dix-huit mesures,' written in 1914 and published in 1915 (this was my first published article), 'Les Principes des Controverses Halachiques entre les écoles de Schammaï et de Hillel,' and one essay in Hebrew 'Hefker, Res Nullius.'" Unfortunately, the present Introduction does not include the summaries of the last three articles written in French and Hebrew, for Dr. Zeitlin was already stricken with illness and found himself very weak and unable to work, though his sharp mind was alert and creative till the very end.

Professor Zeitlin willed that Dr. Abraham I. Katsh, President Emeritus of Dropsie University, and I serve as his literary executors. The devoted task of disseminating Dr. Zeitlin's writings, acquainting the wide world with his genius, is being carried on loyally by Dr. Katsh; whereas I have personally undertaken to review all of Zeitlin's unpublished studies. Dr. Esra Sherevsky, of Temple University, together with Dr. Zeitlin's nephew and niece, Mr. and Mrs. Joel Spector, are assisting in collating his literary remains.

As his closest disciple, I could give an addendum to Zeitlin's summary analysis here. I have refrained from this so that the present Introduction be fully of Dr. Zeitlin's own hand, even in the manner of style, transliterations, and singular presentation. It should be noted, however, that his French article has already been translated into Hebrew in *Bitzaron,* 50, no. 5 (April 1964), in the *Solomon Zeitlin Jubilee Issue* upon his completion of half a century of scholarly activities. Likewise, summaries of the last three essays, in addition to all of his other articles, may be found in my book: *Solomon Zeitlin: Scholar Laureate, Annotated Bibliography 1915–1970,* with an appreciation of his writings, and a special foreword by Zalman Shazar (published 1971). A supplement to this, bringing the listing up to date will soon appear.

Dr. Zeitlin had eagerly awaited the appearance of his fourth volume of *Collected Studies,* but was denied this. He, like Moses, could not enjoy the final glory. A garnishing of his articles written in the *Jewish Quarterly Review* and other scholarly journals could conceivably produce even more than the four volumes published by KTAV, which comprise: Synagogue, Calendar and Liturgy; Canonization, Apocryphal Literature, Pharisees, Proselytism, Who is a Jew? Jewish Rights in Palestine; Judaism and Christianity; and now the Halakhah.

Dr. Zeitlin's life-work and one of his main interests was the Halakhah—its historic development, principles, *takkanot,* texts and editions of the Talmud, elements of rabbinic jurisprudence and controversies, establishment of a code, and the Sanhedrin, ancient and modern. The last pages of his Introduction deal with the problem of the reestablishment of the Sanhedrin in Israel, and Dr. Zeitlin recounts personal contacts in 1952 with Rabbi Maimon, the then Minister of Religion, and with the late Chief Rabbi Isaac Herzog, discussing that subject with them.

His Introduction not only summarizes his articles, explains different passages and controversies in the Talmud, but also presents new and additional insights into the interpretation of Halakhah, its historical background, economic and legal amendments regulating daily life as in Sabbath observance, inheritance, cancellation of debts, slaves, etc. Even after reviewing his own previous writings, Zeitlin here evaluated the opinions of the earlier codifiers and commentators, as Maimonides, seeking to ferret out their sources of interpretation and the correct reading of the basic texts. He held that the Jerusalem Talmud was more reliable than the Babylonian and that the Tosefta had many late additions in it, and the Mekilta of Rabbi Simon ben Yohai was composed in the Middle Ages. Zeitlin gives many illustrations to demonstrate the importance for codifiers to know the historic reasons for the enactment of laws before compiling their codes. He also stresses that there was a continuity of Semicha in Eretz Yisrael. In every phase did Zeitlin add new perspectives and evaluations of old traditions and accepted notions.

Zeitlin stressed again and again that laws and doctrines were not abstractions made for intellectual manipulation. The Halakhah was instituted for the people and not the people for the Halakhah (laws were made for man and not man for the laws). The Halakhah was not rigid but elastic. Full cognizance of the demands of the times were made by amending the Halakhah, thus bringing religion into consonance with life. The different *takkanot* were introduced to amend and *modify* the Halakhah through legal fiction or interpretation, for the purpose of harmonizing religion and life.

Some of the Halakhot were modified to meet material needs, showing that religion could be adapted to practical life. Zeitlin also emphasized constantly that a Talmudic student must and can differentiate between early Tannaitic literature and the later Tannaitic text, and even between the literature of the pre-Hadrianic and post-Hadrianic periods. One must not only be incisive but also steeped in rabbinic literature to distinguish between the factual and homiletical interpretations of the Biblical passages by the rabbis. Zeitlin maintain that after the catastrophe of Bar Kokhba, normative Judaism became well established. When the Rabbis assembled in Usha they laid the foundation for the codification of the Halakhah. He likewise demonstrated that there are two prevalent methods of studying law—the dogmatic and the historical. The first is a probing of the underlying principles; the second is a study of the origin of the laws and the factors which brought about their enactment. Similarly, the Halakhot in the Talmudic or in any later period cannot give a true picture of the Judaism of the Second Commonwealth nor can Miamonides' Judaism represent the nature of Judaism of any other period in history.

There is still room for a collection of Dr. Zeitlin's other works: essays on the Dead Sea Scrolls, Megillat Taanit, Maimonides, Rashi, Hassidism, etc. A summation of the total analysis of his contributions, research, and critical probing of the history of the Second Temple and early Tannaitic period will be found in the three volumes of his *Rise and Fall of the Judean State,* published by the Jewish Publication Society. No student of the Intertestamental period can now pursue any study of this period without resort to Zeitlin's manifold writings found in *History and Collected Studies.* His heritage is vast, and the academic world appreciates this fully.

Dr. Zeitlin was blessed with a long life, bold courage, a keen mind and memory. His writings and teachings have influenced many and even created a school of disciples carrying on his methodology. The words of the ancient Rabbis, to whose teachings he was so devoted, apply unequivocably also to him:

כל מי שנאמרה הלכה בשמו בעולם   הזה שפתותיו דובבות בקבר שנא׳ דובב שפתי ישנים

"If a Halakhah is recited in any person's name in this world, it is as if his own lips would speak forth, as it is written (Song of Songs 7:10)—moving gently the lips of those that are asleep" (*Sanhedrin* 90b).

Professor Solomon Zeitlin continues to live within his teachings, his studies, and his disciples.

Sidney B. Hoenig
Former Dean,
Bernard Revel Graduate School
Yeshiva University
and
Adjunct Professor of Talmudic
Studies,
Dropsie University

INTRODUCTION

Demosthenes, in defining law, said that its purpose was to deter any man from doing what is wrong and punish transgressors to make the rest better men. He further said that next after the gods the law preserves the state. Law is the foundation of society, wrote Cicero: *Est enim ius, quo devincta est hominum societas, et quod lex . . .* (*Laws* 1.15).

There were two types of laws—laws which were set by God through his priests, rulers, kings, and dictators, and other laws which came into vogue, practiced by the people, of which no one knows their origin. A distinction may be drawn between these laws. The former is authoritative and will punish those who will not obey, while the latter is not punishable if one transgresses it. However, the validity of unwritten laws, customs, has been regarded by all peoples. Sophocles made Antigone justify burying her brother Polynices, against the order of King Creon, on the basis of "the immutable unwritten laws of gods. They were not born today nor yesterday; they die not and none knows whence they sprang." Aristotle said that customs are more sovereign than the written laws (*Politics* 3.1287 b.). Cicero likewise maintained that custom had its origin ages before any written law existed or any state was established . . . *quae saeclis omnibus ante nata est quam scripta lex ulla aut quam omnino civitas constituta* (*Laws* 1.6). Philo maintained in his book *The Special Laws* (4.28), "For customs are unwritten laws, the decisions approved by men of old, not inscribed on monuments or leaves of paper, which the moth destroys, but in the souls of those who are partners in the same society."

Each nation cherished its customs and maintained them better than any customs practiced by other people. Herodotus (3.38) writes:

> I will give this one proof among many from which it may be inferred that all men hold these beliefs that their customs (are the best): When Darius was king, he summoned the Hellenes who were with him and asked them what price would persuade them to eat their fathers' dead bodies. They answered that there was no price for which they do it. Then he summoned those Indians who are called Callatiae, who eat their parents, asked them what would make them willing to burn their fathers at death. The Indians cried aloud that he should not speak of so horrid an act. So firmly rooted are those beliefs.

Herodotus wanted to demonstrate that each people cherished their own customs and for no price would they change their customs.

The Judaeans, like all peoples, had two sets of laws—statutory, written laws, and customs, unwritten laws. And they also cherished the unwritten laws as reverently as the written laws. The Judaeans considered the written laws divine, delivered by God to the people through Moses. These written laws were all embodied in the five books of the Laws of Moses, known to us as the Pentateuch. They are religious laws, which were given by God, unlike the laws of the Hellenes and the Romans, which were enacted by dictators, kings, and lawgivers.

Most of the laws in the Pentateuch concerned relations between man and God. Not only was the worship of foreign gods considered a crime against God, but even the profanation of the Sabbath, incest and adultery, homicide and theft were considered crimes against God.

During the first period of the history of the children of Israel, the laws of the Pentateuch were not followed in the Northern Kingdom. The principal tenet of the Pentateuch was that there is one God, Yahweh, and no other god is to be worshipped. This was not adhered to by the kings of Israel, who worshipped foreign gods. Even in the Southern Kingdom many kings worshipped foreign gods. King Solomon, according to the Book of Kings, worshipped foreign gods. King Ahaz and Manassah, the kings of Judaea, brought foreign altars into the Temple for worship.

The observance of the festivals of Passover and Tabernacles occurred only a few times in the Hebrew Bible, while the festival of Weeks is not mentioned at all. It seems that these festivals were not

regularly observed annually. Even the day of the Sabbath was profaned. However, to some Pentateuchal laws we find a following, as
a custom which prevailed in the country. To give an example, according to Deuteronomy, if one committed manslaughter, the nearest member of the family, who was called the Blood-Avenger,
should kill the murderer. In II Samuel (14) a story is related that a
woman who was a widow came to King David and said that she had
two sons and during a quarrel one killed his brother. Now the family
wanted to kill him to avenge the blood of his brother. The woman
complained to the king and said that her dead husband would be
left "neither name nor remnant on the face of the earth." And she
said to the king, "Pray let the king invoke Yahweh your God that
the Blood-Avenger slay no more and my son be not destroyed."
And the king replied, "As Yahweh lives, not one hair of your son
shall fall to the ground." From this story it is evident that the Blood-
Avenger was supposed to kill a murderer. Only by the decree of the
king was the son saved. Also, this story indicates that it was a custom and not a statutory law, as no reference was made to the
Pentateuch.

According to Deuteronomy, if a case is not clear "between one
kind of homicide and another, one kind of legal right and another,
one kind of assault and another, one case within your towns which
is too difficult for you, you shall arise and go to the place which
Yahweh thy God has chosen, and come to the Levites, priests,
and to the judge in charge at that time, and present your problem,
and they shall declare to you the decision. Then you shall do according to what they declare to you from that place which Yahweh
will choose. You shall act in accordance with the instructions given
to you and the ruling handed down to you. You must not deviate
from the verdict that they announce to you either to the right or
to the left."

In Exodus 22:9 it is stated, "For every matter of trespasses,
whether it be for an ox . . . both parties shall come before *Elohim;*
he whom *Elohim* shall condemn shall pay double unto his neighbor." The sages interpreted the word *Elohim* to mean "judges." Thus
the Targum according to Onkelos has "before the judges." In the
Septuagint the word *Elohim* is rendered "to God." In the same

book, 21:5–6, we read, "I love my master, my wife, my children, I will not go out free; then his master shall bring him unto *Elohim*." Here again the sages interpreted the word *Elohim* to mean judges, and so according to Targum Onkelos. The Septuagint renders here the word *Elohim* "the court of God".

In the Book of Exodus it is stated that Moses judged the people. However, his father-in-law, Jethro, advised him to appoint men to judge the people. Only a matter of grave importance, he told Moses, should be brought before him, while small matters should be judged by the appointees.

Was there a court of justice in the early days of Israelite history? There is no historical evidence of such an institution. According to the Bible, Moses was the chief justice. After his death Joshua was the supreme judge. After the death of Joshua, those who saved the Israelites from their oppressors, by military exploits, became judges. In the book of Judges (2:18) it is related: "When God raised them up judges, then God was with the judges, and saved them out of the hands of their enemies all the days of the judges." Othniel, the son of Kenaz, judged Israel because he had defeated the king of Aram (3:9–11). In fact all the men who helped the Israelites defeat their enemies became their leaders and their judges. Among them was a woman named Deborah, who also judged the children of Israel; she had participated in the defeat of Sisera, the captain of the king of Canaan. The Prophet Samuel was also the chief judge of Israel. When he became old he appointed his sons judges of Israel (I Sam. 8:1). However, his sons were not righteous and took bribes and perverted justice. Then, according to the same book, the elders assembled and came to Samuel and said to him: "Behold, you are old, and your sons walk not in your ways; Now make us a king to judge us like all the nations" (8:5).

The duty of the king was not only to rule the people and to defend them against their enemies in war but also to be the judge in their personal quarrels. The author of II Samuel relates that when Absalom plotted for the throne of his father, David, he used to rise early to meet the men who "had a suit which should come before the king for judgment"; then he used to tell the people: "Oh that I were made judge in the land, that every man who has any suit or cause might come to me, and I would do him justice" (15:2–4). Solomon, after ascending the throne of his father, prayed to God that among other things God should grant him an understanding heart to judge (I Kings 3:9). Indeed, to show that God had granted him "a heart to judge" the book relates the well-known story of the quarrel between the two women who were harlots, as to who was the mother of a child each claimed.

The kings who ruled after Solomon were also judges. In the book of II Chronicles, it is related that King Jehoshaphat appointed judges throughout the land and said to them: "Consider what you do; for you judge not for man but for God." In Jerusalem likewise the king appointed judges, instructing them: "And whensoever any controversy shall come to you from your brethren that dwell in their cities between blood and blood, between law and command-ment, statutes and judgment, you shall warn them . . . Thus shall you do, and you shall not be guilty" (19:6–10). Thus, we may surmise that the kings were themselves judges and that they ap-pointed judges in different cities who were subordinate to them-selves. (According to Aristotle, *Politics* III.9, 1285b, it was the custom in all the states where lawful monarchy ruled that the kings were judges. Aristotle further tells us that they had supreme com-mand in war and control over all sacrifices that were not in the hands of the priestly class. In addition to these functions, they were judges. Some gave judgment on oath, and some did not. The oath was taken by holding up the scepter.)

After the restoration, King Artaxerxes granted permission to Ezra to appoint judges "who may judge all the people who are beyond the river," and gave him the right to punish those who transgressed the laws of God and the laws of the king by confisca-tion of goods, by imprisonment, and by death (Ezra 7:25–26). The supreme authority over the Judaeans was invested in the high priest. This authority was confirmed by the subsequent kings of Persia, and later by the Ptolemaic and the Seleucid rulers. Hence the au-thority to judge the Judaeans was transferred from the kings to the priests. The Pentateuch also assigns the authority to the head priest to instruct the people (Deut. 17:8–12, 33:10; Ezek. 44:23–24). In the high priest were vested two authorities, civil as well as ecclesiastical. The polity of the new Judaean settlement was theocracy. How the high priest executed judgment is not known—most likely judgments were issued by the high priest himself together with the *gerousia* (a council of elders).

In the decree in which King Artaxerxes authorized Ezra to appoint judges, the term *dayyan* was used. This term became the accepted one for a judge and the term for court was *Bet Din*. The head of the court was designated *Ab Bet Din*. It is more than probable that a high priest during the period of the theocracy had the title *nasi* (in Ezek. 4:44–46 the high priest was called *nasi*). The high priest derived his authority from the Pentateuch, while his civil authority he derived from the kings who ruled the country.

After the successful revolt by the Hasmoneans, the position of the high priest was radically transformed. Simon the Hasmonean was elected to the high priesthood by the Great Synagogue. He was given authority, however, only over the Temple and its services. His power did not extend into the religious life of the Judaeans.

To deal with matters of religious law involving the entire Judaean community, an independent institution was created, the *Bet Din,* later known by the name *Sanhedrin*. Religious conduct was governed by law. The institution of the *Bet Din* replaced the polity of theocracy. The people were now ruled by men whose authority lay in the knowledge of the law, whereas during the period of theocracy the people were ruled by the high priest, who claimed to function by divine authority. With the establishment of the *Bet Din,* the *gerousia,* which was associated with the high priest, went out of existence. The polity of the community was now nomocracy, the rule of law.

The *Bet Din* was made up of different branches. One was composed of seventy-one members and was called *Bet Din haGadol,* the great court, to differentiate it from the other branches. The *Bet Din* of seventy-one exercised religious authority not only over the Judaeans in Judaea but also over those who lived in the Diaspora. It had the power to fix the calendar, to intercalate the necessary month in a leap year. In general, it attended to the spiritual needs of the Judaeans by introducing *halakot* to guide the people.

In the year 444 B.C.E., when the Pentateuch was canonized and became the constitution of the people, a controversy arose among the Judaeans in regard to customs—unwritten laws. The aristocracy, who called themselves Sadducees, maintained that the written laws of the Pentateuch be enforced, while another group—named by the Sadducees *Perushim,* Pharisees—maintained that the customs (unwritten laws) which were in vogue among the people should be on a par with the Pentateuchal laws. They maintained that the unwritten laws which were practiced should be respected like the Pentateuchal laws.

The *Bet Din haGadol* of seventy-one was a legislative body and enacted laws, but it never tried cases which involved capital punishment or any punishment, no cases which involved criminal or civil matters. It is interesting to note that in Mishnah *Sanhedrin* it is stated that this body had sat as a trial court in a case involving the head of state. This Mishnah emphasizes that the polity of the state was nomocracy. The law was above the head of state. (It is to be noted that the polity of the United States of America is not only a democracy ruled by the people, but is a nomocracy, ruled by law. No one is above the law. If a justice of the Supreme Court commits a felony, even if the President commits such, with Congress is invested the power to judge them.)

The heads of the court of seventy-one were the *zugot,* two men. One bore the title *nasi,* president, and the other *Ab Bet Din,* the father of the court, second to the *nasi.* The president was called *nasi* because in the former days, when the high priest exercised sole religious authority over the Judaeans, he bore the title *nasi.* Now that nomocracy was established, the title *nasi* was transferred to the presiding officer of the court of seventy-one, since this body now had the supreme religious authority over the Judaeans. The reason for having this institution of the *zugot* was due to the fact that there were two factions, one leaning more to the Sadducean view of not enacting new laws, while the other was leaning more to the Pharisaic view. In the early days of this institution, apparently, the prevailing group was more conservative, and hence the president was from this group, while the later period of this institution had the Pharisaic viewpoint as the prevailing one, and the president was from that group. The span of the *zugot* was from the time of its establishment to the period of Hillel (140 B.C.E.-10 C.E.)

* * *

This volume contains thirty essays that have appeared in various publications during a period of over sixty years, in which I deal with the development of the *halaka,* (law), during the Second Commonwealth and the Tannaitic period.

The first halakic controversy recorded was on the *semikah.* Hence I probe this first. The next essay based on a subsequent Mishnah in Hagigah pertaining to a *semikah* controversy between the schools of Shammai and Hillel indeed deals with laying on the hand on the animal which was sacrificed on holidays. This controversy may be the reason for the confusion of the rabbinic commentators and the scholars anent the original *semikah* controversy.

In "The Halaka: Introduction to Tannaitic Jurisprudence," I endeavored to analyze the sources of Tannaitic laws, statutory laws, and unwritten laws, Midrash Torah and Midrash Halaka, *takkana* and *g'zera.* In the essay "Midrash" I demonstrated the development of the concept of Midrash from the early days to the Yavneh period.

In this volume I also include articles which deal with tannaitic jurisprudence: "Intention as a Legal Principle," "Asmakta or Intention—A Study in Tannaitic Jurisprudence," "Studies in Talmudic Jurisprudence—Possession, Pignus and Hypothec," "Testamentary Succession: A Study in Tannaitic Jurisprudence."

The essays which follow deal with *takkana* and *g'zera.* "Takkanot 'Ezra," "The Origin of the Ketubah," "The Takkanot of Erubin," "Prosbol," "Johanan The High Priest's Abrogations and Decrees," in which I endeavored to demonstrate that the term *demai* has the connotation of "farmer." These are followed by the articles "The Am Haarez," "Slavery During the Second Commonwealth and the Tannaitic Period," and "Mar Samuel and Manumission of Slaves."

To be able to deal scientifically with the development of *halaka,* the basic text of the Mishnah, both Talmuds and Tosefta, must be critically examined. Thus, I include my following articles: "A

New Palestinian Edition of the Mishna," "A Critical Edition of the Talmud," "Ginzberg's Studies on the Palestinian Talmud," "The Tosefta," "Maimonides and the Mekilta of Rabbi Simon ben Yochai," followed by the essays "The Need for a New Code," and "Is a Revival of a Sanhedrin in Israel Necessary for Modification of the Halaka?"

I also add here two essays in French. "Les Dix-huit mesures," written in 1914 and published in 1915 (this was my first published article), "Les Principes des Controverses Halachiques entre les écoles de Schammaï et de Hillel," and one essay in Hebrew, "Hefker, Res Nullius," in which I deal with the halakot of properties which were made hefker and also with the laws of derelictio.

I

A Mishnah in Hag. 2.1 reports a controversy between the zugot on the question of semikah. Originally those who were against semikah were presidents of the Bet Din, while the two later zugot for semikah were presidents. All the rabbinic commentators as well as the scholars are of the opinion that the semikah controversy between the zugot pertains to whether or not it is allowed to perform the ceremony of the "laying on of the hands" upon the head of the sacrificial animal on the holidays.

According to the Tosefta there was only one controversy, namely, the question of semikah. It is inconceivable to assume that such a controversy, the laying on of hands on a sacrificial animal brought during the holidays, occupied the minds of all of the five pairs of zugot, five generations, from the time when the Second Commonwealth was established until after Herod's death. Again, we know that there were many controversies between the Sadducees and the Pharisees. It is impossible even to think that the heads of the Great Bet Din did not participate in the controversy. ·

In this essay I advance the theory that the term semikah does not denote the laying on of hands upon a sacrifice but has the connotation to accept the authority of the sages in their innovations of halakot. It is well known that equivocal expressions are frequently misleading, even to scholars. The theory that this controversy had nothing to do with laying hands upon a sacrifice but connotes authority I have demonstrated by analyzing the sources, the Jerusalem Talmud as well as the Tosefta. In this article I endeavor to demonstrate that the controversy between the *zugot* was on the question whether we should accept the new *halakot* innovated by the sages by their interpretation of the Pentateuch.

The second pair was Joshua b. Perahiah and Nittai the Arbelite. The former was against *semikah*, the latter was for *semikah*. In Tosefta (*Makshirin* 3.4) it is stated that Joshua b. Perahiah said that "wheat that is brought from Alexandria is unclean because of *antalion* [water wheel], with which the Egyptians irrigated their fields from the Nile." The sages retorted, "If so, let the wheat be unclean to Joshua b. Perahiah," who disregards the tradition of the sages.

According to the Pentateuch, if water was poured upon *zera*, vegetation, it became susceptible to ritual uncleanliness. The Pentateuch made no distinction between seed attached to the soil and crops detached from it. If this law had been rigidly observed, it would have brought havoc to the economic life of the Judaeans. It would have made it impossible for those who were scrupulous in observing the laws of ritual purity to use grain imported from Egypt, since the Egyptians irrigated their fields, and under this law their *zera*, seed, was thus susceptible to ritual uncleanliness. Grain from Egypt was often a necessity because of frequent poor harvests and famine in Judaea. The sages interpreted the word *zera*, seed, to mean only crops detached from the soil. With this law the sages made possible the importation of grain from the rich granary of Egypt. With this, we can understand Joshua b. Perahiah's contention that the wheat brought from Egypt was unclean because he did not accept the innovation of the law.

The question whether the term "seed" refers to detached seed was a controversy between the Sadducees and Pharisees (M. *Yad.* 4.7). The Sadducees say: "We complain against you Pharisees, because you declared that an object [that is, detached crops] upon which water has been poured is clean." The Pharisees retorted: "We complain against you Sadducees, that you declare clean a stream of water which comes from a cemetery." The Sadducees complained against the Pharisees that they differentiated *attached* and *detached* contrary to the Pentateuchal law. The Pharisees retorted: "You who are interpreting the Pentateuchal laws rigidly, likewise differentiate between what is attached to the ground and what is not attached." The Pharisees said to the Sadducees that they agree that a cemetery is ritually unclean and any water placed in vessels on the cemetery is unclean. However, according to the Pentateuch a stream of water which came from a cemetery would be clean. Thus the Pentateuch also distinguishes between "attached and detached." The argument of Joshua b. Perahiah, who was against *semikah,* as well as the argument of the Pharisees and Sadducees thus take on the full expression of each attitude.

II

In Mishnah *Hagigah* there is recorded a controversy between the school of Shammai and the school of Hillel regarding sacrifices brought on the holidays. The school of Shammai maintained that one may bring on the festival a peace offering but not lay hands thereon; however, no one may bring burnt-offerings. The Hillelites held that one may bring both peace offering and burnt-offering on the festivals. The commentators and the scholars interpret this controversy in relation to *shebut* (a rabbinic Sabbath prohibition). I endeavored to demonstrate that the controversy had an entirely different meaning. The Torah enjoined that a person who brought a sacrifice to the Temple has to lay his hands upon the animal. Laying the hands upon the animal or upon a person was considered, in ancient times, the transference of the iniquity or good deeds and authority. The laying on of the hands upon sacrifices, sin offering, or burnt-offering was to transfer the person's sins to the animal that was to be sacrificed to God.

The Shammaites held that a person might bring a peace offering but might not lay the hands upon the animal; but he might not bring a burnt-offering. The difference between the two types of sacrifices can be that a peace offering is only a gift to God, while a burnt-offering, according to the Pentateuch (Lev. 1:4), is "in expiation of sin," and on holidays there were no individual sacrifices brought, nor was there a sin-offering sacrificed. Since laying the hands on the sacrifice was considered transferring the sins, the Shammaites held that no burnt-offering should be sacrificed on the holidays. The Hillelites, on the other hand, were of the opinion that the laying of the hands on the sacrifice was symbolic; no one could actually transfer his iniquities to the sacrifice. Hillel and his school knew the psychology of the people. They knew that the people really held that by laying hands on the burnt-offering the person would atone for his sin; otherwise, he would not come at all to the Temple. As a matter of fact, when the Shammaites prevailed, there were no pilgrimages to the Temple. The Temple was deserted.

III

The prevailing opinion holds that the period of the *soferim* lasted until the high priest Simon the Just. In this essay it was demonstrated that the period of the *soferim* lasted until the destruction of the Second Temple.

It has been the consensus of opinion among modern scholars that the teaching on the *halaka* as recorded in the *Sifra* and *Sifre,* called by them *Midrash Halaka,* is older than that of the Mishnah; this is historically untrue. In this essay I endeavor to prove that the form of the *halaka* recorded in the Mishnah is older than the form of the *halaka* given in the *Sifra* and *Sifre*. The Midrash form developed during the Yavneh period. The *Sifra* and *Sifre* are not *Midrash Halaka* but *Midrash Torah.*

In this essay the explanation was given of what is a *takkana,* and *g'zera.* A *takkana* is a kind of amendment of an earlier law, either Pentateuchal or early *halaka,* introduced by the sages or by the head of the *Bet Din* for the purpose of harmonizing law and life. It was invoked for the benefit of the people, and was always lenient in tendency. A *takkana* cannot be reversed, and it is universal. The *takkanot* recorded in Tannaitic literature either appeared under the name of the head of the *Bet Din* or attributed to a greater authority of former days and must have support from either a Pentateuchal verse or a *halaka*.

G'zera is a decree—independent legislation by an authority. A decree was promulgated for a particular reason and does not need to be substantiated by the Pentateuch or an early *halaka*. When the reason for it disappeared, the decree automatically became void. In the essay, the difference between *takkana* and *g'zera* was demonstrated. However, in the Talmud we find confusion between *takkana* and *g'zera* (this confusion most likely is *Saboraic*); similarly there is confusion among scholars in their interpretations.

That the *halaka* preceded the Midrash form was illustrated in this essay. To give one example, in the year 31 B.C.E., the 14th of Nisan fell on the Sabbath day, when the Paschal lamb was sacrificed. The Bene Bathayra did not know how to handle the problem. They did not have any tradition on the subject. They were told that there was a man named Hillel who was a disciple of Shemayah and Abtalion, who might know whether the slaughtering of the Paschal lamb takes precedence over the Sabbath. When Hillel was asked, he thought it an opportune time to make the custom (the unwritten law) of the slaughtering of the Paschal lamb on the Sabbath a statutory law. He employed hermeneutic rules to demonstrate that slaughtering the Paschal lamb takes precedence over the Sabbath. He used the principle of *kal wa-homer,* inference *a minori ad maius,* from the less important application of a principle to its more important application. Then he sought to prove it by inference based on analogy, both verbal congruity and equality of subject (in Tannaitic literature called *gezera shawah* and *hekesh*). Hillel's method was too radical for the Bene Bathayra and they rejected it. Only when he said that he had a tradition from Shemayah and Abtalion that the slaughtering of the Paschal lamb takes precedence over the Sabbath, his tradition was accepted. When he was asked how the slaughtering knives were to be carried on the Sabbath, he replied that he had no tradition. However he said: "Leave it to the Israelites; if they are not prophets they are sons of prophets." In fact, those who brought lambs for sacrifice stuck the knives in the fleeces of lambs. The ordinary people, without study in the academies, knew the law that the sacrificing of the Paschal lamb takes precedence over the Sabbath. This indicates clearly that the *halaka* (unwritten law) preceded the statutory laws.

In this essay it is also demonstrated how Tannaitic law shaped and molded the lives of the Judaeans. The Greeks made law a philosophy, the Romans made it a science, the Judaeans made law their religion. Judaism, from the time when it became a nomocracy, became a religion of laws based on equity and high moral principles. As a matter of fact, the word that has the connotation of "religion" is *dat*—"law."

IV

In this essay I again demonstrated that the form of *halaka* supersedes the form of Midrash. Midrash is a derivation from the word *darash,* "to inquire, to interpret." In the early period of Israelite history, when a person was in difficulty, he or she went to inquire of God for a solution. When Rebecca was pregnant, she suffered so much that she said: " 'If it be so, wherefore do I live' and she went to Yahweh to inquire." Also, the Bible relates about Saul that when the asses of his father went astray, he went to the seer to inquire. The Book of Kings relates that when the son of the King Abijah was sick, he told his wife to go to the prophet and inquire what was to become of the child. The Bible relates many instances when the people went to the prophets, seers, the men of God, to inquire.

The sages were actually opposed to prophets. They wanted the people rather to turn to them for interpretation of God's word as recorded in the Torah. That is one of the reasons for the later disappearance of the prophets.

V

This essay deals with the concept of intention as a legal principle in the *halaka,* as was introduced by Hillel. Hillel made a distinction between an *act* which stems from volition and an *event* which does not. According to Hillel, the law may apply the term "act" only to that which follows volition, while nonvolitive actions are to be designated as mere events or incidents. To illustrate: If a person falls from a bridge into the water, it is legally an incident, since there was no volition. However, if one jumps from the bridge into the water, it is legally an act since it followed upon volition. The question may then properly be asked, What prompted the person to do this act? Was it his intention to swim or to commit suicide by drowning? The consequence of the act—in this case, jumping—must be judged by the person's intention. Thus intention is a critical category with regard to the consequence of the act rather than to the act itself. To illustrate further: If a stone falls from a person's hand and in consequence some object was broken, it is legally an incident; but if he threw the stone, it is legally an act since there was volition. If by throwing the stone an object was broken, the breaking was the consequence of the throwing, and the question may now properly be asked, Did the person have the intention of breaking the object? Suppose the person who threw the stone had the intention of breaking the object, but, just as he threw it, someone passed by and was hit and killed by the stone; the person who threw the stone had no intention of injuring or killing this man. The injury or the death of the victim was unintentional, was unpremeditated, and therefore the man who threw the stone was not guilty of manslaughter. The idea of the intention as a legal principle was already recognized by the Hellenes. Demosthenes, in his essay against Aristocratus (53–56), said that the statute clearly states that "if a man kills another in an athletic or prize fight he is not guilty." The reason, said Demosthenes, is that "the intention was not to kill the man but to beat him up and vanquish him."

Hillel's principle of intention was much wider and affects not only the *halakot* regarding homicide but all of the *halakot,* civil and religious. According to this principle, if a man throws a stone and intends the stone to fall on the leg of a person, to injure him, but the stone falls on his heart, the man is not guilty of homicide.

Hillel's principle of intention revolutionized Judaean law. To give an example: according to the Pentateuch, a Jew is not allowed to work on the Sabbath. Picking from a fruit tree was considered work and hence was not allowed. The Hillelites maintained that if a person intended to pick grapes and picked figs, he did not commit a transgression since his intention was not to pick figs, for his intention was not fulfilled.

According to the Pentateuch, food for the Sabbath and holidays had to be prepared the day before. According to the old school, if nature prepared it it may be used on the holiday, like an egg, which the chicken laid on the holiday. However, the Hillelites said that the egg cannot be eaten since the man did not know when the chicken would lay the egg.

An imbecile and a minor have no faculty to intend. Hence if married, the marriage is void. The giving of a ring to the woman does not make the marriage valid. He must give the ring for the intent and purpose of marrying her, and that is what is lacking in an imbecile and minor.

Hillel's innovation was strongly opposed by Shammai, and at the conclave of 65 C.E., when the principle of intention was brought up again, the Shammaites were again rejecting it. Only at Yavneh did Hillel's idea of the concept of intention become an integral part of the *halaka*. In this essay, a range of various *halakot* were cited where stress was laid on intention.

VI

In the Mishnah, *Shabbat* 21.3, a controversy is recorded between the school of Shammai and the school of Hillel. This note intends to prove that this controversy is on the legal principle of intention.

VII

The controversy between Rabbi Judah and Rabbi Jose regarding a case of transaction of a property when the buyer "gives a deposit and says, 'if I retract I shall forfeit my deposit,' and the seller says, 'if I retract I shall return double the amount of your deposit,' Rabbi Jose says the condition holds good; Rabbi Judah, on the other hand, says that if the seller retracts, the buyer may acquire according to his deposit."

I interpret this controversy on the basis of intention. According to Rabbi Jose, the buyer, giving a deposit upon the purchase, had the intention of paying up the balance or else forfeiting his deposit, while the seller, in accepting the deposit, had the intention of turning over the article of sale or else paying double the amount of the deposit. If either of them withdraws, the conditions remain true as indicated. Rabbi Judah, however, who does not take into consideration intention, holds, in case of the buyer's withdrawal, that he must lose his deposit because the giving of the deposit was an act, while in the case of the seller's withdrawal he does not have to give to the buyer double, as he promised, since it was only intention and was not coupled with an act. The seller has to return only the amount deposited, or the buyer may acquire from the property only the value of his deposit.

VIII

My idea that many of the Tannaitic halakic controversies were based on intention was critized by some veteran Jewish scholars. It is interesting to note that one scholar who strongly opposed my idea of intention, some years after I published my article on intention, published an essay regarding the *halaka* in which he pointed out that some of the controversies between the schools of Shammai and Hillel were based on intention, and he cited all of the passages which I quoted to substantiate my idea without referring to my article on intention. Professor Ludwig Blau, of Budapest, also criticized my idea of the principle of intention. In *JQR,* vol. 19, he wrote a review in which he maintained that the controversies between Rabbi Jose and Rabbi Judah were based on *asmakta*. In my reply I substantiated again that many controversies between Rabbi Jose and Rabbi Judah are based not on *asmakta* but on intention. As a matter of fact the term *asmakta* is not found in the Tannaitic literature nor does it occur in the Jerusalem Talmud. This term came into being in Babylon during the Amoraic period.

IX

In this essay I deal with possession, *pignus* and *hypothec*. The principle that a person may acquire property by possession is not referred to in the Pentateuch. In the Pentateuch, acquisition of property was by inheritance or purchase. However, the fact that property may be acquired, also, by physical occupation was an old custom, unwritten law.

This essay deals with the legal requirement for occupation of a property. Possession is not purely physical occupation. Possession not only had to be *bona fide,* but the possessor must have *justa causa,* that the property was purchased by his parents or by himself and the deed of sale was lost. To get the title of the property, the possessor must occupy it for a period of time. The time of occupation must be at least three years. The possessor of real property must make use of it. If it is a house, he must live in it; if it is a field, he must harvest it to make use of its produce. The possessor must have a legal claim on the property; hence a robber of a property could not secure a title of ownership by *usucapio*.

Objects that have no ownership, like fish on the high seas, or things which had owners but they had relinquished their rights, such as things which were lost on the highway and there was no mark of identification, are considered *res nullius, hefker*. Anyone who has taken physical possession of them acquires ownership.

Pignus, mashkan, pawn, refers to the person who borrows money and gives a pawn, a pledge, to the lender for a loan which should be returned when the debt is paid. If the debt is not paid at a certain time, the lender takes possession of the *pignus*. The Pentateuch does not refer to *pignus* at the transaction of the loan.

The passage in Deuteronomy 24:10–13 is translated in the Jewish Publication Society's edition, 1962:

> When you make a loan of any sort to your neighbor, you must not enter his house to seize his pledge. You must remain outside, while the man to whom you made the loan brings the pledge out to you. If he is a needy man, you shall not go to sleep in his pledge, you must return the pledge to him at sundown, that he may sleep in his cloth and bless you; and it will be to you merit before Yahweh our God.

From this rendering it is to be assumed that the Pentateuch refers to the pledge at the time the loan was made. The Jerusalem Bible renders these verses:

> If you are making your fellow a loan on pledge, you are not to go into his house, and seize the pledge whatever it may be. You must stay outside and the man to whom you are making the loan shall bring the pledge out to you.

This again is a wrong translation. These verses in the Pentateuch do not refer to a pledge when the loan was transacted. The Septuagint renders these verses more in the meaning of the Hebrew text:

> If thy neighbor owe thee a debt, any debt whatsoever, you shall not go into his house to take his pledge, you shall stand without, and the man who borrowed shall bring the pledge out unto thee.

From the rendering of the Septuagint it is evident that the Pentateuch does not refer to a pledge when the loan was transacted but to a security when the debtor failed to pay the debt. The rendering of the Septuagint of this Pentateuchal passage is corroborated by Josephus, *Antiquities* 4.7,20 (267–268), as well as in the Talmud, *B. M.* 81–82.

In this essay are presented the different opinions of the sages on the nature of *pignus, mashkan,* whether the *pignus, mashkan,* given by the debtor is a security for the loan or it is an exchange for the debt. The difference would be if the *mashkan* is a security for the debt and the *mashkan* exceeds the value of the debt when the debtor did not pay his debt. The creditor may acquire the *mashkan* of the value of the debt. The excess of the value he has to return to the debtor. Similarly, if the loan was $100 and the pledge was $200, if the creditor lost the pledge he must give the excess $100 to the debtor. If, however, the pledge was of less value than the loan, the debtor must give the creditor the excess. (This opinion regarding *pignus* is in accordance with the Roman law, that *pignus* is a security for payment of the loan.)

Some sages held that *pignus* is an exchange for the loan. According to this opinion, if the *pignus* exceeds the value of the loan, and the creditor lost it, he need not pay the excess value of the *pignus*. On the other hand, if he borrowed $200 and the debtor gave a mashkan worth $100, and the creditor lost it, the debtor does not have to pay him the extra $100 since the *mashkan* is an exchange for the loan; lost the *pignus,* lost the loan.

The Torah enjoined the Jews not only against eating, but even to hold in possession, *hametz,* any leaven product, during the Festival of Unleavened Bread. In the case that some *hametz* was in the possession of a Jew, it was forbidden to derive any benefit from it.

A Mishnah, *Pes.* 2.3, states: if a Jew borrowed money from a Gentile and gave him *hametz* as a security, after Passover it is allowed to derive benefit from it; if a Gentile borrowed money from a Jew and gave him *hametz* as a security, it is forbidden to derive any benefit from it after Passover. The Mishnah of the Jerusalem Talmud reads as follows; if a Jew borrows money from a Gentile and gave him *hametz* as a security, after Passover it is forbidden to derive any benefit from it; if a Gentile borrows money from a Jew and gave him *hametz* as a security, he is allowed to derive benefit from it after Passover. (Confer *The Mishnah On Which the Palestinian Talmud Rests,* ed. W. H. Lowe. This reading is substantiated in the Jerusalem Talmud, *Erubin*). There is evidently a contradiction between the Mishnah in the Jerusalem Talmud and the Mishnah in the Babylonian Talmud. Certainly, it needs an explanation. The Mishnah in the Jerusalem Talmud belongs to an early period and is in accordance with the opinion that *pignus, mashkan,* is a security. Hence, if a Jew borrows money from a Gentile and gives *hametz* as a security, the *hametz* belongs to the Jew; therefore after Passover he cannot derive any benefit from it. If a Gentile borrows money from a Jew and gives him *hametz* as a security, the security is the property of the Gentile and therefore it is allowable to derive benefit from it. The Mishnah of the Babylonian Talmud is of a later period and is in accordance with the opinion that *pignus, mashkan,* is an exchange. Hence, if a Jew borrows money from a Gentile and gives *hametz* as a security, after Passover it is allowed to derive benefit from it since the security is already the property of the Gentile. On the other hand, if a Gentile borrows money from a Jew and gives him *hametz* as a security, after Passover it is forbidden to derive any benefit from it since the security became the property of the Jew.

The view given in the Mishnah of the Babylonian Talmud became the *halaka*. Maybe the reason is due to the fact that the sages were troubled by the question of how the creditor can acquire the security since the debtor never transferred his rights to it, but gives it as a security. However, with the view that the security is actually like an exchange, when the debtor gives a security he transfer his rights. Hence when the debt was not paid, automatically, the security belongs to the creditor and he acquires the title.

When mercantile commerce developed in Judaea, the system of *pignus, mashkan,* faded out. Commerce required a substantial amount of money, and in the place of *pignus* was developed *shtar,* a promissory note in which the debtor wrote that all was mortgaged to the creditor and he may seize the property if the debt is not paid. The system of *pignus, mashkan,* was practiced among the poor people, who needed money for sustenance.

The difference between *hypothec* and *pignus* is the following: *Pignus* was placed in the possession of the creditor while *hypothec* remained in the possession of the debtor and is immovable. The creditor collects his debt from the object which was made *hypothec*. If the debtor assigned his house as *hypothec* and it was burned down or washed away by a hurricane, the creditor cannot collect from other properties of the debtor. Slaves at that period were considered immovable property. If a debtor placed his slave as a *hypothec* to the creditor and later sold him, the sale is not valid and the creditor may seize the slave from the buyer. If, however, the owner manumitted the slave, the *hypothec* ceased to exist, he is no longer a slave; he is in the same category as if a debtor placed his house as *hypothec* for a loan and it was burned down—the *hypothec* was gone. Similarly the slave has no rights, he is an object. After freedom the slave who was assigned as *hypothec* ceased to be a slave; he became a free man.

X

According to the Torah, if a man dies his estate was to be inherited by his sons; if there were no sons, then by his daughters; if there were no sons or daughters, it was to go to the nearest kin. The estate must always remain in the family or the tribe, it cannot be given to a stranger. The firstborn son was to receive a double share of the estate. If one had sold his property, the property was to be returned to the original owner in the Jubilee year. The property always had to remain within the family.

After the Restoration Judaean society was primarily agrarian. With the establishment of the independent state and the conquest of Galilee and Idumea, Judaea developed into a mercantile state. Besides farmers there were artisans, professors, and commercial intercourse. Buying and selling became an important factor in the economic life of the Judaean state. The laws of the Torah that real property cannot be sold forever, and had to be reverted back to the original owner, as well as the laws of inheritance were archaic since the Judaean society no longer was based on clan and tribal relationships. The Judaeans were no longer divided into tribes. The sages sought to amend the laws of the Pentateuch, in accordance with the needs of the people, to make the law into consonance with life. They introduced testamentary succession. A person could write a will in which part of his property could go to his sons, and he may even bequeath to a stranger part of his property. In the Talmud the term for will is *daithke*. The sages were very careful not to trangress the Pentateuchal laws. They believed that the Pentateuchal laws were to be adhered to universally, but interpreted in consonance with life. If a person writes a will, having left sons and a daughter, that the property should go to the daughter, the will was void, since the will is against the law of the Torah. However, they introduced that a person may give his property or a share of his property as a gift to anyone he wanted to, during his lifetime. Since *daithke* goes into effect after the death of the testator, he has the right to change his will at any time and write another will. However, when a man gave his property as a gift and wrote a deed, he cannot disavow the deed. Similarly, if a man wrote a deed of sale he cannot retract.

The law of primogeniture was also considered not in the interest of the economic life of the people. For instance, if a person owned a small farm and limited assets, and had several sons, the firstborn had to inherit a double share, thus leaving the remaining brothers with meager share which often was not sufficient to provide sustenance for their families. It was even more aggravating if the first-born was well-to-do in his own right for he still received a double share of his inheritance. The father could not write a *daithke* dividing the property equally among all the sons. That would be against the law of the Torah, and hence the *daithke* was void. The sages introduced a new law regarding inheritance. The father may write a gift-will. According to the law, the father, in his lifetime, may give a gift to anyone he wanted to, while a will takes effect after death. If the father wanted that all the sons should equally share in his property, he writes that all his property was to be given to his sons "from today and after my death." The father had the use of the property but by writing the gift-will he waived his right to sell it. On the other hand, the sons were not allowed to sell the property during the lifetime of their father. After his death, the property is inherited by all the sons equally since it was a gift-will.

XI

As was said previously, a *takkana* is an amendment either of a Pentateuchal law or a previous law—in order that religion would be nonburdensome on the people. The *takkanot* which were introduced by the early sages were always for the benefit of the people, hence *takkanot* were always lenient.

A *baraita* in both Talmudim ascribes to Ezra the introduction of some *takkanot*. It is axiomatic that the *takkanot* do not go to the time of Ezra. Some of them are quite late after the establishment of the state of Judaea. It is true that the *takkana* concerning the reading of the Torah on the Sabbath goes back to great antiquity, and even the reading of the Torah on Monday and Thursday may also belong to antiquity. Monday and Thursday were market days, when the farmers would come to the city to sell their produce and buy their necessities. These days were known as "days of gathering"; hence the sages introduced the reading of the Torah to acquaint the people with its writings.

Some of the *takkanot* ascribed to Ezra were very heretical, and certainly they were for the benefit of society. In ancient times a person who was afflicted with any kind of disease was ostracized from society. According to the Pentateuch, if a person experienced pollution at night (*noctis pollutio*), he had to leave the city. It seems that this law was practiced during the time of David. The Book of I Samuel 20:24–26 relates that when David failed to appear at Saul's banquet, Saul said: "Something has befallen him; he is not clean, surely, he is not clean." It may be that at the time of Saul, when the state was small, leaving the city and the family for a day was not considered a great hindrance. However, during the time of the Second Commonwealth, when society had progressed, for a person who had *noctis pollutio* to leave the family and the city was considered a great hindrance. The sages amended the law that the person who had *noctis pollutio* had to undergo *tebila,* immersion in water, and that is sufficient to make this person pure.

One of the *takkanot* was that peddlers had the right to go from city to city to sell their merchandise. This was instituted because many cities had issued ordinances forbidding outsiders from establishing businesses. Originally, the peddler went from house to house selling his cosmetics to the women, which was their favorite item. This brought about a lot of domestic unpleasantness since this aroused the jealousy of the husbands. Thus, this is the reason why the sages gave them the right to sell their merchandise in the cities. The ordinances of the cities that did not allow strangers to establish a business was not applied to peddlers.

XII

The economic condition of a woman was bad, to say the least. She had no social status and was not economically protected. When she was a minor her father provided for all her necessities—he fed and clothed her. When she grew up and married, her husband was obliged to feed and dress her, and when sick, seek her recovery by engaging a physician. However, in case her husband died or divorced her, she was left without any support, she became helpless. In order to improve the economic status of women, the sages introduced a *takkana* in the institution of marriage. At the marriage ceremony the groom writes a writ, *ketubah*, in which he declares his obligation to support and her right to continue living in his house when he is dead. He further specified that in the case of a divorce or his death, she would collect the amount of 200 *zuzim*; this amount was the minimum obligatory under the law. The groom could, however, add to this sum any amount he wished, to show his good intent. The *ketubah* was a legal document introduced by the sages to protect the wife financially. The Talmud ascribed this *takkana* to Simon b. Shatah. The *ketubah* is not a marriage contract, it is a *hypothec* which made the husband's property subject to his wife in case of divorce or death. If the property was sold, subsequent to the marriage, she had the right to repossess it from the purchaser.

XIII

The Talmud ascribed the *takkanot* of *Erubin* to King Solomon. Actually these *takkanot* were introduced during the Second Commonwealth and Yavneh period. They were introduced for the purpose that the people should enjoy themselves on the Sabbath day. The sages held that the Sabbath was for men and not men for the Sabbath.

There were three types of *Erubin*. (1) According to the literal meaning of the Pentateuch, the Hebrews had no right to leave their places on the Sabbath. The Septuagint renders the words "his place" as "his house." Later it was interpreted that a Jew may walk 2,000 cubits from his home on the Sabbath. Still later was introduced the law that a Judaean may walk on the Sabbath in the city, regardless of its size. To make the Sabbath more enjoyable, the sages introduced that a person may walk 2,000 cubits outside of the city.

At Yavneh the law of "Sabbath journey" was extended, namely, if a Jew before the Sabbath indicated a desire to make his abode on the Sabbath at a place 2,000 cubits beyond the limits of the city, and deposited food there, at that point, he had the right to walk on the Sabbath 2,000 cubits from the place, i.e., the depository. Thus the *takkana* of *Erub* was actually a legal fiction based on the assumption that the place where he had deposited food on the eve of the Sabbath became his abode (it had more to do with intention rather than action).

(2) The Judaeans lived in houses built like courts. According to the strict laws of the Pentateuch, a Jew may not carry anything from one house to another. That the dwellers should have the right to carry things from one house to another house in the court, the sages introduced a *takkana* that the dwellers in the court contribute their share of the ingredients of a dish to be placed in one of the houses. Thus all the families living in the court were considered partners in all of the houses of the court, the houses became common to all; therefore carrying objects from one house to another house was permitted to all of the dwellers in the court.

(3) According to the old *halaka,* the Jews had no right to cook or prepare any food on the Sabbath. It had to be prepared on the eve, on Friday. Friday was known in the Hellenistic-Roman literature as *paraskeue*—the day of preparedness (in modern Greek Friday is called *parasqievi*). If a holiday fell on Friday, it became impossible to prepare food for the Sabbath. The *halaka* permits cooking on the holidays for the needs of that particlular holiday, but not for another day. The sages introduced a mode of *Erub* giving the right to the Jews to prepare a dish on Thursday and let it lie over until the end of the Sabbath. By this legal fiction all the cooking done on Friday, the holiday, for the Sabbath became merely a continuation of the food from the previous day, which was begun on Thursday, the eve of the holiday.

XIV

According to the Torah, every seventh year was a Sabbatical year in which "Every creditor shall release that which he had lent unto his neighbor; he shall not exact it of his neighbor and of his brother because God's release had been proclaimed." In a mercantile society, this Pentateuchal law was a hindrance for commerce. People were apprehensive to lend in the sixth year since the debtor would not pay back the loan before the Sabbatical year, and thus the loan would be uncollectable. Hillel introduced a *prosbol* (a *prosbol* is a Greek word meaning "before the court"), in which the creditor writes a writ, "I declare before you judges in the place, that I shall collect my debt that I may have outstanding with . . . (name of person) whenever I desire." He deposits it before the judges, and thus the Sabbatical year does not release the debt, and the creditor has the right to collect his loan.

According to the Mishnah, *Sheb.* 10.5, an antedated *prosbol* is valid and a postdated *prosbol* is invalid. According to Maimonides, if the *prosbol* was written before the loan was transacted it is valid, and if it was written after the loan was transacted it was not valid. This certainly was wrong, and he was severely criticized. In explaining he said he followed Gaon Hefez. (It is ironic that Maimonides never quoted sources. When he was confronted with this wrong interpretation, he was forced to explain that he copied Gaon Hefez.)

According to the rabbis and modern scholars, the statement of the Mishnah that an antedated *prosbol* is valid is to be interpreted that if the creditor wrote a *prosbol* in May and affixed the date of April it is valid and the creditor has the right to collect his debt. However, if he wrote the *prosbol* in May and affixed the date of June, such a *prosbol* is invalid and the creditor cannot collect the debt.

In this essay I endeavored to establish that the statement that an antedated *prosbol* is valid and a postdated *prosbol* is invalid does not refer to the loan but to the year, the Sabbatical year. If the *prosbol* was written before the ushering in of the Sabbatical year it was valid, and the creditor had the right to collect his debt. But if the *prosbol* was written after the arrival of the Sabbatical year it is not valid, because all the debts were canceled by the coming of the Sabbatical year, and hence the creditor could not collect his debt. There was another opinion that if a *prosbol* was written during the year of the Sabbatical it was valid since the debts were canceled at the end of the Sabbatical year; thus if the *prosbol* was written a day before the end of the Sabbatical year it was still valid.

Tosefta *Sheb.* 7.10 states that Rabban Simon b. Gamaliel said that if a loan was transacted after the *prosbol* was written, the Sabbatical year does not cancel the debt, hence the creditor has the right to collect the debt. It is untenable that Rabban Simon b. Gamaliel made such a statement, for this would be in opposition to the text of the *prosbol,* which was written in the past tense: "Any debt that is owed to me I shall collect any time I desire." I maintained that the original reading of the text was that such a *prosbol,* which was written before the loan was transacted, was canceled by the Sabbatical year. The rabbis of the Middle Ages like R. Hefez and Maimonides, in his commentary on the Mishnah, who interpreted that an antedated *prosbol,* written before the loan was transacted, was valid, amended the text of Rabban Simon b. Gamaliel from "canceled" to "does not cancel." Here is a clear indication that some sages of the Middle Ages emended the text of the Talmud in accord with their understanding of the *halaka.*

In the Talmud (*Git.* 36) is recorded that Samuel, the founder of the school in Nehardea, said that the *prosbol* was an act of arrogance of the court and that if he had the authority he would abolish it. The rabbis, interpreting this passage, found difficulties. I endeavored to prove that Samuel's statement does not refer to the *prosbol* but to the transaction of the *prosbol,* namely, it could be deposited in a court consisting of two judges. Samuel was of the opinion that a court consisting of two judges was an arrogant court (*Sanh.* 5). He believed that a *prosbol* should be deposited in a court of three.

XV

In this essay I endeavored to establish the original reading of the Mishnah (*Maaser Sheni* 5.15): Johanan the High Priest abolished the confession; i.e., the confession of the farmers when bringing their tithes. (According to the Torah, the farmer had to bring the first fruit to the altar of Yahweh and make the following confession: "I brought the first of the fruit of the land which thou, O Yahweh, hast given me." In the time of Johanan the High Priest, there came into being tenant farmers who farmed the land but did not own the land. Hence they could not make the confession by saying "the land, O Yahweh, which thou hast given me." Thus he abolished the confession.) He decreed *demoi*; i.e., that the consumer had to give the tithe to the Levite (in his days no one needed to inquire about *demoi*); i.e., since the farmers were not trusted in the necessary tithe. The obligation was upon the consumer to give the tithe. He also abolished the "Awakeners" and the "Knockers." (During the persecutions of Antiochus the people appealed to God, knocking with hammers, and the Levites recited the hymn, "Awake, why sleepest thou, O Adonai." During the time of John Hyrcanus the Judaeans were no longer slaughtered as sheep, they were a courageous victorious people. Thus, John abolished both the Awakeners and the Knockers.) "Until his days the hammer used to smite in Jerusalem"; this phrase, as well as the phrase "none needed to inquire about *demoi*," is a later addition.

XVI

In this essay I maintained that the term *Am Haarez* in the early Tannaitic literature had the connotation of farmer, people of the land. I also defined the term *Haberim*. As was pointed out in the previous item (XV), the farmers were suspected of not adhering to the Pentateuchal law to give tithes to the Levites. The life of the *Am Haarez* was very hard. He was busy with constant activity from early morning until late at night in order to extract only a bare living from the soil. He had a constant fight against all kinds of insects as well. Hence it was impossible for him, even if he wanted to, to cultivate himself and be well versed in the *halaka* of purity and impurity. On the other hand, the urban dwellers had more opportunity to educate themselves, and had the opportunity to strictly observe the Pentateuchal laws on levitical purity. The *Haberim* could hardly associate with the *Ame Haarez* because the latter's food was *demoi*. Social intercourse of the *Haberim* with the *Ame Haarez* became impossible as the *Ame Haarez* were held in levitical uncleanliness while the *Haberim* conformed to the Pentateuchal laws of purity.

In later periods the term *Ame Haarez* became synonymous with ignorance and people who lacked morality, while the word *Haberim* became associated with culture and people who were scrupulous with regard to the laws of purity. After the destruction of the Temple, the term *Haberim* was applied to scholars, candidates for membership in the *Great Bet Din*.

In this essay it was also pointed out that the term *Perushim,* Pharisees, was never used in the Talmud in contrast to *Ame Haarez*.

XVII

Slavery was practiced from time immemorial. When a country was conquered, those who were captured were made slaves and sold in the market. The Judaeans did not engage in wars, and hence they did not subjugate other people into slavery.

According to the Pentateuch, we know that people used to sell their female children into slavery. Also we find that some persons, due to their dire necessity, sold themselves into slavery. Also, if a person committed theft and had no money to repay the value of the stolen goods, he was sold into slavery to recompense the amount of the goods stolen. From the Bible we also learn that a debtor who could not pay his debt could be enslaved by the creditor. All these types of slavery were abolished during the Second Commonwealth. The creditor no longer had the right to the person, the debtor. He had no right to enslave the debtor; he only had the right to the debtor's property. He was allowed to seize the property of the debtor if the debt was not paid.

During the Hellenistic period slavery was an important institution upon which the social and economic structure of the society was based. Although the Judaeans did not have *prates lithos,* the stone upon which slaves were sold, common in the Hellenistic world, they did have slaves. They did not differ from other people. Before the destruction of the Second Temple the country was economically developed and thus required the labor of slaves. The wealthy classes employed a large number of slaves for the cultivation of vast tracts of land. A slave was considered an object, a property. He could be acquired by possession or by purchase. A debtor could place his slave as *hypothec* for a loan, and if he did not pay, the creditor could seize the slave, in the same manner as a debtor may place his real property as *hypothec* for his debt. If a debtor sold his property or slave after he received his loan, the sale was not valid and the creditor had the right to seize the property or the slave from the buyer. In the case when the debtor placed the slave as *hypothec* for his debt, and then manumitted him, the *hypothec* ceased to exist. It was in the same category as if a debtor placed his house as *hypothec* for his debt and later the house was burned or swept away by a hurricane—the *hypothec* was gone and the creditor loses. After manumission the slave ceased to exist, he is no longer a slave but a free man.

The sages, like the Stoics, did not condemn the institution of slavery but endeavored to ameliorate the condition of the slaves, by improving their status. They strove to impress the people that slaves were not objects but human beings and should be treated as such.

According to the Pentateuch, an uncircumcised man could not eat of the Paschal lamb; "Every man slave that is bought for money, when you have circumcised him, then shall he eat thereof" (Ex. 12:44). Rabbi Eliezer (R. Ishmael) held that the words "then shall he eat thereof" refer to the slave, that is, when the slave is circumcised he may eat of the Paschal lamb. Rabbi Joshua was of the opinion that the phrase "then shall he eat thereof" refers to the master, that is, if the slave is not circumcised, the master is prevented from eating the Paschal lamb. Thus according to Rabbi Eliezer (Ishmael), a Judaean may keep uncircumcised heathen slaves since doing so will not affect his life, he will not be prevented from eating the Paschal lamb. Rabbi Joshua (R. Akiba) maintained that a Judaean may not keep uncircumcised pagan slaves, the reason being that a slave uncircumcised will affect the master's life in preventing him from partaking of the Paschal lamb. Therefore a Judaean may not keep uncircumcised slaves.

The Talmud (*Git.* 38) records a controversy between Rabbi Ishmael and Rabbi Akiba. The former held that the phrase "You may forever enslave them" is optional, elective. The latter held that he is bound, obligatory. All the commentators of these talmudic passages as well as the scholars held that this controversy refers to the manumission of a slave. Rabbi Ishmael is of the opinion that the master may hold a pagan slave forever or he may set him free. Rabbi Akiba held that a master had no right to set a pagan slave free, he was a slave to him forever. The interpretation rendered by the commentators and the scholars cannot be accepted. We do know that a Judaean did manumit pagan slaves. Furthermore, Rabbi Akiba's point of view would have contradicted his statement when he said that a Judaean may not keep an uncircumcised slave, he must get rid of him either by selling him or by manumission.

In this essay I ventured to explain the controversy between Rabbi Ishmael, who held that the phrase "may forever enslave them" is optional refers to an uncircumcised pagan slave, that he may keep him since the slave does not prevent the owner from eating the Paschal lamb. He does not interfere with the master's obligation. On the other hand, Rabbi Akiba held that a Judaean must sell an uncircumcised pagan slave because his master is prevented from partaking of the Paschal lamb. This is in accordance with his own statement and also of Rabbi Joshua that a Judaean may not keep any uncircumcised pagan slave.

An explanation is required why all the commentators (also the Saboraim) interpret the controversy between Rabbi Ishmael and Rabbi Akiba as referring to the manumission of a pagan slave. Rabbi Akiba held that a pagan slave cannot be manumitted. He had to serve his master all of his lifetime, while Rabbi Ishmael held it to be optional, you may keep him or you may manumit him. The Talmud (*Git.* 38) records a statement of Rabbi Judah in the name of Samuel that one who manumits a pagan slave transgresses the Pentateuchal precept. The commentators interpret that according to Rabbi Akiba it is "obligatory," meaning that the master cannot manumit a pagan slave, while Rabbi Ishmael held it to be "optional," i.e., he may keep the slave all of his lifetime or he may manumit him.

XVIII

In this short article I endeavored to demonstrate that Samuel was never against the manumission of pagan slaves. The Talmud (*Git.* 38) records that Samuel said if a master relinquishes rights over the slave he will become *hefker, res nullius;* he becomes a free person, manumitted, since he has no one to own him. Thus, it would be tantamount to one who manumits a pagan slave. Hence, it would contradict what was cited before that R. Judah said in the name of Samuel that one who manumits a pagan slave transgresses Pentateuchal precepts.

The Talmud *(Ket.* 60a) records that Rami bar Yehezkel, the brother of Rab Judah, said that one must not accept all the statements of his brother (Rab Judah) which he made in the name of Samuel. This is one of the statements. Samuel never held that a Jew who manumitted a pagan slave transgressed a Pentateuchal precept.

XIX

The Mishnah is a compilation of the *halakot,* laws, which the sages of Judaea enacted and introduced. These *halakot* were codified by Rabbi Judah the Prince, at the beginning of the third century C.E. These *halakot,* again, were accepted by all Judaeans, in Judaea as well as in the diaspora, Babylonia. They were revered and held authoritative next to the Torah, and thus the nomenclature of these codified *halakot* is Mishnah, *second* to the Torah. The *halakot* in the Mishnah belong to the category of written laws. They are statutory laws, since they were adopted by the Great *Bet Din.* The term "oral law" is only applicable to customs and laws before they become statutory. After these laws became statutory they were written laws, considered holy as second to the Torah. The term "unwritten laws" is applicable to the customs and the laws which were handed down by tradition but did not become statutory. When these laws were registered as statutory they ceased to be oral but were written laws. These laws, too, were revered and observed as holy, next only to the laws of the Torah.

There were collections of these *halakot*, statutory laws, long before the time of Rabbi Judah. Rabbi Judah collated all the *halakot*
into one code and arranged them in six parts. Many times when
there was a controversy among the sages, in regard to some *halakot,*
Rabbi Judah agreed to the opinion of one of them. Since according
to the principles of Yavneh the law is decided in accordance with
the opinion of the majority, Rabbi Judah did not quote the controversy but he placed the opinion of one as anonymous and thus the
law is according to the anonymous statement. It is generally assumed
that the Mishnah of today is the work of two editions, compiled by
Rabbi Judah.

It is well known that there are two Talmuds, the Talmud of
Jerusalem and the Babylonian Talmud. The Mishnah is found in
both Talmuds. There are some differences in the Mishnah of the
Jerusalem Talmud and the Babylonian Talmud, but that may be
due to different scribes. However, there are *halakot* in the Mishnah of the Jerusalem Talmud which are not found in the Mishnah
of the Babylonian Talmud. To give a few examples; in the Jerusalem
Talmud it is mentioned that the eating of the Paschal lamb, although
allowed to be eaten until dawn, is permitted until midnight. The reason given is to keep the person from transgression. This is not found
in the Mishnah of the Babylonian Talmud. Again, in the Mishnah,
Pes. 10, we find three questions which the son is to ask on the first
night of Passover, while in the Mishnah of the Babylonian Talmud
there are four questions. There are even some contradictions in
the *halakot* between the Mishnah of the Jerusalem Talmud and the
Mishnah of the Babylonian Talmud (see item IX). As was stated
before, Rabbi Judah codified the *halakot* into one code and called it
the Mishnah. How did these additions, lacunae, and opposing statements about particular *halakot* occur? It seems that yet before the
destruction of the Temple there were collections of *halakot,* statutory
laws, upon which the Mishnah of the Jerusalem Talmud is based.
The example, which was cited before, regarding the eating of the
Paschal lamb, which is omitted in the Babylonian Talmud, is due to
the fact that before the destruction of the Temple the sages decreed
that the Paschal lamb, after midnight, defiled the hands; therefore it
simply could not be eaten. But the Mishnah of the Babylonian

Talmud was of the period after the destruction of the Temple; hence the reason for the lacuna in the Babylonian Talmud.

In the same manner can be explained the difference between the Mishnah of the Jerusalem Talmud and the Mishnah of the Babylonian Talmud regarding the questions which are supposed to be asked on the first night of Passover. Before the destruction of the Temple, there were only three questions. At Yavneh, Rabban Gamaliel introduced another question, making it four. Thus the Jerusalem Talmud only has three questions while the Mishnah of the Babylonian Talmud has four. In other words, the Mishnah of the Jerusalem Talmud is based on an earlier collection while the Mishnah of the Babylonian Talmud is based on a later collection.

It must be also noted that there are some Amoraic additions in the Mishnah.

XX

To edit the Talmud one must make use of all available manuscripts. However, the manuscripts must be critically examined and scrutinized. They were copied by human beings who were apt to make mistakes in copying, some of them unwillingly and some due to their ignorance of the text. Rashi already stated that some texts in the Talmud were corrupt due to the ignorance of the scribe (cf. *Ker.* 4.1; *Hul.* 74). Again, the editor must not apply the principle of majority with regard to the authenticity of the text. Even though ten manuscripts have a similar reading and only one manuscript has a different reading, it does not follow that the ten have the correct rendition, for it is possible that these may all come from one source. Certainly the editor must take into account the readings cited in the rabbinic literature, since many passages of the Talmud are recorded in the vast literature, the responsa and novella of the Middle Ages. However, the editor must be on guard, because the rabbis of the Middle Ages emended the text to make it accord with other passages of rabbinic literature or with the accepted *halaka*. Hence the readings of the rabbinic literature of the Middle Ages may be emendations or corrections but not the original readings. The editor must also bear in mind that many passages in the Talmud are not even Amoraic but

Saboraic, a later period. (The term Saboraim has the connotation of clarification, explanation. In many cases the Saboraim, with their clarifications, confused the text.)

In this essay I endeavor to show that the extant text in *Taanit* 2b is corrupt. According to an old tradition, on the Festival of Tabernacles God judged the world, whether there would be a year of sufficient rain or drought. Therefore the Jews are asking God to bless them with ample rain. Rabbi Eliezer maintained that the mentioning of rain should be on the first day of the festival. In the Talmud the question was raised, did Rabbi Eliezer derive his view from the libation of water? The text in the Talmud reads as follows: "Just as the libation may take place on the evening preceding the first day, so the mentioning of the rain will begin on that evening; for it has been said: 'And their meal offering and their drink offering,' even at night, so mentioning of rain is from the evening." The text is meaningless. Apparently the rabbis did not know to which libation the Talmud refers. Was it the libation (of water) brought on the first day of Tabernacles, and prepared on the eve thereof, or the libation (of wine) connected with every sacrifice, which might be brought on the following evening? The standard text confuses both libations. The text should be read this way:

> He (Rabbi Eliezer) derives it from the libation (of water); just as the libation may take place on the evening preceding, so the mentioning of the rain will begin on the eve before the holiday; or he learns it from the libation (of wine); for the libation is at night (the following night) as written, "And their meal offering and their drink offering." Since this is at night, so the mentioning of rain is also at night.

The third method to establish a text is by internal evidence, i.e., by the text itself, from which we could deduce that a particular passage was altered. However, this is a very precarious method since the reconstruction of the text may be due to a superb mind or, on the other extreme, the ignorance of the Talmud. Hai Gaon wrote that the Mishnah and Talmud should not be corrected merely because some passages present difficulties. Only a scholar who is well versed in the Talmud could resort to the third method. He must be also guided by the historical background of the *halaka*. The application of the third method is a *sine qua non* in establishing a scholarly edition of the Talmud. Although this is a Herculean task, to establish a critical edition of the Tannaitic text, we must endeavor to do so. But the editor should not tamper with the extant text. The emendations should be on the margin.

Rashi and Rabbenu Tam utilized all three methods in establishing a text. The latter, even by internal evidence, said many times that the text of the Talmud is not Talmudic but a later interpolation (Cf. Tos. *B.B.*154; *Beccor* 4; 22). Although Rabbenu Tam was sure that the text in the Talmud was an interpolation, he did not tamper with the text. He substantiated his view in the Tosafot.

XXI

The Jerusalem Talmud, unlike the Babylonian Talmud, was not edited, and it came to an abrupt end due to the political, economic conditions which prevailed in Judaea. The Jews suffered much from the early Church of the fourth century. The academies were closed, and due to the great poverty of the people the Talmud was not studied. The center of learning was shifted from Judea to Babylonia.

The Judaeans were very resentful, recognizing the end of their hegmony over their co-religionists in the diaspora. The sages of Judaea did not cherish much love or admiration for the Babylonian Talmud. The verse of Lamentations 3:6, "He has made me dwell in darkness" has a reference to the Babylonian Talmud. They also referred to the Babylonians as those who ate "bread with bread," that is, without ingredients, i.e., they had no taste. The Judaeans held that the rabbis in Babylonia were in confusion and error regarding the *halakot*. It is to be noted that this sarcastic aphorism by the Judaeans toward the Babylonian Talmud does not occur in the Jerusalem Talmud but only in the Babylonian Talmud.

When the center of Jewish learning shifted to Babylonia, the Babylonian Talmud became supreme. The Geonim maintained that the *halaka* must follow the views given in the Babylonian Talmud. The Jerusalem Talmud was not binding. The Geonim of Babylonia strove to establish the hegemony of the Jewish center of learning in Babylonia over that of Judaea. The Jerusalem Talmud was neglected. The rabbis of the Middle Ages occupied themselves with the study of the Babylonian Talmud and not the Jerusalem Talmud. Only very few actually studied the Jerusalem Talmud. Hence, there are no emendations and interpolations in the Jerusalem Talmud as we do find in the Babylonian Talmud. On the other hand, we have gross errors in the Jerusalem Talmud caused by ignorant scribes. Solomon Ibn Adret wrote that there is only one in our generation who could understand the Jerusalem Talmud, due to the corrupted text caused by ignorant scribes. The Geonim maintained that when there is a contradiction between the Jerusalem Talmud and the Babylonian Talmud, the latter is to be followed. Here I dare to take exception. The Jerusalem Talmud is more reliable than the Babylonian Talmud because of its direct continuation of the Tannaim, whereas in Babylonia they had tradition which is not always exact. The Jerusalem Talmud is a mine for the history of the sages and the life of the Judaeans. It is a primary source of the *halaka* and the life of the people after the destruction of the second Temple.

In this essay I gave, succinctly, an evaluation of Louis Ginzberg's monumental work.

XXII

To edit the Tosefta is a Herculean task. Not only must one apply the three methods enumerated previously but also one must probe when and where the Tosefta was composed. The general opinion is that the Tosefta is an addition to the Mishnah. Sherira Gaon rightly asked, If it is an addition to the Mishnah, why did Rabbi Judah the Prince not add it himself?

The Tosefta, as the term indicates, is an addition. There are *halakot* which go back to antiquity and were forgotten. On the other hand, there are many *halakot* which are of a later period after the codification of the Mishnah. Some of them are of the Babylonian period, and some of them are of the Judaean period.

The Tosefta states on a few occasions that animals and heathens are not susceptible to levitical uncleanliness. Thus, it equates heathens with animals. Such *halakot* are not found in the Jerusalem Talmud or the Babylonian Talmud. There was a time when Judaeans looked upon a heathen as a nonhuman, even as the Hellenes considered foreigners barbarians. There must have been some law that levitical purity is not applicable to a heathen. On the contrary, in the year 65 C.E. the sages declared that all heathens are in the status of levitical uncleanliness. Hence the law of animals and heathens not being susceptible to Levitical uncleanliness does not occur in the Talmudim.

The Tosefta refers to Onkelos the Proselyte, who lived during the time of Rabban Gamaliel. The Jerusalem Talmud records that the proselyte Aquila translated the Pentateuch into Greek and was praised by Rabbi Eliezer and Rabbi Joshua. According to the Babylonian Talmud, Onkelos the Proselyte translated the Pentateuch into Greek and was praised by Rabbi Eliezer and Rabbi Joshua. Thus there is a contradiction. Actually, Aquila the Proselyte and Onkelos the Proselyte are the same man. Aquila in Hebrew has *ayin, koph, yod, lamed,* and *samek.* The letter *ayin* was pronounced in Judaea like a *nun;* thus the Babylonians, when they heard the pronunciation Aquila, mistook it for a *nun* and pronounced it Onkelos. Thereby came the confusion of the Jerusalem Talmud and the Babylonian Talmud. The Babylonian Jews, who learned from the Judaeans that Aquila (pronounced Onkelos) had translated the Pentateuch and was praised by the sages, took it for granted that the translation referred to the Aramaic rendering of the Pentateuch and therewith this translation became known as the Targum according to Onkelos. The Targum according to Onkelos was compiled by an anonymous person but does not originate from a particular person. A great part of it was based upon oral Aramaic translations which were in vogue among the people. It may be said with certainty that the Tosefta's use of the phrase "Onkelos the Proselyte" was copied from the Babylonian Talmud, and hence it is a later interpolation.

In the Jerusalem Talmud it is stated that the bridegroom wrote in his marriage contract, "According to the laws of Moses and the Judaeans," i.e., according to the Pentateuchal laws and according to the customs which prevailed in Judaea. In the Babylonian Talmud it is stated that the bridegroom wrote in his marriage contract, "According to the laws of Moses and the Israelites." The reason for the change from Judaeans to Israelites was due to the fact that the people living in Babylonia were not Judaeans but called themselves Israelites. This is the underlying reason for the change from Judaeans to Israelites. The Tosefta used the same phrase as the Babylonian Talmud. This is a strong indication that the Tosefta made use of the Babylonian Talmud.

In this essay it was indicated that the Tosefta made use of both Talmudim, the Jerusalem and the Babylonian Talmud.

Professor Saul Lieberman in his edition of the Tosefta has displayed vast erudition not only of the Tosefta and both Talmuds but in the entire rabbinic literature. He demonstrates his keen observations and ingenuity. However, as I have pointed out in this essay, first and foremost it must be established who, when, and where the Tosefta was composed. There can be no question that the bulk of the Tosefta is Tannaitic; however, there are interpretations and interpolations which are of a later period by Judaean sages and Babylonian sages. Unless we could establish which belongs to the original Tosefta and which are additions, no critical edition of the Tosefta could be accomplished.

XXIII

The Geniza of Cairo (Egypt) was a storehouse for manuscripts of the Middle Ages. Many manuscripts of the Geniza were published by different scholars. A manuscript entitled *Mekilta of Rabbi Simon ben Yochai* was one among the publications.

In this short note I endeavored to demonstrate that this so called *Mekilta of Rabbi Simon ben Yochai* is not Tannaitic but is a concoction of the Middle Ages. I demonstrated this by the terms employed in this Midrash. It is regrettable to note that the scholars who published the Geniza manuscripts did not carefully scrutinize the text. The text definitely proves that they are of the Middle Ages. It is to be noted that some of the Church Fathers actually contended that the Book of Enoch was written by Enoch, the great-grandfather of Noah. As to the question, how did it survive the deluge, which destroyed all things, Tertullian attributed the survival of the Book of Enoch to his great-grandson, Noah, who preserved it by taking it into the ark. The modern scholars took, naively, the titles inscribed on the manuscripts as authentic.

There is a Midrash that Rabban Simon ben Gamaliel and Rabban Jochanan ben Zakkai sent an epistle in which the text reads "from Simon ben Gamaliel and from Jochanan ben Zakkai, to our brethren in the South." This phrase stamps it to be of the Middle Ages. At no time were there two men in Judaean history who simultaneously were called Rabban. Furthermore, ancient letters began with the names of the sender to the addressee. We have hundreds of letters of this period written by Hellenes, Romans, and Judaeans. Josephus, in his book *Vita,* quotes that the provisional government, in the year 67 C.E., sent a delegation to Galilee. When the delegation reached Galilee the letters recorded were from the head of the delegation to Josephus, which begins "Jonathan to Josephus." When Josephus replied the text reads "Josephus to Jonathan." These were contemporary to the time of Simon ben Gamaliel. The preposition "from" at the beginning of a letter was used only in the Middle Ages. In the book *Sefer ha-Yashar,* which is a medieval composition, are given a few letters which begin with the preposition "from"—"From your servant Jacob . . . to the King . . ." Also included is a letter from King Solomon, "From King Solomon . . . to the Queen of Sheba."

In the so-called *Midrash Tannaim* it is stated "When Agrippa was anointed King of Israel." There was no anointment during the Second Commonwealth; neither kings nor high priests were anointed. Furthermore, Agrippa was king over Judaea, not Israel. All of them either ignored the text or were not aware that the text quoted above clearly indicates that it is of the Middle Ages, and thus by holding this Midrash to be of the Tannaitic period scholars are distorting Judaean history. Similarly the Hebrew Ben Sirah and the so-called Zadokite fragment found in the Geniza are of the medieval period; *Siphre Zutta* is also a medieval production.

XXIV

Since the completion of the Babylonian Talmud (*Gemara*) the Jews throughout the ages held that there are three codes of laws which they are obliged to observe: the Torah, which is indeed a code of laws which God gave to the children of Israel through Moses; the Mishnah, which is not a perfect code since there are different opinions; however, Rabbi Judah the Prince, when he codified it, laid down principles regarding the *halakot* which had to be followed. The Talmud is the third basic source for laws.

It may be asked, if Rabbi Judah had intended to codify the Mishnah, why did he employ or quote the views of some sages, individuals, since the law had to follow the views of the majority? It may be explained that Rabbi Judah wanted the Mishnah to be an elastic code, not static. For this reason he recorded minority views so that in the future some sage, some rabbi, may base his decision on a new law (not recorded in the Mishnah) on the basis of the minority view given in the Mishnah.

The Tannaim had no power to disagree or contradict the laws of the Torah. They only had the right to interpret. Similarly, the Amoraim had no power to disagree with the laws quoted in the Mishnah or in the Beraitot. Likewise, no rabbi had the right or power to contradict the laws of the Talmud. He did have the right to interpret but not to disregard. The laws of the Torah, Mishnah, and Talmud were considered binding on every Jew. (In modern times there is still a great segment of the Jewish people [the Orthodox Jews] who consider all the laws of the Torah, Mishnah, and Talmud as binding.)

During the Middle Ages some sages compiled codes: the *Mishneh Torah* of Rambam, the *Turim* by Rabbi Jacob, and the *Shulchan Aruh* by Rabbi Joseph Caro. The *Mishneh Torah* was severely censured by Rabbi Abraham ibn David as well as by Rabbi Solomon Luria. The latter also censured the *Shulchan Aruh* and claimed that Rabbi Joseph Caro based his halakic decisions on wrong readings and hence built a foundation on errors. These so-called codes cannot be binding on the people, though authoritative, since they were written by great rabbis. As a matter of fact, we have thousands of responsa written by the rabbis of the Middle Ages in which we can see that they took the *Mishneh Torah* as authoritative but not as binding. Rabbi Solomon Luria wrote that after the completion of the Babylonian Talmud, no halakic decision coming from the Gaonim or other rabbis can be considered binding, unless it can be proven by the fact that their decision is based on the Babylonian Talmud, Jerusalem Talmud, or even the Tosefta.

After the establishment of the State of Israel, many people believed that it was high time for a new code, because of the existence of a chaotic state in Israeli society regarding civil laws. The chaotic state in the Israeli society regarding the civil laws. For the judges in Israel would utilize different laws in their decisions—Jewish, Ottoman, English, and French. There is no question that there is a great *desideratum* for a new code. The question is whether the time is right for such an undertaking. A new code should not be dogmatic. It should be based on a historical analysis and background of the laws which were enacted. To cite an example, according to the present law, to validate a marriage two witnesses are essential. However, if they are blood relatives to the bride or the groom, the marriage is void. As a matter of fact, according to the Tannaim the reason for witnesses is not to validate or legalize the marriage but to serve as proof against those who may later deny the marriage. This *halaka* was enacted in order to prevent the husband or the wife who might for some reason claim that they were not married. In criminal cases and in civil transactions, two witnesses are required who must be without criminal records and who are not related to the principals. In the case of marriage, however, the necessity of two witnesses was not to validate the marriage but to prevent the later denial of the marriage by either party. Thus if the witnesses are related to the bride or to the groom, there is no reason to disqualify them and render the marriage void, if there were offsprings of this wedlock, to make them illegitimate. This is one example of the many instances where the codifier must be aware of the causes and background of the enactment of laws.

The Babylonian Talmud records controversies between Rabbi Meir, Rabbi Jose, and Rabbi Simon. In the Talmud it was endeavored to explain (most likely by the Saboraim) that the controversy between these sages was based on the principle of *braira*, (retrospective designation). Those who endeavored to explain the controversy on the principle of *braira* encountered great difficulties, since they found confusing and contradictory statements. In this essay I tried to prove that the controvery of these sages was not based on *braira*. As a matter of fact the term *braira* does not occur in Tannaitic literature, nor is it found in the Jerusalem Talmud.

In this essay I also dealt with the concept of *hefker bet din hefker,* that is, the *bet din* had the right to renounce, disown, a person of his control or possession of his property. This concept was introduced after the destruction of the Temple, when the Sanhedrin had both the religious and civil authority over the people.

In Tannaitic literature the term *Haarama* occurs. It was held to be a basis for the sages to introduce *takkanot*. In this essay I maintained that *Haarama* is not a *takkana* and was not introduced by the sages. It is a type of loophole. When the *halaka* is ambiguous, the person had the right to circumvent it.

XXV

After the establishment of the State of Israel in 1948, many of the Neo-Orthodox group, rabbis and laymen, propounded the idea of the reestablishment of the Sanhedrin in Israel. Their spokesman was Rabbi Maimon (Fishman), the ex-Minister of Religion in the Ben-Gurion government. The ultra-Orthodox opposed the idea of the revival of the Sanhedrin. In 1952, when I was in Israel, Rabbi Maimon asked me to talk to Rabbi Isaac Herzog, the chief rabbi, about the revival of the Sanhedrin (Rabbi Herzog was a classmate of mine, 1912–13, in the Sorbonne, Paris). When I visited him and raised the question of the revival of the Sanhedrin in Israel, his face became cold and white, and he told me not to speak about the Sanhedrin. He opposed it. My impression was that he was not personally opposed to the revival of the Sanhedrin, but he was fearful of the ultra-Orthodox, who felt that he was a heretic.

One of the reasons why the ultra-Orthodox opposed the revival of the Sanhedrin was because of the fact that the rabbis had no *semicha* and therefore they could have no Sanhedrin. This is historically wrong. *Semicha* never ceased. The Jews of Babylon did not possess *semicha*. Rabbi Judah the Prince denied the privilege of *semicha* to Babylonian Jewry in order to hold them dependent upon the sages of Eretz Israel. In Eretz Israel *semicha* never ceased. *Semicha* was in practice in Judaea after the death of Rabbi Judah the Prince and continued in Western Europe and later in Poland, where most of the Jews had come from Palestine, while the Jews in Babylonia had no *semicha*. Neither did the Jews of Spain have *semicha* since the bulk of Spanish Jewry migrated to Spain after the year 711, when the Berbers crossed the straits of Gibraltar and conquered Spain. Indeed, the communal life of the Jews in Western Europe was based on the laws and customs that had been in Judaea, while the communal life in Spain, being of Babylonian origin, was fashioned as it had been in Babylonia. Indeed the spiritual leaders in Spain never bore the title "Rabbi," while the spiritual leader in Western Europe and later in Poland and Russia and now in America bore the title "Rabbi," a continuation of the custom in Judaea where the sages bore the title "Rabbi."

Isaac Abrabanel writes that when he settled in Italy he was amazed at the custom of the *semicha* practiced by the Ashkenazim who had come to Italy and called themselves "Rabbis." He thought that the German Jews were imitating the Christians, who conferred a diploma upon a person to show that he was a doctor. Isaac Abrabanel, being a Spaniard, was unaware of the custom of *semicha* practiced among the Franco-German Jews. Similarly, Rabbi Isaac ben Sheshet (born in Barcelona) inquired in one of his *responsa* as to the meaning of the *semicha* which was practiced in France and Germany where the rabbis received it and in turn transmitted it to their disciples. Maimonides, being a Spaniard, was unaware of the fact that *semicha* was practiced by the Jews of France and Germany.

Recognizing that the revival of the Sanhedrin is complex and perplexing, I wonder if the time is ripe for this revolutionary act; and if the spiritual leaders in Israel are foresighted enough and have the capability and the courage to modify the *halaka* in accord to the demands of life; and if the spiritual leaders of the diaspora would adhere to the decisions of the rabbis in Israel? To all of this must be given a negative answer. Israel is a small state surrounded by enemies who want to destroy her. Israel has to fight for political and economic survival. The Israeli army has performed miracles in sustaining the State of Israel. The youth not only glorifies the army but they venerate it. Israel has indeed produced great scientists in every field, including agriculture, but that was a need in order to survive. It cannot be expected that Israel, living in such a milieu, could produce great scholars, spiritual leaders, to build spiritual fortresses for the survival of Judaism. The few scholars who are in Israel are elderly people who came from abroad. The lack of a great spiritual awakening is understandable.

With regard to the present spiritual leaders in Israel, it must be said with regret that most of them still have the mentality and psychology developed among their fellow Jews in the cities of Poland, Lithuania, and Rumania, whence they themselves came. They still seek to preserve the Judaism and the religious practices which were in vogue in Eastern Europe, without recognizing the fact these religious laws were once enacted as a safeguard for Judaism to survive in the ghettos. These laws have outlived their purpose in the free State of Israel. They do not recognize that Israel is now an independent, proud state. In order to perpetuate Judaism in Israel, the spiritual leaders of Israel must follow the principles laid down by their predecessors during the time of the Second Commonwealth.

THE HALAKA

Introduction to Tannaitic Jurisprudence

DEMOSTHENES, in defining law, said that its purpose was to deter any man from doing what is wrong and punish transgressors to make the rest better men.[1] Law is the foundation of society.[2] Since primitive times, when man saw the need of being united, laws came into existence to safeguard the individual as well as society. It is said that the people are worthy of their leaders. Certain it is that the people have the laws that they deserve, of which they are the creators. They may introduce laws which enslave themselves or laws which promote their progress.

The halaka reflects the way of life of the Jewish people. It was the creation of the genius of the Jews of the Second Commonwealth. It was progressive and plastic. The sages strove to bring the halaka into consonance with life.

THE WRITTEN AND UNWRITTEN LAWS

Jewish laws are considered divine, delivered by God to the Children of Israel; some, like the Ten Commandments, revealed by God Himself,[3] others through Moses. They

---

[1] ὧν ἕνεκα πάντες τίθενται οἱ νόμοι τοῦ τε μηδένα μηδὲν ὃ μὴ δίκαιόν ἐστι ποιεῖν καὶ τοῦ τοὺς παραβαίνοντας ταῦτα κολαζομένους βελτίους τοὺς ἄλλους ποιεῖν . . . *Against Aristogeiton*, 1.17.

[2] Next after the gods, the laws preserve the State. Demosthenes, *ibid.* ἐπειδὴ τοίνυν οἱ νόμοι μετὰ τοὺς θεοὺς ὁμολογοῦνται σῴζειν τὴν πόλιν. Est enim ius, quo devincta est hominum societas, et quod lex. . . Cicero, *Laws* 1.15.

[3] See Ex. 20; Shab. 88; comp. also Mak. 24a אנכי ולא יהיה לך מפי הגבורה שמענום.

1

were all embodied in the Code called the Law of Moses,[3a] or
the Law,[3b] commonly known to us as the Pentateuch. Violations of these laws are called sins. Some transgressors are
to be punished either by death or corporal punishment,
while others must bring a sacrifice to God in order to
obtain atonement.

Most of the laws in the Pentateuch concern the relation
between man and God. Every transgression was considered
a crime against God. Not only was the worship of foreign
gods considered such but even the profanation of the
sabbath, incest and adultery. Among the civil laws in the
Pentateuch mention is made of a judge, God himself sometimes acting as a judge. For example — in the Book of
Exodus we read, "What if the servant shall plainly say,
'I love my master, my wife and my children; I will not
go out free; 'then his master shall bring him unto Elohim
(God);"[4] the Septuagint rendering *Elohim* the Court of
God.[5] The rabbis, on the other hand, interpreted this word
to mean judges.

The Law of Moses was canonized by Ezra (the High
Priest) after the Restoration. By this I mean that the
Pentateuch became the constitution of the Jewish people.
While the Law of Moses is referred to in the prophetic
books it was not accepted as the constitution by the Jewish
people.[5a] In the Northern Kingdom (in the State of Israel)
the principal tenet of the Pentateuch, that there is only
one God and no other is to be worshipped, was not adhered
to by the kings of Israel who all worshipped foreign gods.
Even in the Southern Kingdom (in the State of Judaea)

[3a] תורת משה.

[3b] ספר התורה.

[4] Ex. 21, והגישו אדניו.אל האלהים: עד אלהים יבא דבר שניהם אשר ירשיען אלהים.

[5] τὸ κριτήριον τοῦ θεοῦ.

[5a] Comp. also. II Chron. 15. וימים רבים לישראל ללא אלהי אמת וללא כהן
מורה וללא תורה.

many kings were equally guilty. Solomon himself, according
to the Book of Kings, followed foreign gods,[6] while the
kings Ahaz and Manasseh brought foreign altars into the
Temple for worship. If the heads of the nation acted thus
it is evident that the Pentateuch was not the constitution
of the people. No individual could be punished for transgressing the precept of the Pentateuch when the basis of
the Book, that there is only one God, was not accepted by
the kings. After the Restoration the Jewish community of
course did not permit the worship of idols. Monotheism,
the belief in one God, was the guiding principle of the new
community — the Torah became the law of the land.

There is no doubt that parallel with the laws of the
Pentateuch were many not embodied therein. They were
the outcome of customs, unwritten laws — halakot. Philo,
in explaining why Moses added the Book of Genesis to the
Torah, which deals only with the history of the Patriarchs,
said that the Patriarchs actually followed all the laws which
were unwritten but were later given by God to Moses.
According to Philo the written law is the product of the
unwritten law — "One might properly say that the enacted
laws are nothing else than memorials of life of the ancients,
preserving to the later generations their actual words and
deeds."[7] The view that the Patriarchs had observed all
the laws of the Torah is also expressed in the Mishna.[8]
This was the opinion of orthodox Jewry of the Second
Commonwealth. Others had the view that the laws were

---

[6] ויהי לעת זקנת שלמה נשיו הטו את לבבו אחרי אלהים אחרים . . . או יבנה שלמה
במה לכמוש שקץ מואב.

[7] ὁπότε καὶ ἀγράφῳ τῇ νομοθεσίᾳ πρίν τι τὴν ἀρχὴν ἀναγραφῆναι
τῶν ἐν μέρει ῥᾳδίως καὶ εὐπετῶς ἐχρήσαντο οἱ πρῶτοι ὡς δεόντως
ἄν τινα φάναι τοὺς τεθέντας νόμους μηδὲν ἄλλ' ἢ ὑπομνήματα
εἶναι βίου τῶν παλαιῶν ἀρχαιολογοῦντας ἔργα καὶ λόγους οἷς
ἐχρήσαντο. On Abraham, 5. See Wolfson, Philo, II, pp. 180-1.

[8] שקיים אברהם אבינו כל התורה כולה. Kid. 4,

enacted and written on tablets at the time of the Patriarchs
and were held in heaven until God gave the Tables of the
Law to Moses on Mount Sinai. This is told in the so called
Book of Jubilees which I believe was originally called תורת
משה the Law of Moses, and was written in opposition to
the Pentateuch.[9]

The writings of the prophets as well as the Hagiographa
contain references to laws not mentioned in the Pentateuch.
In the Book of Haggai it is stated that God told the
Prophet to examine the priests on the laws of sanctity
and impurity. "Thus said the Lord of Hosts. Ask now
the priests Torah (Law) saying, 'If one bear hallowed flesh
in the skirt of his garment, and with his skirt do touch
bread or pottage, or wine, or oil, or any food, shall it
become holy? And the priests answered and said 'No.'
Then said Haggai, "If one that is unclean by a dead body
touch any of these, shall it be unclean?' And the priests
answered and said, 'It shall be unclean."[10] These two
halakot about which the Prophet Haggai questioned the
priests are not found in the Pentateuch, but apparently
the Prophet thought that they should be familiar with the
laws of sanctification and defilement. In the first question
the priests were asked whether a person carrying holy flesh
קדש with him, could thus transfer his sanctity to other
subjects. The second question was whether a person who
had become unclean by contact with a dead body could
transfer impurity to others.[11]

We learn from the Book of Jeremiah that when the

[9] See S. Zeitlin, *The Book of Jubilees*, 1939.

[10] 2.11–13. כה אמר ד' צבאות שאל נא את הכהנים תורה לאמר הן ישא איש בשר קדש
בכנף בגדו ונגע בכנפו אל הלחם . . . היקדש ויענו הכהנים ויאמרו לא ויאמר חני אם יגע
טמא נפש בכל אלה היטמא ויענו הכהנים ויאמרו יטמא.

[11] Comp. Pes. 17a רב אמר אישתבש כהני ושמואל אמר לא אישתבש כהני. See
also Yer. Sota, חמן אמרין שתי שאילות שאלו חני הנביא אחת השיבו אותו כראוי
ואחת לא השיבו לו כראוי.

Prophet bought a field from Hanamel he wrote a deed in
the presence of witnesses who affixed their signatures.[12] In
the Pentateuch there is no requirement of a deed and witnesses in the transfer of personal property. In the Book
of Tobit it is related that when Raguel gave his daughter
as a wife to Tobit "he wrote an instrument of cohabita-
tion."[13] The author continues, "He gave her to wife according to the decree of the Law of Moses."[14] From the Pentateuch we know that a father had full rights over his daughter, even the right to sell her.[15] If a girl was seduced the
seducer had to pay a penalty for this act but the money
was paid to her father, not to her.[16] The Pentateuch does
not say that if the father gives his daughter away in marriage he must write a deed. The deed which Raguel wrote
was most likely one of transfer of his rights over his daughter, Sarah, to Tobit, her future husband. According to the
Book of Nehemiah the Jews were prohibited from carrying
any burden on the sabbath or buying and selling,[17] while
in the Pentateuch the Jews are forbidden to work on the
sabbath; the nature of the work is not defined. From
Nehemiah, however, we learn that the transaction of any
business on the sabbath formed part of such forbidden
work.

In the Book of Ruth it is stated that Boaz told his kinsman that he would have to marry Ruth when he purchased
the field of Naomi "to raise up the name of the dead upon
his inheritance." "Now this was the custom," we are
informed, "in former time in Israel concerning redeeming

---

[12] 32.9–10, ‎.ואקנה את השדה . . . ואכתב בספר ואחתם ואעד עדים

[13] 7.14. καὶ ἔγραψεν συγγραφὴν βιβλίου συνοικήσεως.

[14] κατὰ τὴν κρίσιν τοῦ Μωυσέως νόμου.

[15] ‎.וכי ימכר איש את בתו לאמה

[16] Deut. 22.28–29, ‎.ונתן האיש השכב עמה לאבי הנער חמשים כסף

[17] 13.15–20. ‎דרכים נתוח בשבת . . . ובשבת . . . ביום השבת . . . ומביאים . . . ומוכרים
‎.בשבת . . . לא יבא משא ביום השבת . . . ומכרי כל ממכר

and concerning exchanging, to confirm all things. A man
drew off his shoe and gave it to his neighbor; and this was
the attestation in Israel."[18] When Boaz acquired the field
the author says, "he drew off his shoe." Among the sages
there was a discussion as to who removed the shoe and who
gave it, whether the kinsman gave his shoe to Boaz, i. e.
as a sign of transfer of the property, or whether Boaz gave
the shoe as a sign of purchase of the property.[19] It is clear,
however, that it was the custom in ancient Israel in the
transfer of immovable property to resort to a symbol of
transfer either by the one who transferred the property or
by the new owner. There is no mention whatsoever in the
Pentateuch of this law or custom.

When Naboth, the Jezreelite, according to I Kings,
refused to give or to sell his vineyard to King Ahab, his
wife Jezebel proclaimed a fast and had two men testify
falsely that Naboth had cursed God and the king. For this
he was put to death and thus King Ahab acquired the vineyard.[20] God then said to Elijah, "Go to Ahab, the King
of Israel, and tell him, "Thus saith the Lord, 'Hast thou
murdered and also inherited?"[21] It is evident that God was
opposed to Ahab's acquiring possession of the vineyard of
Naboth who was put to death on false testimony by a
scheme of Jezebel. If, however, Naboth had cursed God
and the king, Ahab, the King of Israel, would have become
the legitimate heir of the vineyard. Such a law of forfeiture
is not found in the Pentateuch. But in the tannaitic
literature we learn that when a man committed a crime
against the state and was executed his property was

[18] 4.7, וזאת לפנים בישראל על הגאלה ועל התמורה לקים כל דבר שלף איש נעלו
ונתן לרעהו.
[19] See B. M. 47, מי נתן למי בועז נתן לנואל ר' יהודה אומר נואל נתן לבועז.
[20] 21.2–15. ויהי כשמע איזבל כי סקל נבת וימת ותאמר איזבל אל אחאב קום
רש את כרם נבות היזרעאלי.
[21] כה אמר ד' הרצחת וגם ירשת.

not inherited by his children but was forfeited to the state.[22]

From the Book II Kings we may infer that a law existed in Israel in regard to the status of the debtor to the creditor. It is told that, a certain woman of the wives of the sons of the prophets cried to Elisha saying: "Thy servant, my husband, is dead; and thou knowest that thy servant did fear the Lord; and the creditor is come to take unto him my two children to be his bondsmen."[23] From the complaint of the widow we may deduce that in ancient times if a debtor did not pay his debts the creditor had the right to take him into servitude and if he died and the debt was unpaid to take his children into bondage. The principle of *obligatio*, that the debtor was bound to the creditor who had the right to sell him and even his children into slavery or to imprison him, if he did not pay his debt to the obligator is evident from a story in the Gospel according to Matthew.[23a] The law that if a debtor did not pay his debt the creditor had a right not only over his person but also over his children is not in the Laws of Moses.

The principle of *hiyub, obligatio in person*, that the obligator had the right in person and not in property, goes back to the Pentateuch. According to the Torah if a man had stolen property he had to return it to the owner and pay him a fine. If it was an ox his penalty was double, but if he no longer had the ox in his possession that is, if he had slaughtered or sold it, he had to pay a fine five time its value. If the thief did not have the money to pay to the owner for the value of the stolen property he was sold into slavery. From this we can readily see that the *hiyub*,

---

[22] See San. 48b; Tosefta *ibid.* 4, הרוני מלכות נכסיהן למלך, הרוני בית דין‎ ‏נכסיהן ליורשים.

[23] עבדך אישי מת ... והנשה בא לקחת את שני ילדי לו לעבדים‎ 4.1, ; comp. also Neh. 5.

[23a] 18.24–30.

obligatio, to pay for the stolen property, lay in person. According to tannaitic law the thief could be sold only when he was unable to pay the principal of the value but not if he could not pay the fine.[23b] Since *furtum* (theft) was considered *delicta privata*,[23c] the fine which the thief was supposed to pay (for that matter any fine) according to tannaitic law as well as according to the Roman law, could not be collected by the heirs until after *litis contestatio* had taken place.

The few laws which we have just recorded are based purely on customs. They were most likely put into effect by public opinion, because of the antiquity of their practice. After the Restoration they were enforced by the authorities.

The decree which the Persian king gave to Ezra included the authority to appoint judges and to punish those who would not follow דתא די אלהך the law of God and the law of the king. "Let judgment be executed" it read "upon those with diligence whether it be unto death or to banishment or to confiscation of goods or to imprisonment."[24] Thus Ezra received authority to exercise full jurisdiction over those Jews who did not obey all the laws, whether they were the laws of the Torah or unwritten laws. The latter became known in rabbinic literature as halakot. The word halaka means custom, law; it is derived from הלך walk. Similarly the Greek word νόμος law had the original connotation of custom, usage.[25] Hence the laws embodied in the Torah were the written laws, תורה שבכתב and called דברי תורה while those not included in the Pentateuch, which sprang from the customs of the people, and although

---

[23b] Kid. 18a, דתניא בגניבתו ולא בכפילו.

[23c] See below p. 34.

[24] Ezra 7.25–26.

[25] See H. S. Maine, *Ancient Law*, ch. 1, on the meaning of θέμις and νόμος.

sanctioned by the authorities, were called halakot תורה שבעל פה, unwritten laws, or דברי סופרים *jus non scriptum*, ἄγραφοι νόμοι.[26]

At the time of the Restoration many laws not found in the Pentateuch prevailed among the Jews, but many beliefs and doctrines not mentioned there were in vogue. Some of these were established through the influence of the prophets.

One of the main contentions between the Judaeans and the Samaritans was that the former wanted Jerusalem to be the site of the new Temple. The Samaritans objected because the city was not mentioned in the Pentateuch. The importance of Jerusalem above all other cities of Judaea arose through history and the prophetic teachings. The family of David reigned there for centuries and the Temple of God was there.

Although· the new community was established as a Theocracy and the high priest became the vicar of God, who had authority over the entire Jewish community, not only spiritual but also temporal, not all the Jews favored such a government. Many looked forward to the day when the Davidic dynasty would be reestablished,[26a] since God through his prophets had promised David that his dynasty would last forever.

From the tannaitic literature, as well as from Josephus, we learn that the Sadducees rejected the unwritten laws while the Pharisees accepted them. Josephus, in his book, *Jewish Antiquities*, writes as follows, "The Pharisees had passed on to the people certain regulations received from their forefathers but not recorded in the Laws of Moses, for which reason they are rejected by the Sadducaean group, who hold that only those laws should be considered valid which were written down and those which had been handed

---

[26] Cicero derives νόμος from νεμω (to distribute), and *lex* from *lego*.
[26a] See S. Zeitlin, *Religious and Secular Leadership*, Part I, 1943.

down by the forefathers need not be observed."[27] However,
we must assume that the Sadducees could not reject all
the laws which were not the Laws of Moses. No state, large
or small, could function without customs, unwritten laws.[28]
Cicero has well remarked that the law had its origin ages
before any written law existed or any state had been
established.[29] The Sadducees could not reject many laws
in vogue after the Restoration which were in force either
by public opinion or by the vicar, the High Priest. Many
of these customs had become part of the written law and to
this Josephus apparently refers, "Only those laws should
be considered valid which were written down." The
Sadducees particularly opposed the ideas and beliefs of the
Pharisees regarding the Davidic family.

We must assume that the account of Josephus is based on
a source later than the Restoration, when the Pharisees and
the Sadducees were two distinct political and religious
groups. At this time the Pharisees had developed an array
of laws which they held were based not only on tradition
but also on the Pentateuch and which were derived by
hermeneutic rules. The Sadducees opposed these views.
The Pharisees, on the other hand, maintained that the
halakot as well as the Torah were revealed by God. According to the Talmud, "In the days of mourning for Moses

[27] . . . ἐκ πατέρων διαδοχῆς ἅπερ οὐκ ἀναγέγραπται ἐν τοῖς μωυσέος
νόμοις . . . λέγον ἐκεῖνα δεῖν ἡγεῖσθαι νόμιμα τα γεγραμμένα τὰ δ'
ἐκ παραδόσεως τῶν πατέρων μὴ τηρεῖν. (XIII, 10, 6.)

[28] Comp. Philo, *The Special Laws*, IV, 28. ἔθη γὰρ ἄγραφοι νόμοι
δόγματα παλαιῶν ἀνδρῶν οὐ στήλαις ἐγκεχαραγμένα καὶ χαρτιδίοις
ὑπὸ σητῶν ἀναλισκομένοις ἀλλὰ ψυχαῖς των μετειληφότων τῆς
αὐτῆς πολιτείας. "For customs are unwritten laws, the decisions
approved by men of old, not inscribed on monuments or leaves of paper
which the moth destroys but on the souls of those who are partners in
the same society."

[29] . . . *quae saeclis omnibus ante nata est quam scripta lex ulla aut
quam omnino civitas constituta.* Op. cit. 6.

thousands of halakot were forgotten."[30] The same thought
was expressed by a Palestinian Amora of the third century
C. E. when he said, "Many halakot were transmitted to
Moses on Mt. Sinai and all of them are embodied in the
Mishna."[31]

The conception that the unwritten law was really a gift
of God was entertained by the Greeks as well as the
Romans. Demosthenes said that law though made by wise
men was the gift of the gods.[32] Cicero also said that law
came into existence through the divine mind, "The true
and the primal law," he wrote, "applied to command and
prohibition is the right reason of supreme Jupiter."[33] Elsewhere he wrote, "that law which the gods have given to
the human race has been justly praised; for it is the reason
and mind of a wise lawgiver applied to command and
prohibition."[34]

At times the sages considered the halakot the laws enacted by the *Soferim* more important than the laws of the
Pentateuch,[35] and even favored them above the Torah.[36]
A similar opinion of the greater importance of unwritten
laws was held by the Greek philosophers. Aristotle said
that customary laws are more sovereign than the written
laws.[37] There is a statement in the Talmud in the name

---

[30] אמר רב יהודה אמר שמואל שלשת אלפים הלכות נשתכחו בימי אבלו של משה,
Tem. 16.

[31] אמר ר'ז בשם ר' יוחנן . . . שהרי כמה הלכות נאמרו למשה בסיני וכולהן משוקעות
במשנה. Yer. Pea 2.

[32] καὶ μάλισθ' ὅτι πᾶς ἐστι νόμος εὕρημα μὲν καὶ δῶρον ϑεῶν
δόγμα δ' ανϑρώπων φρονίμων. Op. cit.

[33] *Quam ob rem lex vera atque princeps apta ad iubendum et ad vetandum
ratio est recta summi Iovis.* Ibid.

[34] *Ex quo illa lex, quam di humano generi dederunt recte est laudata
est enim ratio mensque sapientis ad iubendum et ad deterrendum idonea.*

[35] חומר בדברי סופרים מדברי תורה, M. San. 10.4.

[36] Yer ibid. וחביבים סדברי תורה.

[37] ἔτι κυριώτεροι καὶ περὶ κυριωτέρων τῶν κατὰ γράμματα νόμων
οἱ κατὰ τὰ ἔϑη εἰσίν. *Politics,* 3, 1287b.

of Rabbi Ishmael that in three instances the halaka super-
seded the Torah. These were cases where the blood of a
beast or a fowl which was slaughtered was to be covered
only with dust, could according to the halaka be covered
with anything at all; where, according to the Pentateuch,
a *Nazir* was forbidden to cut his hair with a razor, was not
allowed to cut his hair with any instrument at all; and
finally where though, according to the Pentateuch, a decree
of divorce had to be written in a book to be valid, it could be
written on anything, on pottery, book or leaves, according
to the halaka.[38]

The Jews, in order to enforce the unwritten laws,
maintained that these like the written laws were revealed
by God. When the unwritten laws were codified they
became written laws and hermeneutic rules were applied
to them to infer new halakot.[38a] While common law — unwritten law — may be enforced by authorities new laws
cannot be inferred from them. Hermeneutic rules may be
applied to written laws but not to customs, unwritten
laws.

The sages of the Talmud who said that many halakot
were revealed to Moses on Mount Sinai held that these
were incorporated in the Mishna.[39] The word Mishna is
derived from the word שנה to study. The term Mishna
has also the connotation of "second" and I think that
these halakot, which were assembled in one collection and

[38] תני דבי ר' ישמעאל בשלשה מקומות הלכה עוקפת [עוקבת] (עוקרת) למקרא
התורה אמרה בעפר והלכה בכל דבר התורה אמרה בתער והלכה בכל דבר התורה
אמרה ספר והלכה בכל דבר. Sota 16a; Yer. Kid. 1.

[38a] Comp. Tosefta Zeb. 1, אף אני אביא . . . אמר לו ר' אליעזר פסח יוכיח
אשם; אמר ר' ישמעאל קל וחומר מה שיריים שאין מכפרין טעונין יסוד תחילה עולה
דבר הלמד בקל וחומר מה, comp. also ibid. שמכפרת אין דין (B. ibid. 51)
ראה את המעשה, שילמד בנזרה שה, and passim.   Comp. also Yer. Pes. 6,
נזכר את ההלכה . . . ר' זעירה בשם ר' אלעזר כל תורה (הלכה) שאין לה בית אב
אינה תורה and passim.

[39] See Note 31.

made into a code were purposely called Mishna to signify that it was the Second Code to the Laws of Moses.

The halakot codified in the Mishna ceased to be unwritten laws; they were now considered *written laws*. The statement in the Talmud that it is permissible to put into writing the Laws of Moses but not the halakot,[40] I venture to say that this refers to the halakot before the codification of the Mishna or to such halakot which were not included in the Mishna. They remained the unwritten law.[41]

One may question, if the Mishna is a code, why are differences of opinion found there in connection with the halakot. A code is a set of laws recorded without any dissension — like the Torah, and the codes of the Roman law like the *Institute of Gaius* for example. We must take into consideration however the fact that Judaism at the time of the codification of the Mishna was a nomocracy, i. e. a government under the rule of the law. The Mishna, being a code, records different opinions but rules are laid down as to which laws are to be observed. Where there is both a majority opinion and a minority opinion the majority opinion must be followed. At times when Rabbi, who was the real architect of the Mishna, thought that the law as interpreted by a particular sage should be followed, he recorded such a view or opinion in the Mishna, either as anonymous or in the name of the sages,[42] i. e. he made it

---

[40] תני דבי ר' ישמעאל כתוב לך את הדברים האלה אלה אתה כותב אבל אין אתה כותב הלכות. Tem. 14b.

[41] . . . . וכן היה הדבר תמיד, הלכות ואין מורין כן, comp. also Maimonides, עד רבינו הקדוש והוא קיבל כל השמועות וכל הדינים וכל הביאורים והפירושים ששמעו מפי משה רבינו ושלמדו בית דין שבכל דור ודור בכל התורה כולה וחיבר מהכל ספר המשנה ושננו לחכמים ברבים ונגלה לכל ישראל וכתבוה כולם, (הקדמה למשנה תורה). Elsewhere I pointed out in the manuscript copy of the Tractate Abodah Zara (Spain, 1291) in the Jewish Theological Seminary of America the reading דהא מכתבא כתביא for לנרסינהו (Ab. Z. 8b).

[42] ראה רבי דבריו של ר' מאיר . . . ושנאו בלשון חכמים. See Hul. 85a. Comp. also Yer. Yeb. 4.11.

the majority opinion. Rabbi set down numerous opinions in the Mishna, even those which he did not accept as the halaka. The reason for this was that if sometime in the future some halakot suggestions should arise the rabbis should be able to support their decisions on those opinions recorded in the Mishna.[43] Hence the Mishna, even though a code, cannot be compared to the Torah. The Torah was revealed by God to Moses and had to be administered by the High Priest, the vicar of God. The code of the Roman law certainly cannot be compared to it. Its authority came either from kings, senate or magistrates. The sages of the Second Commonwealth did not derive their authority from kings, senate or magistrates but from their profound knowledge of the Law and their ability to interpret it. Some of the sages were called דרשנים interpreters.[44]

The halakot in the Mishna are arranged according to the subject matter and generally make no reference to the Pentateuch. The halakot in the *Mekilta Sifra* and *Sifre*, however, are arranged according to the pentateuchal passages and are interpreted by biblical verses. This type of legal interpretations is also found throughout the Talmud.

THE HALAKA AND MIDRASH

The question confronting modern scholars has been what form of law came first, that form of law given in the Mishna or that form of law recorded in the *Mekilta Sifra* and *Sifre?* It has been the consensus of opinion among scholars that the teaching of the law as recorded in the *Mekilta*

---

[43] לעולם הלכה כדברי המרובין לא הוזכרו דברי היחיד בין המרובין אלא לבטלן,
ר' יהודה אומר לא הוזכרו דברי יחיד בין המרובין אלא שמא תיצרך להן שעה ויסמכו
עליהן, וחכמים אומרים לא הוזכרו דברי יחיד בין המרובין אלא מתוך שזה אומר טמא
וזה אומר טהור זה אומר טמא כדברי ר' אליעזר אמרו לו כדברי ר' אליעזר שמעתה.
Tosefta Eduy. 1. Comp. also M. ibid.

[44] שמעיה ואבטליון שהן חכמים גדולים ודרשנים גדולים, Pes. 70b.

Sifra and *Sifre*, which they call *Midrash Halaka*, is older than that in the Mishna.[45] Likewise it has been generally assumed that the teaching of the halaka in the Mishna form took place after the period of the *Soferim*.[46] There is a wide difference of opinion as to when the period of the *Soferim* ended. According to some Simon I was the Just and he was the last of the *Soferim*. Hence this period ended about 300–270 B. C. E.[47] According to others Simon II was the Just, and he was the last of the *Soferim*;[48] hence, according to this view the end of the period of *Soferim* came circa 210–190 B. C. E. Those who held that the teaching of the Midrash form is older than the Mishna find support for their theory in the literature of the Gaonim.[49]

The theory that the teaching of the Midrash form is older than the Mishna is historically untrue. 1 — The Gaonic statement in advancing this view is not sufficient proof. The Gaonim lived centuries after the compilation of the Mishna and therefore the statement is questionable. On the contrary we may deduce from the tannaitic literature that the Mishna form was older and hence the Gaonic statement is refuted. To establish what form of teaching is the older we must go to tannaitic literature, the product of the builders of the Mishna and the Midrash halaka. Only the literature of the Tannaim and the early Amoraim can be conclusive in this matter.

---

[45] N. Krochmal, מורי נבוכי הזמן; Weiss, דור דור ודורשיו; D. Hoffman, המשנה הראשונה; Jacob Lauterbach, *Midrash and Mishnah*. See also G. Aicher, *Das Alte Testament in der Mishnah*; he alone is of the opinion that the Mishna is older than the Midrash.

[46] See Lauterbach *ibid.*

[47] See Oppenheim, (II בית התלמוד) תולדות המשנה; Lauterbach, *ibid.*

[48] Comp. Lauterbach, ibid.

[49] וספרא וספרי דרשי דקראי ניניהו והיכן רמיזי הילכתא בקראי ומעיקרא במקדש see Hoffman, שני ביומיה דרבנן קמאי לפום הדין אורחא הוו תני להון (שרירא גאון) ibid.

Again the theory that the period of the *Soferim* lasted
until Simon I (300–270 B. C. E.) or Simon II (210–190
B. C. E.) is refuted by many passages in tannaitic literature,
according to which the period of the *Soferim* continued
down to the time of the destruction of the Second Temple.
In the Mishna Yad. 3 it is stated that, "the Holy Scriptures
defiles the hands,"[50] was decreed by the *Soferim*. This law
was decreed about the year 65 C. E. a few years before the
destruction of the Temple. Again in the Tosefta Tebul
Yom 2, it is stated that Rabbi Joshua said, "This is new
which the *Soferim* innovated."[51] Rabbi Joshua's statement
refers to the decree which was introduced a few years before
the destruction of the Temple, hence it is quite evident
that the theory that the *Soferim* ceased to exist before the
time of the Maccabees is erroneous and must be disregarded.

The contention that the name *Soferim* designates a group
who occupied themselves with the Book and taught the
Book alone is refuted by the Mishna Yad. 3 and by the
Tosefta Tebul Yom 2. The halaka quoted in this tannaitic
literature is not derived from the Book. We may disregard
the theory that, "This name (Soferim) has been applied to
the earliest teachers of the Halakah, because they imparted
all their teachings in connection with the Book of the Law
either as an exposition of it or as a commentary on it, that
is to say in the form of the Midrash."[52] The halakot just
quoted came not from the "earliest teachers" but from the
teachers of the period shortly before the destruction of the
Second Temple. They are independent halakot. Again it
is not true that the name *Soferim* was applied only to the

[50] כתבי קודש שניים מטמאין את הידים אמרו אין דנין . . . דברי סופרים מדברי
סופרים. See also Tosefta Tebul Yom, 1.10, דברי תורה מדברי סופרים ודנו עליה דברי
תורה ודברי סופרים מדברי סופרים.

[51] אמר ר' יהושע דבר חדש שחידשו סופרים ואין לי מה אשיב.

[52] Lauterbach, *op. cit.*, p. 26.

early teachers while that of the Tannaim was applied to
the later teachers who began to teach the abstract halakot.

The scholars who have dealt with the problem of halakot
have not only failed to see that the term *Soferim*, as applied
to the sages, was used down to the destruction of the
Second Temple but they have not shown a true comprehension of the philosophy of Jewish history during the
Second Commonwealth. Most of these scholars were theologians — academicians. They were accustomed to analyze
written words and thus they applied the same method
to the study of the halakot during the Second Commonwealth. They ignored the fact that the Jews of that period
were a living nation, the creators of the laws. It is well
known that every people besides having statutory laws have
also common laws, customs, which had originated among
the people. In the same way the Jews at the time of the
Restoration, when the Pentateuch was canonized, had
many halakot outside of the Pentateuch which were as old
or even older.

That the halakot preceded the Midrash form is manifest
from two events in the life of Hillel. According to the
Palestinian Talmud there were three reasons for Hillel's
coming to Palestine.[53] He found three contradictory verses
in the Pentateuch:

1. With regard to leprosy one verse reads טהור הוא "he is
clean," which means that a person is considered clean when
his leprosy is cured. In another verse, however it is stated
וטהרו הכהן "the priest shall pronounce him clean," which
means that although a man is cured from leprosy he is
not considered clean unless pronounced so by the priest.
Hillel interpreted these two verses and said that both
conditions were necessary. The one stating that the man

---

[53] Pes. 6. על שלשה דברים עלה הלל מבבל. Comp. also Tosefta Neg. 1.

must be first cured and that the other that he must be pronounced cured by the priest.[54]

2. In one verse it is written that the Pascal Lamb must be brought from the flock and the herd while another passage reads that the Pascal Lamb must be brought from the sheep and the goats. Hillel interpreted this to mean that the Pascal Lamb is to be taken from the flock while the sacrifice called *hagiga* is to come from the herds.[55]

3. In one verse it is stated that unleavened bread is to be eaten for six days but another verse says seven days. Hillel interpreted and reconciled these two verses by referring the seven days to the old harvest while the six days referred to the new harvest.[56] The Jews were not allowed to eat of the new harvest until the sixteenth day if Nisan, i. e. the second day of the Festival of Unleavened Bread. Thus the unleavened bread from the new harvest is to be eaten only six days.

The Talmud continues דרש והסכים ועלה וקיבל הלכה.

Hillel interpreted and reconciled[57] these passages after he arrived in the Land of Israel when he discovered that his interpretations were halakot, i. e. the Jews had been practicing as he had interpreted. Since these three laws were not applicable in Babylonia, for there was no law of leprosy there, nor was there sacrifice of the Pascal Lamb,

---

[54] טהור הוא יכול יפטר וילך לו ח״ל וטהרו הכהן אי וטהרו הכהן יכול אם אמר
הכהן על טמא טהור יהא טהור ת״ל טהור הוא וטהרו הכהן.

[55] כתוב אחד אומר וזבחת פסח לד׳ אלהיך צאן ובקר וכתוב אחד אומר מן הכבשים
ומן העזים תקחו הא כצד צאן לפסח וצאן ובקר לחגיגה.

[56] כתוב אחד אומר ששת ימים תאכל מצות וכתוב אחד אומר שבעת ימים מצות תאכלו
הא כיצד ששה מן החדש ושבעה מן הישן.

[57] והסכים — reconciled. Comp. also Tosefta Zeb. 1.8. אני שמעתי ולא
חורב. See S. Zeitlin, היה לי לפרש ואתה דורש ומסכים להלכה. Comp. also
ודרש מעצמו לשלשה דברים הללו והסכים להלכה ועלה לא״י לדרוש *ad loc.* פני משה
כן, וקבל הלכה, בני א״י קבלו ממנו גם כן להלכה שכך קיבל נ״כ מפי שמעיה ואבטליון.
The commentators did not understand this talmudic passage and hence misinterpreted it.

nor was there any law regarding the new harvest,[58] Hillel interpreted the verses referring to them in accordance with the halaka in vogue in Palestine. Thus it is evident that the halaka supersedes the Midrash.

The other event in Hillel's life from which we may deduce that the halaka preceded the Midrash was in connection with the slaughter of the Pascal Lamb on the sabbath. In both Talmuds it is related that once when the eve of Passover (14th of Nisan) fell on sabbath, the B'ne Bathera did not know whether the Pascal Lamb might be slaughtered on the sabbath. They were advised, there is a man named Hillel, a disciple of Shemaiah and Abatalion, who possibly knows; let us ask him. "They sent for him and asked him whether the Pascal Lamb could be slaughtered on the sabbath." He replied that it could and proved it by hermeneutic rules; by קל וחומר *a minori ad majus*, by גזירה שוה analogy of words, by היקש analogy of subjects. The B'ne Bathera however, did not accept his ruling, but when he said that he had this tradition from Shemaiah and Abatalion they accepted it. Hillel was then appointed Nasi over the Bet Din.[59] The Talmud adds that the B'ne Bathera did not know whether it was permissible to carry the knives for the slaughter of the Pascal Lamb on the sabbath. When they asked Hillel he answered that he had a tradition of "the halaka but that he had forgotten it." However, said he, "leave it to Israel, if there are not prophets there are sons of prophets."[60] The Jews who brought lambs for the

---

[58] Comp. M. Kid. 1. ... כל מצוה שהיא תלויה בארץ אינה נוהגת אלא בארץ
Yer. *ibid.*, החדש אסור מן התורה בכל מקום M. Orla; ר' אליעזר אומר אף החדש
מתניתא דר' אליעזר דתנינן חמן ... ר"א אף ההדש.

[59] זו הלכה נעלמה מבני (מזקני) בתורה פעם אחת חל י"ד להיות שבת ולא היו יודעין
אם פסח דוחה את השבת אם לאו אמרו יש כאן בבלי אחד והלל שמו ששמו את שמעיה
ואבטליון ... התחיל דורש להן מהיקש, וקל וחומר, ומגזירה שוה ... לא קיבלו ככני
עד שאמר להן יבא עלי כך שמעתי מפי שמעיה ואבטליון ... עמדו ומינו אותו נשיא
עליהן. Pes. 66a, Yer. *ibid.* 6.

[60] *Ibid.*

sacrifice stuck knives in the wool of the lambs.[61] It is
evident from this story that although the B'ne Bathera
did not know that the Pascal Lamb could be slaughtered
on the sabbath, and although Hillel to sanction this had to
resort to hermeneutic rules, the farmers knew this and when
preparing to bring the Pascal Lamb for slaughter on the
sabbath they stuck knives in the wool of the lambs. Thus
it is clear that this halaka, i. e. the custom of slaughtering
the Pascal Lamb on the sabbath, was in vogue long before
the time of Hillel. The reason why the B'ne Bathera did
not know of this is that they were new in the *Bet Din*,
having come from outside of Eretz Israel. Hillel sought to
make this halaka — unwritten law — a statutory law by
interpreting the Torah.

It has been suggested that from a particular passage in
the Talmud it is evident that the Midrash form was
older than the Mishna form.[62] The passage referred to
contains a story in which R. Johanan speaks to Simon b.
Lakish about a statement by R. Eleazar b. Pedat, and
remarks: "I see that the son of Pedat interprets in the way
as Moses did from God."[63] Thus the opinion is expressed
that to study or teach in the Midrash form as it is given
in the *Mekilta Sifra* and *Sifre* is as old as Moses. This
interpretation however is erroneous. R. Eleazar b. Pedat
had a reputation for quoting the opinions of others and
not giving original opinions. Simon b. Lakish particularly
criticized him for this.[64] Once R. Eleazar b. Pedat expressed

---

[61] מי שפסחו טלה תוחבו בצמרו . . . ראה מעשה ונזכר הלכה.

[62] Lauterbach, *op. cit.*, p. 32.

[63] Yeb. 72b, ראיתי לבן פדת שיושב ודורש כמשה מפי הגבורה.

[64] Comp. Mak. 5b, . . . א'ל ר' אלעזר אם היא הוחזקה כל ישראל מי הוחזקו
זמנין הוו יתבי קמי דר' יוחנן אתא כי האי מעשה לקמייהו אמר ריש לקיש הוחזקה זו
א'ל ר' יוחנן אם הוחזקה זו כל ישראל מי הוחזקו הדר חזיא לר' אלעזר בישחא אמר ליה
שמעת מילי מבר נפחא ולא אמרת לי משמיה.

an opinion which R. Johanan thought original and told
Simon b. Lakish how much he admired the originality of
b. Pedat who, like Moses, interpreted the law as received
from God without any intermediary. To this Simon b.
Lakish replied that even here b. Pedat was not original
for he took the opinion from the Sifra.[65] Hence there is no
basis whatsoever for the contention that the Midrash form
is older than the Mishna form.

SOURCES OF TANNAITIC LAW

The sources of the law may be divided into the following
categories: The Law of Moses — the written law; halakot
— customs, unwritten laws; *g'zera* — decree; *takkana*; סייג
fence around the law.

The Laws of Moses were the basic laws of the Jews.
However they underwent great modification by interpretation and fiction. The sages declared that some of them
were applicable to the time of Moses only and were not for
posterity.[66]

Halakot which were codified in the Mishna, even those
which before the codification through interpretation of the
Pentateuch were accepted by the Bet Din, became statutory
laws and were used as a basis for new laws. This method
of development of law is called *Midrash Torah* and *Midrash
Halaka*.

G'zera is a decree — independent legislation by an authority. During the Second Commonwealth many laws were
decreed by the authority of the *Bet Din* or by the head of
this institution. A decree was promulgated for a particular

---

[65] See Yeb. 82b, אמר ליה ריש לקיש דידיה היא מתניתין היא היכא תנא ליה . . .
בתורת כהנים.
[66] Comp. Tosefta Pes. 8, פסח מצרים מקום אכילה שם לינה ופסח דורות אוכלין
במקום אחד ולנים במקום אחד. See also S. Zeitlin, The Liturgy of the First
Night of Passover, *JQR*, April 1948.

reason. When the reason for it disappeared the decree
automatically became void. This may be illustrated by an
example from tannaitic literature. It is stated that Jose
b. Joezer and Jose b. Johanan decreed that the land of the
pagans was in a state of levitical uncleanliness.[67] This decree
was issued during the time of the Maccabean struggle for
freedom. It was promulgated to prevent the Jews from
migrating to foreign countries and it was also directed
against Onias's temple. With the decree declaring the land
of the pagans in a state of levitical uncleanliness, it destroyed the rivalry between the temple in Egypt and the
temple in Jerusalem.[68] When both the menace of emigration
and the rivalry of the temple of Onias were thus removed
the g'zera automatically disappeared. When a new cause
arose and the sages thought that, for the benefit of the Jews
and Eretz Israel, the land of the pagans should again be
declared in a state of levitical uncleanliness they decreed
another such g'zera.

From this point of view a perplexing talmudic passage
becomes clear. The question was asked, if Jose b. Joezer
and Jose b. Johanan declared the land of the pagans to
be in a state of levitical uncleanliness why is it said that
the schools Shammai and Hillel had such a decree promulgated?[69] Furthermore, the Talmud says that, according to
tradition, the "rabbis of the eighty years" (i. e. the rabbis
who lived eighty years before the destruction of the Temple)
had promulgated such a decree.[70] The answer given in the

[67] דתני יוסי בן יועזר איש צרידא ויוסי בן יוחנן איש ירושלים גזרו טומאה על ארץ
העמים, Shab. 14b.

[68] See S. Zeitlin, *The History of the Second Jewish Commonwealth,
Prolegomena*, pp. 26–9; comp. also L. Ginzberg, מקומה של ההלכה בחכמת
ישראל, ירושלים תרצ'א.

[69] See Yer. Shab. 1, ... ולא כן א'ר זעירא בר אבונא בשם רב ירמיה יוסי בן
יעזר ... גזרו טומאה.

[70] See Shab. 15a, והא רבנן דשמונים שנה נזור.

Talmud is that although Jose b. Joezer and Jose b. Johanan decreed the land of the pagan to be in a state of levitical uncleanliness the people did not accept their decree; but that when the later rabbis issued such a decree it was accepted by the people.[71] According to our opinion the reason why this decree was repeated three times is not that it was not accepted by the people but that when the reason for the decree vanished, *ipso facto*, the decree became null and void. When the reason arose again the later sages reissued the decree.

Another source of law was *takkana*. *Takkana* is an amendment of early law, either pentateuchal or halaka, introduced by the sages generally for the purpose of harmonizing religion and life. They did not hesitate to amend a pentateuchal law if such was life's demand. Hence *takkana* has a lenient tendency. In introducing a *takkana* the sages sought support for it in the Bible. The *takkanot* recorded in tannaitic literature either appeared under the name of an individual authority, like the *takkana* of *Ketuba*, ascribed to Simon b. Shetah, or the *takkana* of *Prosbol*, ascribed to Hillel, while other *takkanot* were ascribed to Ezra and Solomon. As I have pointed out elsewhere the *takkanot* ascribed to Ezra and Solomon were not introduced by them but were the results of the evolution of the halakot developed during the time of the Tannaim. Some of the *takkanot* were of ancient origin while others came into being shortly before the destruction of the Second Temple and even after that period.[72]

The introduction of takkanot was either by the method of *interpretio* or *fictio* and sometimes by both. To illustrate I shall give an instance of one *takkana*. The Talmud ascribes

[71] אלא מעיקרא גזור ולא קיבלו מיניהו ואתו רבנן דשמונים שנה וגזרו וקיבלו מיניהו; see Tosefot *ibid*. אתו אינהו גזור אנושא לשרוף . . . ואתו רבנן דשמונים שנה.

[72] See S. Zeitlin, Takkanot Ezra, *JQR*, viii.

the *takkana* of Erub to Solomon.[73] In the Book of Exodus we read,[74] "Ye shall sit each of you in his place, let no man go out of his place on the seventh day." Literally the meaning is that the ancient Hebrews had no right to leave their "place" on the sabbath day. The Septuagint however renders the words, "his place" his house.[75] This would mean that the Hebrews had no right to go out of their houses on the sabbath day. They were allowed to walk only four cubits from their homes.[76] Later the words "his place" was interpreted to mean his city. Accordingly they were permitted to walk not only four cubits but two thousand cubits.[77] But if a Jew was, forcibly taken into another city on the sabbath day, i. e. kidnapped by pagans, he could walk only four cubits on the sabbath because that city was not his abode.[78] Similarly if a Jew traveled to Jerusalem on the sabbath day to give testimony on the birth of the new moon, in which case the prohibition to travel was suspended, he had no right to walk around in Jerusalem on the sabbath; he had to stay in one place. Actually there was a court in Jerusalem called Beth-Yazek where the witnesses who arrived on the sabbath to give testimony of the birth on the new moon assembled. Rabban Gamaliel, the Elder, amended the law so that such witnesses were to be considered inhabitants of Jerusalem, (i. e. it was their abode), and have the right to walk two thousand cubits in any direction on the sabbath.[79] The

---

[73] Shab. 14b, ‏בשעה שתיקן עירובין ונטילת ידים‎.

[74] 16.29, ‏שבו איש תחתיו אל יצא איש ממקמו ביום השביע‎.

[75] καθίσεσθε ἕκαστος εἰς τοὺς οἴκους ὑμῶν.

[76] Comp. Er. 51; Yer. ibid., ‏שבו איש תחתיו אלו ארבע אמות‎; see also M. ibid. 4, ‏ר' יהושע ור' עקיבא אומר אין לי אלא ד' אמות‎.

[77] See ibid., ‏נאמר כאן מקום ונאמר להלן ושמתי לך מקום מה מקום שנאמר להלן‎ ‏אלפים אמה אף מקום שנאמר כאן אלפים אמה‎; comp. also Tosefta ibid. ‏ואנשי ...‎ ‏עיר קטנה אין להן אלא אלפים אמה בלבד‎.

[78] M. Er. 4, ‏מי שהוציאוהו גוים או רוח רעה אין לו אלא ארבע אמות‎.

[79] See R. H. 23a ‏חצר גדולה היתה בירושלים ובית יעזק היתה נקראת ולשם כל‎ ‏העדים מהכנסין ... לא היו זזין משם כל היום התקין רבן גמליאל הזקן שיהו מהלכין‎

law was further amended so that a Jew had the right to walk throughout the city on the sabbath and two thousand cubits beyond.

The sages introduced *takkanot* to amend the pentateuchal laws as well as the halaka. From the Talmud we learn that if Rosh Hashana fell on the sabbath the sounding of the *shofar* was suspended. In the Temple however the blowing of the *shofar* took precedence over the sabbath, a custom which was in vogue during the Second Commonwealth. After the destruction of the Temple, Rabban Johanan b. Zakkai introduced a *takkana* that in the city of Jabne, where the *Bet Din* was sitting, the blowing of the *shofar* should take precedence over the sabbath.[80] By this *takkana* Rabban Johanan b. Zakkai sought to demonstrate that the Bet Din took the place of the Temple.

The sages not only amended ritual laws but also laws in relation to the family and civil laws. In the early period of Jewish history, i. e. in the time of the Pentateuch, a woman was considered the property of her father and later of her husband. The father had the right to sell her and give her in marriage; the groom had to pay a certain sum of money, called *mohar*, to the father of the girl.[81] A *takkana* was introduced by Simon b. Shetah to amend this ancient halaka. Instead of the groom paying the father money for taking his daughter in marriage he had to write a writ, *ketuba*, in which he pledged all his property as security for two hundred *zuzim* in the case of his death or divorce. The purpose of this *takkana* was to raise the social and

Comp. אלפים אמה לכל רוח . . . הרי הם כאנשי העיר ויש להם אלפים אמה לכל רוח
also M. Er. 4. מי שיצא ברשות . . . יש לו אלפים אמה.

[80] יום טוב של ראש השנה שחל להיות בשבת במקדש היו תוקעין אבל לא במדינה
M. R. H. 4, ר' אלעזר לא התקין ר' יוחנן בן זכאי אלא אלא ביבנה בלבד כשחרב בית המקדש התקין ר' יוחנן בן זכאי שיהו תוקעין בכל מקום שיש בו ב"ד אמר

[81] Ex. 22.16, see S. Zeitlin, The Origin of the Ketubah, *JQR*, 1933; L. Epstein, *The Jewish Marriage Contract*.

economic life of the woman. She was protected economically in case of divorce or the death of her husband and
she was no longer the property of her father but possessed
rights in herself.[82]

The *takkana* of *Prosbol*, introduced by Hillel, was a modification of a pentateuchal law necessitated by the economic
life of the Jews during the period of the Second Commonwealth.[83]

A *g'zera* is a decree of the authorities absolutely independent of the Torah and for a certain period and may be
local. A *takkana*, on the other hand, is universal and
applicable to all classes like halaka.[83a] It must be supported
by a biblical verse.[83b]

Another source of law was *Minhag* — usage. Some of
the *minhagin* were local, confined to a particular city[84] or
to a particular group, like the usage among shippers,[85]
or among members of a caravan.[86] The difference between
minhag and halaka is that although the origin of halaka is
custom, most customs became laws and were so interpreted in the academies.[87] On the hand *minhag* never became a part of law but was only a custom of a particular
group or locality; hence the members of the group or
locality had to follow the custom. A *minhag* was never
interpreted in the academies.[88] It was pointed out above

[82] S. Zeitlin, *ibid.*

[83] *Idem*, JQR, 1947.

[83a] The Greeks likewise held that law must be universal. Οἱ δὲ νόμοι.
κοινὸν καὶ τεταγμένον ταὐτὸ πᾶσιν, Demosthenes, *op. cit.*

[83b] מכאן סמכו לפרוזבל, Hul. 106; מכאן סמכו חכמים לנטילת ידים מן התורה
מכאן סמכו חכמים לכתובת אשה מן התורה, Yer. Sheb. 10; שהוא מן התורה
Ket. 10a.

[84] מנהג העיר, מנהג המדינה.

[85] כנהג הספנין.

[86] מנהג הולכי שיירא.

[87] מאן דאמר הלכה כר' מאיר דרשינן לה בפירקא, Tan. 26b.

[88] מאן דאמר מנהג מידרש לא דרשינן.

that there was an opinion that halaka even supersedes the Torah.[89] Similarly it was the opinion of some of the Amoraim that a *minhag* sometimes nullifies a halaka.[90]

In the study of tannaitic jurisprudence סיג must be taken into consideration. The term סיג means "a fence around the law." In order to prevent the possibility of transgressing the law the sages introduced what is known as "a fence around the law." Although the term סיג in connection with halaka is found in but a few places in the tannaitic literature, the principle involved shaped many of the tannaitic halakot. It is worth noting that the school of Hillel, which was generally lenient in the interpretation and application of the law, resorted to this principle. According to the halaka fowl and cheese must not be eaten at the same time. There is no law, however, which prohibts them from being placed on the same table. According to the school of Shammai fowl and cheese may be so placed but may not be eaten simultaneously.[91] However, according to the liberal school, the Hillelites, fowl and cheese were not allowed to be placed on the same table,[92] for the reason that one might be tempted to eat both, which was forbidden. Therefore, as a preventive measure, they introduced a fence around the law, not to place fowl and cheese on the same table.

The principle of "a fence around the law" was not used as frequently in the tannaitic literature as *takkana* and *g'zera*. It came to be used as an important principle in the

---

[89] See above p. 12.

[90] See Yer. B. M. 7.1, אמר ר' הושעיה זאת אומרת המנהג מבטל את ההלכה.

[91] Hul. 104b, העוף עולה עם הגבינה על השלחן ואינו נאכל דברי ב"ש ובית הלל אומרים לא עולה ולא נאכל.

[92] Comp. also Eduy. 1, שמאי אומר כל הנשים דיין שעתה והלל אומר מפקידה לפקידה; Beza 1, השוחט חיה ועוף ביום טוב בית שמאי אומרים יחפור בדקר ויכסה. Comp. ובית הלל אומרים לא ישחוט אלא א"כ היה לו עפר מוכן מבעור יום. S. Zeitlin, "Les Principes des Controverses Halachiques entre les écoles de Schammai et de Hillel." *REJ.* 1932.

shaping of the halaka after the Jews had lost their independence, when it became necessary for them to make a
fence around the law.[92a]

INTERPRETATION AND LEGAL FICTION

From time to time the Tannaim, in order to carry out
the current needs of the people, adapted the laws to the
changing conditions of society. They sometimes interpreted
the biblical verses so as to bring the pentateuchal law into
consonance with life. We give an example of such an
interpretation. According to the Pentateuch if water was
put upon the seed the latter became susceptible to levitical
uncleanliness.[93] The word זרע may have the meaning —
seed attached to the ground and seed which is plucked from
the ground. During the period of the Second Commonwealth the Jews of Palestine were dependent on the grain
imported from Egypt, then the granary of the world. It is
well known that the fields of Egypt were irrigated with
water from the Nile, thus water was poured on the seed.
Hence, according to the Pentateuch, the seed was susceptible to levitical uncleanliness. In order to make it
possible for the Jews of Palestine, who were concerned
about the laws of levitical uncleanliness, to import the grain
from Egypt, the sages interpreted the word זרע to mean
seed detached from the ground.[94] Thus the law of levitical
uncleanliness did not affect the grain imported from Egypt
since it was watered while still attached to the ground.
This *takkana* was introduced by the sages in order to
facilitate the economic life of the Jews.

[92a] In the Talmud there are some halakot which are defined as
הלכה למשה מסיני. These are few and are not of a major importance in the
development of halaka.

[93] Lev. 11.38. וכי יתן מים על זרע.

[94] Sifra, 11, כשאחה אומר מחוברים טהורים ותלושים טמאים טמאת מקצת וטהרת
מקצה. See S. Zeitlin, Takkanot Ezra, *JQR*, VIII.

Legal fiction is a process whereby a possible state of things was assumed as actually existing.[95] It was applied throughout the entire tannaitic law. I shall cite two examples. The pentateuchal words, "he shall sit in his place," were, as we have already remarked previously, explained to mean sitting, i. e. a Jew had the right to walk throughout the city on the sabbath and two thousand cubits beyond. Then a new law was introduced that if a Jew deposited food in a place located at a distance of two thousand cubits from the city he had the right to walk that distance from the place of depository on the sabbath. This law was promulgated on the assumption that the place where the Jew had deposited food for the sabbath became his abode. This law, known as *Erubin* is a legal fiction — an assumption that the place where a person deposited food on the eve of sabbath could have been made his abode. Thus the Tannaim considered it a fact that it was his abode, and hence he could walk two thousand cubits beyond it.

The idea of legal fiction was introduced by the Tannaim not only into ritual law but into civil law as well. According to the Pentateuch every seventh year was called the sabbatical year, in which, "Every creditor shall release that which he has lent unto his neighbor; he shall not exact it of his neighbor and of his brother because God's release had been proclaimed."[96] Thus, according to the Pentateuch, if a man made a loan and was not paid before the sabbatical year he could not claim it or sue for it. According to the Mishna if a debtor gave the creditor security for the loan even the security was not equal to the value of the loan he was not entitled to a release of his unpaid debt

---

[95] On legal fiction see *The Institutes* by R. Sohm; T. E. Holland, *The Elements of Jurisprudence.*

[96] Deut. 15.1–3.

because of the sabbatical year.[97] The assumption was that
when the creditor received the security from the debtor
the loan was repaid, being actually in exchange for the
debt, even though the security was not equal in value to
the loan.

Although legal fiction was often applied by the Tannaim
no term for it is found in tannaitic literature. Some students are of the opinion that the word הערמה was the term
used by the Tannaim for legal fiction. They point out the
tannaitic passage where it is stated that, according to
Rabbi Joshua if a dam and its young fall into a pit on a
holiday one may pull out the dam in order to slaughter
it and then change one's mind about which animal to
slaughter, and also pull out the young in order to slaughter
it.[98]

According to the halaka the Jews were allowed to work
on a holiday only for the need of their sustenance. Hence,
if an animal fell into a pit they had the right to lift her out
of the pit for slaughter. However it was not permitted
that a dam and its young be slaughtered on the same day.
Hence, in order to release both of them from the pit, a Jew
may mentally designate the dam for slaughter and then
he may change his mind and decide to slaughter its young
instead; thus he acquires the right to lift the young out of
the pit. Now that both are out of the pit he may slaughter
either one. We have here not a legal fiction but a loophole
in the law. Because of the ambiguity of the law an astute
person may find the loophole and get around the law.[99]

[97] Tos. Sheb. 8.5, המלוה את חבירו על המשכון אף על פי שהחוב מרובה על
המשכון אינו משמט. See also B. M. 82, לבעל חוב שקונה משכון . . .
[98] Beza, 37, אותו ואת בנו שנפלו לבור ר' אליעזר אומר מעלה את הראשון על
מנת לשחטו ושוחטו והשני עושה לו פרנסה במקומו כדי שלא ימות ר' יהושע אומר מעלה
את הראשון על מנת לשחטו ואינו שוחטו וחוזר ומערים ומעלה השני רצה זה שוחט רצה
זה שוחט.
[99] See Pes. 9a, מערים אדם על תבואתו ומכניסה במוץ שלה כדי שתהא בהמתו
אוכלת ופטורה מן המעשר.

Legal fiction is a branch of law and had great influence in molding the halaka, while הערמה is only a loophole to get around the law, and it was a question among the authorities whether a person had the right to take advantage of the ambiguity of the law for his own benefit.[100]

THE SCHOOLS OF SHAMMAI AND HILLEL

Jurisprudence of the time of the Second Temple may be divided into two branches, one dealing with the laws from the time of the Restoration to the time when Simon the Hasmonean was elected high priest and ethnarch, when the Theocracy was abolished and was succeeded by a Commonwealth; and the other relating to the second period from the establishment of the Commonwealth to the suppression of the revolt of Bar Kokba, when the sages assembled in Galilee, in the city Usha. Up to the time of Simon, the high priest had full power over the Jews, both spiritually and temporally, appointing judges and sanctioning and interpreting the laws. After the establishment of the Commonwealth a supreme court — Bet Din — was instituted, most likely by the Great Synagogue which elected Simon as the High Priest and Ethnarch. At the head of the Bet Din were two men, one had the title *Nasi*, and the other *Ab Bet Din.*.

These two, *Nasi* and *Ab Bet Din*, were the representatives of two schools of thought in Jewish law. The first three presidents were of the conservative and the first three *Ab Bet Din* were of the liberal school. The last two presidents were of the liberal and the last two *Ab Bet Din* were of the conservative school.[101] After the death of Hillel and

---

[100] See M. K. 12b, חנאי היא דחניא אין מערימין בכך ר' יוסי בר יהודה אומר מערימין.

[101] Tosefta Hag. סימיהם לא נחלקו אלא על הסמיכה, חמשה זוגות הן שלשה מזוגות הראשונים שאמרו שלא לסמוך היו נשיאים ושנים אבות בית דין, שנים מזוגות

Shammai the office of *Ab Bet Din* was abolished. Gamaliel, the grandson of Hillel, had the title Rabbenu since he was the sole head of the *Bet Din*.

While the schools named after their great masters, Hillel and Shammai, represented liberalism and conservatism respectively, they had their beginning with the 'first pair" Jose ben Joezer and Jose ben Johanan. A parallel instance of origin of similar schools of thought is found in Roman jurisprudence. It is known that in the time of August Caesar there came into being two schools of strongly contrasting characters and tendencies. The actual founders of these two schools were two jurists, Ateius Capito and Antistius Labeo; the former was a strong supporter of imperial despotism and of conservative tendencies, while the latter, who was of an independent spirit, upheld republicanism and was more inclined to break with established institutions if such were life's demands. The schools, however, were named after later jurists, their disciples. The followers of Capito were usually called Sabinians, after his pupil Masurius Sabinus; those of Labeo were called Proculians, after Julius Proculius, a pupil not of Labeo, himself, but of his disciple, Nerva, the grandfather of the Emperor Nerva. For several generations, from the days of Augustus to the days of Antonines, every jurist enrolled himself under one flag or the other and was known as a Sabinian or Proculian. Similarly the schools of Shammai and Hillel were most likely older than their teachers, and many halakot of these two schools had been formulated before the time of Shammai and Hillel.

Some of the sages were not at all in sympathy with the

האחרונים שאמרו לסמוך היו נשיאים ושנים אבות בית דין דברי ר' מאיר וחכמים אומרים
שמעון בן שטח היה נשיא ויהודה בן טבאי אב בית דין ;comp. also Yer. *ibid.* 2.
See S. Zeitlin, The Semikah Controversy between the Zugoth, *JQR*,
VII, *idem*. חורב, תרצ"ט, הפרושים; L. Ginzberg, *op. cit.*

change from high priest to *Bet Din*, i. e. from Theocracy
to Nomocracy. This feeling is reflected in two passages in
the Talmud. One reads: "All the schools (teachers) which
arose in Israel from the days of Moses until the days of
Jose ben Joezer studied the Torah as Moses did, but afterwards they did not study the Torah as Moses did."[102] The
other passage reads: "All the schools (teachers) which arose
in Israel from the days of Moses until the days of Jose ben
Joezer were without reproach but afterwards they were of
reproach."[103] Before the establishment of the *Bet Din*
there were no halakic controversies, the high priest was the
sole authority. He decided the law as Moses did. With
the establishment of the Bet Din there arose halakic controversies. The first controversies recorded were between
Jose ben Joezer, who was the first *Nasi*, and Jose ben
Johanan, who was the first *Ab Bet Din*.[104]

After the establishment of the *Bet Din* Jewish law was
revolutionized. Although the Pentateuch was the basis of
Jewish law and was the constitution of the people, the
sages, in order to bring the halaka into consonance with
life, interpreted and amended the pentateuchal laws. While
the laws of the Pentateuch still had a system of tribal
justice, the tannaitic laws, however, represent the justice
of a great civilization and had far reaching influence on
other civilizations. We refer to that upon the canon law
of the Church in spite of the fact that in the early days of
Christianity the leaders of the Church were opposed to what
they called tradition and the laws of the scribes.

---

[102] Tem. 15b. (שמת) כל אשכולות שעמדו להן לישראל מימות משה עד ימות
יוסי בן יעזר היו לומדין תורה כמשה רבינו מכאן ואילך לא היו לומדין תורה כמ־־
רבינו. The reading עד ימות יוסי, was suggested by Graetz, *Monatsschrift*,
1869.

כל אשכולות שעמדו לישראל מימות משה עד ימות (שמת) יוסי בן יעזר לא היו ג
בהם שום דופי מכאן ואילך היה בהם שום דופי, *ibid.*

[104] See Yer. H. 2, בראשונה לא היתה מחלוקת בישראל אלא על הסמיכה בלבד.

Tannaitic Jurisprudence

Furtum (theft) was regarded in the Pentateuch as among *delicta privata*, that is matters in which the state had no right to interfere. The *actio furti* could only be brought by the victim, not by the state. Even the penalty, a fine paid by the offender, had to be turned over to the injured person and not to the state as in modern laws. Moreover the injured person could forgive the transgressor and refuse to accept any fine. If he acted so the state had no authority to interfere, since the transgressor was not considered a criminal in the eyes of the state. According to tannaitic law, however, the transgressor, besides paying a fine to the victim, was punished by the court.[105] Theft became a crime against society.

Not only theft but maiming or bodily mutilation had been considered a private wrong. The injured person had the right to fix the punishment for the offender, and if the former suffered the loss of an eye or a tooth he was allowed to gouge out an eye, extract a tooth of the offender. That was the law of the Pentateuch, "An eye for an eye, a tooth for a tooth."[106] However the victim could absolve entirely the man who caused the injury. *Talio* was only the extreme satisfaction which an injured person could demand, the state had no right to interfere. The state could not punish the offender; since he was not held guilty of a crime against society. A similar conception was held in ancient Rome. *Si membrum rupsit, ni cum eo pacit talio esto*, (the Twelve Tables) that is, if the injured man did not get any satisfaction he might apply to *talio*.[107]

---

[105] B. M. 91a, לוקה ומשלם.

[106] עין תחת עין שן תחת שן כאשר יתן מום באדם כן ינתן בו.

[107] Compare also Josephus, *Ant.* 4.8, 35. "He that maimeth any one, let him undergo the like himself and be deprived of the same member of which he deprived the other, unless he that is maimed will accept

Even homicide in the Pentateuch was not considered *delicta publica*, a crime against society, but against the family of the victim; hence the kin of the family had to avenge the murder. The authorities had to decide whether a person was killed by accident or deliberately.[108] The execution was carried out by "the avenger of the blood." According to the Pentateuch the slayer could flee to a city of refuge and if he could prove that the dead man had been killed by accident and was not his enemy, he had to remain in the city of refuge until the death of the high priest[109] (the head of the community). There he was to be protected from the "avenger of the blood." However, if it was proved that the accused had killed the man deliberately, the authorities had to deliver him to the "avenger of the blood" who was supposed to kill him. In all primitive society the kin of the victim had the right to take ransom from the murderer and could make private arrangements with him. Such arrangement was called *compositio*. According to the Pentateuch the "avenger of the blood" had no right to take ransom from the murderer but had to kill him.[110] With the establishment of the *Bet Din* homicide became a *delicta publica*, a crime against the state; the institution of the "avenger of the blood" was abolished and the accused was brought before a constituted court. Lynching which was practiced in primitive society became a crime against

of money instead of it; for the law makes the sufferer the judge of the value of what he hath suffered and permits him to estimate it, unless he will be more severe." On the attitude of the Pharisees and of Jesus toward the law of *talio*, see S. Zeitlin, *Who Crucified Jesus* , pp. 114–121.

[108] See Numb. 35.24. ‏והצילו ... נאל הדם ובין המכה בין העדה ושפטו‏

‏ולא ימות ביד נאל הדם עד עמדו לפני‏, Josh. 20.9, ‏העדה את הרצח מיד נאל הדם‏ ‏העדה.‏

[109] ‏וישב בה עד מות הכהן הגדול‏, *ibid*. It is worth while noting that Demosthenes relates that in Greece manslaughter was punished by exile. ἐάν τίς ἐπ᾽ ἀκουσίῳ φόνῳ πεφευγώς, μήπω τῷ ἐκβαλόντων αὐτὸν ᾐδεσμένων αἰτίαν ἔχῃ ἑτέρου φόνου ἑκουσίου. (*Against Aristocrates*, 77).

[110] Numb. 35. ‏נאל הדם ימית את הרוצח ... ולא תקחו כפר לנפש רצח.‏

the state since no individual had the right to administer justice.

In the Pentateuch only a person's act is recognized. The idea of intention is not found there. An act takes place when a voluntary movement of the body is made, while an accident or an event occurs where there is no such voluntary movement. If a man jumps from a bridge it is an act because it is accompanied by volition. If he falls or is pushed from a bridge it is an accident or an event because there is no volition. Similarly if the hand of a person is forcibly guided into writing a signature, this is not considered an act since will is absent. Intention, however, refers only to a future act — the consequence of the first act; in other words to the ultimate purpose — to the end and not to the means. If a person throws a missile in order to break some object or to injure some one; the breaking and the injuring are the consequences of the first act of throwing. The first act resulted from the will of throwing and that was the means to the end of injuring. Intention refers only to the end — to the consequence of the first act and not to the means. The idea of intention as a legal principle was introduced by the school of Hillel and had a revolutionary effect on Jewish jurisprudence.[111]

Tannaitic jurisprudence was progressive, always with a view to the advancement of society. Its legal principles were founded on equity and morals, and revolutionary modifications of the Pentateuch are evident in all its branches. The progressiveness of tannaitic jurisprudence is exemplified in all the halakot. The pentateuchal laws dealing with inheritance indicate that while man is mortal property is permanent. If a person dies his estate is inher-

[111] See S. Zeitlin, Studies in Tannaitic Jurisprudence, *Journal of Jewish Lore and Philosophy*, Vol. 1; *idem*. Asmakta or Intention, *JQR*, V.XIX.

ited by his sons; where there are no sons it passes to his daughters and where there are no daughters it goes to the nearest kin.[112] It must always remain in the family or tribe. If a man sells his real property it must be redeemed and returned to him; if it is not redeemed then it is returned to him in the year of the Jubilee, except if he sells his house in a "walled city" and has not redeemed it within a year, in which case the house remains in the hands of the purchaser,[113] apparently as a punishment for not redeeming it. The idea of testament is not found in the Pentateuch for the simple reason that property cannot be transferred to a stranger. But according to the tannaitic law a man may write a testament[114] so that after his death part of his property may go to a stranger. This law completely reversed the pentateuchal conception of inheritance, wherein a man was considered mortal and property permanent. According to tannaitic jurisprudence man is immortal but the title to property is limitable by time. A man may give away his property by will even ten years after his death and the authorities must carry out his provision.[115]

The conception of partnership, that more than one person may have rights and title to the same property, and the idea of agency, that a person may transfer his rights to another man to act for him, is not recognized in the Pentateuch. The view that a person may acquire property by possession and also that he has the right to relinquish privileges and liabilities connected with a property is not

---

[112] Numb. 27. איש כי ימות ובן אין לו והעברתם את נחלתו לבתו . . . ונתחם נחלתו לשארו הקרוב אליו ממשפחתו.

[113] Lev. 25, בשנת היובל הזאת תשבו איש אל אחזתו . . . ואיש כי ימכר בית מושב עיר חומה והיתה גאלתו עד תם שנת ממכרו . . . ואם לא יגאל עד מלאת לו שנה תמימ— וקם הבית אשר בעיר אשר (לא) לו חמה לצמיתות לקנה אתו.

[114] See B. B. chs. 8-9.

[115] See H. S. Maine, *Ancient Law*, Ch. VI. The early history of testamentary succession.

found. Neither does the Pentateuch speak of *res nullis*.
The entire conception of *jus in rem* and *jus in personam*
was highly developed in tannaitic jurisprudence.

THE HALAKA AS A MODE OF LIFE

Tannaitic law actually shaped and molded the lives of
the Jews. The Greeks made law a philosophy, the Romans
made it a science, the Jews made law their religion. Judaism, from the time when it became a Nomocracy, became
a religion of laws based on equity and high moral principles.
As a matter of fact the word that has the connotation of
religion is *dat* — law. In the tannaitic literature the phrase
המיר את דתו means "he changed his religion."[116] The author
of III Maccabees says that Dositheus, who was by birth
a Jew and later gave up his religion, used the words "he
changed his law."[117] In biblical times the expression used
was changed his god.[118] In the tannaitic period, when
Judaism became a universal religion and the God of Israel
was considered the God of the entire universe, no person
could change his God since there was only one God. Thus,
to say of a person that he left the Jewish people, the term
used was "he changed his law." The term *dat* was used by
the Jews in the same manner as *religio* by the Romans.[119]

---

[116] See Suk., 56b, שהטירה דתה; Pes. 96a המרת הדת.

[117] τοῦτον δὲ' διαγαγὼν Δωσίθεος ὁ Δριμύλου λεγόμενος το γένος
Ἰουδαῖος ὕστερον δὲ μεταβαλὼν τὰ νόμιμα καὶ τῶν πατρίων δογ-
μάτων ἀπηλλοτριωμένος. (1.3) Comp. also Josephus, *Jewish War*, VII;
II Mac. 6.24.

Charles (*The Apochrypha*, Ad. Loc.) translated the words μεταβαλὼν τὰ νόμιμα "abandoned the observance of the law." He did not
recognize that these Greek words μεταβαλὼν τα νόμιμα were actually
a rendering of the Hebrew המיר את דתו "he changed his religion."

[118] Jer. 2.11. ההמיר גוי אלהים.

[119] Modern etymologists are of the opinion that the word *religio* is
derived from the root *ligo* — to tie, bind together. Cicero (*De Natura
Deorum* 11. 28, 72) derives the word *religio* from *relegere*, to relate.
Dr. M. Kaplan in his recent book, *The Future of the American Jew*,

It has been shown above that the Tannaim always bore
in mind that the law was made for man and not man for
the law. One sage expressed it well in saying that sabbath
is for the man and not man for the sabbath;[120] the halaka
was not to be a burden upon the Jews. It has also been
shown that although they deviated from the Pentateuch
they always enacted laws in its spirit. They never abrogated
the biblical law but interpreted it. Some people believe
that the pentateuchal and tannaitic laws are not adjusted
to our present civilization and would like to have them
abrogated, while others do not recognize the fact that some
laws, particularly decrees, are obsolete and are not observed
today. Both groups are mistaken. Jewish law cannot be
abrogated nor can the chain of Jewish tradition be broken.
If one seeks to abrogate the Jewish law one will ultimately
be lost to the Jewish fold, as happened with the Karaites.
Some laws, however, must be interpreted but this must be

1948, made the following assertion, "In fact, there is really no word
for religion in the entire Biblical and Rabbinical literature. Even
in the medieval philosophical literature there is no exact equivalent for
the concept *religion*. The Hebrew word *dat*, which occurs frequently
in Jewish theological writings of the Middle Ages, is wrongly translated
by the word religion; it really means law." Dr. Kaplan is apparently
unaware of the fact that the word *dat* was used in tannaitic literature
in the sense of religion and overlooks the fact that in the Hellenistic
literature the term *dat*, νόμος was used in the sense of changing one's
religion.

Those who believe that Judaism is a civilization are either unaware
of or ignore Jewish history. Judaism is a religion — a nomocracy. In
the bible the term of worship of God, religion, was אמונה *fides*. Likewise
in the New Testament, as well as in the writings of the Church Fathers,
the word religion does not occur. The word πίστεως *fides*, faith, belief
in Jesus, is used. Only the Fathers who wrote in Latin used the word
religio. In the Hellenistic literature the term for worship, religion, was
εὐσέβεια or θρησκεία, ὁσιότης. Thus Kaplan's assertion "there is
really no word for religion in the entire Biblical Rabbinical literature,"
is erroneous.

[120] Yoma 86b היא מסורה בידכם ולא אתם מסורים בידה

done in the spirit of Judaism and by authorities in Rabbinical law — תלמידי חכמים.

Let us hope that the Third Commonwealth, the Republic of Israel, will follow the spirit of the sages of the Second Commonwealth by enacting laws in consonance with life. This must be done in the true spirit of universal Judaism. We should take a lesson from the history of the Second Commonwealth. Let us hope that the Synagogue will not be involved in political struggles. There must be a Religious Court (Sanhedrin) separated from the political Sanhedrin.

MIDRASH: A HISTORICAL STUDY

Considerable confusion prevails on the origin of the Midrash. The general opinion is that the books *Mekilta*, *Sifra* and *Sifre* are Midrash Halaka, while as a matter of fact they are Midrash Torah. Likewise, the theory that the teaching of the Midrash form is older than the Mishna is historically untrue.

As is apparent from the verse, "It is written in the Midrash of the Prophet Iddo"[1] in the Second Book of Chronicles, there was a Midrash in the time of the prophets. Scholars have recognized that this particular Midrash had no connection with the subsequent Midrash of the *Mekilta*, *Sifra* and *Sifre*, or with the Midrash of the Book of Genesis, but they have been unaware of the nature of the earlier Midrash. Claims have been advanced that Midrashim on the prophetic books had been in existence during the Second Commonwealth. This hypothesis is unfounded and can be ascribed only to a lack of knowledge of the origin of the Midrash.

I

The word מדרש Midrash is derived from the word דרש to inquire. We are told in the Book of Leviticus that Moses inquired about the goat of the sin-offering, not knowing it had been burnt, and he became angry with Eleazar and Ithamar, the sons of Aaron, for not eating it in the holy place.[2] When a person was in difficulty he or

---

[1] כתובים במדרש הנביא עדו, 13.22. The LXX has ἐπὶ βιβλίῳ τοῦ προφή-του 'Αδδώ. Comp., however, *Hexapla* ἐν τῇ ἐκζητήσει τοῦ προφήτου; Vulgate, *Scripta sunt diligentissime in Libro Addo Prophetae, in Commentario Prophetae Iddo.*

[2] ואת שעיר החטאת דרש דרש משה 16–7.

41

she inquired of God for a solution. Rebekah, for example,
went to inquire of the Lord, when she was pregnant, "And,"
as the verse in Genesis states, "the children struggled
together within her; and she said, "if it be so, wherefore do
I live?"[3] We have another example in the First Book of
Samuel, about Saul, who, when the asses of his father
went astray and were lost ... went to a man of God to
inquire.[4] Incidentally, it is stated: "Beforetime in Israel,
when a man went to inquire of God, thus he said: 'Come and
let us go to the seer'; for he that is now called a prophet
was before-time called a seer."[5] It is clear then that when
a person suffered a loss or underwent a misfortune, he
went and asked that God foretell the outcome. Apparently,
a particular person called a seer was the intermediary
between God and the person troubled. The queries were
brought to the seer, who was called the man of God. This
function of seer was taken over after the time of Samuel by
a man called a prophet. He answered all the queries in the
name of God. We are told that when Saul was in great
distress after Samuel's death because the Philistines in-
vaded Israel, and he had no prophet to consult, he said to
his servant, "Seek me a woman that has a familiar spirit
that I may go to her and ואדרשה בה inquire of her."[6]

It is related in the Book of Kings that when Abijah, the
son of the King, fell sick, the latter told his wife to go to
the prophet and ask what is to become of the child.[7] The
Lord informed the Prophet Ahijah, "Behold, the wife of
Jeroboam cometh to inquire of thee concerning her son."[8]

---

[3] Gen. 25.22, ‏והאמר אם כן למה זה אנכי ותלך לדרש את יהוה‎.

[4] I Sam. 9.6–10.

[5] ‏לפנים בישראל כה אמר האיש בלכתו לדרוש את אלהים לכו ונלכה עד הראה כי‎
‏לנביא היום יקרא לפנים הראה‎.

[6] Ibid., 28.6–7, ‏וישאל שאול ביהוה ולא ענהו יהוה גם בחלמות גם באורים גם‎
‏בנביאם . . . בקשו לי אשת בעלת אוב ואלכה אליה ואדרשה בה‎.

[7] I Kings 14.1–4.

[8] ‏הנה אשת ירבעם באה לדרש דבר מעמך אל בנה כי חלה הוא כזה וכזה תדבר אליה‎.

In the account of the war between Aram and Israel, we are
told that Jehoshaphat, the king of Judah said to the king
of Israel, "Inquire דרש the word of the Lord today."[9]
When King Ahaziah was injured by falling down through
the lattice of his upper chamber he sent messengers and
said to them, "Go, דרשו inquire of Baal-zebub, the god of
Ekron, whether I shall recover of this sickness."[10] Elijah,
who met the messengers in the name of the Lord, said to
them, "Thus said the Lord. Is it because there is no God
in Israel that thou sendest to inquire of Baal-zebub?"[11]
Further, we are told in the same Second Book of Kings,
that when the king of Israel who was joined by the kings of
Judah and Edom in the war against the king of Moab and
they could find no water for the army and the cattle,
Jehoshaphat, the king of Judah asked, "Is there not here
a prophet of the Lord that we may inquire of the Lord
by him?"[12]

When a Scroll of the Torah was found in the Temple by
the high priest and was brought to the King Josiah and
read to him, the latter rent his clothes and asked the priest
to inquire of the Lord "for them and for the people and for
all Judah."[13] It is clear then from the prophetic books that
people in times of distress went to the prophets to inquire
what the Lord had in store for them.

The author of the Chronicles wrote that King Asa was
a righteous man and followed the ways of God, and that he
commanded the people of Judaea לדרוש "to inquire from
the Lord the God of their fathers and to do the Torah and
the commandments."[14] He further related that the people

---

[9] *Ibid.* 22.5–7, דרש נא כיום את דבר יהוה . . . האין פה נביא ליהוה עוד ונדרשה מאתו.
[10] II Kings 1.2–16, לכו דרשו בבעל זבוב אלהי עקרון אם אחיה מחלי זה.
[11] המבלי אין אלהים בישראל לדרוש בדברו
[12] *Ibid.* 3.11, האין פה נביא ליהוה ונדרשה את יהוה.
[13] *Ibid.*
[14] II Chron. 14.3, ויאמר ליהודה לדרוש את יהוה אלהי אבותיהם ולעשות את
התורה והמצוה.

entered into a covenant to beseech the Lord;[15] however, the author added reproachfully that Asa on becoming sick did not beseech God (the Lord) but the physicians.[16] The author speaking of King Jehoshaphat says that "he walked in the ways of his father, David, and did not inquire of the Baalim." On one occasion he asked,[17] "Is there not here besides a prophet of the Lord that we might inquire of him?"[18] To sum up, we can draw the following conclusions from the biblical books. If there were any problems relating to either the personal life of the king or the welfare of the country during the time of the First Temple, inquiry was made of the seers or prophets who would reply in the name of God. When the wicked kings went to foreign gods to make their inquiries, this was considered a sin, it meant that they did not worship the God of Israel but honored Baal and the other gods.

The seers and the prophets kept records of their prophecies and interpretations of the inquiries of the kings and the people; hence we have such statements as, "the rest of the acts of Solomon . . . are written . . . in the visions of Jedo, the seer, concerning Jeroboam, the son of Nebat;[19] or the statements, "the rest of the acts of Abijah, and his ways, and his sayings, are written in the Midrash of the prophet Iddo;[20] "now concerning his [Joash] sons . . . and the rebuilding of the house of God they are written in the Midrash of the book of the kings.[21] The prophecies which the seers and the prophets delivered to the kings

---

[15] *Ibid.* 15.12–13, וכל אשר . . . ויבאו בברית לדרוש את יהוה אלהי אבותיהם לא ידרש ליהוה אלהי ישראל.

[16] *Ibid.* 16.12, וגם בחליו לא דרש את יהוה כי אם ברפאים.

[17] *Ibid.* 17.3, ולא דרש לבעלים.

[18] *Ibid.* 18.6, האין פה נביא ליהוה ונדרשה מאתו.

[19] *Ibid.* 9.29, ושאר דברי שלמה הראשונים והאחרונים הלא הם כתובים על דברי נתן הנביא ועל נבואת אחיה השילוני ובחזות יעדי החזה על ירבעם בן נבט.

[20] *Ibid.* 13.22, ויתר דברי אביה ודרכיו ודבריו כתובים במדרש הנביא עדו.

[21] *Ibid.* 24.27, ובניו ורב המשא עליו ויסוד בית אלהים הנם כתובים על מדרש ספר המלכים.

were kept in writing and were called the Midrash, i. e., the book in which were recorded the inquiries of the kings and the answers and explanations of the seers and the prophets.

II

The captivity of the Judaeans in Babylonia, although for only a short period, wrought a great revolution in their life. When they were exiled from the Land of Judaea they were idol worshippers. All the kings, with few exceptions, worshipped foreign gods. Even Solomon when advanced in years worshipped foreign gods; however, when the people returned to Judaea, monotheism prevailed. Temples or altars no longer were built to idols. Even the expression "foreign gods" אלהים אחרים which occurs frequently in the Torah, no longer occurs in the literature after the Restoration. The term "idols"[22] was substituted. The God of Israel not only was the God of Judaea but was recognized by the Jews as the only God of the entire universe.

Ezra, who was one of the leaders of the Restoration, was responsible for the canonization of the Pentateuch. While it is true that the Torah of Moses was known to the people in the time of the First Temple, it was not binding on them. It was not considered the constitution of the State. This is evident from the fact that most of the kings of Judah — not to speak of the kings of Israel — worshipped foreign gods; after the time of Ezra, however, the Torah became the constitution of the Jews and the worship of foreign gods disappeared entirely from the land.[23] The seers and prophets disappeared after the canonization of the five books of Moses.

The author of the Book of Ezra relates that "Ezra had set his heart to inquire the law of the Lord, and to do it, and to teach in Israel ordinances and law."[24] The word

---

[22] εἴδωλον, אלילים, ע״ז.   [23] Comp. Yoma 69b.

[24] כי עזרא הכין לבבו לדרש את תורת יהוה ולעשות וללמד בישראל חק ומשפט 7.10.

לדרוש to inquire — which occurs frequently in biblical books of the pre-Restoration period in connection with the inquiring of God or the prophets of God, was applied after the Restoration to the inquiring and interpretation of the Torah.[25]

The word לדרוש has the connotation "to inquire" or "to interpret" the biblical passages. Since the canonization of the Torah, the seers and prophets disappeared. There is a statement in rabbinical literature that prophecies ceased in Israel after the death of Haggai, Zechariah and Malachi.[26] The coincidence of the canonization of the Pentateuch and the disappearance of the prophets was not accidental. There are no accidents in history. Each event, either of a positive or negative character, has its reason and cause. The reason for the disappearance of the seers and prophets, according to my opinion, was due to the canonization of the Pentateuch. These prophets and seers disappeared because there was no longer a need for them, or we may even conclude that the sages were actually opposed to them. The sages wanted the Jews, rather, to turn to them for the interpretation of the words of God, as recorded in the Torah. They also saw harm in resorting to the prophets. As we know, there were false as well as true prophets.

The various Midrashim where the seers and prophets recorded the inquiries made of them, were lost after the Restoration,[27] but the writings of the prophets, like those

---

[25] The word דרש which occurs frequently in the Bible with the meaning of to inquire of God or the prophet never occurs in this sense in the tannaitic literature. This word was employed in the sense of interpreting the biblical verses, first, for the purpose of halaka and later for Agada.

[26] B. B. 14b, הוו נביאים סוף ומלאכי זכריה חני; מיום שהרב בית המקדש נטלה; (ibid. p. 12) מתנבאים מן הנביאים וניתנה לחכמים; עד כאן היו הנביאים מתנבאים ברוח הקדש מיכן ואילך הט אזנך ושמע דברי חכמים (סדר עולם רבא); ומתו נביאים האחרונים חני זכריה ומלאכי באותו היום פסקה נבואה מישראל (סדר עולם ed. Neubauer); (Yer. Mak., B. Yoma 21b) רוח הקדש . . . שחסר דברים חמש אלו; כמשמתו נביאים האחרונים חני זכריה ומלאכי נסתלקה רוח הקדש מישראל (Yoma 9).

[27] Or destroyed, as the writings of the false prophets were destroyed.

of Isaiah, Jeremiah, Ezekiel, Amos and Micah and others
were preserved. The reason is self-evident. The Midrashim
of the seers and prophets dealt with the inquiries put to
them by the kings and other individuals. Their apothegms
and reproaches had personal significance and were not of
national or universal interest. Even the words of Elijah,
who became a legendary figure, not only in Jewish literature
but in the Christian as well, were largely forgotten in spite
of his zealousness for the God of Israel, and his reputation
for the miracles he performed, and the story of his ascen-
sion to heaven. His sayings had only a temporary value
because he dealt with the King of Israel, while, on the other
hand, the prophecies of Isaiah and the others not only had
a national but also a universal appeal. The latter preached
on the universality of God and the relations between man
and his fellow-man; their words had value not only for that
time but for all time, and were to have an everlasting
influence over humanity.

Only the books which were canonized, i. e., considered
holy — as having been revealed by God to Moses, — were to
be inquired into, searched and interpreted. When the books
of the prophets were added to the canon, that is when they
also were considered holy since it was held that the
prophets also received revelations, their writings also were
to be interpreted. The Hagiographa however, were not
included in the canon. They were outside of it and were
not to be interpreted as they were considered as not having
been revealed by God.

A Mishna relates that the high priest was not permitted
to sleep on the eve of the Day of Atonement. In order to
stay awake he used to hold a discourse, interpreting biblical
passages; however, if he was not learned, the scholars
discoursed for him, interpreting biblical verses; but if he
was familiar with the readings of the scriptures, he would
read them. If he could not read, the scholars would read

for him.[28] The question was asked, "From what would they
read before him?" The answer was given that they read
from the book of Job, Ezra and Chronicles. "Zecheriah
ben Kebutal said, "I have often read before him from the
book of Daniel."[29] According to a tannaitic source given
in the Palestinian Talmud, they read for him from the books
of Proverbs and the Psalms,[30] i. e., from all the books which
became known as the Hagiographa. The meaning of the
Mishna is that if a high priest was a scholar, he interpreted
the biblical books, the Pentateuch and the prophetic books,
but if he was not capable of doing so, then other scholars
interpreted these books for him. If he could read but was
not capable of understanding the biblical "interpretations,"
he read certain Scriptures and if he could not read at all,
then others read for him. The reason that the expression
they "read" for him from the books of Hagiographa is
used, was that these books could not be interpreted, because
they had not yet been canonized, and they were not considered as having been revealed by God. They were to be
read only, but the Pentateuch and the prophetic books were
to be interpreted. This is evident from another statement
in the Palestinian Talmud, to the effect that when the Book
of Esther was accepted in the canon, it was allowed to be
interpreted.[31]

The Hagiographa were canonized in the year 65; the
Hebrew canon then contained twenty-two books divided
into three parts, the Torah, The Prophets, and the Hagiographa. The Book of Ecclesiastes was added at the school
of Jabneh (circa 90–100 CE). The Book of Esther was
added at a later time at the Academy of Oushah, making

---

[28] Yoma 1, אם הוא היה חכם דורש ואם לאו תלמידי חכמים דורשים לפניו ואם
רגיל לקרות קורא ואם לאו קורין לפניו.

[29] ובמה קורין לפניו באיוב ובעזרא ובדברי הימים זכריה בן קבוטל אמר פעמים
הרבה קריתי לפניו בדניאל.

[30] תני במשלי ובתילים. Comp. S. Zeitlin, הצדוקים והפרושים, pp. 25–6.

[31] Yer. Meg. 1, זאת אומרת שמגלת אסתר ניתנה להידרש.

the Hebrew canon consist of twenty-four books.[32] The canonization of the Hagiographa at such a late date is the reason that there are no haftarot from the *Ketubim*. When these were canonized haftarot already had been assigned to the Pentateuchal portions.[33]

[32] See S. Zeitlin, *An Historical Study of the Canonization of the Hebrew Scriptures*, 1933.

[33] Dr. Segal, in *JBL*, March 1953, p. 37, dealing with the Promulgation of the Authoritative Text of the Hebrew Bible wrote, "The Synod of Jabneh did not deal with the question of the canon as such. It only touched incidentally on the sanctity of the two late books of the Hagiography, Koheleth and Canticles, in connection with discussion of the application of the so-called decree of the Uncleanliness of the Hands (טומאת ידים), viz. that the touch of a scroll of scripture by the hands required the hands to be washed before they could handle produce of the priestly heave-offering (תרומה)." The Hebrew canon was canonized in the year 65, a few years before the destruction of the Second Temple. In this canon there was included the Song of Songs after a long discussion, but the Book of Ecclesiastes was rejected after debate. Some sages again raised the question at the Academy of Jabneh, of the sanctity of the Song of Songs but this opinion was rejected. It was maintained that the Song of Songs was included in the canon at the conclave of 65, and therefore, the question of its sanctity was closed. The Book of Ecclesiastes which was rejected at the conclave of 65 was canonized at the Academy of Jabneh. The technical term for canonization became טומאת ידים, i. e., the canonized book. These books which defiled the hands were holy. They are part of the Hebrew canon. The books which do not defile the hands were not holy. They are not a part of the Hebrew canon. (See my essay *An Historical Study of the Canonization of the Hebrew Scriptures*, pp. 15–21.

Dr. Segal says, "The so-called uncleanliness of hands (טומאת ידים), viz. that the touch of a scroll of scripture by the hands required the hands to be washed before they could handle produce of the priestly heave-offering (תרומה)." This is not true. Dr. Segal misunderstood the tannaitic literature in reference to the "defilement of the hands" טומאת ידים and the "washing of the hands" נטילת ידים.

It seems Dr. Segal did not grasp the difference between טומאת ידים which is גזרה a decree, and washing the hands נטילת ידים which is a *takkana*. The "defilement of the hands" was decreed in the year 65, a few years before the destruction of the Temple, while the takkana, "washing of the hands" was promulgated after the destruction of the Temple.

It seems that Dr. Segal does not know even the difference between the term מטמא חברתה and מטמא פוסל. ... כתבי הקדש מטמאין את הידים; היד מטמא חברתה; כתבי הקדש שניים מטמאים את הידים and הספר והידים... אלו פוסלין את התרומה; כל הפוסל את התרומה מטמא את הידים להיות שניות.

III

The sages who interpreted the Bible were called *Darshanim*.[34] The methods and the form of the interpretation were called Midrash. The place where the sages assembled to interpret the Bible for the purpose of establishing the halakot was known as the *Bet haMidrash*.[35]

The method of Midrash used in interpreting the biblical verses in order to establish the halakot came into vogue very early; this does not mean however that, the Midrash form is older than the halakot. Halakot — laws — preceded the Midrash form. Some of the halakot recorded in the Mishna are as old as the Pentateuch.[36] The writings of the prophets,[37] as well as the Hagiographa[38] contain references to laws (halakot) not mentioned in the Pentateuch. There were always laws not embodied in the Torah; these were the unwritten laws. That the halakot preceded the Midrash form can be deduced from an episode in the life of Hillel. One of the three reasons for Hillel's going to Judaea was to solve some contradictory verses in the Pentateuch.[39] He noted that it was stated in one verse that unleavened bread was to be eaten for six days,[40] while in another verse it was stated it should be eaten for seven days.[41] Hillel reconciled these verses by showing that the verse wherein it was stated that unleavened bread was to be eaten for seven days refers to the old harvest, while the other verse mentioning six days referred to the new harvest.[42] The Jews were not allowed to eat of the new harvest until the six-

---

[34] שמעיה ואבטליון שהן חכמים גדולים ודרשנין גדולים, comp. Pes. 70b; דרשנים

משמת בן זומא בטלו דורשנים (תוספתא סוטה, טו).

[35] See Yoma 35b, Meg. 27a, *passim*.

[36] שהרי כמה הלכות נאמרו למשה בסיני וכולהון משוקעות במשנה. Yer. Peah 2, see also Tem. 16.

[37] Comp. Hag. 2.11–3.

[38] See Neh. 13.15–20, comp. S. Zeitlin, "The Halaka: Introduction to Tannaitic Jurisprudence", JQR, 1948.

[39] Pes. 6, על שלשה דברים עלה הלל מבבל.

[40] Deut. 16.8, ששת ימים האכל מצות.

[41] Ex. 13.6, שבעת ימים האכל מצות. [42] הא כיצד ששה מן החדש ושבע מן הישן.

teenth day of Nisan, i. e., the second day of the Festival of Unleavened Bread; hence, the unleavened bread from the new harvest was to be eaten only during six days. Hillel, by interpreting the passage in this way, reconciled the contradictory verses. When he went to Judaea he found that his interpretations were halakot, i. e., the Jews in Judaea had been following the laws as he had interpreted them.[43] We see thus these halakot preceded the interpretation. Hillel, who lived in Babylonia, did not know about these halakot since they were not applicable in the Diaspora.

When the Pentateuch was canonized it became the constitution of the Jewish people and was regarded as revealed by God. All the new halakot which were promulgated by the sages, the *Soferim*[44] had to derive support from the Pentateuch. The sages sought such support when the *takkana* of *Ketubah* was introduced,[45] as well as the law for washing the hands.[46] When the law that only "detached seed" are susceptible to Levitical uncleanliness was introduced, the word זרע was interpreted to mean "seed detached" from the ground.[47]

Hillel applied hermeneutic rules in interpreting the Pentateuchal verses for establishing the halakot. He advanced three such rules, *A minori ad majus* קל וחומר, Analogy of words, גזירה שוה, and Analogy of subjects, היקש.[48] These three rules later were developed into seven, and still later into thirteen.

Rabbi Akiba was the *first* to introduce *matres lectionis* in the Bible, maintaining that the pronunciation of the

---

[43] דרש והסכים ועלה וקיבל הלכה.

[44] The period of the *Soferim* continued down to the time of the destruction of the Second Temple. Comp. more S. Zeitlin, *op. cit.*, p. 16.

[45] Ket. 10a, וכאן סמכו חכמים לכתובת אשה מן התורה.

[46] Hul. 106, מכאן סמכו חכמים לנטילת ידים מן התורה; comp. also Yer. Shek. 10, מכאן סמכו לפרוזבול שהוא מן התורה; Suc. 6), אלא כתיבי מי שיעורין הילכתא נינהו וקרא אסמכתא בעלמא.

[47] Sifra 11.   [48] See Pes. 66a, Yer. *ibid.* 6.

words was to be considered.[49] He made use of the *matres lectionis* in interpreting the halakot.[50]

[49] Comp. Kid. 18b, Sanh. 4a, ר' עקיבא סבר יש אם למקרא.

[50] Dr. Segal, in the above mentioned article, writes as follows: "As for the minute exegesis of R. Akiba which is said to have necessitated the fixing by him or by his contemporaries of a standard text, that exegesis was not the invention of R. Akiba or of his generation. He learnt it from his master Nahum of Gimzo, of whom it is related that he subjected every particle to a special exposition. Likewise an older contemporary of this Nahum, Zachariah ben Haqqazzab who ministered as a priest in the Second Temple, deduced *halachoth* from the conjunction *waw*. And their great contemporary Rabban Johanan ben Zakkai is said to have been an adept in this method of exegesis. Thus this method had a somewhat long history before R. Akiba, and it could not therefore have been responsible for the fixation of the text in the generation of R. Akiba."

Rabbi Akiba was the *first* to make use of the *matres lectionis* for the purpose of establishing the halakot. Nahum of Gimzo made use of the particle את. According to Dr. Segal, Zachariah deduced halakot from the conjunction *waw*. But according to the Palestinian Talmud Zachariah did *not* deduce the halakot from the conjunction *waw* but from the word נטמאה which is written twice. שנאמר נטמאה נטמאה דברי ר' עקיבה א"ר · יהושע כך היה ר' דורש ר' זכריה בן הקצב. Even if we should accept Rashi's interpretation of this passage, Zachariah deduced the halakot only from the conjunction *waw* but not from the *matres lectionis*. The Holy Scriptures had the conjunction *waw* in his time but not the *matres lectionis* which were introduced into them in the time of R. Akiba, in the second century CE.

Dr. Segal's statement that Rabban Johanan ben Zakkai had adopted "the method of exegesis" reveals that Dr. Segal fails to distinguish between historical data and legendary tales recorded in the Talmud. The statement recorded about Rabban Johanan ben Zakkai is legendary. It is stated in the same passage that he knew the arguments of Abaye and Raba who lived in the middle of the fourth century. אמרו על ר' יוחנן בן זכאי שלא הניח מקרא משנה נמרא [תלמוד] הלכות ואנדות דקדוקי תורה . . . דבר נדול דבר קטן . . . הוייות דאביי ורבא (Suc. 28). This statement is in the same category as that Methuselah studied nine-hundred orders of the Mishna משותלח צדיק נמור היה והיה שונה ט' מאות סדרי משנה, and Abraham observed the entire Torah, including Erubin. שקיים אברהם אבינו כל התורה כולה, (see Yoma 28b). Dr. Segal failed to realize that the expression אמרו על used in the Talmud regarding great personalities is of a legendary character and cannot be accepted as a historical fact.

Since the so-called discovery of the Hebrew Scrolls by the Bedouins, all who have accepted their antiquity and authenticity have over-night become rabbinic scholars and authorities on the history and liter-ature of the Second Jewish Commonwealth. Men who never occupied themselves in rabbinic literature, some of whom cannot even read it properly without punctuation, have become authorities on this subject.

When the halakot, the unwritten laws, were accepted,
they became the statutory laws. New halakot were
derived from them by hermeneutic rules. To cite one
example, male children, according to the halaka, are
entitled to inherit the property of the father, while the
females have no right of inheritance but only must be
supported. Rabbi Eleazar b. Azariah interpreted the law
to mean that a father is not duty-bound to support his
daughters. True, he said, the sons are entitled to inheritance but the daughters must receive support. But as the
sons are entitled to inheritance only after the death of the
father, the daughters are entitled to support only after that
event.[51] This law, that a father is not duty-bound during
his lifetime to support his daughters was interpreted by
analogy from an old halaka.[52]

IV

When the sages saw that the time had arrived to collect
all the halakot into one corpus which should be *second*
to the Torah, two schools of thought developed. One school
led by Rabbi Meir, held that the halakot should be arranged
according to the subject matter, e. g., the laws connected
with the Sabbath should be embodied in one tractate, the
laws of divorce should be embodied in another tractate
and so on. The other school, which was dominated by
Rabbi Judah, was of the opinion that the halakot should be
arranged in succession according to the Pentateuchal verses.
This is evident from a tannaitic source where, in answer
to the question "What is Mishna?"[53] Rabbi Meir replied

[51] הְאָב אֵינוֹ חַיָּיב בִּמְזוֹנוֹת בִּתּוֹ, זה מדרש דרש ר' אלעזר בן עזריה לפני חכמים בכרם
ביבנה, הבנים יירשו והבנות יזונו מה הבנים אינן יורשין אלא לאחר מיתת האב אף הבנות
אין ניזונות אלא לאחר מיתת האב (Ket. 4.8).

[52] Comp. Yer. Shab. 16, זה מדרשו דרשו ומה להטיל שלום בין איש לאשתו אמר
הכתוב השם שנכתב בקדושה ימחה על המים ספרי מינין שמטילין איבה . . . אינו דין
שישרפו הן ואזכרותיהן; comp. also Yer. Ket. Tosefta *ibid.* 4, דרש הלל הזקן
לשון הדיוט . . . דרש ר' מאיר . . . דרש ר' יהודה.

[53] Kid. 49, אֵיזוֹ הִיא מִשְׁנָה.

"halakot," i. e.,[54] he was of the opinion that the Mishna, the second to the Torah, should be arranged in the form of halakot, according to the subject matter.[55] Rabbi Judah, on the other hand, replied "Midrash-Torah;"[56] he was of the opinion that the second to the Torah, i. e., the halakot, to be arranged according to the Pentateuchal verses.[57]

Fortunately, the school of Rabbi Meir prevailed. The halakot were arranged according to the subject matter; however, the other school did collect and arrange the halakot according to the Pentateuchal verses, and as a result we have the three books, the *Mekilta*, the *Sifra*, and the *Sifre*. These three books were composed either in the time of Rabbi or later, after the Mishna was codified, i. e., at the end of the second century or at the beginning of the third century, CE.

In presenting here the development of the Midrash it becomes quite evident that the Mishna form, i. e., the halakot, preceded the Midrash form. The sages, in order to bestow authority upon many halakot which were promulgated in the period of the Second Commonwealth, supported them by interpreting them through the Pentateuch.[58] The opinion of the scholars who believed that the Midrash form preceded the Mishna form, i. e., the halakot, thus becomes untenable.[59] Most of these Jewish scholars were theologians — academicians. They were accustomed to analyze complicated passages, in like manner as the rabbis of the Middle Ages, and hence they applied the same method to the study of the halakot during the Second Commonwealth. They, however, ignored the fact that the Jews of that period were a living nation, the creators of the laws. It is well known that every nation,

---

[54] ר' מאיר אומר הלכות.

[55] Eru. 96b, כתם מתניתין ר' מאיר; סתם משניות ר' מאיר.

[56] ר' יהודה אומר מדרש תורה.

[57] *Ibid.*, Sanh. 86, כתם ספרא ר' יהודה.   [58] Comp. note 46.

[59] See D. Hoffmann, *Zur Einleitung in die halachischen Midraschim*, Berlin, 1886. J. L. Lauterbach, *Midrash and Mishnah*, New York, 1916.

in addition to having statutory laws, also has common laws, unwritten laws,[60] which had originated among the people. The Jews of the time of the Restoration when the Pentateuch was canonized, likewise had many halakot, unwritten laws, not recorded in the Pentateuch, which were as old or even older than it. In order to make these halakot statutory laws binding upon the people, the sages resorted to interpreting the Torah since the halaka must be supported by biblical verses.[61]

The name Midrash-halakot given or applied to the *Mekilta, Sifra, Sifre*, is erroneous. These books are not *Midrash-halakot* but *Midrash-Torah*. The interpretation of the Pentateuchal passages in them was made for the purpose of establishing the halaka. The term *Midrash-halaka* is to be applied to the interpretation of the old halaka only in order to establish a new halaka.[62] The interpretation of Rabbi Eleazar b. Azariah (Ket. 4.8) as was pointed out above is an example of this.

These three books, *Mekilta, Sifra* and *Sifre* then are *Midrash-Torah* of the four Pentateuchal books, Exodus, Leviticus, Numbers and Deuteronomy. There was no *Midrash-Torah* of the book of Genesis. This is understandable since only very few precepts are recorded there, but a Midrash on Genesis was composed a little later, i. e., in the middle of the third century, or toward the end of that century. This Midrash does not deal with the halaka. It deals rather with theological questions, the creation of the world, reward and punishment after death, and Messianic expectations. The subject is altogether that of eschatology. There were in vogue among the Jews before the composition of this Midrash legends about their forefathers, their kings, their heroes, and generals, though these had no

---

[60] Comp. S. Zeitlin, "The Halaka" *JQR*, 1948.
[61] Comp. Yer. Shek. 1, בשעה שאסרו למקרא כתבו. ובשעה שהתחידו למקרא סתכו
פסח יוכיה . . . אף אני אביא אשם, אמר ר' ישמעאל [62] Comp. Tosefta Zeb. 1,
קל וחומר מה שיריים שאין מכפרין טעונין יסוד תחילה עולה שמכפרת אין דין.

connection with stories in the Pentateuch. To impress these theological ideas upon the people, the rabbis resorted to words and passages on punishment after death found in the Bible. The Midrash on Lamentations like the Midrash of Genesis was also of early composition. The occasion for the composition of this Midrash was that the ninth day of the month of Ab when the Temple was burned by the Romans had been set aside as a national and religious day of mourning. The Jews then assembled to recount the tribulations they had undergone on the Ninth day of Ab and on other days as well, and to offer consolation to one another to bolster their morale and to prepare for the time when the Messiah would appear. They tried to do this by interpreting the passages of the Book of Lamentations. It is said that Rabbi Judah, the patriarch, interpreted the second verse of the Book of Lamentations in 24 ways[63] and thus the Midrash on the Book of Lamentations came into being. It is needless to say that the present Midrashim on Genesis and Lamentations are not altogether of the third century. There are many additions of later centuries; the basic forms of these two Midrashim, however, are of the third century.

The rabbis who occupied themselves with this type of exegesis of the biblical passages were called רבנן דאגדתא, the Rabbis of the Aggada. The earliest Midrashim then, that we have, are on Genesis and Lamentations, and they are not earlier than the third century. Even the *Midrash-Torah*, *Mekilta*, *Sifra* and *Sifre*, belong to the end of the second century and the beginning of the third century. We see, therefore, that there was no Midrash on a prophetic book during the Second Commonwealth.[64]

[63] M. Lamentations 2, ור' הוה דריש כ'ד אפין.

[64] This study, I believe, has shown the absurdity of the view that the Commentary on the book of Habakkuk is a midrash of the period of the Second Commonwealth. Only those who are insufficiently familiar with the history and literature of the Second Jewish Commonwealth can maintain such a hypothesis that this Scroll has reference to personalities of that period or was composed by the Essenes.

STUDIES IN TANNAITIC JURISPRUDENCE

INTENTION AS A LEGAL PRINCIPLE*

Dedicated to My Beloved Teacher
PROFESSOR ISRAËL LÉVI
On Occasion of His Election as
GRAND RABBIN DE FRANCE

IN order to give a clear conception of the development of the Idea of Intention in the jurisprudence of the Tannaites, it is necessary precisely to define and to differentiate Will and Intention. Will in the legal sense, is the determination leading up to the act, whereby we can distinguish it from incident or event; the only objects that can be called acts are immediate consequences of volition; voluntary movements of the body, or, such as follow upon volition, are acts, while involuntary movements of the body are called events or incidents. For instance, if a man plunges into the water purposely, the movement of the body consequent upon the willing would be called an act, but if a man falls into the water without design on his part, that would be called an event, or if a movement is caused by physical compulsion, "vis absoluta," as when the hand of a person is forcibly guided in drawing a signature, there is no act, since will is absent.

*Many scholars have lately striven to discuss Talmudic law. Their discussion lacks consideration of historical development, and, more, they discuss the whole without recognizing the dividing line between Tannaitic and Amoraic jurisprudence. The studies herewith submitted deal with the principles and ideas fundamental to Tannaite jurisprudence, such as: Intention, Possession, Right in Person, Right in Things, etc., which will help us to understand Tannaitic law.

(The idea of intention is usually expressed in the Tannaitic sources by the word כוונה,מחשבה; but not always has the word מחשבה or כונה the meaning of intention.)

As we have said, bodily movements following volitions are acts, but every act is followed by consequences and also attended by concomitants. To desire an act is to will it; to expect any of its consequences is to intend the consequences. In other words, intention relates to the future act, e. g., if a man conceals his grain in water from thieves they become wet, but the man had no desire that the grain should become wet, though he willed the act, he is not pleased with and had no intention to produce the consequences of that act.

Accordingly the consequences of an act are never willed, none but acts themselves are specific objects of volitions. Nor are they always intended, for the person who willed the act may not be pleased with the consequences. If a consequence of the act is in consonance with his desire, the presumption is that it was intended, but an intended consequent is not always desired, e. g., A had an enemy C, and would like to kill him. Once he met C standing near B. In order to kill C, he had to kill also B, although B never was his enemy; he killed B, simply with the intention of killing C; the killing of B, though intended, was not desired.[1]

The Idea of Intention as such we hardly can find in the Bible, neither is the *res divini juris* nor in the *res civilis juris*. The word שוגג in religious laws is *error facto* or *error jure*; e. g., if a man was unclean and entered the sanctuary, he forgot that he was unclean—*error facto*, termed in Pentateuch שגגה, or it may be that the knowing he was unclean, he forgot that an unclean man is prohibited from entering a holy place—*error jure*—also termed שגגה. In the laws of Sabbath, as given in the Mishnah, the same principle is found. If a man wrote on Sabbath, forgetting that writing is forbidden on the seventh, he has committed an error jure. Had that act resulted from forgetting it was Sabbath, it would be an error facto. In both cases he would have to bring a sin-offering.

[1] On "intention" see James Mill, Analysis, II, Tustin Lectures I, Holland, Jurisprudence.

Again, if a man does not realize that what he is eating comes under the head of שרצים, that is an error facto. If, on the other hand, forgetting that the law forbids eating of such שרץ he eats it, that is error jure.

In contrast to שגגה, we find in the Torah זדן. This is *malum in se*, or *malum in prohibitio*. Malum in se is such a mischief as contravenes useful laws, e. g., laws of the Sabbath rest; malum in phohibito is a violation of those laws that prohibit such acts as are pernicious to health or morals.[2]

I. Intention in Ritual Law.

Intention as a factor in Jewish law was first recognized and given a status by Hillel, who insisted that we ought to take into consideration not only the primary act of a man, but also his intention. This innovation was strenuously opposed by his colleague Shammai. This controversy affects all departments of Talmudic law, ritual, civil and criminal:

Grapes which were gathered from the vineyard for the wine-press are made susceptible of levitical uncleanness, according to Shammai, by the juice that runs out of the grapes. For such a case also is implied in וכי יתן מים על זרע. According to Hillel they do not thus become susceptible. For the juice came out upon the grapes without the owner's intention; neither does he use this juice. Now Hillel's reply to Shammai is clear:

Hillel said thus to Shammai: thou sayest that grapes must be gathered in clean vessels because their juice makes them susceptible of uncleanness, though this juice is not used; yet thou sayest that olives need not be gathered in clean vessels because no one desires the liquid that runs out of the olives and it is therefore not implied in כי יתן. Said Shammai to Hillel אם תקניטני, if thou wilt bring the principles of intention to prevail, I shall decree that

[2] See Tosefta Shabbat XI, 19.

olives, too, are made susceptible of levitical uncleanness by their own liquid though no one desires this flow of oil.[3]

The same difference of opinion about Intention we find between the School of Hillel and the School of Shammai.[4]

When the ideas of Hillel and his School gained ground, this principle of Hillel also was accepted,—as can be seen from Machshirin I, 1. Any potable liquid which falls in seed makes it susceptible of טומאה only when the man was pleased that it should so fall. This is according to the Hillelites. When people conceal their fruits in water from thieves, this act does not render them susceptible of ur-

[3] Shabb. 17a; see S. Zeitlin, The Controversy Between the Zugoth, J. Q. R., 1917.

[4] Mikv. IV, 1; Shabb. 16b. See Katzenelsohn, Voschod; S. Zeitlin, "Les Dix huit Mesures" R. E. J. 1914, and "The Controversy Between the Zugoth," J. Q. R.

It is quite possible that not Hillel introduced these ideas which we have cited; they may have been introduced before his time, but, receiving their final form from him, they derived their name also from him. A parallel instance we find in Roman jurisprudence. It is known that already in the time of Augustus there came into being two sects or schools of strongly-contrasted characters and tendencies. The authors of these two schools were two jurists, Ateius Capito and Antistius Labeo; the first one was a warm supporter of the imperial despotism, and of conservative tendencies; while the other was of independent spirit and a strong supporter of the old republicanism, and more inclined to break established rules, if such were life's demands. The schools, however, were named from later chiefs. The followers of Capito were usually called Sabinians, after his pupil Masurius Sabinus; those of Labeo were called Proculians, after Julius Proculius, a pupil, not of Labeo himself, but of his disciple, Nerva, grandfather of the Emperor Nerva. It is worth while to notice that for a series of generations, from the days of Augustus to those of the Antonines, every jurist enrolled himself under one flag or the other, and was known as a Sabinian or a Proculian. Similarly, the schools of Shammai and Hillel may be older than the teachers, and many Halakoth of these two schools have been formulated before Shammai and Hillel.

A full discussion on the School of Shammai and Hillel, I shall give in a work on the History of the Oral Law. About the School of Sabinians and Proculians, see Moscovius, De Sectis Sabinianorum et Proculianorum, Leipsic, 1728, Dirksen, Beitrage Zur Kunde des roem. Rechts, Leipsig, 1825, Hadley, introduction to Roman Law, 1875.

cleanliness, as their intention was not that the fruits should be moistened.[5]

Again: If a man puts a tray on the wall (to expose it to the rain) so it may be rinsed, it comes under the category of כי יותן. If, however, his purpose was to protect the wall, the law of כי יותן does not apply, the washing of the tray or the moistening thereof not being in the intention of the owner.[6]

Likewise: If a person exposes a firebrand to the rain with the object of extinguishing it, this comes not under the category of כי יותן, as his intention was not to make use of the brand. If his object was to make of it a coal, then it *does* come under כי יותן.[7]

This Idea of Intention comes in for consideration also from another aspect of טומאה וטחרה. According to the ancient law, an object can be susceptible of טומאה, when rightly described by the term vessel (כלי), a finished product for the purpose of use; in case, however, it be not thoroughly complete and adaptable to intended use, it is not susceptible of טומאה.

Those Sages who accepted the idea of intention, were cf the opinion that even where the object was not strictly speaking a כלי, by virtue of the expressed (or tacit) intention of the owner to use it for a specified purpose, it comes under the connotation of כלי and is thus rendered susceptible of טומאה. Leather which can be used for many and various purposes, would ordinarily be considered not susceptible, but if he intended that a particular strip should be used for a rug or for a cover, in its unfinished shape and condition, that intention suffices to stamp it as a כלי.[8] They admit, however, that if an object had been used as a כלי and had become unclean, the intention of the owner to adapt it to another use in regard to which its present shape would be unfinished, is not sufficient to

---

[5] Mach. I, 6, הטום פירותיו במים מפני הגנבים אינם בכי יתן.
[6] Ibid. IV, 3.
[7] Tosefta ibid. II, 16.
[8] Kelim, XXVI, 5-8.

render it clean—in that case there is required, in addition, actual change of shape: All *vessels* (כלים) become susceptible of uncleanliness by intention, but cannot be freed from susceptibility of uncleanliness except by actual alteration.[9]

A striking Halaka in Tractate Kelim illustrates how Intention assumed the greatest importance in the ritual laws. Any lid lacking groove would not be susceptible of טומאה, as it is not a כלי. But even if he makes the groove, in case it be without the intention of the maker to cover the pot, it still is unsusceptible, because intention was not there.[10]

The School which differentiates between act and intention as to a future act, quite naturally would differentiate between persons assumed to be possessed of intention and such that are not granted the power of intending as חרש שוטה וקטן, of whom it is taught יש להן מעשה ואין להן מחשבה, that is, their act is valid, but not their intention. If a חרש שוטה וקטן had intention to complete the grooving of the lid for the pot, his intention is not valid or if a חש׳פ removed grain exposed to flies and put it where rain or dew might fall on it, that does not suffice to subject it to the law of כי יותן.[11]

Furthermore, as intention, according to the Hillelites, involves the contemplation of the benefit derived from the future act, it follows that the stranger inasmuch as he cannot have any benefit therefrom, is devoid of intention, which practically puts him (in religious laws) in the same category as חש׳פ.[12]

2. INTENTION IN LAWS OF SABBATH

The Bible forbids מלאכה on Sabbath. It is, however, in Tannaitic sources where a definition of what constitutes a מאכה is found: Only an act which, as already

[9] ibid. XXV, 9.
[10] Thosephtha Kelim,, B. Batra II, 3.
[11] Mach. III, 8, VI, 1; Thosephtha ibid. III, 2.
[12] See note 9.

stated, is consequent of volition, but no involuntary event
or accident. If, for example, with the idea of picking up
grass lying on the ground he actually picked up grass that
was imbedded in the soil, it is not accounted a מלאכה
because of its being involuntary and accidental.[13]

The followers of the Hillelite School brought Intention
to bear upon the laws of Sabbath. Such מלאכה alone is
forbidden in which a man *intends* a particular result; any
מלאכה act—in the doing of which the man contemplated
no particular result is not forbidden;—e. g. פורסין מחצלות
על גביכוורת דבורים בשבת בחמה מפני החמה ובנשמים מפני הגשמים ובלבד
שלא יתכוין לצוד.[14]

One may spread a mat over a beehive on Sabbath in
Summer to protect it from the sun and in the rainy season
from rain, provided he has no intention to catch the bees.
Or: When a lighted lamp is behind the door one may open
or close the door, provided he has no intention to extinguish or to kindle. Even tho' by such opening or closing
he is likely to extinguish or to kindle, still on account of the
fact that he contemplates neither extinguishing nor kindling,
it is not forbidden.[15]

Some of the School of Hillel go even further in this
doctrine of Intention: If a man had intention with regard
to one act which would constitute a מלאכה, but his act
resulted not in accordance with his intention, he is not regarded as having transgressed laws of Sabbath and is not
bound to bring sin-offering.

If, his intention being to pick figs, he picked grapes, or
his intention being to pick grapes, he picked figs, R. Eliezer
says he must bring a sin-offering, R. Joshua absolves him.[16]
R. Eliezer belongs to the school of Shammai, while
R. Joshua was a Hillelite.

The idea of intention as an important factor was upheld by R. Shimon, in this matter representing the Hillelitet
School.

[13] Krit. 19b, passim.
[14] Schabb. 43a.
[15] Jer. Schab. III, 4, see also Babli ibid. 120b.
[16] Krit. 19a and b.   Thosephtha ibid. II, 19.

R. Shimon says a man may (on Sabbath) drag a chair, bed or stool provided he has no intention to make a rut— R. Shimon, as above noted, like the Hillelites, considered as all-important the intention, whereas R. Jehuda, his controversist in the case, considered the act itself as sufficient.[17] With this difference in mind, we are prepared to understand their pronouncements with regard to מלאכה שאינה צריכה כגופיה (work which he personally does not need) and מקלקל (one who spoils). Rabbi Jehuda who considered the act as sufficient held מלאכה שאינה צריכה לנופיה חייב[18] while R. Shimon, who based his judgement on the presence or absence of intention, held that מלאכה שאינה צריכה כגופיה פטור.[19] Their decisions on מקלקל are the reverse; R. Jehuda considered spoiling an object no act, therefore מקלקל פטור; R. Shimon, however, recognizing intention, said המקלקל חייב if he had intention to spoil.[20] As intention depends upon a man himself, and his statements are not always reliable and can not be taken at their face value, R. Shimon had to accept if the act makes clear the intention of a man, no matter whât he says, he is responsible, and of this the Talmud says: מודה ר שמעון בפסיק רישיה ולא ימות i. e. R. Shimon admits that if the intention of any act (even though the man denies it) is as clearly evident as is that of the man who cuts off the head of a person, despite denials of intention to kill him, the act suffices.[21]

מוקצה AND הכנה.

Since we have shown that many controversies between the School of Shammai and the School of Hillel in regard to Sabbath resolve themselves into disputes over the status of Intention as a factor, we will be able better to comprehend the significance of two institutions of Sabbath: הכנה and מוקצה, which have as yet received no adequate scholarly treatment.

[17] Schab. 46b. and passim.
[18] Schab. 73b. and passim.
[19] Schab. 105b. and passim.
[20] Schab. 106a.
[21] ibid. 133a and passim.   See Oruch פסיק

הכנה : According to the law in the Bible, food for Sabbath must be prepared the day before. But the School of Shammai who regard Intention as not essential, anything prepared, even without the intention of the man to use the same on Sabbath or holiday, is allowed to be eaten then. The School of Hillel, however, who require in every act the intention of the person, maintain that anything prepared without intention and knowledge of the man for use on Sabbath or on holiday, is not allowed to be eaten thereon. This difference underlies the following controversy.

The School of Shammai held that an egg laid on Yom Tob was prepared the day before, therefore it may be eaten on the holiday; the School of Hillel maintained that, tho prepared, it was without intention of the man to use it on the holiday, therefore it is not הכנה hence it is forbidden.[22]

The same difference as to the principle of Intention we find in another controversy between R. Jehuda and R. Shimon.

When a first born (cattle) falls into a pit (on a holyday) —R. Jehuda, says, let an expert go down and see whether it has a blemish. In that case he may bring it up and slaughter it (on the holyday), otherwise not. R. Shimon says, even if its blemish was recognizable on the eve of the holyday, but no sage had permitted its use (by a non-priest), they may not slaughter it on the holyday, because it is not considered as "prepared."[23]

R. Jehuda, in conformity with the Shammaite view as to Intention, is of the opinion that the expert's statement that on the בכור there was a blemish establishes the fact of the animal's being prepared for use before the holyday, regardless of absence of intention and knowledge on part of the owner. R. Shimon, on the other hand, adhering to the Hillelite view on Intention, maintains that although the blemish was known on the day before, yet, since no permission had been obtained from a Sage to use the animal,

[22] In the Talmud we find some difficulties in explaining this Mishnah.

[23] Betza 26a; according to the reading of the Thosephtha ibid. III, 3.

intention to use it did not exist, hence the הכנה was not there.[24]

מוקצה: According to the ancient Halacha, any object devoted to a purpose involving an act forbidden by the Sabbath laws, is called מוקצה, and is not allowed to be handled on Sabbath. In the opinion of the Shammaites and R. Jehuda, who ignore the principle of Intention, any object for such purpose, tho without intention of the man, comes under the head of מוקצה. The Hillelites and R. Shimon maintain that only in case the man had the intention to use it for some specific purpose, is the object to be regarded as מוקצה, without such intention, even tho used for the purpose, this use does not render it מוקצה. That is why Judah the Patriarch said to his son Simon אין כר׳שמעון מוקצה אלא גרוגרות וצמוקים בלבד. That is, R. Shimon restricted the term מוקצה to such cases where the intention is as palpable as when a man exposes his figs and grapes to be dried, since in the intermediate stage these have no value or use, and hence his desire clearly is to have dried figs and raisins.[25]

In both Talmudim we find difficulties in the definition of הכנה and מוקצה. In the Palestinian Gemara some authorities find contradiction between the utterance of R. Jehuda, in the above quoted case of the cattle that fell into the pit, and the other Mishna where we read: One may feed a carcass to the dogs (on a holy day). Jehuda says if (the cattle) was not yet carcass on the eve of the holy day, it is forbidden, because it is not "prepared."[26] But there is really no discrepancy in R. Jehudah's statements. In the first Mishna R. Jehuda regards the blemish as pre-existent and therefore מוכן, while Shimon laid stress on absence of intention and consequent non-fulfillment of law of הכנה. In the other Misna R. Jehudah prohibits the feeding in the case the cattle was not dead before Sabbath, there

[24] Schab. 143a.   אנו אין לנו אלא בית שמאי כר׳ יהודה ובית הלל
כר ׳שמעון

[25] Schab. 45a.-b.
[26] Betza III, 4.

being no doubt that it is not included in the category of מוכן.[27]

In the case of מוקצה we find even more difficulties in the Talmud,[27a] as well as in later literature: Missing the significance of R. Shimon's attitude in this law, some of them think that he subscribes to מוקצה מחמת חסרון כים and some that he recognizes מוקצה מחמת or מוקצה מחמת איסור מיאוס (see the discussion of the subject in the late Halachic codes). This because they found apparent contradiction between utterances of R. Shimon. From our viewpoint, however, that Intention was at the basis of R. Shimon's declarations, his מוקצה statements become clear and logically consistent.

So in the Mishna:[28] מותר השמן שבנר אסור...ור"ש...מתיר. "What is left of the oil in the lamp is forbidden to use on Sabbath," the idea being that it was destined for burning, and consequently forbidden. "R. Shimon, however, permitted," on the ground that the man's intention was not that the oil be *consumed*, but that it furnish light, and, therefore, the light having been extinguished, the oil is no longer מוקצה. Likewise in the matter of shifting a lamp on Sabbath. R. Shimon considers מוקצה only when it is evident that he had intention of using the lamp on Sabbaths only.[29]

As a logical sequence in the laws of הכנה the School of Hillel and their successor, R. Shimon, would be strict, לחומרא, while the School of Shammai, and their successor, R. Jehuda, would be lenient, לקולא, whereas in the laws of מוקצה their positions would be reversed.

Intention as a factor we find also in other religious laws. In the laws of כלאים it is stated that dealers in garments made of wool and mingled with linen are permitted to carry their goods on their shoulders, unless they be intentionally so

---

[27] Comp. Schab. 156-b.

[27a] Comp. Schab. 44-45.

[28] Schab. 44a.

[29] ר' שמעון אומר כל הנרות מטלטלין חוץ מן הנר הדולק בשבת; so in Thosephtha Schab. IV, 13; see also Babli ibid. 44a.

carried in the sunny season against the sun or in the rainy season against the rain.[30]

3. INTENTION IN CIVIL LAW.

A still greater part than in the religious laws—those שבין אדם למקום, Intention plays in civil law, the laws שבין אדם לחבירו. Sale of an object under compulsion, or without intention on the part of owner would not entitle the buyer to the possession thereof.[31]

Likewise in Marriage and Divorce, the main consideration was not the act but the underlying intention. The old Halacha states that a wife can be acquired in three ways, בכסף ובשטר ובביאה, but none of these acts is sufficient in the absence of intention to acquire the woman as wife. ביאה without such intention would be accounted ביאת זנות, and not קידושין.[32]

An imbecile or a minor שוטה וקטן, while conceded power of action, is denied power of intention, and as a consequence they would not grant him the right to acquire a wife. If an imbeicle or a minor took a wife and then died without issue, the wife is free from Halitza and from Yibbum.[33]

In re Levirate marriage the law of intention is of particular interest. If a man dies without issue, his wife automatically belongs to his oldest surviving brother, and therefore, intention is not required and the act of ביאה is sufficient to confirm him as husband, even if it be accidental.[34] Accordingly, although the surviving brother be an imbecile or a minor, he may take his sister-in-law as wife, inasmuch as the act is sufficient without intention. If, however, the surviving brother declines to take the woman, he is required by the law of Moses to release her (to give her Halitzah), whereby he gives up the right that inheres in him through his brother's death; accordingly,

[30] Kilaim IX, 5.
[31] Comp. Baba Bathra, 48ab.
[32] Thosephtha Kidushin I, 3.
[33] Thosephtha Yebamoth XI, 10, Babli ibid. 96b.
[34] ibid. 53b-54a.

intention being required to dissolve the bond, an imbecile or minor cannot give Halizah.[35]

4. WRONGS—PRIVATE AND PUBLIC.

What in Modern Jurisprudence is designated as Criminal Law, came in Roman and Tannaitic and other ancient laws under the head of Wrongs (Torts).[36]

The person injured proceeded against the wrong-doer in a civil court, and received compensation in the shape of money damages. This applied not only to the thief who had to pay twofold, fourfold or fivefold, the value of the article stolen, but also one who committed robbery or inflicted personal injury on his neighbor, whose act in modern jurisprudence is regarded as a crime, was in ancient times regarded as guilty of trespass, and if a man injured his neighbor, he had to pay for נזק צער רפוי שבת בושת: damages, pain, medical attendance, enforced idleness, shame.[37]

According to Roman law, any kind of "wrong" was punished as dolus—"injuria qualiscumque scienter admissa." Likewise in Tannaite jurisprudence, any "wrong", was considered a פשיעה on the part of the wrong-doer, even though he may not have had any intent.[38]

Also a man who set fire to another's property, had to pay, even tho he did so unintentionally, by negligence, or carelessness.[39] As Austin has put the matter in regard to Roman Law, so in Tannaite Jurisprudence, this decision results from the impossibility of determining whether the act was due to malice or to carelessness, or rashness, and "such being the case it shall be presumed that he intended and his liability shall be adjusted accordingly provided that the question arise in a civil action. If the question had arisen in the course of a criminal proceeding,

---

[35] Thosephtha ibid. II, 6.

[36] See Th. Maine, Ancient Law, ch. X.

[37] It must be added that sins or violations of divine prescriptions and commands, were considered as crimes in Jewish, Greek and Roman jurisprudence.

[38] אחד שוגג ואחד מזיד See Jer. Baba Kama VIII, 3, and Babli ibid.

[39] Comp. B. Baba Kama pp. 60-62. See ibid. VI, 4.

the presumption would have gone in favor of the party and not against him."[40]

That this view of Austin's holds true of Tannaitic legislation also, is clearly seen in the fact that while in cases of "wrong" they do not discriminate between the liability of a מזיד "Malice" and a שוגג, negligence, in capital cases they took pains to ascertain the presence or absence of intent and inflicted punishment only where the act was proven intentional. As the Talmud[41] formulates it: הני מילי לענין קטלא אבל לענין נזקין חייב

But if it can be demonstrated without a shadow of a doubt that the man through whom the wrong happened was in no wise chargeable with malice or negligence, he is not guilty. If, for instance, a man has securely locked up his ox, and robbers broke in and let the ox escape, or a whirlwind tore down the fence and the ox caused damage, the owner is not responsible.[42] Or, if a man left implements on a roof in such a position that by an ordinary wind they could not be thrown down, but an abnormal disturbance caused them to fall, and they caused damage, the owner is not held accountable.[43]

We have seen in religious laws that the follower of the School of Hillel Rabbi Shimon, wherever possible, urged intention as a determining factor. Even in wrongs, when amercing a man for נזק צער רפוי שבת בושת, Rabbi Shimon urged that, inasmuch as humiliation depends on social status (הכל לפי המבייש והמתבייש) of the two parties,[44] satisfaction for humiliation must be given only when it is clear that the wrong-doer had especially intended to humiliate this man: נתכוין לבייש את זה ובייש את זה פטור[45]

---

[40] Austin, Lectures on Jurisprudence II.
[41] Baba Kama, 28b.
[42] ibid. 54b.
[43] Comp. ibid. 29a.
[44] Comp. ibid. 86a.
[45] ibid.

Accordingly, if a man fell down from a roof—as a result of his own negligence, and inflicted injury on another, he has to pay the first four counts, but not for humiliation.[46]

5. CAPITAL CASES.

According to the Bible, a man killing another man willingly is punished by death, but if the killing was a result of negligence he is only exiled to one of the Cities of Refuge.

The word שגגה in these passages, opposed to צדיה cannot be regarded as "lack of intention," but rather as a distinguishing from malicious acts those due to negligence; since it is clearly stated that those only were intended to refuge by whose negligent act or by accident a man had been killed.[47]

The Tannaites were generally opposed to capital punishment. In fact, they went so far as to stigmatize as חבלנית (murderous) the Sanhedrin that once in seven or seventy years executed a man.[48]   They maintain not only that a man is not guilty of murder because of death caused by his negligence, but even if he had killed his neighbor without intention, i.e., if a man threw a stone against his neighbor's knees, who so hit would not have been killed, but the stone hit the heart and caused death, he is not guilty of murder.[49]   Simon goes farther and says:

If A, intended to kill B, and killed C, he is not guilty of murder, as he had no intention of killing C.[50]

I submit that a more adequate appreciation of the principle of intention as exemplified by the above controversies and orientations, will be helpful in shedding new light on many other passages in Tannaitic Jurisprudence.

[46] ibid.
[47] Numbers XXXV, 22-23; Deut. XIX, 5.
[48] Makkoth 7a.
[49] Sanh. 79a.
[50] ibid.

ASMAKTA OR INTENTION

A STUDY IN TANNAITIC JURISPRUDENCE

THERE are different ways of studying law: The theoretical way, and the critico-historical way. By theoretical way, I mean the study of the laws as they are, without investigation of the underlying reasons for their origin; while the critico-historical way means study of the laws and social forces which brought about these laws, as well as their development in different aspects and stages.

The Jewish Law (Halakah) has never been studied in the critico-historical way. The few works which we have on the Halakah belong to the theoretical class. None of the scholars laid due stress on the development of the Halakah; they did not even differentiate between the Tannaitic Halakah (which came into existence in a period when the Jew lived his own life and had his own jurisdiction) and the Amoraic Halakah (which developed under different circumstances in Babylon).

It is true that for a Rabbi as well as for a Magistrate, in giving out decisions, it is not necessary to go into the origin of the laws or how they came about. The decree of an authoritative jurist, Rabbi or Court is sufficient in deciding a case. But that is not the case with a scholar, or with a Rabbi or jurist who wants to amend the law. A scholar, in studying the law, must know its entire development, when it originated, and the underlying reasons for its origin.

In a previous article I pointed out the importance of the study of the development of the Halakah. I tried to show

263

that many Halakahs which we have in the Talmud and
which are ascribed to the Tannaim, had not yet been
known at the Tannaitic period, as the laws of מוקצה מחמת
איסור, מוקצה מחמת מיאוס.[1] Likewise, it was observed that
many Rabbis, not knowing the origin of different Halakahs, found difficulty in reconciling seemingly contradictory statements of the Tannaim; but if we know the
underlying reasons for the different statements of the
Tannaim, we find no contradiction.[2] To give one example
out of many: in one Mishnah we read, "When a first-born
(cattle) falls into a pit (on a holiday), R. Judah says, let
an expert go down and see whether it has a blemish. In
that case he may bring it up and slaughter it (on the holiday), otherwise not. R. Simon says, even if its blemish
was recognizable on the eve of the holiday, but no sage
had permitted its use (by a non-priest), they may not
slaughter it on the holiday, because it is not considered
'prepared.' "[3] On the other hand we find in another Mishnah: "One may feed a carcass to the dogs (on a holy day).
Judah says, If (the cattle) was not carcass on the eve of
the holy day, it is forbidden, because it is not 'prepared.' "[4]
The compilers of the Palestinian Talmud find a contradiction between the first of R. Judah's statements that if a
first-born (cattle) falls into a pit on a holiday, let an expert

---

[1] "Studies in Tannaitic jurisprudence," *Journal of Jewish Lore and Philosophy*, 1919.

[2] Comp. *ibid.*

[3] בכור שנפל לבור ר' יהודה אומר ירד מומחה ויראה אם יש בו מום יעלה וישחט ואם
לאו לא ישחט ר' שמעון אומר כל שאין מומו ניכר מבעוד יום אין זה מן המוכן, Bezah
III, 4.

An animal may be slaughtered on a holiday, as that is called צרך
אכל נפש. Therefore, if an animal fell into a pit on a holiday, it may be
brought up, as it may be slaughtered. A first-born may not be used
by an Israelite unless he acquire a blemish, which should be ascertained
by an expert.

[4] מחתכין את הדילועין לפני הבהמה ואת הנבלה לפני הכלבים רבי יהודה אומר אם
לא היתה נבלה מערב שבת אסורה לפי שאינה מן המוכן, Shab. XXIV. 4.

73

go down and see whether it has a blemish, and he may slaughter it on a holiday because it is "prepared," while in the second statement he says it is not "prepared."

The compilers of the Palestinian Talmud found that R. Judah's statements are at variance with each other[5]; but when we know the origin of R. Judah's statements we find no contradiction. According to the old Jewish law, no food might be used on a holiday unless it had been prepared on the preceding day. The Shammaiites were of the opinion that everything that was prepared on the eve of a Sabbath or holiday might be used on a Sabbath or holiday, even if prepared by nature without the knowledge of the person. So, if the first-born (cattle) fell into the pit, according to Judah, an expert should go down and see if it has a blemish; and it is lawful to bring it up and slaughter it, since the first-born had the blemish before the holiday. Hence, in R. Judah's point of view, it was actually "prepared" on the eve of the holiday. But in the other Mishnah, in the case of the carcass, if the animal was still alive on the eve of the holiday, it could by no means be considered "prepared."[6]

Asmakta is only another instance of the importance of the study of the development of the Halakah. The subject of Asmakta is one of the most difficult in the Talmud[7]. I refer to the Amoraic discussions, which are known to every student of the Talmud. It is, therefore, unnecessary for me to enlarge upon the subject here, concerned as we are with the Tannaitic, and not the Amoraic jurisprudence.

---

[5] מחלפה שיטתיה דרבי יודה דתנינן תמן רבי יהודה אומר אם לא היתה נבלה מערב Jer. Bezah 62a. שבת אסורה לפי שאינה מן המוכן והכא הוא אמר הכין

[6] Comp. more about intention, S. Zeitlin, *ibid.*

[7] Comp. Rashi, B. Mezia 48b. Maimonides, Mekirah, XI, comp. also M. S. Zuckermandel, *Tosefta Mischna und Boraita*, vol. 2, pp. 294–324.

As Gulak, יסודי המשפט העברי, 1, p. 67, נקרא—חסרין נזירת הדעת. אסמכתא M. Guttman, מפתח התלמוד, 111a; לפעמים בשם אסטכתא

According to the Amoraim, the Tannaim differed in
their point of view regarding the validity of Asmakta. R.
Jose says *Asmakta is valid*: אסמכתא קניא, that is to say, if A,
to strengthen his transaction with B, pledged his property
or money if he should not fulfil the conditions of the
transaction, has the right to claim the pledge, as Asmakta,
a pledge to support a previous deal (Asmakta from the
word סמך to support), is valid. R. Judah was of the opinion
that Asmakta, a pledge to support a previous deal, is not
valid: אסמכתא לא קניא, for when A made the pledge to B, he
expected to fulfil the conditions of the transaction and not
to have to forfeit his property.[8]

The Amoraim based this Asmakta controversy, between
R. Jose and R. Judah, on a baraita and a mishnah.

I. The baraita reads as follows: "If one (the buyer) gives
a deposit and says, If I retract I shall forfeit my deposit;
and the seller says: If I retract I shall return double the
amount of your deposit; R. Jose says the conditions hold
good; R. Judah, on the other hand, says that if the seller
retract, the buyer may purchase according to his deposit."[9]

According to the Amoraim of the Talmud, the controversy between Jose and Judah in this baraita was on the
validity of Asmakta. R. Jose was of the opinion that if a
buyer, to show his good faith in the deal, promises the seller
that if he should retract, he would forfeit his deposit, and
the seller, to show his good faith in the deal, also makes a
pledge that if he should retract, he would double the amount
of the deposit; if either one retract, the pledge would hold
good, as Asmakta (a pledge to support a previous deal) is
valid. R. Judah says that if the buyer retract he should

---

[8] B. Batra, 168a, and passim. Comp. also Maimonides, Mekirah,
XI, about his opinion of Asmakta.

[9] הנותן עורבון לחבירו ואמר לו אם אני חוזר בי ערבני כחול לך והלה אומר אם אני
חוזר בי אכפול לך ערבנך נתקיימו התנאים דברי ר' יוסי—רבי יהודה אומר דיו שיקנה
כנגד ערבנו. B. M. 48b and 77b.

have his deposit returned, while if the seller retract, the
buyer may purchase according to the amount of his deposit.
In either case there would be no forfeit, as Asmakta (a
pledge to support a previous deal) is not valid.

II. The Mishnah reads as follows: "A paid a fraction
of his debt on a note to B and told him to deposit the note
with C, adding, If I do not pay the note by a certain date,
return the note to the creditor to collect the amount of the
note in full. On the due date A did not pay the note. R.
Jose says, C should return the note to B in order that he
may collect the full amount; R. Judah is of the opinion that
the note should not be returned to B." (The note, according
to R. Judah, should be turned over to the Court, and B
may collect only the amount which was not paid on the
note).[10]

In the opinion of the Amoraim, the controversy between
Jose and Judah, in this Mishnah, was also on the validity
of Asmakta. R. Jose says that if A owes money to B on
a note and pays him a fraction of the debt, the balance to
be paid at a certain time; and to prove his good faith,
suggests that the note should be deposited with C, and,
should he fail to pay the balance on due date, the note
should be returned to B for collection in full—if he fails,
his pledge holds good, as Asmakta (a promise to support
a previous transaction) is valid, אסמכתא קניא. R. Judah is
of the opinion that the debtor may collect only the balance
due him, and not the full amount of the note, as Asmakta
(a promise to support a previous transaction) is not valid,
אסמכתא לא קניא.

Owing to many passages in the Tannaitic literature, which
seemingly contradict Jose's or Judah's opinion on Asmakta,

[10] מי שפרע מקצת חובו והשליש את שטרו ואמר לו אם לא נתתי לך מכאן ועד יום
פלוני תן לו שטרו הגיע זמן ולא נתן רבי יוסי אומר יתן רבי יהודה אומר לא יתן.
B. B. X, 5.

we find in the Amoraic literature two conflicting statements about the validity of Asmakta. One statement says, *Asmakta is valid*, והלכת' אסמכתא קניא, Ned. 27b, while the other statement says, Asmakta is not valid, אסמכתא לא קניא, B. M. 66b. The later Amoraim and the Rabbis of the Middle Ages, who were eager to reconcile the two contradictory statements, brought in different conceptions of Asmakta, some of which were valid and others not valid. With these they made the subject of Asmakta the most difficult one in the Talmud as well as in the Rabbinic literature of the Middle Ages (Comp. Rashi, Tosafot, Rambam).

The word Asmakta is not only not mentioned in Judah's and Jose's statements, but is not found throughout the Tannaitic literature. All the Talmudic scholars who dealt with the subject of Asmakta never questioned whether the controversy between Judah and Jose was really on the point of Asmakta.

I venture to say that the principle Asmakta as given in the Talmud, and in the later Rabbinic literature, was not known to the Tannaim; and the controversy between the two Tannaim in the aforestated Mishnahs and Baraita is on the principle of *intention*.

Elsewhere I have pointed out that one of the four principles which were the basis of almost all the disputes between the school of Shammai and the school of Hillel was one of intention.[11]

According to the school of Hillel intention as a factor in law, was not only recognized but insisted upon; that we must take into consideration not only a man's primary act, but also a person's intention. The school of Shammai on the other hand recognized only the act as a factor in law, and did not take cognizance of the intention. This difference

[11] See S. Zeitlin, "The Semikah Controversy Between the Zugoth," *J.Q.R.*, 1917. pp. 515–17.

in view affected all departments of Jewish law—ritual, civil, and criminal. To illustrate a few of the many Halakahs in relation to intention: I. The Bible forbids all manner of work, מלאכה, on the Sabbath; the school of Hillel who maintain that intention is the main factor, are of the opinion that if a man had intention with regard to an act which would constitute a מלאכה but this act did not result in all particulars according to his intention, he is not regarded as having transgressed the laws of Sabbath. According to the school of Shammai, however, the man would be regarded as having transgressed the laws of Sabbath. For example, if a person intended to pick figs and picked grapes instead, or if he intended to pick grapes and picked figs, R. Eliezer says that he must bring a sin-offering; R. Joshua absolves him.[12] R. Eliezer belonged to the school of Shammai, while R. Joshua was a Hillelite. 2. According to the law of the Torah, food for Sabbath must be prepared the day before. The school of Shammai, who regard intention as not essential, were of the opinion that anything prepared even without the intention of using the same on a Sabbath or holiday, is allowed to be eaten thereon. The school of Hillel, however, who require in every act the intention of the person, maintain that anything prepared without the intention or knowledge of man for use on the Sabbath and holiday, is not allowed to be eaten thereon. And that is the controversy between the schools of Hillel and Shammai in regard to an egg laid on a holiday, which naturally is prepared the day before. The school of Shammai say that it may be eaten on the holiday; the school of Hillel forbid it to be eaten on a holiday—although the egg was prepared

[12] מתכוין ללקט תאנים וליקט ענבים ענבים וליקט תאנים—רבי אליעזר מחייב חטאת
ורבי יהושע פוטר. Krit. b. Tosef. ibid., II.

on the eve, it was without intention of the man to use it on the holiday.[13]

Some of the school of Hillel even went so far as to say that even if a person intended to kill A, and killed B, he is not guilty of manslaughter, as his intention was not fulfilled.[14] Or, if a man threw a stone against a person's knees, who thus hit would not have been killed, but the stone hit the heart and cause death, he is not guilty of murder.[15]

The principle of intention was brought into play in the laws of possession. If A holds a property without his intention to make it his own, he does not obtain ownership of this property, it must be an *animus* possession, which means the intention of the possessor to hold the thing possessed as his own.[16]

To possess a thing which is not *res nullius*, does not make the possessor the owner of the property, and as long as the previous owner did not transfer or relinquish his ownership the second one cannot become the owner.[17] (The laws of possession, which require three years, assume that the previous owner had relinquished his ownership). The actual transfer of property from A to B must be by free will and must be intended, as proved by note or witness. In a case where A intends to transfer his title to B, under certain conditions to be fulfilled in the future, the school of

---

[13] ביצה שנולדה ביום טוב בית שמאי אומרים תאכל ובית הלל אומרים לא האכל
Bezah I, 1.

In the Tosefta this controversy is recorded under the name of R. Eliezer and R. Joshua. See tosefta, *ibid.*

[14] ר' שמעון אומר אפי' נתכון להרוג את זה והרנ את זה פטור, Sanh. IX, 2.

[15] See *ibid.*

[16] כל חזקה שאין עמה טענה חזקה אינה חזקה כיצד אמר לו מה אתה עושה בתוך שלי
B. B. III, 3. והוא אמר שלא אמר לי אדם דבר מעולם אינה חזקה.

[17] One may have possession—as in the case of theft—without being the owner, "Furtivae quoque res, et que vi possessae sunt, nec si praedicto longo tempore bona fide possessae fuerint, usucapi possunt," The Institutes of Justinian, Lib. II, Tit. VI, 2, see about יאוש, B. K. 66–67.

Hillel, which recognize intention, are of the opinion that if these conditions are fulfilled, B gets the ownership; while the school of Shammai, which recognize only acts, are of the opinion that A still retains the ownership.

Now we can understand the Baraita above quoted, in reference to deposits. "If one gives a deposit and says, 'If I retract I shall forfeit my deposit', and the seller says, 'If I retract I shall return double the amount of your deposit', R. Jose says that the conditions hold good. R. Jose, who was a Hillelite, maintained that as both the seller and the buyer intended, the conditions hold good; R. Judah said that if the seller retracts, the buyer may purchase according to his deposit." R. Judah was a Shammaiite, and held the opinion that intention was not sufficient; therefore as the seller had intended to double the deposit, he is not bound to do so, but only to return the buyer's deposit.[18]

A similar point of view may be seen in another Halakah, quoted in the Tosefta. "If A pledges to B a house and says 'If I shall not pay you by a certain date, I have nothing in your hands,' and if the date arrives and A does not pay, the condition holds good," according to R. Jose, while R. Judah says, 'How can a man acquire a thing which is not his?'[19] Here the same principle of intention is involved. The house was pledged but still remained in the possession of A; therefore, R. Jose says, his intention is sufficient, but R. Judah holds that intention does not suffice.

---

[18] According to Rashi, לא זה מוחל ולא זה כופל; comp. Maimonides— אם חוזר בו הלוקח קנה זה הערבון שהרי הוא תחת ידו ואם חזר בו המוכר אין מחייבין אלא נותן לו עירבון שלו.—the Tosefta reads: אותו לכפול הערבון שזו אסמכתא It seems to me that the reading of the Tosefta is according to the opinion that עירבון נגד כולו הוא קונה—while the reading of the Baraita is according to the opinion עירבון כנגדו הוא קונה.

[19] מישכן לו בית ומישכן לו שדה ואמר לו אם לא נתתי לך מיכן ועד יום פלוני אין לי בידך כלום הגיע הזמן ולא נתן יתקיים תנאו דברי ר' יוסי, אמר רבי יהודה היאך זוכה זה בדבר שאינה שלו אלא ינתחנו (יתננו) Tosefta B. M. I, 17.

It is interesting to note that if A pawned some "movable"
to B and said to him, "If I pay you not by a certain date,
I have nothing in your hands," and the date came and he
did not pay, then the "movable" which he pawned remains
in B's hands;[20] in this case R. Judah does not hold a different
opinion, as the "movable" was actually pawned and in
possession of B, and not pledged.

The same principle of intention we may see in the second
controversy between R. Jose and R. Judah, which involved,
according to the Talmud, the Rabbis of the Middle Ages,
as well as modern scholars, a controversy of Asmakta. "If
A paid a fraction of his debt on the note to B and told him
to deposit the note with C and adding, "If I do not pay the
note by a certain date, return the note to the creditor to
collect the full amount of the note, and on the due date A
did not pay on the note, R. Jose holds that C should return
the note to B that he may collect the full amount." According to Rabbi Jose, A intended to pay the full amount of the
note, if he should fail to pay on time; therefore B has the
right to collect the full amount. "R. Judah is of the opinion
that the note should not be returned to B." R. Judah, who
does not recognize intention, maintains that B is entitled
to the money said A owes him, but not to the full amount
of the note.[21]

Now I have proved that the two controversies between R. Jose and R. Judah were not on the question of
Asmakta, as the Talmudists and the scholars who followed

[20] המלוה את חבירו על המשכון ואמר לו אם לא נתתי לך מיכאן ועד יום פלוני אין
19. Tosefta, *ibid.* לי בידך כלום והני הזמן ולא נתן הינעו משכון בין רע ובין יפה
[21] מי שפרע מקצת חובו והשליש את שטרו ואמר לו אם לא נתתי לך מכאן ועד יום
B. B. פלוני תן לו שטרו הגיע זמן ולא נתן רבי יוסי אומר יתן רבי יהודה אומר לא יתן
X, 5. Comp. also Tosefta B. M. 1, 16, שנים שנתעצמו זה בזה ואמר אחד לחבירו
אם לא באתי מיכן ועד יום פלוני יהא לך בידי כך וכך היניע זמן ולא נתן יתקיים תנאו
דברי רבי יוסי אמר רבי יהודה היאך זוכה זה בדבר שלא בא לתוך
ידו אלא ינתחנו.

the Rabbis maintain, *but on the principle of intention.* That will not only remove many difficulties which we find in the Talmud, but will give us another, and clearer, conception of the Tannaitic jurisprudence and the development of *intention* as a legal principle.

Asmakta is only one instance of many which prove the importance of the study of the history and development of the Halakah. *No scholarly work on the Talmud which is worth its name can be undertaken unless a thorough study of the history and development of the Tannaitic as well as the Amoraic Halakahs is made.* And again, no scientific Talmudic treatises can be written unless we have a critical edition of the Tannaitic literature as well as the Amoraic, based not only on all the MSS. which are in our possession and on different citations in the vast Rabbinic literature, *but stress must be laid on internal evidence.*

INTENTION AS ONE OF THE CONTROVERSIAL
POINTS BETWEEN JOSE AND JUDAH

PROFESSOR Ludwig Blau in the *JQR*, Vol. 21, pp. 321 ff., discussing
my article "Asmakta or Intention" (*JQR*, Vol. 19, pp. 263 ff.), says that
he agrees with me as to the origin of Asmakta which is of an amoraic
period, but differs with me in the interpretation of the tannaitic law
with which I dealt in my article.

My purpose was not to give the origin of Asmakta, but to show that
the controversies between R. Jose and R. Judah, as recorded in the
Mishna B. B. X, 5. and the Baraita B. M. 48b and 77b (Comp. also
Tosefta Ibid 1), are not based on the principle of Asmakta as the Amoraim
have interpreted. According to the Amoraim, R. Judah holds אסמכתא
קניא לא and R. Jose is of the opinion אסמכתא קניא, while I pointed
out that the controversy between the Tannaim hinges on the principle
of intention. Thus my disagreement with Dr. Blau is not only on the
interpretation of tannaitic Halakah but also on the origin of Asmakta.

Dr. Blau states further that I did not quote the Mishna Baba Mezia
104a and the case which was quoted in the same tractate 104b
"apparently because he considered them as irrelevant to his theory,
while as a matter of fact they form part of it." Dr. Blau is
quite correct in his assertion that I considered them irrelevant to my
theory, but he errs in his other statement that "they form part of it."
My chief contention consists of the fact that the controversy between
R. Judah and R. Jose was one of Intention. In the Mishna Baba Mezia
104a the names of these Tannaim are not mentioned, and therefore
could not be considered relevant to my theory. The other case which
Dr. Blau quotes from Baba Mezia 104b is amoraic and the name of
Raba is given, and this certainly could not be conceived as part
of it. It is true that the Amoraim may have considered it as a part of
the tannaitic Halakah, but those who approach the tannaitic Halakah
from a critico-historical point of view naturally have to disregard the
amoraic interpretation where a critical study of tannaitic Halakah
based on internal evidence goes against it.

The point in which we chiefly disagree is in the interpretation and
the proper understanding of the Baraita B. M. 48b and 77b, which

369

הנוחן עירבון לחבירו ואמר לו אם אני חוזר בו ערבוני מחול לך :reads as follows

והלה אומר אם אני חוזר בו אכפול לך ערבונך נתקיימו התנאים דברי ר' יוסי ר' יהודה

אומר די שיקנה כנגד ערבונו. "If one (the buyer) gives a deposit and says,
if I withdraw I shall forfeit my deposit; and the seller says, if I withdraw I shall return double the amount of your deposit, R. Jose says
the conditions hold good; R. Judah, on the other hand, says that if
the seller withdraws the buyer may purchase according to his deposit."
If the controversy in the Mishna between R. Jose and R. Judah is to
be interpreted on the basis of Intention we then may follow the logic
of their arguments. According to R. Jose the buyer, giving a deposit
upon the purchase, had the intention of paying up the balance or else
forfeiting his deposit, while the seller, in accepting the deposit, had the
intention of turning over the article of sale or else paying double the
amount of the deposit. If either of them withdraws, the conditions
remain true as indicated. But according to R. Judah, who does not
take into consideration the idea of Intention, in case of the buyer's
withdrawal, he must lose his deposit because the giving of a deposit
is an act, while in the case of the seller's withdrawal, he does not have
to double the deposit, since it was only a promise—Intention—and
was not coupled with an act, and he had to return only the amount
deposited, or the buyer may acquire from the property the value of
his deposit. If, on the other hand, we accept Dr. Blau's point of view
as regards the controversy of R. Jose and R. Judah, based on "a fine by
agreement," we fail to understand why R. Judah held that in case the
buyer withdraws he is fined, since his deposit is forfeited, while if the
seller does so he is not fined, since he only returns the purchaser's
deposit. (Rashi's interpretation לא זה מוחל ולא זה כופל is based on the
amoraic interpretation of the Mishna which was erroneously construed. On the other hand, compare Maimonides Mekirah, XI, who
gives the right interpretation of the said Mishna אם חוזר בו הלוקח קנה
זה הערבון שהרי הוא תחת ידו ואם חוזר בו המוכר אין מחייבין אותו לכפול הערבון.
That this controversy is based on the principle of Intention may
also be seen from the Tosefta B. M. 1, 17. The Tosefta reads as follows:
מישכן לו בית ומישכן לו שדה ואמר לו אם לא נתתי לך מיכן ועד יום פלוני אין לי בידך
כלום הגיע הזמן ולא נתן יתקיים התנאים דברי ר' יוסי אמר ר' יהודה האיך זוכה זה
בדבר שאינה שלו אלא [ינחתנו] (יחננו). "If A transfers his house as security
to B and says 'if I shall not pay you by a certain date I have nothing
in your hands,' and if the date arrives and A does not pay, the condition holds good," according to R. Jose, while R. Judah says, "How
can a man acquire property which is not his, but should (cut off) divide

(ינתחנו). Namely: B has an equity in this property to the extent of his loan." Here, likewise, the principle of Intention is involved. When A borrowed the money from B giving him the house as security A had the full intention that if he should fail to repay when the time fell due the house was to remain with B. In this case there were both *act* and *intention* on the part of A. Rabbi Judah, who ignored the principle of Intention, said "How can B get the house which was not his, since the property was mortgaged to him for a certain amount? Therefore, if the amount was not paid to him (ינתחנו), i. e., he is to take out of the property the amount due him, and the rest he was to return to the owner."

Dr. Blau may be correct in his assertion that the Babylonian law exercised some influence on Jewish Halakah, which may be true with reference to the Babylonian Talmud, but has nothing to do with our Mishna and Tosefta. We must also remember that there is a great distinction between the Halakot in Mahuza on the Tigris and in Pumbiditha and those in Jerusalem, Jabnia, Usha.

As regards Dr. Blau's statement that "according to Jewish law words are not sufficient, there must be possession (קנין), which assumes definite forms," that is not the case, however. According to the tannaitic law possession is not necessary for acquiring property, as *res immobiles* can be acquired בכסף בשטר ובחזקה. Writing the deed of sale or transferring the money is enough to acquire property, and possession is not required. נכסים שיש להם אחריות נקנין בכסף בשטר ובחזקה, ושאין להם אחריות אין נקנין אלא במשיכה. Only in order to acquire *res mobiles* or *res nullius* is possession essential.

As to Dr. Blau's objection to my idea of Intention and to the interpretation of the Mishna ביצה שנולדה ביום טוב see the writer's answer in an article entitled, "Les Principes de Controverses Halachiques entre les écolés de Schammaï et de Hillel. Études sur la Jurisprudence Tannaitique," in *REJ*, XCIII (1932), 73–83.

A NOTE ON THE PRINCIPLE OF INTENTION
IN TANNAITIC LITERATURE

A Mishna in the Tractate Shab. 21 reports the following controversy between the Schools of Shammai and Hillel. בית שמאי
אומרים מעבירין (מנביהים) מעל השלחן עצמות וקליפין ובית הלל אומרים
מסלק את הטבלא כולה ומנערה. The School of Shammai say: Bones
and shells may be taken up from the table (on the Sabbath)
and the School of Hillel say: The entire table must be taken
and shaken. In the Tosefta the opinions of these two
schools are reversed.[1] We cannot assume that this is a scribal
error as the same reading is recorded in the Mishna of the
מתניתא דתלמודא דבני מערבא, ed. W. H. Lowe.

The contradiction between the Mishna and the Tosefta was
noticed by the rabbis of the Middle Ages, but they did not clarify
which source records the opinions held by the two schools correctly. Rashi apparently was of the opinion that the reading of our
Mishna is not the correct one and the opinions of the two schools
are to be reversed.[2]

To understand the underlying reasons for the difference
between these two schools and also to define which source has
the correct version, I shall make the following observations.
The difference of opinion between the two schools hinges on the
principle of intention.

I pointed out in my article "Studies in Tannaitic Jurisprudence"[3] that the controversy between the schools of Shammai
and Hillel, recorded in the first Mishna of Beza, as to whether

[1] בית הלל אומרים מנביהין מעל השלהן עצמות וקליפין ובית שמאי אומרים מסלק את
הטבלה כולה ומנערה. (Shab. 143a)
[2] אין אנו סומכין על משנתינו כמות שהיא שנויה אלא כוהלפת שיטהה וב׳ש כר׳ יהודה.
[3] *Journal of Jewish Lore and Philosophy*, Vol. 1, 1919; *idem*, "Asmakta or
Intention," *JQR*, Vol. XIX; "Les Dix-Huit Mesures," *REJ*, 68 pp. 22–34.

631

an egg laid on *Yom-tov* may be eaten on the holiday, in which the
School of Shammai decided in the affirmative and the School of
Hillel in the negative,[4] is based on the principle of intention.
According to the School of Hillel no act was considered valid
unless it was intended by the person, while the School of Shammai
disregarded intention.   Therefore many controversies between
these two schools, such as that recorded in the first Mishna of
Beza, would be the result of their differences on the principle
of intention. According to the Pentateuch any food to be eaten
on the Sabbath had to be prepared on the day previous.[5] For
this reason in the Hellenistic literature Friday was called
$\pi\alpha\rho\alpha\sigma\kappa\epsilon\upsilon\dot{\eta}$,[6] Friday was known as the day of preparation.
The same principle applied with respect to anything to be eaten
on holidays; it had to be prepared the day before. The School
of Shammai regarded an egg laid on a holiday as already prepared
before and hence permitted it to be eaten on the holiday, while
the School of Hillel laying stress on the person's intention or
lack of intention prohibited the eating of the egg on the holiday.

We also find the same difference as to the principle of intention
in the controversy between Rabbi Judah and Rabbi Simon.
We refer to the Mishna Beza 3.4 בכור שנפל לבור רבי יהודה אומר
ירד מומחה ויראה אם יש בו מום יעשה וישחוט ואם לאו לא ישחוט רבי שמעון
אומר כל שאין מומו ניכר מבעוד יום אין זה מן המוכן. If a firstling fell
into a pit (on a holiday) Rabbi Judah says: Let an expert go
down and look at it; if it has a blemish he may bring it up and
slaughter it, otherwise it may not be slaughtered. Rabbi Simon
says: If the blemish was not perceived on the day before, it
may be regarded as having been prepared (thus it cannot be
slaughtered on the holiday). Rabbi Judah, being a Shammaite,
held that the owner may slaughter the firstling on the holiday
because it has a blemish and was really prepared to be used
before the holiday, even though the owner was not aware of the
blemish before the holiday. Intention was not a prerequisite.

---

[4] ביצה שנולדה ביום טוב בית שמאי אומרים תאכל ובית הלל אומרים לא האכל.
[5] והיה ביום השישי והכינו, Ex. 16.5.
[6] *Ant.* XVI. 6, 2; John 19,14.
[7] See further "Studies in Tannaitic Jurisprudence", pp. 302–308.

Rabbi Simon, being a Hillelite, maintained that since the blemish was not known to the owner a day before the holiday he had no intention of using it on the holiday. Therefore it was not in the category of "prepared". According to the Tosefta Rabbi Simon was of the opinion that even were the blemish known the day previous and no expert had pronounced his opinion on the matter the animal could not be slaughtered on the holiday,[8] since the intention of the owner to use it on the holiday was lacking.

In the Halakot, where the principle of הכנה "prepared" is involved, the School of Shammai would be לקולא "lenient" while the School of Hillel would be לחומרא "strict".

The controversy in the Mishna Shab. 21 where according to the School of Shammai a person may take up the bones and shells from the table and where according to the School of Hillel he must remove the board and shake off the bones is indeed based on the principle of intention. According to the School of Shammai when an animal is slaughtered before the Sabbath and since the flesh is thus prepared for human beings it follows that the bones also have been prepared to be fed to the dogs.[9] One may therefore pick the bones from the table on the Sabbath and feed the dogs. But, according to the Hillelites, who stress the principle of intention, the person had no intention before the Sabbath of giving the bones to the dogs and therefore has no right to feed them, however he may take up the entire board and empty the contents on the floor.

To this Mishna the Gemara adds a statement of R. Nachman in which he says that the Shammaites were in agreement with R. Judah while the Hillelites were in agreement with R. Simon.[10] Rashi took R. Nachman's statement to mean that we cannot rely on this Mishna as it is recorded, but that we must reverse

---

[8] בכור שנפל לבור רבי שמעון אומר אפילו שמומו ניכר מערב יום טוב ולא התירו מומחא אין שוחטין אותו ביום טוב לפי שאינו מן המוכין.

[9] Comp. Tosefot Shab. 143a, עצמות וקליפין. לא כפי' הקונטריס דפי' אפילו קשין ואין ראוין לאכילת כלבים דהאי הנא אמרינן בגמרא דכרבי שמעון סבירא ליה ור' שמעון פ'ה אע'ג דאין ;... see also Tosefot Beza 2a, בעי לכל הפחות ראוית למאכל בהמה ראוין לא למאכל אדם ולא למאכל בהמה ולא נהירא ... לכך נ'ל שהם ראוים למאכל בהמה.

[10] אמר רב נחמן אנו אין לנו אלא בית שמאי כרבי יהודה ובית הלל כרבי שמעון.

the controversy.[11] However the statement in the Mishna is in order and R. Nachman meant to say that R. Judah was a Shammaite and followed the principle of this school, namely that intention of the person is not necessary in the laws of הכנה. R. Simon, on the other hand, was a Hillelite and held that the intention of the person is a *sine qua non* in the laws of הכנה.

In the case where a firstling fell into a pit (on a holiday) Rabbi Judah was of the opinion that if an expert descended into the pit and declared that the firstling had a blemish it might be slaughtered on the holiday since it had incurred the blemish before the holiday and therefore could be slaughtered by an Israelite, although the owner was not aware of the blemish before the holiday. Rabbi Simon maintained that although the animal may have incurred the blemish before the holiday, of which the owner was unaware, it meant he had no intention of slaughtering it. The animal, therefore, may not be slaughtered on the holiday.

Both R. Judah and R. Simon would agree that dogs could be fed with the flesh of a carcass if the animal had died before the Sabbath because, even according to the Hillelites, it would have been מוכן "prepared". R. Judah, who did not take into consideration any intention of a person, would also maintain that if the animal died on the Sabbath one would not be allowed to feed the dogs from the flesh of its carcass since the animal was still alive on the eve of the Sabbath, and could not be considered מוכן "prepared".[12]

The Palestinian Talmud found a contradiction in the words of R. Judah in the above mentioned statement.[13] It was maintained that R. Judah's opinion, as recorded in tractate Beza, must be reversed since it was at variance with his statement as recorded in tractate Shabbat. However, as we have explained, the controversy between these two sages was on the principle of intention. R. Judah was not at variance with his statement

---

[11] See above note 2.

[12] מהכין את הדילועין לפני הבהמה ואת הנבלה לפני הכלבים רבי יהודה אומר אם לא היתה נבלה מערב שבת אסורה לפי שאינה מן המוכן, Shab. 24.4.

[13] כהלפה שיטתיה דר' יהודה דתנינן תמן ר' יהודה אומר אם לא היתה נבלה מערב שבת כו' אסורה לפי שאינו מן המוכן והכא הוא אמר הכי, Beza 62a.

in tractate Shabbat and it is unnecessary to reverse his statements.

In conclusion I may say that the Mishna Shab. 21, as recorded
in the Babylonian Talmud, is the correct version and that which
was before. R. Nachman. The controversy was between the
Schools of Shammai and Hillel on the principle of intention.
The School of Shammai would be לקולא "lenient" while the
School of Hillel would be לחומרא "strict". The question has
already been raised why this controversy was not quoted in the
Tractate of Eduyyot where all the קולי בית שמאי וחומרי בית הלל
are recorded.[14] This may be readily explained. Many controversies between these two schools where the Shammaites were
lenient and the Hillelites strict were not recorded in this tractate.
The Palestinian Talmud of *Ket.* 8 remarked that apparently
only those controversies where the Shammaites were lenient
and the Hillelites strict from every angle were recorded.[15]   In
our instance the main controversy was: May a person take the
bones and shells from the table and feed the dogs, or may he
lift the entire board and shake its contents on the floor. In any
case the dogs would be fed and the controversy was only regarding the act of the person. Therefore there is no leniency and
strictness from every angle.

The version as recorded in the Tosefta[16] and the Palestinian
Mishna is faulty. We must assume that this change in the reading was made at a very early period. But why? I believe that
this also may be explained. The rabbis in the Talmud as well as
the rabbis of the Middle Ages explained that this controversy
between the Schools of Shammai and Hillel was not on the
principle of הכנה but on the principle of מוקצה.[16]   In the latter

---

[14] Comp. Tosefot Shab. 143a, במסכת עדיות לא מיתניא בהדי קולי בית שמאי וחומרי
וי"ל דבעדיות לא תני לה טקולי בית שמאי Tosefot Beza 2b; בית הלל והיינו כרב נחמן
ומחומרי בית הלל.

[15] ר' פנחס בעא קומי ר' יוסי ולמה לא תניתה טקולי בית שמאי ומחומרי בית הלל אמר
ליה לא אהינן מיתני אלא דבר חמור משני צדדין וקל משני צדדין ברם הכא חומר הוא מצד
אחד וקל מצד אחר. Comp. also Yer. Pe'a 6.2. See also Tosefot Ket. 78a
[16] בית הלל אומרים מנביהין מעל השולחן עצמות וקליפין ובית שמאי אומרים סלק את
הטבלה כולה ומנערה.

[16] Comp. Beza 2a, כאי טעמייהו דבית שמאי מוקצה היא ומאי קושיא דילמא בית שמאי
ליה להו מוקצה... אכר רב נהכן בתרנגולת העומדת לנדל בצים ודאית ליה מוקצה

90

case the Hillelites were always lenient[17] while the Shammaites
were strict. Hence the reading was reversed. Furthermore we
may assume that since this controversy between the Shammaites
and the Hillelites, as recorded in our Mishna, is not found among
the מקולי בית שמאי ומחומרי בית הלל in the Tractate Eduyyot,
therefore it was thought that our reading was faulty and was
changed. But the version of our Mishna is correct and that of
the Tosefta and the Palestinian Mishna is faulty.

The controversies between the Schools of Shammai and Hillel
as well as those between R. Judah and R. Simon on the principles
of הכנה and of מוקצה are very complicated and in many passages
of the Talmud the Amoraim made them still more so.

In this note I hope I have shed some light on the Mishna
Shab. 21. I am aware that in many passages of the Talmud
the reader will find some complications, and even contradictions
to my theory. My theory is based *only* on the tannaitic literature, the product of the Tannaim, and it is my belief that the
controversies between the two Schools were not fully understood
and hence the meanings were confused.[18]

אית ליה נולד ודלית ליה מוקצה לית ליה נולד בית שמאי כרבי שמעון ובית הלל כרבי יהודה
וכי אמר רב נחמן הכי והתנן בית שמאי אומרים מגביהין מעל השולחן עצמות וקליפין ובית
הלל אומרים מסלק את הטבלא כולה ומנערה ואמר רב נחמן אנו אין לנו אלא בית שמאי כרבי
יהודה ובית הלל כרבי שמעון.

[17] Comp. Shab. 45a, ... אין מוקצה לרבי שמעון אלא שמן שבנר בשעה שהוא דולק
אין מוקצה לרבי שמעון אלא גרוגרות וצימוקים בלבד.

[18] In a future study on the history of the tannaitic halaka I hope to shed
more light on these principles.

THE SEMIKAH CONTROVERSY BETWEEN
THE ZUGOTH *

IT is a well-known fact that equivocal expressions are
frequently misleading even to scholars. The semikah
controversy between the Zugoth is an illustration of such
an equivocal expression that has given rise to error. This
controversy is of great significance, because it is the first
one recorded in the Talmud, and because, although it was
continued through the administration of all the successive
Zugoth, no agreement was reached on the subject.

The word סמיכה has various meanings in the Talmud:

(a) It is used in the sense of proximity as: אין סומכין
לשדה תבואה, חרדל וחריע. אבל סומכין לשדה ירקות חרדל וחריע
(Kil'oim, II, 9). 'It is not allowed to sow mustard and
bastard saffron closely adjoining to a field which was sown
with grain, because this is a forbidden junction (כלאים); but
it is allowed to sow mustard and bastard saffron closely
adjoining to a field which was sown with herbs, for this is
not a forbidden junction.'

(b) It is also used in the sense of laying on of hands as:
בית שמאי אומרין מביאין שלמים ואין סומכין עליהם . . . . . . וב״ה אומרין
מביאים שלמים ועולות וסומכין עליהם (Ḥagigah II, 3). 'The school
of Shammai says, It is allowed to bring peace-offerings on
the holidays, but the laying on of the hands must not be

* Zugoth (זוגות), meaning Pairs, is the Talmudic appellation for the two
leaders of the Sanhedrin from the days of Jose b. Joezer and Jose b. Joḥanan
(about 160 B.C.E.) till the time of Hillel and Shammai.

done on the holidays. The school of Hillel says, It is allowed to bring both peace-offerings and burnt-offerings on the holidays and to lay the hands on them.'

(c) It is used, again, in the sense of relying upon an authority as : נסמוך על דברי זקן (Erubin 65 b). 'We may rely upon the authority of the aged man (R. Hanina b. Joseph)', or הלכות שבת חגיגות.....שהן מקרא מועט והלכות מרובות יש להן על מי שיסמכו הן הן גופי תורה (according to the Munich MS.) (Ḥagigah I, 8). 'The laws concerning the Sabbath and the festive sacrifices which are numerous although only a few of them are Biblical, are nevertheless essential parts of the Law because we have them on good authority.' (From this also developed the 'Semikah' which is given to a scholar, thus investing him with authority.)

In all places where a dispute concerning semikah occurs, we can easily see from the context in what sense the word is used. In the case of the semikah controversy between the Zugoth, however, the Mishnah says obscurely לסמוך and שלא לסמוך without stating explicitly the sense in which the word is used, thus giving rise to misunderstanding. The Mishnah reads as follows : יוסי בן יועזר אומר שלא לסמוך יוסי בן יוחנן אומר לסמוך. יהושע בן פרחיה אומר שלא לסמוך נתאי הארבלי אומר לסמוך. יהודה בן טבאי אומר שלא לסמוך שמעון בן שטח אומר לסמוך. שמעיה אומר לסמוך אבטליון אומר שלא לסמוך. הלל ומנחם לא נחלקו יצא מנחם נכנס שמאי.¹ הלל אומר לסמוך שמאי אומר שלא לסמוך. הראשונים היו נשיאים ושניים להם אבות בתי דינין (Ḥagigah, II, 2).

All the commentators are of the opinion that the semikah controversy between the Zugoth is identical with the controversy between the schools of Shammai and Hillel

¹ Hillel before Shammai. So is the version in P. Ḥag. II, 2, and B. Shabb. 15 a.

recorded in the succeeding Mishnah as to whether or not
it is allowed to perform the ceremony of the 'laying on of
hands' upon the head of the sacrificial animal in the
temple-court on holidays.[2]   It seems to me, however, that
the identification of those two controversies, which is
evidently based on the mere fact that the editors of the
Mishnah placed them contiguously, is still an open question.
For it would appear surprising, indeed, that all the Zugoth
should not have been able to find a solution for a halakic
problem which is a mere *shebot* (שבות).

This was indeed noticed by Frankel in his דרכי המשנה,
pp. 43–4, and by Weiss in דור דור, pp. 103–4.   They nevertheless did not abandon the traditional interpretation.

It would also be strange that while in the case of the
schools of Shammai and Hillel the Mishnah states explicitly
the problem of their controversy, in the case of the Zugoth
the problem is stated obscurely by the words לסמוך and
שלא לסמוך.

A close examination of the Tosefta and Palestinian
Talmud will show that the dispute between the Zugoth is
not identical with that of the schools of Shammai and
Hillel as is generally assumed; that the controversy of the
Zugoth centred around an important general principle
rather than on the question of the propriety of performing
the semikah ceremony in the temple-court on holidays.
The Tosefta reads: מימיהם לא נחלקו אלא על הסמיכה. חמשה
זוגות הן שלשה מזוגות הראשונים שאמרו שלא לסמוך היו נשיאים ושנים
אבות בית דין. שנים מזוגות האחרונים שאמרו לסמוך היו נשיאים ושנים
אבות בית דין..... אמר ר' יוסי מתחילה לא היו מחלוקות בישראל
אלא בבית דין של עשרים ושלשה וכו'..... איזו היא הסמיכה שנחלקו

ב"ש אומרים מביאין שלמים ואין סומכין עליהם אבל לא עולות וב"ה[2]
אומרים מביאין שלמים ועולות וסומכין עליהם (Hag. II, 3; Bes. II, 4).

94

עליה ב״ש וב״ה. ³ ב״ש אומרים אין סומכין ביו״ט שלמים שחנג בהן
סומך עליהן מערב יו״ט וב״ה אומרים מביאין שלמים ועולות וסומכין
עליהן (Tosef. Ḥagigah, II, 8–10). 'Never was there a controversy in Israel except the one concerning semikah.
There were five Zugoth.   Three of the earlier Zugoth who
were of the opinion שלא לסמוך were presidents (of the
Sanhedrin) and their opponents were vice-presidents ; two
of the latter Zugoth who held the view לסמוך were presidents
and their opponents were vice-presidents . . . . . Said R. Jose,
Formerly no controversy occurred in Israel except in a
court (בית דין) of twenty-three members . . . . .   Over which
semikah were the schools of Shammai and Hillel divided?
The school of Shammai said that the laying on of hands
on the festive sacrifices must not be done on a holiday ;
the semikah ceremony should be performed a day before
the holiday.   The school of Hillel said, It is allowed on
a holiday to bring peace and burnt-offerings and lay the
hands upon them.'

The fact that the Tosefta asks 'over which semikah
were the schools of Shammai and Hillel divided' and not
over which semikah were the Zugoth divided,⁴ clearly
shows that the two controversies were not considered
identical.   The P. Talmud reads : בראשונה לא היתה מחלוקת
בישראל אלא על הסמיכה בלבד ועמדו שמאי והלל ועשו אותן ד׳. כשרבו

---

³ See הנהות הגר״א on the Tosef.

⁴ מעשה בהלל הזקן שהביא את עולתו לעזרה וסמך עליה ביו״ט חברו
עליו תלמידי ב״ש . . . לאחר ימים נברה ידן של ב״ש ובקשו לקבע הלכה
כדבריהם והיה שם בבא בן בוטא מתלמירי ב״ש ויודע שהלכה כב״ה
(J. Ḥag. II, 78 a ; B. Beṣ. 20 a).   There is no evidence in this passage, as
some think, that the controversy of the Zugoth is identical with that of the
schools of Shammai and Hillel. The Talmud says here 'ויודע שהלכה
כבית הלל' ; but not שהלכה בהלל or כזוגות שאמרו לסמוך, which would
have been more proper if the two controversies were considered identical.

95

תלמידי ב״ש וב״ה ולא שמשו את רביהן כל צרכן רבו המחלוקות בישראל
(P. Talm. Ḥagigah II, 2).

It is evident from this passage that according to the P. Talmud the semikah was the only subject of contention that was debated during the administration of all the Zugoth (as a matter of fact we do find other controversies between the Zugoth, as for instance the controversy between Judah b. Tabbai and Simon b. Shataḥ [5] and the one between Joshuah b. Peraḥah and the Ḥakamim [6]).

The commentators have erred in considering the words לסמוך and שלא לסמוך, that are used in the case of the Zugoth, identical with the words סומכין and אין סומכין that are used in the case of the controversy between the schools of Shammai and Hillel.[7] The words לסמוך and שלא לסמוך do not denote here to lay on the hands on an object, but express the derivative meaning of the verb, as in the phrase נסמוך על דברי זקן (Erub. 65 b), מיסמך סמיכא דעתיהו (Ḥag. 20 b), יש להם על מי שיסמכו (ibid., Mishnah I, 8), i. e. to depend, to rely, to accept the authority of,[8] and the question discussed by the Zugoth was whether we could depend upon the authority of the Ḥakamim.

It is very probable that this Mishnah, which is the second of the second chapter of Ḥagigah, is closely related to the last Mishnah of the first chapter which contains the statement that the laws concerning the Sabbath and festive sacrifices, &c., which are numerous although few of them

[5] Hag. 16 b; Mak. 5 b; Tosef. Sanhed. V, VI.

[6] Tosef. Makširin, III, 4.

[7] See Frankel, דרכי המשנה, ff. 43-4; Weiss, דור, V, I, ff. 103-4.

[8] A. Sidon, 'Die Controverse der Synhedrialhäupter' in *Gedenkbuch für Erinnerung an David Kaufmann*, ff. 355-64. He was the first to interpret the semikah of this Mishnah in the sense of relying upon authority and not in the sense of 'laying on of hands'.

are Biblical, are nevertheless essential parts of the Law because we have them on good authority. This Mishnah developing the subject further, informs us that the question as to whether or not we ought to rely upon the Ḥakamim in their innovations has not always been generally accepted; but it was rather the subject of contention during the administration of all the Zugoth.

Three of the earlier and two of the latter Zugoth say: שלא לסמוך, i. e. we ought not to rely on the Ḥakamim in their innovations upon the Torah. Their colleagues say: לסמוך, i. e. we rely entirely upon the Ḥakamim even in their innovations upon the Torah.

An examination of the few halakic statements of the Zugoth which have been transmitted to us corroborates this interpretation of the controversy of the Zugoth.

We shall also be able to understand their obscure halakoth which were transmitted to us.

The first pair which was divided over the semikah question was Jose b. Joezer and Jose b. Joḥanan. יוסי בן יועזר אומר שלא לסמוך יוסי בן יוחנן אומר לסמוך. Now, no halakah is recorded of Jose b. Joḥanan, excepting the decree which he issued together with Jose b. Joezer declaring Gentile territory and glass vessels as levitically unclean.[9] It is undoubtedly to be assumed that his halakic opinions are included in the anonymous ancient halakoth of the Talmud. Of Jose b. Joezer, however, we have three halakot as testimonies (עדיות) from which the inference may be drawn that by these testimonies he set himself in opposition to the ordinances of the Ḥakamim: העיד יוסי בן יועזר על איל קמצא דכן ועל משקה בית מטבחיא דכן ודיקרב במיתא מסאב וקרי ליה יוסי שריא (Ed. VIII, 4).

[9] Shabb. 14 b.

97

The content of this Mishnah is puzzling indeed. For, what is the purpose of his testimony? Is it not explicitly stated in the Torah: 'He that toucheth the dead body of any human person shall be unclean seven days' (Num. 19. 11)? The Talmud in fact wonders at this Mishnah: 'and they called him "Jose the permitter" (יוסי שריא), they ought to have called him "Jose the forbidder" (יוסי אסרא מבעי ליה)'! (Ab. Zar. 37 b). Should we assume, however, that by שלא לסמוך Jose b. Joezer meant that we ought not to rely upon the authority of the Ḥakamim in their innovations upon the Torah, the purpose of his testimonies will become clear to us. For with these testimonies Jose b. Joezer opposed the tradition of the Ḥakamim who decree what was not to be found in the Torah. This was in accordance with his own view that 'we ought not to depend upon' the decrees and traditions of the Ḥakamim (שלא לסמוך).

The meaning of these testimonies thus becomes clear:

I. איל קמצא דכן (the locust) il ḳamṣa is clean and may be eaten. For, Biblically, those locusts are clean 'that go upon all fours, which have jointed legs above their feet', ההלך על ארבע אשר לו כרעים ממעל לרגליו (Lev. 11. 21). But the Ḥakamim said that the marks of cleanness in locusts are: four legs, four wings, hindlegs for leaping and the wings covering the greatest part of the body, ארבע רגלים ארבע כנפים וקרצולים וכנפיו חופין את רובו (Ḥul. 59 a; ibid., 65 a). In this matter, therefore, he opposed the decree of the Ḥakamim requiring those additional marks of cleanness, and maintained that the locust il ḳamṣa which had only the marks pointed out in the Torah, was clean [10] and might be eaten.

[10] Ab. Zar. 37 a, b.

II. ‏משקה בית מטבחיא דכן‎ The liquid of the slaughtering-place is clean. Biblically, 'All drink in every such vessel that may be drunk shall be unclean' ‏כל משקה אשר ישתה בכל‎ ‏כלי יטמא‎ (Lev. 11. 34). Thus only water is susceptible to levitical uncleanness. The Ḥakamim, however, decreed that blood and five other kinds of liquids are also susceptible of levitical uncleanness [11] (Sifra Shemini, VIII ; Pes. 17 a). To oppose this decree Jose b. Joezer testified that ‏משקה‎ ‏בית מטבחיא‎, i.e. blood, is ‏דכן‎, clean. For blood and the other liquids are not implied in the verse ‏משקה אשר ישתה‎ and therefore are not susceptible to uncleanness.[12]

III. ‏ודיקרב במיתא מסאב‎ One that touches a corpse becomes unclean. According to the Torah : 'He that toucheth the dead, even any man's dead body, shall be unclean seven days' ‏הנגע במת לכל נפש אדם יטמא שבעת ימים‎ (Num. 19. 11). The Ḥakamim decreed ‏חרב הרי הוא כחלל‎ [13] that the sword with which a person was killed had the same levitical status as the slain body, i.e. one who touches such a sword becomes unclean for seven days. Against this Jose b. Joezer testified that only ‏דיקרב במיתא‎ the one who touches the corpse becomes unclean, but not the one who touched a sword with which a person was slain.

It is because of these three testimonies that he was called 'Jose the permitter' ‏יוסי שריא‎, as in all of these he

[11] ‏אין לי מים מנין הטל והיין והשמן והדם והדבש והחלב ת״ל וכל‎ ‏משקה‎ (Sifra Šmini, IX).

[12] The Talmud (Pes. 17 a) has two different versions of this statement: ‏רב תני משקי בית מטבחיא ולוי תני משקי בית מדבחיא‎. According to our interpretation, however, it makes no difference. For by ‏משקי בית מטבחיא‎ is meant water and blood, and by ‏משקי בית מדבחיא‎ wine and oil.

[13] Pes. 14 b: ‏בחלל חרב. חרב הרי הוא כחלל‎. See Katzenelenson, *Sadducees and Pharisees*, Voschod ; S. Zeitlin, ' Les dix-huit Mesures ', *RÉJ.*, LXIII, 1914.

99

opposed the decrees of the Ḥakamim. This explains also the statement of the Mishnah מטפחתו היתה מדרס לקדש [14] that his towel was considered unclean of the first degree (מדרס) for those who observed the levitical laws prescribed for the handling of the sacred food. Obviously they declared it unclean because he did not subscribe to the decrees of the Ḥakamim in matters pertaining to the laws of levitical uncleanness.

This throws light upon an obscure narrative which R. Judah tells in the name of Jose b. Joezer: אמר ר' יהודה קורות נעץ (יוסי בן יועזר) להם ואמר עד כאן רשות הרבים עד כאן רשות היחיד (Ab. Zar. 37 b).

R. Judah who was engaged in the study of antiquity, and all of whose statements were undoubtedly based on tradition, tells us that Jose b. Joezer had erected beams and demonstrated: here the limits of the public road (רשות הרבים) end; here the limits of the private ground (רשות היחיד) end. It is rather strange that Jose b. Joezer, the president of the Sanhedrin, should personally go out in the streets of the city to erect beams for the purpose of fixing and demonstrating the limits of the private and public ground. This narrative, however, contains another instance of the application of Jose b. Joezer's principle not to accept the authority of the Ḥakamim in their innovations upon the Torah. For the law formerly recognized two classes of territory with regard to the Sabbath laws: public territory (רשות הרבים) where carrying on the Sabbath day was forbidden (as we find in Nehemiah's order to lock the gates of the city before the Sabbath, so that 'there should be brought in no burden on the Sabbath day', Neh. 13. 19); and private territory where carrying on the Sabbath was

[14] Ḥag. 18 b.

100

allowed (Shab. 96 b). The Ḥakamim, however, added
another class, namely, the Karmelith (כרמלית), i. e. private
territory used by the public, and forbade the carrying of
objects from it to the two other classes of territory and vice
versa. The Talmud, indeed, regarded the Karmelith as
a mere Rabbinical restriction (מדה) (Shabbat 11 b). Rejecting this new enactment of the Ḥakamim, Jose b. Joezer said:
Here the limits of the public ground end; here the limits
of the private ground end. I recognize two classes of
territory with regard to the Sabbath laws and no more.

Now, if we assume that the controversy between the
Zugoth was regarding the validity of the innovations of the
Ḥakamim, we shall be able to understand the only halakah
which has been transmitted to us from the second pair.

The second pair was Joshua b. Peraḥah and Nittai
the Arbelite. יהושע בן פרחיה אומ' שלא לסמוך נתאי הארבלי אומר
לסמוך. No halakah is accredited to Nittai the Arbelite;
but undoubtedly, as indicated above, his halakic opinions
were included among the anonymous ancient halakoth.

Of Joshua b. Peraḥah we have the following halakah:
יהושע בן פרחיה אומר חטים הבאים מאלכסנדריא טמאות מפני אנטליא
שלהן. אמרו חכמים אם כן יהיו טמאות ליהושע בן פרחיה וטהורות לכל
ישראל (Tosef. Makshirin, III, 4).

The argument of the Ḥakamim 'let the wheat be
unclean for Joshua b. Peraḥah but clean for all Israel', is
strange indeed. If it is considered clean for all Israel, why
should it be unclean for Joshua b. Peraḥah? But it becomes
clear when we realize that in this halakah Joshua b. Peraḥah
opposed the decree and tradition of the Ḥakamim.
Biblically, 'if any water be put upon the seed' וכי יתן מים על
זרע it becomes susceptible to levitical uncleanness (מכשר
לקבל טומאה), and no distinction is made between seed which

101

is fixed to the ground (מחובר לקרקע) and that which is
plucked (תלוש), for this is the implication of the phrase על זרע.
This, then, is the contention of Joshua b. Peraḥah: 'Wheat·
that is brought from Alexandria is unclean מפני אנטליא שלהן.'
אנטליא (= ἀντλίον) is the water-wheel with which the
Egyptians irrigated their fields from the Nile. Thus, water
was poured on the seed and it became susceptible to levitical
uncleanness. Whereupon the Ḥakamim answered: if so
'let the wheat be unclean for Joshua b. Peraḥah' who
disregards the tradition of the Ḥakamim, 'but clean to all
Israel' who accept the ordinance of the Ḥakamim: that
seed becomes susceptible to levitical uncleanness when
water has been poured over it only when it was already
detached from the earth (תלוש), but not while still fixed to
the ground (מחובר).[15]

The third pair was Judah b. Tabbai and Simon b.
Shataḥ יהודה בן טבאי אומר שלא לסמוך שמעון בן שטח אומר לסמוך.
Of Simon b. Shataḥ several laws and decrees have been
transmitted. A narrative of Judah b. Tabbai has come
down to us reflecting his attitude toward tradition:
אמר יהודה בן טבאי אראה בנחמה אם לא הרגתי עד זומם להוציא מלבן
של צדוקים שהיו אומרים אין עדים זוממים נהרגין עד שיהרג הנידון.
אמר לו שמעון בן שטח אראה בנחמה אם לא שפכת דם נקי שהרי
אמרו חכמים אין עדים זוממים נהרגין עד שיזומו שניהם.[16]

Judah b. Tabbai, who did not accept the decrees of
the Ḥakamim in their innovations upon the Torah, executed
one עד זומם. For according to the Bible, 'if a witness of
violence rise up against any man to testify against him for
any wrong . . . . . and the judges shall inquire diligently;
and behold, if the witness be a false witness, he hath testified

[15] Sifra T. K. Šmini 11; Tosef. Makširin, I.
[16] Ḥag. 16 b; Mak. 5 b; Tosef. Sanhed. VI.

a falsehood against his brother: then shall ye do unto him
as he hath purposed to do unto his brother', כי יקום עד שקר
באיש ... והנה עד שקר העד שקר ענה באחיו ועשיתם לו כאשר זמם, &c.
(Deut. 19. 16–19). This implies that even if one witness was
proved זומם, he is to be executed. Simon b. Shataḥ, on
the other hand, who accepted the innovations of the
Ḥakamim upon the Torah, reproached Judah b. Tabbai
for having shed innocent blood (שפכת דם נקי), for the
Ḥakamim said: עדים זוממים do not incur the penalty unless
both were found זוממים. ע"פ שנים עדים יומת המת' מה עדים'
שנים אף זוממים שנים (Tosef. Sanhed. VI, 6).

The fourth pair was Shemaiah and Abtalyon: שמעיה אומר
לסמוך אבטליון אומר שלא לסמוך. Of this pair, several halakoth
were transmitted by others in their name;[17] but no halakoth
have come down from them directly from which their
attitude toward tradition might be inferred. In the
testimonies that others made in their name they always
concur.[18]

[17] Yebam. 67 a; Edu. I, 3.

[18] There is a passage in the Talmud attributed to Shammai the elder:
האומר לשלוחו צא הרג את הנפש הוא חייב ושולחיו פטור. שמאי הזקן
אומר משום חגי הנביא שולחיו חייב שנאמר אותו הרגת בחרב בני עמון
(Ḳid. 43 b). 'If any one said to his agent: go slay a person, the agent is
liable for the crime but the instigator is not responsible. Shammai the elder
said in the name of Ḥaggai the prophet: the instigator is liable for the crime,
for it is written: "Him hast thou slain with the sword of the children of
Ammon" (2 Sam. 12. 9). (Nathan the prophet charged David with the
crime of killing Urijah, although David only gave the order to expose him
in the battle front.)' To my mind the attribution of this statement to
Shammai is open to question. For from the Talmudic discussion (*ibid.*, 42 b)
it appears that the school of Shammai held that the instigator is free from
penalty (שולחיו פטור) : על כל דבר פשע ב"ש אומרים שחייב על המחשבה
כמעשה וב"ה אומרים אינו חייב עד שישלח בו יד שנאמר אם לא שלח
ידו. אמרו ב"ש לב"ה והלא נאמר על כל דבר פשע אמרו להם ב"ה
לב"ש והלא נאמר אם לא שלח ידו כו' אמרו ב"ש לב"ה אם כן על כל

The fifth and last pair was Hillel and Shammai. Aside from the semikah controversy of all the Zugoth we find

דבר פשע למה לי? שיכול אין לי אלא הוא אמר לעבדו ולשלוחו מניין ת״ל על כל דבר פשע. It is thus evident from this passage that the school of Shammai held that שולחיו פטור. Now if Shammai is the author of the statement that the instigator is liable (שולחיו חייב), deriving his opinion from the verse אותו הרגת, the school of Shammai would have replied to the school of Hillel that the opinion that the instigator is liable one may derive from the verse אותו הרגת and thus revert to their argument על כל דבר פשע למה לי?. This proves the fact that the school of Shammai did not know that שולחיו חייב is derived from the verse אותו הרגת. But would this be possible if Shammai was the author of the statement? As a matter of fact it is very doubtful if Shammai ever used the method of deriving halakic opinions from Biblical intimations (דרש פסוקים). The law derived from the verse עד רדתה which the Talmud attributes to Shammai, וכן היה שמאי אומר עד רדתה אפילו בשבת (Shabb. 19 a) is quoted in the Tosef. (MS.) in the name of Hillel: הלל הזקן דורש אפילו בשבת (Erub. III, 7). The Sifre brings this statement in the name of Shammai, and continues: זו אחד מג׳ דברים שדרש שמאי הזקן (Sifre Šoftim 203). We do not find, however, in the entire Talmud the other two cases. Should we accept the version of the Tosefta, the statement of the Sifre could be referred to Hillel rather than to Shammai. For we do find Hillel deriving laws from Biblical intimations in two other instances: (1) ונוגע בנבלתם יטמא. הלל אומר ונרפא הנתק. הלל אומר ולא (2); (Sifra Šmini); אפילו הם בתוך המים שניתק נתק בתוך נתק (Sifra Tazria 9). We also find elsewhere that Hillel went up from Babylon because of three things על שלש׳ דברים עלה הלל מבבל (J. Talmud Pesaḥ, VI, 33 a). It is highly probable, therefore, that in the case of the law derived from the verse אותו הרגת we should read שמעיה אומ instead of שמאי. This agrees with the narrative of Josephus (Antiq., XIV, 9, 4), that Sameas, reprimanding his colleagues for suppressing their opinion in the case of Herod, said that Herod deserved capital punishment for instigating his men to kill Hezekiah and his followers. For according to his own view : 'האומר לשלוחו צא הרג את הנפש שולחיו חייב'. The narrative of Josephus is identical with the Talmudic narrative : עבדיה דינאי מלכא קטל נפשא אמר להם שמעון בן שטח לחכמים תנ' עיניכם ונדוננו (Sanhed. 19 a). Here, surely, we ought to read שמעיה instead of שמעון בן שטח ; ינאי מלכא here = הרדוס. See Derenbourg, Histoire de la Palestine depuis Cyrus jusqu'à Adrien, Paris, pp. 146-8 ; Graetz, Geschichte der Juden, vol. 3 II, note 16.

several other disputations between Shammai and Hillel. According to the Palestinian Talmud, Shammai and Hillel were divided upon four issues;[19] according to the Babylonian Talmud they disagreed upon three issues.[20]   It is highly probable that the two versions are not contradictory.   The Babylonian Talmud may have omitted the semikah controversy, considering it as included in the controversy of the Zugoth.   The first Mishnah of Eduyoth records three controversies between Shammai and Hillel: שמאי אומר כל הנשים דיין שעתן. והלל אומ' מפקידה לפקידה. שמאי אומר מקב לחלה והלל אומר מקבים. הלל אומר מלא הין מים שאובין פוסלים את המקוה שחייב אדם לומר בלשון רבו [21] שמאי אומר ט' קבים.

[19] בראשונה לא היתה מחלוקת בישראל אלא על הסמיכה בלבד ועמדו
שמאי והלל ועשו אותן ד' (J. Ḥag. II, 2).

[20] אמר רב הונא בג' מקומות נחלקו שמאי והלל (Shabb. 15 a).

[21] After the Munich manuscript.   In our printed editions the reading is שחייב אלא.   The word אלא, however, has no meaning here.   The traditional interpretation of the Mishnah is that Hillel said מלא הין instead of הין in order to quote the exact expression of his teachers Shemaiah and Abtalyon, who being descendants of proselytes (בני גרים) pronounced הין like אין, and for this reason they said מלא הין to distinguish it from אין. (See Maimonides' Com. to this Mishnah; also J. Brüll, מבוא המשנה, note 14). The legend that Shemaiah and Abtalyon were descendants of Gentiles (Gittin 57 b), misled the Talmudic commentators and scholars in the interpretation of another Mishnah (see Yoma 71 b מעשה בכהן גדול וכו', the expression 'ייתן בני עממין' does not necessarily mean sons of Gentiles. It may refer to the people over against the priest): עקביה בן מהללאל העיר ד' דברים . . . . . .הוא היה אומר אין משקין לא את הגיורת ולא שפחה משוחררת. וחכמים אומרים משקין. אמרו לו מעשה בכרכמית שפחה משוחררת שהיתה בירושלים והשקוה שמעיה ואבטליון. אמר להם דוגמא השקוה. ונדוהו ומת בנדוי (Eduyoth, V, 6).   All the Talmudic commentators and scholars (see Weiss, דור דור, ver. 1, p. 176; I. Levi, Wörterbuch, on the word דוגמא; also Aruk) are of the opinion that Akabya was excommunicated because he showed disrespect to Shemaiah and Abtalyon by saying דוגמא השקוה, which they interpreted to mean : they showed favoritism to their own class in giving the 'testing water' to one who was a proselyte like

Another controversy between Shammai and Hillel is found in Shabb. 15 a: הבוצר לגת שמאי אומר הוכשר לקבל טומאה והלל אומר לא הוכשר.

In these four controversies four principles are involved with which Hillel proposed to start a new development in the Oral Law: (1) סיג לתורה, i. e. where an apprehension exists lest a Biblical law may be transgressed we ought to take a preventive measure. (2) Leniency in law (צד קולא)· (3) Semikah. (4) Subjectivity, i. e. we ought to reckon with the intention of the person. In these four principles Shammai was his opponent.

These were the issues between them:

(1) שמאי אומר כל הנשים דיין שעתן והלל אומר מפקידה לפקידה.

Thus, according to Shammai, the sacred food which a woman handled a moment before her menstruation is levitically clean; but according to Hillel all the sacred food which she handled since her last בדיקה is unclean. Here a very rigorous law as נדה is involved, and since it may be feared that she might err, we ought to take the preventive measure of declaring all the sacred food that she handled since her last בדיקה levitically unclean. But Shammai maintained that

themselves. This interpretation, however, is erroneous. The version in the P. Talmud is דוכמה instead of דוגמא (P. Talm. Moed katan, III, 81 d), and the explanation there given of the word דוכמה is that it is equivalent to דכוותה. The interpretation of our Mishnah thus becomes apparent. Akabya b. Mehalalel said דוכמה השקוהו, i. e. Shemaiah and Abtalyon gave the 'testing waters' not to an emancipated handmaid (שפחה משוחררת), but to one who is like unto her (דכוותה), namely, a Hebrew handmaid (אמה עבריה). Akabya thus contradicted the Ḥakamim who cited the case of Karkemith to corroborate their opinion and denied the fact that she was a proselyte. Akabya was not excommunicated for this halakah alone, but for all the four halakoth in which he stubbornly resisted the opinion of the Ḥakamim. R. Eliezer b. Hyrcans was excommunicated for a similar attitude toward the opinion of the Ḥakamim.

we do not entertain such fears and there is no need of any
preventive measure. Let the strict law prevail. It is
incumbent upon the woman to guard herself. A similar
issue was disputed between the schools of Shammai and
Hillel: העוף עולה עם הגבינה על השלחן ואינו נאכל דברי ב"ש וב"ה
אומרים לא עולה ולא נאכל (Edu. V, 2; Ḥul. 104 b).

The school of Hillel contended that fowl should not be
allowed to be placed on the same table with cheese, because
if the fowl and the cheese would lie on the same table, one
might forget and eat them together. Therefore it is
necessary to take the preventive measure and forbid to
place them on the same table. The school of Shammai, on
the other hand, permitted it because no preventive measures
were necessary. For a human being ought to know what
is permitted and what is forbidden.

(2) שמאי אומר מקב לחלה והלל אומר מקביים. Hillel adopting
the principle of leniency maintained that dough of less than
two *Kabbim* is not to be considered technically an עיסה
subject to the law of חלה. Shammai, on the other hand,
maintained that dough of one *Kab* also constitutes technically
the עיסה which is subject to the law of חלה. For the strict
law must prevail.

(3) The following controversy involves the question of
semikah: הלל אומר מלא הין מים שאובין פוסלים את המקוה שחייב[22]
אדם לומר בלשון רבו. שמאי אומר ט' קבים. According to Hillel
a Hin of 'drawn water' (מים שאובין) is sufficient to make the
pond unfit for ritual immersion, שחייב אדם לומר בלשון רבו,
because one must use his teacher's words, i. e. one 'must
depend upon' the teaching and tradition of his master.[23]

---

[22] See the previous note.

[23] The word לשון is used in the Talmud in the sense as: אין לנו
בעירובין אלא כלשון משנתנו' Erub. 66 b).

Shammai opposing this tradition of Hillel maintained that nine *Kabbim* of 'drawn water' made the pond unfit. For since such an amount of water can be used for the purification of a בעל קרי or for a sick person,[24] it is sufficient to make the מקוה unfit.[25]

(4) Intention: whether we ought to reckon with the intention of a person. הבוצר לגת שמאי אומר הוכשר לקבל טומאה,

[24] Berak. 22 a ; Mikw. III, 4.

[25] The Ḥakamim accepted neither the opinion of Hillel nor that of Shammai until they heard a testimony in the name of Shemaiah and Abtalyon : וחכמים אומרים לא כדברי זה ולא כדברי זה עד שבאו שני גרדיים משער האשפה שבירושלים והעידו משום שמעיה ואבטליון שג' לוגין מים פוסלין את המקוה, וקיימו חכמים את דבריהם (Eduy. I, 3). It would appear that a tradition of Shemaiah and Abtalyon had so much weight with them that they relied upon it even though it was transmitted by two weavers. Similarly, when the Bne Bthera, in their perplexity as to whether the Passover offering suspended the Sabbath laws (Pes. 66 a ; J. VI, 1), heard that there was a Babylonian present who had *served* Shemaiah and Abtalyon, they immediately sent for him. The decision of Hillel the Babylonian that the Passover offering suspended the Sabbath laws, arrived at by means of the ק"ו, גז"ש, and היקש, was, however, entirely disregarded until he said : 'so I heard from the mouth of Shemaiah and Abtalyon'. It is probable that Hillel proposed to introduce an innovation in the Oral Law, that in a case where there was no precedent, every Beth Din should have the right to decide by means of three hermeneutic rules : the inference from minor and major (קל וחומר), analogy of expression (גזירה שוה) and comparison (היקש). Unwilling to agree to this innovation, the Bne Bthera did not accept his decision until he quoted Shemaiah and Abtalyon. The reason why the Bne Bthera were perplexed in this case, was, perhaps, because they had no tradition on the matter. The difficulty of the P. Talmud : והלא אי אפשר לשני שביעית שׁ[לא]יחול ארבעה עשר להיות בשבת ולמה נתעלמה הלכה מהן? (J. Pes. VI, 1, 33 a). 'Since it is impossible that the fourteenth of Nisan should not fall at least once in fourteen years on a Sabbath day, why, then, did they forget the law?' (see Slonimsky, העיבור, Warsaw) may thus also be explained. The administration of the Bne Bthera followed upon the administration of the Zugoth who were divided over the semikah question. The Bne Bthera, therefore, either had no tradition on the matter or did not 'depend upon' tradition.

הלל אומר לא הכשר. Grapes which were gathered from the field for the wine-press are susceptible to levitical uncleanness, according to Shammai, by the juice that runs out of the grapes. For such a case also is implied in וכי יתן מים על זרע. According to Hillel they do not thus become susceptible. For the juice came out upon the grapes without the owner's intention ; neither does he need this juice. Now Hillel's reply to Shammai is clear : אמר לו הלל לשמאי מפני מה בוצרין בטהרה ואין מוסקין בטהרה. אמר לו שמאי להלל אם תקניטני גוזרני טומאה אף על המסיקה (Shabb. 17 a).

Hillel said thus to Shammai : thou sayest that grapes must be gathered in clean vessels because their juice make them susceptible to uncleanness, though this juice is not needed; yet thou sayest that olives need not be gathered in clean vessels because no one desires the liquid that runs out of the olives [26] and it is therefore not implied in כי יתן. Said Shammai to Hillel אם תקניטני, i.e. if thou wilt bring the principle of intention to prevail, I shall decree that olives are also made susceptible to levitical uncleanness by their own liquid though no one desires this superfluity. Like the others it would appear that this view of Hillel was not adopted at that time, for the same dispute was continued by the schools of Shammai and Hillel : המניח כלים תחת הצנור לקבל מי גשמים .... פוסלין את המקוה. אחד המניח ואחד השוכח דברי ב"ש וב"ה מטהרין בשוכח [27]. The school of Hillel, following the principle of its founder that we must reckon with a person's intention, maintained that the rain-water made the מקוה unfit only when the vessels were placed there intentionally. Otherwise, if the vessels were left under the pipe through forgetfulness and were not intended

[26] Tosef. Toharoth, X, 2.
[27] Mikv. IV, 1 ; Shabb. 16 b

to receive the rain-water the latter does not render the מקוה unfit. The school of Shammai not accepting the principle of intention, declared that in either case the מקוה became unfit.[28]

These are the four controversies between Shammai and Hillel. They mark the beginning of the development of the controversies between the schools of Shammai and Hillel.

[28] See Katzenelenson, *Sadducees and Pharisees*, Voschod; S. Zeitlin, ' Les dix-huit Mesures', *RÉJ.*, LXIII, 1914.

THE SEMIKAH CONTROVERSY BETWEEN THE
SCHOOL OF SHAMMAI AND HILLEL

IN AN ARTICLE PUBLISHED IN APRIL 1917, in this *Review*, I dealt with the problem of the Semikah Controversy between the Zugoth. [1] In it I endeavored to show that this controversy did not revolve around the question of laying the hands on the animal brought for sacrifice during the festivals. I ventured to advance the theory that the controversy between the Zugoth over the Semikah was over Semikah tradition. I substantiated my view on internal evidence, on the halakot recorded in the name of the *Zugoth*. [2]

The Semikah controversy between the schools of Shammai and Hillel was, however, on the laying of hands on the sacrifice. The school of Shammai maintained that one may bring on the festivals a peace offering but not lay the hands thereon, but no one may bring burnt-offerings. The school of Hillel held that one may bring both peace offerings and burnt-offerings on the holidays and lay his hands thereon. [3] This controversy between the two schools took place during the time of Hillel. It is recorded that Hillel once brought a burnt-offering on the holiday with the intention of laying his hands thereon. However, the Shammaites, having gained the upper hand, forced Hillel to change his sacrifice from a burnt-offering to a peace offering. [4] When the view of the

[1] The Semikah Controversy Between the Zugoth, *JQR*, 1917, pp. 499-517.

[2] Cf. pp. 504-513.

[3] Hag. 2. 3. בית שמאי אומרים מביאין שלמים ואין סומכין עליהן אבל לא עולות ובית הלל אומרים מביאין שלמים ועולות וסומכין עליהן.

Cf. also M. Betzah 2. 4.

[4] Yer. Hag. 2. מעשה בהלל הזקן שהביא עולתו לעזרה וסמך עליה חברו עליו תלמידי בית שמאי התחיל מכשכש בזנבה אמר להן ראו נקיבה היא ושלמים.

Cf. Tosefta *ibid.*

111

Shammaites prevailed, the people ceased to bring offerings on the holidays. It is stated that when Baba ben Buta came to the Azarah during a holiday, he found it deserted and he was deeply affected. He placed the blame on those who maintained that one cannot lay his hands on the offering brought on the holiday. [5] Although he was a Shammaite he ordered that animals be brought, and declared that anyone who wants to bring sacrifice, either peace offering or burnt-offering they might bring them and lay their hands thereon The Talmud continues that the law was accepted in accordance with the view of the Hillelites. [6]

The problem which confronts us—what was the underlying reason for the controversy between the two schools. The Talmud explains that the laying of hands on the sacrifice was in the category of שבות Shebut, [7] which is not permitted on the Sabbath nor on the holidays. Shebut is merely a rabbinical injunction. [8] It is surprising that a person could bring an animal to be sacrificed but was prohibited from laying his hand thereon. When a person brought the animal for sacrifice, it was unavoidable for him not to lay hand upon it. Further-more, from the story given in the Talmud, once when Passover fell on a Saturday, the people brought their lambs and placed the knives in the wool of the animal. [9] Thus it would have been unavoidable for them not to lay their hands on it. One Amora seeks to prove from this injunction of laying the hands on the animal on a holiday that the laying on of hands must

[5] Yer. ibid. והיה שם בבא בן בוטא פעם אחת נכנס לעזרה ומצאה שוממת
אמר ישמו בתיהן של אלו שהושמו בית אלהינו מה עשה שלח והביא שלשת
אלפים טלי ··· ואמר להן ··· כל מי שהוא רוצה יביא עולות יביא ויסמוך יביא
שלמים ויסמוך.

Cf. Tosefta ibid.

[6] באותה השעה נקבעה הלכה כבית הלל.

[7] Hag. 16.

[8] Cf. Betzah 36. אלו הן משום שבות לא עולין באילן ולא רוכבין
על גבי בהמה ··· לא עולין באילן גזירה שמא יתלוש, ולא רוכבין על גבי
בהמה שמא יצא חוץ לתחום

[9] Yer. 4. מי שהיה פסחו טלה היה היה תוחבה בגיזתו גדי היה קושרה בין
קרניו.

be with full force; [10] but this is not mentioned in the tannaitic literature.

Another problem confronts us which has to be elucidated. When the view of the Shammaites prevailed that one might bring a peace offering on the holidays but might not lay his hands upon the animal—why did the people not only cease bringing burnt offerings and peace offerings but also cease making pilgrimages to the Temple so that the *Azarah* was deserted? It has been suggested that laying hands on the animal to be sacrificed was cherished by the people. But why? There must have been a valid reason for the custom to be cherished by the people.

To fully comprehend the controversy between the school of Shammai and the school of Hillel requires a historical survey of the custom of *Semikah*, the laying of hands on the sacrifice. The Pentateuch enjoined that a person who brought a sacrifice to the Temple has to lay his hands upon the hands upon the animal. [11] Laying the hands upon an animal or upon a person was considered, in ancient times, the transference of iniquity or good deeds and authority.

When God told Moses that he should delegate his authority to Joshua, He ordered Moses to lay his hands upon him. [12] Moses followed this injunction of God, he laid his hands upon Joshua. [13] By laying his hands upon Joshua, Moses delegated his authority and responsibility to Joshua. [14] This is the origin of the ceremony of the ordination of rabbis by laying the hands upon the candidate. [15] The laying of hands on the sacrifices, sin offering, or burnt offering, was to transfer the person's sins to the animal that was to be sacrificed to God. [16]

[10] Hag. 16. אמר רמי בר חמא שמע מינה סמיכה בכל כוחו בעינן דאי
סלקא דעתך לא בעינן מאי קא עביד לסמוך.
[11] Lev. 1.4. וסמך ידו על ראש העולה ונרצה לו לכפר עליו.
[12] Num. 27. 18. וסמכת את ידך עליו.
[13] *Ibid.* 23. ויסמוך את ידיו עליו.
[14] *Cf.* also *Ibid.* 8. 10-12. וסמכו בני ישראל את ידיהם על הלוים ... והלוים
יסמכו את ידיהם על ראש הפרים.
[15] See S. Zeitlin, *Religious and Secular Leadership,* I. pp. 67-71.
[16] *Cf.* M. Yoma 3. 8.

On the Day of Atonement two bullocks were sacrificed, one a communal sacrifice the other the high priest's personal sacrifice. After laying his hands on the latter sacrifice he confessed his sins and asked God to forgive the iniquities, transgressions and sins committed by him and his family.

After sacrificing his bullock, the high priest continued the service by laying his hand on the goat to be sent to the Azazel and made confession for the entire people. He said, "O God, Thy people, the House of Israel, have committed iniquity, transgressed, and sinned before thee. O God forgive, I pray, the iniquities and transgressions and sins which thy people, the House of Israel have committed and transgressed and sinned before thee". [17] By laying the hands upon the goat the people believed that they had transferred their sins to the animal which was sent into the wilderness. [18]

On the Sabbath and on the holidays no individual sacrifices were brought, no sin offerings were sacrificed. Since the laying of hands on the sacrifice was considered transferring the sins, the Shammaites held that a person might bring a peace offering but might not lay his hands upon the animal: but he might not bring a burnt offering (whole-offering). The difference between the two types of sacrifices can be explained by the following: According to the Pentateuch if a person brought a burnt offering he should lay his hands upon the head of the animal "and it shall be accepted for him to make atonement for him". [19] With regard to the peace offering the Pentateuch enjoined the laying of hands upon the animal, but this was not for atonement. The phrase "to make atonement for him" is not given. This was the underlying reason for the view of the Shammaites; since the laying of hands on the burnt offering was for atonement and no supplication was permitted during the holidays and therefore they prohi-

[17] Lev. 16. 21-22. וסמך אהרן את שתי ידיו על ראש השעיר החי והתודה עליו את כל עונות בני ישראל ... ונשא השעיר עליו את כל עונתם אל ארץ גזרה.
[18] M. Yoma 6. 2. בא לו אצל שעיר המשתלח וסומך שתי ידיו עליו ומתודה וכך היה אומר אנא השם עוו פשעו חטאו עמך בית ישראל.
[19] Cf. note 10.

bited the bringing of burnt offerings. Since a peace offering was a gift to God and was connected with the festival, one might bring it, but hands should not be laid upon it.

When the Shammaites prevailed, the people, believing that by laying their hands on the animals their transgressions and iniquities would be transferred to the sacrifice, ceased to bring their sacrifices and refrained from making pilgrimages to Jerusalem and the Temple. The Hillelites, and Hillel himself, were of the opinion that the laying of hands on the sacrifice was symbolic.—no one could actually transfer his iniquities to the sacrifice. To encourage the Judaeans to make pilgrimages to Jerusalem and to the Temple the Hillelites maintained that one who brought a peace offering or a burnt offering might lay hands upon the sacrifice. Hillel and his followers endeavored to make the Temple the center of the Judaean religion. While the people were in Jerusalem they undoubtedly attended gatherings, (synagogues), where the Torah and its interpretations were expounded.

Hillel lived during Herod's time when the Judaeans underwent great physical and mental suffering. Many Judaeans shunned coming to Jerusalem. The Hillelites endeavored to encourage pilgrimages to Jerusalem and to the Temple. That was the underlying reason for the controversy between the schools of Shammai and of Hillel over *Semikah*, the laying of hands upon the sacrifice on the holidays.

115

TAKKANOT 'EZRA

AN ancient Baraita in the Talmud[1] ascribes to Ezra
ten *takkanot*. These, as explained by the compilers of
the Talmud, are not definitely clear to us. In fact, for
a long time many have been astonished by the Baraita's
ascribing them to Ezra. Moreover, when we investigate
Rabbinic sources, we find that to the editors of the Talmud
the *takkanot* presented difficulties, as some of these *takkanot*
had been considered as already contained in the Torah.
However, it is evident that the sources of these *takkanot*
were unknown to the Rabbis,[2] and also the underlying causes
and reasons. As we investigate these *takkanot* carefully and
thoroughly we realize their significance in Jewish religious
life. The Pharisees, who, animated by the general purpose
to harmonize religion and life, brought about reforms in
religious life, e. g. the laws of *Erub* that made the Sabbath
less burdensome,[3] also made important reforms in the laws
of clean and unclean, that were extremely burdensome to
Israel if literally construed and enforced according to the
Torah. For example, such as were suddenly affected by
bodily impurity (*noctis pollutio*, קרי) or defiled by contact
with a corpse would, by literal interpretation of the Torah,

[1] B. Baba kamma 82 a ; Pal. Megillah IV, 1, 75 a.

[2] See Weiss, *Dor Dor we-Doreschaw*, II, 66.

[3] Concerning the time when Solomon introduced the device of ' erubin '
(Erubin 21 a and Shabbat 14 b) see Geiger in he-Ḥaluṣ, VI, and also
Derenbourg, *Essai sur l'Histoire de la Palestine*, p. 144.

61

have to depart from the city,[4] the law being as severe in
their case as in the case of those having a contagious
disease like leprosy. It would have been impracticable
in the period, when the Jewish people were at the pinnacle
of their intellectual and material development, that a
person merely by reason of such an occurrence should be
constrained to give up communal life and leave the city.
So the Sages amended the law in accordance with the new
requirements. Such men as these, having no contagious
disease (including those affected by *noctis pollutio,* and
others), were merely incapacitated from entering the
Temple-court or the Sanctuary, but were not compelled
to keep apart from their fellow citizens and leave the city.[5]

Now we will examine the *takkanot* themselves, that the
Baraita ascribes to Ezra. This is the list: (1) Reading
from the Scroll at Sabbath afternoon service; (2) Reading
from the Scroll at morning service on Mondays and
Thursdays;[6] (3) Holding court on Mondays and Thursdays;
(4) Ritual bath (*tebilah*) for בעלי קרי ; (5) Eating garlic on
Eve of Sabbath; (6) Washing clothes [giving them out to
be washed] on Thursdays; (7) That a woman should rise
early and bake; (8) That a woman should gird herself
with a belt; (9) That pedlars should carry about their
wares in the cities; (10) That a woman should dress her
hair before immersion.

The first three, concerning the reading from the Pentateuch on Sabbath afternoon, and on Monday and Thursday

---

[4] Num. 5. 2; Deut. 23. 11.   [5] Pesaḥim 67 and 68.

[6] In Pal. Megillah, *ibid.,* the *takkanot* to read from the Scroll during
Minḥah of Sabbath and on Monday and Thursday are reckoned as one
takkanah ; and there is another to complete the list, viz. שיהו הנשים
מדברותזו עם זו בבית הכסא. But this, we are informed in the Talmud
Babli (Sanhedrin 19 a), was a ruling of R. Jose in Sepphoris.

mornings, and sessions of court on Mondays and Thursdays, are fairly intelligible to us.[7] The fourth *takkanah* concerning the requirement that a בעל קרי must receive or undergo *ṭebilah*, seems thus to have been understood by the compilers of the Talmud, and so ·the Gemara asks in reference thereto: 'Is this not known from the Torah— that one who has experienced pollution should undergo *ṭebilah*?'[8] But such is not the real purport of the *takkanah*; there is involved in it a reform in the laws of purification. As we have noted above, originally it was incumbent on the בעל קרי to leave the camp, to undergo *ṭebilah*, and thereafter to wait until evening (after sunset he became clean).[9] For historical evidence that such was at one time the Jewish law, note what King Saul said when David failed to appear at his father-in-law's table: מקרה לא טהור הוא;[10] the expressions he uses are quite consonant with the obligation of a man suddenly confronted with pollution to leave the city, and the observance of such a law might not be felt as a hardship or obstacle in such a small kingdom.

However, what was not felt to impede progress in the days of Saul was felt by the Pharisees to be a great hindrance in their desire to bring about agreement between religion and a larger life. By their method of exegesis they explained מחנה (camp) as מחנה שכינה (camp wherein the Shechinah resided); therefore the law of temporary banishment could apply only to the Sanctuary proper, and to the 'Azarah, known also as מחנה לויה 'camp of the Levite group', and not to the whole city.[11]

---

[7] See Derenbourg, *ibid.*, pp. 22-3.
[8] Lev. 15. 16; Deut. 23. 12.   [9] *Ibid.*   [10] 1 Sam. 20. 24-6.
[11] See Zeitlin, 'Les dix-huit Mésures', *Revue des Études Juives*, LXVIII, p. 29; Pesaḥim 68 a; Sifre, 255.

Similarly in the matter of *sunset.* For according to the Torah, mere bathing of the body in water would not have been deemed sufficient to render a person pure, unless the sun had set on him thereafter, and he is called by the Talmud טבול־יום. The Sages then ordained that, if he had taken the prescribed bath, he was *ipso facto* pure, and relieved of the necessity of waiting until sunset.[12] This reform the Talmud ascribes to Ezra in these words, הוא תיקן טבילה לבעלי קרי, meaning to say, that it is sufficient for him to undergo *ṭebilah,* as he need not leave the city nor concern himself as to when the sun will set.

The law of טבול יום, according to which *ṭebilah* alone does not suffice, but it is necessary to wait for sunset, the Pharisees made, by their decree, apply in cases of *terumah*—if a priest was unclean, he would not only have to undergo *ṭebilah,* but be inhibited from eating *terumah* until night.[12a] This is one of the 'Eighteen Measures' that were decreed by Bet Shammai and Bet Hillel.[13] And

---

[12] Sifra Emor 4, 1 : מה ישראל שאינם אוכלים בתרומה במעורבי שמש מעשר נאכל. Tosefta Parah 3, 6 : הרי הן אוכלים במעשר טבולי יום בטבול יום.

[12a] יטמא עד הערב . . . טהור לחולין מבעוד יום ולתרומה משתחשך. Sifra Shemini 8.

[13] See Zeitlin, *ibid.* This decree was a consequence of the Pharisees' hostility to the priesthood, which was particularly strong in the last days of the Second Temple, so strong indeed that they virtually decreed that almost everything disqualified *terumah,* and *terumah* disqualified had to be burnt (see my article, *ibid.*); and also that almost everything rendered the priest unclean and unfit to eat *terumah* and *ḳodesh,* going so far as to say that if any man (of the priesthood) carried any object on his shoulder, though it touched nothing unclean, still some object polluted might be lying underground as far down as the spade might dig—and who knows but that there might be some pollution at that depth?—consequently it would also render unclean the man who carried the object (see Ohalot 16. 1). In line, possibly, with this general principle, they made the ruling that the

now we are able to understand the controversy between the Pharisees and the Sadducees in the matter of the burning of the Red Heifer. The Sadducees, adhering as they did to the old Halakah, and basing their arguments on the plain meaning of Scripture, said: When is a man purged of his uncleanness? After sunset. *Tebilah* alone does not render him pure. As the priest who burns the Red Heifer must be pure,[14] and we are apprehensive lest by accident he come under the head of מקרה לא טהור, or lest his brother priests have touched him, in which case the *tebilah* (ablution) would not have the immediate effect of purging him and qualifying him to burn the Heifer—therefore the Sadducees considered it necessary to defer that burning until after sunset.

The Pharisees, however, who had adopted the principle that, if one took the prescribed bath, he is rendered pure without waiting for the sun to set, said the priest may burn the Heifer before ṣunset, immediately after *tebilah*.

As for the pomp wherewith the ceremony of the Red Heifer was surrounded, the purpose of the Pharisees was

priests should not eat of *terumah* until after sunset, apprehending that the priest might have been contaminated by some object, and maintaining, as they did, that for eating of *terumah* immersion did not suffice, but that setting of the sun was necessary, consequently *terumah* could not be eaten in the day-time. This makes intelligible the first Mishnah of the Talmud, as, after asking from what time we are allowed to read שמע, it says, when the priests begin to eat *terumah*: מאימתי קורין את שמע בערבית משעה שהכהנים נכנסים לאכול בתרומתן. The Talmud is astonished, asking why the Mishnah does not in so many words say 'from the appearance of the stars'. But if we say that the Sages decreed that the priests should not eat *terumah* until after sunset, that is, until nightfall, the Mishnah very clearly indicates to us when we can read the שמע, when the priests gather to eat their *terumah*, which did actually serve the people as a criterion whereby, the sun having set, they might know that they could read the שמע.

[14] Num. 19. 5-9.

120

to demonstrate in public that their view had won recognition. They actually defiled the priest who was to burn the Heifer. ובית טבילה היתה שם—A pool was there in which he could immerse his whole body, after which he might burn the Heifer, without waiting for the sun to set—all this the Pharisees did, מפני הצדוקים שלא יהו אומרים במעורבי שמש היתה נעשית[15] 'so that the Sadducees should not have occasion to say that it had to be done at sunset'.

This is the reason underlying the difference between the Pharisees and the Sadducees in the matter of the burning of the Red Heifer, namely, the principle of טבול יום, and not, as is generally believed, that the Sadducees were more exacting in the matter of the purity of the priest who burned the Heifer, and the Pharisees less exacting, less scrupulous.

The fifth *takkanah* is 'to eat garlic on the eve of the Sabbath'. The Talmud's explanation, that garlic is a מכנים אהבה, induces love, and that Friday night is the זמן עונה, makes thereof a strange, grotesque *takkanah*, and long ago many expressed surprise that a Baraita should ascribe it to Ezra, particularly as the making Sabbath eve the זמן עונה is one of the most recent things in the Talmud.[16] This *takkanah* has, in my opinion, no connexion with עונה, but was really a great and significant reform in the development of the laws of clean and unclean. Originally, they did not permit the eating of garlic, because before plucking it from the ground they moistened it with water,[17] and by this pouring of water upon it they rendered it susceptible

[15] Parah 3. 7 ; Tosefta, *ibid.*   [16] Ketubot 62 b.

[17] Tosefta Makshirin 3. 3 : חילפתא בן קוניא אומר שום בעל בכי טמא מפני שמרבצין עליו במים ואחר כך קולעין אותן. They evidently were in the habit of pouring water upon it before plucking, as it was so sharp as to produce tears in those who ate it.

121

of becoming unclean. For in Leviticus 11. 38 the expression
occurs ‏וכי יתן מים על זרע‎. However, the earlier Sages so
revised the Law, that seed is rendered susceptible of receiving impurity through the pouring of water thereon, only
when detached, not when attached (by nature) to the soil
(Sifra Shemini 11, 3); and this *takkanah* the Talmud
ascribes to Ezra.[18] What hitherto was obscure now becomes
clear—we are able to understand a Mishnah in Yadaim 4
which brings in a disputation between the Sadducees and
the Pharisees : ‏אומרים צדוקים קובלים אנו עליכם פרושים שאתם‎
‏מטהרים את הנצוק ; אומרים הפרושים קובלים אנו עליכם צדוקים שאתם‎
‏מטהרים את אמת המים הבאה מבית הקברות‎ ' The Sadducees say,
We complain against you, Pharisees, because ye declare
clean the ‏נצוק‎. The Pharisees say, We complain against
you, Sadducees, that ye declare clean the stream of water
that comes from the cemetery.' All the commentators
who have discussed this Mishnah, and all the scholars who
have spoken about the matters of dispute between the
Pharisees and the Sadducees, have taken for granted that
the word ‏ניצוק‎ implies pouring from one vessel into another,
and hence they interpret the Sadducees as saying, ' We
find fault with you, O Pharisees, because in case a man

[18] This enables us to understand the answer the Sages gave Ḥalafta
ben Ḳonia : ‏אם כן יהא טמא לחילפתא בן קוינא וטהור לכל ישראל‎
(Tosefta, *ibid.*), equivalent to saying, ' Ye who do not avail yourselves
of the *takkanah*, that seed never becomes susceptible of uncleanness through
pouring thereon of water save when detached from the soil, have occasion
to investigate, but not the great bulk of Israel who abide by that *takkanah* ;
for them it is clean and unquestionably permissible as food '. Similarly
they disposed of the objection that Joshua ben Peraḥiah made to importing
wheat from Egypt, where, as no rain falls, water is necessarily poured upon
the seed, making it, according to that teacher, susceptible of uncleanness.
The Sages, applying to Egyptian wheat the ruling concerning that which
was attached to the soil, observed that it might be unclean for Joshua
ben Peraḥiah but not for the vast body of Israel who abided by the *takkanah*.

122

pours a liquid from a clean vessel into a vessel that is
unclean ye maintain that what is left in the upper vessel
remains clean', and that the Pharisees rejoin thereto, 'We
have as much right to find fault with you that ye declare
clean the stream of water that issues from a cemetery'.
This interpretation of the Mishnah appears to me unacceptable. For, aside from our not being able to find
any evidence that the Sadducees ever declared unclean
the water that remained in the upper vessel when part
thereof had been poured into an unclean vessel, and aside
from inability to see whereon they could base such a
view—according to this interpretation, the answer that the
Pharisees give does not fit in with the question that the
Sadducees propound. The Sadducees are thus represented as asking why they (the Pharisees) declare clean
the water in the upper vessel when a part has been poured
therefrom into an unclean vessel, and the Pharisees are
represented as answering with the query, why they (the
Sadducees) declare clean the water that issues from the
cemetery—which is wholly irrelevant and bears no relation
to the original question.

The word נִצּוֹק which almost everywhere has the connotation of pouring out from one vessel into another, has,
it appears to me, misled the commentators; they thought
that in this passage also it had that connotation. Here,
however, נִצּוֹק, nif'al of יצק, refers to the status of that which
has received the water. The dispute resolves itself thus:
'The Sadducees say, We object to your declaring seed
clean in case water has been poured thereon—we mean
that ye make distinction (as far as the Law is concerned)
between that which is attached to the soil and that which
is detached—which is above the ground, and claim that

in case water is poured on the seed while it is attached
to the soil, that seed does not become susceptible of
receiving pollution; that only when the seed has been
removed from the ground does the pouring of water thereon
render it susceptible of impurity.' To this, the answer
of the Pharisees appears to be directed, and in fact proves
that to have been the purport and burden of the question;
for the rejoinder is virtually, 'Do ye not also make a
similar distinction in the matter of defilement between that
which is attached to the ground and that which is detached,
when ye admit that the stream of water, though coming
from a cemetery (than which nothing is more unclean), is
clean, because the stream of water is attached to the soil?'[19]

That the eating of garlic served as a means of emphasizing
some principle we can see from another Mishnah, also very
ancient.[20] He that forswears benefit from 'men who rest
on the Sabbath' is forbidden to derive benefit from
Cutheans as well as Israelites, since the Cutheans, though
they do not regard as binding the *takkanot* and *gezerot*
added by the Sages (e. g. the *Erub*), do rest on Sabbath in
conformity with the Torah. He that forswears benefit
from 'men who eat garlic' is forbidden in case of Israelites,
and permitted in case of Cutheans. The reason in the latter
case is that the Cutheans adhered to the old Halakah
based on Scripture, and consequently did not eat garlic,
because before plucking it from the ground, it was
customary to wet it, pouring water upon it, and thereby

---

[19] R. Leszynsky, *Die Sadduzäer*, pp. 38–43, says that ניצוק in this
passage means 'honey'. See also Geiger, *Urschrift*, p. 147; Derenbourg,
Essai, p. 134.

[20] Nedarim 3. 10: הנודר בשובתי שבת אסור בישראל ואסור בכותים,
מאוכלי שום אסור בישראל מוחר בכותים is the correct reading. See
Bet Joseph, Tur Yoreh Deʾah, § 214.

it was rendered susceptible of becoming unclean ; and since the Torah makes no distinction between detached from and attached to the soil, and the emendation of the Sages, that only such seed as is detached is susceptible of receiving defilement, but not that which is attached to the soil, had not been adopted by the Samaritans. Hence, he who had forsworn benefit from people who ate garlic was regarded as not having included Cutheans in his vow, since they did not eat garlic, whereas he was forbidden benefit from Israelites, who having accepted the *takkanah* of the Sages, did eat garlic. Now we can understand why this (fifth) *takkanah* was considered so important as to be ascribed to Ezra.[21]

The sixth *takkanah*, שיהיו מכבסין בחמישי בשבת, evidently permitted giving garments to the launderers on Thursdays. This accords well with the Hillelite Halakah that allows giving work to a Gentile three days before the Sabbath, though it is probable that he may not finish it before Sabbath. See Shabbat 11 a.[22]

The seventh *takkanah*, שתהא אשה משכמת ואופה, is explained in the Talmud to mean, the housewife should get up early to bake in order to give of her bread to the poor man. According to my opinion, this *takkanah* also bore some relation to Sabbath observance, particularly as in the Palestinian Talmud, the reading is שיהיו אופין פת בערבי שבתות ; that is, this regulation had for its purpose, that on Fridays baking should be begun in time for a crust to be

---

[21] In ordaining that garlic be eaten on Sabbath eve the Sages appear to have availed themselves of a custom that already existed (Nedarim 8. 6), and by sanctioning it to have given concrete expression to their views.

[22] R. Zadok says that in Rabban Gamaliel's house they used to give clothes to the launderer three days before Sabbath, see *ibid*.

formed on the bread while it was still day (see Shabbat 19 and last Mishnah of Shabbat 1). This *takkanah* emanated from the Hillelite school; the Shammaite school, however, insisted that the work must be completely finished before sunset (Shabbat 1. 4–11).

The eighth *takkanah*, שתהא אשה חוגרת בסינר, the Talmud regards as designed to promote modesty in behaviour. The etymology of סינר is a bit obscure. Rashi says that ʿSenarʾ is a pair of *trousers*. Apparently the purpose of the *takkanah* was, as explained in the Talmud, to promote modest behaviour; the essence thereof accordingly would have been: though trousers are originally included in men's garments which are *ipso facto* forbidden to women, still since the wearing of them by women will be promotive of modesty, we commend and even recommend the new custom. Or it is possible that the *takkanah* was required by reason of the סינר being a garment of foreign origin, whether in vogue among the Persians (زناری) or identical with the ζωνάριον (belt) in vogue among the Greeks; however, צניעות, or feminine delicacy, motivated the reform in dress.

The ninth *takkanah*, שיהיו רוכלין מחזרין בעיירות, is regarded in the Talmud as facilitating the sale of women's ornaments. It seemed better that the pedlars should carry their stock into all parts of the cities rather than that by their coming into the houses jealousy of the husbands be aroused, and domestic unpleasantness result—so the sales should be negotiated on the street.[23] In the Yerushalmi,

---

[23] Yebamot 24 b. In case a pedlar is seen leaving the house and his wife girding herself with a ʿSenarʾ, the husband has the right to divorce her without dower. See *ibid.*, 63 b, where the Talmud quotes Ben Sira as saying: רבים היו פצעי רוכל המרגילים לדבר עברה.

in connexion with the pedlars hawking their wares in the open, the expression is used מפני כבודן של בנות ישראל 'on account of the dignity of the daughters of Israel', and after this they made a regulation that the citizens must not prevent these pedlars from freely moving about to sell their wares.[24]

The tenth *takkanah*, שתהא אשה חופפת וטובלת, evokes expressions of surprise in the Babylonian Talmud, to this effect: Since according to the ordinance of the Torah a woman must dress her hair before taking the ritual bath, wherein does the *takkanah* consist? what new element does it contain? Had the redactors of the Babylonian Talmud been aware in this case of the Palestinian Gemara, they would not have asked this question, for there they would have seen הוא (עזרא) התקין שתהא אשה חופפת קודם לטהרתה שלשה ימים 'He (Ezra) amended the law, so that a woman might dress her hair three days before her purification'.

The reason for the *takkanah* was as follows: When a woman at the close of her separation period desired to cast off her uncleanness, she had to take the prescribed ritual bath at night;[25] the dressing of her hair had (originally) to be on the day immediately preceding her *ṭebilah*.[26] However, if her time for *ṭebilah* fell on Saturday night or on a Sunday night, Sunday itself being Yom Ṭob, and so she could not by reason of the sanctity of Sabbath or of Yom Ṭob cleanse and comb her hair—what was

---

[24] This *takkanah*, that the citizens should not hamper the pedlars in their efforts to sell their goods, was made because these men, who had formerly entered houses, were now, out of regard for the reputation of Jewish women, disallowed to enter houses ; the merchants of the city were, therefore, not to hinder them from exercising the privilege granted by the other *takkanah* of going about in the cities to sell their wares. See Baba batra 22 a.

[25] Yoma 6 a.   [26] See Niddah 67 b and 68 a.

127

there for her to do? Then the Sages ordained that in
case the night for *ṭebilah* of a Niddah was at the conclusion
of Sabbath, or at the close of the festival of Rosh-ha-
Shanah that fell on Thursday and Friday, making it impossible for her to cleanse and comb her hair immediately
previous to her *ṭebilah*, she might instead cleanse and
comb her hair on Friday, that is, three days before her
purification.[27] This was· the *takkanah* that the Talmud
ascribed to Ezra.

Now we can fully understand why just these *takkanot*
were ascribed to Ezra, inasmuch as we have seen their importance and their value in the development of the laws of
טומאה וטהרה, the laws of the Sabbath, and in domestic life.

As for the time of these *takkanot*, Weiss[28] has well
shown that they do not go back to Ezra's day. In my
opinion, they were instituted neither by one man nor in one
period, but were the results of the evolution of the ancient
Halakot according to the demands of the time, some of these
takkanot being very ancient, and others not quite so ancient.
The *takkanot* in the matter of טומאה וטהרה are very ancient,
e. g. the '*takkanot shum*', that the only time that seed
becomes susceptible of receiving pollution is when it is
detached from the soil. That it is very old is seen by
what is stated of Joshua ben Peraḥiah as opposed thereto.[29]
The *takkanot* or amendments in the laws of Sabbath
enabling the Jews to give clothes to the launderer on
Thursday, and to bake bread on Friday while it was day,
are from the times of Bet Hillel and Bet Shammai ;[30]

[27] The Babylonian Amoraim were divided in opinion on this matter.
See Niddah, *ibid.*

[28] *Dor Dor we-Doreschaw*, II, p. 66.

[29] See Tosefta Makshirin 3. 4.

[30] It is very likely that this *takkanah* about reading from the Scroll

therein we can see traces of how the ancient Halakot were remoulded, and how the Pharisees strove to bring the religion into consonance with life, and to amend the Pentateuchal law, if such were life's demands.

during the Sabbath afternoon service was instituted at the close of the period of the Second Temple, the purpose being (on Sabbaths) to restrict it to the afternoon, as the Sages preferred that the people free from work should go to the Bet-ha-Midrash to hear the exposition of the Sages and not read the Holy Scriptures, and therefore they decided that reading of the Scriptures was permissible on Sabbath from Minḥah and after. And this we find in a Tosefta (Shabbat 14): אף על פי שאמרו אין קורין בכתבי הקדש, and we also find in the Talmud that it is not allowed to read the Scriptures until the afternoon service: אין קורין בכתבי קדש אלא מן המנחה ולמעלה (Pal. Shabbat 15 c); and also the question arose among the Amoraim: If the fifteenth of Adar falls on a Sabbath, what should be done in regard to reading of Megillat Esther, as it is forbidden to read from the Scriptures before Minḥah (J. Megila 74 b)? See S. Zeitlin, 'Les dix-huit Mesures', RÉJ., LXVIII, pp. 34-5.

THE ORIGIN OF THE KETUBAH

A Study in the Institution of Marriage

WE find recorded in the tannaitic literature two documents in relation to marriage, *Shetar Ḳiddushin* שטר קדושין
and *Ketubah* כתובה. Neither of these documents is mentioned in the Bible. A Mishna in the tractate Ḳid. states
that a woman may be acquired in one of three ways, either
by *Kesef*, by *Shetar*, or by *Bi'ah*.[1]

Some scholars are of the opinion that the *Ketubah* is
identical with *Shetar Ḳiddushin* mentioned in the Mishna,
and therefore they believe that the *Ketubah* is the oldest
form of a marriage contract.[2] This point of view is not
borne out by tannaitic literature, and I believe that the
contrary is the case. The *Ketubah* and the *Shetar* שטר are
not one and the same thing. The *Shetar* is a much older
document than the *Ketubah*. The Mishna employs merely
the term *Shetar*. If the *Shetar* and the *Ketubah* were identical, why then did not the Mishna use the term *Ketubah*
or *Shetar Ketubah*? In the entire tannaitic literature we
do not find *Shetar* referring to *Ketubah*. What we do find is
that the word *Shetar*[3] or *Sefer*[4] sometimes is appended to

---

[1] האשה נקנח בשלש דרכים . . . בכסף בשטר ובביאה. Ḳid. I, 1.

[2] See L. Epstein, *The Jewish Marriage Contract*, pp. 5–31. In this
book Dr. Epstein has displayed great learning and has shown that he
is at home, not only in the Talmud, but in the entire field of rabbinic
literature. This book is undoubtedly the most important book on the
study of the institution of marriage as it was developed among the Jews
since the talmudic period. It is my intention to deal, not with the
development of the *Ketubah* during the rabbinic period, but only to
trace its origin.

[3] Tal. Ket. 104b, שטר כתובה.

[4] Mishna Yeb. XV, 3. ספר כתובתה. Eduy. I, 12. Tos. Eduy. I, 6.

1

the term *Ketubah*. Generally speaking, the term *Ketubah* is invariably used in the tannaitic and amoraic literature without any addition.

Again, we know from the tannaitic literature that *Ketubah* was instituted as a תקנה (*Takkana*), reform,[5] while the *Shetar* was not a *Takkana*. Furthermore, the *Ketubah* had to be written by the groom, while the *Shetar Kiddushin* was required to be written by the father of the bride. That the *Shetar Kiddushin* was written in the early days by the father of the bride, and not by the groom, may be proven from the second Mishna in the same tractate where the phrase is עבד עברי נקנה בכסף ובשטר, namely, that a Hebrew slave may be acquired in one of two ways: either the buyer pays in money, or the seller signs a bill of sale.[6] Therefore we may safely assume that the *Shetar* mentioned in the first Mishna, where it is said that a woman may be acquired in one of three ways, of which one is by the *Shetar*, was required to be written by the father of the girl as a bill of sale. That this was the practice of the early Hebrews may be seen from the story which is recorded in the Book of Tobit, where it is said that Raguel gave his daughter Sarah to Tobit. And Raguel "called her mother, and told her to bring a book, and he wrote an instrument of co-habitation, even that he gave her to him to wife according to the decree of the law of Moses."[7]

דבית שמאי דרשין מספר כתובתה, Yer. Yeb. 14d.

[5] שמעון בן שטח תיקן כהובה לאשה, Tal. Shab. 14b. Comp. Ket. 82b; Tos. Ket. XII, 1; Yer. Ket. 32b.

[6] Ḳid. 16a. Comp. also the third Mishna of the same tractate, where we read עבד כנעני נקנה בכסף בשטר ובחזקה. A Gentile slave may be acquired in one of three ways: either the buyer pays the money בכסף, or the seller signs a bill of sale בשטר, or by possession בחזקה.

[7] Tobit VII, 11–14. The word συγγραφὴν stands for the Hebrew word שטר נישואין or שטר קידושין. Comp. the *Introduction to the Book of Tobit*, Ed. Charles, p. 184; also Rosenman, *Studien z. B. Tobit*, Berlin, 1894.

Finally, we may say that what the Mishna meant by *Shetar* is wholly unidentical with *Ketubah*, because one of three ways in which a woman may be acquired as a wife was sufficient to make the marital union legal.[8] *Shetar Kiddushin* alone was sufficient to make the marriage valid, whereas a *Ketubah* alone was not sufficiently binding.[9]

Since the *Shetar* and the *Ketubah* were not one and the same thing, what then was the *Ketubah*? The Mishna in Ḳid. says that a woman may be acquired as a wife by purchase. Such was the custom among the early Hebrews. Jacob paid Laban in menial labor to marry his daughters. Similarly for Michal, David paid her father, King Saul, with two hundred foreskins of the Philistines.[10] The money the groom paid the father for the girl is termed *Mohar* in the Bible. Shechem offered any amount of *Mohar* for the hand of Dinah.[10a] According to the biblical law, anyone who seduces a girl must pay a fine to the father, an amount equal to the *Mohar* for virgins.[11] In the Elephantine Papyri a marriage document is recorded, (dated about 441 B.C.E.), which reads in part as follows: "She is my wife and I her husband, from this day forever. I have given you *Mohar* for your daughter, Miphtahiah, the sum of five shekels."[12]

The word *Kesef*, in the Mishna, was already interpreted by the schools of Shammai and Hillel (which illustrates the

[8] Ḳid. 8b, and passim.

[9] אסור לו לאדם שישהא את אשתו אפילו שעה אחת בלי כתובה, B. Ḳ. 89a. The rabbis were of the opinion that a man should not live with his wife without a *Ketubah*, but never considered that marriage without the *Ketubah* is void.

[10] Sam. 18.25–27.

[10a] Gen. 34.12.

[11] Exod. 22.15–16.

[12] See Cowley, *Aramaic Papyri of the Fifth Century B. C.*, 1923, הי אנתתי ואנה בעלה מן יומא זנה ועד עלם יהבת לך מהר ברתך מפתחיה [כסף] שקלו ||||||.

132

antiquity of the statement). The Shammaites, who interpreted the letter of the Law, maintained that the word
Kesef, referred to in the Mishna, stood for silver, hence a
woman might be acquired with a dinar, which was the
smallest silver unit of the time, or with the value of a dinar.
The Hillelites who interpreted the Law according to its
spirit maintained that the word *Kesef* in the Mishna had
the meaning of money in general, and therefore a man could
acquire a wife with anything that has the value of money.[13]

A woman might also be acquired as a wife with a *Shetar*,
i.e., a bill of sale or a deed of gift, which was to be written
by the father of the girl. In the story of Tobit, we are told
that when Raguel gave his daughter Sarah to Tobit for
a wife, he wrote a contract συγγραφὴν and that alone was
considered sufficient and binding. The third way in which
a girl could be acquired as a wife is by ביאה *usus*. Likewise,
the old Roman law provided that a woman might be
acquired in one of three ways, namely, by *coemptio*, by
confarreatio, or by *usus*.

The early Tannaim of the Hellenistic period, who were
interested in raising the status of women in society,
protected them by introducing a reform in the marriage
contract. Formerly, the Halakah did not provide for the
economic welfare of the wife in the case of divorce or of her
husband's death. She was subject to the caprice of her
husband, for he could in time of anger divorce her, without
any hesitation on his part, though normally had he thought
it over he might not have done it. To obviate this evil, the
early Tannaim introduced a *Takkana* in the institution of
marriage, by introducing a *Ketubah*, namely, that a groom
should contribute two hundred zuzim to the father of the

בית שמאי אומרים בדינר ובשוה דינר בית הלל אומרים בפרוטה ובשוה פרוטה [13].
Comp. L. Ginzberg, מקומה של הלכה בחכמת ישראל, ירושלים, where the
correct interpretation is recorded.

girl, to be turned over to her in case of divorce or death of her husband.[14] This *Takkana* only partially improved the situation, for the woman was only protected on the economic side by the two hundred zuzim which she was to receive at the time of the death of her husband or of divorce. The divorce, however, still remained an easy matter for the husband. The Palestinian Talmud puts it: והיתה קלה בעיניו לגרשה,[15] it was easy for him to divorce her.

This *Takkana* of *Ketubah*, which aimed to improve the status of woman, wrought havoc on the poorer element which encountered difficulty in producing the two hundred zuzim, and therefore postponed marriage indefinitely, as it is clearly stated in the Talmud.[16] In order to remove the economic burden of the groom, and at the same time not to undermine the economic protection of the woman, the Tannaim went a step further and modified the *Takkana*— that the groom should not have to pay the two hundred zuzim for the girl, but be allowed to keep that money in his business, and instead he was required to write a writ כתובה, in which he pledged all his properties as security for the two hundred zuzim.[17] With this last form of the *Ketubah*, the Tannaim met the requirements of their time; the woman was provided economically in case of divorce or death of her husband; the financial burden was lifted from the shoulders of the groom, for he was relieved of providing two hundred zuzim at the time of marriage. Yet at the same

---

[14] Yer. Ket. 32b. בראשונה היתה מונחת כתובתה אצל אבותיה.

[15] Ibid.

[16] Ket. 82b. תניא נמי הכי בראשונה היו כותבין [נותנין] לבתולה מאתים ולאלמנה מנה והיו מזקינין ולא היו נושאין נשים.

[17] This *Takkana* the Talmud ascribed to Simon b. Shetaḥ. עד שבא שמעון בן שטח ותיקן שיהא כותב לה כל נכסי אחראין לכתובתה, Yer. Ket. 32c, בראשונה שהיתה כתובה אצל אביה והיתה קלה בעיניו להוציאה התקין B. ibid. 82b. שמעון בן שטח שתהא כתובתה אצל בעלה והיה כותב לה כל נכסיי דאית לי אחראין וערבאין לכסף כתובתיך, Tos. Ket. XII, 1.

time the divorce was made more difficult for the husband than heretofore. He had only to produce cash in time of divorce, which naturally made it less likely for him to hastily procure a divorce.

We are now in a better position to understand the controversy between Rabbi Meir and Rabbi Judah.[18] According to Rabbi Meir, the difference between a wife and a concubine is that a wife has a *Ketubah* and a concubine has none. According to Rabbi Judah a concubine also had a *Ketubah*. That is, in the case of the man's death, she was to receive money. For the wife, however, it is stipulated in the *Ketubah* that all his property is pledged as security for the two hundred zuzim. This clause is not to be written in the *Ketubah* of the concubine. She can get money if there is an estate left, and is entirely dependent on the good-will of the heirs.

The *Takkana* was instituted primarily for the protection of those women who would be left without means in case of divorce or the death of their husbands. The Tannaim felt that the women of wealth might not avail themselves of this *Takkana* and marry without a *Ketubah*, and thus they would invalidate the universality of the *Takkana*. In order to give this *Takkana* a tone of permanency and general applicability,[19] the Tannaim forbade the husband to live with his wife without a *Ketubah*[20]—even if she surrendered her privilege of the *Ketubah*.

---

[18] איזו היא אשה ואיזוהיא פלנש ר' מאיר אומר אשה יש לה כתובחה פלנש אין לה כתובה
ר' יודה אומר אחת זו ואחת זו יש לה כתובה אשה יש לה כתובה ותנאי כתובה פלנש יש לה
כתובה ואין לה תנאי כתובה, Yer. Ket. 29d.

[19] A *Takkana* in its very nature is universal, permanent and applicable to all classes. Its object is the amendment or the modification of the Law, through a fiction, or interpretation of the biblical law, or the early Halakah, for the purpose of harmonizing religion and life. See S. Zeitlin, "The Halaka in the Gospels," *H. U. C. Annual*, Vol. I, 365; idem "Takkanot Ezra," *JQR*, 1917.

[20] B. Ḳ. 89a.

Since a *Takkana* must find some support in either biblical or early halakic lore, the *Ketubah* reform was therefore deduced from an early Halakah.[21] One of the three ways in which a woman may be acquired as a wife is by *Shetar*. Formerly the *Shetar* was written by the father of the girl and became ultimately a part of the religious ceremony as we have seen above in the story of Tobit. This *Shetar* corresponded to the *confarreatio* in Roman law. The Tannaim in introducing the *Ketubah* reform interpreted that the *Shetar* had to be written by the groom,[22] and should consist of two parts; one relating to the *Kiddushin* and the other was the stipulation regarding the two hundred zuzim. Thus, the *Ketubah* is a reform and was necessitated by the economic considerations of the times.

[21] According to a talmudic statement (Ket. 10. Comp. Yer. Ket. 36b) the *Takkana* of the *Ketubah* was deduced from the biblical verse כסף ישקול כמהר הבתולות, מכאן סמכו חכמים לכתובה אשה מן התורה. This statement refers to the clause of the 200 zuzim which is to be written in the *Ketubah*. Comp. Mek. 17. ואין מהר אלא כתובה. The *Shetar Ketubah*, however, was deduced from an early Halakah.

[22] The statement found in the Tos. Ķid. I, 2. אפילו כתב לה על החרס ונתן לה על שטר פסול.., refers to the time when the *Ketubah* was already introduced.

THE TAKKANOT OF ERUBIN

A Study in the development of the Halaka

AN AMORA of the third century ascribed the takkanot of Erubin to Solomon and also that of washing the hands to him.[1] The takkana of washing the hands however was not instituted by Solomon.[2] It really was a gradual development of the laws of purity and impurity during the Second Commonwealth; having in fact been introduced either a few years before the destruction of the Second Temple or shortly thereafter. Nor were the takkanot of Erubin instituted by Solomon but they were also gradually developed during the time of the Second Commonwealth. As the takkana of washing the hands was a great reform in the religious life of the Jews, so also were the takkanot of Erubin, being introduced to bring religion in consonance with life to render the Sabbath less burdensome and make it a day of delight.

The Talmud uses the word Erubin in the plural and not the singular, Erub. There are really three types of Erubin. (1) In connection with a person's movements on the Sabbath, עירוב תחומין. (2) In connection with carrying an object on the Sabbath, עירוב חצירות. (3) In connection with the preparation of food for the Sabbath when a holiday falls on the eve of it, עירוב תבשילין. These three types of Erubin were introduced at different periods and all of them have great significance in Jewish life.

---

[1] 'Erub. 21b, אמר רב יהודה אמר שמואל בשעה שתיקן שלמה עירובין ונטילת ידים.
[2] See S. Zeitlin, *HUCA* 1, pp. 365–371.

In order to clarify the import of the takkana of Erub
in connection with a person's movements on the Sabbath
we shall first give the pentateuchal laws in regard to the
Sabbath. In the Book of Exodus it is stated, "You shall
sit each of you in his place, let no man go out of his place
on the seventh day."[3]

According to the literal meaning the ancient Hebrews
had no right to leave their places on the Sabbath. The
Septuagint, however, renders the words "his place" "his
house."[4] This would mean that a Hebrew had no right to go
out of his house on the Sabbath. They were, however,
allowed to walk four cubits from their homes.[5] Their movements on the Sabbath, however, could not be considered a
matter of pleasure; they were actually confined in their
homes, or nearby for the entire Sabbath day.

The fact that the Jews could not travel on the Sabbath
became a by-word even among the gentiles. Ovid, in his
essay, *The Remedies of Love*, said, "Nor let foreign sabbaths
stay you."[6] In order to make the Sabbath less burdensome
the sages introduced two reforms. One allowed a Jew to
walk, instead of four cubits, two thousand cubits from his
home;[7] another permitted him to walk throughout the
entire city.[8] From the tannaitic sources it is difficult to
determine which reform came first, but it seems to me
that the regulation that a Jew be allowed to walk two
thousand cubits from his home was the first to be intro-

---

[3] 16, 29, שבו איש תחתיו אל יצא איש ממקומו ביום השביעי.

[4] תחתיו, οἴκους ὑμῶν.

[5] Comp. Mishna 'Erub. 4.1; *ibid.* 51a שבו איש תחתיו אלו ארבע אמות;
comp. also Yer. *ibid.* 4.

[6] *Nec te peregrina morentur sabbata.*

[7] Comp. 'Er. 4.2. Tosefta *ibid.* 7.5. See also *ibid.* 3.9. . . . הרועים
יובזמן שדרכן ללון בשדה אין להם אלא אלפיים אמה בלבד נאמר כן מקום . . . אף
מקום שנאמר כאן אלפיים אמה.

[8] Comp. *ibid.* M. 4.1. . . . הוליכוהו לעיר אחרת . . . רבן גמליאל ור' אליעזר
בן עזריה סהלך את כולה.

duced. That this is so, is evident from a passage in the
Talmud which states that before the time of Rabban
Gamaliel the Elder, the people who saw the birth of the
new moon were allowed to travel on the Sabbath but after
testifying before the Court were not permitted to walk in
the city of Jerusalem on the Sabbath and were confined
in one place, called Beth Yazek. Gamaliel the Elder
amended the old law so that such witnesses have the same
privilege as the inhabitants of Jerusalem, of walking two
thousand cubits on the Sabbath.[9] We may hence conclude that the regulation that an inhabitant of a city had
the right to walk two thousand cubits was introduced in
the time of Rabban Gamaliel the Elder, i. e. 20–50 C. E.

The privilege of walking two thousand cubits on the
Sabbath was granted only to the residents of the city
wherein they dwelt. If a Jew was forcibly taken into
another city on the Sabbath, i. e. kidnapped by pagans,
he could walk only four cubits on the Sabbath because
that city was not his abode.[10] An exception was made by
Rabban Gamaliel the Elder only for those who came to
Jerusalem to testify on the birth of the new moon, and
so by a legal fiction Jerusalem was declared to be their
abode.

If a Jew arrived in a city before the Sabbath day for
the purpose of remaining over the Sabbath, he did not
have the privilege of latitude of a resident of that city as
he was still a member of the community whence he came.
Thus if he came from a small town to a large city he did
not have the privilege of walking throughout the city but
only two thousand cubits from his temporary abode.
However, if a Jew went from a large city to a small town

[9] R. H. 23b. חצר גדולה היתה בירושלים ובית יעוק היתה נקראת ולשם כל העדים
מתכנסין . . . בראשונה לא היו זזין משם כל היום התקין רבן גמליאל הזקן שיהו מהלכין
אלפיים אמה לכל רוח.

[10] ‘Er. 4.1, מי שהוציאוהו נכרים או רוח רעה אין לו אלא ארבע אמות.

he had the right to walk throughout the town.[11] Similarly,
if a Jew was travelling and had to stop on the road because
of the approaching Sabbath, he was allowed to walk two
thousand cubits from his temporary resting place.[12]

These takkanot introduced by the sages, that a Jew may
walk two thousand cubits on the Sabbath, were further
extended, and the word *makom*, place, was taken to mean
the city. Thus a Jew had the right to traverse the entire
city on the Sabbath even if it extended more than two
thousand cubits. The sages went even further in their
interpretation of the laws pertaining to the Sabbath. In
the early days when the word *makom* was interpreted as
meaning "house," the right was given to walk two thousand
cubits from it; the word *makom* was soon interpreted to
mean city. The sages applied the principle to give a
person the right to walk two thousand cubits beyond the
city limits.[13]

In order to make the Sabbath still more pleasant, the
sages further amended the law and introduced the law of
Erub, namely, that if before the Sabbath a Jew indicated
a desire to rest on the Sabbath at a place two thousand
cubits beyond the limits of the city and deposited food at

[11] Tosefta *ibid.* 7. בראשונה היו בני טבריא מהלכין את כל חמתא ואין בני חמתא
באין אלא עד מקום הקופא בלבד, עכשיו בני טבריא ובני חמתא חזרו להיות עיר אחת.
אנשי עיר גדולה מהלכין את כל עיר קטנה ואין אנשי עיר קטנה מהלכין את כל עיר
גדולה כשהיו בתוך אלפיים אמה שלהן, לא היו בתוך אלפיים אמה שלהן אין להם אלא
אלפיים אמה ואנשי עיר קטנה אין להם אלא אלפיים אמה. The Mishna reads as
follows: אנשי עיר גדולה מהלכין את כל עיר קטנה ואין אנשי עיר קטנה מהלכין את
כל עיר גדולה, כיצד מי שהיה בעיר גדולה ונתן את עירובו בעיר קטנה או בעיר קטנה
ונתן את עירובו בעיר גדולה מהלך את כולה וחוצה לה אלפיים אמה.
We should bear in mind that the Mishna was codified by Rabbi
Judah, and that it reflected the later *halaka*, while the Tosefta records
the earlier *halaka*.

[12] Comp. n. 7. See also Mishna 4.5, מי שישן בדרך ולא ידע עד שחשיכה
יש לו אלפיים אמה לכל רוח דברי ר' יוחנן בן נורי וחכמים אומרים אין לו אלא ארבע
אמות.

[13] Yer. 'Er. 4.1. מה מקום שנאמר להלן (ערי מקלט) אלפיים אמה אף מקום
שנאמר כאן אלפיים אמה.

that point, he had the right to walk on the Sabbath two thousand cubits from the place, *i.e.*, the depository.[14] Thus the takkana of Erub was a *legal fiction* based on the assumption that the place where a Jew had deposited food on the eve of the Sabbath became his abode.

With regard to the laws of the Sabbath, the limits of the city itself were extended. It is well known that in olden days no less than today, cities had suburbs — houses were built outside the city limits. These houses, or any other buildings used as dwelling places were considered within the city limits, and the counting of the two thousand cubits began from the remotest house in the farthest suburb. Opinions differed among the early Amoraim as to whether these houses were added to the city or the city extended to them; the city, they said, became full like a pregnant woman.[15] These different opinions had no effect in connection with the laws of Sabbath but may have made a difference in the social and economic structure of the community.

The takkana of Erub was indeed a *legal fiction* and it had more to do with intention rather than with action. By depositing the food in a particular place on the eve of Sabbath the person was presumed really to make it his abode. Thus while he could appoint an agent to deposit his food at a particular place, he could not appoint an imbecile or a minor[16] since they could not carry out duties connected with intention.[17] An imbecile or minor, for

---

[14] It was called ריפתא דערובא. Ber. 39b.

[15] See Yer. 'Er. 5.1. רב אמר מאברין ושמואל אמר מעברין מאן דמר מאברין מוסיפין לה אבר ומאן דמר מעברין כאשה עוברה; see also Tosefta *ibid.* 6.

[16] 'Er. 31b, אינו עירוב . . . השולח עירובו ביד חרש שוטה וקטן. If a Jew appointed an agent to execute the Erub for him, i. e., to place the Erub in a particular location, he could send the Erub to him by a minor or imbecile since they do not have the power of intention and thus they could not change the will of the sender.

[17] Tosefta Maksh. 3.2, חרש שוטה וקטן . . . יש להן מעשה ואין להן מחשבה.

example, could not consummate a marriage because the
act requires intention to marry, to make a particular
woman his lawful wife; nor could an imbecile give a divorce
to his wife because it also requires intention to make her
free and thereby give her the right to marry another
man.[18] Neither could an agent be appointed who did not
recognize the law of Erub.[19] It is logical that a man who
denies the validity of this takkana should not be allowed
to perform it.

The takkana of Erub by which a person may deposit
food in a particular place on the eve of the Sabbath allows
him to walk four thousand cubits from the city on the
Sabbath. This takkana could apply only to a person who
was in his home on Friday and not to one who was on
the road. Thus the takkana was extended further that if
a person was on the road on Friday at the distance of
four thousand cubits from his city and he could not reach
the city before sunset, he could if he knew of a definite
tree or another particular object in a distance of two
thousand cubits, designate either as his abode which the
Talmud calls קונה שביתה "acquired residence." Hence a
person may walk the two thousand cubits to the definite
object and two thousand cubits further to the city on the
day of the Sabbath.[20] The sages differed as to which type
of the Erub was the original. Rabbi Meir was of the
opinion that the former type was the original, while Rabbi
Judah was of the opinion that the latter was.[21]

The takkana of Erub is concerned with a person's ideas

[18] *Ibid.* Yeb., Babli *ibid.* 96b, סוטה וקטן שנשאו נשים ומתו נשותיהן פטורות
מן החליצה ומן היבום.

[19] מי שאינו מודה בעירוב.

[20] מי שבא בדרך וחשכה והיה ירא שמא תחשך והיה מכיר והיה מכיר אילן או נדר ואמר שביתתי
תחתיו לא אמר כלום שביתתי בעיקרו מהלך ממקום רגליו ועד עיקרו אלפיים אמה
סעיקרו ועד ביתו אלפיים אמה נמצא מהלך משחשיכה ארבעת אלפים אמה, אם אינו
סכיר או שאינו בקי בהלכה ואמר שביתתי במקומי זכה לו מקומו אלפיים אמה לכל רוח.

[21] ר' מאיר סבר עיקר עירוב בפת . . . ור' יהודה סבר עיקר עירוב ברגל

or thoughts, in other words with his intention. Thus, if a Jew expecting a scholar (his teacher) to arrive on Sabbath, to a point four thousand cubits from his city, and wanted to meet him but did not know from which direction of the city he would arrive, from the east or from the west, he could put an Erub in the two different places. If the scholar arrives from the east, the Erub placed there is valid; if he comes from the west, the Erub placed there is valid,[22] the person may walk two thousand cubits from the place where the Erub had been deposited. Similarly, if a person fearing that the city will be attacked on the Sabbath and he will have to flee, but does not know from what direction, the east or the west, the enemy will approach, he may place two Erubin in these two opposite places. If the enemy arrives from one side, the Erub placed in the opposite direction is considered valid and vice versa.[23]

Besides the takkana of עירוב תחומים, there was, as we pointed out before, another takkana עירוב חצירות. According to the old *halaka* the carrying of any object from one's location into the property of another one was prohibited.[24] This law was burdensome since at the time of the Second Commonwealth the Jews lived commonly in a kind of court, and of course they could not carry anything from one house to another. To make the Sabbath more pleasant an עירוב חצירות was introduced, i. e., the dwellers in

---

[22] מתנה אדם על עירובו . . . ואומר אם בא חכם מן המזרח עירובי למזרח מן המערב עירובי למערב, בא לכאן ולכאן למקום שארצה אלך [לא בא] לא טיכן ולא טיכן הרני כבני עירי.

[23] אם באו נכרים מן המזרח עירובי למערב ואם באו מן המערב עירובי למזרח אם באו טיכן וטיכן למקום שארצה אלך לא בא לא טיכן ולא טיכן הרני כבני עירו.

The Babylonian Talmud explained these *halakot* on the principle of *Bre'ra*; however, the Palestinian Talmud does not mention it. The entire principle of *'Bre'ra* is amoraic, these *halakot* really are based on the principle of intention.

[24] Jer. 17.21-2, ואל תשאו משא ביום השבת . . . ולא תוציאו משא מבתיכם ביום השבת.

143

the court contributed their share of the ingredients of a
dish to be placed in one of the houses. Thus, all the
families living in the court were considered partners in all
the houses in the court. In other words, the houses became
common to all; therefore, the carrying of objects on the
Sabbath from one house to another was permitted to all
the occupants. All the dwellers in the court had to share
in the Erub. If a person did not join them the carrying of
the objects from one house to another was prohibited, if
his property lay between them.[25] However, the man could
give up his property or transfer it to his neighbor,[26] and
in such case, full permission to carry the object in the
court was granted. If a pagan lived in the court, this did
not prohibit his Jewish neighbors from carrying an object
from one house to another.[27] This law was, however,
amended later so that the residing of a pagan in a court
in the midst of the Jews prohibited his neighbors from
carrying an object on the Sabbath day in the court;[28] the
property of the pagan had to be rented from him. He
could not give it up or present it to his neighboring Jews
as a Jew could.[29] Similarly, a Jew who openly profaned
the Sabbath was considered a pagan and could not give
up his property for the day of the Sabbath.[30] If such a
Jew lived in the court in the midst of other Jews, it was
necessary to rent the property or purchase it from him

[25] Tosefta 'Erub. 7.12, אנשי חצר ששכח אחד מהם ולא עירב עליו לבטל רשות;
comp. Mishna ibid. 6.2, see also Rashi 26a ודאי מתני' בשיבטל להן רשות
שהיה לו בחצר מיירי דאי לא בטיל אף בחצר אסורים לטלטל מבתיהן.
[26] נותן רשות ומבטל רשות.
[27] Tosefta 'Erub. 8.1, חצר של גוים הרי היא כדיר של בהמה מותר להכניס
ולהוציא מן החצר לבתים ומן הבתים לחצר.
[28] Comp. Mishna ibid. 6.1, הדר עם הנכרי [גוי] בחצר או עם מי שאינו מודה
בעירוב [בשבת] הרי זה אוסר עליו.
[29] Tosefta 'Erub. 7.18, הלכה ישראל מבטל, ובגוי עד שישכור, Yer. ibid. 6.3
ישראל נוטל רשות ונותן רשות; comp. also B. ibid. 69b, והעכו"ם [והגוי] משכיר
ובנכרי עד שישכור.
[30] Tosefta ibid., ישראל המחלל שבת בפרהסיא אינו צריך לבטל רשות; B. ibid.
69b, ישראל . . . שאינו משמר שבתו בשוק אינו מבטל רשות.

before acquiring the right to carry an object in the court on the Sabbath. If a Jew profaned the Sabbath secretly, he was still regarded as a Jew:[31]

The third type of Erub was called עירוב תבשילין. According to the old *halaka* the Jews had no right to cook or prepare any food on the Sabbath. It had to be prepared on the eve, i. e., on Friday.[32] This day was known in the Hellenistic-Roman literature as παρασκευή,[33] "the day of preparedness." If, however, a holiday fell on Friday, it became impossible to prepare food for the Sabbath. The law permits cooking on a holiday for the needs of that particular day, but not for those of another day; food prepared and cooked on Thursday for the Sabbath in a hot climate like Palestine would most likely become putrid. Therefore, there was introduced עירוב תבשילין, i. e., giving the right to a Jew to prepare a dish on Thursday and let it lie over until the end of the Sabbath. By this fiction all the cooking done on Friday, the holiday, for the Sabbath becomes merely a continuation of the preparation of the food from the previous day which began on Thursday.[34]

It is difficult to determine which of these three types of Erubin was instituted first, although there is a statement in the Talmud that Abraham already knew of Erubin and observed it,[35] and another statement that King Solomon instituted the takkanot of Erubin. We may, however, say definitely that the institution of Erubin came into being

---

[31] Tosefta *ibid.*, ושאין מחלל שבת בפרהסיא צריך לבטל רשות.

[32] See Ex. 16.5, ויהי ביומא; comp. Targum J., והיה ביום הששי והכינו; B. 'Erub. 38b, והיה ביום שתיתאי ויזמנון מה דייתהון לקטיהון למיכל ביומא בשבתא; see also Pes. 46b. הששי והכינו חול מכין לשבת . . . ואין יו'ט מכין לשבת.

[33] See Josephus, *Ant.* 16.6, 2; John 19.14.

[34] Bez. M. 2.1, יום טוב שחל להיות ערב שבת לא יבשל אדם בתחלה מיום טוב לשבת אבל מבשל הוא ליום טוב ואם הותיר הותיר לשבת ועושה תבשיל מערב יום טוב וסומך עליו לשבת.

[35] Yoma 28b, קיים אברהם אבינו אפילו ערובי תבשילין.

at the earliest in the last three or four decades before the
destruction of the Second Temple.

In a Mishna in the tractate of Erubin it is stated that
Rabban Gamaliel related a story about his father Rabban
Simon in connection with עירוב חצירות.[36] This Rabban
Gamaliel, undoubtedly, is the second, since he says that
the story happened when they lived in Jerusalem.[37] The
emphasis on Jerusalem shows that without a doubt it
refers to the second Gamaliel who lived in Jabneh, and
the event to which he refers happened when he was a
young man and lived with his father in Jerusalem. From
this we may see that the institution of עירוב חצירות had
already been in existence at the time of Rabban Simon who
lived shortly before the destruction of the Temple. It
cannot be definitely stated when עירוב תחומין was instituted.
It certainly was not known in the time of Rabban Gamaliel
the first;[38] he introduced the תחום שבת, i. e., to give a Jew
permission to walk on the Sabbath two thousand cubits
from his own city, which was called תחום שבת, a Sabbath
Day's journey.[39] It is clear, however, that in the time of
Rabban Gamaliel *the second*, the takkana of עירוב תחומין
was already in vogue.[40] It is impossible to ascertain when
the third type of Erubin was instituted, but we may say
with certainty that all these three types of Erubin were
instituted before the time of Bar Kokba; in other words,
from the middle of the first century C. E. until the first
quarter of the second century.

---

[36] אמר רבן גמליאל מעשה בצדוקי (מומר) אחד שהיה דר עמנו במבוי בירושלם
ואמר לנו אבא מהרו והוציאו את הכלים למבוי.

[37] שהיה דר עמנו במבוי בירושלים.

[38] See above p. 353.

[39] Hag. 15, עד כאן תחום שבת; 'Er. 4.1, והיינו בתוך התחום; comp. also
Acts 1.12, σαββάτου ἄπεχον ὁδόν.

[40] Comp. 'Er. 4.1, פעם אחת לא נכנסו לנמל עד שחשיכה אמרו לו לרבן גמליאל
מה אנו לירד אמר אמר להם מותרים אתם שכבר הייתי מסתכל והיינו בתוך התחום עד שלא
חשיכה.

I have here sought to show merely how the institution of Erubin came into being. I have not dealt with all the *halaka* of Erubin which are of a later development. My purpose was only to show the origin of these great takkanot. The sages of the Second Jewish Commonwealth down to the time of Bar Kokba strove to make the law applicable to the Jews, and therefore they instituted different takkanot. It is true that from time to time the sages had instituted prohibitionary laws, גזירות, that were for emergencies, to safeguard either the Jews or Judaism. There is always a difference between a decree *g'zera* and a takkana. A decree is only temporary; when the reason for the decree vanished, *ipso facto*, the decree became null and void. A takkana, on the other hand, is universal and applicable to all classes like *halaka*.[41] A takkana is an amendment of early law, either pentateuchal or *halaka*, introduced by the sages generally for the purpose of harmonizing religion and life. Hence a takkana has a lenient tendency. In introducing a takkana the sages usually sought support for it in the Bible.[42] The takkanot of Erubin were introduced because it was held that the Sabbath was for man, and not man for the Sabbath,[43] and that men should enjoy themselves on the Sabbath day.

It is said that people are worthy of their leaders. It is certain that people have the laws that they deserve. Leaders may on one hand introduce laws which enslave people and make them law-breakers, and on the other hand enact laws which promote their progress and make them cherish their institutions. This refers to civil law and to religious law as well.

[41] See S. Zeitlin, "The Halaka, Introduction to Tannaitic Jurisprudence," *JQR*, 1948, pp. 21–6.

[42] מכאן סמכו חכמים; Beza 15b; מכאן סמכו חכמים לעירוב תבשילין מן התורה, Hul. 10b, לנט' ידים מן התורה.

[43] כי תשא, Mekilta לכם שבת מסורה ואי אתם מסורים לשבת; comp. Yoma 85b.

PROSBOL

A Study in Tannaitic Jurisprudence

TANNAITIC jurisprudence, or, for that matter, any jurisprudence, can be studied by two methods, the dogmatic
and the historic. By dogmatic method I mean the study
of the Halaka as codified in the Mishna or in later codices,
and by the historic method I mean the study of the origins
and causes which led to a particular Halaka. A judge or a
rabbi must follow the dogmatic method in deciding the
law. He has to follow the law as it was codified, as it was
decided by previous authorities. A student of the law,
however, cannot follow the dogmatic method. He must investigate the causes which brought about the enactment
of the law.[1] We know that some laws were enacted as a
result of social, political and economic conditions, and,
therefore, we recognize in the Jewish law the differences
between the Babylonian Talmud and the Palestinian Talmud. These differences are not due merely to those of
interpretation or to various versions of the previous law,
but are related to diverse social and economic conditions
in the given countries.[2]

I

According to the Pentateuch, every seventh year was
called the sabbatical year, in which "every creditor shall
release that which he had lent unto his neighbor; he shall
not exact it of his neighbor and of his brother because God's

[1] See S. Z., ‏הפקר ויאוש‎, ‏לפלאות לו שבעים שנה‎, ‏לכבוד לוי גינצבורג‎, ‏ספר היובל‎
‏נ.י. ירק, תש"ו, האקדימה האסרקנית למדעי היהדות‎.
[2] *Ibid.* p. ‏ט"ז‎.

341

148

release had been proclaimed."[3] From tannaitic sources, we learn that Hillel had introduced Prosbol,[4] by which the sabbatical year does not release the debt, and the creditor has the right to demand his loan. According to the same source, the Prosbol reads as follows: "I declare before you, judges in the place, that I shall collect my debt that I may have outstanding with . . . whenever I desire."[5] From the Mishna we also learn that if the creditor deposited his notes with the court, he may collect his loan from the debtor והמוסר שטרותיו לבית דין אינן משמטין. The sabbatical year does not apply to such a loan.[6]

Various questions confronted the rabbis of the Middle Ages. Is Hillel's *Takkana* of Prosbol the same as המוסר שטרותיו, which is mentioned in the Mishna, or does the *Takkana* of Prosbol differ from המוסר שטרותיו? If it is the same, what was the purpose of Hillel's *Takkana*? And if it is not the same, then what is the difference, and why did Hillel introduce the Prosbol, since, according to the Mishna, if a creditor deposited his notes with the court, the law of the sabbatical year does not apply to his loan and he may collect it? The rabbis of the Middle Ages were divided on this point. Some maintained that Hillel's *Takkana* of Prosbol does not differ from the Halaka given in the Mishna, where it is stated that המוסר שטרותיו לבית דין אינן משמטין,[7] while others held that Hillel's *Takkana* of Prosbol did differ from this Halaka.[8]

---

[3] Deut. 15.1–3.

[4] Sheb. 10.2, פרוזבל אינו משמט זה אחד מן הדברים; התקין הלל הזקן פרוזבל; Git. 4.3, שהתקין הלל; Sifre, קס״ח, הלל התקין פרוזבל; מיכן אמרו הלל התקין פרוזבל . . . .

[5] Sheb. ibid., זה נופו של פרוזבל מוסר אני לכם איש פלוני ופלוני הדריינים שבמקום פלוני שכל חוב שיש לי שאונבנו כל זמן שארצה.

[6] *Ibid.* 10.1.

[7] Rashi, Mak. 3b, Ket. 89a, מוסר שטרותיו לבית דין, הוא פרוזבל שהתקין הלל; הלל התקין פרוזבל כדי שלא תשמט שביעית שמוסר שטרותיו לבית דין.

[8] R. Nissim, (on Alfasi), Git. 4, וכ״ח כיון דטדרייתא במסירת שטרות סניא למה הוצרך לתקן פרוזבל.

There are other difficulties in connection with the *Takkana* of Prosbol. In the text of the Prosbol, the creditor declares: "I shall collect my debt that I have outstanding with . . . ," from which it is clear that the Prosbol can take effect only after the loan was made. Yet, according to the Halaka פרוזבל המוקדם כשר, an antedated Prosbol is legal, which is in contradiction to the wording of the Prosbol itself.

II

Before establishing how the institution of the Prosbol arose, we should give a short survey of the development of שטר חוב — creditor's note. In the Bible, there is no mention of any written document connected with a loan. According to the biblical law, as well as the Roman law, a debtor was bound over to his creditor if he did not fulfill his *obligatio ex contractu*, that is, if he did not pay his debt to his creditor. The latter had the right to take the debtor or his children in bondage. According to the Roman law, the creditor had the right to even kill the debtor if he did not fulfill his *obligatio ex contractu*.[9] That the creditor had certain rights over his debtor or over his children is shown by the story in the II Kings. We are told that "a certain woman of the wife of the sons of the prophets cried to Elisha saying: 'Thy servant, my husband, is dead, and thou knowest that thy servant already feared God and the creditor has come to take unto him my two sons for bond men!'"[10] From her complaint, we may conclude with certainty that in Israel in ancient times if the debtor did not pay his debts, his creditor had the right to take him into servitude, or, if he had died, to take his children into bondage.

[9] Comp. Gaii *Institutionum Iuris Civilis* III.
[10] 4.1, והנשה בא לקחת את שני ילדי לו לעבדים.

From Nehemiah we learn that the Jews complained thus: "We have borrowed money for the king's tribute upon our fields and our vineyards. Yet now our flesh is as the flesh of our brethren, our children as their children; and, lo, we bring into bondage our sons and our daughters to be servants, and some of our daughters are brought into bondage already; neither is it in our power to help it; for other men have our fields and our vineyards."[11] Hence, after the Restoration, the debtor's *obligatio* was in the person as well as in the property.

The *obligatio in personem* — the creditor's right over the debtor, even to kill him, was abolished by the Romans in 313 B. C. E. by the *Lex Poetelia*.[12] The sages, after the Restoration, abolished the *obligatio in personem*. They introduced the *shtar*, which the debtor gave to the creditor, by which he placed his property as a hypothec. In this manner, they removed from the creditor the right over the person of the debtor. It became only an *obligatio in rem*. The creditor had the right to seize the property of the debtor, if he did not pay the debt, but he did not have the right to take him or his children in bondage.

As we learn from the papyri, as early as the year 456 B. C. E., the debtor used to give the creditor a note in which he not only obligated himself to pay the debt but also, if the debt was not paid, he gave the creditor the right to seize his property. If the debtor died before the debt was paid, his children had to pay it. A promissory note, written in the ninth year of Artaxerxes (456 B. C. E.) reads in part as follows: "You, Meshullam, and your children, have the right to take for yourself any security which you may find of mine, till you have full payment of

---

[11] ‏...והנה אנחנו כבשים את בנינו ואת בנתינו לעבדים ויש מבנתינו נכבשות‎ 5.1–5, "
‏ואין לאל ידנו ושדתנו וכרמינו לאחרים.‎

[12] See Gaii, *op. cit.* III.

your money and interest thereon, and I shall have no power
to say to you that I have paid you your money and the
interest on it while this deed is in your hand, nor shall I
have power to lodge a complaint against you before governor or judge on the ground that you have taken from me
any security while this deed is in your hand. If I die
without paying you this money and interest thereon, my
children are to pay you this money and interest thereon.
If they do not pay you this money and interest thereon,
you Meshullam have a right to take for yourself any food
or security that you may find of theirs until you have full
payment of your money and interest thereon, and they
shall have no power to lodge a complaint against you before
governor or judge while this deed is in your hand."[13]

III

Early tannaitic jurisprudence does not speak of שטר חוב,
creditor's note.[13a] According to the tannaitic law, real property can be acquired in three ways;[14] by money, that is,
when the buyer pays the vendor the value of the property;
by writ, that is, when the vendor transfers the title by writ;
and by possession, that is, by acquiring property through
holding it for a period of time, when the property was previously *res nullius*,[15] or if there was no claim against it.[16] By

[13] . . . אנת משלם ובניך שליטן שליטן למלקח לך כל ערבן זי תשכח לי בי זילבנן כסף ודהב
והן מיתח ולא שלמתך בכספא זנה ומרבית בני הטו ישלמון לך . . . ולא יכלין וקבלין
עליך קדם סגן ודין וספרא זנה בידך, No. 10. *Aramaic Papyri of the Fifth
Century B. C.* Edited, with translation and notes, by A. Cowley.
Oxford, at the Clarendon Press. 1923.

[13a] Comp. also B. K. 175b, אמר עולא דבר תורה אחד סלוה בשטר ואחד מלוה
ע'פ גובה מנכסים משועבדים, מה טעם שעבודא דאורייתא . . . ר' יוחנן ור' שמעון בן
לקיש דאמרי תרוייהו מלוה על פה גובה מן היורשין ומן הלקוחות מאי טעמא שעבודא
דאורייתא.

[14] Kid. 1.5, נכסים שיש להם אחריות נקנין בכסף ובשטר ובחזקה.

[15] Also if the buyer held the property for a period of time.

[16] מחאה. Comp. also Mishna B. B. 3.3, כל חזקה שאין עמה טענה אינה חזקה.

these methods, a pagan slave could be acquired,[17] as well as a wife.[18]

By introducing שטר חוב, the sages not only changed the rights of the creditor over the debtor but also modified the biblical laws of releasing the debts in the sabbatical year. According to the Bible, any debt which outlasted a sabbatical year could no longer be collected. However, with the introduction of the שטר חוב, the creditor could collect his debt even though it was not paid before the arrival of the sabbatical year, on the principle that the property of the debtor was mortgaged to the creditor at the time when the note was written, and thus before the sabbatical year arrived. However, such a note had to be deposited with the court.[19]

Such notes were usually kept in the archives of the record office in the Temple. Josephus relates that the Sicarii, in order to win the debtors over to their cause, destroyed the money-lenders' bonds, kept in the record office[20] near the "bouleuterion," council chamber (courthouse).[21] And the Mishna refers to this when it says that the sabbatical laws do not apply to those who deposit creditor's notes with the court. On the same principle, if a loan is given on security, the laws of the sabbatical year do not apply because, when the debtor gives a pledge or security to the creditor, it is exchanged for his debt. If the debtor does not fulfill his obligation, the pledge becomes the property of the creditor.[22] The latter really acquired the pledge at

---

[17] Kid. 1.3.

[18] Ibid. 1, האשה . . . נקנית בכסף בשטר ובביאה.

[19] Comp. Git. 37a, ר' יוחנן ור' שמעון בן לקיש דאמרו תרוייהו . . . שטר שיש בו. Comp. אחריות נכסים אינו משמט . . . תנן התם . . . והמוסר שטרותיו לב"ד אין משמטין also ibid. שטר העומד לנבות כנבוי דמי.

[20] B. J. II, 427, μεθ᾽ ἃ τὸ πῦρ ἐπὶ τὰ ἀρχεῖα ἔφερον ἀφανίσαι σπεύδοντες τὰ συμβόλαια τῶν δεδανεικότων καὶ τὰς εἰσπράξεις ἀποκόψαι τῶν χρεῶν.

[21] . . . ἀρχεῖον καὶ τὴν ἄκραν καὶ τὸ βουλευτήριον. Ibid. VI.354.

[22] המלוה את הבירו על המשכון אף על פי שהחוב מרובה על המשכון אינו משמט,

the time when it was given to him in exchange for the lien.[23]

Thus, a loan to secure which the debtor gave the creditor a nóte to be deposited in the archives or in the court was not released by the sabbatical year, and the creditor had the right to collect it. However, a loan for which no note was given and which was only transacted in the presence of witnesses, or a loan made without any witnesses, was to be forfeited if not paid before the sabbatical year. Even when the debtor gave a note to the creditor which was not deposited in the archives or in the court, (because the creditor wanted to negotiate the note) the loan could not be subsequently collected if it was not paid before the arrival of the sabbatical year.

To avoid such complications and to encourage loans to the needy, Hillel introduced the Prosbol.[24] The term Prosbol is Greek προς βουλη meaning a declaration by the creditor before the court (or προσβολη meaning "application") in which the creditor states before the court that any debt which A owes him may be collected at any time the loan is called.[25] Thus, the Prosbol had a two-fold application in protecting the creditor from losing his loan; first

---

המלוה על המשכון . . . אינו משמטין . . . שמואל אומר אפילו על 8.5; .Tosefta Sheb
משכון דקני . . . דאמר רבי יצחק ,Yer. Sheb. 10. Comp. also Git. 37a
סניין לבעל חוב שקונה משכון ולך תהיה צדקה. אם אינו קונה צדקה סניין סכאן לבעל
חוב שקונה משכון.

[23] According to Samuel if one lends one's neighbor a thousand zuz and receives as a pledge the handle of a saw, the loan is forfeited, if the creditor loses the handle, אמר שמואל האי סאן דאוחפיה אלפא זוזי להבריה וסשכן
לו קחא דמגלא אבד קתא דמגלא אבד דמגלא אבד אלפי זוזי (Shebuot 43b). Samuel's opinion is in accordance with the view משכון נגד כולו הוא קונה

[24] See also R. Nissim (on Alfasi) Git. 4, כיון סדאריתא במסירת סטרות סני
לסה הוצרך לתקן פרוזבל י"ל מפני שאין הכל רוצין למסור שטרותיהן ועוד שלפעמים
אינם בידם ועוד דפרוזבל מהני אף למלוה על פה.

[25] Comp. also L. Blau, Prosbol im Lichte der Griechischen Papyri und der Rechtsgeschichte. *Festschrift zum 50 Jahrigen Bestehen der Franz-Josef-Landesrabbiner-Schule in Budapest.* 1927.

when the creditor received a note which he did not deposit with the court, secondly when the loan was transacted without witnesses.

IV

According to the Mishna Sheb.[26] a שטר מוקדם, an ante-dated note, is invalid, i. e. if the note was written before the loan was transacted. A postdated note, i. e. if the loan was transacted in January but the note was written in February, is legal. The Mishna also says that if a Prosbol was antedated, פרוזבל המוקדם, it is valid and that a post-dated Prosbol is invalid, והמאוחר פסול. The general inter-pretation of this Mishna is that if a Prosbol was written in February and was dated January, it is valid, because it is only valid for a loan transacted before January but not valid for a loan transacted between January and February, al-though the Prosbol was written in February, and the credi-tor would lose the benefit of the Prosbol for the loans transacted between January and February. However, a postdated Prosbol, i. e. one written in January and dated February, is not valid, and the creditor cannot collect the loans.[27]

According to Maimonides פרוזבל המוקדם כשר והמאוחר פסול is to be interpreted that if the Prosbol was written before the loan was transacted it is valid, and if it was written after the loan was transacted, it is not valid.[28] According

---

[26] Sheb. 10.5, שטרי חוב המוקדמים פסולים והמאוחרים כשרים.

[27] See the Commentary of R. Samson b. Abraham, on Sheb. ad loc.; Bertinoro, ad loc., פרוזבל המוקדם כשר, שזמנו מוקדם שנכתב בכסליו וזמנו הכתוב בתוכו מתשרי קודם כשר . . . אבל פרוזבל המאוחר פסול שאיחר זמנו.

[28] פרוזבל מוקדם הוא שיכתוב הפרוזבל תחילה ואחר כן ילוה לו הממון. המאוחר שילוה הממון תחילה ונעשה חוב ואח"כ כתב פרוזבל והוא פסול. פ' המשניות להר"ם.

Maimonides, however, retracted in his *Mishne Torah*, and said that if the Prosbel was written before the loan had been transacted, it was not valid. כתב הפרוזבל תחלה ואח"כ הלוה הלוה אינו מועיל, אלא משמט עד שיכתוב הפרוזבל אחר שהלוה. נמצאת אומר שכל מלוה הקודמת לפרוזבל אינה נשמטת בפרוזבל זה. ואם הפרוזבל קודם למלוה נשמטת בפרוזבל זה. לפיכך פרוזבל המוקדם כשר

to others פרוזבל המוקדם כשר is to be interpreted if the loan was transacted, let us say, in February, and the Prosbol was handed in to the court in April but was dated March, such a Prosbol was valid, because that would be to the disadvantage of the creditor, since the loans made from March to April were not included in the Prosbol. However, המאוחר פסול i. e. if the loan was transacted, let us say, in February, the Prosbol was handed in to the court in March and was dated April, such a Prosbol was not valid, because it would be to the advantage of the creditor since loans made from March until April were included in the Prosbol.[29]

כיצד כתבו בניסן והקדים זמנו מאדר כשר . . . אבל אם איחר זמנו וכתבו מאייר פסול
(ה' שמיטה ויובל, פ'ט כ'ב). This contradiction between his Commentary on the Mishna and between his statement in the *Mishne Torah* was noticed by his contemporaries, who asked him for an explanation. He replied that his statement in the *Mishne Torah* was correct, while that in the Commentary on the Mishna represented a first draft and was made without due deliberation. שאלה, תורנו הדרתו הדין בפירוש פרוזבל
המוקדם והמאוחר כיצד הוא לפי שראינו שהאדון כתב דברים בחיברו ומצינו בפירושו
למשנה בהפך מזה . . . תשובה, מה שכתבנו בחיבור הוא הנכון שאין בו ספק וכן כתבנו
בפירוש המשנה, ומה שהגיע לידכם פירוש המשנה ומצאתם בו הפך מדברי שכתבתי בחבור
זה שהגיע אליכם הוא המהדורא קמא שיצאה מתחת ידינו קודם שעיינינו ודקדקנו היטב
ונמשכנו באותו פירוש על מה שכתב בעל ספר הדינים רב חפץ נ'ע והטעות הוא מעל
הספר הזה ונמשכנו אחרי דבריו מפני שלא עיינינו בדבר היטב אבל אחר שדקדקנו בדברינו
ועיינינו בהן נתבאר לנו מה שכתבנו בחיבור. ודעו כי כן נם כן יש במהדורא קמא זו של
פירוש המשנה שהגיע לידכם מקומות רבים כיוצא בזה בעניינים שנמשכנו מהם בכל דבר
מאותם הדברים לדעת גאון מהגאונים ואח"כ נתבאר לנו הענין ואינו מהחייות הדחיות שיש לאותם
הדעות וההסברות של אותם הגאונים באותם הדברים ודחינו אותם . . . וכתב משה.
(תשובות הרמב'ם, אברהם חיים פריימן, ירושלים).

This responsum is of great interest. It reveals that Maimonides acknowledged that some of the interpretations given in his Commentary on the Mishna were incorrect, and that this was due to his reliance on the Geonim. It also shows that he did not altogether admire some of the Geonim. Comp. also, כסף משנה (ה' שמיטה ויובל פ'ט), כתב הפרוזבל חלה. See also בתוספתא אלא ששנויה בהפך ונר' שט'ס הוא שהטעם מהופך וקל להבין ומסהברא דכל מלוה שנעשית אחר זמן הפרוזבל אינה משמטת, Isaak ben Abba Mari, בשעה שמוציא הפרוזבל בבית דין כחוב בו וכל חוב שיש לו ולישנא מעליא נקט והא דרשב'ן דתוספתא עיקר . . . והיינו דתנן פרוזבל המוקדם כשר שאם הלוה לוה ממנו בניסן וציוה הלוה לדיינין לכתוב הפרוזבל באדר שלפניו . . . ואם לוה בניסן ואיחר זמן פהרוזבל באייר פסול. See S. Lieberman, ח'א, תוספה ראשונים, ספר העטור.

[29] Comp. also R. Nissim Gaon, quoted by R. Isaak ben Abba in
היכא שהלוה בניסן בשנה אחת של שביעית, והלוה לו מלוה אחרת בניסן. ספר העטור

It is impossible to accept these interpretations because
in the Mishna the Prosbol is given alongside of the note.
The antedated note,[30] שטר מוקדם which is invalid, refers to
the loan. The note was written before the loan was transacted.[31] In the same manner, a postdated note שטר מאוחר
is valid. It does not mean that the date in the note is later
than the writing of the note, but it means that the note
postdated the loan, and such a note is valid. In the same
manner, we must assume in regard to the Prosbol that it
cannot refer to the difference between the time of the writ-

בשנה ששית של שביעית, והודיע לדיינים שתי הלוואות אלו, והדיינים הקדימו הפרוזבל שני
באדר שלפני ניסן דהוה ליה פרוזבל מוקדם למלוה שניה כשר ... אבל אם הודיע
לדיינים באדר בשנה ששית והלוה הממון בניסן של ששית, ואיחרו הדיינים את הפרוזבל
וכתבו זמן הפרוזבל באייר של אחר ניסן, סניסן של שנה ששית, הרי זה פסול, ואפילו
סלוה ראשונה אין נובין בו.

[30] פרוזבל המוקדם כשר והמאוחר פסול. שטרי חוב המוקדמים פסולים, והמאוחרים
כשרים.

[31] Comp. Rashi, Sanh. 32a, שטרי חוב המוקדמים, ליכתב קדם המלוה B. M.
72a, המוקדמים למלוה; R. H. 2a, לשטרות, להבחין איזה שטר חוב מוקדם למלוה
ואיזה מאוחר.
Maimonides, in his Commentary on the Mishna, interprets שטר
מוקדם to mean that if A borrowed money and gave to the creditor a
note and repaid the loan without getting his note back and then obtained another loan for the same amount, this note is called שטר מוקדם
and is invalid. ועניין שטרי חוב המוקדמים פסולין ... כנון שלוה ראובן משמעון
ממון וכתב לו שטר, אחר כן החזיר ראובן לשמעון ממנו שהלוה וכתב לו שמעון מחילה
ונשאר השטר בידו ... ואחר כן לוה ראובן משמעון ממון שני, ואמר לו ראובן אל תצרכני
לכתיבת שטר אחר השטר הראשון שהיה לך עלי יהיה בידך אחרי שכך הממון אחד,
שהשטר ההוא הוא מוקדם ... ונעשה פסול ... ואמרו מאוחרין כשרין סבואר והוא שיקח
המלוה ויכתב השטר אחרי כן ... זה פירוש מוקדמין וסאוחרין ויש לך להתבונן בו מפני
שרבים כשלו בו וחשבו שכל מי שיכתוב שטר חוב מזמן ואחר כך לקח הממון ההוא בשטר
... לאחר זמן ארוך שזהו שטרי חוב המוקדמין וזה אינו אמת. R. Isaak ben Abba
Mari correctly pointed out that this interpretation of Maimonides is
incorrect. ור' משה בן מיימן דחק עצמו ופי' מוקדמין שטר שלוה בו וחזר ולוה בו.
וליתא דההוא מכללא נפקא כדטוכח בפ' שנים אוחזין, שטר שלוה בו ופורעו אינו חוזר
ולוה בו, אימת אלימא לטחר וליומא אוחרי, תיפוק לי' דהוה מוקדם ותנן שטרי חוב
המוקדמין פסולין, ואם איתא, לימא לי' תנינא שטרי חוב המוקדמין פסולין ולא הל"ל
(עטור, זמן) ... תפוק לי'. Maimonides in his *Mishne Torah* apparently retracted what he wrote in his Commentary on the Mishna. שטרי חוב
המוקדמים פסולין שהרי לקוחות בהן לקוחות שלא כדין ולפיכך קנסו אותו חכמים ולא
ינבה בשטר מוקדם אלא מבני חורין גזרה שמא יטרוף מזמן ראשון שהקדימו, שטרי חוב
המאוחרין כשרין שהרי הורע כחו של בעל השטר שאינו טורף אלא מזמן השטר וה' מלוה
ולוה, כ'נ.

ing of the Prosbol and the affixed date of the Prosbol.
Certainly, we cannot assume that an antedated Prosbol
means that it was written before the loan was transacted,
because a Prosbol written before a loan was transacted
could not be valid since the text of the Prosbol reads "any
loan which I have." Therefore, it is quite clear that the loan
must precede the Prosbol and not the Prosbol the loan.[32]

In the same Tosefta it is stated that Rabban Simon ben
Gamaliel said כל מלוה שלאחר פרוזבל הרי זה אינו משמט; in the
case of a loan transacted after the Prosbol was written the
sabbatical year does not apply, and the creditor has the
right to collect the loan. There is another variant, however,
which reads that a loan transacted after the Prosbol was
written is משמט i. e. it is cancelled by the sabbatical year;
such a Prosbol is not valid.[33] This reading undoubtedly is
correct, in spite of the fact that all the great rabbis of the
Middle Ages give the reading הרי זה אינו משמט.[34] It is impossible to assume that Rabban Simon ben Gamaliel held
that a Prosbol, written before the loan is transacted, is
valid, for this would contradict the text of the Prosbol.
The text of the Prosbol, as we said before, is in the past
tense כל חוב שיש לו.[35] However, we must explain how such
a change was made in the words of Rabban Simon ben
Gamaliel from משמט to אינו משמט. It seems that the change
was brought about by the erroneous interpretation by some

---

[32] שצריך כתיבתו אחר הלואה מדגרסינן במשנה כל שיש לי, ולא קתני שיהיה לי
Rav Nissim Gaon, quoted in העטור.

[33] See Saul Lieberman, תוספת ראשונים ח"א, ad loc.: בחוון יהזקאל מניה כאן.
הרי זה משמט, והנהה זו ולמרות זה שהוא נתלה באילן גדול, אין לה שחר, כי נירסתנו
מתאשרת ע"י רב חפק, ר"ן נאון, הרסבם, ריבמק, הר"ש העטור והאו"ז.

[34] ולפיכך נירסתנו: אינו משמט היא למעלה מכל כפק ופקפוק, ולפי זה יוצא
שהפרוזבל צריך להיות לפני ההלואה. ועכשיו מתעוררת השאלה איך להתאים תוספתא
זו למשנתנו: פרוזבל המוקדם כשר והמאוחר פכול, ועל מדוכה זו ישבו כבר הגאונים
והראשונים ... סוף דבר, הגירכא הנכונא בתוספתא, היא כמו שהיא לפנינו, והפשט
במשנה הוא כפי הירושלמי שפרוזבל המוקדם הוא שהקדים את זמנו ... והפשט הפשוט
הוא כרשב"ג הולק על כשנתנו וכן הולק הוא נם על הרישא של התוספתא. Ibid.

[35] See note 32.

of the rabbis of the Middle Ages of the passage פרוזבל המוקדם כשר that a Prosbol written before the loan was given is valid, and והמאוחר פסול that a Prosbol written after the loan was transacted, is invalid. The present reading in the Tosefta is due to the interpretation of the rabbis of the Middle Ages that if the Prosbol was written before the loan was transacted, the Prosbol is valid.

V

Some readings in the tannaitic literature reveal that they were changed to comply with the views held by the Amoraim and even by the Geonim. It is worth while giving a few examples.

A Mishna in Eduyyot reads: "In case a needle was found in meat the knife and the hands were clean, while the meat was defiled. If, on the other hand, it is found in the dung, everything is clean."[36] In the Talmud a statement by Rabbi Akiba is appended to this. It reads as follows: "We prove our point that there is no defilement of hands in the temple."[37] This statement was incomprehensible to the Amoraim. They asked, "Why does he say only, there is no defilement of the hands in the temple?[38] He should have included vessels, since the knife also is declared clean." From explanations given by the Babylonian rabbis it is evident that the underlying reasons for R. Akiba's statement were unknown to them.

The Mishna, in my opinion, had the original reading: המחט שנמצאת בבשר שהסכין טהור והבשר טמא. "In case a needle was found in the meat the knife was clean, while the meat was defiled." Now we can understand R. Akiba's state-

[36] אף הוא העיד (ר' חנינא סגן הכהנים) . . . על מחט שנמצאת בבשר שהסכין והידים טהורות, והבשר טמא, ואם נמצאת בפרש הכל טהור.

[37] Pes. 19a, אמר ר' עקיבא זכינו שאין טומאת ידים במקדש

[38] ibid, ונימא שאין טומאת ידים וכלים במקדש

ment.[39] The meat is unclean, because of the needle; the knife is clean since hands do not defile in the temple. The schools of Shammai and Hillel decreed that hands defile every vessel in the temple.[40] From this Mishna declaring the knife clean, R. Akiba deduces זכינו that there is no defilement of hands in the temple, for, did not the hands hold the knife? Some compilers of the Talmud, having before them the statement of R. Akiba שאין טומאת ידים במקדש and not having the word ידים in the Mishna, inserted ידים so as to read שהסכין והידים טהורות and this impelled later rabbis to ask, Why does not R. Akiba refer to vessels as well?"[41]

Another example may be quoted. It is stated in the Palestinian Talmud that R. Johanan said that if a master renounces his right to his slave, he is no longer permitted to use the services of the latter and has no power to issue a writ of freedom.[42] According to the Babylonian Talmud, R. Johanan held that if the master renounces his rights to his slave, the slave regains his freedom, and the master must issue a writ of freedom to him.[43] There is a contradiction between the Palestinian and the Babylonian Talmuds in the statement by R. Johanan as to the status of a slave. There is no question that in the Babylonian Talmud the statement by R. Johanan was changed. According to the Palestinian law (Roman law), if a master renounces his rights to a slave, the latter does not regain his freedom but becomes a *res nullius*.[44] R. Johanan, who was a Pales-

---

[39] אין טומאת ידים במקדש.

[40] משעבר הרגל והיו מעבירין, Sheb. 13b; Yer. *ibid.*; Hag. 3, 7, הספר והידים; Yer. *ibid.* 79d, על טהרת עזרה . . . ואמרין להם הזהרו שלא תגעו בשלחן [במנורה] פעם אחת הטבילו את המנורה אמרו צדוקים ראו פרושים מטבילין נלנל חמה ומאור והלבנה.

[41] See S. Zeitlin, The Halaka in the Gospels, *HUCA* I, 365–69.

[42] ר' אבהו בשם ר' יוחנן אמר המפקיר את עבדו אינו רשאי לשעבדו ואינו רשאי לכתוב לו נט שיחרור, Yer. Git. 4.

[43] Git. 39, והאמר עולא אמר ר' יוחנן המפקיר עבדו יצא לחירות וצריך נט שיחרור.

[44] Rudolph Sohm, *The Institutes of Roman Law*, p. 173.

tinian, followed the Palestinian law. Therefore, according
to him, if a master renounces his rights over his slave, he
is no longer entitled to his services nor does he have the
right to issue a writ of freedom, since the slave is no longer
his property. The slave is a *res nullius*. In Babylonia,
however, there was a different law. Therefore, the statement of R. Johanan was modified to read that the slave
regains his freedom if the owner renounces his rights over
him, but needs a writ of freedom from his owner.[45]

Another striking example may be cited where the
Geonim changed the reading of the Talmud in accordance
with their theories. In the tractate Sanhedrin of the
Babylonian Talmud, we have a statement that an authorization obtained from the Babylonian Exilarch is valid
both in Babylonia and in Palestine. However, an authorization obtained from the authorities of Palestine is valid
'there,' i. e. Palestine, but not 'here,' i. e. Babylonia.[46]
But, according to the reading, recorded in the *Midrash
Wehishir*, which is a Palestinian product, anyone who
received an authorization in Palestine could render decisions
in Palestine and in Babylonia. However, if he obtained an
authorization in Babylonia, it is valid for Babylonia but is
void in Palestine.[47] We may say with certainty that the
present text, which we have in the Talmud Sanhedrin,
was tampered with, and that the original reading was
מהתם להכא מהני that the authorization obtained in Palestine
was valid in Babylonia. This change was brought about
by the opinion held by the Babylonian authorities that
they were superior to the Palestinian scholars.[48]

---

[45] See S. Zeitlin, הפקר ויאוש.

[46] פשיטא מהכא להכא ומהתם להתם מהני ומהכא להתם מהני דהכא שבט והתם
ש"ט. מחוקק, p. 5. ... מהתם להכא מאי ... ש"ט מהתם להכא לא מהני ש"ט

[47] לפי ... אבל נטל רשות מראש ישיבה שבבבל ודן בארץ ישראל אינו מועיל ...
שבארץ ישראל נאמר שבט ... אבל בבבל נאמר בה מחוקק ... ועוד הלכה למעשה ...
שאין מועיל רשות בבל בארץ ישראל (ספר והזהיר, משפטים).

[48] See S. Zeitlin, *Religious and Secular Leadership*, pp. 105–112. It

VI

From the Tosefta, we learn that the time for writing the Prosbol was on the eve of the New Year of the post-sabbatical year, i. e. the beginning of the eighth year.[49] However, we have another variant of the same Tosefta, which states that the time for writing the Prosbol was on the eve of the New Year of the sabbatical year.[50] This reading is unquestionably correct. According to a Mishna if a debtor returns his loan to the creditor during the sabbatical year, the sages will be pleased with him.[51] It is

had already noticed by such authorities as the Tosafists that hypothetical passages exist in the Talmud. Comp. Nidah 24a, אמר רב פפא בפניו מוטמטין כ"ע לא פליני. והא דקאמר איתיבה ר' יוחנן לריש לקיש לא היו דברים מעולם ;comp. also Yeb. 35b, הא דקאמר לעיל איתיבה כולי עלמא לא פליני, ; B. B. 154b, נמיהבי הכונס יבסתו לא היו דברים מעולם והא דפריך לעיל ריש לקיש לר' יוחנן מטשנת בר קפרא ואמר לו ר' יוחנן שאני אומר מודה בשטר שכתבו א"צ לקיימו, לא אמר דבר זה מעולם וכולה סוניא דלעיל ליתא לפי מסקנא זו.

[49] אימתי כותבין עליו פרוזבל ערב ראש השנה של מוצאי שביעית. See Nachmanides' Commentary on Deut. 15.1, שכן מצינו בתוספתא שכותבין פרוזבל ער'ה שו'ח הרשב'א ח'ב של מוצאי שביעית. Comp. also

[50] אימתי כותבין פרוזבל ערב ראש השנה של שביעית כתבו ערב ראש השנה של כדתנן אימתי כותבין עליו פרוזבל ערב, ספר העטור מוצאי שביעית. Comp. also ראש השנה של שביעית ... והא דנרס' אימתי כותבין פרוזבל ערב שביעית לא בא למעט אלא שאין כותבין אותו מטשנכנס שביעית אבל קודם שביעית כותבין אותו בכל שעה עד כדתנן אימתי כותבין פרוזבל ערב ראש השנה ,כפתור ופרח, פרק חמשים ;ערב שביעית שלפני שביעית. וכן נמי כתב הר' בן מלכי צדק פרוזבל דינו ליהכתב עד שלא תכנס אהבת ציון השטיה ... והוא יום ערב ר'ה של שנה השביעית Comp. also Ratner, וירושלים, ad loc.

[51] המחזיר חוב בשביעית רוח חכמים נוחה הימנו. R. Samson, in his commentary on this Mishna, interprets בשביעית to mean the last day of the sabbatical year, ביום אחרון של שביעית אי ניטו בשמינית. Rashi likewise, gives the same interpretation (Git. 37b). However, the term שביעית in the Talmud always has the connotation of the sabbatical year, and not the post-sabbatical year or the end of the sabbatical year. Rashi and the other authorities were apparently compelled to interpret the term שביעית as meaning the end of the sabbatical year because, according to the *Sifre*, the sabbatical year released debts only at the end of the sabbatical year. (Comp. Rashi *ibid*.) מקץ שבע סנים יכול מתחילת השנה או בסופה הרי (S.fre Deut.). Comp. also אתה דן ... אף קץ האמור כאן בסופה ולא בתחילתה Ar. 28b; Yer. R. H. 3, 5. See העטור, המחזיר חוב לחבירו דוקא בשביעית, מקץ אבל לאחר שביעית לא. See also Abraham ibn Ezra, Deut. 15.1, שבע סנים תעשה שטיטה בתחלת השנה. Similarly, the rabbis interpret the Mishna (Sheb. 10, 2) השוחט את הפרה וחלקה בראש השנה אם היה החדש מעובר

certain from this Mishna that the sabbatical year releases
the loan, and, therefore, it is impossible to assume that
the time for writing the Prosbol was on the eve of the
New Year of the post-sabbatical year. How could a creditor
write a Prosbol to declare that he would collect any debt
due him when the sabbatical year released all debts? Hence,
it is obvious that the reading of the Tosefta, specifying
the time for writing the Prosbol on the eve of the New
Year of the sabbatical year, is correct. The reading of
the Tosefta is as follows: אימתי כותבין פרוזבל ערב ראש השנה
של שביעית, כתבו ערב ראש השנה של מוצאי שביעית, אע'פ שחוזר וקרעו
[52],לאחר מכן נובה עליו והולך אפילו לזמן מרובה the time of writing
the Prosbol was the eve of the New Year of the sabbatical
year. However, if the Prosbol was written on the eve of
the New Year of the post-sabbatical year and was later
destroyed, the creditor still could collect his debt.

The statement, פרוזבל המוקדם כשר והמאוחר פסול, an antedated Prosbol is valid and one postdated is invalid, does not
refer to the loan at all but to the sabbatical year. The ex-

משמט as referring to the New Year of the postsabbatical year. In my
opinion the rabbis had to resort to this explanation because of the
Halaka that only the end of the sabbatical year released debts.

Maimonides interprets the Mishna (*Mishne Torah*) as follows: את שחט
הפרה וחלקה על דעת שהיום ראש השנה של מוצאי שביעית ונתעבר אלול, ונמצא אותו
אם היה החדש אברו הדמים. Maimonides renders the words היום סוף שביעית
מעובר as referring to the month of Elul. However, this is questionable.
According to the Palestinian Talmud (Sheb. 10; Sanh. 1), Rab said that
Tishri was never intercalated רב אמר תשרי לא נתעבר מימיו. This statement
was questioned by some authorities והא תנינן, because the Mishna said
אם היה החדש מעובר, which indicates clearly that the phrase החדש
מעובר in the Mishna refers to the month of Tishri and not Elul.

In my opinion, the Mishna השוחט את הפרה,והלקה בראש השנה אם היה החדש
מעובר משמט does not refer to the New Year of the post-sabbatical year
but to the New Year of the sabbatical year. The phrase מעובר החדש
certainly does not mean the month of Elul but the month of Tishri.
Comp. also Yer. Mak. 1, 2, מכיון שאינו ראוי לתובעו כמי שאינו ראוי להאמינו.
וכיון שאינו ראוי להאמינו כמי שאינו ראוי ליתן לו מעות, וכאן הואיל והוא ראוי ליתן לו
מעות ולא נתן נעשית הראשונה מלוה See שטיטת כספים. יצחק זאב כהנא'
[52] See note 50. Comp. also Ratner, *op. cit.*

פרובל המוקדם כשר והמאוחר פסול is to be interpreted pression
to mean that if the Prosbol was written before the arrival of
the sabbatical year it was valid, and the creditor could collect his debt. But, if the Prosbol was written at the end of
the sabbatical year i. e. on the eve of the New Year of the
post-sabbatical year, it is not valid, because all the debts
were cancelled by the sabbatical year.[53] However, there
was another opinion that even such a Prosbol was valid,
and that is what the Tosefta says: כתבו ערב ראש השנה של
מוצאי שביעית, אע'פ שחוזר וקרעו לאחר מכן נובה עליו והולך אפילו
לזמן מרובה. This opinion that a postdated Prosbol מאוחר
is valid is also recorded in the Palestinian Talmud: והתני
פרובל בין מוקדם בין מאוחר כשר.[54] The statement in the
Palestinian Talmud is the same as that in the Tosefta.

Those who hold that פרובל המוקדם, a Prosbol written
before the loan was executed, is valid in contrast to שטר
המוקדם פסול a promissory note given before the loan was
executed which is invalid, find support in the Tosefta,[55]
where it is stated כשר בנט פסול בפרובל כשר בפרובל פסול בנט.
They interpret the word נט to mean a promissory note and
explain the Tosefta in the following manner: A postdated
promissory note is valid, while a postdated Prosbol i. e.
a Prosbol written after the loan was transacted, is invalid;
an antedated Prosbol i. e. a Prosbol written before the loan
was executed is valid, while an antedated promissory note
i. e. a note given before the loan was executed, is invalid.[56]

---

[53] Comp. ספר ראבי'ה, [השמיטה] פירושה מוקדם לסוף שנת — פרובל המוקדם
כשר, והמאוחר לאחר סוף שביעית פסול, ספר הישר לרבנו חם.
[54] See Yer. Sheb. 10, ואין מונה אלא) והתני פרובל בין מוקדם בין מאוחר כשר
משעת הכתב).
[55] Comp. ספר העטור; מלאכת שלמה Mishna Sheb. ad loc.
[56] Comp. ספר השטרות להרב ר' יהודה הברצלוני, ed. S. J. Halberstam.
ובשאלה להגאון והא דתנא בתוספתא הכשר בנט פסול בפרובל, הכשר בפרובל פסול
בנט . . . בשלמא הכשר בנט פסול בפרובל שהניתן היא שטרי חוב המוקדמין פסולין
וההיא דאמר בתוספתא כשר; והמאוחרין כשרין, פרובל המוקדם כשר והמאוחר פסול
בנט פסול בפרובל, כשר בפרובל פסול בנט בנט חוב כאמר (ריטב'א, נטין, י"ח).

While it is true that the word *get* in the Talmud has also the connotation of any kind of writ, however, in this Tosefta, the word *get* applies only to a writ of divorce. This is substantiated by the text of the Tosefta in its entirety. The text of the Tosefta reads as follows: כשר בגט פסול בפרוזבל, כשר בפרוזבל פסול בגט. כשר באשה פסול ביבמה, כשר ביבמה פסול באשה. כשר בגרושה פסול בחלוצה, כשר בחלוצה פסול בגרושה. This Tosefta, in my opinion, is to be interpreted in the following manner: "כשר בגט פסול בפרוזבל," "a writ of divorce on condition is valid,[57] while a Prosbol on condition is not valid;" כשר בפרוזבל, a creditor may include in his Prosbol the loans which he made to five different people;[58] פסול בגט, a writ of divorce may be issued by the husband only against one wife.[59] כשר בפרוזבל פסול בגט may be also interpreted in this way: a Prosbol must be written in the past tense;[60] but a writ of divorce in the past tense is invalid.[61]

כשר באשה פסול ביבמה, a woman may be acquired in one of three ways, either by money, by *usus* or by a writ.[62] A יבמה a levirate marriage may be consummated only by *usus*.[63]

ונט מאוחר ודאי כשר כדקתני: (חדושי הרשב"א נטין, יז) .Comp. also Ibn Adret בתוס' חולין, כשר בגט פסול בפרוזבל, כשר בפרוזבל כשר בגט, נט מאוחר כשר ובתוספתא דחולין נמי תניא כשר בגט פסול בפרוזבל, כשר בפרוזבל; ופרוזבל פסול פסול בגט [כשר בגט] דהיינו מאוחר פסול בפרוזבל דפרוזבל מאוחר פסול וטעמא דמילתא משום דנופו של פרוזבל מוסרני לכם ... כל חוב שיש לי אצל פלוני וכשהוא מאחרו נמצא שבכלל פרוזבל זה חובות שהלוה לאחר מכאן ולפיכך פסול ... אבל אחרים אומרים דנט מאוחר פסול וכן דעת הרסב"ם ... והא דתניא בתוספתא כשר בגט R. Nissim on .פסול בפרוזבל כשר בגט חוב קאמר דאף [שאר] שטרות נקראים נט Alfasi, *ibid.* See Saul Lieberman, *op. cit.* ח"ב.

[57] Comp. .הרי זה ניטך על מנת שתתני לי מאתים זוז הרי זו מנורשת Git. 7.74, also Mordecai, Git. 4.

[58] Sheb. 10, חטשה לווין מן אחד אינו כותב פרוזבל אחד לכולן.

[59] Comp. Mishna Git. 3, passim. Comp. also כל נט ... וכחב לה לשמה .שנכחב שלא לשם אשה פסול

[60] כל חוב שיש לי.

[61] .גופו של נט הרי את מוהרת לכל אדם

[62] .האשה נקנית בנ' דרכים בכסף בשטר ובביאה

[63] Yeb. 54a, passim. .ביאה נוטרת בה ואין כסף ושטר נוטרין בה

165

כשר ביבמה פסול באשה, a levirate marriage by an imbecile or a minor is valid,[64] however, a marriage by a minor or imbecile is not valid.[65]

כשר בגרושה פסול בחלוצה, a writ of divorce made out under compulsion is valid;[66] a halitza (levirate divorce) under compulsion is invalid,[67] כשר בחלוצה a halitza under false assumption is valid;[68] פסול בגרושה a writ of divorce under false assumption is invalid.[69] Thus, we can see from the wording of the Tosefta that it deals with divorce and marriage. Hence the expression כשר בגט refers to a writ of divorce.

VII

I believe that we have cleared up the confusion in the tannaitic literature in regard to Prosbol and are able to summarize the *Takkana* of Prosbol, which was introduced by Hillel. Before his time, the creditor in order not to lose the money which he had loaned to his fellowmen on account of the sabbatical year, deposited with the court the promissory note given to him by the debtor. Such a promissory note had a clause to the effect that the real property of the debtor was mortgaged to the creditor. In such a case, the creditor had the right to collect the debt

[64] הרש שוטה [וקטן] שבעלו קנו ופטרו את הצרות. Tosefta *ibid.* 10, 11. Or יבמה יבוא עליה בין בשוגג בין במזיד, בין באונס ובין ברצון.

[65] שוטה וקטן שנשאו נשים ומתו, נשיהם פטורות מן החליצה ומן היבום, *ibid.* Or הכשר בגרושה, ספר העטרות. Comp. כל ביאה שהיא אינה לשם קדושין אינה ביאה פסול בחלוצה איסחבר לה [נט שעושה כשר חליצה שעושית פסולה כשר בחלוצה פסול בגרושה] חליצה שוטעת כשרה נט שוטעה פסול יליף סינן אי הכי אי הוא ופירש הכשר באשה פסול ביבמה לא קאסינא על קאמינא על בירורית, הכי חזינן לענין חלוצה ונרושה כראסתחבר לכון, והכשר באשה שאם באתה ואמרה סת בעלי תנשא לפום הלכתא. ופסול ביבסה דתנן אינה נאמנה לוטר כת יבוסי שתנשא.

[66] נט שעושה כשר, Yeb. 106a.

[67] חליצה שעושית פסולה, *ibid.*

[68] חליצה שוטעית כשרה, *ibid.*

[69] נט שוטעה פסול, *ibid.*

even after the sabbatical year, on the premise that the
property of the debtor was already mortgaged before the
sabbatical year. According to the opinion of the school of
Shammai, anything which ultimately has to be collected is
considered as already collected.[70] However, that was only
a custom and had not as yet been sanctioned. Hillel introduced the *Takkana* that the creditor may write a writ —
a Prosbol, even without the knowledge of the debtor,[71]
in which he declares that he will collect all the debts people
owe him. The Prosbol is valid, whether or not the creditor
has a promissory note, and whether or not the note was
deposited with the court.[72] This *Takkana* Hillel made a
law by supporting it by a verse in the Pentateuch.[73] A
Takkana must always be based on the Pentateuch.[74]

Since the Prosbol, in some ways, took the place of
a promissory note, it had to be similar to it. Since a
promissory note is valid only when it has a clause of
אחריות נכסים,[74a] so the Prosbol was valid if the debtor has real
property.[75] However, if the debtor has no real property,
but the creditor has, the latter may, by legal fiction, assign
part of his property to the debtor and thus write a Prosbol.[76]

The Prosbol was supposed to be written before the eve of
the sabbatical year.[77] However, according to some later

---

[70] Git. 37a, בית שמאי הוא דאמרי שטר העומד לינבות כנבוי דמי.

[71] See Tosefta B. B. 11, 7, שאין כותבין פרוזבלין אלא מדעת המלוה.

[72] See above p. 347. The phrase ואפילו נחונים ברומי, should be interpreted "if the notes are in Rome" and not "if the judges are in Rome."
See R. Nissim, Git.; see also, שמיטת כספים, מאת יצחק זאב כהנא.

[73] See Yer. Sheb. 10.2, מכאן סמכו לפרוזבל שהוא מן התורה; ופרוזבל דבר
תורה? כשהתקין הלל סמכוהו לדבר תורה Comp. also Sifre, Deut. ואת אחיך
תשמט ידך ולא המוסר שטרוחיו לב'ד, סיכן אמרו הלל התקין פרוזבל.

[74] Comp. S. Zeitlin, The Origin of the Ketubah, *JQR*, 1933.

[74a] Comp. B. M. 13a, דאמר שמואל אומר היה ר' מאיר שטר חוב שאין בו אחריות
אחריות טעות סופר הוא בין בשטרי הלואה; נכסים אין נובה לא ממשעבדי ולא סבני חורי
בין בשטר מקח וממכר (*ibid.* 15b).

[75] אין כותבין פרוזבל אלא על הקרקע.

[76] אם אין לו מזכהו בתוך שדהו כל שהוא.

[77] See above p. 356.

rabbis, it was to be written before the eve of the post-sabbatical year. This opinion is due to the new Halaka that the sabbatical year released debts only at the end of the year.[78]

The Prosbol was written before a court of two persons.[79] The Talmud relates that Samuel said that the Prosbol was an act of arrogance of the court; he further said that if he had authority he would abolish it.[80] The rabbis of the Talmud had difficulty in explaining Samuel's statement.[81] It seems to me, however, that there is no difficulty whatsoever. Samuel was of the opinion that the decision of a court of two persons, while it was valid, was an arrogant act of the court.[82] Thus, the Prosbol which was transacted before a court of two was, according to Samuel, an act of arrogance.[83] To the statement of Samuel, the Talmud adds that Rab Nahman remarked that he would confirm a Prosbol.[84] The rabbis of the Talmud again found difficulty in explaining the words of Rab Nahman.[85] In my opinion the words of Rab Nahman are clear. He considered a court of two persons bona fide[86] and he said that he had tried monetary cases alone.[87]

[78] See above p. 357.

[79] See Git. 32b, ורב נחמן בפני ב', לבי תרי נמי בית דין קרו להו, אמר רב נחמן מנא אמינא להדרתנן מוסרני לפניכם פלוני ופלוני הדייניןׁ.

[80] *Ibid.* 36b, ... דאמר שמואל הא פרוזבל עולבנא דדיינא, אם אייישר חילי אבטלינה איבעי להו האי עולבנא לישנא דחוצפא הוא ... הא שמע דאמר עולא עלובה כלה שזינתא בקרב חופתהׁ.

[81] Comp. *ibid.*

[82] Sanh. 5b, אמר שמואל שנים שדנו דיניהם דין אלא שנקרא בית דין חצוף; Yer. Ber.

[83] האי פרוזבלא עולבנא (חוצפא) דדיינאׁ.

[84] Git. 36b, רב נחמן אמר אקיימנהׁ.

[85] Comp. ibid.

[86] See note 79.

[87] Sanh. 5a, אמר רב נחמן כגון אנא דן דיני ממונות ביחידיׁ.

Many theories advanced in relation to the Prosbol were erroneous due to lack of knowledge of the Talmud. As an example note the following: "Even a progressive like Mar Samuel denounced this abrogation of a biblical law as an 'arrogance', because he himself was remote from

168

Although I have dealt with the origin of the Prosbol and its application during the tannaitic period, and have presented the difference between המוסר שטרותיו לב״ד and the *Takkana* of Hillel, I have not discussed the laws of the Prosbol after the tannaitic period, since my purpose was to treat only tannaitic jurisprudence.

the sphere of the Palestinian Sabbatical year and acquainted only with the less capitalistic Babylonia." We also find the following statement by another writer: "A serious panic was thus averted, and credit once again operated normally." (*Journal of Religion*, Oct. 1946). It is indeed unfortunate that some writers who have no knowledge of the Talmud write on Jewish history of which theTalmud is the source.

STUDIES IN TALMUDIC JURISPRUDENCE

I

POSSESSION, PIGNUS AND HYPOTHEC

JURISPRUDENCE, OR, AS CICERO NAMED IT, *prudentia juris* [1] signifies knowledge of law. The Institute of Justinian defines jurisprudence: *jurisprudentia est divinarum atque humanarum rerum notitia, justi atque injusti scientia.* Jurisprudence is the knowledge of things divine and human; the science of the just and the unjust.

Knowledge of the law is of great importance for the understanding of law and its application. Society is ruled by laws, however laws are made by men. The Code of Theodosia and the Institute of Justinian is the result of men, kings and assemblage by jurists. This is true of the Napoleonic Code. The enactment of laws reflects the period when they were promulgated. The knowledge of jurisprudence is of great aid to the understanding of society. It presents a panorama of the social, economic, cultural and political life of the people. To a great degree the people are responsible for the laws, their leaders enacted them. The people live by them.

Jewish law has a long history. The first code is the Pentateuch. The laws therein are considered to have been revealed by God to Moses. Other nations believed that their laws were revealed by their gods. Plato put in the mouth of Athenaios, "Minos used to go every ninth year to hold converse with his father (Zeus) and that he was guided by his divine oracles in laying down the laws of your cities." [2]

---

[1] *De Oratore, 60, et prudentiam iuris.*

[2] ὡς τοῦ Μίνοω φοιτῶντος πρὸς τὴν τοῦ πατρὸς ἑκάστοτε συνουσίαν δι' ἐνατοῦ ἔτους καὶ κατὰ τὰς παρ' ἐκεινοῦ φήμας ταῖς πόλεσιν ὑμῖν θέντος τοὺς νόμους. *Laws, 1.*

170

The Pentateuch, use the terms, מצוה, משפט, חק for law which the Septuagint respectively renders δικαίωμα, κρῖμα, ἐντολή, ordinance, legal decision and command. Not all the laws which were in vogue among the Israelites are included in the Pentateuch. There are references to laws in the prophetic books which are not referred to in the Pentateuch.[3] The Talmud correctly remarks that thousands of laws in existence at the time of Moses were forgotten during the period of mourning for him. All or most of these laws are incorporated in the Mishneh.[4] the prophet Haggai applied the word Torah to law.[5] The Septuagint rendered the word תורה by νόμος, law.

The second code is the Mishneh which was compiled and codified by Rabbi Judah the Prince in the early third century CE. In the Mishneh are laws which go back to great antiquity, long before the Hasmonean period. Even some texts in the Mishneh are of a very early period, and can be traced to the late persian period or the early Hellenistic time. The term mishneh has different connotations, study, repetition and second. The laws which were compiled and codified by Rabbi Judah and his court was named Mishneh, i.e. the second to the Torah.[6] The terms מצוה, משפט, חק in the Pentateuch for law are not used in the Mishneh. The term for law in the Mishneh is הלכה halakah. The word halakah has the meaning of walking, going in the way of the forefathers. Similarly the word νόμος which has the connotation of practice, usage, custom became the standard term for law.

The sages who lived during the Second Commonwealth were called Soferim, whereas those who lived after the destruction of the Temple down to the codification of the Mishneh were called Tannaim. The sages had no right to abrogate

---

[3] Cf. S. Zeitlin, "The Halakah" *JQR* July, 1948.
[4] Talmud Tem. 16; Yer. Pea 2.
[5] Hag. 2.11; cf. S. Zeitlin, *op. cit.* p. 4.
[6] Cf. S. Zeitlin, *JQR*, Oct. 1954; Jan. 1955, pp. 274-76.
[7] Idem., "The Halaka" *JQR*, July, 1948.

any Pentateuchal law. To make the laws in cognizance with life the sages amended many Pentateuchal laws by interpreting them. This can be exemplified by the following: According to the Pentateuch if one takes out an eye from his fellow man the culprit had to be punished by having his eye taken out, "an eye for an eye". The sages interpreted that the Pentateuch did not mean eye for an eye literally but that the culprit had to compensate the victim with money.[8] By this interpretation the sages abolished *lex talionis*. This was done by interpreting that it was the original intent of this Pentateuchal law.[9] In their minds the sages did not abrogate the Pentateuchal law. According to the Pentateuch the Sabbatical Year released all debts which had not been paid before its approach.[10] The sages interpreted that this law refers only to a loan which was exacted orally or before witnesses. If the debtor has given a promissory note to the creditor, and the creditor had deposited this note with the court, the Sabbatical Year does not apply to this loan and the creditor had the right to collect it.[11] This is on the assumption that when the debtor gave a promissory note and the creditor deposited it with the court before the approach of the Sabbatical Year it was considered collected [12] and the law of the Sabbatical Year was no longer applicable to this loan. The sages did not abrogate the Pentateuchal law but modified it by interpreting the biblical verse.

The Mishneh attained canonical authority soon after its completion. Rabbi Judah collected the halakot which he maintained should be observed by the people. Many halakot which had been in vogue at one time but became inapplicable due to the social and religious changes that had occurred in the life of the Jews were collected by his disciples under the

---

[8] B.K. 83b.
[9] S. Zeitlin, "Pharisees and the Gospels" *Studies in Memory of Linda R. Miller*, 1938.
[10] Deut. 15.1-2.
[11] Cf. Yer. Sheb. 10. 1. תשמט ידך ולא המומר שטרותיו לב"ד.
[12] Cf. Git. 37a. כגבוי דמי.

name of Tosefta and Baraitoth, i. e. additions and outside
halakot of the Mishneh.[13]

The sages who lived after the compilation of the Mishneh
were called Amoraim, interpreters. The Amoraim did *not*
have the authority to differ with the laws laid down in the
Mishneh nor could they differ with the laws pronounced by
the Tannaim. To expound new laws they interpreted the
halakot propounded by the Tannaim. They had the right if
there was a controversy between two Tannaim to choose the
opinion of one sage and disregard the other. However there
was a limitation. In the controversies between the Schools of
Hillel and Shammai the laws propounded by the School of
Hillel had to be followed. To give another example: If there
was a controversy between Rabbi Eliezar and Rabbi Joshua
the opinion of the latter was the accepted law.

The studies of the Amoraim resulted from their endeavors to
interpret the laws of the Tannaim and the promulgation of
new laws embodied in the work known as the Talmud.

The Mishneh is a compilation of laws which were laid
down in Palestine. There are two Talmuds—the Palestinian
(Talmud Yerushalmi), and the Babylonian (Talmud Babli).
The latter was compiled at the end of the fifth and the beginning of the sixth century. The Palestinian Talmud never
came to a natural completion. The talmudic academies in
Palestine fell into decay because of the political conditions.
By the end of the fourth century all the academies in Palestine ceased to exist due to the persecution of the Church
and the compilation of the Palestinian Talmud came to an
abrupt end.[14]

The Babylonian Talmud became the standard text of
Jewish law and is called *Gamara*. The term *Gamara* has the
connotation of study,[15] tradition [16] and final.[17] The Baby-

[13] Cf. S. Zeitlin, "Talmud" *Encyclopaedia Britannica*, 1963, 1967.
[14] Idem., ibid.
[15] Cf. Ab Zara 19, ‎אבל גמרא מחד רבא‎.
[16] Cf. Yoma 33 ‎משמיה דגמרא‎.
[17] Sanh. M. 6. 1, ‎גמר דין‎.

lonian Talmud is named *Gamara* as it is the final codification of Jewish law. The halakot in the *Gamara* were considered divine. No rabbi could differ from them, he could only interpret.

The halakot recorded in the Babylonian Talmud in many instances are in opposition to the halakot stated in the Palestinian Talmud. This is due to the difference in the economic and political life of the two Jewries.

There are three codes,—the Pentateuch, the Mishneh and the Gamara. From the legal point of view the Pentateuch is a code in the full sense. No differences of opinion are recorded in the Pentateuch. The laws were presented by Moses in the name of God.

The Mishneh is a code but is not comparable to the Pentateuch. The Mishneh records different opinions of the sages and their dissentions. However principles were laid down as to which laws are to be observed. Where there is a majority opinion and a minority opinion the majority opinion must be followed. Where differing opinions on a particular law are quoted and followed by an anonymous opinion the latter is accepted law.[18] At times when Rabbi Judah taught that the law as interpreted by a particular Tanna should be followed, he recorded his view in the Mishneh either as anonymous or in the name of the sages, i. e. he made it the majority opinion.[19] In many cases Rabbi Judah agreed with the opinions of Rabbi Meir although his views were not accepted. To make Rabbi Meir's views binding he recorded his views in the Mishneh anonymously.[20] Rabbi Judah set down numerous opinions in the Mishneh, even those which he did not accept

[18] Cf. Yebam. 42.
[19] See Hul. 85.
[20] Cf. Tos. Shab. 3.5: Talmud B.K. 71.

המבשל בשבת בשוגג יאכל במזיד לא יאכל דברי רבי מאיר רבי יהודה אומר
בשוגג יאכל למוצאי שבת במזיד לא יאכל [עולמית] רבי יוחנן הסנדלר אומר
בשוגג יאכל למוצאי שבת לאחרים ולא לו במזיד לא יאכל עולמית לא לו ולא
לאחרים•

In Mishneh Ter. 2.3. Rabbi Judah the Prince reorded R. Meir's opinion
anonymously. .והמבשל בשבת שוגג יאכל מזיד לא יאכל.

as halaka. The reason for this was that if some time in the future some halakot suggestions should arise the rabbis would be able to support their decisions on those opinions recorded in the Mishneh.[21]

The Gamara is a code but it is not comparable to the Mishneh. There are principles laid down to guide which halakot in the Gamare are to be followed. To ilustrate: Where there are differences of opinion between Rab and Samuel in ritual matters the law is in accordance with the opinion of Rab. In civil matters the law has to be followed in accordance with Samuel's opinion.[22] In the halakic controversies between Raba and Abbaye with the exception of six cases the opinion of Raba is the accepted halaka.[23]

After the close of the period of the Talmud the sages were called Saboraim, Gaonim. There were great sages during the Middle Ages who compiled halakot in the form of code and many of them wrote responsa to expound the halakot. There were great rabbis in Spain, the Levant, in the Franco-German communities and in Poland. Their halakot decisions varied due to the difference in the social and economic conditions of the countries. Their works are considered authoritative but not binding. Their works are authoritative due to the great learning and piety of the authors. Their decisions however were not unanimously accepted. Maimonides in his *Mishneh Torah* unhesitatingly rejected many of halikic decisions of the Gaonim. In his *Mishne Torah* he often expresses, "This is the view of the Gaonim but I do not adhere." [24] Rabbi Abraham ben David (RaBad) severely critized the *Mishne Torah* using such terms, "This is not true"—"This is a mistake,"—"This reason has no sense." In another place, he said, "It seems to me that he (Maimonides) came only to

[21] Tosefta Eduy. cf also M. ibid., לעולם הלכה כדברי המרובין לא הוזכרו דברי היחיד בין המרובין אלא לבטלן ר' יהודה אומר לא הוזכרו דברי יחיד בי המרובין אלא שמא תיצרך להן השעה ויסמכו עליהן.
[22] Cf. Bekh. 49b. הילכתא כרב באיסורי ושמואל בדיני
[23] Cf. Sanh. 27a, passim.
[24] See S. Zeitlin, *Maimonides A Biography*, ch. VIII.

confuse the whole world." [25] A rabbi of the twelfth century Zerachiah ha-Levi severely criticized the halakic decisions of Alfasi. A rabbi of the sixteenth century in Poland Solomon Luria castigated Joseph Caro for some of his halakic decisions. He also criticized him for his dependence on the Spanish rabbis and ignoring the French rabbis.[26] Joseph Caro was the author of the *Shulchan Aruch*, hence Rabbi Solomon Luria held that many decisions in the *Schulchan Aruch* were based on wrong readings of the Talmud.

During the Middle Ages rabbis were engaged in writing responsa to develop and elucidate Halakot. These works are extremely important for the development of Jewish law and for the social, economic and religious history of the Jews in the Diaspora. However a word of caution must be uttered. A modern scholar who endeavors to present the history of Jewish law cannot group in one page (as is done by many) the Talmudic laws, Palestinian, Babylonian, laws of the responsa of the Middle Ages, disregarding where the responsa were written, Spain, France and Poland. Compilation of such works, to my mind, does not present a true development of Jewish law, which has a long history from the Pentateuch to the responsa, but blurs it.

POSSESSION

In the Pentateuch the acquisition of property was either through purchase or by inheritance. Abraham in order to bury his wife Sarah bought a cave from Ephron.[27] The sons of Jacob sold their brother Joseph into slavery. The transaction was made with money.[28] Jacob paid Laban in manual labor to marry his daughters.[29] Property was also acquired by inheritance. At the death of a person his property auto-

[25] Cf. Idem., ibid.
[26] See his Introduction to B.K.
[27] Gen. 23. 9-16.
[28] Gen. 37. 26-28; cf. also II Sam. 24. 21-24.
[29] Cf. Gen. 29. 18.

matically went to his sons, if there were no sons it went to the nearest kin.[30] The mode of acquisition of *usucapio* (taken by use), possession in which, a person who used a property for a determined length of time becomes the owner of the property, is not recorded in the Pentateuch. From the book of Jeremiah we may deduce that the mode of possession was practised in Judaea. In it is stated that on the command of God Jeremiah bought a field from his uncle Hanamel for which he paid seventeen shekels of silver. The deed of purchase had the signatures of witnesses and was sealed. It is further stated that God said to Jeremiah that the deed should be put in an earthen vessel, "that they may continue many days." [31] Jeremiah further relates that he prayed to God and said, "Behold the mounds, they are come into the city to take it, and the city is given into the hands of the Chaldeans . . . O Adonai Yahweh: You have said unto me buy the field for money, and called witnesses; whereas the city is given into the hands of the Chaldeans." [32] The answer of God was that good days will come to Judaea. "Men shall buy fields for money and subscribe the deeds and seal them and call witnesses, in the land of Benjamin, and in the places around Jerusalem." [33] The fact that Jeremiah deposited the deed in an earthen vessel to be preserved for a long time was for the purpose that when he would return to the city he would be able to present the writ of sale and dispossess any one who had taken possession of the field. This indicates that the mode of possession was in vogue during the early time of the Judaean people.

Possession is not purely physical retention or occupation of a property, it is a legal mode for the acquisition of a property. It must be *bona fide* on the part of the possessor; he must act in good faith that he was really entitled to the property

[30] Cf. Num. 27. 8-11.
[31] Jer. 32. 7-14.
[32] Ibid., 16-25.
[33] Ibid., 44.

possessed; his belief must be founded on *justa causa*, (a legal grant of possession). The Mishneh clearly states that usucaption where the possessor does not advance any claims to the property, i.e. he does not claim that he purchased it but the deed of sale was lost, or he does not claim that he inherited it is not considered usucaption.[34]

An old text preserved in the Mishneh states that a man can acquire a woman for his wife in one of three ways,—by silver, [money], if the groom pays money to the father of the girl; or by *shtar*, a writ in which the father signified that he gave the daughter to the man for marriage; or by *usu capio* intercourse,[35] The *usu capio* must be intent to take her to a wife. By *usu capio* of the woman the *patria potestas*, authority of the father over his daughter, ceased and was transferred to the man, husband, who acquired all the rights over her.[36] In the later tannaitic literature the term "acquire a wife" does not occur but is substituted by the term *kiddushin*, consecration.[37] However, according to the law, if a man had intercourse with a women with the intention of making her his wife it was considered a legal marriage.

In another Mishneh it is stated that a heathen slave may be acquired by money, that is by purchase, or by writ which the owner gave, or by usucaption.[38] If a man took possession of a slave and the owner did not protest then the possessor acquired all the rights over the slave.

Possession not only had to be *bona fide* and the possessor must have *justa causa* but the possessor to get title to the property must occupy it for a period of time in order to enable the supposed owner to protest the occupation of the property. According to the XII Tables immovable property

---

[34] M. B.B. 3. 4., ‏כל חזקה שאין עמה טענה אינה חזקה‎.

[35] M. Kid. 1.1. ‏האשה נקנית בשלש דרכים בכסף בשטר ובביאה‎. Cf. also S. Zeitlin, "The Origin of the Ketuba", *JQR*. July, 1933.

[36] See S. Zeitlin, *The Rise and Fall of the Judaean State*, Vol. II. (Second Edition) pp. 289-291.

[37] *Kiddushin*, Cf. M. Kid. 2.1. ‏האיש מקדש‎.

[38] M. Kid, 1.3. ‏עבד כנעני נקנה בכסף בשטר ובחזקה‎.

can be acquired after two years of possession, *Usu capio audem mobilium quidem rerum anno completur fundi vero et aedium biennio; et eita lege XII tabularum cautum est.*[39]

According to the Mishneh possession of real property must be three complete years in order to be considered valid.[40] There is another opinion that a field which produces fruits a complete year and two fractional years is sufficient for the possessor to claim ownership of the property.[41] The reason is that the possessor has made three harvests.

The possessor of real property must make use of it,—if it is a house he must live in it,—if it is a field he must harvest it and make use of the produce. Usucaption of an orchard or a vineyard during the period of *orla* was not considered valid possession.[42] (*Orla* is the fruit of the trees of the first three years. According to the Pentateuch if a person planted trees he may not use the fruit of the first three years, this is called *orla*.)[43] Thus a person who held possession of a vineyard or orchard during the period of *orla* could not use the fruit. Thus his possession of the three years is not valid and the plaintiff may seize the property. In the Diaspora, where the law of *orla* was not applicable, possession of an orchard during the three years of *orla* is *bona fide* usucaption.[44] Similarly, if a person used an orchard or field during the Sabbatical year, or if one used a field which had *kilayim* (forbidden junction of heterogenous plants in the same field) was not considered usucaption as he could not make use of the fruits.[45] In the Diaspora the law of the Sabbatical year is not applicable.

---

[39] Gaius, II. 42.

[40] M. B.B. 3, חזקת הבתים ··· שלש שנים מיום ליום.

[41] Ibid., רבי ישמעאל אומר שלשה חדשים בראשנה ושלשה חדשים באחרונה ושנים עשר חדש באמצע.

[42] B.B. B.B. 36. אכלה ערלה אינה חזקה.

[43] Lev. 19.23.

[44] Ket. 80 אמר רב יהודה אכלה ערלה הויא חזקה. Cf. S. Zeitlin, "Some Reflection on the Text of the Talmud" *JQR* July, 1968.

[45] B.B. 36. אכלה ערלה שביעית וכלאים אינה חזקה.

The usufructuary has mere detention, occupation, but not usucaption; he is using the fruit of a property which belongs to another. A husband has no usucaption on the property which his wife brought to him.[46] He had the right of usage and of the fruit but the property had to be returned to her heirs in case of her death, or to her *in specie* in the event of her divorce. Usucaption is inapplicable to an *aris*, a tenant, who tills the owner's field for some share in the produce.[47] A craftsman cannot secure title by usucaption.[48] Guardians cannot claim usucaption.[49] Partners cannot secure title of ownership by usucaption.[50] In order that ownership of a thing should be acquired by usucaption it was necessary that the thing itself should be susceptible of being held in *dominio*. A craftsman, a guardian, a partner cannot claim *dominio* over the property. There is another opinion that a craftsman cannot secure title of ownership by usucaption but a partner could.[51]

The property of a fugitive who has fled the city on account of a capital offence cannot be secured by usucaption, since the fugitive cannot protest as in doing so his whereabouts would be revealed. However if a fugitive has fled on account of a civil matter a person who has used the property for three years acquires the title of ownership,[52] since the fugitive if he had legitimate claims on the property would have protested against the possessor. One who robbed a property cannot secure to title of ownership by usucaption. אין גזלן לו חזקה.[53] *Furtive quoque res, et quae vi possessae sunt nec si praedicto longo tempore fide possessae fuerint usucapi possunt.*[54]

[46] M. M. B.B. 3. 5. אין לאיש חזקה בנכסי אשתו.
[47] Ibid. אריסין.
[48] אומנין is not mentioned in the האומנין Palestinian Mishneh.
[49] M. B.B. ibid.
[50] Ibid.
[51] B.B. 42b. שמואל תני אומן אין לו חזקה אבל שותף יש לו.
[52] Cf. B.B. 38b; cf. also Yer. ibid. 3.3.
[53] B.B. 47.
[54] Things stolen, or seized by violence, cannot be acquired by

Objects that have no ownership, like fish on the high seas and animals in the jungles, or things which had owners but they had relinquished their rights, as if things were lost on a highway and there was no mak of identification, these things are considered *hefker*, *res nullius*; any one who has taken physical possession of them acquires ownership.[55]

In the Mishneh B. M. 1. 4 is stated that if a man saw a lost object and fell upon it and another person came and took physical possession of it, that person acquired the property. ראה את המציאה ונפל עליה ובא אחר והחזיק בה זה שהחזיק בה זכה בה• The reason is that the second person has taken physical possession of the object with the intention of acquiring it. The sole intention of a person to acquire a lost object is not sufficient of the person to claim ownership. According to the Mishneh if a person saw a lost object and said to a man "pick it up and give it to me" and the man took possession of it and said "I acquired this object for myself" the man who picked up the object acquired it. היה רוכב על גבי בהמה וראה את המציאה ואמר לחברו תנה לי נטלה ואמר אנו זכתי בה זכה בה אס משנתנה לו אמר אני זכיתי בה תחלה לא אמר כלוס• The intention of acquiring an object which has no owner is not sufficient without physical possession.

In dealing with usucaption the Mishneh does not refer to Pentateuchal verses since there is no alllusion in the Pentateuch to usucaption. The mode of acquiring property by possession is based on customs, halakot, which were in vogue among the Judaeans. These halakot, unwritten laws, go back to a very early period.[56]

---

possession, although they have been possessed *bona fida* during the length of time above prescribed.

[55] *Quod si vis fluminis partem aliquam ex tuo praedio detraxerit et vicini praedio attulerit palam est eam tuam permanere. Plane, si longiore tempore fundo vicini tui haeserit arboresque quas secum taxerit, in eum fundum radices egerint ex eo tempore videntur vicini fundo adquisitae esse. Institutionum Justiniani*, Lib. II.

[56] *Jus non scriptum.* Cf. S. Zeitlin, "Halaka" *JQR*, July, 1948.

Pignus and Hypothec

Pignus, pawn, is the transfer of a property, movable or immovable, for a loan and is returned when the debt is paid. In the early Roman period the form of a pawn, pledge, was effected by a *nexum* (voluntary assignment of the person for the debt) with a *fiducia* (in trust, a pawn). The Pentateuch does not refer to a pignus, pledge, at the transaction of the loan. In Deuteronomy is stated כי תשה ברעך משאת מאומה לא תבא ביתו לעבט עבטו בחוץ תעמד והאיש אשר אתה נשה בו יוציא אליך את העבוט החוצה ואם איש עני הוא לא תשכב בעבטו. [57] The translation of the Bible by the Jewish Publication Society, 1917, renders these verses, "When thou dost lend they neighbor any manner of loan, thou shalt not go into his house to fetch his pledge. Thou shalt stand without and the man to whom you dost lend shall bring forth the pledge without unto thee." The modern translation of the Torah (Jewish Publication Society, 1962), renders thes verses, "When you make a loan of any sort to your neighbor, you must not enter his house to receive his pledge. You must remain outside, while the man to whom you made the loan brings the pledge out to you." From these renderings it is to be assumed that the Pentateuch refers to the pledge at the time the loan was made. (The same rendering is in the revised standard version).[58] The Septuagint renders these verses, כי תשה ברעך משאת מאומה לא תבא אל ביתו לעבט עבטו בחוץ תעמד והאיש אשר אתה נשה בו יוציא אליך את העבוט החוצה ἐὰν ὀφείλημα ἡ ἐν τῷ πλησίον σου ὀφείλημα ὁτιοῦν οὐκ εἰσελεύσῃ εἰς τὴν οἰκίαν αὐτοῦ ἐνεχυράσαι τὸ ἐνέχυρον ἔξω στήσῃ καὶ ἄνθρωπος οὗ τὸ δάνειόν σού ἐστιν ἐστιν ἐν αὐτῷ ἐξοίσει σοι τὸ ἐνέχυρον ἔξω. "If thy neighbor owe thee a debt, any debt whatsoever, you shall not go into his house to take his pledge. You shall stand without, and the man who borrowed shall bring the

[57] Deut. 24. 10.13.

[58] *The Jerusalem Bible* renders these verses, "If you are making your fellow a loan on pledge, you are not to go into his house and seize the pledge whatever it may be. You must stay outside, and the man to whom you are making the loan shall bring the pledge out to you."

pledge out unto thee.[59] From the rendering of the Septuagint it is evident that the Pentateuch does not speak of a pledge when the loan was made but of a security when the debtor failed to pay his debt.

The correct rendering of these verses in the Septuagint is corroborated by Josephus and the Talmud. Josephus in describing the Pentateuchal laws in connection with loans writes, "Those who have borrowed whether silver or produce of any kind, liquid or solid, if their affairs through God's grace proceed to their liking, shall bring back and with pleasure restore these loans to the lenders, as though they were laying them up with their own possessions and would have them again at need. But if they are shameless concerning restitution, one must not prowl about the house to seize a pawn before judgment has been given on the matter; the security should be asked for at the door, and the debtor should bring it of himself, in no wise gainsaying his creditor who comes with the law to support him. If he from whom the pawn has been taken be well-to-do, the creditor should take possession of it until restitution be made; but if he be poor the creditor should return it before sun-down." [60]

From Josephus' interpretation of these verses in the Pentateuch it is evident that the Pentateuchal law about a pledge for a loan refers to a pledge of a loan which was not paid and the creditor wants to seize a security for it.

The Talmud speaks of two types of pledges,—one made when the loan was transacted and the other when the debtor

[59] The Douay Bible has "When thou shalt demand of thy neighbour any thing that he oweth thee, thou shalt not go into his house to take away a pledge. But thou shalt stand without: and he shall bring out to thee what he hath."

[60] Οἱ δὲ λαβόντες εἴτε ἀργύρια εἴτε τινὰ τῶν καρπῶν ὑγρὸν ἢ ξηρῶν κατὰ νοῦν αὐτῖος τῶν παρὰ τοῦ θεοῦ χωρησάντων κομίζοντες μεθ' ἡδονῆς ἀποδιδοῦσαν τοῖς δοῦσιν ὥσπερ ἀποθέμενοι εἰς τὰ αὐτῶν καὶ πάλιν εἰ δεηθεῖεν ἕξοντες ἄν δὲ ἀναισχυντῶσι περὶ τὴν ἀπόδοσιν μὴ περὶ τὴν οἰκίαν βαδίσαντας ἐνεχυριάζειν πρὶν ἢ δίκη περὶ τουτοῦ γένηται τὸ δ' ἐνέχυρον αἰτεῖν ἔξω καὶ τὸν ὀφείλοντα κομίζειν δι' αὐτοῦ μηδὲν ἀντιλέγοντα τῷ μετὰ νόμου βοηθείας ἐπ' αὐτὸν ἥκοντι. *Ant.* 4. 7. 26(267-268).

did not pay his loan and the creditor sought assistance from
the court to get a pledge for his loan.[61] The second type is based
on these Pentateuchal verses. Thus we may safely conclude
that the Septuagint rendering is well attested by Josephus
and the Talmud. The *JPS* translation is not in accordance
with the spirit of the halaka, law. In the Pentateuch there is
no reference to a pledge given at the time of the transaction
of a loan. Neither does the Pentateuch refer to a deposit,
earnest money where the purchaser of a property gives
a deposit to the seller and in case the buyer does not fulfill the
contract the deposit is forfeited. In the story of Judah and
Tamar it is related that she asked him to give her a pledge,
earnest, until he will send her a kid of his flock.[62] The pentateuch uses the word ערבון pledge. The Greek word ἀρραβών
arrabon has the connotation of pledge, earnest money.

Pignus משכן *mashkan* was given by the debtor to the
creditor when the loan was transacted. The creditor not only
took possession of the *mashkan* but eventually he could acquire ownership of it if the debt was not paid. He had the
right to sell it and obtain his satisfaction from the proceeds.
With this right went an obligation on his part,—to restore

[61] Cf. B.M. 81-82. כאן שמשכנו בשעת הלואתו כאן שמשכנו שלא בשעת
המלוה את חבירו לא ימשכנו אלא .Cf.M. B.M. 9.12. pp. 113-114; הל ואתו
בבית דין This Mishneh refers to a loan which was not paid. Cf. Rashi
ad. loc.; לא תבא אל ביתו לעבוט עבוטו B. M. 113b; ותגיע זמן ולא פרע לו;
הרי בעלחוב אמור; בעל חוב שבא למשכנו לא יכנס לביתו למשכנו אלא עומד
בחוץ ibid., Tos. B.M. והלה נכנם ומוציו לו משכנו שנאמר בחוץ תעמוד;
10.8 המלוה את חבירו (the loan was not paid) אינו רשאי למשכנו ואם
מישכנו צריך להחזיר לו · · · שליח בית דין הבא למשכן הוא עומד בחוץ והן
מוציאין את המשכן שנאמר בחוץ תעמוד · · ·
The Mishneh in Shekalim states that on the first of Adar announce-
ment was made regarding the payment of the half Shekel to the Temple.
On the fifteenth of that month pledges were extracted from those who
did not pay, באחד באדר משמיעין על השקלים · · · בחמשה עשר בו ישבו
במקדש משישבו במקדש התחילו למשכן.
If a person who borrowed money and did not pay, the creditor with the
aid of the court had the right to exact a *mashkan*. Similarly the community had the right to exact a *maskan* from those who did not pay
the half shekel.
[62] Gen. 38. 17-18.

the *mashkan* unharmed in case the debt was paid. According to Roman law if the pignus was worth more than
the debt and the debt was not paid the creditor had to
give the debtor the excess of the value of the debt. According to Roman law if the creditor lost the pignus thorough
accident, by fire or shipwreck, he was not accountable for it.
*Creditor quoque qui pignus accepit re obligatur, qui et ipse de
ea re quam accepit restituenda tenetur actione pigneratitia.
Sed quia pignus utriusque gratia datur et debitoris quo magis
pecunia ei crederetur et creditoris quo magis ei in tuto set creditum placuit sufficere quod ad eam rem custodiendam, exactum
diligentiam adhiberet quam si praestiterit et aliquo fortuito casu
eam rem amiserit securum esse nec impediri creditum petere.*[63] "A
creditor also who has received a pignus is bound *re*, for he
is obliged to restore the thing he has received by the *actio
pigneratitia* but as much as the pignus is given for the benefit
of both parties, of the debtor that he may borrow more
easily, and of the creditor that repayment may be better
secured, it has been decided that it will suffice if the creditor
employs his utmost diligence in keeping the thing pledged; if,
notwithstanding this care, it is lost by some accident the
creditor is not accountable for it, and he is not prohibited
from suing for his debt".

The Talmud records different views regarding the responsibility of the creditor over the pignus. According to Rabbi
Eliezer if the pignus was lost the creditor had to take an
oath and had the right to collect the debt. Rabbi Akiba was
of the opinion that if the pignus was lost the creditor lost his
right to collect the debt.[64]

The sages differed in their conception of the nature of
pignus, *mashkan*. Whether the *mashkan* given by the debtor
is an exchange for the debt or a security for the debt. The

---

[63] *Institutionum Justiniani*, Lib. III, 15.
[64] Sheb. 43b. המלוה את חבירו על המשכון ואבד המשכן ישבע ויטול את
מעותיו דברי רבי אליעזר, רבי עקיבא אומר יכול הוא שיאמר לו כלום הלותני
אלא על המשכון אבד המשכן אבדו מעותיך.

difference would be: If the *mashkan* is an exchange for the debt and exceeds the value of the debt when the debtor did not pay the debt the creditor had the right to sell the *mashkan* and may appropriate the money which is in excess of the value of the debt. If the *mashkan* is a security for the debt and the creditor has sold it for the non payment of the debt he excess of the value has to be given to the debtor.

Rabbi Eliezer's opinion regarding *mashkan* is in accordance with the Roman law that pignus, *mashkan*, is a security for the payment of the debt. If the creditor lost the *mashkan* not through negligence but to circumstances beyond his control he has to take an oath that it was stolen or lost and he is entitled to collect the debt.

The sages who held that a *Mashkan* is a security for a loan were of the opinion that the creditor had the right on the *Mashkan* to the amount of the loan which he made. כנגדו הוא קונה. If the *Mashkan* had greater value than the and loan the the creditor lost the *Mashkan* he has to refund to the debtor the money which the *Mashkan* was in excess of the loan. If the *Mashkan* had less value than the loan and the creditor lost it he forfeits the money of the value of the *Mashkan*. The debtor has to pay the creditor the money which is in excess of the value of the *Mashkan*.

The sages who were of the opinion that the *Mashkan* is in exchange for a loan held that if the *Mashkan* was of less value than the loan and the creditor lost it he forfeited the loan. On the other hand if the *Mashkan* is in excess of the value of the loan and the creditor lost it the debtor forfeited the amount in excess of the loan.[65]

---

65 המלוה את הברו על חמשכן ואבד המשכן אמר לו סלע הלויתיך עליו

ושקל היה שוה והלה אומר לא כי סלע הלותני עליו וסלע היה שוה פטור סלע

הלויתיך ושקל היה שוה והלה אומר לא כי אלא סלע הלותני עליו ושלשה

דינרים היה שוה חייב סלע הלויתני עליו ושתים היה שוה והלה אומר לא כי.

The question whether pignus, *mashkan*, is an exchange for a loan or a security for a debt is the underlying principle of the controversy between Rabban Simon, son of Gamaliel, and Rabbi Judah the Prince.

According to the Pentateuch the Sabbatical year cancels all debts. If the debtor has not paid his loan before the Sabbatical year the creditor cannot collect the debt. It is stated in the Pentateuch, "Every creditor shall release that which he had lent unto his neighbor; he shall not exact it of his neighbor and of his brother." [65a]

Rabban Simon, son of Gamaliel, held that even if the *mashkan* is worth only half of the money borrowed the law of the Sabbatical year is not applicable to this loan and the creditor has the right to collect the loan.[66] Rabbi Judah the Prince was of the opinion that if the *mashkan* has the same

אלא סלע הלויתיך עליו וסלע היה שוה פטור סלע הלויתני עליו ושתים היה
שוה והלה אומר לא כי אלא סלע הלויתיך עליו וחמשה דינרים היה שוה חייב
ומי נשבע מי שהפקדון אצלו שמא ישבע זה ויוציא הלה את הפקדון

Shebu. 43-44.

If a man lent his fellow money on a pledge, *mashkan*, and the pledge was lost, and the creditor said' I lent you a *sela* and the *mashkan* was worth a shekel (ahalf a sela)' and the debtor said that the loan was a *sela* and the pledge was worth a *sela*, the debtor is exempt from taking an oath. If the creditor said the loan was a *sela* and the pledge was worth a *shekel*, and the debtor maintain that the loan was a *sela* but the pledge was worth three *denars* (four denars-sela) the debtor has to take an oath that pledge was worth three *denars* and pay to the creditor one *denar*. Similarly if the debtor said I borrowed a *sela* and the *mashkan* was worth two and the creditor claimed that the *mashkan* was worth one *sela* the creditor is exempt from taking an oath. If the debtor said to the creditor you gave me a *sela* and the pledge was worth two and the creditor claimed that the pledge was worth five *denars* the creditor has to take an oath, the debtor has to take an oath that the pledge exceeded the value of the loan, and the creditor has to take an oath that the *mashkan* was lost, the creditor take the oath first; if the debtor shall swear first as to the value of the pledge the creditor may produce the pledge to prove that the debtor has sworn falsely.

[65a] Deut. 15.v2.

[66] B.M. 48b המלוה את חבירו על המשכון ונכנסה השמיטה אף על פי
שאינו שוה אלא פלג אינו משמט דברי רבי שמעון בן גמליאל.

187

value as the loan the law of the Sabbatical year is not applicable and the creditor may collect the loan. But if the loan exceeds the value of the *mashkan* the Sabbatical law is not applicable to that part of the money covered by the *mashkan*,—however the creditor forfeits the excess money above the value of the *mashkan*, the law of the Sabbatical year is applicable to the amount of money which is in excess of the value of the *mashkan*.[67]

The view of Simon, son of Gamaliel, is due to the fact that he held that a *mashkan* is an exchange for a loan regardless of its value. This view was well expressed by Samuel who said that if a person borrowed a thousand *zuz* and gave as *mashkan* a handle of a saw, which is worth little, if the creditor lost the handle of the saw he cannot collect the thousand *zuz*.[68] The handle of the saw was in exchange for the thousand *zuz*. Rabbi Judah the prince held that the *mashkan* is a security for the amount of the loan.[69] Thus if the amount of the borrowed money is in excess of the *mashkan* the law of the Sabbatical year is applicable only to the money covered by the mashkan but not to the excess.

It is to note that Rabbi Judah the Prince, architect and compiler of the Mishneh, recording in the Mishneh the laws of the Sabbatical year in connection with *mashkan*, gave the opinion of Rabban Simon, son of Gamaliel. To make this opinion a law he recorded it as an anonymous opinion.

המלוה על המשכן והמוסר שטרותיו לבית דין אין משמטין [70]

The Tosefta is more specific where it is stated את המלוה

חבירו על המשכן אף על פי שהחוב מרובה על המשכן אינו משמט [71]

---

[67] Ibid., רבי יהודה הנשיא אומר אם היה המשכן כנגד הלואתו אינו משמטואם לאו משמט.

[68] Sheb. 43b. אמר שמואל האי מאן דאוזפיה אלפא זוזי לחבריה ומשכן לו קתא דמגלא אבד קתא דמגלא אבד אלפי זוזי. Cf. Yer. Sheb. 10.1. משכן Simon, son of Gamaliel held that שמואל אומר אפילו על המחט, כנגד כולו הוא קונה.

[69] R. Judah's opinion is that משכן כנגדו קונה.

[70] M. Sheb. 10.1.

[71] Sheb. 8.5.

"One who makes a loan to his fellow man on a *mashkan*, although the debt exceeds the value of the *mashkan*, the Sabbatical year does not release the debt."

The sages who were of the opinion that a *mashkan* is an exchange for a loan held that the mortgagee is in the category of שומר שכר [72] a paid guardian who is responsible for the property entrusted to him. Thus if the mortgagee lost the *mashkan* he lost the money which he loaned. The sages who held the opinion that a *mashkan* is a security for a loan, regarded the mortgagee as שומר חנם, an unpaid guardian who is not responsible for theft or loss. In this case if the mortgagee lost the *mashkan* he has to take an oath and collect the money.[73] (The rabbis in the Talmud had difficulty in explaining the views of Rabbi Eliezer and Rabbi Akiba. It seems to me that in presenting the principles upon which their controversies were based that their conceptions of mashkan become clear).

A Mishne in Baba Metzia states that if a person received a pledge for a loan he is accounted an unpaid guardian.[74] Rabbi Judah held, "If he lend him money he is accounted an unpaid guardian; if he lend him fruit, produce, he is accounted a paid guardian." [75] Rabbi Judah's opinion is difficult to comprehend. If a person borrowed fruit what was the purpose? If a person borrowed an object then after it was used he had to return it. If fruit or produce is borrowed after usage how can it be returned. I may suggest that teh word פירות has the connotation usufruct,[76] the right of temporary possession and usage of something belonging to another and which has to be returned to the owner in due time without damage or injury. Now we can understand Rabbi Judah's opinion. If a person borrowed money and gave a *mashkan* the

[72] In accordance with the view משכון נגד כולו הוא קונה.
[73] Corresponds to the opinion משכון נגדו הוא קונה.
[74] 6.5., הלוהו על המשכון שומר שכר.
[75] Cf. Rashi *ad loc.* הלוהו מעות שומר חנם הלוהו פירות שומר שכר דדרך פירות להרקיב.
[76] Cf. Gitin 47b קנין פירות כקניין הגוף דמי. Possession of the usufruct is like ownership of the field.

creditor is an unpaid guardian, the *mashkan* is a security for the loan. However when some one borrowed an object as usufruct and gave a *mashkan* the creditor is a paid guardian since the debtor received an object and gave the creditor a *mashkan*, an object—actually there is an exchange: one object for another object. Therefore the creditor is a paid guardian: if he lost the *mashkan* he cannot demand anything from the person to whom he gave the object for usufruct.

In the Mishneh it is stated that the Abba Saul said, "A man may rent a poor man's *mashkan* and so by degrees reduce the debt, for so he like to one restored lost property.[77] In the Palestinian Talmud, Abba Saul's statement was questioned, that hiring out would be antichresis.[78] Antichresus in Roman law was a substitution of usufruct for interest. Jewish law prohibits interest, usury.

In many localities in Babylonia pignus assumed different characters. In Sura pignus was given to the creditor for a certain period of years and after the lapse of this period the property was returned to the owner without payment. It was called משבנתא דסורא *mashkanta* of Sura.[79] In other localities the debtor had the right to repay the loan at any time and reclaim the *mashkan* as soon as the value of the creditor's usufruct equaled the amount of the loan, but if the usufruct amounted to more than the loan the balance could not be claimed by the debtor.[80]

HYPOTHEC

Hypothec is a derivation from the Greek ὑποθήκη which has the meaning pledge. The difference between hypothec and pignus is,—pignus was placed in the possession of the creditor while hypothec remained in the possession of the

[77] B. M. 6.5 אבא שאול אומר רשאי אדם להשכיר משכנו של עני להיות
פוסק והולך עליו מפני שהוא כמשיב אבידה·
[78] הדא אנטיכרסיס, ἀντιχρῆσις.
[79] Cf. B.M.67 משכנתא דסורא דכתבי בה הכי במשלם שנין אילין תיפוק
ארעא דא בלא כסף·
[80] הא משכנתא באתרא דמסלקי·

debtor[81] Originally if an object was made hypothec to the
creditor he has the right to seize only this object if the loan
is not paid.[82] If a person made his house or field a hypothec
and it was swept by flood or burned the creditor cannot
collect from other properties of the debtor.[83] In a later period
there were two types of hypothec,—One was written that a
particular object was assigned as hypothec. The creditor
has the right only to this object if the loan was not paid.
If the object was lost the creditor had no legal right to any
other properties of the debtor.[84] In the other type when the
debtor did not specify in writing a particular assignment the
creditor had the right to size the hypothec. If the hypothec
is lost the creditor had the right to seize any other real
property of the debtor. Only immovable, real property can be
made as hypothec.[85] If a person had made his heathen slave
hypothec and sold him the creditor had the right to seize him
from the buyer. (A heathen slave was considered real property). If a person made his ox hypothec and sold it the sale
is valid and the creditor cannot seize it from the buyer. If a
person had assigned a particular property to his wife as
hypothec for her ketubah and sold the property the wife had
the right to seize it from the buyer in case of divorce or the
death of her husband.[86]

The Sabbatical year canceled all debts even if a promissory
note was given to the creditor [87] unless it was deposited in the

---

[81] When the thing over which the right was given passed into the
possession of the creditor, the right of the creditor was expressed by
the term pignus; when the thing remained in the hands of the debtor,
the right of the creditor was expressed by the term hypothec
Justinian's Institutes.

[82] Cf. B. K. 96. דשוייה ניהליה אפותיקי דאמר ליה לא יהא לך פירעון
אלא מזה.

[83] Git. 41. ••• העושה שדהו אפותיקי ושטפה נהר

[84] Ibid. B. B. 44.

[85] B. K. 11, עשה עבדו אפותיקי ומכרו בעל חוב גובה, שורו אפותיקי
ומכרו אין בעל חוב גובה הימנו.

[86] Tos. Ket. 12 העושה שדה אפותיקי לכתובת אשה מכרה לאחר ידה
על העליונה רצה גובה ממנה רצה גובה משאר נכסים.

[87] M. Sheb. 10.1. השביעית משמטת את המלוה בשטר ושלא בשטר.

court.[88] However if in the promissory note one property was assigned as hypothec the law of the Sabbatical year was not applicable to this loan.[89]

If a person assigned his heathen slave as hypothec and then manumitted him [90] the hypothec ceased to exist. It was in the same category if a debtor placed a house or field as hypothec for a loan and later on a hurricane swept it away— the hypothec is gone and the creditor loses. The property has no rights, it is an object. Similarly the slave has no rights, he is an object. After manumission the slave who was assigned as hypothec ceases to be a slave, he becomes a free man. If, however, the creditor seized the ex-slave he is compelled to free him and the ex-slave has to write a *shtar*, promissory note for the money, which his previous owner borrowed. Rabban Simon, son of Gamaliel, held that the ex-slave owes nothing to the creditor. When the ex-slave had been assigned by his master he was an object and now the object ceased to be. The creditor has to free him and the old master, the debtor, has to write a *shtar*, promissory note to the creditor for the money borrowed.[91]

In this short essay I have endeavored to demonstrate the underlying principles of the Tannaim regarding possession, pignus and hypothec. In some interpretations of their controversies I deviated from the accepted views of even the later sages. After careful scrutiny of the historical and socio-economic background of these institutions I became convinced, with all due respect to the rabbis, that their views cannot be accepted.

---

[88] Ibid. המלוה על המשכון והמוסר שטרותיו לבית דין אין משמטין.

[89] Tos. ibid. המלוה את הבירו ··· בשטר שיש בו הפותקי הרי זו אינו משמט.

[90] Cf. Yer. Git. 4.4 העושה עבדו אפותיקי מכרו אנו מכור שחררו משוחרר.

[91] M. ibid. 4.4, עבד שעשאו רבו אפותיקי לאחרים ושחררו שורת הדין איו העבד חייב כלום אלא מפני תיקון העולם כופין את רבו ועושה אותו בן חורין וכותב שטר על דמיו רבן שמעון בן גמליאל אומר אינו כותב אלא משחרר·

TESTAMENTARY SUCCESSION:
A STUDY IN TANNAITIC JURISPRUDENCE

THE LAWS REGARDING testamentary succession are not found
in the Pentateuch, because pentateuchal law decreed that
the estate of a deceased person was to be inherited by his
sons. In a family where there were no sons, the estate was to
pass to the daughters; and in a family where there were no
daughters or sons, it was to go to the nearest of kin. [1] The
law stated that the estate must always remain in the family
or tribe; it could not be given to a stranger. In the story given
in the Pentateuch about the daughters of Zelophehad whose
father died without male issue (Num. 27. 1-11), the daughters
complained before Moses: "Why should the name of our father
be done away from among his family, because he had no son?
Give unto us a possession among the brethren of our father."
And God told Moses that the daughters of Zelophehad were
right: that they should inherit the possession of their father,
and that the property of a man must remain within his family
and cannot go to a stranger. [2] If a man sold his real property,
it had to be returned to him in the Year of Jubilee. [3] If a
person gave part of his property as a gift, he could give it
only to members of his family. If a man presented a gift to
his slave, at the time of the slave's manumission the property
had to be returned to the master of his children. [4] In sum,
the property always had to remain within the family. Thus
we find no laws of testamentary succession in the Bible.

[1] Numb. 27. 8-9. איש כי ימות ובן אין לו והעברתם את נחלתו לבתו ואם
אין לו בת ונתתם את נחלתו לאחיו ... ונתתם את נחלתו לשארו הקרב אליו
ממשפחתו וירש אתה.

[2] Numb. 27. 4.

[3] Lev. 25. 25-28.

[4] כי יתן הנשיא מתנה לאיש מבניו נחלתו היא לבניו ... וכי יתן מתנה מנחלתו
לאחד מעבדיו והיתה לו עד שנת הדרור ושבת לנשיא אך נחלתו בניו להם תהיה.
Ezek. 46. 16-17.

193

During the Second Commonwealth, however, the Judaean people were no longer divided into tribes. The entire conception of tribes and the family went through a revolutionary change. Due to the development of commerce, buying and selling became an important factor in the economic life of the Jew. The pentateuchal law that real property cannot be sold forever and always had to revert back to the original owner was both archaic and a hindrance to commerce. Judaean society was no longer based on tribal and clan relationships. Thus the pentateuchal laws of inheritance were amended. The sages introduced a new law of inheritance which they based on testamentary succession, and which stated that a person could make a will διεθήκη (daithke) whereby part of his property could go to whomever he designated, even to a total stranger. [5]

The fact that a will was designated in the Talmud by the Greek term *daithke* does not necessarily prove that the Judaeans adopted the principle of testamentary succession from the Greeks or the Romans. When the principle of a will (testamentary succession) was developed in Judaea, there was no Hebrew term for it because the idea of testamentary succession was unknown in the Bible. Therefore the word *daithke*, or will, was borrowed from the Greek, and is a loanword. The principle of testamentary succession is Judaean.

The use of the Greek word *prosbol* by the Tannaim is another case in which a foreign term was borrowed by the Jews to describe a new law for which there was no extant Hebrew phrase. According to the old halaka, in a case where a creditor did not have a promissory note from a debtor, the debt was voided in the sabbatical year and the creditor had no right to demand payment. [6] Hillel introduced a *takkanah*, that is, a new regulation whereby a writ could be composed by the creditor in which he states to the court: "I declare before

[5] See M.B.B. 8.6; 9.6; Tos. *ibid.* 8.8. Cf. S. Zeitlin, *The Rise and Fall of the Judaean State*, pp. 433-4.
[6] Deut. 15.1-3.

you ... and ... , the judges of ... (the place) that I shall collect the debt I have outstanding with ... whenever I desire". [7] The creditor deposited this writ with the court. The biblical precepts concerning the sabbatical year did not apply to such a loan. [8] The later Tannaim named this writ *prosbol*, [9] "before the court". But there is no evidence in the tannaitic literature that Hillel himself employed the term *prosbol*.

Originally, a will in which property was bequested to one who was not a member of the family, or in which it was specified that a particular son should be denied inheritance, was void. [10] According to pentateuchal law, the first-born son was to receive a double share of the inheritance from his father. [11] If it was specified in the will that the first-born son should share the inheritance equally wilh his brothers, such a will was also void, since it violated the pentateuchal laws. [12]

With the changeover in Judaean society from agriculture to commerce as a primary occupation, and as the urban population greatly increased, other modifications were made in the pentateuchal laws with regard to real property. A person was permitted to sell his property to anyone, and it did not have to be returned to him in the Jubilee Year. Only when a person rented property for a specified period of time was it returned to the previous owner at the expiration of that time. When a property was sold, the transfer of title went to the purchaser, and the seller lost title to the property. Similarly, a person was permitted to present his property as

---

[7] מוסר אני לכם איש פלוני ופלוני שבמקום פלוני שכל חוב שיש לי שאגבנו כל זמן שארצה·

[8] See M. Sheb. 10.3.

[9] πρoς βoυλη

[10] B.B. 8.5. ··· האומר איש פלוני ירשני במקום שיש בת לא אמר כלום שהתנה על מה שכתוב בתורה·

[11] Deut. 21.17. כי את הבכור בן השנואה יכירלתת לו פי שנים·

[12] M.B.B. 8.4. האומר איש פלוני בני בכור לא יטול פי שנים לא אמר כלום שהתנה על מה שכתוב בתורה·

a gift to anyone, and once it was given away it became the permanent property of the recipient. When a person wrote a deed in which he gave a way some property as a gift, he could not retract his deed, nor could he disavow a deed of sale of his property. [13] In the case of a *daithke* a man could retract or change his will. [14] since a *daithke* did not go into effect until after his death. While the testator was alive, he could write another *daithke* which annuled a previous one. [15]

If a person who was desperately ill wrote a document bequesting his property to someone, and later recovered and claimed that the writ was a *daithke* will, he thus had the right to retract. The person to whom the property was bequested claimed that the man who had made him the bequest was well at the time he made it, and thus that it was a gift and as such could not be retracted. It was the general opinion of the sages that as long as the property was in the possession of the testator, one who laid claim to the property as a gift had to prove that the testator was well when he composed the writ. [16]

When a man bequested his property to his slave, by virtue of this bequest the slave was manumitted and received the property. However, if the bequest had the limitation that not all of the property was to go to the slave, then he was not manumitted. [17] If the master later made a *daithke* in which he bequested the rest of his property to someone else, then that person received not only the property bequested to him, but also the slave and the property which had formerly

[13] Yer. *ibid.* 8. ·אין מתנה מבטלת מתנה

[14] *Ibid.* ·דייתיקי מבטלת דייתיקי

[15] Cf. Tos. B.B. 8.10. הכותב דייתיקי יכול לחזור בו מתנה אין יכול לחזור בו איזו היא דייתיקי דא תהא לעמוד ולהיות אם מתי ינתנו נכסיי לפלוני איזו היא מתנה מן היום ינתנו נכסיי לפלוני·

[16] M.B.B. 9.6. הוא אומר שכיב מרע היה והן אומרים בריא היה צריך להביא ראיה שהיה שכיב מרע דברי רבי מאיר וחכמים אומרים המוציא מחבירו עליו הראיה
Cf. Tos. *ibid.* 10.11.

[17] M. Pea 3.8. הכותב נכסיו לעבדו יצא בן חורין שייר קרקע כל שהוא לא יצא בן חורין·

37

been bequested to the slave. In a case where the master possessed two slaves, and bequested to one all that he possessed
with the exception of one property, the slave was not manumitted. If he had bequested the one remaining property to
the second slave, and the second slave was manumitted,
he acquired both the first slave and the larger share of the
property originally bequested to him by the master. [18]

If a man was stricken with severe illness, and he made a
gift of his property to people who were not members of his
family, if he did not give away all of his property, the gift
was valid. However, if he gave away all of his property the
gift was void. [19] Since he had given away all of his property
while he was very ill, it was to be assumed that he had made
a will and the property had not been given as a gift. Upon
his recovery, he had the right to make another will, thus
nullifying his previous gift.

As stated above, a will which contradicted the laws of
inheritance, as given in the Pentateuch, was invalid. If a
testator who had daughters wrote a will in which he assigned
his property to someone outside his family, such a will was
void because it was contrary to the pentateuchal law. Similarly, the will of a person who had sons but bequeathed his
property to a daughter was void, [20] since, according to pentateuchal law, where there are sons still living in a family,
daughters may not inherit property.

In the second century, Rabbi Jochonan ben Baroka held
that if a testator wrote a will in which he bequeathed his
property to a potential heir, his will was valid. [21] (A potential
heir was considered a person who had no actual right to inherit

[18] Tos. B.B. 9.14. האומר כל נכסיי נתונין לפלוני עבדי והשאר לשני זכה
שני בראשון.
[19] M. ibid. 9.6. שכיב מרע שכתב כל נכסיו לאחרים ושייר קרקע כל שהוא
מתנתו קיימת לא שייר קרקע כל שהוא אין מתנתו קיימת.
[20] Ibid. 8.5. האומר איש פלוני יירשני במקום שיש בת תירשני במקום
שיש בן לא אמר כלום שהתנה על מה שכתוב בתורה.
[21] Ibid. רבי יוחנן בן ברוקה אומר אם אמר על מי שהוא ראוי ליורשו
דבריו קיימין.

the property of the deceased, but had the potentiality to inherit it.) If a man had two sons, one of whom had a daughter, and the son who had the daughter died during the lifetime of his father, there remained one son and the granddaughter. In this case, the property would be inherited by the remaining son. The granddaughter, however, was a potential heir. If the son died after his father, the daughter (granddaughter) would be the actual heir of her father, and thus receive the property which he had inherited from his father. Rabbi Jochonan ben Baroka thus held that if a testator wrote a will bequeathing his property to his granddaughter, the will was valid since she was a potential heir. Similarly, if a person had two daughters, and one of them had a son, and this daughter died during her father's lifetime, the property of the deceased father would go to the surviving daughter. The son of the deceased daughter was, however, a potential heir. If his mother died after the death of her father, her son (grandson) would inherit the share of the property which she had received from her father. If a grandfather wrote a will bequesting his property to his grandson, this will was also valid, therefore, since the grandson was a potential heir. [22]

Further, if a man in good health wrote a deed in which he made a gift of all his property to people other than members of his own family, the gift was valid, although in so doing he had disinherited his own children. But the sages disapproved of such action. Rabbon Simon, son of Gamaliel, was of the opinion that if the children had not behaved well, the father should be commended for such an action. [23]

If a person made a gift of his property, including his heathen slaves, the recipient of the gift might maintain that he could not accept the slaves [24] because in doing so he would be

---

[22] Cf. Talmud *ibid*. 130-131.

[23] *Ibid*. הכותב את נכסיו לאחרים והניח את בניו מה שעשה עשוי אלא
אין רוח חכמים נוחה הימנו דבי שמעון בן נמליאל אומר אם לא היון בניו נוהגים
כשורה זכור לטוב·

[24] Cf. Tos. *ibid*. 8.1. הכותב נכסיו לאחד והיה בהם עבדים אף על פי
שאמר הלה אי אפשי בהם

deprived of certain religious privileges. Some sages held that if a Jew owned heathen slaves who were not circumcised, he was not allowed to participate in the slaughter and eating of the pascal lamb. [25] However, it was the general opinion of the sages that the gift was valid, and that if the receiver was a *kohen* the slaves had the right to eat *terumah*, the sacred food of the priests. [26] Rabban Simon, son of Gamaliel, held the view that if the person to whom the gift was assigned refused to accept a part of it, the heirs acquired the entire property. [27]

A *daithke* was written in Hebrew, Aramaic and Greek. The witnesses could be either Judaeans or Hellenes. [28] At the Conclave of 65-66, it was decreed that the Greek language should not be used by the Judaeans. [29] Rabban Simon, son of Gamaliel, declared that a *daithke* written in Greek lost the validity of a will and became a writ of gift. [30] Greek was then the language employed in the writing of all commercial deeds, so that it can be inferred from this ruling that sanctity was attached to a testamentary document or *daithke*.

Despite the introduction of testamentary succession, the law of primogeniture hindered the economic development of the country during the Second Commonwealth. If a person owned a small farm and limited assets, and had several sons,

---

[25] אחד פסח מצרים ואחד פסח דורות מי שהיו לו עבדים Pes. 8.18.
שלא מלו ··· מעכבין אותו מלאכול בפסח׃
S. Zeitlin, "Slavery during the Second Commonwealth and during the Tannaitic Period" *JQR*, Jan. 1963, pp. 201-205.
[26] Tos. B.B. הרי אוכלין בתרומה׃
[27] רבן שמעון בן גמליאל אומר כיון שאמר הלה אי אפשי בהן זכו בהם ירשין׃
[28] משנין שטרות מעברית ליוונית ומיוונית לעברית T.B.B. II. גט שכתבו
עברית ועדיו יונית יונית ועדיו עברית M. G. 9. 8.
[29] שמונה עשר דבר גזרו ··· על לשון Yer. Shab. 1.4.
Cf. S. Zeitlin, "Les Dix-huit Mesures" *REJ*, 1915.
[30] רבן שמעון בן גמליאל אומר הכותב דייתיקי בלעז Tos. NB.B. 9.14.
הרי זו מתנה׃
רבן שמעון בן גמליאל אומר אף הכותב דיאתמון בלעז הרי זו מתנה רבי הנין
בשם רבי יהושע בן לוי חזרתי על כל בעלי לשונות לידע מה דיאתמון ולא
אמר לי אדם דבר Yer. *ibid*. 8.8. διατίθημι disposition of property by will)

the first-born had to inherit a double share according to the pentateuchal law. [31] This left the remaining brothers with a meager share which often was not sufficient to provide sustenance for their families. It was even more unjust if the first-born was well-to-do in his own right, for he still received a double share of the inheritance. The father could not divide his property equally among his sons, since that was counter to the pentateuchal law. If a father wrote a *daithke* dividing his property equally among his sons, it was void. [32] To circumvent this law, the sages introduced a new regulation whereby the testator who wanted to divide his property equally among his sons could write a gift-will. In it he wrote that all his property was to be given to his sons "from today and after my death". [33] The father had the use of the property, but by writing the gift-will he waived his right to sell it. On the other hand, the sons were not allowed to sell the property during the lifetime of their father. [34]

In this essay we have attempted to demonstrate how the principle of testamentary succession—that a person may give real property to a stranger by writing a will or by bestowing it as a gift—was introduced during the Second Commonwealth to meet the needs created by the changes in the social and economic life of the people.

[31] Cf. above n. 11.
[32] Cf. M. B.B. 8.4.
[33] *Ibid.* הכותב נכסיו לבניו צריך שיכתוב מהיום ולאחר מיתה
[34] האב אינו יכול למכור מפני שהן כתובין לבן והבן אינו יכול מפני שהן ברשות האב

JOHANAN THE HIGH PRIEST'S ABROGATIONS AND DECREES

IT IS STATED in a Mishne (Maaser Sheni 5: 15) that "Johanan the High Priest removed the confession in connection with the tithe. He also abolished the Awakeners and the Knockers. Until his days, the hammer used to smite in Jerusalem. And in his days no one needed to inquire concerning *demoi*." [1]

יוחנן כהן גדול העביר הודיית המעשר אף ביטל את המעוררין ואת הנוקפין עד ימיו היה פטיש מכה בירושלים ובימיו אין אדם צריך לשאול על הדמאי

One must establish the text in order to understand the underlying reason for the abrogations by Johanan the High Priest, John Hyrcanus I. The text of the Mishne reads: העביר הודיית המעשר "He removed the confession in connection with the tithe." The text at the end reads: אין אדם צריך לשאול על הדמאי "No one needed to inquire concerning *demoi*." The text in a Baraita, however, reads as follows ביטל את הודוי וגזר על הדמאי. "He abolished the confession (in connection with the tithe) and decreed on the demoi." [2] It will be shown in the course of the essay that this is the correct text.

The social and economic conditions prevailing at that period must be outlined to make intelligent the full import of John Hyrcanus' abrogations and decrees.

From the time of the Restoration to the period of John Hyrcanus, the Jewish community had undergone revolutionary changes in its social and economic structures. Judaea after the Restoration was a small, obscure country consisting of villages and one important city, Jerusalem. In the main, the inhabitants were divided into two classes: on the one hand priests and Levites engaged in the temple service, and on

[1] Maaser Sheni, 5.15; Sotah, 9.10. *Cf.* Yer. Demoi, 1.2
[2] Sotah 48a

the other landed folk, the *ame ha-arez*. [1] Priests and Levites received no monetary remuneration for their work in the temple other than a tithe from the crops of the landed folk, *ame ha-arez*, and gifts from the sacrifices brought to the temple. The Hebrew name for the priests' tithes was *Terumah*, for that of the Levites, *Maaseroth*. The priests received an additional *Terumah* over and above the regular tithe. To this tax which the farmers paid to the priests and Levites they also, during the Seleucid period and probably during the Ptolemaic rule over Judaea, had to give one-third of their crops and one-half of their fruit to the state. [2] These taxes were paid either with the products of the crop or with money equivalent. Hence the burden of taxation was indeed heavy on the farmers, the *ame ha-arez*. These taxes, paid by the farmers to the Seleucids, were retained by the state of Judaea when it gained its independence. Thus the farmer's tax burden was not relaxed in the time of John Hyrcanus I.

The life of the *ame ha-arez*, the farmer folk, was hard. They had to labor incessantly in the field from early morning until sunset to extract a mere living from the soil. They struggled constantly with inclement weather, suffered from destructive insects and, in some years, had to wage war against locusts. Water was often lacking and the heat intense. As long as the Jewish community consisted of two classes, the farmers supported the priests and the Levites in accordance with the biblical law. However, after the conquest of Judaea by the Ptolemies, a new social class emerged which did not engage in agriculture but in trade and manufacturing. Many Jews held high positions in the Ptolemaic court as tax collectors. They helped and encouraged the middle class of artisans and traders. Hence during the time of the Ptolemies there was a change in the social structure in Judaea. In addition to the existing two classes, there now emerged a third class, the traders.

[1] *Cf.* S. Zeitlin, "The 'Am Ha-arez,'" *JQR*, 1932, vol. xxiii, pp. 45-61.
[2] *Cf.* I Mac. 10. 29-33.

With the establishment of the Commonwealth this third class grew in prominence and power. Seafaring became an important factor after the conquest of Joppa by Simon, the Hasmonean. Now for the first time after the Restoration the Judaeans acquired a port, an outlet to the Mediterranean Sea. [1] The traders thereby gained a stronghold over the community. John Hyrcanus I was the first to engage mercenaries. [2] These were led by Jewish officers. A permanent army came into being in Judaea, and a corps of Jewish officers constituted a new social group.

Simon, the Hasmonean, and particularly his son, John Hyrcanus, conquered many cities which they colonized with Judaeans. John Hyrcanus undoubtedly followed the policy of the Seleucids who colonized newly conquered cities by settling Greeks in them. The land, however, belonged to the state. One may, therefore, assume that when John Hyrcanus conquered new territories and settled them with Judaeans, the land remained state property, and those who occupied the land were tenants. Some of them had the status of hereditary tenants; i.e., while the land belonged to the state, the colonists were entitled to live on these lands and their children had the right of occupancy by the law of inheritance. Another type of tenancy came into being. Men who had distinguished themselves in the wars, particularly the leaders of the military caste, received large tracts of conquered lands. This group did not cultivate the land but placed it in the hands of tenants who tilled it for a certain share in the produce, or who paid a fixed rental in kind.

According to the Pentateuch, the farmer had to bring the first fruit to the altar of the Lord and to make a confession while presenting this offering. The following words were included in the confession: "And now, behold, I brought the first of the fruit of the land which Thou, O Yahweh, hast given me." [3] Some of the farmers who brought the first fruit were only

[1] *Cf. ibid.* 14.34.   [2] *Cf. Ant.* 13.8, 4 (249).
[3] Deut 26: 10.

tenants, the land belonging to the state or the landowners, so the uttering of this phrase by them would have been false. Johanan the High Priest, therefore, abolished the confession.

John Hyrcanus also abolished the confession in connection with the *Maaser*. According to the Pentateuch, the man who brought the *Maaser* to Jerusalem in the third year had to confess, saying, "I have put away the hallowed things out of my house, and also have given them unto the Levites and to the stranger and to the orphan and to the widow according to all Thy commandments which Thou hast commanded: I have not transgressed any of Thy commandments, neither have I forgotten them." [1]

It will be recalled that before the establishment of the Second Commonwealth the Judaean society consisted primarily of two classes—the *ame ha-arez* and the priests and Levites. But later new classes emerged—artisans, traders, a military caste, and a working class who tilled the fields for the landowners. Many of the *ame ha-arez* resented the fact that they alone had to carry the burden of supporting the priests and the Levites, a burden which the urban population was not required to share. Many of the *ame ha-arez*, therefore, withheld the *Maaser*, the tithes, [2] and the priests and the Levites did not receive their due allotment. The truth is that the farmers refused to take into account the fact that when they gave their tithes they raised the prices for their grain to meet their tax obligation and, actually, the burden of taxation was distributed among the consumers as well as the farmers. Since the *ame ha-arez* were suspected of not giving the God-ordained tithe to the Levites and conceivably might perjure themselves in saying they "also have given them unto the Levites," John Hyrcanus ביטל את הודוי abolished the entire ceremony of confession for the *Maaser*. [3]

[1] *Ibid.* v. 13.
[2] Sotah 48. מקצתן מעשרין מקצתן אין מעשרין
[3] *Cf.* Yer. Demoi, 1.2 העביר, המעשר הודיית העביר גדול כהן יהנן שלא יתוודו.

The economic status of the Levites began to deteriorate. To improve their condition, John Hyrcanus גזר על הדמאי, decreed that those who purchased from the farmers should give the prescribed tithe to the Levites. [1] In order to avoid any adverse effect on commerce, the religious leaders limited this decree only to those who purchased produce from the *ame ha-arez* for personal consumption; but those who purchased for purposes of trade remained exempt. They also exempted those who purchased grain for the feeding of cattle from giving the tithe to the Levites. [2]

The word דמאי, generally interpreted to mean *doubt*, refers to produce upon which there was doubt as to whether the tithe had been taken from it. Elsewhere I have maintained that the word דמאי *demoi* has the connotation "common people," *ame ha-arez*, as the word δῆμος means "common people." [3] The word דמאי never occurs in the entire tannaitic literature in the sense of doubt, but only in reference to the produce of *ame ha-arez*. We may, therefore, say with certainty that the word *demoi* could not have the connotation of doubt.

The question may be raised that the decree of John Hyrcanus referred to the produce of the *ame ha-arez* while the text has it that he decreed on the *demoi*, the common people, produce not being mentioned in the decree. This is easily explainable on the basis of the short form of expression characteristic of the early tannaitic period. The following examples will suffice. According to the Talmud, Simon ben Shetah introduced a *Ketubah*, a writ, [4] but he really did not introduce a writ. What he did introduce was the formula that the groom should write a *Ketubah*, a writ, in which he pledged all his properties as security for the two hundred

---

[1] *Cf.* Sotah, 48 הלוקח פירות מעם הארץ מפריש.

[2] Tos. Demoi, 1.15 הלוקח לבהמה ולחיה ולעוף פטור מן הדמאי; *Cf.* also Mishne, *ibid.*, 1.3

[3] *Cf.* S. Zeitlin, *The History of the Second Jewish Commonwealth Prolegomena* 1933, pp. 69-70.

[4] שמעון בן שטח תיקן כתובה לאשה Shab. 14.

zuzim to be paid to his wife in case he should divorce her or in the event of his death.[1] The *Takanah* of Simon ben Shetah was to provide for the woman's economic security in the event of divorce or the death of her husband. The main object of the *Takanah* is not referred to.

Again, Hillel introduced the *Takanah* of *Prosbul*.[2] The word *Prosbul* is borrowed from the Greek προς βουλῇ, before the council (court). The substance of Hillel's *Takanah* of *Prosbul* was that the creditor should write a declaration (note) before the court.[3] The note, the principal object of Hillel's *Takanah*, is not referred to. In a like manner the produce of the *ame ha-arez* is not referred to in the decree of John Hyrcanus; simply the word *demoi* is given. The use of *Prosbul* and *Ketubah* as well as *demoi* shows the characteristic manner of expression of the early tannaim.

The well-founded suspicion that many of the *ame ha-arez* did not give the tithe gave rise to the *Haburah*, a new association in Judaea. The *ame ha-arez*, the farmers, were suspected of being personally unscrupulous both in relation to levitical laws of purity and impurity and with regard to their products. Consequently, many of the city dwellers, who were scrupulous in their observance of the laws of levitical purity and the laws of the tithe, would not partake of bread with them or associate with them. This group was called *Haberim*, associates; *i.e.*, Jews who joined together. This association was named *Haburah* in the early tannaitic literature.

The city dwellers, particularly the *Haberim*, were a cultured group and laid great stress on the observance of the biblical laws, particularly those with regard to levitical purity and tithes. On the other hand, the *ame ha-arez*, the farmers, found it impossible to develop the degree of culture and the knowledge of the laws attained by the city folk. There was

---

[1] *Cf.* Yer. Ket. 8.11; B. *ibid.* ותיקן כל נכסיו אחראין לכתובה.

[2] הלל הזקן תיקן פרוזבל M. Sheb. 10.3. *Cf.* S. Zeitlin, "Prosbol." *JQR* 1947, pp. 341-62,

[3] שכל חוב שיש לי שאגבנו כל זמן שארצה.

a wide gap between these two groups. The observance of levitical purity and the giving of the required tithes affected the daily life of the people. Hence a *Haber*, who was scrupulous in the observance of these laws, could not partake of bread with an *am ha-arez* or associate with him. [1] Consequently tannaitic literature uses the term *Haberim* always in opposition to *ame ha-arez* but only in reference to the laws of agriculture and levitical purity.

Needless to say, the *am ha-arez*, the farmer, strongly resented the attitude of the *Haberim*. The *Haber* could not invite the *am ha-arez* to dine in his house—neither could he accept such an invitation from the *am ha-arez* to dine in his house. This resentment of the *ame ha-arez* developed into hatred towards the *Haberim*. On the other hand, the *Haberim* looked down upon the *ame ha-arez*, the farmer folk, as being the lower class in Judaean society. The antagonism between these two groups developed more and more and led to acrimonious social strife.

In time the term *ame ha-arez*, which originally meant farmer folk, came to be synonymous with "ignorance and immorality." It became an epithet of contempt and reproach for those who were ignorant, crude, immoral and who did not observe the Jewish laws. The word pagan, from the Latin *paganus*, originally also meant "countryman" but later became the appellation of the irreligious. Similarly the word "boor" or "hick" is occasionally applied not only to a farmer but to a rude and ill-bred person.

The word *Haber* later was applied to a learned man, a scholar. After the destruction of the Second Temple the term *Haber* was applied to a candidate of the *Bet Din*, Sanhedrin. [2]

The bitter feeling between the different social classes in Judaea derived from their economic difference and their

---

[1] ואינו מתארח אצל עם הארץ Tos. Demoi, 2.

[2] חבירים מהו ליכנס לקידוש החדש; אמר רבי הושעיה חבר הוינא
ואעלי אמר רב כהנא חבר הוינא Cf. Yer. Sanh. I.

social distinctions. Class conflict was unavoidable where such tension and antagonism flourished.

John Hyrcanus also abolished the "Awakeners" and the "Knockers." In the Talmud it is well explained that the Awakeners were the Levites who daily recited the following hymn in the temple:

"Awake, why sleepest Thou, O Adonai?
Arouse Thyself, cast not off forever
Wherefore hideth Thou Thy face
And forgettest our affliction and our oppression?
For our soul is bowed down to the dust
Our belly cleaveth unto the earth
Arise for our help and redeem us for Thy mercy's sake." [1]

The Levites sang daily in the temple during the wars against the Seleucids. They appealed to God to awake and redeem the people for His mercy's sake. They also recited the following hymn:

"Nay, but for Thy sake are we killed all the day;
We are accounted as sheep for the slaughter." [2]

These appeals to God were superfluous after the great victories of the Hasmonean family and the establishment of the Jewish Commonwealth and the great military success of Hyrcanus which added large territories to Judaea. The Jews were no longer slaughtered as sheep and their souls were no longer bowed down to the dust. They were a courageous, victorious people who possessed dignity and pride. The abolishing of the awakeners was due to the confidence of John Hyrcanus in the stability of the Judaean State. The

---

[1] Ps 44: 24-27 עורה למה תישן אדני הקיצה אל תזנח לנצח למה
סניך תסתיר תשכח ענינו ולחצנו כי שחה לעפר נפשנו דבקה לארץ בטנו
קומה עזרתה לנו ופדנו למען חסדך
כי עליך הרגו כל היום נחשבנו כצאן טבחה

[2] Ps 44: 23

hymns sung by the "Awakeners" were later incorporated in the Book of Psalms.

John Hyrcanus also abolished the "Knockers." The "Knockers" according to the Talmud are those who used to strike upon the calf between his horns. Johanan the High Priest said to them, "How long will you feed the altar with *nebelot*?" [1] The Babylonian Talmud renders the passage somewhat differently. "They used to knock him (the victim) as they do in idol worship. He [Johanan the High Priest] said 'How long will you feed the altar with *nebelot* (carrion)?'" How, asks the Talmud, could Johanan the High Priest say to them that they fed the altar with *nebelot* when the victim had been slaughtered? The answer was that Johanan said that they fed the altar with *terefot*, prohibited both for the altar and for human consumption. [2]

The talmudic explanation for the abolition of the "Knockers" by John Hyrcanus does not give the real historical reason. The explanation there is late. It seems that the "Knockers" were correlated with the "Awakeners." Prior to the time of Judah the Maccabeean the Temple had been defiled having been in the possession of Antiochus Epiphanes and his Jewish adherents. The religious followers of the Hasmoneans had no access to the temple. Appealing to God they *knocked with hammers* and recited a hymn, "Awake, why sleepeth Thou, O Adonai?" They cried that they were being killed daily for observing His laws. Even when the Temple was later rededicated by Judah, many Jews still

---

[1] Yer. Sotah, 9. את הנוקפין אותן שהיו מכין על גבי העגל בין קרניו
אמר להן יוחנן כהן גדול עד מתי אתם מאכילין את המזבח נבילות

[2] מאי נוקפין אמר רבי יהודה אמר שמואל שהיו מסרטין לעגל בין קרניו
כדי שיפול דם בעיניו אתא איהו בטיל . . . . שהיו חובטין אותו במקלות כדרך
שעושין אתו לפני ע״ז אמר להם עד מתי אתם מאכילין נבילות למזבח, נבילות
הא שחיט להו אלא טריפות .Cf. Tos., *ibid* עד מתי אתי אתם מאכילין את
המזבח טריפות

The text given in the Tosefta is based on the emendation in the Babylonian Talmud. *Cf.* also S. Lieberman, *Hellenism in Jewish Palestine*, 1950, pp. 139-143.

continued to recite prayers for victory, accompanying it by knocking with hammers and reciting the hymn "Awake...." John Hyrcanus abolished the "Awakeners," the Levites, who sang in the temple the hymn, "Awake" and the "Knockers" who knocked with hammers beseeching God to awaken and to help them to observe the laws of God and to overcome their enemies.

This is the meaning of the words in the Mishne, "Until his days/John Hyrcanus'/ the hammer used to strike in Jerusalem"; *i.e.*, by the Knockers. The Talmud explains that the smiting of the hammer refers to the middle days of the Feasts--Passover and Tabernacles [1]—and that John Hyrcanus forbade any work which necessitated the wielding of the hammer on the middle days of the feast. We may say with certainty from internal evidence of the Talmud, Moed Katan, that the knocking of the hammer, mentioned in this Mishne, had no relation to kinds of labor which were forbidden on the middle days of the feast. [2] The statement, "From his days the hammer was not struck in Jerusalem," is an explanation of the fact that the "Knockers" were abolished by John Hyrcanus. Similarly the phrase, "and in his days none needed to inquire about *demoi*" explains the decree of John Hyrcanus that the consumer has to give the tithe.

The original text of the Mishne was יוחנן כהן גדול ביטל את הודוי ומר על הדמאי ובימיו אין אדם צריך לשאול על הדמאי; אף הוא ביטל את המעוררין ואת הנוקפין עד ימיו היה פטיש מכה בירושלים Johanan the High Priest abolished the confession; *i.e.*, the confession of the *ame ha-arez* when bringing the tithes. He decreed *demoi*; *i.e.*, that the consumer had to give the tithe to the Levites. In his days no one needed to inquire about *demoi*; *i.e.*, since the *ame ha-arez* were not trusted in the necessary tithe.[3] He also abolished the "Awakeners" and the

---

[1] Sotah, 48. עד ימיו היה פטיש מכה בירושלים, בחולו של מועד

[2] M. M. K. 1.10 שנשברו מתקנן במועד ••• הצינור והקורה, *Cf.* Talmud, *ibid.*, 11.

[3] Yer. Sotah, 9 שהעמיד זונות.

"Knockers," hence from his day on no hammer was smitten in Jerusalem.

The words עד ימיו היה פטיש מכה בירושלים "Until his days the hammer used to smite in Jerusalem," and the words ובימיו אין אדם צריך לשאול על הדמאי "In his days none needed to inquire on *demoi*" were grouped at the end of this Mishne by a later editor because of the similar words ובימיו and ימיו.

The decrees and abrogations made by John Hyrcanus I reflect the political as well as the socio-economic conditions prevailing shortly after Judaea became an independent state.

THE AM HAAREZ

A Study in the Social and Economic Life of the Jews before and after
the Destruction of the Second Temple

EVERY student of the Talmud is aware of the animosity
which existed between the Tannaim and the Am haarez.
Who were the Ame haarez? What caused this animosity?
The consensus of opinion among modern scholars is that
the term Ame haarez, found in the tannaitic literature,
refers to the ignorant, or to the people who did not observe
the Jewish Law.[1] There is never great sympathy between
the intellectual class and the masses of a nation. But the
animosity which the Rabbis felt toward the Am haarez, and
the intense hatred the Am haarez had for the scholars, cannot be ascribed to the mere ill feeling of the classes. There
must have been a more profound cause for this antagonism.

The term Am haarez occurs quite frequently in the Bible,[2]
and means literally "the people of the land." It never occurs
in the sense of ignorant people, or those who did not observe
the law. In the biblical literature of the post-exilic period,
the term Am haarez usually referred to the people of the
land who were not of Jewish origin.[3] In the early tannaitic
literature the word Am haarez is mentioned mostly in con-

---

[1] E. Schürer, *Geschichte*, 1898, VII, 400. Bousset, *Die Religion Des
Judentums*, 1926, 187. Bacher, *Theol. L.*, 1910, N. 22. Comp. also C.
Montefiore, *Hibbert Lectures*, 1892, 495–502.

[2] A very ingenious and most stimulating book on the Am haaretz in
the Bible was written by the late Judge Mayer Sulzberger, *The Am
Ha-aretz*, Philadelphia, 1909; See also S. Daiches, "The meaning of am
haares in the Old Testament." *J. of Theol. Studies*, XXX, 245–8.

[3] Esther, VIII, 17, ורבים מעמי הארץ מתיהדים Ezra, VI, 21; IX, 1
Nehemiah, X, 31. לא נתן בנתינו לעמי הארץ.

210

nection with the law of *maasrot* and *terumah* and the laws
of levitical uncleanness, but is not found in connection with
the laws of Sabbath, Passover or any of the major laws.
Therefore we may assume that Am haarez does not refer
to the person accused of not observing the Jewish law. The
statement quoted in the Tosefta ‪בן חבר שלמד אצל עם הארץ‬[4]
likewise disproves the notion that the term Am haarez refers
to ignorant people.[5]

I venture to suggest that the term Am haarez used in
the early tannaitic literature refers to the people of the land,
the farmers who tilled the soil. This theory is substantiated
by a Baraita, where it is stated that the laws of *hekdesh*,
terumah and *maasrot* are the body of the Torah, and they
are transmitted to the Am haarez.[6] The laws of *hekdesh*,[7]
terumah and *maasrot* are agrarian, and the Baraita states
they are transmitted to the Am haarez, which shows conclusively that the Am haarez in the Baraita can be interpreted only as referring to a *farmer*. From the tannaitic
literature we infer that the Boethusians (Sadducees) were
against the use of the willow branch on the seventh day of
the Succot festival, if it fell on the Sabbath.[8] A Baraita
relates the following story: Once the seventh day of the
Succot festival fell on the Sabbath. The Boethusians hid
the willow branch under heavy stones on the eve of the
Sabbath so that it should not be used on the Sabbath. The

---

[4] Tos. Demai 1, 18. "A Son of a *Ḥeber* who studied under Am haarez."

[5] See A. Büchler, *Der Galilaische Am-ha Ares*. Büchler is of the
opinion that the animosity against the Am haarez developed after the
Hadrianic period. Comp. however, J. Klausner, ‪היסטוריה ישראלית חלק‬
‪ג', ע' 185‬ D. Chwolson, *Beitrage Zur Entwicklungsgeschichte des Judentums
vor ca. 400, v. Chr. bis ca. 1000, n. Chr.,* 1910; L. Katznelson, "The
Sadducees and Pharisees," (Russian) *Voschod*, 1898.

[6] Shab., 32, ‪תניא ר"ש בן גמליאל אומר הלכות הקדש תרומות ומעשרות הן הן‬
‪גופי תורה ונמסרו לעמי הארץ.‬

[7] Lev. XIX, 23, 24. Deut. XV, 19.

[8] Tos. Suc. III, 1; T. Ibid., 43b. ‪שאין ביתוסין מורין שחיבוט ערבה דוחה שבת.‬

Ame haarez discovered this and removed the willow branch
from under the stones on the Sabbath and brought it to the
altar.[9] The question now arises what particular interest
had the Ame haarez in the willow branch to remove the
stones on Saturday, which is generally not permissible. If
we should, however, assume that Am haarez has the meaning of farmer, we can understand the full significance of the
story. According to the Jewish tradition, on the feast of
Tabernacles the world is judged as to whether it should have
rain.[10] The four species, the lulab, ethrog, myrtle and the
willow branch are used in order to obtain the favor of God,
so that He may give rain.[11] We can now understand why
the Ame haarez, the farmers, took special pains in bringing
the willow branch to the altar for the prescribed ceremony,
as this ceremony of the willow branch was of vital importance
to the fields.

After the Restoration, during the Persian and the early
Hellenistic periods, the Jewish population was divided into
two major classes: the farmers, who tilled the land, and the
Priests and the Levites, who were engaged in the service
of the Temple. These did not receive remuneration in money
for their services, but regularly were given in payment from
the crops which were supplied by the farmers. They also
received various gifts from the sacrifices which were brought
to the Temple. The Priests received *terumah*, and the
Levites, *maasrot*, the Priest an additional *terumah*.[12] The
Jewish population consisted principally of the Am haarez.[13]
The number which lived in cities was very insignificant,
with the exception of those who lived in Jerusalem. The

---

[9] מעשה וכבשו עליה ביתוסין אבנים גדולות מערב שבת וידעו בהן עמי הארץ ונררום
והוציאם מתחת אבנים בשבת. Tos. Ibid.; Tal. Ibid.

[10] M. R. H. 1, 2. בחג נידונין על המים.

[11] Tal. Tan. 2b.

[12] תרומה מעשר.

[13] Comp. Josephus, *Against Apion*, 1, 60.

people who could not find work on the land migrated to
Egypt, and many joined the Hellenistic armies as mercenaries.[14] As long as the Am haarez constituted the bulk of
the nation, and there was no urban life of any significance,
they did not withhold the Tithe, and sustained the Priests
and the Levites. After the Ptolemaic Conquest, and particularly after the successful revolt of the Maccabees, the
situation changed. Cities on the coast were added to Judea
either by conquest or by penetration. Trade and commerce
began to flourish. The urban population rapidly expanded
and developed. So to the Jewish people which consisted of
two classes up to the Maccabean period, the Am haarez
and the priestly caste, was added another class, the urban
population.

The Am haarez no longer constituted the bulk of the
people because a great part of the Jewish population dwelt
in the cities. Under the biblical law the Am haarez, and
they alone, had to support the Priests and the Levites, as
the *terumah* and *maasrot* were given by them. Since the
Priests and the Levites were maintained entirely at their
expense, the Am haarez began to resent the fact that the
urban population did not share at all in the maintenance,
and hence many of the farmers tried to withhold the Tithe.[15]
The Priests, and particularly the Levites, did not receive
their due allotment. The Am haarez failed to take into
consideration that when giving the Tithe, he increased the
prices on his grain to cover his loss, hence the burden of the
Tithe was shared by the consumer as well. To this period we
may trace the first clash which occurred between the Am
haarez and the urban population. The leaders of the Jews

---

[14] See E. Bevan, *A History of Egypt Under the Ptolemaic Dynasty*,
London, 1914, 111–112.

[15] מקצתן מעשרין ומקצתן אין מעשרין. Sot. 48a, Comp. Tos. Ibid., XIII,
10; Yer. Ibid. 24a.

suspected the Am haarez of withholding the *maasrot*. (They did not suspect him of withholding the *terumah*, as anyone outside of the Priests who eats *terumah* merits death). They could not improve the economic status of the Levites, since the biblical law requires the farmer and not the buyer to give the Tithe.[16]

Beginning with the time of John Hyrcanus (136–105 B. C. E.), the economic condition of the Priests and Levites was improved, as he decreed upon *demai* גזר על הדמאי[17] i. e., he who purchases from the Am haarez should give the Tithe because the farmer was not trusted in reference to *maasrot*. This is what the Mishna tells us. "Since his (John Hyrcanus) days nobody has to inquire about *demai*."[18] ומימיו אין אדם צריך לשאל על הדמאי. The meaning of this statement is quite clear. For, John Hyrcanus ordered the purchaser to give the Tithe to the Levites, disregarding the word of the Am haarez. To question the farmer in reference to the *maasrot*, was useless.

According to the biblical law, the tiller of the land, when he gave his *maasrot*, was to go to the Temple and thus confess before God, "I have brought away the hallowed things out of mine house, and also have given them unto the Levite,

---

[16] Comp. Deut. XIV, 22–29, XXVI, 1–15.

[17] The word *Demai* is borrowed from the Greek word δῆμος-δῆμοι meaning common people, Am haarez. John Hyrcanus' decree refers to the fruit of the people. The word fruit is not mentioned in the decree. The short form of expression is characteristic of the early Halakah, and it is found in many old Halakahs. One example will suffice. Hillel introduced the Takkana of *Prosbul* הללל פרוזבל. The word *Prosbul* is likewise borrowed from the Greek πρὸς βουλῇ, before the Council (court). The substance of Hillel's Takkana of *Prosbul* is to make a written declaration (note) before the court. The note, the principal object in Hillel's Takkana, is not mentioned at all. In the Talmud, the word *demai* has the meaning of doubt, i. e., it is not known if the Am haarez gave his tithe to the Levites. Comp. Yer. Maas. Sh., 56, Yer. Sot. 24B. מי תיקן, ומי לא תיקן. Comp. ערוך the word דמאי.

[18] The reading in the Mishna is ובימיו or כל ימיו. The reading should be amended to ומימיו.

and unto the stranger, to the fatherless, and to the widow,
according to all Thy commandments which Thou hast commanded me: I have not transgressed Thy commandments;
neither have I forgotten them."[19] Since John Hyrcanus
declared that the Am haarez could not be trusted in reference to *maasrot*, and the purchaser of the food from the
farmer had to give the *maasrot*, it was impossible for the
Am haarez to confess before God and say, "I did as You
had commanded," since the *maasrot* had yet to be given by
the consumer. On the other hand, the man who purchased
could not confess, for the Law in the Bible stated that the
tiller of the land was the only one to confess. Therefore,
John Hyrcanus abolished the confession of *maasrot*.[20]

The Jewish State up to the Maccabean revolt was Theo-
cratic. It was the belief of the people that God is the Governor of the Universe, and the High Priest is to administer
in the name of God.[21] After the great victory of the Maccabees over the Greeks, a revolutionary change took place
in the minds of the Jewish people concerning the re-organ-
ization of the Jewish State.

In the year 143 B. C. E., a great synagogue[22] was called
together to set up a form of government. This assembly
changed the system of the government from a Theocracy
to a Commonwealth. Simon, the last survivor of the Has-
monaeans, was appointed High Priest and Head of the
Jewish Nation; "forever, until a faithful prophet should
arise."[23] His son, John Hyrcanus, who succeeded him had

---

[19] See Deut. XXVI, 1-15.

[20] חניא אף הוא ביטל את הודאי וגזר על הדמאי, לפי ששלח בכל נבול ישראל וראה
שאין מפרישין אלא תרומה נדולה בלבד ומעשר ראשון ומעשר שני מקצתן מפרישין
ומקצתן אין מפרישין . . . . עמד והתקין להם הלוקח פירות מעם הארץ מפריש מהם
מעשר ראשון ומעשר שני מעשר ראשון מפריש טמנו תרומת מעשר . . . . ביטל וידוי
דחברים וגזר על דמאי של עמי הארץ. Sota 48a. Comp. also Yer. Demai, 21d.

[21] Josephus *Against Apion*, II, 16.

[22] ἐπὶ συναγωγῆς μεγάλης. כנסת הנדולה.

[23] 1, Macc., XIV, 41, 42.

the title "High Priest and Head of the Jewish Commonwealth."[24]   The Jewish Commonwealth was called חבר
היהודים. Some of the cities were granted autonomy, and
were ruled by their own Senate (Boule)[25] *Ḥeber*. Such cities
were called חבר העיר. The inhabitants of the cities were
divided into two categories. Those who had full citizen
rights, and participated in the city government were called
חברים *Ḥaberim*.[26] The other category consisted of foreigners
who did not belong to the Jewish race, proselytes, and anyone who lived in the city but was not a citizen of that city
and could not enjoy its privileges. They were called Townsmen אנשי העיר, בני העיר. So the Jewish State became divided
mainly into two classes. The *Ḥaberim*, חברים, the privileged
class, the Patricians, and the Am haarez, tiller of the land,
the plebeians. The *Ḥeber* could hardly associate with the
Am haarez, since the latter's food was *demai*.[27] Intercourse
of the *Ḥeber* with the Am haarez became almost impossible,
as the Am haarez was held in levitical uncleanness,[28] and
the *Ḥeber*, who conformed to the laws of Purity, could not
associate with the them.[29] The Am haarez undoubtedly

[24] יהוחנן הכהן הגדל וחבר היהודים, or יהוחנן הכהן הגדל וראש חבר היהודים.
See E. Schürer, *Geschichte*, v. I, 269. Madden, *History of Jewish Coingae*,
1864, 51–61.

[25] Comp. B. J., II, 15, 6; 16, 2. Apparently the city council consisted
of seven men. See B. J., II, 20, 15. They were probably called פרנסי
העיר. Comp. Tos. Meg. III, 1. It is worthwhile to note that according
to Eusebius, *The Church History*, II, 1, there were 70 Apostles and 7
Deacons. The Sanhedrin consisted of 70 men, while the members of the
City Council comprised 7. The Christian Apostolic Institution and
Diaconate were undoubtedly taken over by the early Christians from
the Jews.

[26] On the question of חבר See M. Weinberg and S. Kraus, *Jeschurun*,
1929, 1930.

[27] Comp. Tos. and Mishna Demai, Yer. Demai. Most of the citations
on Am haarez are quoted by Büchler, Der *Galilaische Am-ha Ares*.

[28] Tos. Demai כליו של עם הארץ, see, Hag. 22b. כליו של עם הארץ ואינו מתארח אצל עם הארץ
טמא או טהור אמרו לו טכא.

[29] ספק בנדי עם הארץ ... לא יאכל זב פרוש עם זב עם הארץ בנדי, Shab. 13a,
עם הארץ סדרם לפרושׁין, Hag. II, 7. The garb of the Am haarez is a

resented this attitude bitterly, and a hatred sprang up among the Am haarez for the *Ḥaberim*. On the other hand, the *Ḥaberim* looked down on the Am haarez as the lower class of Jewish society.[30]

In the century before the destruction of the Temple by the Romans, two factions came into existence, offshoots of the Pharisees. These sects were of the opinion that all Jews are equal before God, and there is no lordship of man over man, but they differed in their method of realizing their ideas. We have reference here to the Fourth Philosophy and to the Apocalyptists (the apocalyptic pharisaic sect, the forerunners of Christianity). The former faction was mainly revolutionary in character. They strove to get rid of the Roman tyranny and Herodian dynasty by force. This sect maintained that the Jewish State should be along democratic

source of uncleanness to the Perushin. The word Perushin in this Mishna, as well as in Shab. cannot be taken as referring to the Pharisees. The term Perushin in these passages refers to the people who had separated themselves from the Am haaretz, and ate their meals על טהרת הקדש. See S. Zeitlin, "The Pharisees," *J. Q. R.*, 1926, p. 388. Moore, is of the opinion: "That in the tannaitic literature and Amoraic sources, the name of Perushin is used only in contrast to Am ha Ares, the ignorant and negligent vulgus." *Judaism*, 1, 60. This theory, however, is without foundation. The word Perushin in the aforementioned Mishna does not apply at all to the Pharisees. Perushin in this passage refers to the people who had separated themselves from the Am haarez and ate their meals in accordance with levitical purity. Therefore the garments of the Am haarez are a source of uncleanliness to Perushin because the Am haarez were suspected of not observing the levitical laws of purity. This interpretation is supported by the text itself, where it is stated, "The garments of the Perushin are a source of impurity to the eaters of Terumah," which means that the people who ate their meals in accordance with the Levitical laws of purity can still transmit impurity to the eaters of Terumah. Am haarez in the tannaitic literature is used only in contrast to חבר or to תלמיד חכם but never to the word פרושים Pharisees.

[30] Ned. 20a. The Pharisees who strove to abolish the distinction between the Priests and the Israelites, could not obliterate the differences between the חברים and the Am haarez, as the latter were under suspicion of not giving the tithe, and not observing the Levitical laws of Purity which made impossible the association of the חברים with them.

lines, and there should be equality among all the classes.[31] It is most likely that the dictum found in the Mishna: "He who says, Mine is thine, and thine is mine, is an Am haarez,"[32] has reference to the followers of the Fourth Philosophy, or to the Apocalyptists, who favored economic and social equality.

The followers of the Fourth Philosophy were recruited mostly from the Am haarez, the masses, *Demos*. They had joined the revolutionary party in the revolt not only against the Romans, but also against the Jewish State, as well as against the rich.[33] The masses were particularly attracted by the principles of the Fourth Philosophy,—that there is no overlordship of man over man, and all Jews are equal before God, irrespective of rank and knowledge. Some of the Am haarez, the masses, joined the Apocalyptists, who preached the same Gospel as that preached by the sect of the Fourth Philosophy, that all the Jews are equal before God.

It is interesting to note, that what happened in Jewish history during the Second Commonwealth, re-occurred in the history of the Jews in Poland during the Eighteenth Century. It is a known fact, that the leaders in the time of "The Committee of the Four Lands"[34] disliked the Jewish masses who lived in the small towns and villages. The Rabbis and the scholars considered the masses who lived in the villages of Ukrania not only ignorant, but a disgrace to Judaism. The masses were forbidden to wear the same type of clothes as the Rabbis, so as to differentiate them from the intellectual class. On the other hand, the masses

[31] Ant. XVIII, 1, 6, B. J. II, 8, 1. Comp. Ibid, II, 17, 6, "to win over a host of grateful debtors and to cause a rising of the poor against the rich."

[32] Ab, V, 10. שלי שלך ושלך שלי עם הארץ

[33] B. J. II.

[34] ועד ארבע ארצות.

envied the scholars, and hatred for the intellectual aristocracy ensued. When Hassidism arose, as a revolt against the intellectual class, the masses joined the Hassidic movement, which preached the principle of equality of all Jews before God. There was to be no distinction between the man who knows the Talmud and studies it all day, and the man who does not know the Talmud and is completely ignorant, but is ready to serve God with his entire heart and soul.[35]

In the year 65 C. E., the Jewish revolutionary army had a great victory over Cestius, the Roman general. A provisional government was established in Jerusalem, under the leadership of Ananias, the High Priest, a Sadducee, and Simon, son of Gamaliel, a Pharisee.[36] This provisional government did not remain in power for a long time. It was overthrown by the radical parties. A new government was organized, consisting of seventy men of the *demos*.[37] The position of High Priest had heretofore been inherited or given to members of the most aristocratic families. The new government manoeuvered that a farmer, *Am haarez*, be invested with the office of High Priest. Thus Josephus tells us, "They accordingly summoned one of the high priestly clans, called Eniachin, and cast lots for a high priest. By chance the lot fell to one who proved a signal illustration of their depravity; he was an individual named Phanni, son of Samuel, of the village of Aphthia, a man who not only was not descended from high priests, but was a *farmer* ϑὶ ἀγροικίαν . . . They dragged their reluctant victim out of the field." (χώρας).[38]

---

[35] See S. Zeitlin, "Chassidism: A Revolt of the Masses," *The Jewish Tribune*, August 1st, 1930.

[36] B. J., II, 20, 3., IV, 3, 9; Vita, 38, 44, 60.

[37] B. J. IV, 5, 4.

[38] Ibid., IV, 3, 8; Comp. Tos. Yoma, 1, 6. אמרו עליו על פנחס איש חבתא שעלה גורלו להיות כהן גדול והלכו עליו נזברין ואמרכלין ומצאהו כשהוא חוצב ומלאו עליו את המחצב דינרי זהב אמר ר' חנינא בן גמליאל לא הסתח היה והלא חתנינו היה אלא מצאוהו כשהוא חורש.

With the overthrow of the provisional government, civil war broke out in Jerusalem between the various factions of the Jews. The City fell into the hands of the radical parties, and a reign of terror was established by the new government. Anyone who belonged to the nobility or to the families of the High Priests was tortured and murdered.[39] The cause for such wholesale massacre was not only due to the fact that the leaders of the radical parties suspected that the High Priests and nobility sided with Rome, but there was another reason, I believe, which brought about this bloodshed; the revenge of the masses against the old oppressors. This thought is borne out by Josephus, "They thirsted above all for the blood of the brave and the nobility, massacring the latter out of envy."[40] The student of history will note that the struggle which occurred in little Judea between the masses and the upper classes, is analogous to what happened in the revolutions of recent times, such as the French and Russian.[41] When the masses snatched the power from the existing government, they were over-zealous to annihilate the clergy and nobility, not only because the latter opposed the ideas of the masses, but also to avenge themselves. The annihilation of the upper class during the civil war in Jerusalem was largely due to the animosity existing between the Am haarez,—the masses,[42] and the upper classes.

When Jerusalem was captured by the Romans, and the

---

[39] B. J. IV, 5, 2, 3.

[40] ibid., IV, 6, 1.

[41] See S. Zeitlin, *La Revolution Juive de 65–70, La Revolution Francaise & La Revolution Russe*, Paris, 1930.

[42] After the conquest of Galilee by the Romans, the farmers of Galilee whose fields were laid waste, went to Jerusalem to assist the people of Jerusalem to defend the Holy City against the Romans. When the provisional government was overthrown, they joined the different radical parties, and many of them were instrumental in instituting the reign of terror which took place during the civil war.

Temple destroyed, the Jews were helpless. It is a psychological consequence that in a period of distress a nation like an individual, turns to God for assistance. Thus, the ideas of the Fourth Philosophy were abandoned, and the ideas of the Jewish Christians, the followers of the Apocalyptists, gained a number of adherents among the Jews. Many of the Am haarez—the farmers of Galilee, and the masses generally, formed the rank and file of the new Christian sect. The Gospel, according to John, tells us that the Pharisees claimed that none of the leaders, or any of the Pharisees, joined Jesus, but the masses who do not know the Law are accursed.[43]

Before the destruction of the Temple, the Am haarez hated the learned and privileged class, as the latter would not associate with them, and many religious laws were enacted against them. The aristocracy looked down on the Am haarez, but did not hate them. After the destruction of the Temple an intense animosity for each other sprang up in both classes. The reason for the hatred which the Rabbis felt toward the Am haarez is due to the fact that the leaders of the Jews considered the sect of the Fourth Philosophy as responsible in the main for the destruction of Jerusalem. Josephus usually refers to them as bandits and robbers and blames them for the catastrophe which befell the Jews.[44] The leaders considered the Apocalyptists, the forerunners of Christianity, equally responsible for this calamity. Thus Josephus says, "Besides these there arose another body of villains, with purer hands but more impious intentions, who no less than the assassins ruined the peace of the city. Deceivers and impostors, under the pretence of divine inspiration fostering revolutionary changes."[45]

[43] John, VII, 49.
[44] See B. J. Ant. XVIII, I, 6. "and laid the foundation of our future miseries, by this system of philosophy, . . . brought the public to destruction." Comp. B. J. VII, 8, I.
[45] Ibid., II, 13, 4.

The mutual animosity is well illustrated in the early tannaitic literature. Rabbi Eliezer[46] said it is lawful to stab an Am haarez on the Day of Atonement that falls on a Sabbath. On the other hand, Rabbi Akiba said, "When I was an Am haarez I used to say, 'I wish I had one of those scholars. I would bite him like an ass.'" His disciples said "You mean like a dog." He replied, "An ass's bite breaks the bones, and a dog's does not."[47] The antagonism of the early Jewish Christians and the Rabbis is clearly demonstrated in the New Testament. Even the pagan writers have made comment on this animosity. Tacitus tells us, "It is said that Titus first called a council and deliberated whether he should destroy such a mighty temple . . . Titus himself, . . ., holding the destruction of this temple to be a prime necessity in order to wipe out more completely the religion of the Jews and the Christians; for they urged that these religions, although hostile to each other, nevertheless sprang from the same sources; the Christians had grown out of the Jews; if the root were destroyed, the stalk would easily perish."[48]

---

[46] Pes. 49 b. The reading is undoubtedly אליעזר and not אלעזר and this reading is supported by the MSS.

[47] Ibid. אמר ר' אליעזר עם הארץ מותר לנוחרו ביום הכיפורים שחל להיות בשבת
אמרו לו תלמידיו אסור לשוחטו אמר להן זה טעון ברכה וזה אינו טעון ברכה . . . .
תניא אמר ר' עקיבא כשהייתי עם הארץ אמרתי מי יתן לי תלמיד חכם ואנשכנו כחמור
אמרו לו תלמידיו ר' אמור ככלב אמר להן זה נושך ושובר עצם וזה נושך ואינו שובר עצם.

[48] "At contra alii et Titus ipse evertendum in primis templum consebant quo plenius Iudaeorum et Christianorum religio tolleretur: quippe has religiones, licet contrarias sibi, isdem tamen ab auctoribus profectas: Christianos ex Iudaeis extitisse: radice sublata stirpem facile perituram." Suplicius Severus, Chron. 30.6. According to Josephus, B. J. VI, 4, 6, Titus was against the burning of the Temple. It appears to me that Tacitus had historical data to the effect that Titus was anxious for and commanded the burning of the Temple. Josephus who wrote his book B. J. in honor of his patron, the Emperor Titus, and to glorify the Flavian family, misrepresented the historical fact in his book, stating that Titus was anxious to save the Temple from destruction. Comp. also Dio Cassius, 66.6. See Cyrus Adler, The Memorandum on the Western Wall, Phila., 1930, pp. 10–11.

The term Am haarez was applied frequently (in the tan-naitic literature of the first century) to the Jewish-Christians. This is evident from the definition of Am haarez given by the Rabbis of the first generation after the destruction of the Temple. "An Am haarez is he who does not read the *Shema* evening and morning," said Rabbi Eliezer. Rabbi Joshua says, "He who does not put on the the phylacteries," Ben Azzai says, "He who has no fringes (*Zizit*) on his garb."[49] It is well known, from the New Testament and the Church Fathers, that the early Christians objected to the *Shema*, phylacteries and fringes.[50] This animosity between the Jews and Jewish-Christians became more intense during and shortly after the war of Bar Kokba, as the Jewish-Christians did not assist them in their great and last upris-ing against the Romans. The Jews were suspicious that the Jewish-Christians were betraying them.[51] After the war of Bar Kokba, particularly beginning with the third century, the Jewish-Christians became more and more a definite, segregated sect, the Jews no longer regarded them as Jews, and the animosity of the Jews for the Christians progres-sively diminished.

The word Am haarez in the later tannaitic literature did not always refer to farmers or to the Jewish Christians. It became a byword of contempt and reproach for those whom

[49] Ber. 47 b. ‏איזהו עם הארץ כל שאינו קורא קריאת שמע ערבית ושחרית דברי‎ ‏רבי אליעזר רבי יהושע אומר כל שאינו מניח תפילין בן עזאי אומר כל שאין לו ציצית‎ ‏בבגדו.‎

[50] Mat. XXIII, 5, Comp. Justin Martyr, *Dialogue with Tyrpho.* 46. "For He enjoined you to place around you a fringe of purple dye, in order that you might not forget God; and he commanded you to wear a phylactery . . . and we know that the ordinances imposed by reason of the hardness of your people's hearts, contribute nothing to the per-formance of righteousness and of piety."

[51] Idem. *The First Apology of Justin,* 31, "Bar Kokba, the leader of the revolt of the Jews, gave orders that Christians alone should be led to cruel punishments." Comp. also Eusebius, *Church History,* IV, 8.

the Rabbis considered crude, immoral, or those who did not observe the Law.[52]

It is stated above the word Am haarez originally applied to the farmers who lived in the villages. Because the farmers had a very busy life which required constant activity from early morning until late at night in order to extract only a bare living from the soil, and the constant fight against all kinds of insects, it was impossible for them, even if they wanted to, to cultivate themselves and become educated in Jewish lore. The city-dwellers, on the other hand, through their varied contacts through trade, commerce, or even the more elegant arts and industries, could more easily educate themselves, as well as their children. Thus the differentiation between the two classes, the Am haarez, the farmers, and the city-dwellers, was not only social and economic, but also cultural. The Am haarez under these circumstances was ignorant, while the city-dweller was more cultured. Hence, in the later periods, the word Am haarez became synonymous with ignorance. The word *Ḥeber*, before the destruction of the Temple designated the man who shared in the city government. After the destruction of the Temple, when the Jews had no city government, the word *Ḥeber* applied to those who were cultured, observed the Law, and were scrupulous with regard to the laws of Purity. The word תלמיד חכם or חכם applied to scholars, and to men who specialized in the Jewish Law and Lore. There is a probability that the word תלמיד חכם or חכם applied only to those men who occupied a definite position in the Academies of learning.[53]

---

[52] Comp. Pes. 49 b.

[53] The question of חברים and תלמיד חכם will be discussed at length in a separate article on the Constitution of the Jewish State during the Second Commonwealth.

APPENDIX

אוצר של ישראל וגוים מטילין בו אם רוב גוים ודאי ואם רוב ישראל
דמאי (Tosefta Demai, I, 12.)

A storehouse used by Jews and Gentiles for their deposits
(the grain), if the majority of the depositors are Gentiles,
the grain is in a state of certainty (i. e., untithed). On the
other hand, if the majority of depositors are Jews, the
grain is *demai* (in a state of doubt). Here the Tosefta
has the word demai in contrast to certainty.

כל העיר מוכרין ודאי ואחד מוכר דמאי לקח ואינו יודע איזה לקח
הרי זה אסור Ibid. IV, 6. Here again the word *demai* is in
contrast to ודאי which shows that demai has the meaning
of doubt.

שלשה שאכלו כאחת חייבין לזמן אכל דמאי . . . והכותי מזמנין
עליהם Mishna Ber. VII, 1. Three who ate together are
required to say grace (Zimun) after the meal. If they
ate *demai* or a *Cuthi* was in their midst, the common
grace should be said. In the Talmud (ibid 47B) it is
related that some of the Amoraim questioned the privilege
of a *Cuthi* partaking in the grace since a Baraita tells us
that an Am Haarez can not be included in the Benediction
(Zimun). והכותי מזמנין עליו אמאי לא יהא אלא עם הארץ ותניא
אין מזמנין על עם הארץ.

In the Talmud various explanations are offered. It
seems to me, however, that there is no contradiction between the Mishna and the Baraita. The Mishna which
states אכל דמאי . . . והכותי מזמנין עליהם is according to the
School of Hillel, who were of the opinion that one may
feed the poor people with demai דמאי העניים את מאכילין.
Therefore, if demai was used in the meal, you have to
offer the common grace (Zimun). The statement in the
Barita, אין מזמנין על עם הארץ is the Shammaite point of view,
which is that one may not feed the poor with demai, בית

שמאי אומרים אין מאכילין את העניים ואת האכסניא דמאי and so if an Am Haarez partook in the meal, no common grace is to be offered. It is interesting to note that the word Am Haarez is on a par with demai.

תניא ר' שמעון בן אלעזר אומר בעון שני דברים עמי הארצות מתים על שקורין לארון הקדש ארנא ועל שקורין לבית הכנסת בית עם (Shab. 32a,) Simon ben Eleazer said for two sins the Ame Haarez died young, because they called the Holy Ark ארנא and because they called the Synagogue the People's House. The Jewish masses looked upon the synagogue as a popular institution, and called it the "People's House." The reason the Ame Haarez called the Synagogue the "People's House" was due to the fact that the institution of the Synagogue had developed from the assemblies which met in the towns and villages for social, economic and religious purposes.

ישיבת בתי כנסיות של עמי הארץ מציאין את האדם מן העולם (Ab. III, 10). Sitting in the assembly houses of the Am Haarez is one of the things that takes men out of the world (cause their death).

ממזר תלמיד חכם קודם לכהן גדול עם הארץ (Hor. III). Here the Mishna has the word Am Haarez in contrast to תלמיד חכם. Comp. also B. B. 8a.

The term Am Haarez, as we have noticed, occurs quite frequently in tannaitic literature, and is to be interpreted in various ways. Only from internal evidence of the text where the term Am Haarez occurs, can we get at the real meaning of the word and know to what particular class of people it refers.

SLAVERY DURING THE SECOND COMMONWEALTH
AND THE TANNAITIC PERIOD

SLAVERY AS AN institution goes back to great antiquity. The weak were conquered by the strong who made them slaves, ruling them with an iron hand as they did cattle. There were also those who through poverty sold themselves into slavery. Regretably the traffic is still in existence in parts of Africa. The Stoic philosophers and the Jewish sages taught that slaves are human beings and should be accorded humane treatment but they did not advocate their abolition. Slavery was deeply rooted in society upon which its economic structure and social life were fundamentally based.

We learn from the admonition of Seneca to the Romans of his attitude to the institution and the deplorable status of the slaves, "I do not wish to involve myself in too large a question," he wrote, "and to discuss the treatment of slaves, towards whom we Romans are excessively haughty, cruel and insulting. But this is the kernel of my advice: Treat your inferiors as you would be treated by your betters. And as often as you reflect how much power you have over a slave, remember that your master has just as much power over you. "But I have no master" you say. You are still young; perhaps you will have one. Do you not know at what age Hecuba entered captivity, or Croesus, or the mother of Darius, or Plato, or Diodenes?" [1]

---

[1] *Nolo in ingentem me locum immittere et de usu servorum disputare, in quos superbissimi, crudelissimi, contumeliosissimi sumus. Haec tamen praecepti mei summa est: sic cum inferiore vivas, quemadmodum tecum superiorem velis vivere. Quotiens im mentem venerit, quantum tibi in servum liceat, veniat in mentem tantundem in te domino tuo licere. "At ego" inquis, "nullum habeo dominum." Bona aetas est; forsitan habebis. Nescis, qua aetate Hecuba servire coeperit, quae Croesus, qua Darei mater, qua Platon, qua Diogenes? Ep. 47.*

13

By Roman law slaves were under the domination of their owners. According to *jus gentium* the owners were invested with the power of life and death over them. [2]

The Bible as well as the tannaitic literature also sanctioned the institution of slavery and stressed that slaves should be humanely treated. The Bible refers to different classes of slaves. Slavery in the Pentateuch could be readily defined as bondage since the services were limited by time. Jewish slaves had to serve six years and were to be freed in the seventh year.

The Bible speaks of a father who sells his daughter into bondage [3] and also of a man who sells himself because of poverty. [4] If a person was convicted of larceny he had to make restitution not only of the property but also to pay a fine. If the thief had no money to pay he was sold into slavery. [5] In the story of Joseph and his brethren we have a reference to a silver goblet found in the sack of Benjamin which was supposedly stolen from Joseph. Then it is stated that Joseph said to Judah, ,,He with whom it is found [the silver goblet] shall be my slave." [6] This story shows that there was an old custom that a thief was punished by being made a slave. According to the Twelve Tablets theft was considered a capital offence *furtum fecerat*. A freeman was first scourged and then by judgment of the magistrate delivered to the person from whom he had stolen. [7] (Whether the thief was to be made a slave by delivery, or reduced to the condition of an insolvent judgment debtor was an old question). Later the severity of this punishment was modified, "Theft, whether by a slave or by freeman, was punished by the praetorian edict with fourfold damages." [8]

[2] Cf. Gaius, I. 52.
[3] Ex. 21, 7.
[4] Lev. 25, 39.
[5] Ex. 22, 2.
[6] Gen. 44, 17.
[7] Gaius, 3, 189.
[8] Ibid.

In dealing with the laws of theft Josephus wrote, "He that stealeth a head of cattle shall pay fourfold as a penalty, save in the case of an ox, for which he shall be fined fivefold. He that hath not the means to defray the imposed amount shall become the slave of those who have had him condemned." [9] The scholars who dealt with the question of slavery saw a contradiction between Josephus' statement and the law as recorded in the Talmud, [10] which held that a thief was sold into slavery only if he could not pay the principal but not if he could not pay the fine. [11] This contradiction is easily resolved as the talmudic law is of a later period, after the destruction of the Second Temple. Josephus recorded the law which prevailed in the early part of the Second Commonwealth. [12] Another contradiction was noted in the law as given by Josephus and that as is stated in the Pentateuch. According to the latter if a thief had not the money to pay for stolen goods he was sold into slavery. [13] According to Josephus if the thief had not the money to pay, "He shall become the slave of those who had him condemned," thus he became the slave of the one from whom he had stolen. Actually there is no contradiction. According to the Pentateuch theft, *furtum*, was considered *private delict* private wrongs, [14] and held that delinquents should be punished by becoming liable to personal action at the suit of the injured party. The object of such action was either to recover damages or a penalty, or to recover both damages and penalty; the State had no power to interfere. It was a case entirely between the man who suffered the loss and the thief. He had the right to absolve the thief, enslave

[9] *Ant.* 4, 8, 27 (272).
[10] Cf. Boaz Cohen, "Civil Bondage in Jewish and Roman Law" *Louis Ginzberg Jubilee Volume*, p. 117.
[11] Kid. 18.
[12] Cf. also E. Urbach, *Zion*, 1960, pp. 151-2.
[13] Ex. 22, 2.
[14] A *private delict* gives rise to an obligation; the law intends that delinquents shall be punished by becoming liable to a personal action by the injured party, the object of such action being either to recover damages or a penalty קנס, ot both.

him or sell him into slavery. This was the extreme satisfaction that the plaintiff might demand. Josephus states that the plaintiff had the right to enslave the thief. The Pentateuch gives as the extreme punishment for the thief that the plaintiff has the right to sell him into slavery.

Injury and bodily mutilation likewise were considered private wrongs. The injured person had the right to fix the punishment. If he suffered the loss of an eye or a tooth he was provided with the right to take out an eye or a tooth from the offender. The law of *talio* as given in the Pentateuch, "an eye for an eye", was the extreme satisfaction which the plaintiff might demand. He might obtain satisfaction with money or entirely absolve the man who caused the injury. The plaintiff was the sole judge. It was a matter between the man who was injured and the person who inflicted the injury. The State had no right to interfere. [15] Josephus, in dealing with the law of injury, wrote, "He that maimeth anyone, let him undergo the like himself, and be deprived of the same member of which he had deprived the other, unless he that is maimed will accept money instead of it; for the law makes the sufferer the judge of the value of what he had suffered, and permits him to estimate it, unless he will be more severe." [16] Josephus here again records that the injured person had the right to get satisfaction with a milder punishment, to obtain money for his injury, "unless he will be more severe", the maimed person had the right to apply the law of *talio*. On the other hand the Pentateuch records only the extreme punishment, i.e., *talio*. During the Second Commonwealth the Pharisees abolished *talio*. The injured person had only the right to demand satisfaction with money for the loss of his eye or tooth, also for the pain incurred, for medical care, for disability and humiliation. The abolishment of *talio* was made through legal fiction as the man who suffered the loss of an eye had the right only to take out an eye exactly like his, in size and color.

[15] Cf. S. Zeitlin, "The Malaka" *J.Q.R*, 1948, p. 34.
[16] *Ant.* 4, 8, 45 (280).

Since it is impossible for two men to have precisely the same organs in every respect the injured could not make use of the law of *talio*. [17]

In relating the history of King Herod Josephus said that the king enacted a new law in regard to thieves which was contrary to the original laws. He wrote as follows, "He (Herod) made a law, no way like our original laws, and which he enacted of himself, to expose housebreakers to be ejected out of his kingdom; which punishment was not only grievous to be borne by the offenders, but contained in it a dissolution of the laws of our forefathers; for this slavery to people of other religions, and such as did not live after the manner of the Judaeans, and this necessity that they were under to do whatsoever such men should command, was an offence against our religion, rather than a punishment to such as were found to have offended, such a punishment is not found in our laws; for those laws ordain that the thieves shall restore fourfold; and that if he have not so much, he shall be sold indeed, but not to people of foreign religion, nor so that he be under perpetual slavery, for he must have been released after six years. But this law, thus enacted, in order to introduce a severe and illegal punishment, seemed to be a piece of insolence in Herod, when he did not act as a king but as a tyrant, and thus contemptuously, and without any regard to his subjects, did he venture to introduce such a punishment. Now this penalty, thus brought into practice, was like Herod's other actions and became a part of his accusation and an occasion of the hatred he lay under." [18]

[17] B. K. 83. Cf. S. Zeitlin, "Talmud" *Encyclopaedia Britannica*, 1963.

[18] *Ant.* 16, 1, 1 (1-15). Ἐν δὲ τῇ διοικήσει τῶν ὅλων πραγμάτων ἐσπουδακὼς ὁ βασιλεὺς τὰς κατὰ μέρος ἀδικίας ἀναστεῖλαι τῶν περὶ τὴν πόλιν καὶ τὴν χώραν ἁμαρτανομένων τίθησι νόμον οὐδὲν ἐοικότα τοῖς πρώτοις, ὃν αὐτὸς ἐβεβαίου τοὺς τοιχωρύχους ἀποδιδόμενος ἐπ' ἐξαγωγῇ τῆς βασιλείας ὅπερ ἦν οὐκ εἰς τὴν τιμωρίαν μόνον τῶν πασχόντων φορτικόν, ἀλλὰ καὶ κατάλυσιν περιεῖχεν τῶν πατρίων ἐθῶν. τὸ γὰρ ἀλλοφύλοις καὶ μὴ τὴν αὐτὴν δίαιταν ἔχουσιν τοῦ ζῆν δουλεύειν καὶ βιάζεσθαι πάνθ' ὅσα προσέταττον ἐξ ἀνάγκης ἐκεῖνοι ποιεῖν ἁμαρτία πρὸς τὴν θρησκείαν ἦν οὐ κόλασις τῶν ἁλισκομένων,

Josephus, or rather the author of his source, condemned Herod for selling thieves to pagans outside of Judaea. This he considered to be the act of a tyrant not of a king—a direct transgression of Judaean law which did not permit the selling of a thief outside of the country to non Jews. It has been suggested that Herod, in his zeal to eradicate thievery and burglary which were rampant in the early years of his reign, followed the Roman law pertaining to house breakers. It has also been pointed out that the Roman law prohibited the enslavement of a citizen within the boundary of the City of Rome, and for this reason citizens were sold into slavery outside of the city. The theory has been advanced that a Judaean could not be sold into slavery within the boundaries of Judaea. Therefore when Herod introduced the law that a housebreaker should be sold into slavery consequently he had to be sold outside of Judaea. It has also been maintained that Herod, being king of Judaea was also a client king of Rome and shared an obligation to Caesar. The law enacted by him was not the whim of a tyrant but of a ruler who had the double responsibility of the country entrusted to him and to Caesar. His duty was that order should prevail in the country and, being a client king, all his acts had to be understood in the perspective of Rome. Hence the law of the housebreaker, enacted by Herod, is connected with the *pax Romana*. [19]

It was held that the "housebreakers", referred to by Josephus, were really not ordinary thieves, criminals, but were political opponents of Herod. When Herod conquered Judaea

πεφυλαγμένης ἐν τοῖς πρώτοις τῆς τοιαύτης τιμωρίας· ἐκέλευον γὰρ οἱ νόμοι τετραπλᾶ καταβάλλειν τὸν κλέπτην, οὐκ ἔχοντα δὲ πιπράσκεσθαι μέν, ἀλλ' οὔτι γε τοις ἀλλοφύλοις οὐδ' ὥστε διηνεκῆ τὴν δουλείαν ὑπομένειν ἔδει γὰρ ἀφεῖσθαι μετα ἑξετίαν. τὸ δ' ὥσπερ ὡρίσθη τότε χαλεπήν καὶ παράνο-μον γενέσθαι τὴν κόλασιν ὑπερηφανίας ἐδόκει μέρος, οὐ βασιλικῶς ἀλλὰ τυραννικᾶς αὐτοῦ καὶ πρὸς τὰ κοινὰ τῶν ἀρχομενων ὀλιγώρως θεῖναι τὴν τιμωρίαν νενοηκότος ταῦτα μὲν οὖν καθ' ὁμοιότητα τοῦ λοιποῦ τρόπου γιγνό-μενα μέρος ἦν των διαβολῶν καὶ τῆς ἐπ' αὐτῷ δυσνοίας.

[19] Cf. A. Schalit, הורדוס המלך pp. 124-128; I. Gutman, שעבוד נופו של אדם בחוביותיו בתורת ישראל. *Sefer Dinaburg.*

he did not succeed in annihilating all who had opposed him and were adherents of the Hasmoneans. The so called "house-breakers" were those who opposed him politically. It has been suggested that ordinary criminals joined the "housebreakers" for personal gain. To establish peace and impress Augustus with his capacity as a ruler Herod had to eradicate the trouble makers. He did not slay them as he was apprehensive of the reaction of the people and he therefore decided to treat the offenders as ordinary criminals, thieves. According to the Torah as previously stated thieves sold into slavery served only six years and then were freed, thus able to return to their previous illegal acts. Herod hence decided to sell thiefs outside of Judaea to pagans which meant that they would be in perpetual slavery. [20] The view has even been advanced that Herod established a special *Bet Din* which tried offenders. This *Bet Din* had his authority and may be named the ''*Bet Din* of Herod" as the Talmud makes reference to the bet din of the Hasmoneans. [21] Although the view that Herod in selling thieves into slavery outside of Judaea based his action on Roman law was ingeniously defended nevertheless it cannot be accepted historically. As portrayed by Josephus, Herod was a tyrant. Many of his actions were not based on legal principles. Even granting that Herod in selling thieves outside of Judaea into perpetual slavery he based himself on Roman law this does not prove that his actions were based on legal principles. To sell a Jew as a slave to a non Jew outside of the borders of Judaea into perpetual slavery was against the spirit of the Judaeans. The *Sifra* as well as the *Sifre* in interpreting the passages of Leviticus and Deuteronomy made it clear that a Jew could be sold into slavery only to a Jew within the borders of Judaea. [22] Philo

[20] Ibid., pp. 128-130.
[21] Ibid., p. 132.
[22] כשבית דין מוכרים אותו אינו נמכר אלא לך
The Sages enacted a law that if one sells a slave to a non Jew or outside the boundary of Judaea the slave regains his freedom. It is probable that the purpose of this law to conteract Herod's action. See below.

also condemned those who sold slaves into a foreign land, "Never to return, never even to dream of again saluting the soil of their native country or to know the taste of comforting hope". [23] Josephus, or his source, following the spirit of the Judaeans condemned Herod for his act, saying, "He did not act as a king but as a tyrant, and thus contemptuously and without any regard to his subjects, did he venture to introduce such a punishment. Now this penalty, thus brought into practice, was like Herod's other actions and became a part of his accusation, and an occasion of the hatred he lay under."

It has been maintained that Herod was apprehensive of public opinion. He was aware that when he killed Hezekiah in the time of John Hyrcanus II the people arose against him and he was compelled to appear before the *Bet Din* to defend his act. Herod, now in order not to arouse the animosity of the Judaeans, sold the thieves into perpetual slavery rather than to slay them. [24] This theory is untenable. When Herod killed Hezekiah he was a commoner officially under the jurisdiction of Hyrcanus. He was now king and did not hesitate to act as he thought fit without regard for the feelings of the Judaeans. [25]

---

[23] Laws IV. 17. Cf. also S. Belkin, *Philo and the Oral Law*, pp. 89-96.
[24] Schalit, Ibid.
[25] The verses in Exodus 22, 1-2 אם במחתרת ימצא הגנב והכה ומת אין
לו דמים אם זרחה השמש עליו דמים לו שלם ישלם אם אין לו ונמכר בגנבתו
which is traditionally and correctly rendered, "If a thief be found breaking in, and his smitten and dies, there shall be no blood guilt for him (i.e. for the owner who has smitten the thief) but if the sun has risen upon him there shall be blood guilt for him (if the owner killed the thief); he shall make restitution (the thief); if have nothing he shall be sold for his theft." These verses were rendered, If a thief be found breaking in, and his smitten and dies, he should not pay (the thief should not pay for the damages since he paid with his life) but if the sun has risen upon him he has to make restitution with money, he has to pay; if he has nothing he shall be sold for theft. אם במחתרת
ימצא הגנב והוכה ומת אין לו דמים כלומר; במקרה זה אין הגנב חייב לשלם
פיצוי על הנזק שגרם שהרי הוא מת ואין לתבוע מן המת כלום הואיל ומותו הוא
כפרתו ופיצוי מספיק על הנזק; אם זרחה השמש עליו דמים לו שלם ישלם,,
אם אין לו ונמכר בגנבתו כלומר אם נתפס הגנב לאור השמש ולא נהרג חובת

Besides the class of slaves heretofore mentioned there were the debtors, known in Roman law as *nexi*. If one borrowed money and could not pay his debt the creditor had the right to take him and his children into bondage. It is true that this class of slaves is not mentioned in the Pentateuch but from the biblical books we know of its existence. It is related in II Kings that a certain woman cried to the prophet Elisha, saying, "Thy servant, my husband, is dead; and thou knowest that thy servant did fear Yahweh; and the creditor is come to take unto him my two children to be his bondsmen." [26] Thus the creditor had the legal right to the person of the debtor and, if the debt was not paid, he could be taken into bondage or sold into slavery. [27] The legal right to the person of the debtor is evident in the book of Nehemiah where it is written that many of the Judaeans came to Nehemiah to complain against the money lenders, "We have borrowed money for the king's tribute upon our fields and our vineyards, they cried to him; some of our daughters are brought into bondage already." [28] We can deduce from other biblical passages the existence of this type of slavery. It is stated in the book of Isaiah that Yahweh said, "Or which of My creditors is it to whom I have sold you?" [29] We have in the book of Proverbs, "And the debter is slave to the lender." [30] Whether a man who was enslaved for an unpaid debt re-

---

הפיצוי על הנזק שנגרם על ידיו רובצת עליו והוא חייב לשלם ואם לו יימכר

This rendering and interpretation is totally incorrect. First the word דמים never occurs in the sense of money in the Bible but has the connotation of blood, blood guiltiness. דמים בראשו Again to interpret the verse אם במחתרת ימצא הגנב והכה ומת אין לו דמים

"If the thief be found breaking in and be smitten that he died he should not pay" does not make sense. Certainly if the thief was killed on the spot how can he or some one else pay for a theft which was not perpetrated?

[26] II Kings, 4, 1.
[27] Cf. S. Zeitlin, "The Halaka," *JQR*, 1948.
[28] Neh. 5, 1-5.
[29] Is. 50, 1.
[30] Prov. 22, 7.

gained his freedom with the approach of the sabbatical year
or had to serve in bondage until the value of the loan was
repaid and be unaffected in his status by the sabbatical year
is not clear. Philo wrote that debtors who did not pay their
debts were freed in the seventh year. [31] However we may conjecture that such a slave had to remain in bondage in accordance with the value of the loan.

It is stated in one place in the Talmud that Jewish slaves
continued as long as the Jubilees existed, [32] but we learn from
another passage that the Jubilees ceased to exist before the
establishment of the Second Commonwealth. [33] We may
conclude from this that there were no Jewish slaves during
the Second Commonwealth. This contradicts everything that
we learned from the tannaitic literature. There is ample evidence in this literature that slavery did exist among the
Judaeans during the Second Commonwealth. How can we
reconcile these contradictory statements? I venture to say
that the statement in the Talmud that Jewish slaves ceased
to exist with the abolishment of the Jubilees referred only
to those who had not paid their debts and could be enslaved
by the creditors. This type of slavery was abolished. The
creditor no longer had the right to the person of the debtor;
he had no right to enslave the debtor or his children for an
unpaid debt. He only had the right to the property of the
debtor. He had the right to seize the property of the debtor
if the debt was not paid, and if the property had been sold
after the loan was contracted the creditor had the right to
seize the property from the buyer. The change in the law came
about when a *shtar* was introduced, when the debtor gave a
promisory note to the creditor for the loan which he contracted. When the debtor gave the *shtar* to the creditor he
placed his property as a hypothec. [34]

[31] *Laws*, 2, 122; *De Virtutibus*, 123.
[32] Kid. 69; Ar. 29.
[33] Ar. 32.
[34] S. Zeitlin, *The Rise and Fall of the Judäean State*, Vol. I, pp. 311-2.

The right of the creditor to the person of the debtor was abolished in Rome by *lex poetelia* in the year 311 BCE. [35] From Philo and the Gospel according to Matthew we may conjecture that during the Roman period the creditor had the right to enslave their debtors for unpaid loans. Philo, in his book, *De Virbutibus* 123, wrote, "As for the debtors, who through temporary loans have sunk into bearing both the name and the painfulness which their cruel situation entails, and those whom a more imperious compulsion has brought from freedom into slavery, he [Moses] would not allow them to remain for ever in their evil plight, but gave them total remission in the seventh year. For creditors who have not recovered the debt, or have gained possession in some other way of those who were formerly free should be content, he [Moses] says with six years as a time for their service, and those who were not born to slavery should not be altogether deprived of comforting hope, but should pass back to the old independence of which they were deprived through adverse circumstances."

We learn from the tannaitic literature that during the Second Commonwealth that a debtor could not be enslaved by a creditor for an unpaid debt. The creditor only had the right to seize his property. Philo, on the other hand, speaks of the right of the creditor to enslave the debtor if he did not pay his loan. Here there is a contradiction. Furthermore the law that a slave has to serve six years but becomes free in the seventh year was applied to those who sold themselves because of dire need or to a thief, but not to a debtor who was enslaved by his creditor. He was enslaved to the creditor whom he served according to the value of the debt. The law of the sabbatical year was not applicable to him. According to Philo, however, a debtor had to serve his creditor six year and received his remission in the seventh year. Here is another contradiction.

At the time of Jesus, or rather at the time of the composition

[35] Cf. Livy, 8, 28.

of the Gospel according to Matthew, debtors who did not pay their loans were either sold or put in prison. This may be deduced from the account given in Matthew about a man who owed a thousand talents which he did not repay, "His master commanded him to be sold," Matthew relates, "and his wife and his children and all that he had and payment to be made." On the pleading of the servant the master had compassion and forgave him the debt. Matthew continues, "But the same servant went out and found one of his fellow servants which owed him a hundred pence and he laid hands on him and took (him) by the throat saying 'pay me that thou owest' and his fellow servant fell down on his feet and besought him saying, 'have patience with me and I will pay thee all', and he would not but went out and cast him into prison till he should pay his debt." The Gospel continues that when this was told to the master he called his slave and said unto him, "O thou wicked servant I forgave thee all thy debt because thou desiredest me: Shouldest thou no also have had compassion on thy fellow servant, even as I had pity on thee? And his lord was wroth, and delivered him to the torments until he should pay all that was due him." [36] Philo's statement and the story recorded in the Gospel, that debtors who did not pay their debts could be imprisoned or enslaved, contradicts what we learned from the tannaitic literature, namely that creditors could not enslave or imprison their debtors for unpaid debts but only had the right to seize their property.

Diodorus, in writing about debtors, stated, "The lawgiver ruled that the repayment of loans could be exacted only from a man's estate, and under no condition did he allow the debtor's person to be subject to seizure, holding that whereas property should belong to those who had amassed it or had received it from some earlier holder by way of a gift, the bodies of the citizens should belong to the state, to the end that the state might avail itself of the services which its citizens owed it, in times of both war and peace. For it would be

[36] Matt. 18, 24-34.

absurd, he felt, that a soldier, at the moment perhaps when he was setting forth to fight for his fatherland, should be haled to prison for an unpaid debt, and that the greed of private citizens should in this way endanger the safety of all." He continues by saying, "It appears that Solon (594 BCE) took this law also to Athens, calling it *Seisachtheia*, (shaking off of burdens)." [37] From Diodorus we learn that the law of the creditor having the right to the person of the debtor was abolished on the principle that the citizens belonged to the state and were subject to the state in time of war or peace; that no one had the right to enslave a fellow citizen or imprison him for unpaid debt. Thus according to the Judaean law as well as the laws of Rome and Athens the creditor had no right to the person of the debtor.

Philo's statement and the story given in the Gospel according to Matthew can be explained on the theory that although the law of the right of the creditor to the person of the debtor was abolished it nevertheless was practiced in Egypt and Syria and both authors record that the practice still prevailed in these two countries. Or it can be explained on the theory that these two authors did not base their accounts on the law which prevailed but had in mind a message presenting the ethical side of the law and the people. Philo, as an ethical teacher, emphasized that although slavery was a degradation Jewish law tried to allay its severity. He claimed that among other nations the debtor became a slave to the creditor while in Jewish law the crditor had the right to keep the debtor as bondsman for only six years. Philo either did not know or did not record that according to early halakah the debtor had to serve the creditor only according to the value or the debt and the principle of the sabbatical year was not applicable in this case. Furthermore in the time of Philo the law that the creditor had the right to the person of the debtor had been abolished.

In the Gospel according to Matthew the story about the

[37] Diodorus, I. 79.

debtor is a homily. The author conveyed the religious principle that God would forgive the inequity of a man if he would
forgive a fellow man the sin committed against him. Thus
when the master heard that the slave whom he had forgiven
indebtedness had imprisoned his fellow man for not paying
his debt to him, the master now delivered his slave to the
tormentors until the debt was paid to him. The author of the
Gospel concludes, "So likewise shall my heavenly Father do
also unto you if you from your hearts forgive not every one his
brother their trespasses." [38]

While there were Jewish slaves during the Second Commonwealth the sages always laid stress on humane treatment
towards them. Judaea did not have πρᾶτής λίθος the stone
upon which slaves were sold, which was common among
other nations. Actually Jewish slaves were bondsmen. This
was due not only to the humane treatment towards them but
also to a time limit of service.

During the Hellenistic period slavery was an important
institution upon which the social and economic structure of
the country was based. The Judaeans did not differ from
other peoples. After the establishment of the Commonwealth
its economic development required the labor of slaves. The
wealthy classes, particularly, employed a large number of
slaves for the cultivation of vast tracts of land. Josephus
tells us that at the funeral of Herod hundreds of slaves participated in the procession. Both the writings of Josephus
and the tannaitic literature speak of the slaves employed by
the high priestly families. [39] The sages warned the people not
to employ too many slaves, [40] but the people did have slaves.
A gentile slave was an object acquired in the same manner
as real property. [41]

The condition of the slaves in the Roman Empire is por-

[38] Matt. 18, 35.
[39] Cf. *Ant.* 20, 9, 2 (206); Talmud Pes. 57, Tos. Men. 13, 21.
[40] Cf. Abot 2, 7.
[41] Cf. M. Kid. 1, 3, 5.

trayed by Juvenal. He writes as follows; „Crucify the slaves!"
says the wife. 'But what crime worthy of death has he committed?' asked the husband; 'Where are the witnesses?'
Who informed against him? Give him a hearing at least; no
delay can be too long whan a man's life is at stake.' What, you
numskull? You call a slave a man, do you? He has done no
wrong, you say? Be it so; but this is my will and my command.
Let my will be the voucher for the deed." [42] Thus the whim of
a woman was sufficient to have a slave killed. Slaves were in
the power of their owners. This was recognized by *ius gentium*.
The owner was vested with the power of life and death
over their slaves. Slaves were regarded as impersonal men,
"A slave who is manumitted, having no rights, cannot lose
any, for all his rights date from the day of his manumission."
*Cum servus manumittitur, quia servile caput nullum jus habet,
ideo nec minui potest, eo die enim incipit statum habere.* [43]
There was another Roman maxim, "A slave by manumission
loses no rights, having none to lose." *Servus manumissus
capite non minuitur quia nullum caput habet.* In Roman society
slavery was an institution by *ius gentium*, making one man
the property of another in contravention of Natural law. [44]
In the later imperial Rome the status of slaves was greatly
improved. Hadrian (117-137) deprived the masters of the
power to put slaves to death without a judicial sentence. [45]
Antoninus Pius (138-161) ordained that if a master was excessively cruel to his slaves he should be compelled to sell them;
also that one who killed his slave should be liable to punishment as was one who killed someone else's slave. [46]

---

[42] Sat. 6, 219-224. *"Pone Crucem servo" meruit quo crimine servus
supplicium? quis testis adest? quis detulit? audi; nulla umquam de morte
hominis cunctatio longa est "o demens, ita servus homo est? nil fecerit,
esto: hoc volo, sic iubeo, sit pro ratione voluntas."*

[43] Dig. 4, 5, 4.

[44] *The Institutes of Justinian,* 1, 16, 4.

[45] Spartian, *Hadrian,* 18.

[46] A proprietor who killed a slave was subject to the penalty of
the *lex Cornelia de sicariis.*

GENTILE SLAVES

A clear differentiation between the Hebrew slaves and the gentile slaves is given in the Pentateuch only in the following; —the former served his master for a definite period while the latter had no limitation to his service. The gentile slave was a permanent possession of his owner and, as a property, was inherited by his children on his death. [47] The status of the gentile slave and the rights of his owner is not clearly stated in the Pentateuch. The sages who strove to elevate the status of the slaves maintained that if an owner intentionally killed his slave he was liable to punishment. [48] The verses in the Pentateuch, Exodus 25, 20-21, "If a man smite his man slave or female slave, with a rod, and he die under his hand, he shall surely be punished. Notwithstanding if he continue a day or two, he shall not be punished; for he is his money," was assumed as referring to gentile slaves. I believe that the sages who held that if a master killed his slave he was liable to punishment supported their views by interpreting these verses as referring to gentile slaves. However this pentateuchal section refers to only one type of slave, namely the Hebrew slave. It does not refer to gentile slaves. Similarly the pentateuchal command, "And if a man smite the eye of his man slave, or the eye of his female slave, and destroy it he shall let him go free for his eye's sake." [49] refers also to a Hebrew slave. Likewise the sages interpreted this verse as referring to a gentile slave. However they injected their views in order to support the halakah, which was indeed revolutionary for their time. In reality the maining or the killing of slaves, recorded in the Pentateuch, refers to Hebrew slaves. The words כי כספו הוא "for he is his money" [50] have been taken to refer to a gentile slaves but this is not sufficient proof. The Pentateuch

---

[47] Lev. 25, 45-46.
[48] Tosefta B.K. 9, 24; Kid. 24.
[49] Ex. 21, 26-7.
[50] Cf. Sifre (Mekilta) Mishp. 8. בכנעני הכתוב מדבר מהם תקנו•

refers to a Hebrew slave by the term "buy". [51] Thus the
phrase "for he is his money" could well be applied to a Hebrew slave.

In the eraly days of the Second Commonwealth a gentile
slave was considered property. He was acquired in the same
way as real property,—by purchase, by a deed from the previous owner or by possession. [52] A debtor could place his slave
as hypotheca for a loan which if unpaid could be seized by
the creditor [53] in the same manner as a debtor placed real
property as hypothec for his debt. If a debtor sold his property or his slave after he received the loan the sale was not
valid and the creditor had the right to seize the property
or the slave from the buyer. In the case when the debtor
placed the slave as hypothec for his debt and then manumitted
him the hypothec ceased to exist. It was in the same category
as if a debtor placed his house or field as hypothec for his debt
and later on a storm swept it away—the hypothec was gone
and the creditor loses. The property has no rights it is an
object. Similarly the slave has no rights, he is an object. After
manumission he has ceased to exist as a slave. However
if the creditor has seized the ex slave he is compelled to free
him and the ex slave has to write *shtar* for the money which
his previous owner borrowed. [54] We can see from the above
halakah that the sages had invested the slave with some
rights since he had to pay for the amount for which he had
been hypothec. Raban Simon ben Gamaliel said that the ex
slave does not owe anything to the new master, the creditor—
the new master has to free him the old master who had manumitted him had to write a *shtar* for the money borrowed. [55]

A gentile slave was considered the property of the owner. If
the owner was a kohen the gentile slave had the right to eat

---

[51] Cf. Ex. 21, 2. כי תקנה עבד עברי‧

[52] Cf. M. Kid. 1, 3, 5.

[53] Cf. M. Git. 4, 4.

[54] Ibid. Yer. ibid. העושה עבדו אפותקי מכרו אינו מכור שיחררו משוחרר‧

[55] Ibid. רבן שמעון בן גמליאל אומר אינו כותב אלא משחרר‧

14

terumah, [56] sacred food, just as the cattle. If the kohen married an Israelite she was entitled to eat terumah, [57] as in the olden days she was considered the property of her husband. If she was divorced and the slave was manumitted they no longer had the right to eat terumah. [58]

The Pentateuch specified that the uncircumcised could not eat of the pascal lamb. It further said, "Every man slave that is bought for money, when thou has circumcised him, then shall he eat thereof." [59] Rabbi Eliezer held thst the words אז יאכל בו "Then shall he eat thereof," refers to the slave, that is when the slave is circumcised he may eat of the pascal lamb. Rabbi Joshua was of the opinion that these words אז יאכל בו "Then shall he eat thereof," refers to the master, that is if the gentile slave is not circumcised the master is prevented from eating the pascal lamb. [60] The difference in the views of these two sages may be explained. Rabbi Eliezer, who was of the old school, followed literally the pentateuchal injunction that only the circumcised may partake in the eating of the pascal lamb. Rabbi Joshua, who was

[56] M. Yeb. 8, 1.
[57] Ibid.
[58] Cf. M. Ter. 8, 1; Tosefta ibid. 10, 18.
[59] Ex. 12, 44, וכל עבד איש מקנת כסף ומלתה אותו אז יאכל בו׃
[60] Cf. Sifre(Mekilta) Be 15. רבי אליעזר אומר אין מילת עבדיו
מעכבתו לאכל בפסח ומלתה אותו אז יאכל בו (רבו) עבדו מצינו שהוא רשאי
לקיים לו ערלים עבדים׃
Cf. Rashi, Ex. 12, 44. מגיד שמילת עבדיו מעכבתו מלאכול בפסח דברי
רבי יהושע רבי אליעזר אומר אין מילת עבדיו מעכבתו מלאכול בפסח אם
כן מה תלמוד לומר אז יאכל בו חעבד׃
See Tos. Yeb. 70 b. ורבי אליעזר גופיה דרש במכלתא דמילת עבדיו
אין מעכבת אדם מלאכול בפסח ודרש אז יאכל בו העבד׃
Urbach, Zion, 1960, p. 162 has, שמר רבי אליעזר גם במקרה זה על
המסורה הקדומה שאין אדם רשאי לקיים עבדים ערלים״ ושמלת עבדיו
מעכבת את אדון העבד מלאכול בפסח this text is totally wrong. ⋯
Apparently Prof. Urbach overlooked the fact that the schooles of Shammai and Hillel continued for some time after the destruction of the Second Temple. Cf. Tos. Kel. 1, 4. הלכו וקצצום ובאו ושאלו ביבנה׃
See also Yer. Ter. 5, 4. אמרו מי פגע בכם אינו אלא מתלמידי בית שמאי׃

of the school Hillel which strove to elevate the status of the
slaves, interpreted the pentateuchal passage to mean that the
slave has a relationship with his owner and that if uncircumcised his owner may not partake in the eating of the pascal
lamb. By our interpretation of the controversy between these
two sages we may explain another controversy. According
to Rabbi Eliezer a master may keep uncircumcised gentile slaves
since doing so will not effect his life, he will not be prevented
from eating of the pascal lamb. Rabbi Akiba, the follower of
Rabbi Joshua, maintained that the master may not keep uncircumcised slaves, [61] the reason being that since a slave has a
relationship with his master and affects his life in that being
uncircumcised his master is prevented from partaking of the
pascal lamb. Therefore an owner may not keep uncircumcised slaves.

We find a statement in the Tosefta that male slaves who
were not circumcised and female slaves who were not baptized
prevent their master from partaking of the pascal lamb. Rabbi
Eleazar ben Jacob said that this law refers only to the pascal
lamb which was slaughtered in Egypt in the time of Moses. [62]
The law that an uncircumcised slave prevents his master from
partaking of the pascal lamb is in accordance with the view
held by Rabbi Joshua and Rabbi Akiba who maintained that
that uncircumcised slaves prevented their master from eating
of the pascal lamb, there is however no basis for the law that
an unbaptized female slave prevents her master from partaking of the pascal lamb. There is no indication in the
Pentateuch of baptism in connection with the pascal lamb.
It seems to me that this law apparently was enacted after the
destruction of the Second Temple when a male proselyte had
to undergo both circumcision and baptism and a female pro-

---

[61] Yeb. 48. תנו רבנן מקיימין עבדים שאינן מלין דברי רבי ישמעאל [אליעזר]
רבי עקיבא אומר אין מקיימין•

[62] Pes. 8, 18. אחד פסח מצרים ואחד פסח דורות מי שהיו לו עבדים שלא
מלו ושפחות שלא טבלו מעכבין אותו מלאכול בפסח, רבי אליעזר בן יעקב
אומר אני בפסח מצרים הכתוב מדבר•

selyte had to be baptized. [63] This law given in the Tosefta refers to slave proselytes. On the other hand Rabbi Eleazar ben Jacob was of the opinion that the said law refers to the time of the Exodus but not to the pascal lamb of all time. He followed the view of Rabbi Eliezer who maintained that uncircumcised slaves may not eat of the pascal lamb but that they do not prevent their master from partaking of it.

A controversy is recorded in the Talmud between Rabbi Ishmael and Rabbi Akiba. The former held that the phrase in Lev. 25, 46 והתנחלתם אותם לבניכם ··· לעולם בהם "You may forever enslave them" is רשות optional, elective. The latter held is חובה bound, obligatory. [64] All the commentators on this talmudic passage as well as the scholars held that this controversy refers to the manumission of a slave. Rabbi Ishmael is of the opinion that the master may hold a gentile slave forever or he may set him free. Rabbi Akiba held that the master had no right to set a gentile slave free, he was a slave to him forever. The interpretation rendered by the commentator cannot be readily accepted. We do know that Jews did manumit gentile slaves. Furthermore Rabbi Akiba held that a Jew may not keep uncircumscribed slaves. [64a] The Talmud records a statement of Samuel that a Jew who manumitted a gentile slave transgresses a Pentateuchal precept. [65]. The Talmud questioned this from a story given in the name of Rabbi Eliezar. Once Rabbi Eliezer came to the synagogue and not finding the needed quorum, being only nine men including himself, he freed his slave in order to make the necessary quorum. [66] The Talmud removed the contra-

---

[63] Cf. S. Zeitlin, "L'origine de L'Institution du baptême pour les Proselytes" *REJ*, 1934.

[64] Git. 38. תנו רבנן לעולם בהם תעבדו רשות דברי רבי ישמעאל,
רבי עקיבא אומר חובה·
רבי ישמעאל אומר עבד כנעני אין לו פדיון לעולם ואינו יוצא אלא לרצון·
[64a] See above note 61.

[65] Ibid. אמר רב יהודה אמר שמואל כל המשחרר עובר בעשה·

[66] Ibid. מתיבי מעשה ברבי אליעזר שנכנס בבית הכנסת ולא מצא עשרה
ושחרר את עבדו והשלימו לעשרה מצוה שאני·

diction between Samuel's [67] statement and the action of
Rabbi Eliezer, explaining that Rabbi Eliezer acted as he did
for the sake of a mitzvah. After reconciling this contradiction
the Talmud quotes the controversy between Rabbi Ishmael
and Rabbi Akiba previously referred to with regard to
gentile slaves. The Talmud advances the possibility that
perhaps Rabbi Eliezer, who freed his gentile slave, adhered to
Rabbi Ishmael's view that it is optional for a Jew to free his
gentile slaves. The answer given is that Rabbi Eliezer held
"it is prohibited." [68]

In the Talmud Ber. 47 the account of Rabbi Eliezer's action
and the statement by Samuel were given in reverse order. The
account of Rabbi Eliezer who freed his gentile slave to make
a quorum is related first. The Talmud then questions how
could he do this? Samuel said that any one who frees his
gentile slave transgresses a pentateuchal precept. The answer
given is that Rabbi Eliezer did this for the sake of a mitzvah. [69]
The Talmud does not make reference to the fact that Rabbi
Eliezer said "it is prohibited." To say that the Amoraim
were not aware of this statement cannot be entertained. Most
likely Rabbi Eliezer's statement "it is prohibited" is apocryphal,—he never made this statement. [69a] We do not find
this statement anywhere in the Talmud. Furthermore it was
against his view. He held that a Jew may keep uncircumcised

---

[67] תנו רבנן לעולם בהם תעבדו רשות דברי רבי ישמעאל רבי עקיבא
אומר חובה

[68] ודלמא רבי אליעזר סבר ליה כמאן דאמר רשות לא סלקא דעתך דתני
בהדיא רבי אליעזר אומר חובה.

[69] מעשה ברבי אליעזר שנכנס לבית הכנסת ולא מצא עשרה ושחרר עבדו
והשלימו לעשרה . . . והיכי עביד הכי והאמר רב יהודה [אמר שמואל] כל
המשחרר עבדו עובר בעשה לדבר מצוה שאני.

[69a] There are many hypothetical passages in the Talmud. Cf.
Tosafet Nidah 24a, Yeb. 35a, B.B. 154b והא דפריך לעיל ריש לקיש
לרבי יוחנן ממשנת בר קפרא ואמר לו רבי יוחנן שאני אומר מודה בשטר שכתבו
אין צריך לקיימו לא אמר דבר זה מעולם.
Cf. also S. Zeitlin, "Prosbel" *JQR*, 1947, pp. 354-355.

slaves. Again, in removing the contradiction between the action of Rabbi Eliezer and the statement of Samuel, why did not the Talmud explain that Rabbi Eliezer perhaps adhered to the view held by Rabbi Ishmael that a Jew had the option to free his gentile slaves?

I venture to say that the said controversy between Rabbi Ishmael and Rabbi Akiba does not refer to the manumission of a gentile slave but to the sale. Rabbi Ishmael held that a Jew had the option to sell his uncircumcised gentile slave. This is in accordance with his view that a gentile slave does not interfere with the life of his owner, he does not prevent his owner from eating of the pascal lamb. Thus, as we mentioned before, according to Rabbi Ishmael and Rabbi Eliezer a Jew may keep uncircumcised gentile slaves. On the other hand Rabbi Akiba held that a Jew must sell an uncircumcised gentile slave because his master is prevented from partaking of the pascal lamb. This is in accordance with his own statement and that of Rabbi Joshua that a Jew may not keep uncircumcised gentile slaves. [70]

According to pentateuchal law if a master maimed his slave either by smiting his eye or knocking out a tooth the slave has to be set free. [71] It is related in the Talmud that Rabban Gamaliel (of Jabneh) told Rabbi Joshua and joyously that Tabi, his slave was now free because he had blinded his slave in one eye. Rabbi Joshua disagreed with him on the ground that since there were no witnesses [72] and that freedom of a slave by smiting his eye is only a penalty imposed upon the master, therefore the slave is not automatically free. He held that the law in the Pentateuch is not mandatory; the slave had the right to demand his freedom by evidence that

---

[70] Cf. note 61. The words לעולם בהם תעבדו were added later to explain the statements of Rabbi Ishmael and Rabbi Akiba.

[71] Ex. 21, 26-27.

[72] B.K. 74. מעשה ברבן גמליאל שסימא את עין טבי עבדו והיה שמח שמחה גדולה מצאו לרבי יהושע אמר לו אי אתה יודע שטבי עבדי יצא לחירות אמר למה אמר לו שסימתי את עינו אמר לו אין בדבריך כלום שכבר אין לו עדים·

his master maimed him purposely, not by accident. [73] Since
Tabi apparently did not demand his freedom he wanted to
remain a slave. As a matter of fact Tabi died a slave. [74] A
Hebrew slave had to serve six years and was to be freed on
the seventh. However if he wanted to remain a slave and serve
his master, because he became attached to him, his ear had
to be pierced as a sign of punishment. [75] There was no regulation regarding a gentile slave who refused freedom when
granted by the master. There was no mandatory law en-
forcing a gentile slave to accept freedom.

The pentateuchal laws regarding injury, tort, and theft were
matters between the person who was injured and the one who
inflicted the injury, between the person from whom the property was stolen and the one who committed the theft. The
injured person could entirely absolve the one who had committed the injury. The state had no right to interfere. The
injured person could also demand satisfaction for his injury in
which the culprit had to pay for damage, pain, medical care,
idleness incurred and humiliation. [76] This payment was called
קנס penalty. The injured person had to prove that the injury
was committed intentionally and then the court imposed the
payment of the penalty. Similarly the person from whom
property was stolen had the right to demand double the value
of the theft. This also was a matter between the two parties.
The man who was the victim of the theft could absolve the
thief. The double payment was called קנס penalty. In the
same vein the freedom of the slave because he was injured was
a penalty to be paid by his master and it was a matter between the master and his slave. The court had no right to
interfere. Only when the slave brought the case to the court

[73] חחובל בעבדו ובשפחתו הכנענים בינו לבינו פטור מפני שהוא קנס.
Tosefta B.K. 9, 21.
[74] Ibid., ibid. המכה את עבדו בין שמתכוין לו ובין שאין מתכוין לו יצא בן
חורין רבן שמעון בן גמליאל אומר במתכוין יצא לחירות ובשאין מתכוין לא
יצא לחירות.
[75] Cf. Tosefta B. K. 7, 5; Kid. 21.
[76] Cf. S. Zeitlin, "The Halaka" *JQR* 1948, pp. 34-37.

did the court have the right to force his owner to free him.
The freeing of the slave because he was maimed was a קנס, a
penalty imposed upon the master.

A different version of the incident of Rabbon Gamaliel's
maiming of his slave is given in the Palestinian Talmud and is
connected with the law whether a master is permitted to
manumit his gentile slave. [77] This connection with the law of
manumission is of a later period, amoraic. The Babylonian
Talmud makes no reference to it. Rabbi Joshua's disagreement
with Gamaliel and holding that the slave is not free is based
on the fact that the slave did not ask to be freed and there
were no witnesses to the maiming.

The Tannaim were divided on the point whether a slave who
had gained his freedom because of maiming by his master
needs a writ of manumission. Rabbi Akiba and others maintained that the slave needed it while Rabbi Meir and others
were of the opinion that it was unnecessary. [78] The underlying reason for this controversy can be explained in the
following: Those who maintained that the maimed slave
needs a writ held that the freeing of the slave was a קנס penalty imposed upon the master, while those who maintained
that the slave does not need the writ held that the maiming
made him free,—this is the pentateuchal law. We may add
that Rabbi Akiba held that the maimed slave had to have a
writ of manumission from his master to protect him and his
descendants, since through the attainment of his freedom he
might marry an Israelite and his children might be Jews.
Thus the writ of manumission protected the manumitted
slave and his descendants from suspicion and ill talk.

According to a Mishne if a Jew sells a slave to a gentile the
slave automatically attains his freedom. Similarly if a slave
was sold to one who lives in a foreign land that slave obtains

[77] Yer. Ket. 3, 10. רבן גמליאל כמאן דאמר מותר לשחררו אמר ליה כל
גרמה אמרה שאסור לשחררו
[78] Git. 42. בכולן עבד יוצא לחירות וצריך גט שיחרור מרבו, דברי רבי
ישמעאל רבי מאיר אומר אינו צריך · · · רבי עקיבא אומר צריך·

his freedom. [79] These statements are ambiguous. The Jewish court had no authority over the pagans or over those who resided outside of Judaea. How could the slave obtain his freedom without the consent of his new master? It seems that this law was enacted during the reign of Herod when he sold the "housebreakers" into slavery to gentiles outside of Judaea. [80] The law that such slaves regain their freedom became imperative,—it was a *mitzvah* for the Jews to ransom them. Later Simon ben Gamaliel introduced the law that it is a *mitzvah* for the Jews to ransom slaves. [81]

The Mishne records a controversy between the Pharisees and the Sadducees in regard to slaves. The Sadducees complained against the Pharisees by saying that if an ox or an ass have done injury the owners are culpable, while if a slave has done injury the owner is not culpable. They argued that an animal is not in the category of those who perform *mitzvoth*; nevertheless if an animal committed an injury his owner was responsible; in the case of a slave who was obliged to perform *mitzvoth* his owner should be responsible. The Pharisees replied that there was no comparison. An animal they said has no understanding, it is an object, therefore if it has committed injury the owner is culpable. However a slave has understanding, and furthermore he may be provoked by his master and commit an injury. Therefore the Pharisees held that the master is not responsible—the slave is responsible for committing an injury. [82] The controversy between the Sadducees and the Pharisees may be stated thus:—the former held that a slave is an object, the property of the owner, having no

[79] M. Git. 4, 6. המוכר את עבדו לגוים או לחוצה לאדץ יצא בן חורין·

[80] See above p. 191

[81] Tos. Git. 4, 2. כשם שישראל מצווין לפדות את בני חורין כך מצווין לפדות את העבדים·

[82] M. Yad. 4, 7. אומרים צדוקים קובלין אנו עליכם פרושים מה אם שורי וחמורי שאיני חייב בהם מצות הרי אני חייב בנזקן עבדי ואמתי שאני חייב בהן מצות איני דין שאהא חייב בנזקן אמרו להם לא אם אמרתם בשורי וחמורי שאין בהם דעת תאמרו בעבד ואמה שיש בהן דעת שאם יקניטם ילך וידליק גדיש של אחד ואהא חייב לשלם·

status rights or liabilities. The Pharisees, endeavoring to raise
the status of the slaves, maintained that a gentile slave is not
an object, that he is a human being with status and if he
commits an injury he should be held responsible.

The Mishne states that the Sadducees held that gentile
slaves were obliged to perform mitzvoth. It is strange that
they, the Sadducees, should have entertained this view. From
what we know of them we may rightly assume that they held
that a gentile slave is an object without any rights or obli-
gations. The halaka that a gentile slave had to undergo circumcision was enacted much later. [83] This was not the view of
the Sadducees. During the Second Commonwealth when
the Sadducees and the Pharisees flourished a gentile slave
could not perform mitzvoth, he was in the category of an
animal. Upon his death the master could not accept condolence as would be the case in the death of his cattle. Rabbon
Gamaliel had to excuse himself when he accepted condolence
on the death of his gentile slave by saying that his slave was
different, a righteous person. [84] The Sadduccean statement
that slaves had to perform mitzvoth actually referred to
Noachite mitzvoth, *jus gentium.*

The conception of partnership, that two or more persons can
share one property, does not appear in the Pentateuch. The idea
of partnership and its laws was introduced and developed during
the Second Commonwealth. [85] Each partner could relinquish
his rights in a property or sell it. If two men share the ownership of a gentile slave. One partner has the right to manumit
his share of the slave and if he does so the man became half
slave and half free. According to the School of Hillel the half
slave had to serve his master one day and was free the other
day. The School of Shammai objected to this since it would
place the half slave at a disadvantage. He could not marry the
daughter of an Israelite because he was a half slave—he could

[83] Cf. Yeb. 48.
[84] M. Ber. 2, 7.
[85] See S. Zeitlin, *The Rise and Fall of the Judaean State,* pp. 431-2.

not marry a female slave because he was half free. [86] In
support of their view they quoted a verse from Isaiah. "He
created it not a waste, He formed it to be inhabited." [87] The
fact that the Shammaites quoted this verse and not the
Pentateuch where it is stated "Be fruitful and multiply" [88]
reveals that their objection to the Hillelites was not based on a
mitzvah but on their regard for the welfare of the half slaves.
The Hillelites recognised the soundness of the Shammaite
view and followed it. [89]

A private property can become a *res nullius*. If the owner
publicly relinquishes his rights over it anyone can acquire it.
A property gives its owner privileges and liabilities. He has
sole rights over the property but he is also liable to any damage caused by it. The Tannaim were divided in their opinion
as to when the owner who declared his property *res nullius*
is removed from any responsibility for it. Rabbi Meir held that
when the owner declared his property *res nullius* his privileges and responsibilities came to an end. Rabbi Jose held
that the owner was responsible until the property was ac-

---

[86] מי שחציו עבד וחציו בן חורין עובד את רבו יום אחד ואת .M. Git. 4, 5
עצמו יום אחד דברי בית הלל, בית שמאי אומרים תיקנתם את רבו ואת עצמו
לא תיקנתם לישא שפחה אינו יכול בת.חורין אינו יכול•
[87] והלא לא נברא העולם אלא לפרייה ורבייה שנאמר לא תוהו בראה לשבת
יצרה•
[88] Gen. 1, 28. פרו ורבו•
[89] כופין את רבו ועושה אותו בן חורין וכותב שטר על חצי דמיו חזרו בית הלל
כדברי בית שמאי•   In the case when the owner of a
slave who half freed him, Rabbi held that the slave was half free and
half slave, while the sages were of the opinion that he remained a slave.
תנו רבנן המשחרר חצי עבדו רבי אומר קנה וחכמים אומרים לא קנה
(Git. 41, cf. also Yer. ibid. 4, 5; Kid. 1, 3). Here is reflected the views
of the sages regarding slavery. Those who held that a slave could be
half slave and half free held a slave to be an object, property. If a
person owned property he had the right to give it away or renounce
his right to hald of it,—thus half of the property belonged to him and
the other half did not. Those who adhered to the view that a slave was
a human being held that he could not be divided in half-half slave and
half free.

quired by another person. [90] In the case of a person relinquishing his rights over a slave and declaring him *hefker, res
nullius* Rabbi Jochanan declared the slave thus becomes free
but still needs a writ of manumission to establish his freedom. [91] However Samuel was of the opinion that the act of
the owner made the slave free and that the writ of manumission was unnecessary. [92] Rabbi Jochanan followed the view of
Jose that in declaring of a property *hefker* the owner still has
liability over the property and that itis still attached to him.
Samuel followed the view of Rabbi Meir—that when the
owner declares that relinquishes his rights over the property
he has no liability and the property is no longer attached to
him. Rabbi Jose would have held that if the owner made his
slave *hefker* the slave became free but to make it complete he
has to obtain a writ of manumission. Rabbi Meir would have
held that when the owner relinquishes his rights the slave
becomes free and did not need the writ. [93]

The Palestinian Talmud gives another version of Rabbi
Jochanan's view. According to it if the owner relinquishes his
rights over a slave and makes him *hefker* the slave becomes
hefker, res nullius and the owner has no right to write a writ
of manumission. [94] When the owner declares the slave *hefker*

[90] Cf. Yer. Ned. 4, 10; Pea 6, 1. תנא רבי מאיר אומר כיון שאדם מבקיר
יצא דבר מרשותו, רבי יוסי אומר אין הבקר יוצא מתחת הבעלים אלא בזכיה•
[91] Git. 39. אמר עולא אמר רבי יוחנן המפקיר את עבדו יצא לחירות
וצריך גט שיחרור•
[92] Ibid. 38. דאמר שמואל המפקיר את עבדו יצא לחירות ואינו צריך גט
שיחרור•
[93] Cf. S. Zeitlin, הפקר ויאוש: ספר היובל לכבוד לוי גינצבורג•
[94] Yer. Git. 4.4. אבהו בשם רבי יוחנן אמר המפקיר את עבדו אינו רשאי
לשעבדו ואינו רשאי לכתוב לו גט שיחרור•

The text in the Palestinian Talmud reads as follows: אמר לו רבי
זעירא כל עמא אמרין דהוא צריך ואת אומר אינו צריך• We are confronted with a great difficulty. It was stated in the name of Rabbi
Jochanan that if an owner makes his slave *hefker* he is not allowed to
keep him as a slave nor is he *allowed* to give him a writ of manumission.
Rabbi Zeira retorted כל עמא אמרין דהוא צריך ואת אומר אינו צריך
"Everyone said that he needs (to give the slave a writ of manumission)

his ownership and authority over the slave ceases and consequently he cannot write a writ of manumission. The slave is

and you said he does not need to do so." The retort is not in accord
with the statement of Rabbi Jochanan. He said אינו רשאי "it is not
allowed" while in the retort it is staed אינו צריך "he does not need to
do so." There is a distinct difference between the words רשאי "allowed" and צריך "needed."

I pointed out (in mine article) that Iben Adret in his *novella* has
another version of this text which reads as follows: והכי איתי בירושלמי
רבי איל בשם רבי יהושע בן לוי, רבו המתיאש מעבדו אינו רשאי לשעבדו
וצריך לו גט שחרור שמע רבי יוחנן ואמר יפה למדנו רבי ישוע בן לוי כלום
למדו גט שחרור אלא מאשה מה אשה אינה יוצאת משום יאוש וצריכה ממנו
גט אף עבד אינו יוצא משום יאוש וצריך לכתוב לו גט שחרור רבי איל בשם
רבי יהודה · · · המתיאש מעבדו אינו רשאי לשעבדו ואינו צריך לכתוב
לו גט שחרור אמר ליה רבי זעירא כל עמא אמרין דהוא צריך ותימר אינו.
צריך שמא אינו מעכבו מלאבול בפסח (חדושי הרשבא גיטין) Thus Rabbi
Zeira's statement was *not* a retort what Rabbi Jochanan said המפקיר
את עבדו אינו רשאי לשעבדו ואינו רשאי לכתוב לו גט שחרור but to the
statement given in the name of Rabbi Judah המתיאש מעבדו אינו רשאי
לשעבדו ואינו צריך לכתוב לו גט שחרור "An owner who has abandoned
his rights המתיאש over his slave is not allowed to hold him as a slave
and does not need to give him a writ of manumission." To this Rabbi
zeira retorted that all say דהוא צריך that the owner needs to give his
slave a writ of manumission "and you said that he does not need it."
The text quoted by Iben Adret is the correct one while the text which
we have in in the Palestinian Talmud is faulty--there is a lacuna.
Fortunately Iben Adret supplied the full text.

Prof. Urbach, his article on slavery, *Zion*, 1960, p. 173 n. 150,
wrote, ודברי ש׳ צייטלין, הפקר ויאוש בסה״י לכבוד ל׳ גינצבורג עמ׳
שע״ב הע׳ 33 אין להם ימוד. He does not explain why there is no "basis"
for my statement. It seems that he did not fully comprehend the text
of the PalestinianTalmud. Furthermore he did not grasp the distinction
between the word רשאי and the word צריך. There is a vast difference
in the implications of these two terms. Again he did note that Rabbi
Jochanan is quoted differently in the Babylonian Talmud and the
Palestinian Talmud. The Babylonian text reads as follows, אמר עולא
אמר רבי יוחנן המפקיר את עבדו יצא לחירות וצריך גט שחרור, while that
in the Palestinian Talmud is רבי אבהו בשם רבי יוחנן אמר המפקיר את
עבדו אינו רשאי לשעבדו ואינו רשאי לכתוב לו גט שחרור.
Prof. Urbach wrote further הרשב״א אומר במפורש ׳ורב ורבי יוחנן
דאמרו צריך גט שחרור״ ואין הוא מעיד על נוסח שונה בירושלמי.
It is well known that when there was a difference in text between

res nullius without an owner. This is in accordance with
Roman law. [95] I believe that the Palestinian Talmud has the
correct version. Hence there are three views with regard to a
slave whose owner made him *hefker*. According to Rabbi
Jochanan the slave is *hefker* and the owner does not possess
the right to give him a writ of manumission. [96] According to
Rab he is *hefker* but needs a writ of manumission. [97] According to Samuel the owner in declaring his slave *hefker* has
made him free and he needs no writ of manumission. [98]
Though these controversies are between Amoraim, their
views are based on the tannaitic principles which prevailed in
Judaea. Rabbi Jochanan followed the customs which prevailed in Judaea while Rab and Samuel followed the Babylonian customs.

According to tannaitic law a man may lose his rights to a
property even without bequeathing it or relinquishing
it,—he did not declare his property to be *hefker*—but lost it
or it was stolen or robbed from him; if he is reconciled to the
fact that he will never get it back; then the person who found
the property or the thief or robber acquires the property. [99]
The thief or robber has to recompense the value of the property
but not return it. In The Talmud it is classified under the
principle of יאוש. The principle of יאוש was applicable only to
movable property, not to immovable. [100] It was not applicable to land. There was a difference of opinion as to whether
the principle of יאוש was applicable to slaves. If a slave was
robbed and was advanced in age his value diminished. According to an opinion of the Tannaim the robber has to recompense the owner for the value of the slave at the time that

the Palestinian and the Babylonian Talmuds the rabbis of the Middle
Ages followed the latter and ignored the former.

[95] Rudolp Sohm, *The Institutes of Roman Law*, p. 173.
[96] See note 94.
[97] Git. 38. אמר רב המפקיר עבדו יצא לחירות וצריך גט שחרור•
[98] See note 92.
[99] Cf. M. Kelim, 26, 8; S. Zeitlin, *op. cit.* p. 12.
[100] B.K. 117; Yer. ibid. 10, 6.

he was forcibly removed because the robber had acquired the slave who aged while in the robbers possession. Rabbi Meir, however, held that the robber returns the slave although he is of lesser value than when he was forcibly taken. [101] Rabbi Meir was of the opinion that the slave always belonged to the master and never belonged to the robber.

If a slave ran away and his owner was reconciled to the loss and the slave later returned, the master lost his right over him. However a runaway remained in the status of a slave and could attain his freedom only by a writ of manumission from his master. [102] Similarly if a slave was imprisoned or in captivity and escaped, the master no longer has any rights over him because he became reconciled to the loss. The runaway is still in the status of a slave and could attain his freedom only if his master gave him a writ of manumission. [103]

The Mishne states that when a slave was taken captive and was ransomed—he remained a slave and had to serve if he was ransomed as a slave ; however, he does not serve as a slave if he was ransomed as a free man. Rabban Simon ben Gamaliel was of the opinion that in either case he had to serve. [104] The Mishne is ambiguous äs to to whom he had to serve— the first master or the second who ransomed him. Most of the authorities of the Middle Ages held that the word ישתעבד referred to the first master. [105] Elsewhere I pointed out that the word ישתעבד refers to the second master. [106] This Mishne refers to the master who was reconciled to the loss when his slave was taken captive and therefore he had no right to hold him as a slave, though the slave was still under his domain.

[101] M. B.K. 9, 2. גזל בהמה והזקינה עבדים והזקינו משלם כשעת הגזילה רבי מאיר אומר אומר לו בעבדים הרי שלך לפניך.

[102] Git. 39; Yer. ibid. 4, 4.

[103] Ibid. 38.

[104] M.Git. 4, 4. עבד שנשבה ופדאהו לשם עבד ישתעבד לשם בן חורין לא ישתעבד רבן שמעון בן גמליאל אומר בין כך ובין כך ישתעבד.

[105] בין כך ובין כך ישתעבד לרבו הראשון.

[106] הפקר ויאוש .

The Tosefta refers to the same case but elaborates on it. [107] In the case of a slave taken into captivity and later ransomed—if he was ransomed as a slave he had to serve and his master, i.e., the first one, had to recompenses the man who ransomed him and to free the slave. But if the slave was ransomed as a free man the man who ransomed him could not keep him as a slave. However he remained in the status of a slave and his former master freed him without recompensing the ransomer. Simon ben Gamaliel was of the opinion that in either event the ransomer had the right to keep the slave as such and that the former master frees him and recompensed the ransomer. He explained that it is a mitzvah to ransom a free man as well as a slave. [108]

According to tannaitic law a slave obtains his freedom when his master gives him a writ of manumission. [109] Also if a master

[107] עבד שנשבה ופדאהו אם לשם עבד ישתעבד ורבו נותן את דמיו אם לשם חירות לא ישתעבד ואין רבו נותן דמי רבן שמעון בן גמליאל אומר בין כך ובין כך [לא] ישתעבד ורבו נותן דמיו כשם שישראל מצווין לפדות בני חורין כך מצווין לפדות עבדים·

[108] Prof. Urbach in his article, n. 179, followed the general view that referred to the first master. נסיונו של ש·צייטלין, הפקר ויאוש, ס·היובל לכבוד לוי גינצברג, עמ' שע''ט העי 60 להוכיח דווקא מן התוספתא ש''בין כך וכך משמע דווקא דווקא לרבו השני ולא לרבו הראשון'' אין לו על מה שיסמוך והוא מנוגד לפשוטה של התוספתא וכבר נדחה על ידי אלבק·
Although he supports his view on Albek we must reject it. As I have pointed out in my article n. 60, the word ישתעבד refers to the second master. This is evident from other statements in the Talmud. If the owner abandoned התיאש is reconciled to the loss of his slave, he can no longer hold him as a slave. Thus if a slave escaped from prison the master no longer had rights over him. Similarly, if a slave escaped from captivity the master could no longer hold him as a slave. Thus if a slave was taken in captivity and was ransomed by another man the Mishne stated ישתעבד he has to serve; this could refer only to the second master, since we assume that the first master is reconciled to his loss. The first master may recompense the man who ransomed the slave and set him free. However if the person who ransomed the slave for the purpose of freeing him, then the ransomer has no right to hold him as a slave, and the first master does not need to recompense him. Cf. also Yer. Git. 4, 4. אמר רבי יוחנן אין לך משחרר אלא רבו רבו הראשון· ומה שאמר לשם עבד ישתעבד הוי פירש לרבו שני (רשד''ם יורה דעה קצד)
[109] Git. 20.; M. ibid. 1, 4; Yer. ibid.

makes a will leaving his entire estate to his slave by this a slave attains his freedom. [110] If a slave marries an Israelite with the consent of his master it was considered an act of manumission. [111] If a master had made a writ of manumission and asked that it be given to his slave and the master died before it was delivered the slave was not manumitted because there was a possibility that the master had retracted. [112]

When a gentile slave received manumission he could marry an Israelite but his status was not on a par with a proselyte.[113] The priests who were scrupulous as to pedigree did not regard a manumitted slave as the equal of an Israelite. It is related in a Mishne that once when Tobiah, the physician, together with his son and his manumitted slave witnessed the birth of the new moon the priests disqualified the manumitted slave as a witness but the *Bet Din* disqualified the son from giving testimony and accepted the testimony os the manumitted slave. [114] The testimony regarding the birth of the new moon was only a ceremonial. The *Bet Din* knew the precise time of the birth of the new moon. The institution of testifying about the birth of the new moon was introduced in the early days of the Second Commonwealth when the calendar was changed from a solar to a lunar-solar. It was for the purpose of combatting the strong opposition against the change. [115]

To sum up— in this essay it was demonstrated that slavery existed in Judaea during the Second Commonwealth and the tannaitic period. The sages like the Stoics did not condemn the institution but endeavored to ameliorate the condition of the slaves by improving their status. They strove to impress the people that slaves are human beings and should

[110] M. Pea 3, 8.
[111] Git. 40.
[112] M. Git. 1, 5. Cf. however ibid. האומר תן גט זה לאשתי ושטר שיחרור זה לעבדי אם רצה להחזיר בשניהן יחזיר דברי רבי מאיר וחכמים אומרים בגיטי נשים אבל לא בשיחרורי עבדים.
[113] Cf. M. Git. 4, 5; Tosefta Kid. 5, 3; 13. Cf. ibid. 4, 14.
[114] M.R.H. 1, 7.
[115] S. Zeitlin, *The Rise and Fall of the Judaean State*, pp. 222-3.

be treated humanely. The sages were opposed to the sale of Judaean slaves outside of Judaea and to foreigners and favored the manumission of gentile slaves.

In this essay I have differed not only from my predecessors who wrote on slavery but have also deviated from the commentators and even from the amoraic interpretations. I hold that for the history of the Second Commonwealth and the tannaitic period the primary source is the tannaitic literature. We must analyze the tannaitic literature both critico-historically and independently of the interjection of the amoraic interpretation. The Amoraim injected their views in the tannaitic halakot as the Tannaim injected their views in the Pentateuch.

MAR SAMUEL AND MANUMISSION OF SLAVES

IN MY ARTICLE ON SLAVERY (*JQR*, January, 1963) I maintained that Rabbi Akiba held that a Jew may not keep an uncircumcised slave, as he would prevent him from eating the paschal lamb. I rejected the generally accepted view that he meant by the word חובה obligatory, that a master must keep a pagan slave in slavery forever. I suggested that the controversy between Rabbi Ishmael and Rabbi Akiba did not refer to the manumission of a pagan slave but to the sale. Rabbi Ishmael held that a Jew had the option to sell his uncircumcised slave. This is in accordance with his view that a pagan slave does not interfere with the life of his owner, it does not prevent his owner from eating the paschal lamb. On the other hand Rabbi Akiba held he must sell his uncircumcised slave because his master was prevented from partaking of the paschal lamb. I may further suggest that Rabbi Akiba's statement חובה obligatory, meant that he held that a Jew is bound to manumit his uncircumcised slave because he interferes with his master's religious right. I wrote that the words לעולם בהם תעבדו "You may take your bondman forever" were added later. For any reading in the Talmud, no matter how faulty it may be, explanation is required as to how this reading was inserted.

The Talmud states that Rab Judah said in the name of Samuel that a Jew who manumits a pagan slave transgresses a pentateuchal precept. (אמר רב יהודה אמר שמואל כל המשחרר עבדו עובר בעשה[1] Samuel could hardly have held such a view; he held that if an owner of a pagan slave relinquishes his rights over the slave and declares him *hefker, res nullius*, the slave becomes free and a rite of manumission is unnecessary.[2] On the other hand, Rab held that though in such a case the slave becomes free a writ of manumission is necessary.[3] If Samuel held that if an owner who frees his pagan slave transgresses a pentateuchal law, how could Samuel hold that if the owner makes his pagan slave *hefker* the slave becomes free and even a writ of manumission is unnecessary? The act of making the slave *hefker, res nullis*

---

[1] Git. 38.
[2] Ibid. דאמר שמואל המפקיר עבדו יצא לחירות ואינו צריך גט שיחרור·
[3] Ibid. אמר רב המפקיר את עבדו יצא לחירות וצריך גט שיחרור·
אמר עולא אמר רבי יוחנן המפקיר את עבדו יצא לחירות וצריך ,ibid 39
אבהו בשם רבי יוחנן אמר המפקיר את עבדו Cf. Yer. ibid. גט שיחרור·
אינו רשאי לשעבדו ואני רשאי לכתוב לו גט שיחרור·

See *JQR*, 1963, pp. 212-214.

is tantamount to freeing him; the owner by so doing does not transgress a pentateuchal law. Hence the two statements contradict each other.

I venture to say that Rab Judah's statement in the name of Samuel, that a master who frees his pagan slave transgresses a pentateuchal law was not made by Samuel. This is not surprising. There are many statements made by Rab Judah in the name of Samuel which the Talmud questions that Samuel ever made. Upon several occasions M'remar, brother of Rab Judah, said that one must not accept the statements of his brother (Rab Judah) which were made in the name of Samuel.[4] The statement of Rab Judah in the name of Samuel that a master who frees his pagan slave transgresses a pentateuchal law was also not made by Samuel. This statement of Rab Judah was expressed as a homily. He did likewise when he said that any one who migrated from Babylon to Eretz Israel transgresses a precept, quoting Jeremiah דאמר רב יהודה כל העולה מבבל לארץ ישראל עובר בעשה (5 שנאמר בבלה יובאו ושמה יהיו עד יום פקדי אותם. "They shall be carried to Babylon and there shall they be, until the day that I remember them said Adonai." Rab Judah did not mean this as halaka. He was opposed for some reason to his students leaving Babylonia for the academies in Eretz Israel. This statement was meant to be sermonic. The words of Jeremiah could not be taken as a precept.

The Talmud does have the statement that Rab Judah made in the name of Samuel, that a master who frees his pagan slave transgresses a pentateuchal precept because it is written שנאמר לעולם בהם תעבדו. The Saboraim expounded and interpreted a great part of the Talmud. Their interpretations and explanations became a part of the Talmud. When the Saboraim had before them Rab Judah's statement in the name of Samuel that if an owner when he frees his pagan slave transgresses a pentateuchal law where it is stated לעולם בהם תעבדו "you may forever enslave them." In the controversy between Rabbi Ishmael and Rabbi Akiba wherein the former said רשות optional, and the latter said חובה obligatory, the Saboraim mistakenly thought that the controversy between Rabbi Ishmael and Rabbi Akiba referred to the manumission of a pagan slave. Rabbi Ishmael was of the opinion that a master may hold a pagan slave forever or he may manumit him. Rabbi Akiba held that it was obligatory for the master to keep the pagan slave forever. The Saboraim having before them Rab Judah's statement based on the pentateuchal words לעולם בהם תעבדו added

---

4 רמי בר יחזקאל אמר לא תצתינהו להני כללי דכייל דכיי אחי משמיה דשמואל · Ket. 2¹.

5 See ibid. 10-111.

the same words to the controversy between Rabbi Ishmael and Rabbi Akiba. Thus these words לעולם בהם תעבדו רשות דברי ר׳ ישמעאל in connection with the controversy between Rabbi Ishmael and Rabbi Akiba are Saboraic. Some of the Saboraic interpretations help in the understanding of intricate passages in the Talmud, others lead to confusion.

THE HALAKA IN THE GOSPELS
AND ITS RELATION TO THE JEWISH
LAW AT THE TIME OF JESUS

SOLOMON ZEITLIN,
Isaac Elchanan Theological Seminary, New York, U. S. A.

Dedicated to my Friend Dr. Louis Ginzberg
on the occasion of His fiftieth Birthday

ALMOST ALL New TESTAMENT students admit, as a matter of course, that a comparative study of Jewish law will lead us to a better understanding of the Halakhas which are discussed by Jesus and the Pharisees, but in their comparative studies none of them lay stress on the evolutionary character and the historical development of the Jewish Halakhas, so as to inquire if these Halakhas as found in the New Testament were in existence among the Jews before or even in the time of Jesus. Such an investigation would certainly result in understanding of the historical value of the New Testament.

A close examination of the Halaka mentioned in the Gospels will show that many of them as e. g., the institution of hand-washing before the meals which, according to the statement in the Gospels, was a subject of controversy between the Pharisees and Jesus, as well as the institution of baptism for proselytes, were not in existence among the Jews at the time of Jesus. Therefore we are constrained thereby to conclude that the statements in the Gospels which allude to these Halakhas and to the institution of baptism for proselytes were not based on written or oral sources but on the customs existing at the time of compilation of the Gospels.

Baptism for proselytes in the Gospels and its origin.

In the New Testament we find evidence of the fact that in the time of the Apostles and even of Jesus, baptism was

262

required in the name of Jesus for such as wished to be admitted into the Christian Community. This can be seen from Mark 16. 16, "He that believeth and is baptised shall be saved"[1] and also Matthew 28. 19 where we find that Jesus instructed his disciples: "Go therefore, make disciples of all the nations, baptizing them into the name of the Father and of the Son, and of the Holy Ghost."[2] In the Acts we find that Philip's converts were baptized (8. 12. 38) and Peter said "Be baptized every one of you in the name of Jesus Christ" (2. 38).[3]

The opinion of almost all New Testament Scholars is that baptism among the Jews had been in vogue long before Jesus, although they admit that it is not mentioned either in the Bible or in the Apocrypha, and that Philo and Josephus are silent on the subject. They nevertheless contend that baptism among the Jews as initiation of proselytes existed before Jesus' time, since from the beginning of Christianity the Jews were hostile to the new sect, and we can hardly conceive of their adopting that institution from them.[4] It appears to me that although it is evident that the Jews would not have borrowed any institution of this character from the new Christian sect, upon whom they looked as heretics, nevertheless this alone does not suffice to show that the Jews had baptism for proselytes before the advent of Jesus, for, upon historical investigation of the Talmudic passages bearing on this subject and a full investigation of the origin of this institution, we shall find that the Jews did not adopt it until shortly before the destruction of the second Temple.

---

[1] Ὁ πιστεύσας καὶ βαπτισθεὶς σωθήσεται.

[2] Βαπτίζοντες αὐτοὺς εἰς τὸ ὄνομα τοῦ Πατρὸς καὶ τοῦ υἱοῦ καὶ τοῦ ἀγίου Πνεύματος. On the text, see Allen, l. c. (The International critical Commentary). Comp. Conybeare, ZNTW (1901) 275.

[3] Comp. Acts 10. 48; 19. 5. Baptism itself was no longer a simple sign of purity or repentance, as it was in the time of John the Baptist; it was now a public confession of faith in the name of Jesus Christ.

[4] See Edersheim, *The Life and Time of Jesus*, Ap. 12. Schürer, *Geschichte des jüdischen Volkes*, III. 131. M. Schneckenburger, "Über das Alter der jüdischen Proselytentaufe", Berlin, 1828; see also E. Bengel, *Über das Alter der jüdischen Proselytentaufe*, Tübingen, 1814. Comp. also Harnack, *Hist. of Dogma* I. 79.

As we noticed before, all the scholars admit that no trace of baptism for proselytes is found in the Bible or in the Apocrypha, Philo or Josephus,[5] yet they claim that the argument of silence is not strong enough, as no occasion for mention thereof presented itself.—But Josephus, it would appear to us, had, occasion to mention baptism of proselytes had it really existed among the Jews.

We refer to his account of the conversion of Izates, King of Adiabene, when Eleazar reproached the king for not being circumcised, and he felt compelled to undergo this rite, though he incurred danger from his family and his nation. Had baptism at this time been required, Josephus would not be silent on this point.[6]

In my opinion, in the time of the Second Commonwealth until shortly before the destruction of the Temple, baptism was not required for entry of any Gentile into the Jewish community.

We, indeed, find passages in the Bible relating to the rite of baptism, but as admitted by all scholars, these have reference to persons who wished to be purified from sin and from uncleanliness. Baptism, as we know, was practiced also among the Essenes and the טובלי שחרית, but we cannot in all Tannaitic literature find any trace of baptism for those who wished to enter into Jewish communities until shortly before the destruction of the Temple. The Rabbis of the Talmud sometimes ascribe antiquity to baptism by referring it to Pharaoh's daughter[7] or to Jacob or to Moses,[8] but admittedly without historical foundation.

We do find a controversy about baptism between the Schools of Shammai and Hillel,[9] but these schools existed for more than a century and lasted some time after the destruction of the Temple. We will show that this controversy belongs

---

5 See Schneckenburger, ibid. Edersheim, ibid. Schürer, ibid.

6 *Ant.* XX. 2.4. Comp. also Schneckenburger, ibid. pp. 113—116.

7 T. *Sotah* 12b.

8 *Ker.* 9a.

9 נר שנתגייר בערב פסח ב"ש אומרים טובל ואוכל את פסחו לערב וב"ה אומרים הפורש מן הערלה כפורש מן הקבר, *Pes.* VIII.

to a later period.[10] It has been noted that baptism for proselytes is mentioned in the *Sibyllino Oracles* (B. IV)[11] and also in Arrian's writings we find the statement that baptism was demanded of proselytes.[12] These writings, however, are known to belong to the Second Century and hence prove nothing for the time of Jesus.

Some of the New Testament Scholars, who have rejected the antiquity of proselyte baptism, have contended that the Jews naturally required baptism from a convert, who had never undergone Levitical purification, and they argue thus: If a Jew was frequently to bathe to attain ceremonial purity, a Gentile, whose whole life up to that moment had been lived in pollution, upon becoming a proselyte would be in greater need of it.[13] This, however, does not hold good; for, we know that in early times of the Tannaim, the Gentiles in this regard were held to be *unsusceptible* of impurity, and were never subjected to the laws of טומאה וטהרה. Many statements to this effect are found in the Tannaitic literature, such as, Gentiles are not susceptible of impurity הבהמה והגוים אין מקבלים טומאה[14] also, Gentiles who are affected by leprosy do not impart impurity.[15] Therefore, a Gentile not being considered unclean was not

---

[10] See below note 19.

[11] 'Εν ποταμοῖς λούσασθε ὅλον δέμος ἀενάισι.

[12] Ὅταν τινὰ ἐπαμφοτερίζοντα εἴδωμεν, εἰώθαμεν λελειν οὐχ ἔστιν 'Ιουδαῖος ἀλλ' ὑποχρίνεται ὅταν δ' ἀναλάβῃ τὸ πάθος τὸ τοῦ βεβαμμένου καὶ ἠρημένου, τότε καὶ ἔστι τῷ ὄντι καὶ καλεῖται 'Ιουδαῖος. Arrian, *Disert. Epic.* II. 9.

[13] Edersheim, ibid. Schürer, ibid. Marcus Dods, *Dict. of Christ and the Gospels*, Art. *Baptism*. A. Plummer, "Dict. of the Bible", Art. *Baptism*, about the literature on Baptism for Proselytes, see Schürer, ibid. Tertullian also tells was that the Jews had to bathe often (every day) to attain purity, "Judaeus quotidie lavat, quia quotidie inquinatur". De Bapt. XV. The statement of Tertullian has no value for the time of Jesus, as Tertullian lived in the second century (155—222 C. E.). If is true for his own time when in consequence of the 18 measures which were promulgated shortly before the destruction of the Temple, the Jews owing to the fact that almost every object was considered unclean had to bathe frequently in order to attain purity.

[14] *Neg.* VII. 10.

[15] Ibid. II. 14, טהור . . . בהרת בגוי עד שלא נתגייר ואחר כך נתגייר.
Tosefto ohalot, I. 4, תגוי והבהמה הנוגעים במת . . . . כלים הנוגעים בהם טהורין.

obliged to receive baptism on becoming a proselyte; as a matter of fact, he was regarded as a new-born child.[16] גר שנתגייר כילד שנולד דמי.

Only in the time of the great revolution against the Roman domination in the end of the year 65 C. E. when the Jewish national spirit was awakened, the influence of the School of Shammai, favorable to the promoting of organized resistance, and therefore prevailing at that period, tended to dissever Jews from all Gentile connections.[17] Among other measures designed for this purpose, they made the pronouncement that all Gentiles are *ipso facto* unclean [18] כזבין לכל דבריהם and on this basis they prohibited all the Jews to associate with them. In consequence of these pronouncements, any Gentile now being regarded *ipso facto* unclean, baptism become a *sine qua non* for entering into the Jewish Community. Baptism for proselytes was therefore introduced into Jewish law after the assembly which adopted the 18 measures. All the controversies about baptism for proselytes are later than this period.[19]

הגוים והגור התושב אינן ממטאין בויבה Zabhim II. 1 ומהרתם אתם ושביכם מה אתם בני ברית מקבלים הזייה אף השבויה כשתבוא לברית ותטמא מקבלת הזייה.

Siphre Zutta (ed. H. Horwitz) XXXI. 19. Comp. ibid. XIX. 10. Comp. also the statement of the Talmud, יצא כותי [נוי] שאין לו טומאה. *Naz.* 61b.

[16] *Yeb.* 22a passim.

[17] See S. Zeitlin, "Les dix-huit mesures", RÉJ (1914) 22—29. Also idem, *Meg. Täʿän.* as a source for Jewish chronology and history in the Hellenistic and Roman periods, p. 108, note 286.

[18] *Tos. Zab.* II. 1, see also S. Zeitlin, "Les dix-huit mesures", RÉJ 1914.

[19] גר שנתגייר בערב פסח בית שמאי אומרים טובל ואוכל פסחו לערב   ובית הלל אומרים הפורש מן הערלה כפורש מן הקבר. *Pes.* VIII.

The School of Shammai held that a Gentile circumcised and baptised on the 14th of Nisan could on the following evening eat the Paschal Lamb, while the School of Hillel was of the opinion that he had to wait seven days. The underlying motives of these schools were as follows:

The Hillelites, carrying out the principle of עשו סינלתורה, "make a fence around the law", took cognizance of human nature. A Gentile who on the 14th of Nisan had taken his ritual bath and who in his state of paganism might have defiled himself by touching a corpse, if he were allowed, according to the law, to eat the Paschal Lamb that same evening, he might think on some other occasion, after touching a corpse that he would not have to wait the seven days required by law; thus by eating the Paschal Lamb in impurity

As any Jew who was unclean in the degree of a זב was obliged after purification to bring a sacrifice,[20] so the Gentile who was declared unclean in the degree of a זב and wished to become a Jew, after being baptized, had to bring also a sacrifice.[21] As a result of the above-mentioned pronouncement he was regarded as unclean and, as a *sine qua non,* had to be baptized and also to offer a sacrifice after undergoing such purification. Some Rabbis of the Talmud misunderstood the reason of baptism and sacrifice for the proselytes and were led to consider as indispensable essentials for proselytes-circumcision, baptism, and sacrifice.[22] The Rabbis have been followed in this by modern Talmudists as well as by New Testament Scholars; the reason for baptism having gradually become unknown was that it had been put on a par with circumcision as a symbol.[23]

As we said above, it is generally admitted that the institution of baptism for proselytes was adopted from the Jews by the early Christians. This could have taken place only after the

he would incur excision. The Hillelites thought fit, in consequence of the principle of "make a fence around the law" עשו סיג לתורה and determined that he must wait seven days. Although when he was a Gentile he was not susceptible of Levitical impurity, but only upon the adoption of the Eighteen Measures, he *qua* Gentile, being acknowledged as unclean, in the degree required one day for purification. The School of Shammai, holding the principle, "Let the strict Law prevail". יקוב הדין את ההר were of the opinion that if a Gentile is baptized on the 14th of Nisan he may eat on that very evening of the Paschal Lamb. In future years if he should touch a corpse, he would have to wait seven days as would any Jew in the same manner. Compare *Pes.* 92a and *Jer.* ibid. 36 b, about the principles of the School of Shammai and Hillel, see Schwartz, "Die Controversen der Schamaiten and Hilleliten", Vienna, 1893, and S. Zeitlin, "the Semikah Controversy Between the Zugoth", JQR VII. 511—517.

[20] Lev. 15. 14.

[21] *Tos. Šek.* III, *Ker.* 98 b. It is interesting to note that the sacrifice which the proselytes had to bring, was the same as that which the Jews had to bring after purification from the uncleanliness of a זב.

[22] *Ker.* 9 א.

[23] In the first generation after the destruction of the Temple, we find a dispute between Eliezer and Joshua as to circumcision and baptism "which is sufficient"? גר שמל ולא טבל טבל ולא מל רבי אליעזר אומר הרי זה גר .... טבל ולא מל רבי *Yeb* 45 .... יהושע אומר הרי זה גר.

Introduction of the 18 measures in the end of the year 65 C.E. when all Gentiles were delared *ipso facto* unclean and so baptism for the proselytes became *sine qua non*.

Now, as we have come to an understanding cf the origin of baptism, we are bound to conclude that all passages in the New Testament referring to baptism in the name of Jesus and the instruction of Jesus to the disciples "Teach all nations, baptizing them in the name of the Father and of the Son and of the Holy Ghost", as well as the narrative of the author of the Acts that Philip's converts were baptized cannot refer to the time of Jesus or to the time of Peter and Paul (Apostolic age), when baptism for proselytes was not required or thought of.

THE INSTITUTION OF WASHING THE HANDS IN THE GOSPELS

From the Gospels we learn Jesus had a controversy with the Pharisees about washing of hands before meals. According to Mark: "And when they saw some of his disciples eat bread with defiled (common) that is to say, with unwashen hands, (they found fault). For the Pharisees and all the Jews, except they wash their hands oft, eat not, holding the tradition of the elders. And when they come from the market, except they wash, they eat not. And many other things there be, which they have received to hold, as the washing of cups and pots, brazen vessels and of tables. Then the Pharisees and scribes asked him, 'Why walk not thy disciples according to the tradition of the elders, but eat bread with unwashen hands?' He answered and said unto them, 'Well hath Esaias prophesied of you hypocrites, as it is written, this people honoureth me with their lips, but their heart is far from me! . . For laying aside the commandment of God, ye hold the tradition of men, as the washing of pots and cups; and many other such like things ye do'." [24]

[24] Καὶ ἰδόντες τινὰς τῶν μαθητῶν αὐτοῦ κοιναῖς χερσί, τουτ' ἔστιν ἀνίπτους, ἐσθίοντας [ἐσθίουσιν] (τοὺς) ἄρτους (ἐμέμψαντο). Οἱ γὰρ Φαρισαῖοι

All the students of the New Testament as well as of rabbinics have taken as a matter of course that the Pharisees and all the Jews of the time of Jesus had already adopted the institution of hand-washing before meals. According to some of the students of the New Testament, Jesus, in attacking this institution, was assailing the very stronghold of Pharisaism and Judaism of that time.[25] It seems to me that the students of the New Testament, in dealing with this passage, have followed blindly some of the Jewish scholars who had no historical understanding of this institution. The expression טומאת ידים and נטילת ידים in the *Talmud* have been considered interchangeable, owing to misconception of the whole subject on the part of some of the later Rabbis. This can be seen from the *Talmud Šab.* 14b, where it is stated that the schools of Shammai and Hillel, when they accepted the eighteen measures, included among them that hands are defiled. The Amoraim were perplexed, by this decree because according to their opinion it was instituted by Shammai and Hillel; and according to the understanding of some Rabbis, Solomon had already declared that hands are defiled.[26] We see that in their opinion, טומאת ידים of the eighteen measures is one and the same as נטילת ידים which is ascribed

---

καὶ πάντες οἱ Ἰουδαῖοι ἐὰν μὴ πυγμῇ νίψωνται τὰς χεῖρας οὐκ ἐσθίουσι, κρατοῦντες τὴν παράδοσιν τῶν πρεσβυτέρων. Καὶ (ἐρχόμενοι) ἀπὸ ἀγορᾶς ἐὰν μὴ βαπτίσωνται, οὐκ ἐσθίουσι καὶ ἄλλα πολλά ἐστὶν ἃ παρέλαβον κρατεῖν βαπτισμοὺς ποτηρίων, καὶ ξεστῶν, καὶ χαλκίων (καὶ κλινεῶ) Ἔπειτα (καὶ) ἐπερωτῶσιν αὐτὸν οἱ Φαρισαῖοι καὶ οἱ γραμματεῖς. Διατί οἱ μαθηταί σου οὐ τεριπτοῦσιν κατὰ τὴν παράδοσιν, τῶν πρεσβυτέρων ἀλλὰ ἀνίπτοις (κοιναῖς) χερσὶν ἐσθίουσι τὸν ἄρτον. Ὁ δὲ (ἀποκριθείς), εἶπεν οὗτοῖς ὅτι καλῶς [καλω] προεφήτευσεν Ἡσαῖας περὶ ὑμῶν τῶν ὑποκριτῶν ὡς γέγραπται ὅτι ὁ λαὸς οὗτος χείλεσί με τιμᾷ ἡ δὲ καρδία αὐτῶν πόρρω ἀπέχει ἀπ' ἐμοῦ ......
Ἀφέντες (γὰρ) τὴν ἐντολὴν τοῦ Θεοῦ, κρατεῖτε τὴν παράδοσιν τῶν ἀνθρώπων, καὶ βαπτισμοὺς ξεστῶν ἀποτηρίων ἃ ἄλλα παρόμοια τοιαῦτα πολλὰ ποιεῖτε. Mark 7. 2–8, comp. Matthew 15.2 according to Luke 11. 37–39, Jesus himself ate without washing the hands before.

25 Compare Edersheim, *The Life at the Time of Jesus*, Ch. XXXI, and the literature there quoted. Even the radical theologians and historians who contested the historical value of the Gospels never had investigated historically the Halakas which are reported in the New Testament.

26 ‏ידים תלמידי שמאי והלל נזור‎ ‏שמאי והלל נזור‎ . . . . ‏ואכתי שלמה נזור דא"ר‎
Šab. 14 b. ‏והודה אמר שמואל בשעה שתיקן שלמה עירובין ונטילת ידים‎.

to Solomon, and this confusion between טומאת ידים and נטילת ידים produced the general misunderstanding among scholars as to the institution of washing the hands.

In reality, they have no connection, owing to the fact that טומאת ידים is a גזרה whereas נטילת ידים is a תקנה. Every Talmudist realizes the great distinction between גזרה and תקנה.

A *Taḳḳana* has for its purpose to amend the law or to modify it when the need is felt of harmonizing religion and life, through a fiction (e. g.; *Taḳḳana* of *'Eruḇîn*) or inter-pretation of the Biblical law (e. g.; טבילה לבעל קרי), of Tradition, or Common Law, such as is seen in most of the *Taḳḳanôt* of Ezra and other *Taḳḳanôt* found in Tannaitic literature,[27] though some of them at first sight, may not seem susceptible to such analysis, through the historic facts being unknown. A גזרה, however, is a decree of the Sages, absolutely independent of and unconnected with any law in Bible or Tradition, but which they found necessary to enact, and at times it is intended to remain in force for a certain period.

I shall, however, demonstrate that the institution of נטילת ידים had no connection with the decree: טומאת ידים, one of the eighteen measures, and then it will be evident that in the time of Jesus, this institution was not in existence.

DECREE OF DEFILEMENT OF HANDS

The decree of defilement of hands טומאת ידים, issued in the famous gathering of the schools of Shammai and Hillel, as one of the גזרות, was directed against the priests, as well as ספר, וטבול יום, as I have shown elsewhere.[28]

The *Mishna* in *Ḥag.* II. 8, tells us that after every holiday all the vessels in the 'Azara were dipped into water.[29] The priests said to the worshippers: Be careful not to touch the vessels, as they cannot be readily dipped, e. g. golden altar, or the candelabra.[30] But the Pharisees, who were opposed to

[27] See S. Zeitlin, *Taḳḳanôt Ezra*, JQR.
[28] Ibid. idem, *Les dix-huit mesures*, REJ (1914).
[29] Ḥag. III. 7. משעבר הרגל (היו) מעבירין על טהרת עזרה.
[30] Ibid. III. 8. ואמרין להם הזהרו שלא תגעו בשלחן [ובמנורה].

distinctions between the priests and ordinary Israelites, insisted that even vessels touched by priests required such purification, that is the significance of their pronouncement as to "hands", namely, that in the sanctuary, priests' hands are unclean as the hands of others. Once, indeed, according to the *Talmud* they purified the golden candelabrum (מנורה)[31] to carry out their principle. The Sadduccees then perpetrated the jest: It will soon come to their purifying the disk of the sun.[32] Their idea in purifying the Menorah was not, as the scholars think, to be overstrict,[33] but simply to protest against the teaching of the priests (mostly Sadduccees) and place them on the same footing as the masses. This decree was approved of by both Shammai and Hillel, but was not adopted in practice by reason of the fact that most of the high priests were Saducean. After the defeat of Cestius, when the power was restored to the Sanhedrin, and on the gathering of the כנישתא a platform was adopted for war against the Romans, and in Opposition to the Sadduccees,[34] the decree of defilement of hands of the priests in the sanctuary was confirmed, and that is the meaning of the decree that hands are defiled.

A *Mishna* in *'Eduyyôt* reads: "In case a needle was found in meat, the knife and the hands were clean, while the meat was considered defiled. If, on the other hand, it is found in the dung, everything is clean.[35] In the *Talmud* there is appended to this Rabbi Akiba's amendment. Rabbi Akiba says, "We prove our point that there is no defilement of hands in the sanctuary".[36] This statement of R. Akiba's was incomprehensible to the Amoraim; they asked, why does he state only, no defilement of the hands in the sanctuary on the basis of the Mishna? He should have included vessels, since the knife also

---

[31] Jer. Ḥag. III, p. 79 d פעם אחת הטבילו את המנורה.

[32] Ibid. אמרו צדוקים ראו פרושים מטבילין גלגל חמה (מאור הלבנה).

[33] Graetz, *Geschichte der Juden* III, note 12. Derenbourg, *Histoire de la Palestine*, 133.

[34] See Graetz, *Geschichte* III. S. Zeitlin, *Les dix-huit measures*, RÉJ (1914).

[35] מחט שנמצאת בבשר שהסכין והידים טהורות והבשר טמא נמצא בפרש הכל טהור *'Eday.* II. 3.

[36] *Pes.* 19 a. אמר ר' עקיבא זכינו שאין טומאת ידים במקדש.

is declared clean.[37] From the reasons assigned by them it is evident that the purpose of R. Akiba's statment was unknown to the Rabbis. Aside of the difficulty experienced by the Amoraim, it is hard to understand the statement: "We have proven our point". Where do we find, before Akiba's time, anyone declaring that hands in the sanctuary are unclean? The whole subject of טומאת ידים presents difficulties. If the hands have touched any טומאה is not the whole body as well as these members defiled?

The *Mishna* must in my opinion be amended to read: המחט שנמצאת בבשר שהסכין טהור והבשר טמא . . . אמר ר' עקיבא וכינו שאין טומאת ידים במקדש. "In case a needle was found in the meat, the knife was clean, while the meat was considered defiled." Now we can understand Akiba's point. The meat was unclean, because of the needle, the knife is clean since hands do not defile. As before stated, Shammai and Hillel declared hands defile every vessel in the sanctuary. From this *Mishna* declaring the knife clean, Akiba deduces that the hands are not defiled in the sanctuary, for, did not the hand hold the knife?

Later, some compilers of the *Talmud*, having no conception of historic background to the decrees of the schools of Shammai and Hillel *in re* defilement of hands, having before them the statement of Akiba זכינו שאין טומאת ידים במקדש, they mistakenly inserted ידים so as to read הסכין והידים מהורות and this impelled later Rabbis to ask, "Why doesn't Akiba refer to vessels as well?" Through their unfamiliarity with the underlying historical reasons they concluded that hands as such may be defiled without defilement of the body, and sought for explanations.

This idea of hands being defiled without the rest of the body, we cannot, I am convinced find in early Tannaitic sources, before the adoption of the eighteen decrees. We do find that before entering the sanctuary the priest had to bathe his hands and feet,[38] this was called in the *Talmud* קדוש ידים ורגלים. The

---

[37] Ibid. 19b ונימא שאין טומאת ידים וכלים במקדש.

[38] *Ex.* 21. 18-21.

custom prevailed among many nations, in entering their sanct-
uaries.[39]

The defilement of hands as distinct from the rest of the
body is intimated in the expression "Holy Writings defile the
hands".[40] Among the eighteen measures we find that the Scroll
is to be considered defiling.[41] As I have shown in another
place, the reason for this pronouncement is opposition to the
priestly cast, for the Scroll is but one of the many things
which were declared to defile the *T:rumah*.[42] Later, we find
that all Holy Scriptures defiled the hands. This decree surely
was directed against the Sadduccees, for they are said to have
protested, "Why do the Holy Scriptures defile the hands,
whereas the books of Homer do not"?[43] From this protest
we see that the Sadduccees felt it was directed against them.
The Sadduccees believed in the Written Law alone, while the
Pharisees ascribed authority also to Tradition in order to snatch
away this weapon from their opponents, a large number of
whom were priests. They declared that the Holy Scriptures
defiled the hands so as to render unpermissible the eating of
T:rumah. With a similar object in view they do not allow
reading of Scriptures on Sabbath, until after *Min'ha*. For the
sages felt that when the people were free from work they
should, rather than read the Bible, hear the exposition of the
Law in the Schools.[44]

39 In Egypt, while the ritual required that the priests bathe the whole body
before offering sacrifices, it laid stress on washing the hands. See G. Maspero,
The Dawn of Civilization. Similar custom prevailed in Babylon, when the *barû*
must wash their hands before approaching the gods, or taking part in sacrificial
rites. Maspero ibid. Among the Greeks and Romans it was customary to wash
hands before entering the temple, and a vase full of water stood in the entrance
to the temple. It was customary for the Greeks and Romans to wash their
hands before various magical rites.

40 כתבי הקדש מטמאין את הידים.

41 *Šab.* 13b הספר והידים.

42 S. Zeitlin, *Les dix-huit mesures*, REJ (1914), idem *Täkkonôt* Ezra, JQR
(1917).

43 אומרין צדוקין קובלין אנו עליכם פרושים שאתם אומרים כתבי קודש מטמאין את
Yad. IV. 6. הידים וספרי המירס אין מטמאין.

44 *Šab.* 14 אף על פי שאמרו אין קורין בכתבי הקדש אין קורין בכתבי קדש אלא מן
Jer. *Šab.* 15c. המנחה ולמעלה.

As we have shown the motive of declaring hands to be defiled by the Holy Scriptures, was to disqualify such priests as handled them from touching the Terumah, and hence the priest, Sadduccee, was prevented from reading the Holy Scriptures; for this purpose it sufficed to declare defilement of hands, but in all other cases of defilement by touching a corpse or any minor contamination if the hand was contaminated, the whole body shared that contamination.

THE TÄKKANA OF WASHING THE HANDS BEFORE MEALS AND ITS ORIGIN

According to Talmudic statement, Solomon instituted [45] נטילת ידים. We can hardly believe that this תקנה goes back to the time of Solomon.[46] This institution undoubtedly was of great importance at the time when the Pharisees sought to harmonize the laws with the living conditions, and, therefore, they found it proper to ascribe this just to Solomon, as at other times, it can be shown, important תקנות adopted shortly before the destruction of the Temple were ascribed to Ezra.[47]

The real purport of this תקנה, as we will show, is a modification of the laws of טומאה וטהרה. From the Bible, wo know that בעלקרי or one disqualified by a minor impurity had to leave the town and undergo T:bîlah, and thereafter to wait until evening (after sunset he became clean).[48]

For historical evidence that such was at one time the Jewish law, note what King Saul said when David failed to appear at his father-in-law's table. מקרה לא טהור.[49] The expressions he uses are quite consonant with the obligation of a man suddenly confronted with pollution to leave the city, and

---

[45] Šab. 19b. אמר ר׳ יהודה אמר שמואל בשעה שתיקן שלמה עירובין ונטילת ידים.
[46] In the Talmud Ḥul. 106 is Solomon's name not mentioned with the connection of נטילת ידים. Ḥul. 106a. מאי מצוה מצוה לשמוע דברי ר׳ אליעור בן ערך.
[47] See S. Zeitlin, Täkkonôt Ezra, JQR.
[48] Lev. 15. 16; Deut. 23. 12.
[49] Sam. 20. 24–6.

24

the observance of such a law might not be felt as a hardship or obstacle in such a small kingdom.[50]

However, what was not felt to impede progress in the days of Saul was felt by the Pharisees to be a great hindrance to their desire to bring about agreement between religion and a larger life. By their method of exegesis they explained מחנה (camp) as מחנה שכינה (camp wherein the Š:ḥînah resided); therefore the law of temporary banishment could apply only to the Sanctuary proper, and to the 'Azarah, known also as מחנה לויה camp of the Levite group', and not to the whole city.[51]

Similarly in the matter of sunset. For according to the Torah, mere bathing of the body in water would not have been deemed sufficient to render a person pure, unless the sun had set on him thereafter, and he is called by the *Talmud* טבול יום. The Sages then ordained that, if he had taken the prescribed bath, he was *ipso facto* pure, and relieved of the necessity of waiting until sunset.[52] This תקנה the *Talmud* ascribes to Ezra in these words: הוא תיקן טבילה לבעל קרי, meaning to say, that it is sufficient for him to undergo T:ḅîlah, and he need not leave the city nor wait until sunset.

The law of טבול יום, according to which T:ḅîlah alone does not suffice, but it is necessary to wait for sunset, the Pharisees made, by their decree, apply in cases of T:rumah. If a priest was unclean, he would not only have to undergo T:ḅîlah, but be inhibited from eating T:rumah until night.[53] After the schools

---

50 So Josephus tell us that any one who had gonorrhoe had to leave the city. Ἀπήλασε δὲ τῆς πόλεως καὶ τοὺς λέπρα τὰ σώματα κακωθέντας καὶ τοὺς περὶ τὴν γονὴν ῥεομένους. *Ant.* III. 11. 3.

51 *Pes.* 68a; *Sifre* 255; S. Zeitlin, ibid.

52 *Sifra Š:mini* 8. יטמא עד הערב... מהור לחולין מבעוד יום ולתרומה משתחשך *Tos. Parah* III. 6 מעשר נאכל במבול יום מה ישראל שאינם אוכלים בתרומה במעורבי *Sifra 'Ĕmâr* IV. 1. שמש הרי הן אוכלים במעשר טבולי יום.

53 A I said, after the adoption of the eighteen measures, the priests, as well as the laymen were put into a state of uncleanliness. The Jews, to eat חולין על מהרת הקרש, washing the hands before the meals became a condition *sine qua non*, while for the priests who wish to eat T:rumah, immersion did not suffice, but that setting of the sun was necessary; consequently, T:rumah could not be eaten in the day-time. This makes intelligible the first *Mishna* of

of Shammai and Hillel had adopted the ד"ה ד"ה which put
every Jew in a state of Ritual uncleanliness, life for the
Jews became impracticable. Therefore the Rabbis declared that
it would be sufficient to wash the hands and that טבילה is
unnecessary. This was the purport of the נטילת ידים ascribed
to Solomon, an index of the importance attached thereto.
Eleazer b. Arach, survivor of the destruction of the Temple,
speaks of נטילת ידים as a new institution and declares that
such נט"י ידיו לא שמך במים מכאן, quoting טבילה, quoting מכאן
סמכו לנט"י מן התורה.[54] Some Rabbis were averse to the alleviation
contained in this תקנה, among them Eleazer B. Hanoch who
was excommunicated for non-acceptance of the rabbinical
decree.[55]

We have shown that this תקנה of hand-washing before
meals נטילת ידים is a modification of the laws טומאה וטהרה
and comes after the famous eighteen measures passed by the
Sanhedrin after the victory of Cestius in the end of 65 C. E.
When after the adoption of the eighteen measures, every Jew
was considered in a state of pollution. Consequently to wash
the hands before meals became a condition *sine qua non* for
them. We are constrained thereby to conclude that no institution
of hand-washing before meals was known in the time of
Jesus.[56]

the *Talmud*, as, after asking from what time we are allowed to read שמע, it
says, when the priests begin to eat *T:rumah*: מאמתי קורין את שמע בערבית משעה
שהכהנים נכנסים לאכל בתרומתן. The Amoraim were perplexed, asking why the
Mishna does not in so many words say, "from the appearance of the stars".
But if we say that the Sages decreed that the priests should not eat *T:rumah*
until after sunset, that is, until nightfall, the *Mishna* very clearly indicates to
us when we can read the שמע, when the people as a criterion whereby, the
sun having set, they might know that they could read the שמע. Comp. S. Zeitlin,
Täkkanât Esra, JQR (1917).

54 *Ḥul.* 106 a.

55 .אלא את מי נדו את ר' אלעזר בן חגיד שפפפק בנטילת ידים [בשפפפק במהרת ידים]
Ber. 19 a, comp. *J. M. K.* III. 81 d.

56 That the eighteen measures were adopted shortly before the destruction
of the Temple, is to my opinion beyond doubt, as we find that Rabbi Joshua,
who was a survivor of the destruction of the Temple, calls טבול יום a new
decree, and also his colleague, Rabbi Eleazer b. Arach, speaks of the institution
נטילת ידים, as a new institution. See also S. Zeitlin, *Dix-huit mesures*, REJ (1914).

THE GOSPELS AS WITNESSES OF THE HISTORICITY OF JESUS

The main witnesses of the historicity of Jesus are the Gospels. The statement of Josephus concerning him are not taken seriously by the most conservative scholars;[57] the Talmudic statements are also rejected by many scholars as not having any historical bearing.[58] The data of pagan historians, Suetonius and Tacitus, regarded as proofs of the historicity of Jesus are considered doubtful.[59] Even Paul's epistles have awakened the question, does he speak of a real historical personage or as an idea?[60] The main sources for the historicity of Jesus, therefore, are the Gospels. We find, it is true, discrepancies even in the Synoptic Gospels, but these may readily be explained as due to the variety of sources from which they drew. The many legends about Jesus cannot disprove the historicity, just as the legends about Alexander, Charlemagne, and Washington do not prove these heroes unhistorical. In the Gospels great importance was attached to the primitive Mark and the *Logia* of Matthew and above all to the sayings of Jesus and disputes with the Pharisees which are regarded by scholars so unique and so permeated with personality that none could consider them otherwise than authentic.

Eusebius tells us in the name of Papias (150 C. E.) who gives as his authority John the Presbyter, that Mark never saw Jesus, nor was among his followers, that he met Peter later. According to Papias, Mark was Peter's interpreter and he carefully wrote down all that he heard from Peter and the

---

57 See Schürer, *Gesch. d. jüd. Volkes* I. 544, and the literature there quoted.

58 See Joel, *Blicke in die Religionsgeschichte* II (1883). Lublinski, *Die Entstehung des Christentums aus der antiken Kultur* (1910). Drews, *The Witnesses to the Historicity of Jesus* III. (1912, eng. tr.)

59 Bruno Bauer, *Christmus und die Caesarum* (1879). Drews, *The Christ Myth* (1910, eng. tr.). Norden E., *Josephus and Tacitus*, NJKA (Berlin, 1913).

60 Bruno Bauer, *Kritik der Paulinischen Briefe* (1852). Jensen P., *Hat der Jesus der Evangelien wirklich gelebt?* Reitzenstein, *Die hellenistischen mysteriösen Religionen* (1910). Drews, work quoted.

words of Jesus. He was concerned only to omit nothing that he had heard, or to admit no untruth into his writings . .[61]

We have seen that even the Halakic controversies reported by Mark and the other Gospel writers, which have been considered hitherto as most positive evidence of the historicity of Jesus and which Papias claims the primitive Mark to have derived from Peter's times, had not arisen. Hence it becomes clear that these Halakic references were based neither on written nor on oral sources traceable to Peter, but on customs prevalent in the times of the Gospel-writers. So we are right to assume that even the Gospels have no value as witnesses of the Historicity of Jesus. The question therefore remains: If are there any historical proofs that Jesus of Nazareth ever existed?

---

[61] *Eccl. Hist.* III. 39. Καὶ τοῦθ' ὁ πρεσβύτερος ('Ιωάννον) ἔλεγεν. Μάρκος μὲν ἑρμηνευτὴς Πέτρου γενόμενος, ὅσα ἑμνημόνευσεν, ἀκριβῶς ἔγραψεν, οὐ μέντοι τάξει τὰ ὑπό τοῦ κυρίου ἢ λεχθέντα ἢ πραχθέντα. Οὔτε γὰρ ἤκουσεν τοῦ κυρίου οὔτε παρηκολούθησεν αὐτῷ, ὕστερον δέ, ὡς ἔφην, Πέτρῳ. Ὃς πρὸς τὰς χρείας ἐποιεῖτο τὰσ διδασκαλίας ἀλλ' οὐχ ὥσπερ σύνταξιν τῶν κυριαχῶν ποιούμενος λογίων, ὥστε οὐδὲν ἥμαρτεν Μάρκος οὕτως ἕνια γράψας ὡς ἀπεμνημόνευσεν 'Ενὸς γὰρ ἐποιήσατο πρόνοιαν, τοῦ μηδὲν ὧν ἤκουσεν παραλιπεῖν ἢ ψεύσασθαι τι εν αὐτοῖς. Besides the reference to the origin of the Gospel of Mark, we have in Eusebius also one to the origin of the Gospel of Matthew, and again in the name of Papias: Ματθαῖος μὲν οὖν 'Εβραΐδι διαλέκτῳ τὰ λόγια συνετάξατο, ἡρμήνευσεν δ'αὐτὰ ὡς ἦν δυνατὸς ἕχαστος.

A NEW PALESTINIAN EDITION OF THE MISHNA

THE Harry Fischel Institute of Palestine, which has published some important books in rabbinics, has recently issued another work, *The Mishnah: Berakoth, Peah, Demai*.[1] These three Mishnayot, alongside of the text, are supplied with the commentary of R. Obadiah of Bertinoro. J. D. Herzog has furnished a translation of the text, as well as a commentary in English. Variant readings and notes in Hebrew have also been added.

The general introduction, which is in English, deals with the nature and subject matter of the Oral Law and the redaction of the Mishna. Since the author of this introduction is an orthodox Jew, it is natural that he should cite only the views on the Mishna advanced by those scholars who professed orthodoxy. This procedure is not in accordance with true scholarship. He should have presented to the readers the views of other scholars as well and shown wherein they erred, if they erred at all. The author has presented one side only, and one may question whether even this side is well presented. There are understatements and misstatements; for example, on page iii the author writes as follows: "The Oral Law may be viewed as consisting, in its essence, of the following. In the first place, it contains a number of precepts, both positive and negative, whose title recalls their origin, הלכה למשה מסיני. In these one finds further details in regard to laws set forth in the Pentateuch." However, the expression הלכה למשה מסיני does not apply to the entire Oral Law. As a matter of fact, the Talmud only applies the expression הלכה למשה מסיני to very few Halakot[2] and to

[1] משניות ברכות פאה דמאי, עם פירוש רבינו עובדיה מברטנורה ז"ל, תרגום ומבואות ופירוש חדש באנגלית מאת יעקב דוד הלוי הרצג. הערות נוסחאות וציונים, מאת חברי מכון העֲרי פישל. *The Mishnah Berakoth Peah Demai*, text with commentary of R. Obadiah of Bertinoro. Translation and New Commentary in English by Jacob David Herzog. Variant Readings and Short Exegetical Notes in Hebrew, by Fellows of Harry Fischel Institute, Jerusalem, 5705/1945.

[2] For example, אסר. Yoma 80a; א"ר יוחנן שעורין ועונשין הלכה למשה מסיני. Suk. 34, ר' אסי אמר ר' יוחנן עשר נטיעות ערבה וניסוך המים הלכה למשה מסיני. Comp. also Kid. 38b, ערלה הלכה והכלאים מדברי סופרים, מאי הלכה אמר רב. Comp. יהודה אמר שמואל הילכתא מדינא, עולא אמר ר' יוחנן הלכה למשה מסיני. also B. M. 112b, אמר רב יהודה אמר שמואל הלכות גדולות שנו הני הילכתא נינהו הני תקנות נינהו. (הני הלכה נינהו וכי הילכות למשה מסיני הם, רש"י). Yer. Shab. 3b, באמת הלכה למשה מסיני.

those for which there is no support in the Pentateuch. Again, the
Halakot to which the Talmud refers as הלכה למשה מסיני, are positive
only, not negative. According to the Talmud, during the seven days
of mourning for Moses, thousands of Halakot were forgotten but all of
them are found in the Mishna.[3] The view inherent in the Mishna is
that all the Halakot were really transmitted to Moses. However, the
expression הלכה למשה מסיני does not apply to all of the Oral Law.

Again, on page V, the author writes: "The competent religious
authority to whom the tradition of the original Oral Law and the
machinery for its expansion were entrusted, was the Great Sanhedrin,
the seventy-one foremost masters of the law in Israel who met first in
the sanctuary of pre-Temple days, then in the Temple, and, after the
destruction of the latter, in synods outside Jerusalem. The appointment of the earliest Sanhedrin is recorded in the Pentateuch." According to the author, the Great Sanhedrin, during the Temple period, met
in the Temple, while, in the pre-Temple days, it met in the sanctuary.
Is this history or homiletics? What is the author's authority that the
Great Sanhedrin held its sessions in the sanctuary during the pre-
Temple period? As the term Sanhedrin is of Greek derivation, it could
not be applied to any group which flourished during the pre-Temple
period. Although the Talmud sometimes uses the term Sanhedrin in
connection with the period of Moses, such references are Agadic. ואין
סומכין על אגדה.

Further, in quoting Halevy's theory on the redaction of the Mishna,
the author writes as follows: "For the best illustration of his theory
Halevy points to those Mishnahs, considerable in number, in which
Hillel and Shammai, the first of the Tannaim, appear." Hillel and
Shammai were not Tannaim. The period of Tannaim began after the
destruction of the Temple, while the scholars of the preceding period
were called Soferim, not Tannaim. That the sages before the destruction of the Temple were called Soferim is borne out by many passages
in the Mishna and Tosefta. In the Mishna Yodayim, a controversy is
recorded between Rabbi Joshua and the sages on the defilement of
hands. Rabbi Joshua said to the sages that the Holy Scriptures are
second (i. e. of the second degree in defilement) and render hands un-

---

[3] אמר רב יהודה אמר שמואל שלשת אלפים הלכות נשתכחו בימי אבלו של משה.
אמר ר' זעירא בשם ר' יוחנן אם באת הלכה תחת ידיך ;Tem. 16a; Yer. Pea 17a
ואין אתה יודע מה טיבה אל תפליגנה לדבר אחר שהרי כמה הלכות נאמרו למשה בסיני
וכולהן משוקעות במשנה, ibid. Hag. 76d.

clean. The sages answered: "Ye may infer nothing about the biblical laws from the laws of the Soferim and nothing about the laws of the Soferim from the biblical laws and nothing about the laws of the Soferim from the laws of the Soferim."[4] It will be noted that Rabbi Joshua called this law that the Holy Scriptures defiled hands, which was enacted by the school of Shammai and Hillel[5] shortly before the destruction of the Temple, one of the laws of the Soferim. From this we may infer that the period of the Soferim lasted until the destruction of the Second Temple, while the period of the Tannaim began after the destruction of the Second Temple.

In regard to the compilation of the Mishna, scholars differ as to whether the Midrash-form preceded the Mishna-form. Herzog quotes the theories of Halevy, Fraenkel and Hoffman. He does not mention the theories of other scholars.

The translation of the Mishnayot in this work is generally accurate. However, some individual Mishnayot are ambiguously translated and some are even faultily rendered. In the last Mishna of the first chapter Berakoth, the phrase ולא זכיתי שתאמר יציאת מצרים בלילות is translated as "yet I failed to make my opinion prevail" etc. It seems to me that a better translation would be ולא זכיתי "I did not prove my point that *the* passage referring to Exodus should be said at night until Ben Zoma interpreted the biblical passage . . ." That the term זכיתי has also the meaning 'proving' is evident from another Mishna. In Eduyot (2, 3), a Mishna reads as follows: מחט שנמצאת בבשר שהסכין והידים טהורות. In the Talmud Pes. 19a, there is appended a statement of Rabbi Akiba אמר ר' עקיבא זכינו טומאת ידים שאין טומאת ידים במקדש who deduces from this Mishna that the hands are not defiled in the Temple. Using the word זכינו, he says: "We prove our point that there is no defilement of hands in the Temple." Since many sages maintained that the decree of defilement of hands

---

4 כל הפוסל את התרומה מטמאין את הידים להיות שניות, היד מטמא את חבירתה דברי ר' יהושע וחכמים אומרים אין שני עושה שני אמר להם והלא כתבי קדש שניים מטמאין את הידים אמרו לו אין דנין דברי תורה מדברי סופרים ולא דברי סופרים מדברי תורה ועל כולן א"ר. Comp. also Tebul Yom, 4 ,6, ולא דברי סופרים מדברי סופרים אמר ר' ,10 ,1. Tosefta *ibid.* יהושע דבר חדש חדשו הסופרים ואין לי מה להשיב יוסי ראה הלכה זו האיך נחלקו עליה אבות הראשונים ודנו עליה דברי תורה מדברי סופרים ודברי סופרים מדברי סופרים.

5 Comp. Shab. 13b, אלו פוסלין את התרומה . . . והספר והידים והטבול יום; Kelim 15, 6. אומרים צדוקים; כל הספרים מטמאין את הידים חוץ מספר העזרה, Yed. 4, 6. קובלין אנו עליכם פרושים שאתם אומרים כתבי הקודש מטמאים את הידים

applied to the Temple as well,[6] Rabbi Akiba proved from this Mishna that there was no such defilement in the Temple.

The text of the Mishna Peah 6, chapter 11, reads as follows: מעשה שזרע ר' שמעון איש המצפה לפני רבן גמליאל ועלו ללשכת הגזית ושאלו אמר נחום הלבלר מקובל אנו . . . Herzog renders this in the following words: "R. Simeon of Mizpah once sowed his field in the time of Rabban Gamaliel and they went up to the Hall of Hewn Stone and inquired." In the commentary, he adds: "Lit. in the presence of R. Gamaliel ·i. e. during his term of office as President of the Sanhedrin." He com- ments upon the expression ועלו, (and they) as follows: "R. Simeon and his colleagues." Since he furnishes many variant readings of the Mishna, it is surprising that he does not record all the different variants of this Mishna. As a matter of fact, there is another reading of this Mishna, מעשה שזרע ר"ש איש המצפה ובא לפני רבן גמליאל.[7] In this case, we should translate that Rabbi Simeon of Mizpah once sowed his field and came before Rabban Gamaliel and they went up to the Hall of Hewn Stone and inquired. In any event, Herzog's statement that Simeon and his colleagues went up to the Hall of Hewn Stone is untenable, since there is no mention of colleagues in the Mishna.

In his introduction to the tractate Demai, Herzog has made state- ments which cannot be supported by the Talmud, and which cer- tainly have no historical foundation. According to him, John Hyrcanus instituted Demai. However, the truth is that John Hyrcanus decreed Demai גזר על הדמאי i. e. he who purchases from the *Am haarez* should give a tithe, because the farmer was not to be trusted with regard to *Maasrot*.[8]

In connection with the Pharisees, Herzog makes the following asser- tion: "Somewhere about this time groups of devoted men, anxious for the preservation of the Law, banded themselves together with that object in view. Known as Pharisees (*Perushim* from פרוש 'to separate,' i. e. persons keeping themselves apart from uncleanness) or *Haberim* ('associates'; see Demai 2[3]), they took scrupulous care to observe the law in every detail, particularly such ordinances as Tithes and ritual purity, in regard to which *amme-haaretz* were particularly lax."

_____

[6] Shab. 15b, הזהרו שלא תגעו והלל נזרו טומאה על הידים; Hag. 3, 7, שמאי בשלחן.

[7] Comp. also ובא לפני רבן גמליאל, שנות אליהו.

[8] Sota 48a, Yer. Demai 21d, ביטל וידוי דחברים ונזר על דמאי של עמי הארץ. See S. Zeitlin, The Am Haarez, *JQR*, 1932.

The view that the term Pharisees is derived from the word פרוש 'to separate' and that *Perushim* and *Haberim* are synonymous had been advanced by Geiger and by the German Christian theologians. But this view is erroneous. In the Talmud, the term *Perushim*, Pharisees in contrast to the term *Amme-haaretz* is not found even once.[9] The term *Perushim* is always in contrast to *Zeddukim*, and the term *Haberim* in contrast to *Amme-haaretz*. The notion that the term *Haberim* is synonymous with *Perushim* is incorrect. On the contrary, we may infer from the Talmud that the term *Haberim* was not used synonymously with the term *Perushim*. Compare Talmud Nidah 33b . . . ת"ר מעשה בצדוקי אחד אמר אביי בצדוקי חבר. From this passage, it is evident that the term *Haber* was applied to one who was scrupulous in the laws of cleanliness and uncleanliness and was in opposition to *Am-haaretz*. Again, from this passage it is evident that a *Zedduki* may be a *Haber*, as long as he is scrupulous in the laws of purity and impurity. Thus, the term *Perushim* is not synonymous with *Haberim*.

There are other lapses, particularly in the introduction. However, in many places Herzog shows his great erudition in rabbinic literature. He displays originality in handling rabbinic sources. This he displays in his English commentary. It is especially evident in his commentary on the tractate Demai.

Mr. Fischel has always been a great patron of rabbinic literature. Through his encouragement rabbinic lore has received a great impetus.

---

[9] In the Mishna Hag. 2.7 we have the following text בגדי ע"ה מדרס לפרושין. The word פרושין does not have the connotation Pharisees but "separatists," people who separated themselves from uncleanliness and ate their meals with purity. That the word פרושין cannot be associated with Pharisees can be proven from the text itself. טבל לחולין הוחזק לחולין אסור למעשר, טבל למעשר הוחזק למעשר אסור לתרומה, טבל לתרומה הוחזק לתרומה אסור לקודש, טבל לקודש הוחזק לקודש אסור לחטאת . . . בגדי עם הארץ מדרס לפרושין בגדי פרושין מדרס לאוכלי תרומה בגדי אוכלי תרומה מדרס לקודש. בגדי קודש מדרס לחטאת. From this text we see that the Mishna designated the different degrees of purity and impurity. Comp. also Shab. 13a; Pes. 70a.; B. B. 60b כשחרב הבית בשניה רבו פרושין בישראל שלא לאכול בשר.

A CRITICAL EDITION OF THE TALMUD

An Appreciation of Malter's Text of Tractate Ta'anit*

IT IS well known that the Talmud is an encyclopedia of Jewish knowledge and lore, and not only deals with halakic problems, but also records various historical events, and gives the views of the rabbis on every subject which they consider of importance. The bulk of the Talmud is the work of the Amoraim, but it also embraces a great Tannaitic literature, apart from the Mishnah proper. I refer here of course to the numerous Baraitot which are found only in the Talmud, and also to the equally numerous citations from the Mishnah and other Tannaitic literature. On the other hand, it is also well known that the Rabbanan Sabora'e made additions to the text as late as the seventh century. Consequently the literature embodied in the Talmud represents the period from Hellenism to Islam, from the Soferim to the Geonim, a stretch of nearly a millennium.

The text of the Bible, after it had once been canonized, was sacredly guarded against change, and every letter in the Pentateuch was counted. Until the discovery of printing, however, the Talmudists of various periods often suggested and actually made changes in their text, sometimes in marginal notes, and sometimes in the text proper, either on the basis of internal evidence, or of comparative study

מסכת תענית מן תלמוד בבלי הוגהה על פי כתבי יד שונים והוצאות עתיקות ונעתקה*
ללשון אנגלית על ידי צבי כלטר. *The Treatise Ta'anit of the Babylonian Talmud* critically edited an the basis of manuscripts and old editions and provided with a translation and notes by HENRY MALTER, Ph.D. Professor of Rabbinical Literature at Dropsie College, Philadelphia. The JEWISH PUBLICATION SOCIETY OF AMERICA, 1928. Pp. XLVII+480+Index.
61

of other copies. Every student of the Talmud is well aware
of this fact from the commentaries of Rashi and of his
grandson R. Tam, who complain bitterly against this practice, although they themselves frequently indulged in it.
Their changes were not merely glosses, but were embodied
in the text, of which they have now become an often in-
distinguishable part. In more recent times, great Talmudic
scholars like Solomon Luria (1510–73) and Samuel Edels
(1555–1631) incorporated in their larger works on the
Talmud thousands of textual corrections which were subsequently embodied in the text. Not only was the Talmudic
text changed by successive generations of rabbis, but even
the Tannaitic literature was subjected to many changes
and interpolations at the hands of the Amoraim.

It goes without saying that a text of this nature cannot
be utilized for scientific or legal research until a critical
edition is available. A man like Solomon Luria objected
to Joseph Caro's בית יוסף because he claimed that many of
Caro's halakic conclusions were based on faulty readings.[1]

Such a critical edition must be based on external as well
as internal evidence. By the former I mean all the MSS.
in our possession, as well as the citations in the vast rabbinic
literature. But in addition to these, due attention must be
paid, in every case where the text is in question, to the
probable intent of the passage, as determined by all the
collateral historical-critical knowledge at our command.

To reproduce the original texts of the Tannaim and
Amoraim is sometimes impossible because of changes which,
it can be proved, were introduced in the tannaitic parts
by the Amoraim and in the amoraic by the Rabbanan
Sabora'e, although we háve no external evidence of such
change. For example, a Mishnah in Eduyyot reads: ועל

ועוד אחרת לא היו לפניו ספרים מונהים והעתיקם בטעות כאשר ימצאו בדפוס [1]
ולפעמים בנה יסוד על הטעות ההוא, ים של שלמה, הקדמה שניה חלין.

מחט שנמצאת בבשר שהסכין והידים טהורות והבשר טמא נמצאת בפרש
הכל טהור, "When a needle is found in the flesh (of an animal),
the knife and the hands are clean, but the meat is defiled;
when it is found in the entrails, every thing (including the
meat) is clean."[2] A baraita adds R. Akiba's dictum: אמר
ר' עקיבא זכינו שאין טומאת ידים במקדש "Our point is proved—
there was no defilement of hands in the Temple."[3] This
dictum of R. Akiba was incomprehensible to the Amoraim,
who ask: "Why does he state merely that there was no
defilement of hands, and not mention defilement of utensils?
Does not the Mishnah read, שהסכין והידים טהורות?"[4] Aside
from the difficulty raised by the Amoraim, it is hard to
understand R. Akiba's זכינו, because we find no statement
before his time as to the defilement of hands in the Temple.
Again, if the hands had been defiled by an unclean object,
then the rest of the body would likewise have been defiled.

The Mishnah must therefore, in my opinion, originally
have read: מחט שנמצאת בבשר הסכין טהור והבשר טמא. This
would explain R. Akiba's dictum: The meat is defiled by
the needle; but the knife is clean, because hands *do not
defile* objects in the Temple. The word זכינו was to combat
the statement of Shammai and Hillel, who decreed that
the hands do defile vessels in the Temple. Akiba used this
old Halakah to show that hands do not defile, since otherwise the knife, which had been touched by the hands,
would also have been unclean. The Amoraim, having before
them R. Akiba's dictum, זכינו שאין טומאת ידים במקדש, and
not seeing the word ידים in the Mishnah, added it, so as to
make it read, שהסכין והידים. It was this which impelled
the later Amoraim to ask why Akiba spoke only of the
defilement of hands, and not of the utensils.

[2] Edu. II, 3.
[3] Pes. 19a.
[4] *Ibid.*

Another striking example will suffice. A Mishnah in Erubin reads: הדר עם עכו"ם בחצר או עם מי שאינו מודה בעירוב הרי זה אוסר עליו רבי אליעזר בן יעקב אומר לעולם אינו אוסר עד שיהיו שני ישראלים אוסרין זה על זה אמר ר' גמליאל מעשה בצדוקי אחד שהיה דר עמנו במבוי בירושלים.[5]

According to the old Halakah, where Jews dwelt in houses having a common court, it was forbidden to carry any object into such a house or out of it on the Sabbath day, unless the dwellers had resigned their rights to the court, or leased them to the man who wishes to do the carrying. Where a Jew shared such a court with a Gentile, it was not necessary to obtain a relinquishment of the Gentile's rights, on the old principle הבהמה והגוים[6] and their houses were considered כדיר וסהר של בהמה.[7] However, shortly before the great revolt against the Romans, the entire attitude towards the Gentiles was changed, the Halakah likewise was altered, כזבין לכל דבריהם[8] and thereafter if a Jew shared such a court with a Gentile, and wished to use it as his own during the Sabbath, it was necessary to lease such rights from the Gentile, who could not validly relinquish them gratuitously. Such is the meaning of the first part of the Mishnah, הדר עם עכו"ם בחצר.

With the הדר עם עכו"ם the Mishnah classifies מי שאינו מודה בעירוב, i. e., a Jew who does not believe in the laws of Erub. To this R. Gamaliel adds מעשה בצדוקי, which perplexed the Amoraim, since there is no mention of צדוקי in the first part of the text. The whole מי שאינו מודה בעירוב is inexplicable, because according to the Halakah only a Jew who openly violated the Sabbath was considered as a Gentile for this purpose. On the other hand, a Jew who did not accept the

---

[5] Eru. VI, 1.
[6] Neg. VII, 10.
[7] Tosef. Eru. V, Yer. *ibid.*, 24b.
[8] Tosef. Zab. II, 1.

legal fiction of Erub was one who kept the Sabbath very strictly, and could not be classified with the Gentile.

There is no doubt therefore that the original reading of the text was מי שאינו מודה בשבת, i. e., one who does not believe in the *Sabbath*. Such a man, who violated the Sabbath openly, was put on a par with a Gentile, and this would explain the points raised by R. Eliezer b. Jacob and R. Gamaliel. The former, who lived before the destruction of the Temple, objected because he shared the view of the old Halakah, חצר של גוי כסהר של בהמה and הבהמה והגוים[9]. R. Gamaliel objected to the second point, מי שאינו מודה בשבת, i. e., a Jewish Christian, who did not believe in the Sabbath, and quoted a story of his father, Simeon, to prove that the Jewish Christians were considered Jews for this purpose.

That the R. Gamaliel here mentioned was the second of that name, and that therefore the word צדוקי does not refer to the Sadducees but to the Jewish Christians is clear from the story itself. He says: "My father lived in a court with a צדוקי in Jerusalem." If R. Gamaliel I would have told this story, he would not have specified Jerusalem, where he and his father lived; this could only have been said by Gamaliel II, who lived in Jabneh, whereas his father had lived in Jerusalem. By that time, moreover, the sect of the Sadducees was no longer in existence, and therefore the word צדוקי originally referred to the Jewish Christians.

These two examples seem to me to show conclusively from internal evidence that the text has been altered; nevertheless, in the absence of external evidence, it cannot safely be reconstructed on this basis. However, in studying the history and development of the Halakah, such internal evidence must be given an important part.

Where such internal evidence is directly supported by another Talmudic reading, the text in question must be

[9] Comp. Eru. 24b and c.

reconstructed.   Thus, according to the Talmud Babli,[10] Shammai was of the opinion that the siege of a city may be continued even on the Sabbath day, which he deduced from the Biblical phrase עד רדתה. This same statement is found in the Sifre; while in the Tosefta (Erub., iii, 7), it is attributed to Hillel.   The latter reading must be accepted against the other two, for the following reasons: first, Shammai never based Halakah on Biblical hermeneutics. Further, the Sifre, after attributing the opinion to Shammai, adds: זו אחד מג' דברים שדרש שמאי הזקן.[12]   There are no such other cases in Talmudic literature ascribed to Shammai; on the contrary, if we accept the Tosefta reading, there are two other cases ascribed to Hillel.[13]

Again, when internal evidence discredits a reading in all the manuscripts and printed editions, but there is direct evidence that there was at one time a reading in harmony with the internal evidence, the text must likewise be reconstructed.   Such a case is found in the Mishnah, Yadaim, iv, 8, which I have discussed elsewhere.[14]

When the manuscripts have diverse readings, and there is no internal evidence in point, we can in a few cases arrive at a conclusion from indirect references in nonrabbinic literature.   According to all the editions, and most of the manuscripts, the Mishnah in Taanit, which gives the days of the Wood Festivals, names the 20th of Elul, while one or two manuscripts read 10th of Elul. Josephus, in Bell. Jud. II, 17, 6, says that the 14th of Lous was a Wood Festival in the year 65.   The 14th of Lous that

---

[10] Shabb. 19a, וכן היה שמאי אומר עד רדתה אפילו בשבת.

[11] הלל הזקן דורש אפילו בשבת.

[12] Sifre Shoftim 203.

[13] (1) Sifra Shemini. וונוע בנבלתם יטמא, הלל אומר אפילו הם בתוך המים.
(2) Sifra Tazria. ונרפא הנתק הלל אומר ולא שניתק נתק בתך נתק.
(3) Sifra Shoftim. עד רדתה הלל דורש אפילו בשבת.

[14] *Megillat Ta'anit as a Source for Jewish Chronology*, pp. 99–100.

year fell on the 9–10 of Elul, and therefore we must reject the overwhelming evidence of the manuscripts and accept the minority reading. These cases are naturally very rare.

In the ordinary case of disagreement among manuscripts, therefore, the editor must consult any citations which he may find in rabbinic literature. If such citations are only incidental, they can be taken only at their manuscript value. Only when they occur in discussions of the passage in point can they carry greater weight. And in such cases the editor must be on his guard against changes possibly introduced by such later authorities as more in conformity with their respective codes.

Every student of the Talmud is familiar with the confusion which the text presents in reference to the names of the various Tannaim and Amoraim, and an editor must likewise be on his guard, so far as is possible, to determine the correct names, drawing on his knowledge of the genealogy, history, and geography in question.

It is needles to emphasize the difficulties which attend the study of any aspect of the Talmudic period in the absence of a critical edition of the text, Tannaitic as well as Amoraic. Strangely enough, however, there has heretofore been no systematic effort to prepare such a critical edition. A first step in textual criticism, in many ways epoch-making, was taken by Raphael Nathan Rabbinovicz in his voluminous דקדוקי סופרים (*Variae Lectiones*, Munich-Przemysl, 1867–97), but this work, while it evinced great scholarship and laid the foundation for a critical edition, did not itself constitute such an edition. The first tractate of the Talmud to be edited critically is Ta'anit, which has been issued by the Jewish Publication Society of America, as part of the series of Jewish Classics made possible by Jacob H. Schiff. The volume was entrusted to Professor Henry Malter, and was published posthumously, having been completed just before his untimely death.

The Society is to be commended for this choice of a tractate and of an editor, because the volume is in every way a fitting inauguration of this great task. The tractate Ta'anit deals not only with Halakah, but also with Jewish history, liturgy, and folkore. It gives a full description of the institution of public fasts, the divisions of the Priests and the Levites, and the congregational services connected therewith.

In preparing this tractate, Malter utilized all the extant manuscripts, and all the printed readings, rare as well as standard. The volume reminds us once more of his amazing erudition, and his complete mastery not only of the Talmud itself, but of the whole province of rabbinic literature. Again and again throughout the text, his decision as to a reading bears testimony to his profound knowledge of Hebrew and Aramaic philology. The introduction gives an extended description of the manuscripts and first editions of numerous medieval works which he consulted in the course of the study. This published text is based on the conclusions at which he arrived in his *editio major*. The latter, with the full critical apparatus, will be issued shortly by the American Academy for Jewish Research.

In many passages, Malter has completely revised and re-arranged the accepted text. Many Talmudists will at first glance be reluctant to adopt his readings, but in nearly every case it will be seen upon examination of his notes that the new readings are entirely sound. Certain passages naturally must always remain open to discussion, and partly from a subjective point of view. A few examples will illustrate the difficulties inherent in such cases:

On page 3a, instead of כי רמיזי מים בשביעי הוא דרמיזי he reads שביעי אמר רחמנא ולא שמיני.

291

On page 13a the usual text reads, איניש אחרינא לא, Malter's edition has כולי עלמא לא. Likewise he has changed אי הכי אימא סיפא on the same page to אי הכי היינו דקתני עלה.

On page 18a, the older editions read עשאוהו כיו"ט עצמו ואפילו בהספד נמי אסור. Malter ommits the words: ואפילו בהספד נמי אסור.

On page 26b, for the usual לא שכיח שכרות לא גזרי בהו רבנן he reads לא שכיחא שכרות לא גזרינן. He explains that the expression לא גזרו בהו רבנן is used by the Amoraim, while the Tannaim would have said לא גזרינן. This latter observation is quite correct, but R. Meir, R. Judah and R. Jose were referring to an incident which occurred while the Temple was still in existence, and therefore the reading לא גזרו בהו רבנן is quite correct.

It is most deplorable that Professor Malter was taken from us while in the midst of his labors, and that he could not see this work in its final form. So far as I know, he had read only the first proof, and the *editio major* had not even been finally prepared for printing. I feel almost certain, from my conversations with him, that he still had certain changes in mind, and therefore some of the readings which seem particularly questionable should not necessarily be taken as representing final conclusions on his part. In this category I include such cases as the following:

On page 2b, the standard text reads: או דילמא מניסוך המים נמר לה מה ניסוך המים מאורתא דאמר מר ומנחתם ונסכיהם אפילו בלילה, Malter's version: או דילמא מניסוך המים נמר, אף הזכרה מאורתא לה מה ניסוך המים מאורתא אף הזכרה נמי מאורתא דאמר מר ומנחתם ונסכיהם בלילה ומנחתם ונסכיהם אפילו למחר. Neither of these readings is acceptable. The rabbis apparently did not know which ניסוך המים was meant. Was it the libation brought on the Feast of Tabernacles, and prepared on the eve thereof,[15] or the libation connected with every sacrifice,

[15] Talmud Suk. 51a. See Rashi Ta'anit 2b.

which might be brought the *following* evening, or even on the morrow?[16] The standard text represents both points of view. מה ניסוך המים מאורתא refers to the former libation, as the word מאורתא means "from the eve thereof;" the other phrase מנחתם ונסכיהם בלילה refers to the second libation. Therefore the text must be read to refer to either of the two forms of libation: מניסוך המים נמר לה מה ניסוך המים מאורתא. Or: אף הזכרה מאורתא. מניסוך המים נמר לה מה ניסוך המים בלילה, דאמר מר ומנחתם ונסכיהם בלילה, אף הזכרה נמי בלילה.

On pages 4a–4b, the standard text reads: סברוה שאלה והזכרה חדא מלתא היא מאן תנא אמר רבא רבי יהושע היא דאמר משעת הנחתו אל אביי אפי' תמא רבי אליעזר שאלה לחוד והזכרה לחוד, ואיכא דאמרי לימא רבי יהושע היא דאמר משעת הנחתו אמר רבא אפילו תימא ואיכא, Malter, instead of רבי אליעזר שאלה לחוד והזכרה לחוד סברוה שאלה לחוד והזכרה לחוד, reads: דאמרי לימא ר' יהושע. . . . מאן תנא אמר רבא ר' אליעזר היא דאמר מיום טוב הראשון הוא מזכיר אמר ליה אביי אפילו תימא רבי יהושע שאלה והזכרה חדא מלתא היא. This follows the Oxford manuscript, and Malter prefers it to the standard text because the latter is based on Rashi's emendation, which he does not accept. Following Rabbinovicz, he points out that Rashi says ולא גרסינין סברוה שאלה לחוד והזכרה לחוד, דהא לא משתמע ממתנ', whereas the statement סברוה שאלה לחוד והזכרה לחוד is in accordance with the Mishnah, which makes it clear that שאלה and הזכרה are separate. Apparently Rabbinovicz erroneously took it for granted that Rashi's words דהא לא משתמע ממתנ' refer to the hypothesis סברוה שאלה לחוד והזכרה לחוד. In fact Rashi must have referred to the מסקנא from this hypothsies, namely, שאלה הזכרה חדא מילתא. It then becomes impossible to accept the Oxford reading. The rabbis were always willing to accept an erroneous assumption for argument's sake—if it were finally reduced *ad absurdum*; but we never find in the Talmud a correct סברוה—הוה אמינא leading to

[16] Men. 44b. Zeh. 84a.

an erroneous מסקנא, and the Oxford reading would be precisely that.

On page 18b, Malter's text reads as follows: מאי טורינוס אמרו כשהרג טורינוס את לולינוס ואת פפוס אחיו בלודקיא אמר להם אם מעמו של חנניה מישאל ועזריה אתם יבא אלהיכם ויציל אתכם מידי כדרך שהציל את חנניה מישאל ועזריה מיד נבוכדנצר אמרו לו חנניה מישאל ועזריה צדיקים גמורים היו (וראויין היו ליעשות להם נס) ונבוכדנצר מלך הגון היה וראוי ליעשות נס על ידו ואותו רשע הדיוט הוא ואינו ראוי ליעשות נס על ידו ואנו נתחייבנו הריגה למקום ואם אין אתה הורגנו הרבה הורגים יש לו למקום הרבה דבים הרבה נמרים והרבה אריות יש לו שפוגעין בנו והורגין אותנו אלא לא מסרנו הקדש ברוך הוא בידך אלא שעתיד ליפרע דמנו מידך אמרו לא זז משם עד שבאו דיופלי מרומי ופצעו את מוחו בגזירין.

From the translation it is clear that Malter identifies טורינוס with Trajan, and לולינוס and פפוס with שמעיה and אחיה, the latter being the הרוגי לוד. Assuming that טורינוס was Trajan, the reading ופצעו את מוחו בגזירין is probably incorrect, as we know that Trajan died a natural death, and the reading should therefore follow tractate שמחות, which reads לא מתו עד שראו מחטטין בעיניו. Likewise, the reading ואותו רשע הדיוט must be dropped, as Trajan was not a הדיוט, but the Emperor. The reading should be מלך רשע, following שמחות and the scholion to Megillat Ta'anit. Finally, the word כשהרג should read כשתפס, again following שמחות and the scholion.

Malter's text is quite acceptable if we do not identify טורינוס with Trajan, and it is entirely likely that the Talmud confused the day of יום טירון with the martyrdom of שמעיה or לולינוס and פפוס or אחיה, who were killed by Trajan's general, Quietus. It says plainly that the festival יום טירון was abolished because that was the day when שמעיה—לולינוס and פפוס—אחיה were killed.[17] Quietus was in fact

---

[17] בטל יום טירון יום שנהרג לולינוס ופפוס, Yer. Ta'anit 66a, Megillah 70c, יום טורינוס בטולי בטלוה הואיל ונהרגו שמעיה ואחיה. Rashi, Ta'anit 18b.

killed by Hadrian in 117, which explains the phrase ופצעו
את מוחו בגזירין. Similarly ואותו רשע הדיוט becomes acceptable
if it refers to Quietus.

Students of history will be especially grateful for the
scholarly treatment which Malter has given to the passages
dealing with the משמרות and מעמדות, and for the flood of
light which the Hebrew notes have thrown upon this
important institution. At an early time the Priests and
Levites had respectively been divided into twenty-four
משמרות, so that all of them might have equal opportunity
to share in the functions of the Temple. The Israelites
had no need of such a division, as the sin-offerings and
purification-offerings were brought by individuals, and
even the daily sacrifices had not yet become communal
institutions יחיד מתנדב ומביא תמיד Men., 65a. Only in later
times, when the Pharisees established the daily offerings
as a communal sacrifice, to be brought from public treasury,
שיחיו כולן באין מתרומות הלשכה,[18] did there arise a need for
divisions among the Israelites, so that through their representatives they might take part in the daily sacrifices.
The Israelites therefore were likewise divided into
twenty-four divisions which were called מעמדות.

The new edition is supplied with an enlarged מסרת הש"ס
ומדרשים, which refers not only to the Talmud, but to the
whole Halakic and Midrashic literature. In a way, the
most important part of his work will be fully appreciated
when scholars have an opportunity to examine his extended
notes in the *editio major*. The volume which has already
appeared in the Schiff Library of Jewish Classics shows
clearly not only the need but the feasibility of a complete
edition of the Talmud, and sets a very worthy standard for
future scholars to follow in completing the work. It will
remain a monument to Malter's learning and acumen.

[18] Men. 65a.

As Malter recognized, the completion of this great task is not to be expected from individual scholars. It must be carried out by organized efforts. The Jewish Publication Society is to be congratulated upon this splendid beginning, and we must hope that all our institutions of learning, here and abroad, will unite in the effort to make possible a critical edition of the Tannaitic and Amoraic literatures.

GINZBERG'S STUDIES ON THE
PALESTINIAN TALMUD

THE Mishna which is a compilation of the Oral Law is a work of importance, second only to that of the Bible. The name Mishna may have a double meaning — "study" and "the second." Since the Sadducees did not believe in the Oral Law, the sages laid more importance upon the study of the Mishna than upon the Bible.[1] They even said that the laws of the Soferim were to be given preference to the words of the Bible.[2]

The Mishna is a code, even if an imperfect one. Since there are many contradictory points of view on the Halakah recorded in the Mishna, principles were laid down as to which were binding. For instance, if a law was recorded first anonymously and then later made the subject of a disputation between authorities, the anonymous statement was not valid. The law was decided according to the opinion of the majority. When Rabbi Judah, the compiler of the Mishna, however, was of the opinion that a law should be decided according to a single authority, he incorporated the law in the name of the sages so as to make the law binding. From this we may see that the Mishna was indeed a code.

The origin and the compilation of the Mishna were in Palestine. After the death of Rabbi Judah, when the laws of the Mishna became codified, the later rabbis under the name of Amoraim — the expounders — interpreted the

[1] חומר דברי סופרים מדברי תורה, Sanh. 11.3.

[2] דתניא ר'ש בן יוחוי העוסק במקרא מידה שאינה מידה במשנה מידה שנוטלין ממנה שכר העוסק בתלמוד אין לך מידה גדולה מזו, Yer. Shab. 16.

83

297

Halakot of the Mishna. These interpretations are known to us by the name Talmud. The disciples of Rabbi Judah continued to interpret the Mishna in Palestine. Two disciples of Rabbi Judah, Rab and Samuel, returned to their homeland, Babylonia, and established academies of higher learning there. They brought the Palestinian Mishna with them. The Babylonian Amoraim continued to discuss and interpret the Mishna. Thus, we have two sets of interpretations of the Mishna, i. e., two Talmudim — the Palestinian Talmud and the Babylonian Talmud — which are very much dissimilar in character, presentation and language.

The Palestinian Talmud was written in western Aramaic while the Babylonian Talmud was written in eastern Aramaic. There are even some different readings in the Mishna itself.[3] Some scholars have tried to find a solution to the problem as to why the Mishna in the Babylonian Talmud differs from the Mishna in the Palestinian Talmud.

The Babylonian Talmud was compiled at the end of the fifth century C.E., and was later expounded by the Saboraim. There are some additions of the Geonim in the Babylonian Talmud. It became the most important book of the Halakah in the Academies of Sura and Pumbedita. On the other hand, the Palestinian Talmud was never edited, owing to the persecutions which the Jews suffered in the third and fourth centuries, first, from the Romans and, in later centuries, from the Christians. The study of

---

[3] For example, in the Mishna in the Palestinian Talmud, Ber. 1, we have the reading ואיכלת פסחים (comp. מתניתא דבני מערבא; see also Ginzberg, I, 100). The Mishna in the Babylonian Talmud omits the words ואיכלת פסחים. The Mishna in B. M. 4 has the reading הכסף קונה את הזהב while the Mishna in the Babylonian Talmud reads הזהב קונה את הכסף. The text of the Mishna in 'Ab. Zarah 4 in the Palestinian Talmud reads נכרי מבטל ע״ז שלו ושל ישראל while the Mishna in the Babylonian Talmud has the following reading: נכרי מבטל ע״ז שלו ושל חבירו.

the Talmud was even prohibited by the Christian authorities, and the schools were closed.

The center of Jewish learning was well established in Babylonia. There was no opposition or rivalry from Palestine. The Geonim strove to make the Babylonian Talmud the final word in the Halakah, a sort of code like the Mishna itself. They laid down principles as to how to decide the Halakah. If there were controversies in the Talmud between the Amoraim, they made rules as to whose opinion should be followed in the decision of the Halakah. It is well known that there are hundreds of controversies in the Babylonian Talmud between the two great Amoraim, Abbaye and Raba. According to the principles which were accepted, the law was always decided according to the opinion of Raba with few exceptions. In compiling the Babylonian Talmud, the Amoraim incorporated many Halakot and Aggadot from Palestinian authorities. For example, there are many Halakot in the Babylonian Talmud by Palestinian rabbis like R. Jochanan and Resh Lakish.

The Babylonian Talmud was named Gemara. The word Gemara like the word Mishna has two meanings. Gemara has the connotation —"study" and "final." Most likely, the Geonim meant that the Babylonian Talmud was the final word in the Halakah. (In many places the word Talmud was deleted by the censors who erroneously substituted the word Gemara.)

The relationship of the Palestinian Talmud to the Babylonian Talmud is the same as that of the Tosefta, the Sifra, the Sifre and the Mekilta to the Mishna. The Mishna is binding; the Tosefta, the Sifra, the Sifre and the Mekilta are only authoritative, i. e., new laws might be deduced from them, provided that they were not in contradiction to the Mishna. Thus these works had a

great influence on the Halakah, but not as great as the
Mishna had. In the same manner the Palestinian Talmud
was only authoritative, but not binding. By this I mean
to say that the law as expounded by the Saboraim and
the Geonim of the Babylonian Talmud was the final
Halakah. The Palestinian Talmud may be accepted only
as authoritative when there is no contradiction from the
Babylonian Talmud. This was well pointed out by Hai
Gaon, one of the greatest Geonim: ומלתא דפסיקא בתלמוד
דילנא לא סמכינן בה על תלמודא דבני ארץ ישראל (תשובות הגאונים,
מאת שמחה אסף). The same point of view was expressed by
Alfasi: דעל גמרא דילן סמכינן דבתראי הוא ואינהו הוו בקיאי
מינן טפי מערבא דבני בגמרא (Eur. 10). The same attitude
was maintained by Zerachiah ha-Levi: ומצאתי בתלמוד
4.ירושלמי ואנו אין אנו סומכין על התלמוד ההוא. (המאור הגדול, גיטין)

The Geonim and the great rabbis of the Middle Ages
called the Babylonian Talmud their Talmud. Hai Gaon
referred to the Babylonian Talmud as "our Talmud," בתלמוד
דילנא. Alfasi likewise called the Babylonian Talmud "our
Talmud," גמרא דילן. In Ramban we find the same expression, 5.ומוחזק בתלמודנו Likewise, Zerachiah ha-Levi called the
Babylonian Talmud, "our Talmud," ומפני שלתלמדנו תלמוד
6.בבלי Rashi also spoke of the Babylonian Talmud as "our
Gemara," 7.בגמרא שלנו

Since the Babylonian Talmud became the final word in
the Halakah, the rabbis studied it and wrote commentaries
upon it. They also compiled novellae upon the Babylonian
Talmud. The Palestinian Talmud, on the other hand,
remained neglected. Only a few rabbis in the Middle
Ages, in Germany and Poland, studied the Palestinian

4 Comp., המאור הקטן, ומצאתי בתלמוד ירושלמי ... ואין אנו סומכין בכל זה, המאור הקטן
פסחים, ג' אלא על התלמוד שלנו.
5 4 מלחמות, כתובות.
6 4 המאור הגדול, כתובות.
7 Gen. 15.3, ibid. 17.2, בגמרא בבלית שלנו.

Talmud, and hence no great work until now has been written on the Palestinian Talmud.

The Palestinian Talmud, however, as a source of the development of the Halakah and Jewish history is indispensable. Its value for the development of the early Halakah is even more important than the Babylonian Talmud since it represents a continuation of the Halakah in the same country where the Mishna was compiled. The Palestinian Talmud is a mine of information for the history of the Jews of Palestine, the history of religion, Jewish customs and liturgy. Jewish scholarship has not utilized the Palestinian Talmud. This is due to the fact that Jewish scholarship in Germany and France has not in our times produced any great Talmudists. There were rabbis of note in Lithuania and Poland who mastered the Palestinian Talmud but no Jewish scholars.

Prof. Louis Ginzberg has just published three volumes of novella on the first four chapters of the first Tractate of the Palestinian Talmud.[8] Dr. Ginzberg has a reputation as a great Talmudist. In his novellae on the Palestinian Talmud he may be compared to the Talmudists of the Middle Ages who wrote novellae on the Babylonian Talmud. He displays vast erudition not only in the Palestinian Talmud, but in the entire rabbinic literature. His keen observations and ingenuity remind us of the great novellae which were written by our great rabbis in the Middle Ages.

[8] פירושים וחדושים בירושלמי, מיוסדים על מחקרים בהשתלשלות ההלכה והנדה
בארץ ישראל ובבל, מאת לוי בן טרנו הרב יצחק זצ"ל נינצבורג. חלק ראשון, ברכות
פרק א' וב', חלק שני ברכות, פרק נ', חלק שלישי ברכות פרק ד'. *A Commentary on the Palestinian Talmud.* A Study of the Development of the Halakah and Haggadah in Palestine and Babylonia. By Louis Ginzberg. I, Berakot I and II: pp. 420+lxxii+קלב. II. Berakot III: pp. 325. III, Berakot IV: pp. 444. New York: The Jewish Theological Seminary of America, 1941.

To review his work in the pages of this magazine is almost impossible, because one cannot give sufficient examples of the remarkable acumen displayed by Dr. Ginzberg on every page.

The three volumes of Ginzberg contain interpretations of difficult passages and establish correct readings of the text. They present very important material for the history of the Sanhedrin and also deal with its functions. They likewise give a full exposition of the Levitical law of uncleanliness and its observance. They also throw light on the difference of the liturgy, particularly of the Amidah. They give us a clearer view of the Jewish communities as they were organized in Palestine.

GINZBERG'S STUDIES ON THE
PALESTINIAN TALMUD

(Continued from JQR, N. S. XXXIII [1942], 83–88)

By SOLOMON ZEITLIN, Dropsie College

IN ORDER to write a commentary on the Talmud, a perfect text must first be established. It is well-known that even the Babylonian Talmud has no authoritative text. Scholars from time to time have added various readings, either on the margin or in the text itself; sometimes they even emended the text. In many cases the copyists themselves changed the text by adding or omitting words. When Rashi decided to write a commentary on the Babylonian Talmud, he sought first to establish a correct text of the Talmud.

Two methods may be applied in establishing the text of the Talmud — one by external evidence and the other by internal evidence. The external evidence consists of the manuscripts in our possession, as well as the citations of the Talmud in the vast rabbinic literature, and all of this must be utilized. The internal evidence is in the text itself, from which it is quite evident that a particular passage was altered. However, this is a very dangerous method in establishing a talmudic reading, since the reconstruction of the text may be due to an over ingenious interpretation or, at the other extreme, to ignorance of the talmud. Hai Gaon said that the Mishna and the Talmud should not be corrected merely because some passages present difficulties.[9]

---

[9] See שיטה מקובצת, to Ket. 68, ואין לנו לתקן את המשניות ואת התלמוד בעבור קושיא שקשה לנו, quoted by Ginzberg in the מבוא, p. 18.

419

Thus, only a talmudic scholar of the highest repute, similar to the type of our great rabbis of the Middle Ages, could resort to the second method. To safeguard the text, however, from such ingenious corrections, it is advisable that the text proper should not be tampered with, but emendations should be recorded on the margin.

Rashi, in his commentary on the Talmud, applied both methods. In emending the text of the Talmud, he not only made use of other rabbinic literature like the Tosefta and the books of the geonic period, but he also utilized all the different manuscripts which were used in the schools of his teachers — particularly the manuscript of Rabbenu Gershom, for which purpose he went to Mayence and Worms. Rashi, in his monumental work on the Talmud, sometimes used the expression הכי גרסינן לה; sometimes he quoted different readings from his teachers which he either accepted or rejected.[10] In many cases he proved only from internal evidence that the text was faulty. He did not hesitate to say in his commentary that, although a particular reading was found in all the books, nevertheless it was erroneous.[11] Sometimes, judging by internal evidence, he emended the text and said that the present reading had been corrupted by גרסנין.[12]

Prof. Louis Ginzberg, in his commentary on the Palestinian Talmud, followed the same methods as his great predecessor, Rashi, in his commentary on the Babylonian Talmud. Prof. Ginzberg not only utilized all the readings of the vast rabbinic literature and the corresponding

---

[10] Comp. Suk. 40a; Shab. 93.

[11] Zeb. 23b, ... ובספרים שלנו נירסא זו משובש' בכ'מ בהש'ס; ibid. 63b, ...אע'פ שהוא בכל הספרים אמת ,Hullin 74b; יודע אני שנירסה זו שיבוש שהרי הדבר שהוא שיבוש...

[12] Zeb. 115a, ... והגרסנין שינו את הלשון ;.ibid, 104, ה'נ והלכה כדברי חכמים ותו לא מידי ותוספתא זו נירס' דתלמידי תרביצאי היא וטעו .Comp. also Kid. 22a; Sota, 19b.

passages in the Tosefta and other tannaitic literature, but resorted as well to internal evidence in establishing the text of the Palestinian Talmud. In his emendations of the text, Ginzberg shows not only his genius in emending the Palestinian Talmud, but he gives evidence of his phenomenal erudition in the entire rabbinic literature. He has shown a remarkable faculty in deciding what is the proper text. For this he utilized all the necessary apparatus which is a prerequisite for establishing a text. His argumentation is so extensive and convincing that it leaves no doubt in the mind of the talmudic scholar as to the correctness of his ingenious emendations. Prof. Ginzberg, however persuasive he may be in arguing for a change of the text, does not venture to emend the text proper. He lets it stand as we have it in the printed Palestinian Talmud, but in his commentary he presents valid reasons for the necessary emendations.

To show Prof. Ginzberg's method in establishing the text of the Palestinian Talmud, I shall demonstrate with a few examples. The text of the Palestinian Talmud reads as follows: סימן לדבר משיצאו הכוכבים ואף על פי שאין ראיה לדבר זכר לדבר ואנחנו עושים במלאכה ... מעלות השחר עד צאת הכוכבים. The first part סימן לדבר refers to the statement in the Mishna in regard to the time when the priests may eat Terumah, while the second part of the talmudic statement זכר לדבר refers to the time which may be considered the beginning of nightfall. Prof. Ginzberg remarks very well that the construction is illogical and, moreover, he says that the words סימן לדבר have the same connotation as the expression ראיה לדבר. Hence he advances the theory that there is a mingling of two different readings — a short one which occurred in some manuscripts סימן לדבר צאת הכוכבים and a longer text found in other manuscripts ואע״פ שאין ראיה לדבר זכר לדבר ואנחנו ... עד צאת הכוכבים. Thus, our text is a

combination of two different readings. He also very con-
vincingly establishes that the original reading was not
משיצאו הכוכבים but צאת הכוכבים since it refers to the verse in
Nehemiah, ואנחנו עושים במלאכה ... מעלות השחר עד צאת
הכוכבים.[13]

The Talmud tells us a story that when the father-in-law
of R. Jannai, who was also his teacher, died, R. Jannai
(who was a priest) asked if he might participate in the
funeral of his father-in-law and thus defile himself. R. Jose
prohibited him from doing so.[14] The text continues ר' יוסי
נטמאו לו תלמידיו ואכלו בשר. Prof. Ginzberg rightly remarks
that the text as we have it ר' יוסי נטמאו לו תלמידיו is untenable since the same Rabbi Jose prohibited R. Jannai
from participating in the funeral of his father-in-law. It
would be quite illogical to assume that when R. Jose died
his disciples would defile themselves by participating in his
funeral since he did not allow R. Jannai to defile himself
at the funeral of his father-in-law. Therefore Ginzberg suggests that the reading in our text is erroneous and should
be שמע ר' אחא ומר יטמאו לו תלמידיו ונטמאו לו תלמידיו.[15] The
story would be as follows: When R. Jannai's father-in-law
died he asked R. Jose if he might participate in the funeral,
thus defiling himself. R. Jose did not permit him to do so.
However, R. Aḥa did allow him to participate in the
funeral. Thus the disciples of the father-in-law of R. Jannai,
including R. Jannai himself, participated in the funeral and
defiled themselves. Apparently some of the disciples were
priests. This textual emendation of Ginzberg is supported

---

[13] V. 1, p. 13. Comp. also Tosefta, ibid. 1: כיצן לדבר צאת הכוכבים
ואף על פי שאין ראיה לדבר זכר לדבר ... ועד צאת הכוכבים.

[14] ר' ינאי זעירא דמך חמוי הוא היה חמוי והוא היה רביה שאל לרבי יוסי ואסר לי'
שמע ר' אחא ומר יטמאו לו תלמידיו.

[15] V. 2, pp. 80–1.

by another passage of the Palestinian Talmud. (Nazir 7, 1.)[16]

Another original emendation by Ginzberg may be cited. Our text reads: תני ר' יודה אומר היו כולם שורה אחת העומדין משום כבוד חייבין משו' אבל פטורין ירדו לספוד הרואים פנים פטורין וכ'.[17] The same statement is found in שמחות.[18] There the reading is ירדו לפסגן instead of ירדו לספוד. Ginzberg ably points out that our reading is unacceptable and that Elijah Gaon of Vilna had emended the text in שמחות to read לנחמן instead of לפסגן. Ginzberg suggested that the primary reading was לספפן and in our text was corrupted to לפסגן and לספוד.

Some *Baraitot* which are recorded in the Palestinian Talmud have different readings in the Babylonian Talmud. Prof. Ginzberg explains that the different readings were not due to copyists' error, but rather reflect Jewish life. I shall cite one example. The text of the Palestinian Talmud reads as follows: עשרה כוסות שותין בבית האבל .... עוד שלשה אחד לחזן הכנסת ואחד לראש הכנסת.[19] However, in the Babylonian Talmud we have the following reading: חזני העיר ופרנסי הצבור. Prof. Ginzberg explains the reason that the Palestinian Talmud reads חזן הכנסת ראש הכנסת is due to the fact that in Palestine each synagogue was autonomous, and the head of the synagogue was the only one who supervised its needs, while in Babylonia there was a city-wide community which supervised the different synagogues and hence the Babylonian Talmud has the following reading: חזני העיר ופרנסי הצבור.

---

[16] ר' ינאי זעירא דמך חמוי .... שאל לר' יוסי ואסר ליה שמע ר' אחא (חמא) ואמר יטמאו לו תלמידיו נטמאו לו תלמידיו.

[17] Ibid., pp. 121–8.

[18] 10, 7.

[19] V. 2, pp. 63–66.

Ginzberg advances another hypothesis for the variance in the said readings of these Talmuds, suggesting that the Babylonian Talmud records the conditions of an earlier period (the time before the destruction of the Temple), while the text in the Palestinian Talmud records the conditions in the Jewish communal life of the later period (the time after the destruction of the Temple).

Some difficult passages in the Palestinian Talmud, according to Ginzberg, are due to errors of the copyists, who misunderstood the abbreviations recorded in the text. One example will suffice. Our text reads תני אפי' בתי כנסיות ובתי מרחציות.[20] According to Ginzberg the reading should be כסאיות instead of כנסיות, but originally this was abbreviated by the letters ב'כ and copyists thought that these letters were the abbreviation of the word בתי כנסיות.[21]

All the commentators have found difficulty in explaining דרקק איצטלין ... אסור. Some even changed the word אסור to מותר.[22] However, Ginzberg suggests that איצטלין is a Greek word στῦλος. With this philological explanation he removes all the difficulties.[23]

Every student of Rabbinics knows that the words אכילת פסחים are not found in the Mishna of the Babylonian Talmud. The Talmud explains that the reason that the Mishna does not have the two words אכילת פסחים is that the Mishna is according to R. Eleazar ben Azariah who was of the opinion that the time limit at midnight for the eating of the Pascal Lamb is biblical.[24] However, in the Mishna of the Palestinian Talmud the words אכילת פסחים do appear.[25] The Palestinian Talmud explains that this

---

[20] Pes. 4, 4.   [21] V. 1, מבוא, יט.
[22] See פני משה, ad loc. Also מראה הפנים, ad loc.
[23] V. 2, p. 309.
[24] See Ber. 9a.
[25] See Mechilta, פ' בא, כאן אמרו אכילת פסחים ואכילת זבחים והקטרו' חלבים ... מצותן עד שיעלה עמוד השחר.

Mishna is according to the sages who were of the opinion
that the midnight limit for the eating of the Pascal Lamb
is only a rabbinical decree, not biblical. The Palestinian
Talmud continues to say אמר רבי חונה ולית כן אכילת פסחים
אפילו כרבנן דתנינן הפסח אחר חצות מטמא את הידים. This statement of R. Ḥuna is complicated. The author of the פני
משה explains this dictum of R. Ḥuna in this manner: Even
according to the sages who were of the opinion that the
Pascal Lamb might be eaten the whole night, nevertheless
אכילת פסחים could not be in the Mishna, since according to
another Mishna the Pascal Lamb after midnight defiled
the hands and so the Pascal Lamb might be eaten only up
to midnight. The Gaon of Vilna, who was aware of
the difficulties connected with this talmudic statement,
emended the reading as follows: לית כאן אכילת פסחים דתנינן
הפסח אחר חצות מטמא את הידים omitting the word אפילו.
According to his emendation, R. Ḥuna's words would be
interpreted in this way: The Mishna could not have the
words אכילת פסחים and be in accordance with the view of
the sages, since we learn from another Mishna that the
Pascal Lamb after midnight defiled the hands; thus one
Mishna would contradict the other. Ginzberg advances a
very original thought as to how the word אפילו came into
the Talmud. According to him the words אכילת פסחים were
abbreviated by the letters א"פ. One copyist wrote out this
abbreviation אכילת פסחים on the margin; then another
copyist inserted these two words in the text and allowed
the abbreviated letters to remain; then there came a third
copyist who read these abbreviated letters אפילו, and so we
have the text אכילת פסחים אפילו.

Ginzberg suggests another explanation of R. Ḥuna's
statement. In the Mechilta of R. Simon the following
statement is found in reference to the time limit of the
Pascal Lamb: בלילה הזה, מה לילה הזה הנאמר למטה עד חצות אף

לילה הזה הנאמר כאן עד חצות, אמר לו ר' עקיבה מה אני צריך והלא
כבר נאמר ואכלתם אותו בחפזון בשעת חפזון ...[26] According to
both R. Eleazar ben Azariah and R. Akiba the time limit
for the eating of the Pascal Lamb by midnight is biblical.
They differ only as to the text from which the law is
derived. Thus, we have two versions. According to the
Mechilta of R. Simon there was a unanimous opinion that
the midnight limit for the eating of the Pascal Lamb is
biblical; while, according to another source, there was a
controversy — one scholar maintaining that it was biblical
while others were of the opinion that the midnight limit
for the eating of the Pascal Lamb is only a rabbinical injunction. According to Ginzberg if we assume that R.
Ḥuna knew of the Mechilta of R. Simon, R. Ḥuna's statement is very clear. In the statement לית כן אכילת פסחים
אפילו כרבנן, R. Ḥuna opposed the version that there was a
division of opinion as to the midnight limit for the eating
of the Pascal Lamb. To support his point of view, R. Ḥuna
quotes from another Mishna that the Pascal Lamb after
midnight defiled the hands.[27]

Prof. Ginzberg, besides elucidating the different passages
in the Palestinian Talmud, has given us excellent essays
dealing with the Sanhedrin, the communal life of the Jews
in Palestine, and prayers.[28] Ginzberg, in Volume 3, pp.
189–220, proves successfully that the Sanhedrin consisted
of 71 members, not 72, as some maintain. On page 208 he
advances the hypothesis that the words ומנו אותו אב בית דין
are actually a misreading; originally the text had וכנו אותו
אב"ד, אחת בארבע. Thus, R. Eleazar ben Azariah was not an
Ab Bet Din, but he lectured once in four weeks. However,
Ginzberg says that it is possible that the reading of the

---

[26] Mechilta of R. Simon, ed. Hoffmann, p. 11.
[27] V. 1, 101–10.
[28] V. 3, 238–86.

Palestinian Talmud as we have it is correct and thus R. Eleazar ben Azariah was an *Ab Bet Din*. I believe that the second hypothesis of Ginzberg is more acceptable since the word ומנו means appointment and thus we must accept the present reading of the Palestinian Talmud.

On pp. 213–217 Ginzberg deals with the מופלא. According to him, the word *mufla* means "learned." According to Tosafot the מופלא was not of the 71 members of the Sanhedrin.[29] Ginzberg, with great ability and skill, sets forth the reasons that caused the rabbis to hold the opinion that the מופלא was not a member of the Sanhedrin. Ginzberg, on the other hand, asserts that the מופלא was a member of the Sanhedrin. Elsewhere I advance the theory that the מופלא was actually the pleader of the court who presented the case against the defendant before the Sanhedrin and thus he was not a member of the Sanhedrin.[30] The Tosefta Hor., 1, 2,[31] is to be interpreted to mean that, according to the sages, if the court rendered a decision while one of the members of the court was not present the decision was considered void. Rabbi, however, was of the opinion that the decision of the court could be considered void only when the מופלא was absent, although he was not a member of the Sanhedrin. The reason for his opinion was that, since the מופלא was the one who presented the case before the court, the decision should not be considered valid unless he had been present. The Mishna which reads הורו ב"ד וידע אחד שטעו ואמר להן טועין אתם או שלא היה מופלא של ב"ד שם או שהיה אחד מהן גר או ממזר ... ה"ז פטור is to be interpreted as follows: The Mishna is in accordance with Rabbi's point of view, that the decision of the court may

[29] San. 3b, מופלא שבב'ד שלא היה מן החשבון.

[30] *JQR*, XXXII (1942), pp. 300–1.

[31] הורו ב"ד וידע אחד מהן שטעו או שהיה אחד מן התלמידים וותיקין יושב לפניהן וראוי להוראה כשמעון בן עזאי והלך ועשה על פיהם הרי זה חייב ..... הורו בית דין ואחד מהן אין שם פטורין ורבי אומר אני עד שיהא מופלא שבהן.

be void in the following three eventualities: 1. If the court was not legally constituted as in the instance where one member was a proselyte or of illegitimate birth. 2. If one of the members pointed out that the court erred in its decision. 3. If the *mufla* was not present. However, if an ordinary member was absent the decision was valid.

Dr. Ginzberg is right in accepting Rashi's point of view against the opinion of the Tosafot that R. Judah's state-ment [32] ר' יהודה אומר אחד ממונה על כולן refers to the Sanhedrin of 71 which was supreme.[33] This Sanhedrin of 71 had the right to supervise the decisions of the smaller Sanhedrins.

Dr. Ginzberg, in dealing with the statement דשמואל אמר אנא מן יומי לא צלית דמוספא אלא חד זמן דמית בריה דריש גלותא ולא צלו ציבורא וצלייתי [34] not only gives a definition of the term חבר עיר, but he also presents a very illuminating and comprehensive study of the חבר עיר. Much has been written on the חבר עיר. The early rabbis like Hai Gaon, Rashi and Maimonides gave different interpretations.[35] All of these interpretations of the rabbis, as well as those of the modern scholars, still present difficulties. Dr. Ginzberg gives the nine instances in which the term חבר עיר occurs and successfully explains every one of them.[36] According to him חבר עיר is a society of men, appointed or elected by the people, to supervise the activities of Jewish life in the city such as prayers, charities, funerals and consoling the mourners. In reference to the Tosefta Meg. 4, where we read כהן שיש בו מומין בידיו וברגליו לא ישא את כפיו מפני שהעם מסתכלין בו אם היה חבר עיר הרי זה מותר he rightly says that the term חבר עיר in the Tosefta could apply only to a scholar. However, Ginzberg suggests that the reading may be cor-

[32] San. 16b, אחד ממונה על כולן, פ'ה ב'ד הגדול שבירושלים ולא משמע הכי.
[33] V. 3, p. 216, א'לב המעיין היטב בדברי התלמוד והספרי וראה שאין לזו מפרושו.
של רש'י שאחד בדברי ר' יהודה משמעו בית דין אחד — סנהדרין גדולה, ולא איש אחד.
[34] V. 3, 410–28.   [35] See idem., ibid.   [36] Pp. 421–25

rupt and instead of חבר עיר the original words were הכר which means that everybody knew that he had physical defects.

Dr. Ginzberg very ingeniously interprets the statement עולין בחבר עיר על האיש ואין עולין בחבר עיר ,(11, 2), in שמחות על האשה, that if a man died the members of the society חבר עיר came officially as representatives of the city to console the mourners. When a woman died, however, the society חבר עיר did not come as a body to represent the city, but came as individuals to console the mourners. Ginzberg connects the חבר עיר with the institution of פרנסי העיר.[37] It seems to me that the term חבר עיר does have a connection with חבר היהודים. The word חבר originally meant "together." When the Jews gained their indepen dence they established a Commonwealth under the name חבר היהודים. The members of the city were called חבר עיר. The men who had the right to supervise the activities of the city were called חברים. Ginzberg himself shows that many words of the Talmud went through a development, so the word חבר which originally meant a city-dweller acquired the connection of learned man in contrast to the farmer עם הארץ. Later, the word חבר even assumed the connota- tion of scholar (comp. the Palestinian Talmud Sanhedrin, 1). חברים מהו ליכנס לעיבור שנה נישמעינה מהדא מעשה ברבן גמליאל שאמר יקרוני שבעה זקנים לעליה ונכנסו שמונה אמר מי הוא שנכנס שלא ברשות עמד שמואל הקטן על רגליו ואמר אני עליתי. The word חברים here undoubtedly means a scholar who was not yet ordained while the man who received his ordination was called זקן.[38]

[37] והנה כבר עלה בידינו לעמוד על משטעו האמתי של חבר העיר שאינו לא חבורת אנשים שבעיר (צבור) ולא חבורה שמתקבצת לפני חכם העיר . . . , אלא שבכל מקום שדברו בו כוונו לחברת אנשים שמנו עליהם בני העיר לצרכי העיר, כתפלה וצדקה הלויית המת ותנחומי אבלים (p. 425).

[38] See Palestinian Talmud, Hor. 3, אמר ר' זעירא הדא אמרה שממנין זקנים בפה.

Ginzberg, in his Commentary and his interpretations of the first four chapters of the Palestinian Talmud, did not follow the method of his predecessor Rashi in writing a continuous Commentary. Ginzberg only interprets those passages which are complicated. He follows the method of those rabbis who wrote חדושים, particularly the method of Ibn Adret, and that may explain why in these three volumes Ginzberg gives only the text of the Palestinian Talmud which he interprets. He follows the method of the rabbis who in their חדושים gave only the passages of the Babylonian Talmud which they interpreted.

Dr. Ginzberg has written two Introductions — one in English and one in Hebrew. The English Introduction consists of 72 pages, written in popular vein, to give the general reader an idea of the history of Rabbinic Literature. In this Introduction Ginzberg tells the reader what the Mishna is; he gives the history of the compilations of the two Talmuds — Palestinian and Babylonian. He sets forth the relationship between the two Talmuds, and he also introduces the reader to the different commentaries written on the Palestinian Talmud.

The Hebrew Introduction is lengthier, consisting of 132 pages, and is, indeed, we may say, more than an ordinary introduction — it is a book about the composition and the history of the Palestinian Talmud.

He deals with the text of the Palestinian Talmud and explains why its text is more corrupt than the text of the Babylonian Talmud; he emphasizes the importance of being thoroughly familiar with the language of the Palestinian Talmud for the understanding of the text. He deals with the relationship of the Tosefta to the Talmuds, particularly to the Palestinian Talmud; and with the attitude of the Geonim to the Palestinian Talmud. He explains why the Babylonian Talmud became the authoritative Talmud.

He well points out that the lack of authority of the Palestinian Talmud was due not only to the fact that it was not edited properly because of the Jewish persecutions in Palestine. He is of the opinion — and I believe he is right — that the center of Jewish learning in the geonic period was in Babylonia and therefore the Babylonian Talmud became supreme. This Talmud became supreme even in Palestine, supplanting the Palestinian Talmud. The reason may be ascribed to the following causes: The Geonim of Babylonia strove to establish the hegemony of the Jewish center of learning in Babylonia over the Palestinian Jews, and furthermore the Palestinian Jews were economically and politically dependent on Babylonia. Many Babylonian Jews settled in Palestine and thus helped to establish the supremacy of the Babylonian Talmud.

In his Introduction, Dr. Ginzberg, very well propounds the theory that the Mishna in the Babylonian Talmud was the earlier redaction of Rabbi while the Mishna in the Palestinian Talmud was a later redaction.

Dr. Ginzberg in this Introduction gives an account of those who studied the Palestinian Talmud. Above I pointed out that the reason why the Palestinian Talmud was neglected[39] was that the Palestinian Talmud was accepted only as authoritative[40] when there was no contradiction from the Babylonian Talmud. This is the reason why the rabbis of the Middle Ages occupied themselves with the study of the Babylonian Talmud and not the Palestinian Talmud. Only very few actually studied the Palestinian

---

[39] *JQR*, pp. 85–6.
[40] See Ginzberg, מבוא, ע' פד-ו.

Talmud. In Spain, Maimonides and Ibn Adret, and especially Nachmanides, made extensive use of the Palestinian Talmud. According to Ginzberg, the earliest scholars of France knew very little of the Palestinian Talmud. Even Rashi, according to Ginzberg, did not have before him the entire Palestinian Talmud, but only had some tractates of it.[41] We may accept Ginzberg's view as correct. Elsewhere I pointed out that Rashi, without any doubt, made use of the Palestinian Talmud.[42] However, Ginzberg's point of view as to Rashi's usage of the Palestinian Talmud remains correct. Of the later period Ginzberg singles out particularly the Gaon of Vilna and his disciple Hayyim of Volozhin. Of the scholars who contributed to the study of the Palestinian Talmud he mentions Z. Frankel, Israel Lewy and B. Ratner.

At the end of this Introduction Dr. Ginzberg makes a very interesting and profound observation on the study of the Talmud in the 19th century, which is of great significance for the proper evaluation of Jewish scholarship in America. Ginzberg well remarks that the 19th century was the golden period of talmudic study in Lithuania while during this same time in Germany the study of the Talmud declined (with few exceptions). It is true, he says, that many important books of great scholarly achievement were produced in Germany during this period. However, owing to insufficient knowledge of Rabbinics on the part of some of the authors, their works could not be of any value for a proper valuation of Jewish history.

Dr. Ginzberg is not only profoundly right in his severe judgment, but he sounds a note of warning to Jewish

---

[41] יאיך שהיה הדבר הזה, ברור הוא שכשחבר רש״י פרושו על התלמוד לא Ibid., קי,
היה לפניו הירושלמי אלא לעתים רחוקות, ואפשר שלא ראה כימיו ירושלמי שלם.

[42] See תש״ב ,הורב, פירוש רש״י על התורה והירושלמי.

scholars in America as to the indispensability of the knowledge of Rabbinics for Jewish scholarship.

It is regrettable to note that many authors in this country are the spiritual successors of the German school — *Iuedische Wissenschaft* — either dismissing Rabbinics or being ignorant of it.

After the destruction of the Second Temple, Jewish life was not only guided by the rabbis, but dominated by them. Thus, the vast responsa of the rabbis are not only a mine of information, but are indeed indispensable for a proper evaluation of Jewish life. However, to make use of this vast literature, a profound knowledge of the Talmuds is quite necessary.

There are those who will not accept all the interpretations of Dr. Ginzberg — I, myself, am not in agreement with some of them. However, this is to be expected of a work of such magnitude. Not all of the interpretations of Rashi, the Tosafists or Ibn Adret are accepted. Ginzberg's work on the Palestinian Talmud is not only a monumental work, but epoch-making. It is the first and only serious rabbinic work published so far in this country. Ginzberg is the first to give us a thorough, scholarly treatment of the Palestinian Talmud from the old rabbinic and also scholarly point of view. It is true that there have been attempts to explain some passages of the Palestinian Talmud. However, they were feeble and unsuccessful.

Solomon ibn Adret said there was only one in a generation who could understand the Palestinian Talmud.[43] Prof. Ginzberg, I believe without exaggeration, has no equal in our generation and is one of the greatest authorities on the Palestinian Talmud since the time of the Gaon of Vilna.

כבר ידעת שרבו השבושים בנוסהאות שבירושלמי והסבה הגדולה למעוט השנחה 43 הלומדים בו ואין עוטדין עליו רק אחד בדור (תשובות הרשב"א הטיוחסות להרכב"ן, צ"ו)

Ginzberg, in his work, shows a combination of the old rabbinic erudition — the product of the Yeshiva of Telzh —
and scholarly discipline acquired in a European university.

Dr. Ginzberg's work פירושים וחדושים בירושלמי is indispensable not only for all serious rabbinical students for the
study of the text and the history of the Halakah, but also
for anyone who works in the history of the Jewish Institutions of the talmudic period. Ginzberg's work is indeed a
credit to the Jewish Theological Seminary of America where
he has been serving as Professor of Talmud for forty
years. Jewish scholarship in America may well be proud
of this epoch-making work.

This work will undoubtedly become a classic on a par
with the חדושים of the great rabbis of the Middle Ages.

THE TOSEFTA

The Tosefta is mentioned frequently in the Talmud. It is stated there wherever an anonymous opinion is expressed in the Tosefta, that is of R. Nehemiah, כתם תוספתא ר' נחמיה.[1] According to tradition, the author of the Tosefta was R. Hiyya, a pupil of R. Judah, the codifier of the Mishne. The first to ascribe the authorship to him was Sherira Gaon. The Jews of Kairowan had asked him about the authorship of

[1] Sanh. 86.

the Tosefta and if R. Hiyya was the author, why had it been necessary for him to make additions to the Mishne?[2] In his reply Sherira Gaon said according to the Epistle which bears his name that there could be no doubt that the Tosefta had been compiled by R. Hiyya,[3] but that it was not certain whether the Tosefta had been compiled during the lifetime of R. Judah or after his death. He stated unequivocally that the Tosefta had been compiled after the compilation of the Mishne.[4] In the same Epistle, Sherira sought to explain why R. Judah himself did not compile the Tosefta.[5]

The view that the Tosefta is a supplement to the Mishne and that it was compiled by R. Hiyya was accepted by the rabbis of the Middle Ages. Maimonides also was of the same opinion.[6] Modern scholars, however, do not share this view. The first attempt to explain the composition of the Tosefta was made by Zechariah Frankel who held that the Tosefta was a compilation of two independent Baraitot collections, one by R. Hiyya and the other by R. Hoshaya. He believed that additional material was freely interpolated into these collections from both Talmuds.[7] Other scholars who followed Frankel advanced various views on the authorship and compilation of the Tosefta. H. Dünner advanced the theory that the Tosefta was compiled after the conclusion of both Talmuds.[8] I. H. Weiss stated that the compiler of the Tosefta was a Palestinian by birth who lived in Babylonia in the latter part of the fifth century, and that he drew his material from different sources, making use of the discussions in both Talmuds.[9] Dr. D. Hoffmann,[10]

[2] והתוספתא ששמענו כי ר' חייא כתבה לאחר המשנה נכתבה או בזמן אחד עמה

[3] ומה ראה ר' חייא לכתבה אם לתוספת דברים שהן מפרשין את עניני המשנה אמאי לא כתבן רבי. (אגרת שרירא גאון, בנימין מנשה לוין)

[3] ולעיינין תוספתא ודאי דר' חייא תרצה.

[4] ומילי דתוספתא בריךין דבהר מתניתין אינון ועליהון תניאן ולא פשיט לן ביומוי דרבי נח נפשיה דר' חייא או דבתריה:

[5] ודאמריתון מה ראה ר' חייה לכותבה ואמאי לא כתב ר' טעמיה אלו בקש ר' לומר כל מה שהיה שנוי ארוכן מילי ואיתיקרן אלא רבי עקרי הדברים תיקן... ואתא ר' חייה פשט בבריתא... ואילו היכא דאתי ר' חייה בבריתיה לאיפלוני על רבי אין שומעין לו.

[6] ראה אחר מתלמידיו והוא ר' חייא לחבר ספר וללכת בו אחר רבו ולבאר מה שנשתבש מדברי רבו והוא התוספתא ועניניו לבאר המשנה. (הקדמה לפירוש המשניות). ור' חייא חיבר התוספתא. (הקדמה למשנה תורה) התוספתא היא שיור המשנה (מבוא התלמוד, לר' שמואל הנגיד).

[7] דרכי המשנה, pp. 304–08.

[8] MGWJ, 1870.

[9] דור דור ודורשיו, 2.

[10] MGWJ, 1882.

A. Schwarz,[11] and M. Brüll[12] also dealt with the problem of the compilation of the Tosefta.

M. Zuckermandel set forth a novel theory on the origin and compilation of the Tosefta. He held that the Tosefta really was the original Mishne compiled by R. Judah, and that our text of the Mishne was not the original compilation of R. Judah, but a version that was altered and modified by the Babylonian Amoraim. Hence the Babylonian Talmud could not have been based on the original Palestinian Mishne of R. Judah. The Tosefta, Zuckermandel maintained, was the original form of the code which R. Judah compiled.[13] This view of the origin of the Tosefta has no validity. My purpose in quoting here the traditional point of view and the views of the modern scholars is to show that the authorship of the Tosefta and the time of its compilation is still a moot question.

Many of the halakot in the Tosefta are in contradiction to those recorded in the Mishne; others are merely elaborations. Many halakot recorded in the Tosefta are not found in the Mishne but in the Baraitot in both Talmuds. Some of them are in agreement with the Baraitot while others are not. Again, we find halakot in the Tosefta which date from a very early period of the Second Jewish Commonwealth, and yet they are not recorded in the Mishne. Why were they omitted by R. Judah? On the other hand we have some halakot in the Tosefta which were enacted in the time of R. Judah, and others even in a later period. It is evident that the origin of the Tosefta and its relationship to the Mishne and the Baraitot are still unsolved.

The Tosefta, though studied by the sages during the Middle Ages, was never held to be on a par with the Mishne in authority. Incidentally, this is one of the reasons why the text of the Tosefta is replete with mistakes and lacunae.

The Erfurt Ms. was edited by Zuckermandel with variants.[14] The traditional Tosefta was printed in Vilno by the Romm family.[15] In addition to the most ingenious emendations by the Gaon of Vilno, and different readings recorded in some mss., it contained an excellent

[11] *MGWJ*, 1875.

[12] See *Zunz Jubelschrift*, p. 94.

[13] *Tosefta Mishna and Baraitha*, 1908; comp. also Henry Malter, *JQR*, 1911.

[14] *Tosefta, nach den Erfurter und Wiener Handschriften mit Parallelstellen und Varianten*, 1880.

[15] בדפוס והוצאת ראם, ונלוו עליה, הגהת הגר״א, מנחת בכורים, מצפה שמואל, אור הגנוז, נוסחאות כתבי יד.

commentary by David Fardo, חסדי דוד. There are two other valuable commentaries on the Tosefta, one by יונה ב'ר נרשון, and the other by יחזקאל אברמסקי.

Prof. Saul Lieberman has recently published a work on the first *Seder* (Zeraim) of the Tosefta, in three volumes. The first volume is entitled: *The Tosefta, According to Codex Vienna, with Variants from Codex Erfurt, Genizah Mss. and Editio Princeps (Venice 1521) Together with References to Parallel Passages in Talmudic Literature.* He calls the other two volumes *Tosefta Ki-Fshuṭah, A Comprehensive Commentary on the Tosefta.* This work was published by the Louis Rabinowitz Research Institute in Rabbinics at the Jewish Theological Seminary of America, New York, 5715 — 1955.

Prof. Lieberman's edition of the first *Seder* of the Tosefta is a storehouse of all the various readings found in the vast rabbinic literature of the Middle Ages. He has collected all the variants in the different manuscripts in our possession; all of which required not only diligent labor but great learning. In his edition of the Tosefta Prof. Lieberman has shown his mastery of the entire medieval rabbinic literature. His edition of the Tosefta is superior to the edition which was published by Romm where among the commentaries were included the חסדי דוד and the readings by the Gaon of Vilno. It is also superior to Zuckermandel's edition. Prof. Lieberman's work is on a par with the great work of Rabinovitz, the דקדוקי סופרים on the Talmud. Rabbinic students will be very grateful to Prof. Lieberman for his edition of the Tosefta.

The first volume has a brief introduction of seven pages dealing with the different manuscripts of the Tosefta. The second volume contains a short introduction of nine pages about the commentaries written on the Tosefta.

One would have welcomed from Professor Lieberman an introduction to the Tosefta itself which would deal with basic questions such as, who was the actual compiler of the Tosefta and when it was compiled. What is its relation to the Mishne and the Baraitot? As long as these fundamental problems are not cleared up, no adequate commentary can be written. If the Tosefta was compiled by R. Hiyya, as tradition tells us, then it is one of the most important documents of the tannaitic period, and the Amoraim made use of it. If it was compiled in Babylonia at the end of the amoraic period, or even later, it loses its importance as a source for the tannaitic literature. An editor or a commentator on the Tosefta must first decide the problem of its origin. Without this clarification, a satisfactory commentary is impossible.

To edit critically the Tosefta, or any other tannaitic or amoraic text, one must of course make use of all available manuscripts. However, the majority rule must not be applied in regard to authenticity.[16] Even though ten manuscripts have similar readings, and one manuscript only has a different reading it does not follow that the ten have the correct rendition for it is possible that they may all revert to one source. An editor must apply the following principles: 1. He must examine all available manuscripts; 2. He must furthermore take into account the readings to be found in later rabbinic literature as many passages of the Tosefta are recorded in the vast rabbinic literature of the Middle Ages. However, he must be on guard too. For the rabbis of the Middle Ages may have purposely emended the text to make it accord with other passages in the rabbinic literature or with the accepted halaka. Hence the readings in the rabbinic literature of the Middle Ages may be emendations or corrections and not the original reading. 3. Finally establish original readings, i. e. where there are multiple variants one must apply internal evidence and also be guided by the historica₁ background of the halakot. This third method (internal evidence) was very well employed by Rashi.[17]

In his edition of the Tosefta Professor Lieberman applied the first two principles but not the third. This is a serious shortcoming. Without the application of internal evidence, it is impossible to provide a critical-scholarly edition of a problematical tannaitic text. However Herculean the task to establish the original reading of a tannaitic text, the editor must endeavor to do so.

I shall illustrate the defects which result from the failure to apply these critical tests by a few examples. Thus Tosefta Peah 3.3, reads as follows: העומר שהחזיק בו להוליכו לעיר ונתנו על גב חבירו ושכח את שניהם התחתון שכחה והעליון אינה שכחה (התחתון) ר' שמעון אומ' שניהם אין שכחה [התחתון מפני שמכוסה והעליון מפני שוכח בו. This Tosefta is recorded in the Palestinian Talmud with slight changes. In the former the reading is: שהחזיקו בו להוליכו לעיר while the Palestinian Talmud has שנטלו להוליכו לעיר. This difference is not of great importance. However, this Tosefta is also recorded in the Babylonian Talmud[18] where we find a different version of great importance. In the Tosefta the reading is ר' שמעון

[16] The principle of "majority rule" was applied by Dr. Lieberman.

[17] וכשכחבו בספרים ולשטו' מפרש טועה כתבו (זבחים 115) ברייהא זו מ שובשת בספרים; נירסא זו הכתובה בספרים משובשת היא ועל ידי פרשנים טועין שלא היו בקיאין בשמועה ופירשה בשיבוש בהך הנרסא (Ker. 4).

[18] Sota 45, עוסר שהחזיק בו להוליכו לעיר והניחו על נבי חבירו ושכחו התחתון

אומר שניהם אין שכחה התחתון מפני שטכוסה והעליון מפני שזכה בו. Rabbi Simon
said both [the two sheafs] do not come under the law concerning the
forgotten sheaf. The lower because it is covered, and the upper, because
the owner acquired it. The text in the Babylonian Talmud has שניהם
אינן שכחה התחתון מפני שהוא טמון והעליון מפני שהוא צף, the lower is not in the
category of שכחה while the upper sheaf cannot be considered שכחה
because he is floating, i. e., it is not on the ground of the field. Now,
in the Tosefta we have מפני שזכה בו while the Babylonian Talmud has
מפני שהוא צף. These two terms had different meanings. R. Simon could
have given only one reason for his opinion and we are confronted with
the question, what is the original reason of R. Simon. Prof. Lieberman
records only the readings and does not solve the problem, as to what
was R. Simon's reason for stating that the upper sheaf is not in the
category of שכחה.

From internal evidence we may say with certainty that the reading
of the text, as recorded in the Babylonian Talmud, is the original
reading. First, we note that the Amoraim already had the reading
והא מפני שהוא צף כאמר, אימא מפני שהוא צף שהוא צף. The reading in our
Tosefta as well as in the Palestinian Talmud was emended on the basis
of the interpretation given in the Babylonian Talmud on R. Simon's
dictum. מפני שהוא טמון אבל בעליון דברי הכל לא הואי שכחה, שאני התם כיון דאחזיק
ביה זכה ביה אי הכי טאי איריא על נבי חבירו אפילו בשדה נמי אין הכי נמי והא
דקתני על נבי חבירו משום התחתון והא מפני שהוא צף קאמר אימא מפני שהוא כצף.
Second, we may also conclude from internal evidence that the original
reading was מפני שזכה בו and not מפני שהוא צף. R. Simon was a Hillelite
who maintained that a sheaf which is forgotten in the field is not in the
category of *hefker*, *hence* he could not have used the term מפני שזכה. It
seems that Prof. Lieberman did not fully realize the underlying reason
for the controversy between the Shammaites and the Hillelites.

The sages divided property into the following categories, private
property, נכסי יחיד, property which belonged to many, communal
property, נכסי רבים, property which belonged to the State, and was
called נכסי בני בבל[19]; or נכסי נבוה or נכסי הקדש, Divine property, i. e., property
which belonged to The Temple, and הפקר *res nullius*, property which
had no owner. Anyone had a right to relinquish his rights to private

---

שכחה והעליון אינו שכחה ר' שמעון בן יהודה אומר משום ר' שמעון שניהם אינן שכחה
התחתון מפני שהוא טמון והעליון מפני שהוא צף.
[19] ואיזהו דבר של עולי בבל כנון הר הבית והעזרות והבור שבאמצע הדרך: חזקה
דרכים של עולי בבל.

property and declare one's property *res nullius*, and anyone could
appropriate such property and become the sole owner of it. On this
principle was based the law of מציאה that if a person loses something
which has no identification marks, the finder becomes the owner on the
assumption that the previous owner was reconciled to its loss and
inferentially relinquished his rights to it. A forgotten sheaf in the
field according to the Torah belongs to the poor. The owner is considered to have forfeited his rights and cannot return later and appropriate it. The Torah invalidated his ownership of the sheaf. A
forgotten sheaf belongs only to the poor; a rich person cannot take
possession of it. It belonged to only a segment of the Jewish people.

The question then arose: Is this forgotten sheaf in the category of
res nullius, or is it a property which belongs to (a restricted group)
many? The sages were divided on this point. The Shammaites were of
the opinion that since the Torah made the forgotten sheaf the property
of all the poor people, therefore it is in the category of *hefker*. The
Hillelites held that any property which belongs to [only] a segment of
the people could not be in the category of *hefker*.[20]

R. Simon, being a Hillelite, could not have used the words מפני
שזכה בו, since a forgotten sheaf is not in the category of *hefker*. Hence,
we may say with certainty that the authentic statement of R. Simon
was מפני שהוא צף in accord with this Tosefta reading in the Babylonian
Talmud.

The lack of critical analysis of the text is apparent throughout this
edition of the Tosefta.

The Tosefta [Peah 3.2] records the following: אמ' ר' אלעאי שאלתי
את ר' יהושע על אילו עומרין נחלקו בית שמיי אמ' לי התורה הזאת על אילו העומרין
הסמוך לנפא ולנדיש לבקר ולכלי' ושכחו וכשבאתי ושאלתי את (ר' ליעזר אמ' ר'
ליעזר) ר' ליעזר אמ' לי סודים באילו שאין שכחה על מה נחלקו על העומר שהחזיק
בו להוליכו לעיר ונתנו בצד גדר ושכחו שבת שמאי או' אין שכחה מפני שזכה בו ובית
הלל אומ' שכחה וכשבאתי והרציתי דברים לפני ר' לעזר בן עזריה אמ' לי התורה
אילו דברים נאמרו בסיני. R. Ilai asked R. Joshua what sort of forgotten
sheaf was the subject of the controversy between the Shammaites and
the Hillelites. The reply was that the controversy was over a sheaf
which had been left near a fence or near a heap of other sheaves. The
Shammaites were of the opinion that this sheaf was not in the category
of a "forgotten sheaf" hence the poor people could not have it; the

<hr>

[20] בית שמאי אומרים הפקר לעניים הפקר ובית הלל אומרים אינו הפקר עד שיפקיר
אף לעשירים.

Hillelites were of the opinion that this sheaf was in the category of a "forgotten sheaf" and hence the poor could have it. R. Ilai then asked R. Eliezer about the controversy and he answered that both schools were in agreement, that such a sheaf could not be considered in the category of "having been forgotten." The controversy turned on whether or not a farmer took a sheaf to carry it to the city and left it near a fence, etc. The Shammaites maintained that such a sheaf was not, strictly speaking, "forgotten," whereas the Hillelites considered that such a sheaf was in the category of "forgotten" and therefore the poor could take it.

The Tosefta further states that R. Ilai related the words of R. Eliezer to R. Eleazar ben Azariah and the latter said, "That is the truth as it was given on Sinai." The Palestinian Talmud has a similar account to that in the Tosefta; however, there are some variations. A minor variant is the fact that the Tosefta reads מודים whereas in the Palestinian Talmud we have לא נחלקו. More important and significant is the following difference. The Tosefta states that R. Eliezer said that both schools were in agreement that the sheaf which was left near the fence could not be in the "forgotten" category, שאין שכחה, while in the Palestinian Talmud we have a statement to the contrary, שהוא שכחה,[21] they can be considered "forgotten." Now, which has the correct version? R. Eliezer could not make both statements, שאין שכחה and שהוא שכחה. Professor Lieberman in dealing with this text quoted all the readings and also showed that Maimonides also had the reading in the Palestinian Talmud,[22] שאינו שכחה. However, according to Lieberman, Maimonides later retracted and had the words שהוא שכחה.[23] However, the Gaon of Vilna emended the text of the Tosefta.[24] To establish the original reading of R. Eliezer's statement, we must clarify again the controversy between these two schools in relation to the forgotten sheaf. The Shammaites considered a "forgotten sheaf" in the category of *hefker*, that is to say, they held that the law of *hefker* was applicable; therefore, if the sheaf was left near a fence it could not be considered *hefker* and was not a "forgotten sheaf." Similarly, if someone found a

---

[21] כשבאתי אצל ר' אליעזר אמר לי לא נחלקו בית שמאי ובית הלל על העומר שהוא סמוך לגפה . . . שהוא שכחה.

[22] הרי לך ברור שה"ם גרס בירושלמי כמו שהוא לפנינו בתוספתא ופירש שאם העומר היה מלכתחילה אצל הגפה והגדיש כ"ע מודים שאינו שכחה.

[23] אבל בפיה"ם להר"ם מהדורא בהרא חזר בו רבינו וכתב (הוצ' הרצג עמ' 27) וכבר בארו בנמרא שהם לא נחלקו כנראה מן המשנה הזאת שהיא שכחה.

[24] שהיא שכחה.

lost article near a fence he did not have the right to touch it.[25] It was
not *hefker*. The Hillelites were of the opinion, as we said before, that
a forgotten sheaf was not in the category of *hefker* since only poor
people could take it. Hence, regardless of where the owner left the
sheaf and had forgotten about it, the poor people may take it.

R. Joshua, a Hillelite, recorded the controversy about the "forgotten
sheaf" near a fence. R. Eliezer, who was a Shammaite[26] stated that in
this case the Hillelite agreed with the Shammaites that a sheaf which
had been left over near a fence was to be considered a "forgotten sheaf"
which the poor people might take. Hence the reading in the Palestinian
Talmud is the correct one and retains the original words of R. Eliezer.
Although R. Eliezer said that the Hillelites agreed with the Shammaites
and in this statement he was supported by R. Eleazar ben Azariah,
yet R. Judah, when he compiled the Mishne disregarded it and accepted
the statement of R. Joshua the Hillelite that the controversy between
the Shammaites and the Hillelites was over a sheaf which was left near
a fence.[27]

With all due respect to the sages of the Middle Ages, we must say
their readings were not always authentic. In many cases they emended
the text to harmonize with the halakot which they accepted. A scholar
must courageously reject such emendations, if internal evidence
negates them.

The Tosefta Peah 4 has the following statements: מעשר ראשון חזקה
ללוים. If it is known that a particular person received the first tithe,
he is considered a Levite. The reading in the Erfurt edition is, מעשר
ראשון חזקה לכהונה, that the receiving of the first tithe places one in the
status of a priest. The same reading is given in both the Babylonian
and Palestinian Talmud, Ket.[28] According to Lieberman, the authentic
reading is that given in the Vienna Ms.[29] It seems to me that this
reading is questionable. R. Eleazar ben Azariah maintained that

---

[25] מצא אחר הגפה או אחר הנדר . . . לא ינע בהן.

[26] ור' ליעזר לאו שמותי הוא (ירושלמי תרומות ה, ד,).

[27] העומר שהוא סמוך לנפה . . . ושכחו בית שמאי אוסרים אינו שכחה ובית הלל
אומרים שכחה.

[28] כך מעשר P. Talmud 2.7. מעשר ראשון חזקה לכהונה, B. Talmud 26,
ראשון חזקה לכהונה.

[29] וכנראה שהגירסא שלפנינו נכונה . . . וכיצד אפשר לומר שמעשר ראשון חזקה
לכהונה. The Vienna ms. is inferior to the Erfurt ms.

the first tithe should be given to the priest[30] (he himself was a priest).[31]
The reading in the Erfurt Ms., as well as in Talmud is in accord with
R. Eleazar ben Azariah's opinion,

Another example is (ibid.) the Tosefta has בראשונה כשהיה שם בית דין.
Prof. Lieberman believes that this may refer to an historical date, to
the *Bet Din* before the time of Trajan.[32] It is strange that Prof. Lieberman who always diligently quoted variant readings did not refer to
the Palestinian Talmud, Ket. 2, where the reading is שתי חזקת
לכהונה... אף באלכסנדריה בשעה שבתי דינין יושבין שם, "in Alexandria when
the courts were in session." The text of the Palestinian Talmud does
not refer to any historical date. The reference to the Palestinian
Talmud Suk. and Er. seems to me to be irrelevant.

Again, Tosefta Shebiit 8 states: רבן שמעון בן גמליאל אומ' כל מלוה
שלאחר פרוזבל הרי זה אין משמט, Rabban Simon ben Gamaliel said, any
loan transacted after the Prosbul was written is not affected by the
Sabbatical year; the debtor had to repay his loan. This reading, as was
well pointed out by Prof. Lieberman, is attested by all the great sages
of the Middle Ages;[33] however, there is another reading to which
Prof. Lieberman referred משמט viz. such a loan is annulled if it is not
repaid before the Sabbatical year. Prof. Lieberman accepted the reading
of the sages without any hesitation; however, in my opinion there is
not only merit in the other reading which says משמט, but by internal
evidence we may say it was the original statement by R. Simon ben
Gamaliel, הרי זה משמט.

According to Prof. Lieberman, if a Prosbul were written in April
and the money which was borrowed in May was not repaid before the
time of the Sabbatical year, the debtor had to repay the loan because
it was not annulled by the Sabbatical year. The question which confronts us is, why should the Sabbatical year not annul such a loan. It

---

[30] Comp. — ורא' בן עזריה אמר נותנין מעשר לכהונה ,Yer. Ma'as. Sh. 5.
B. Ket. 26, לכהן ולא ללוי מי אמר אין. The statement בתר דקנסינהו עזרא
ללוים "After Ezra punished the Levites," is only a legal fiction to divert
the first tithe from the Levites to the priests. There is a grave doubt
that any tithe was given, to the Levites or to priests during the First
Temple.

[31] Ber. 27, והוא עשירי לעזרא.

[32] אפשר שהכוונה היא עד זמנו של טריינוס הרשע ע' ירושלמי סוכה פ"ה ה"א,
ירושלמי ערובין ספ"נ.

[33] וגרסא זו מקויימת ע"י רב חפץ, ר'ן גאון, ר' טוביה ב"ר אליעזר, ר' מנחם בר'
שלמה ר"ש הריבמ"ץ, הר"ס, ר"א בן הר"ם הר"ש, העיטור והאו"ז.

was not protected by the Prosbul. The context of the Prosbul refers to
a debt previously transacted כל חוב שיש לי and not to a future loan.[34]
Suppose, for instance, A made a loan to B in March, and to make
certain that the Sabbatical year would not annul his loan, he wrote a
Prosbul in April in which he stated that he would collect all the debts
due him. Then, let us assume that in May he made a loan to B or to C;
how could the Prosbul which was written in April protect the loan which
he made in May? We must accept the single reading which has משמט
against the one which is recorded in the vast rabbinic literature.

The rabbis of the Middle Ages emended the text of the Tosefta to
read אין משמיט instead of משמט which was the original reading of R. Simon
ben Gamaliel. They emended the text of the Tosefta because of an
erroneous interpretation of the clause פרוזבל המוקדם כשר which they
interpreted to mean that a Prosbul written before the loan was made is
valid, and of the clause פרוזבל המאוחר פסול, a Prosbul written after the
loan was transacted is invalid.[35] I have pointed out elsewhere[36] that
Rabenu Tam had interpreted that the words פרוזבל המוקדם, והמאוחר
do not refer at all to the loan but to the time, i. e., if a Prosbul was
written before the approach of the Sabbatical year, it was valid,
פרוזבל המוקדם כשר. If it was written at the end of the Sabbatical year,
i. e., on eve of the new year of the post-Sabbatical year, it was not valid,
והמאוחר פסול, because all debts were cancelled by the Sabbatical year.
There was, however, another opinion that even such a Prosbul was

---

[34] זה נופו של פרוזבל . . . שכל חוב שיש לי שאנבנו כל זמן שארצה.

[35] Comp. Maimonides, com. to Mishne, פרוזבל מוקדם הוא שיכתוב
הפרוזבל החילה ואחר כך ילוה לו הממון, המאוחר שילוה הממון החילה ונעשה חוב
ואח"כ כתב פרוזבל והוא פסול. Maimonides, however, recognized the
erroneousness of his statement and retracted in his *Mishne Torah* where
he said that if the Prosbol was written before the loan had been transacted, it was not valid. כתב הפרוזבל החלה ואח"כ הלוה אינו מועיל, אלא
משמט עד שיכתוב הפרוזבל אחר שהלוה, נמצאת אומר שכל מלוה הקודמת לפרוזבל
אינה נשמטת בפרוזבל זה, ואם הפרוזבל קודם שמלוה נשמטת בפרוזבל זה, לפיכך
פרוזבל המוקדם כשר כיצד כתבו בניסן והקדים זמנו מאדר כשר . . . אבל אם איחר
זמנו וכתבו מאייר פסול (ה' שמיטה ויובל פ"ט). שצריך כתיבתו אחר הלואה מדנרסינין
(הוספתא), Comp. Lieberman, p. 202 במשנה שיש לו, ולא קתני שיהיה לו. (העטור)
שלאהר פרוזבל וכו', כלומר, אפילו לוה אהרי שכתב את הפרוזבל אינו משמט. It
seems that Prof. Lieberman did not fully comprehend the absurdity of
such statement. See note 37. See further S. Zeitlin, "Prosbol," *JQR*,
April, 1944.

[36] *Ibid.*, p. 357.

valid,[37] and that is what the Tosefta said. כתבו ערב ראש השנה של מוצאי
שביעית אע"פ שחזר וקרעו לאחר מכן נובה עליו והולך אפילו לוסן טרובה.

The time of the writing of the Prosbul was the eve of the New Year
of the Sabbatical year. However, if the Prosbul was written on the
eve of the New Year of the post-Sabbatical year, the creditor could
collect the debt. R. Simon ben Gamaliel said that any debt contracted
after the Prosbul was written, regardless of time, was annulled by the
Sabbatical year.[38] He agrees with the previous opinion recorded in the
Tosefta.[39] The opinion that a Prosbul written after the approach
of the Sabbatical year is valid is also recorded in the Palestinian
Talmud.[40]

According to the Tosefta and also the Mishne, if a loan was made on
a pledge of security although the debt exceeded the amount of the
pledge, the laws of the Sabbatical year do not apply to this loan. Prof.
Lieberman says that the משכון the pledge, or security, must be of real
estate,[41] but this is not borne out by the statement of Samuel who said
that any loan made on a pledge which is worth only a needle, the law of
the Sabbatical year is not applicable to such a loan.[42]

The Tosefta in Ma'as. Sh. 1 has the following text: לוקחין חיה
ועוף לבשר תאוה אבל לא לובחי שלמים מי שנזרו שיהא בשר תאוה מטמאת את הידים
בשר תאוה מטמא את. After the decree that אמרו אין לוקחין חיה לבשר תאוה
הידים, "defiles the hands," it was said that no animal should be bought
with the redemption money for the second tithes secular meat. Prof.
Lieberman in his commentary said: לפי גזרה זו לא היו אוכלים בירושלים
בשר תאוה אפילו של הולין. According to this decree secular meat was not
eaten in Jerusalem even if it were hulin.

It is strange that Prof. Lieberman did not attempt to explain what
was the conception of טומאת ידים in this respect; neither did he seek to
explain why בשר תאוה should defile the hands. The principle of defiling
the hands is applicable only in the following four cases. The Holy
Scriptures defile the hands,[43] and this is also applicable to the casing

---

[37] והתני פרוזבל בין פוקדם בין מאוחר כשר.
[38] כל מלוה שלאחר הפרוזבל הרי זה משטט.
[39] כתבו ערב ראש השנה של מוצאי שביעית . . . נובה.
[40] See note 37.
[41] (p. 201 תוספתא) על המשכון וכ' כלומר, על משכנתא, על קרקע.
[42] Comp. Yer. Sheb. 10, המלוה על המשכון . . . אינן משמטין שמואל אמר
אפילו על המחט.
[43] כתבי הקודש מטמאין את הידים.

as well as to the thongs of the books,[44] the paschal lamb after mid-night defiles the hands,[45] and so הפגול והנותר,[46] i. e., a sacrifice which became unfit due to improper intention of the mind and the part of the sacrifice left over beyond the prescribed time. The law of the defiling of the hands is not applicable to any other subject. Why then should the בשר האוה be included among these which defile the hands?

Dr. Lieberman did not clarify the principle of the טומאת ידים "defiling of the hands," and why only the above mentioned subject defiles the hands and not others. He fails to interpret this passage properly. He says, שכן הגת שנעשת על גבי בשר האוה וכ'. כלומר, אם המתעסק בנת אכל בשר חולין טמאים כאילו אכל דינו כאילו, האוה. The correct meaning of this passage is as follows: a vat, the liquid of which was pressed on בשר האוה defiles *kadosh* but not *terumah*. The reason thereof is that טומאת ידים is in the *second* category of uncleanliness, שני לטומאה; thus, it defiles *kadosh* but not *terumah*.

In the Vienna Ms. the reading is טמאה לקודש טמאה לתרומה. Prof. Lieberman is inclined to accept this reading in preference to the other reading wherein it is stated טהורה לתרומה. He says, טמאה לתרומה, בד: וטהור לתרומה, ובכו"ע: טהורה לתרומה, וכ"ה להלן נדה... ולכאורה אינו מובן שהגת תהיה טהורה לתרומה וטמאה למעשר. אבל לני' כי"ו היא טמאה לתרומה ולמעשר, ע' במשנת פרה פי"א מ"ה. ברם קשה להגיה את רוב הנוסחאות והכוונה היא שבירושלים עיר שעושה את כל ישראל חברים היו כולם טהורים לקודש. This inter-pretation is erroneous, because he evidently did not take into account the historical background of the decree of the "defilement of the hands."[47] It is interesting to note that the law that בשר האוה defiles the hands is not found in the Mishne, whereas the other instances פסח אחרי חצות פגול ונותר מטמא את הידים are recorded. Dr. Lieberman did not connect the law of בשר האוה, recorded in the Tosefta, with those mentioned in the Mishne. Apparently he did not see that there was a connection between them.

(I dealt with the origin of the "defiling of the hands" in my essay, *A Historical Study of the Canonization of the Hebrew Scriptures*.)

Again, Tosefta Ma'as. Sh. 5, reads as follows: מעשה ברבי אליעזר שהיה לו

---

[44] הכשיחות והרצועות... מטמאין את הידים היק הספרים מטמאות את הידים.
[45] הפסח אחר חצות מטמא את הידים (Pes. 10.9).
[46] *Ibid.*
[47] Comp. Tosefta Niddah 9.18, בראשונה היו אומרים בשר התאוה טהור חזרו וגזרו עליו שיהא מטמא את הידים חזרו וגזרו עליו שיהא מטמא במנע חזרו וגזרו שיהא כנבלה עצמה וטמטא במשא חזרו ואמרו כל הגת שנעשית על גבי בשר התאוה טמאה לקודש וטהורה לתרומה.

כרם בצד כפר טבי במזרח לוד ולא רצה לפדותו אמרו לו תלמידיו ר' משנזרו שיהא
R. Eliezar .נפדה זה כסוך לחוטה אתה צריך לפדותו עקר ר' אליעזר ובצרו ופדאו
had an orchard near *K'far Tabi* in the east of Lydda and he did not
want to redeem the crops of fourth year's. When his pupils told him
that it had been decreed that the fourth year's crop should be redeemed
outside of Jerusalem, he complied with this decree and cut the grapes
and redeemed them. A similar incident is given in the Babylonian
Talmud, where it is stated that when Eliezar wanted to make the
fourth year's crop *hefker*, i. e., *res nullius*, his pupils told him that his
colleagues had permitted the crops to be redeemed.[48] Prof. Lieberman
mentioned the different versions, without elaborating on the subject, apparently not realizing that the version was of great importance.
The text of the Tosefta reads, ולא רצה לפדותו, he did not want to redeem
the crops of the fourth year, while the text of the Babylonian Talmud
has ובקש להפקירו לעניים, he wanted to declare the crops *res nullius*,
which is a very important difference indeed. There is an even more
vital difference between these two texts in relation to the orchard of
R. Eliezar. We read in the text of the Tosefta that his pupils told
R. Eliezar "it was decreed" משנזרו. The term decree has the connotation
that that which was permitted previously now is prohibited. The term
g'zerah has the connotation of stringency. We are told in the text of
the Talmud that the pupils of R. Eliezar told him that his colleagues
התירו, permitted which means that that which previously had been
prohibited is now allowed. This is diametrically opposite to that which
is stated in the Tosefta.

It is not the purpose of the present reviewer to be an interpreter of
the Tosefta, nevertheless I shall try to clarify the seeming contradiction
between the text in the Tosefta and the text in the Babylonian Talmud.
It seems that they did not refer to the same orchard of R. Eliezar. The
Tosefta refers to the orchard which R. Eliezar had near *K'far Tabi*,
northeast of Lydda, while the Babylonian Talmud refers to an orchard
which R. Eliezar had near *K'far Tabi* southeast of Lydda.

According to the old Halaka, the harvest of the fourth year of any
orchard, which is located within one day's journey of Jerusalem, had
to be brought to Jerusalem. The fourth year's harvest of an orchard
which is beyond this limit had to be redeemed. The Mishne says that

---

[48] Bezah 5, כרם רבעי היה לו לר' אליעזר בטורח לוד בצד כפר טבי ובקש
Comp. also להפקירו אמרו לו תלמידיו רבי כבר נמנו עליך [עליו] הבריך והתירו
R. H. 31.

to the west of Jerusalem Lydda was the terminal of one day's journey. Thus, the crops of the fourth year of any orchard above, i. e. to the north of Lydda, had to be redeemed, whereas the crops of the orchards located below, i. e. to the south of Lydda, could not be redeemed but had to be brought to Jerusalem.[49]

After the destruction of the Temple the first *Bet Din*,[50] i. e., Rabban Jochanan ben Zakkai did not deal with the problem of the crops of the fourth year. The later *Bet Din*, i. e., the court of Rabban Gamaliel, decreed that all the crops of the fourth year of the orchards located beyond one day's journey should be redeemed. R. Eliezer who had an orchard located near *K'far Tabi*, northeast of Lydda refused to redeem the fourth year's crops because the Temple had been destroyed. When his pupils told him it had been decreed that the crops of the fourth year had to be redeemed, he complied. The story recorded in the Babylonian Talmud refers to the orchard which R. Eliezer had near *K'far Tabi* to the southeast of Lydda, i. e., in the area of one day's journey. According to the old Halaka such a crop could not be redeemed but had to be brought to Jerusalem. R. Eliezer who could not take the crop to Jerusalem wanted to make it *hefker*.[51] However, his pupils told him that his colleagues permitted the crops to be redeemed. The reason R. Eliezar did not know of these changes in the halakot was due to the fact that he did not attend the sessions at the Academy having been excommunicated by his colleagues.[52]

The text of the Tosefta reads, זמן עצי הכהני' והעם בתשעה.[53] Again, the printed text of the Tosefta reads, בתשעה באב, "on the ninth of Ab."[54] The Erfurt Ms. has also בתשעה and ellipses which means that the scribe omitted a word. Dr. Lieberman assumes that the reading should be בתשעה באב, on the ninth of Ab. He supports himself on Lichtenstein's edition of the Scholia on the *Megillat Ta'anit* where the reading is מפני כשעלתה גולה בראשונה התקינו להם את יום תשעה באב שיהו מביאין

---

[49] כרם רבעי היה עולה לירושלים מהלך יום אחד לכל צד ואיזו היא תחומה אילת מן הדרום ועקרבה מן הצפון לוד מן המערב.

[50] משחרב הבית בית דין הראשון לא אמרו בו כלום בית דין האהרון נזרו שיהא זה נפדה סמוך לחומה.

[51] According to the Shammaites הפקר הוה לעניים הפקר. R. Eliezar was a Shammaite.

[52] Comp. B. M. 59, comp. also R. H. 31, אי סלקא דעתך רבן יוחנן בן זכאי חביריו דרבי אליעזר מי הוה רבו הוה.

[53] Lieberman, בתשעה באב :צ"ל.

[54] Bik. 2.9. Comp. however, מנחת בכורים, ... ה"ג זמן עצי כהנים והעם תשעה כנוסחת הגר"א ולא גרסינן בתשעה באב.

קרבן עצים.[55] However, the text in the Talmud upon which the Scholia are based does not have on the ninth of Ab.[56] Furthermore, the Mishne says that there were nine times in the year when wood was supposed to be brought to the Temple by a particular branch of the priesthood and the people,[57] and these days are enumerated, but the ninth day of Ab is not included among them. The Scholia on the *Megillat Ta'anit* were composed during the geonic period and have no historical value for the history of the Jews during the Second Commonwealth.

Prof. Lieberman in explaining the text of the Tosefta Ber. 6, 'ר, יורה או' המברך על החמה הרי זה דרך אחרת, "R. Judah says when one pronounces a blessing over the sun he is following an unorthodox point of view," says that R. Judah's statement refers to one who blesses the sun anytime he sees it after some cloudy days.[58] The word cloudy is not mentioned in the Tosefta. According to the Talmud when one sees the sun in its *tekufah*, and the moon in its strength, i. e., when the moon is full, and the stars in their constellations, he should pronounce a benediction.[59] R. Judah's opinion was that anyone who pronounces a benediction only on the sun and not on the moon or stars was unorthodox.

The text in the Tosefta (*ibid.*) has באל״ף למ״ד וחותם באל״ף למ״ד הרי זה דרך אחרת; however, in the Erfurt edition the reading is באל״ף ולא בדל״ת וחותם באל״ף ולא בדל״ת הרי זה דרך אחרת. The Palestinian Talmud has the following reading, ביו״ד ה״א וחותם באל״ף למ״ד הרי זה דרך אחרת. Prof. Lieberman is of the opinion that the reading of the Tosefta is unquestionably right, although it varies from the reading in the Palestinian Talmud, and he asserts והגירסא בסיפא של התוספתא כמעט בטוחה

---

[55] זמן עצי הכהני' והעם בתשעה. בכי״ע זמן עצי הכהנים בתשעה (ואח״כ יש שם ריווח ושלש נקודות). והנכון הוא בד: זמן עצי הכהני' והעם בתשעה באב. ובמשנתנו (תענית פ״ד מ״ה) זמן עצי הכהנים והעם תשעה, כלומר, בתשעה זמנים סביאים קרבן עצים... וכבר העיר הרי״ן אפשטיין שבמשניות מטיפוס א״י... אף בתענית הגירסא: בתשעה, והכוונה לתשעה באב... וכן הביא מן הנמרא למנילת התענית (פ״ה הוצ' ליכטנשטין עמ' 76) ספני שכשעלתה נולה בראשונה התקינו להם את יום תשעה באב שיהו סביאין בו קרבן עצים. אמרו חכמים כשיעלו למחר הנליות הן אף הן צריכין, התקינו להם את יום חמשה עשר באב.

[56] זמן עצי כהנים והעם תשעה, ת״ר למה הוזרכו לומר זמן עצי כהנים והעם אמרו כשעלו בני הנולה לא מצאו עצים בלשכה.

[57] זמן עצי .כהנים והעם תשעה... בחמשה באב בני פרעוש... בחמשה עשר בו בני זתו...

[58] ונראה שהר״ח פירש את התוספתא שלנו כפשוטה, והיינו מי שרואה את החמה ואת הלבנה וכו' אחרי שלא ראה אותם במשך זמן ידוע, מפני העננים מברך עושה בראשית.

[59] תנו רבנן הרואה חמה בתקופתה לבנה בנבורתה וכבבים במסילהם ומזלות כסדרן אומר ברוך עושה בראשית (Ber. 59).

לנמרי, שהרי ני' כי"ו פקוויימת ע"י כי"ע והרוקח, ואעפ"י שבירושלמי מסורת אחרת,
כבר הוכחנו בכ"מ שאין לתקן מקור אחד ע"פ השני במקום שהניראות בשניהם יש
להם על מה לסמוך. We cannot correct, he says, the reading of one text
by another when both have valid support. Prof. Lieberman failed to
explain how there came to be various readings in the Tosefta and in the
Palestinian Talmud. Were they due to different points of view held by
by the Tannaim. If so, which was the earlier and which was the later?
Is the reading in the Tosefta the earlier opinion and that in the Palestinian Talmud the later, or vice versa? What were the underlying reasons
for the different readings? Answers to these questions are very important
in establishing a text. The reading in the Palestinian Talmud is superior
to that in the Tosefta.

Prof. Lieberman in his work תוספת ראשונים, in referring to the Tosefta
said, לפי גרסא זו יש חשש של דרך אחרת רק אם לא הזכיר את השם כלל ונגד אלה
שנזהרו שלא להזכיר את השם אפילו בברכה תיקנו במשנה שיזכירו את השם אפילו
בשאילת שלום, וכאשר האריכו בעניין זה החכמים האחרונים אבל לא נתברר לי בוודאית
למי כיוונו חז"ל. In his article in the *PAAJR*, 1951, he wrote, "With
those people in mind who were careful not to mention the substitute for
the Tetragrammaton even in prescribed benedictions, the Mishna
ordained that a man greet his fellow with (the use of) the Name of
Lord. However, I do not know for certain of whom the Rabbis were
thinking." Prof. Lieberman in the present edition of the Tosefta still
adheres to his original view, that the Mishne and the Tosefta refer to
those extremists whom he calls חסידים שוטים[60] who were careful not to
mention even *alef dalet* in the blessing and instead used *alef lamed*.
It is surprising that Prof. Lieberman did not recognize the absurdity
of such a statement. The sages certainly would not use the words
עת לעשות ליי' הפרו תורתך . . . הפרו תורתך עת לעשות ליי', "It is time to work
for the Lord and they rendered the law void." The sages would not
have rendered the law void for fear of extreme Hasidim, חסידים שוטים.
The reference in the Mishne and Tosefta is to the Judean Christians.[61]

According to Prof. Lieberman the clause ברוך אתה אלי, "Blessed be
Thou O my God," which is found in the so-called Manual of Discipline
bears a relation to this Tosefta. He says, ובמגילות שנתגלו בזמן האחרון
ביריחו אנו מוצאים ברכה המתחילה: ברוך אתה אלי וכו'. In the scrolls which
were discovered in Jericho lately we find a blessing which begins,
'Blessed be Thou O my God.' "[62] He is apparently unaware of the fact

---

[60] I, p. 122.
[61] Comp. S. Zeitlin, *The Zadokite Fragments*, pp. 25–27.
[62] I, p. 122.

that such a blessing is not found anywhere in ancient Jewish literature, neither in rabbinic or apocryphal, or in the New Testament. The blessing always began ברוך אתה אדני, Blessed be Thou, O Lord, and not "my God." Prof. Lieberman apparently did not recognize the fact that the author of the so-called Manual of Discipline who wrote the words, "my God," in the blessing was a semi-literate who took the *yod* at the end of the word *Adonai* to be the possessive "mine," and since he was apprehensive of writing *Adonai* he wrote *Eli.*

These passages are only a few of the many which show that the neglect to apply the principle of internal evidence in examining the text, and the failure to recognize the historical background of the halakot leads to errors and false hypotheses.

We hope that Prof. Lieberman will continue to edit the subsequent sections of the Tosefta. We hope, also, that Prof. Lieberman will supply an introduction to the opus: the origin of the Tosefta, its purpose, its compiler, and the date of its composition. We should find answers to the basic questions: What is the relation of the Tosefta to the Mishne, and to the Baraitot? Was R. Hiyya the compiler, as Sherira Gaon held? Or was it compiled in the fifth century, as maintained by some scholars? The age and purpose of the compilation of the Tosefta are *sine qua non* for a proper understanding of this classic rabbinic work. It is to be hoped that Prof. Lieberman will fill these lacunae in the forthcoming volume.

MAIMONIDES AND THE MEKILTA OF RABBI SIMON BEN YOCHAI

It is well known that Maimonides in his *Mishne Torah* did not mention the sources upon which he based his decisions. The sources which he used for the compilation of the *Mishne Torah* were not only the Babylonian and Palestinian Talmudim but such *Halakic Midrashim* as the *Sifra*, *Sifre* and the *Mekilta*. He likewise used the different *Targumim* and the *Geonic* literature. Some of the source material used by Maimonides is still unknown to us. Many scholars have searched the vast rabbinic literature to find the origin of some particular *Halaka* given by Maimonides.

Rabbi Kasher in his book *Maimonides and the Mekhilta of Rabbi Simeon Ben Johai*[1] endeavors to show that many of Maimonides's *Halakot* for which the rabbis could find no source were actually based on the *Mekilta of Simon Ben Yochai*. The so called *Mekilta of Rabbi Simon Ben Yochai* was edited by Dr. Hoffmann nearly forty years ago. Some part of the *Mekilta* was incorporated in the מדרש הגדול which was edited previously by Dr. Schechter. (See the introduction to the *Mekilta* by Dr. Hoffmann as well as the introduction of Kasher to the book under review.)[2]

Rabbi Kasher, with great ability and knowledge of rabbinic literature, shows the dependence of Maimonides's decisions upon the *Mekilta*. However not all of Kasher's assertions are correct. Some of the statements found in the *Mekilta* which he believes were the source of Maimonides's decisions in his *Mishne Torah* are on the contrary actually taken from the *Mishne Torah* and not vice versa.

To cite a few examples: No. 69 — Kasher quotes the *Mishne Torah* which reads as follows: אין לנין דיני נפשות אלא בפני הבית, והוא שיהיה בית דין

מקורי הרמב"ם והמכילתא דרשב"י, מאה הלכות במשנה תורה שמקורן במכילתא[1] דרבי שמעון בן יוחאי לספר שמות שנתעלמה מאתנו זה מאות בשנים ונתגלתה בתקופתנו בכתבי היד סתימן, במדרש הגדול על התורה ומכהבי היד של הגניזה במצרים ועוד. עם מבוא באורים והערות, מאת מנחם כשר, ניו־יארק, תש"נ. American Torah Shelemah committee. 1943.

[2] Comp. also Israel Lewy, *Ein Wort über die Mechilta des R. Simon, Jahresbericht des Jüdisch-Theolog. Seminars zu Breslau*, 1889; Louis Ginzberg, *Der Anteil R. Simons an der ihm zugeschriebenem Mechilta*, Festschrift zu Israel Lewy's 70. Geburtstag, 1911.

487

הנדול שם בלשכה שבמקדש . . . ומפי השמועה למדו שבזמן שיש כהן מקריב על נבי המזבח יש דיני נפשות, והוא שיהיה בית דין הנדול במקומו. In Kasher's opinion the foregoing statement of Maimonides is based on the *Mekilta*, which reads as follows: ומניין שאין ממיתין אלא בפני הבית ת'ל מעם מזבחי תקחנו למות, הא אם יש מזבח אתה ממית, ואם לאו אין אתה ממית, מכאן אמרו· ארבעים שנה קודם חרבן בית שני בטלו דיני נפשות מישראל, מפני שנלו סנהדרין ולא היו· במקומן במקדש ³.
However, the paragraph of the *Mekilta* which reads: ארבעים שנה קודם חרבן בית שני בטלו דיני נפשות מישראל מפני שנלו סנהדרין ולא היו במקומן במקדש ארבעים שנה קודם חרבן בית שני בטלו דיני· is taken from the *Mishne Torah*: נפשות מישראל אף על פי שהיה המקדש קיים מפני שנלו הסנהדרין ולא היו שם במקומן במקדש.

The expression בית שני found in the *Mekilta* of Rabbi Simon Ben Yochai proves conclusively that it cannot be tannaitic. The Tannaim never used the expression בית שני. They always used the word הבית. Comp. Joma 39b, חנו רבנן ארבעים שנה קודם חורבן הבית; R. H. 31b, ותניא שאמרת לנו משום אביך . . . ק'פ שנה; Shab. 15a, ארבעים שנה קודם שנחרב הבית עד שלא חרב הבית . . . פ' שנה עד שלא חרב הבית . . . ארבעים שנה עד שלא חרב הבית; A. Z. 9b, אמר ר' חנינא אחר ארבע מאות לחורבן הבית; Tosefta, Mo'as. Sh. 5, 15, משחרב הבית ב'ד הראשון. Sometimes we find in the tannaitic literature the phrase: שחרב בית המקדש but never בית שני ⁴.

The Tannaim who lived during the destruction of the Temple or shortly after never used the term *Second Temple*. For them it was the destruction of *The* Temple. Only in the amoraic period or later, did the Jews begin to use the term — *Second Temple* to differentiate it from the *First Temple*, since neither the Amorain, their fathers nor their grandfathers could have witnessed the catastrophic event of the destruction of the temple. For them it was only history. Thus the term בית שני *Second Temple*, used in the *Mekilta*, reveals without the slightest doubt that the passage cannot be tannaitic. Thus, Maimonides did not use the *Mekilta* but the *Mekilta* made use of the *Mishne Torah*.

No. 5 — Kasher quotes Maimonides, אין כל הדברים האלו אמורים אלא בזמן שנלו ישראל לבין האומות או שיד עכו'ם [נוים] תקיפה על ישראל, אבל בזמן שיד ישראל תקיפה עליהם אסור להניח עכו'ם (נוי עובד עבודה זרה) בינינו אפילו יושב ישיבת עראי. On this he comments that the rabbinic scholars could not find the source upon which Maimonides based the said decision.

³ Comp. also Naḥmanides' commentary on Num. 35.29: ושנו במכלתא מנין שאין ממיתין אלא בפני הבית שנאמר מעם מזבחי תקחנו למות מזבח אתה ממית ואם לאו אין אתה ממית.

⁴ B. B. 60b, ת'ר כשחרב הבית בשניה, see, however, דקדוקי סופרים *ad loc.*, כשחרב בית המקדש, comp. also Tosefta, Sota, 15, 5, כשחרב הבית המקדש.

Kasher adds that we are now fortunate in finding the source upon which Maimonides has based his *Halaka*. It is his opinion that Maimonides based the said Halaka on the *Mekilta*, which reads as follows: לא ישבו בארצך זו אזהרה שלא ישיבו גוי עובד עבודה זרה. However, Kasher failed to notice that the phrase: גוי עובד עבודה זרה cannot be tannaitic. The Tannaim did not use the phrase גוי עובד עבודה זרה. For them the word גוי meant עובד עבודה זרה. Sometimes we do find the expression גוי עובד עבודה זרה. Here again but not ע"ז של גוי or הגוי והעבדה זרה שלו the passage which Kasher thought was a part of the *Mekilta* and used by Maimonides as a basis for his decision was actually copied from the *Mishne Torah*.

No. 76 — Kasher quotes Maimonides, בשלשה דברים נכנסו ישראל לברית במילה וטבילה וקרבן... וכן לדורות כשירצה העכו"ם להכנס (ליכנס) לברית ולהסתופף תחת כנפי השכינה ויקבל עליו עול תורה צריך מילה וטבילה והרצאת קרבן. He believes this passage is based on the *Mekilta* which reads as follows: והיה כאזרח הארץ מה אזרח אינו לברית אלא בשלשה דברים במילה וטבילה ובהרצאת קרבן, אף גר אינו נכנס לברית אלא בשלשה דברים במילה ובטבילה ובהרצאת קרבן. In this again the compilers of the so called *Mekilta* made use of the *Mishne Torah*. Comp. Ker. 9, רבי אומר הם כאבותיכם מה אבותיכם לא נכנסו לברית אלא במילה וטבילה והרצאת דם אף הם לא יכנסו לברית אלא במילה וטבילה והרצאת דמים ... ת"ר גר בזמן הזה צריך שיפרש רובע לקונו אמר ר' שמעון (בן יוחאי) כבר נמנה ר' יוחנן בן זכאי ובטלה.

There is no question that in some cases Maimonides actually based his decisions in the *Mishne Torah* on the *Mekilta*, and so in many instances Kasher is correct.

In his introduction Kasher says that he hopes the present book will evoke the interest of rabbis and rabbinic scholars and encourage them in the study of the *Mekilta of Rabbi Simon Ben Yoḥai*, *Halakic Midrashim* and other *Geonic literature* which have been discovered. But a note of warning should be sounded. In the study of the book under review, as well as the study of the *Mekilta* and other *Midrashic literature* lately discovered, great care should be taken to ascertain their authenticity, as many passages found in them are not of the tannaitic period but of the later rabbinic period so that one may avert error and confusion.

SOME REFLECTIONS ON THE TEXT
OF THE TALMUD

IN THE ARTICLE "TOSEFTA" [1] I pointed out that in order to edit critically the Talmud one must apply three different methods.

1. All available manuscripts must be examined. However the majority rule must not be applied in regard to the establishing of the correct reading. Even though ten manuscripts have similar reading and one manuscript only has a different reading it does not follow that the ten have the correct rendition, for it is possible that they may all revert to one source. Although the copyists were conscientious and pious persons nevertheless they resorted to changing the texts because of their lack of understanding of the Talmud. As a matter of fact we do note many readings in the manuscripts which demonstrate that the copyists misunderstood the text.

2. The editor must take into account the readings of the Talmud found in the later rabbinic literature as many passages of the Talmud are recorded in the vast rabbinic literature of Middle Ages. However he must be on guard. The rabbis of the Middle Ages may have purposely emended the Talmudic text to make it accord with other passages in the rabbinic literature or with the accepted halaka. Hence the readings in the rabbinic literature of the Middle Ages may be emendations or corrections and not the original text.

3. Where there are textual variants the editor must apply internal evidence in order to establish the original text. By internal evidence I mean that if a reading is connected with the name of a particular sage one must scrutinize his views

[1] *JQR*, 1957, pp. 386-400.

throughout the Talmud in order to ascertain which variant
would be in accordance with his views. The editor also must
be guided by the historical background of the halakot. It is
to be noted that Rashi in his commentaries on the Talmud
employed internal evidence in establishing the text of the
Talmud.[2]

It is well known that the Mishne was codified by Rabbi
Judah the Prince at the beginning of the third century. However he only collated and codified. Many parts of the Mishne
go back to antiquity. On the other hand there are many
interpolations and additions in the Mishne which are of the
Amoraim.[3] The Gemora was edited by Rab Ashi at the end
of the fifth century. However there were many additions
made by the Saboraim, who flourished in the sixth and first
part of the seventh century, who interpreted many passages.
Their interpretations and explanations became a part of the
Talmud. While some of their interpretations helped in the
understanding of intricate passages, others lead to confusion.
To ascertain which passages in the Talmud are not Amoraic
but Saboraic and also to detect the additions which the
Amoraim interpolated in the Mishne one must carefully
scrutinize the text and employ internal evidence. Examination
of manuscripts will be of no avail since there are no manuscripts
of the time of Rab Ashi. Neither will the study of the rabbinic
literature of the Middle Ages be of any value. The rabbis of
the Middle Ages mostly did not differentiate what passages in
the Talmud were Amoraic and what were Saboraic. The only
scientific criterion that remains is that of internal evidence.

In this short essay I shall try to establish the correct text
of some of talmudic passages by internal evidence. In the
Talmud B. B. it is stated in the name of Rab Judah that if a

---

[2] Cf. Zeb. 23b ··· ובספרים שלנו נירסא זו משובשת בכ"מ בהש"ם
ibid. 63 ··· ה"ג והלכה ,ibid. 104 ;יודע אני שגרסא זו שיבוש שהרי
;כדבר חכמים ותו לא מידי ותגיספתא זו נירסא דתלמידי תרבצאי היא וטעו
.Hullin 74 ;אע"פ שהוא בכל הספרים אמת הדבר שהוא שיבוש·

[3] Cf. S. Zeitlin, *HUCA*, 1924.

man used *orlah*,[4] i.e. if a person occupied [5] an orchard or a vineyard during the period of *orlah*, it was not considered possession. *Orlah* is the fruit of the trees of the first three years. According to the pentateuchal law if a person planted trees he may not use the fruits of the first three years,[6] this is called *orlah*. According to the tannaitic law a person may acquire property in three different ways,—by purchasing, the purchaser paid money for the property; by deed, i.e. the owner wrote a deed in which he assigned the property to a person; a person may also acquire a property by possession.[7] According to the Talmud the minimum time to acquire possession must be three years [8] and during this time the possessor must use the property. According to the standard text of the Talmud Rab Judah was of the opinion that if a person possessed an orchard for three years but this period was *orlah*, i.e. he was prohibited the use of the fruits of the trees, and consequently he did not make use of the orchard. Hence the law of possession is not applicable. The alleged owner had the right to sieze the orchard from the possessor.

The Talmud supports Rab Judah's opinion from another statement where it is said that if a person used an orchard or a field during the period of *orlah* or during the Sabbatical Year, or if one used a field which has *kilayim* (forbidden junction of hetrogenous plants in the same field) it is not considered a valid possession, the possessor had no legal power on the field. The alleged owner had the right to seize the property from the possessor. This passage in B. B. presents a difficulty. In Tractate Ket. 80 it is stated that Rab Judah said that if a person used the field during the period of *orlah* or during the Sabbatical Year or if one used a field which had *kilayim* it is considered a valid possession. Thus

---

[4] B.B. 36. אמר רב יהודה אכל ערלה אינה חזקה
[5] מאי בעית בהאי ביתא אמר לו מינך זבינתיה ואכלית שני חזקה
[6] Lev. 19.23-24.
[7] Cf. Nishne Kid. 1.5.
[8] Mishne B.B. 3.1.

there is a contradictory statement. In B. B. Rab Judah said אכלה ערלה אינה חזקה while in Ket. 80 Rab Judah said דאמר רב יהודה אכלה ערלה שביעית וכלאים הרי זו חזקה. If a person used an orchard during the period of *orlah* it is considered a valid possession.

The rabbis of the early Middle Ages in recognizing this contradiction emended the text in B. B. to read אכלה ערלה שביעית וכלאים אינה חזקה. However other rabbis maintained that the correct reading is אכלה ערלה··· הויא חזקה. In Tos. Men. 58b where are enumerated the contradictory passages found in the Talmud these two passages are cited. Thus the rabbis of the Middle Ages had the contradictory statements of the two passages in the Talmud. Hence it is clear that to ascertain the correct opinion of Rab Judah, manuscripts are of no avail. Nor can the rabbinic literature of the Middle Ages solve this difficulty since the rabbis themselves were divided as to the correct reading of the text in B. B. Only by internal evidence can we ascertain as to what was Rab Judah's opinion regarding a person who occupied an orchard for three years during the period of *orlah*.

The Mishne in tractate Orlah states that the laws of *orlah* outside of the land of Israel is halaka.[9] Samuel, a Babylonian sage, interpreted the word halaka to mean the custom of the country. Rabbi Jochanan, a Palestinian, interpreted the word halakah in the Mishne in the sense of an old oral law given to Moses at Sinai.[10]

According to Samuel the Pentateuchal laws regarding *Orlah* are *not* applicable to lands outside of Israel. Rab Judah, a Babylonian and a disciple of Samuel, adhered to the opinion of his mentor, namely that the laws of *Orlah* are not applicable in Babylonia. Thus a man may use the fruit of the trees of the first three years of planting. Hence a person who possessed a

---

[9] 3.9. החדש אסור מן התורה בכל מקום והערלה הלכה

[10] Yer. ibid., הלכה, שמואל אמר כהלכות המדינה ר' יוחנן אמר הלכה B. Kid. 38, מאי הלכה אמר רב יהודה אמר שמואל הילכתא למשה מסיני מדינה·

field for three years during the period of *Orlah* has bona fide possession and the alleged owner can not disposses him. The correct reading in the Talmud B. B. is אמר רב יהודה אכלה ערלה הויא הזקה.

As noted before, the sages of the Middle Ages had difficulty in establishing the correct textual reading of the Talmud.[11] I am somewhat surprised that they did not recognize that many Pentateuchal agrarian laws were not applicable in Babylonia.

II

We read in the Mishne Taanit that, "Rabban Simon b. Gamaliel said: The Israelites never had such joyful days as the fifteenth of Ab and *Yom Hakipurim* (the Day of Atonement). . . . The daughters of Jerusalem used to go out on these days and danced in the vineyards, saying, 'Young men, lift up thine eyes and consider what thou wilt select for thyself (as a wife); do not fix thine eyes upon beauty, but consider the family.' " [12]

There were two Rabban Simon b. Gamaliel, The first Simon was the head of the *Bet Din* approximately between the years 40 C.E. and 60. The second was the head of the *Bet Din* approximately between the years 145 C.E. and 170. I believe it most probable that the Rabban Simon b. Gamaliel given in the Mishne is the later one since he used the name "Israelites." During the Second Commonwealth the people living in Judaea were called Judaeans not Israelites. Only after the destruction of the Temple did they apply to themselves the name Israelites.[13]

[11] Cf. Rashbam, B.B. 36, אכלה ערלה אחת מן השלשה שנים הויא שנת ערלה אינה חזקה · · · ובפירוש ר"ח גרסינן אכלה ערלה · · · הרי זו חזקה ולא נהירא· Cf. Tos. ibid. הכי גרים ר"ח אכלה ערלה הויא חזקה וכן נראה לר"י עיקר ואיירי כשאכל ה זמורות·

[12] Tan. 4.8, אמר רבן שמעון בן גמליאל לא היו ימים טובים לישראל כחמישה עשר באב וכיום הכפורים שבהן בני ירושלם יוצאץ בכלי לבן שאולין שלא לבייש את מי שאין לו · · · ובנות ירושלם יוצאת וחלות בכרמים וכך היו אומרות בחר בחור שא נא עיניך וראה מה אתה בורר לך·

[13] Cf. S. Zeitlin, *The Jews: Race, Nation, Or Religion?* pp. 30-36.

Rabban Simon b. Gamaliel said that "the Israelites never had such *good days* as the fifteenth of Ab and the Day of Atonement." The word *yom tov* (good day) never occurs in the Pentateuch. The Pentateuchal festivals were termed חגים,[14] מועדים [15] and רגלים.[16] During the Second Commonwealth the festivals were also termed זמנים. The term *yom tov* first occurs in the book of Esther where it is written, "The days wherein the Judaeans had rest from their enemies, and the months which was turned unto them from sorrow to gladness, and from mourning into a *yom tov* (good day) they should make them days of feasting and gladness." [17] The word *yom tov* was applied to the days when the people rejoiced in commemoration of joyful events, but these were not regular festivals and were not sanctioned by the law. However after the destruction of the Temple the word *yom tov* was applied to the three Pentateuchal festivals.[18] The Day of Atonement (*yom hakipurim*), according to the Pentateuch, was a day of affliction,[19] the day that the people had to deprive themselves of any pleasure. It can hardly be assumed that on that day, the Day of Atonement, the daughters of Jerusalem would go to the orchards, dance and look for mates.

Philo's description of the Day of Atonement is as appropriate to Jewish observance of modern times as it was in the time of the Second Commonwealth. He said that the Day of Atonement

> ... is carefully observed not only by those zealous for piety and holiness but also by those who never act religiously in the rest of their life. For all stand in awe, overcome by the sanctity of the day, and for the moment the worse vie with the better in self-denial and virtue. The high dignity of this

[14] Cf. Deut. 16.16 passim.
[15] Lev. 23.2; Numb. 29.39.
[16] Ex. 23.14.
[17] Esther 9.22, בימים אשר נחו בהם היהודים מאויביהם והחדש אשר נהפך להם מיגון לשמחה ומאבל ליום טוב.
[18] Cf. Mishne Bezah 1.1, passim.
[19] Cf. Lev. 23.27-29.

day has two aspects: One as a festival, the other as a time of purification, an escape from sins for which indemnity is granted by bounties of the gracious God who has given to repentance the same honor as to innocence from sin.[20]

The Day of Atonement came to be the most solemn day in the Jewish calendar. The Judaeans stood in awe, denying themselves food and drink on it. The entire day was devoted to repentance, supplication and prayer, not only for themselves but for all the people. Consequently it cannot be accepted that during the Second Commonwealth the maidens of Jerusalem went to the orchards to dance and enjoy themselves on the Day of Atonement.

On the other hand the statement of Rabban Simon b. Gamaliel that the maidens of Jerusalem went to the orchards to dance on the fifteenth of Ab and *yom hakipurim* (Day of Atonement) refers to the time before the Restoration, i.e. during the time of the first Temple, cannot be seriously considered. The name of the month Ab was introduced after the Restoration.[21] Before that period the months were called by numbers, i.e. the first, the second, the third, the fourth and the fifth, etc. After the Restoration the fifth month was named Ab.

The foregoing arguments convince me that the original reading was not הכפורים but כיומי הפורים days of Purim. The fifteenth of Ab and the days of Purim were joyful days. These days are recorded in the Megillat Taanit as days of joy.

According to the Mishne there were nine days on which the priests and the people used to bring wood offerings.[22] Among the nine days was the fifteenth of Ab. The Megillat Taanit records only the fifteenth of Ab as the day of the wood offering and as a semi-holiday.[23] It is probable that the fifteenth

---

[20] *The Special Laws*, I. 186-187.
[21] Yer. R.H. 1.2.
[22] Tan. 4.1.
[23] בחמשה עשר באב זמן אעי כהניא די לא למספד

of Ab was celebrated anciently because from that day on the sun, in approaching the autumnal equinox seems to lose its strength, while in the middle of Adar, the days of Purim, the rays of the sun, in approaching the vernal equinox, appear to become stronger. These days which originated as pagan celebrations were made to commemorate religious events.[24] The fifteenth of Ab may well have been the occasion of the priests: bringing wood to the Temple; but it also was held to be in commemoration of many events which, according to tradition, happened to the Israelites in the early days.[25]

The amendment of the text in the Mishne לא היו ימים טובים לישראל כחמישה עשר באב וכיומי הפורים can also be supported by the fact that the phrase *yom tov* does not occur in the Bible. It is found the first time in the book of Esther in connection with Purim. This supports my contention that the original reading was כיומי הפורים. The words יום הכפורים came into the Mishne at a very early period and the sages in the Talmud gave varied reasons why on that day the maidens of Jerusalem went to the orchards to dance on that day.

---

[24] Cf. S. Zeitlin, *The Rise and Fall of the Judean State*, I. p. 254.
[25] Cf. Talmud B. Tan. 30; Yer. ibid. 4.7.

KORBAN: A GIFT

IN THE PENTATEUCH THE word *korban* has the connotation
of an animal sacrifice to God. It was also applied to a meal
offering. In Nehemiah the offering of the woods was also
called korban.[1] The Septuagint rendered the word korban
δῶρον gift. The word korban in the tannaitic literature has
also the connotation of a vow, that is a person takes a vow
to do or not to do a particular thing.

In the Gospels it is recorded that Jesus charged the Pharisees that they were rejecting the laws of God in keeping up
their own tradition. "And he said unto them full well ye
reject the commandment of God, that ye may keep your own
tradition. For Moses said, honor thy father and thy mother;
and whoso curseth father or mother, let him die the death.
But ye say, if a man shall say to his father or mother, it is
korban, that is to say, a gift, by whatsoever thou mightest be
profited by me; he shall be free." [2] All the commentators of
the Gospel maintain that the word korban means a gift to God.
The Jerusalem translation of the New Testament renders this
passage in Mark as follows: "Anything I have that I might
have used to help you is Corban, that is dedicated to God."
In a note the editor wrote, "Corban, an Aramaic word,
meaning an offering, especially to God."

The word korban, however, referred to in the Gospels does
not have the meaning of gift to God but a vow, — a person took
it upon himself not to perform a particular act. In this sense
the word korban is referred to in tannaitic literature. Thus the
passage in Mark should be translated accordingly. "What ye
say, if a man shall say to his father and mother, it is Korban

[1] Neh. 13. 31.
[2] Mark 7. 11.

(a vow) by whatsoever thou mighest be profited by me (shall not honor his father)".[3]

Josephus, in *Contra Apionem*, makes reference to korban as a thing devoted to God.[4] In *Bellum Jud.* Josephus relates that Pilate confiscated "the sacred treasury known as *Korbonas.*"[5] The word korban is an allusion to the chamber or box where was kept the money given to the Temple particularly to the repair of the Temple. Thus the word korban has the notation—a gift to the Temple. This gift is not as sacred as a korban—a sacrifice to the altar. The Talmud makes a disitinction between a korban to the altar and a korban for the repair of the Temple.

A Mishne in Maaser Sheni states, "If a man found a vessel and on it was written Korban, Rabbi Judah says: If it was of earthenware the vessel is to be deemed profane but its contents Korban." Since the earthenware vessel has no value it must be assumed that the person gave its contents, a korban, a gift. The Mishne continues, "If it was (the vessel) of metal it is to be deemed Korban but its contents are profane."[6] The reason is that since the metal vessel has a value the word Korban written on it refers to the vessel and not to the contents. Some saw difficulty in this Mishne—how could one

[3] Apparently the scribe thought that the word korban had the meaning of a gift, and so he added in Mark the words ὅ ἐστιν δῶρον that is a gift. In Matthew he left out the word korban entirely, and he gave the interpretation of it as δῶρον, a gift. However, in some versions of the gospel, according to Mark, the phrase ὅ ἐστιν δῶρον is not found, and in some versions of the gospel, according to Matthew, we have the reading κορβὰν ὅ ἐστιν δῶρον. From this we can readily see that the word korban was in Matthew as well. Cf. Tischendorf, N. T. Lipsiae.

[4] 1. 22. 106. Josephus wrote that Theophrastus said that "the laws of the Tyrians prohibit the use of foreign oaths, in enumerating which he includes among others the oath called korban. Now the oath will be found in no other people except the Judaeans, and, translated from the Hebrew, one may interpred it as meaning 'God's gift' ". διαλέκτου δῶρον θεοῦ.

[5] 2. 9. 4 (175), καλεῖται δὲ κορβωνᾶς.

[6] 4. 10. חרם של היה אם אומר יהודה רבי קרבן עליו וכתוב כלי המוצא
הוא חולין ומה שבתוכו קרבן ואם היה של מתכת הוא קרבן ומה שבתוכו חולין,
אמרו לו אין דרך בני אדם להיות כונסין חולין לקרבן.

use profane things in a sacred vessel, that would be *meilah*, i.e. unlawful use of sacred things. However the laws of *meilah* refer to korban sacrifice to the altar, or other sacred things for the Temple or priests but did not apply to korban a gift for charity, which was kept in the Temple.[7]

In digging at the base of the wall of the Temple ruins the renowned archaeologist Prof. Benjamin Mazar discovered a limestone fragment bearing the inscription Korban. It was assumed and so recorded in the press that the word korban had the connotation of sacrifice. To my mind this is an erroneous rendering. In this instance the word korban has the meaning of gift. This limestone with the inscription of korban is a small fragment of a larger object which some person presented as a gift to the Temple for a charitable or sacred purpose. Or it may be a fragment of a larger object, a case in which money was contained, a treasury for the Temple.

The discovery of the limestone fragment with its inscription of korban does not add knowledge to what we know about the Temple from the tannaitic literature. However it is a significant and important discovery since for the first time there was found an inscription dating from the Herodian Temple. Prof. Mazar should be highly congratulated for this archaelogical discovery.

---

[7] מצא כלי חרס וכתוב עליו [קוף] קרבן, הוא קרבן Cf. Tosefta ibid. 5.2.
ומה שבתוכו קרבן דברי רבי מאיר וחכמים אומרים אין דרך בני אדם להיות
מקדיש כלי חרס, מצא כלי מתכות וכתוב עליו קרבן אם היה ריקן אסור
להשתמש בו עד שיודע שהוא של הקדש ונפדה·

The text in the Tosefta is at variance with the text in the Mishne. The word הקדש is not found in the Mishne. In the Mishne it is stated, "It is not the custom of men to place *hulin* into what is korban." In the Tosefta is stated, "It is not the custom of men to consecrate earthenware." In the Tosefta it is further stated, "(If a man) found a metal vessel and on it was written korban, if it was empty he was not allowed to use it until he knows that it is of *hekdesh* and was redeemed." It is difficult to comprehend this text. Elijah Gaon emended the text to read מלא instead of ריקן. The text of the Tosefta is corrupt. It was apparently assumed that the word korban has the connotation of sacrifice and therefore the Tosefta used the term מקדיש. The term korban in the Mishne has the connotation of a gift.

350

THE NEED FOR A NEW CODE

FAMILY MATTERS IN Israel, like marriage and divorce, are vested in the *Bet Din*, rabbinical court, but in civil matters the courts follow the Ottoman, English and French laws. This is an unhappy state of affairs for a young nation. Professor Silberg, Justice of the Supreme Court of Israel, in his book, *Principia Talmudica*, [1] laments this situation and eloquently states that it must not endure. He adds that the State of Israel must have its own laws and he suggests a code to be based on the sources of Hebrew law. To forestall criticism which may arise against codification of a new code, since there are already codes, the *Mishne Torah* by Maimonides, *The Tur* and the *Shulchan Aruch*, he maintained that life has not stood still since the compilations of these codes. The economic and social life of the Jews since the Emancipation has greatly developed particularly in Israel where the people have their own state. To legally regulate the different problems between individuals, judges have applied various systems of laws which were in practice in the country before Israel's independence. He held that it is high time to have a code based on rabbinic law. He said that this code should not be an "abridged *Shulchan Aruch*"; that it would not have the aura of religious sanctity but would rather be of a secular character, embodying all the principles of the Hebrew law, utilizing the vast rabbinic responsa.

Justice Silberg is of the opinion that the collection of material for such a code should be dogmatic, i.e., contain all the laws in the vast rabbinic literature. He is opposed to

1. כך דרכו של תורה, ירושלים.

351

the historical method in the application of the code, saying
that this method is valuable and important for a scholar
engaged in historical research, but not for a judge. [2] While
in general I agree with him on the advisability of having a
code in Israel, I differ with him on the method of codification.
It is true that a judge in giving a decision on the law is not
bound to investigate the reasons therefor and its origin. To
paraphrase a talmudic axiom, the judge has to decide the law
as he sees it in the books. A codifier, however, must not do so.
He has to apply critical historical analysis of the laws given
in rabbinic literature, designating those which are to be codified
and those which are not. We shall show presently the *sine
qua non* for the historical method to be applied by the codifier.
I do not mean to say that the dogmatic method should be
ignored. However the codifier must know the reasons for the
enactment of laws. Many laws enacted by the early rabbis are
in oblivion due to historic and social changes.

The Mishne is not a perfect code. However, Rabbi Judah,
the Prince, in compiling it applied a critical method. He did
not include laws that were already in oblivion. It is well
known that when there was a halakic controversy between
the sages the law followed the opinion of the majority. It is
also well known that the law was not decided in accordance
with Rabbi Meir's view. [3] However when Rabbi Judah, the
Prince, thought that the law should be decided in accordance
with Rabbi Meir's view, although the majority of the sages
were opposed to him, he gave his halakic view anonymously
and ignored the majority. [4] To give two examples of many:

הגישה אל החומר צריכה להיות דוגמאטית פירושה של דבר עלינו לראות [2]
המשפט העברי כמות שהוא ··· ידיעת דרכי ההתפתחות השובה לנו אמנם מאד
מאד אבל מבחינה הדרכתית בלבד ··· היא לא מחקר מדעי הימטורי·
שאין בדורו של ר' מאיר כמותו ומפני מה מה לא קבעו הלכה [3] Eur. 46.
כמותו·
ראה רבי דבריו של ר' מאיר ושנאן בלשון [4] Hul. 85; Yer. Yeb. 4. 11.
חכמים·

In the Tosefta Demoi it is stated that if a man buys wine
from the Kutem he may say that he will set apart two *logs* ...
After he set apart the redemption money Rabbi Meir held
that he may drink the wine. Rabbi Judah, Rabbi Jose and
Rabbi Simon held that he may not drink the wine. [5] Rabbi
Judah, the Prince, who thought that the law should follow
Rabbi Meir's view incorporated it anonymously, ignoring
the view of the other sages although they were in the majority. [6] In the Tosefta it is stated that if a person through error
cooked anything on the Sabbath he may eat it, but if he did
so wantonly he may not eat it. This is Rabbi Meir's view.
According to Rabbi Judah if a person through error cooked
anything on the Sabbath he may eat the food after the
Sabbath, but if he cooked the food wantonly he may not
eat it at all. Rabbi Johanon haSandler (from Alexandria) [7]
said that if a person through error cooked food on the Sabbath
he may not eat it but others may eat it after the Sabbath.
However if a person cooked food on the Sabbath wantonly
neither he nor any other may eat of it at any time. [8] It is
stated in the Mishne that if one through error cooked food on
the Sabbath he may eat of it, but if he did so wantonly he

הלקח יין מבין הכותים בערב שבת ושכח ולא הפריש אומר שני לוגין [5]
שאני עתיד להפריש הרי הן תרומה עשרה הבאים אחריהם מעשר ראשון תשעה
הבאים אחריהם מעשר עני ומיחל ושותה מיד דברי רמאיר רי יהודה ור'
יוסי ור' שמעון אוסרים אמרו לו לר' מאיר אי אתה מודה ישאם יבקע ששותה
טבל אמר להם לכשיבקע (7 .Tosefta Demoi, 8).

הלוקח יין מבין הכותים אומר שני לוגן שאני עתיד להפריש הרי הן תרומה [6]
ועשרה מעשר ותשעה מעשר עני מיחל ושותה (4 .M. Demoi, 7).

[7] Yer. Hag. 3. 1.   אמרו רבי יוחנן הסנדלר אלכסנדרי לאמתו הוא.

המבשל בשבת בשוגג יאכל במזיד לא יאכל דברי ר' מאיר ר' יהודה [8]
אומר בשוגג יאכל למוצאי שבת במזיד לא יאכל ר' יוחנן הסנדלר אומר בשוגג
יאכל למוצאי שבת לאחרים ולא לו במזיד אל יאכל עולמית לא לו ולא
לאחרים. Tos. Shab. 3. 5.

may not eat of it. [9] This was Rabbi Meir's view, and was
given in the Mishne anonymously. Rabbi Judah the Prince
ignored the views of the other two sages. This is another
example of the many halakot where in the Mishne Rabbi
Meir's view was given anonymously and the views of his
opponents were ignored. If we assume that Rabbi Judah the
Prince simply collected halakot he may be accused, and
rightly, of doctoring them and concealing views of other
sages,—an act of culpability. This is far from the character
of Rabbi Judah as we know him. However if we should say
that his real purpose was to give decisions of the halakot, to
codify them, then he was right in ignoring the views of the
sages with whom he did not agree, giving Rabbi Meir's views
anonymously in order to make them the laws.

Supporting himself on Albeck, Justice Silberg maintained
the the Mishne is simply a collection of halakot, and that
Rabbi Judah the Prince did not intend it to be a codification
of halakot. This view is based on many references in the Tosefta where Rabbi Judah differs with the halakot given anonymously in the Mishne. [10] This argument does not carry much
weight. First we know that Rabbi Judah the Prince changed
his mind on a number of occasions regarding the halakot and
this is reflected in the Mishne itself. The Mishne given in the
Palestinian Talmud differed from the Mishne given in the
Babylonian Talmud. This is due to the fact that Rabbi
Judah the Prince changed his mind. One halakah is from an
early edition of the Mishne while the other halakah is from a
later edition. One characteristic fact is that in the Mishne of
the Palestinian Talmud there are three questions to be asked

[9] M. Ter. 2. 3.   המעשר והמבשל בשבת בשוגג יאכל מזיד לא יאכל

[10] לא התכוון לפסוק ולא פסק הלכה למעשה וכבר הוכח הדבר בראיות
מוצקות על ידי. אלבק וראיותו החזקה והמשכנעת ביותר היא כי במקומות
רבים בתוספתא ובברייתא חולק רבי גופו על "סתם משנה" שהיא לדעת
מתנגדיו של אלבק ההלכה הפסוקה· (P. 16).

on *Seder* night while in the Mishne of the Babylonian Talmud there are four questions. Furthermore the Mishne in the Palestinian Talmud gives the questions in a different order. [11] This can be attributed to the different editions of the Mishne. We also have to bear in mind that the Mishne was compiled by Rabbi Judah the Prince and his Court. [12] In many instances he disagreed with a particular view of a sage which was nevertheless accepted by his Court and given anonymously in the Mishne. This explains why the Tosefta records halakot wherein Rabbi Judah the Prince was opposed to those halakot given anonymously in the Mishne. The views of Rabbi Judah the Prince given in the Tosefta are of an early period.

Rabbi Judah the Prince was not the first compiler of halakot. Many halakot were compiled before the destruction of the Temple. Rabbi Akiba was the first to compile halakot according to subject matter and his disciples continued this method. Rabbi Judah the Prince later collected all the halakot which he thought should be a standard for the religious and social life of the Jews, a code which was named Mishne, second to the Torah. Thus we have in the Mishne halakot which go back to great antiquity. Rabbi Judah the Prince did not change the style nor the wording. There are layers even in a single section of the Mishne, some of which date back to great antiquity while others are of the period of Rabbi Judah. In compiling the Mishne when Rabbi Judah thought that the law should be decided according to the view of one particular sage, although there was some difference of opinion,

[11] ‏שבכל הלילות אנו אוכלין חמץ ומצה ··· אנו אוכלין שאר ירקות ···‏

‏אנו אוכלין בשר צלי ··· אין אנו מטבילין אפילו פעם אחת·‏

Bab. M. Pes. 10. 4.

‏שבכל הלילות אין אנו מטבילין אפילו פעם אחת ··· אנו אוכלין בשר‏

‏צלי ··· אנו אוכלין חמץ ומצה·‏ Pal. M. ibid.

[12] ‏רבי ובית דינו·‏

he gave the view of that sage anonymously or in the name of "sages" in order to make it the law. At times he recorded conflicting views and sometimes he did not. Rabbi Judah was the real architect of the Mishne. We do, however, find some Amoriac additions. [13] These have not changed the essence of the Mishne. The final collection of halakot of Rabbi Judah the Prince was called the Mishne, i.e., second to the Torah.

If Rabbi Judah had intended that the Mishne should be a code the question may arise why he embodied in it the views of individuals, of a minority, since the law had to follow the views of the majority. The answer is that he wanted the Mishne to be an elastic code not static. For this reason he recorded minority views so that in the future some sage, some rabbi, may base his decision on a new law on the basis of the minority view given in the Mishne. [14] Similarly the Supreme Court of the United States records both the majority and dissenting minority opinions although the decision is in accordance with the opinion of the majority. Rabbi Judah was aware that life does not stand still, that it progresses and develops, that new halakot had to be enacted which could be based on the minority views recorded in the Mishne. It may be said that the Mishne is not as perfect a code as possible, still it is a code.

Justice Silberg makes reference to the Code of Maimonides, the *Mishne Torah*, wherein no discussions nor names are given. It is indeed a code, but static. Maimonides was strongly assailed for this by Abraham ibn David. He was also critcized by the great talmudist and rationalist Rabbi Solomon Luria for not giving the sources and authorities for his decisions on

---

[13] Cf. S. Zeitlin, *JQR* 1947, pp. 352-54.

[14] לעולם חלכה כדברי המרובין לא הוזכרו דברי היהיד בין המרובין

אלא לבטלן ר׳ יהודה אומר לא הוזכרו דברי היחיד בין המרובין אלא שמא

תיצרך להן השעה ויסמכו עליהן. Tosefta Ed. 1. 4.

the halakot. Luria said that no one knows whence Maimonides derived the halakic decisions, whether from the Talmud, other sources, or whether they represent his own views. Luria further said that many of Maimonides' decisions have been based on wrong readings. [15] It is a fact that Maimonides many times decided the halakah contrary to the Talmud, basing himself on extra-rabbinical literature. To give one example: According to the Talmud there is a biblical injunction against cooking meat and milk together. If one cooks them together he is not permitted to eat thereof nor may he derive benefit therefrom. These prohibitions were deduced from the Pentateuch where the verse forbidding the seething of a kid in its mother's milk is recorded three times. [16] Maimonides accepted the talmudic injunction against the eating of meat and milk together as a Pentateuchal law. He derived this prohibition from a *kal vo-homer*—a *mnori ad majus*. Since the Pentateuch prohibited the cooking of meat and milk together certainly the eating of it was prohibited. [17] He

[15] ולאמת לפי דעתו ושכלו כתב כל התורה כאלו קבל משה מפי הגבורה הלכה למשה מסני מבלי ראייה ברורה ומכל מקום הוא מקובל בשכל הנקנה מאחר שאינו ידוע מקורו ובאמת כתב עליו ר' משה מקוצי שהוא כחלום בלא פתרון ... כי מי יודע מה הוא כוונתו אם מחמת ראיית מהתלמוד שלנו או מהירושלמי או מהתוספתא או מהגאונים או מסברת עצמו או טעות סופר הוא כאשר יש בכמה מקומות•

כי מימות רבינא ורב אשי אין קבלה לפסוק כאחד מן הגאונים או מן האחרונים אלא מי שיכשרו דבריו להיותן מיוסדים במופת חותך על פי התלמוד והירושלמי ותוספתא במקום שאין הכרע בתלמוד (הקדמה ב״ק, חולין)•

[16] Hul. 115. תנא לא תבשל גדי בחלב אמו שלש פעמים אחד לאסור אכילה אחד לאיסור הנאה ואחד לאיסור בישול•

[17] בשר בחלב אסור לבשלו ואסור לאכלו מו התורה ואסור בהנאה ומי שיבשל משניהם כאחד לוקה שנאמר לא תבשל גדי בחלב אמו וכן האוכל כזית משניהם מהבשר וחלב שנתבשלו כאחד לוקה ואף על פי שלא בשל לא שתק

357

rejected the talmudic prohibition of deriving benefit from
meat and milk cooked together as being Pentateuchal.
Maimonides based this halakah on the Targum according
to Jonathan. [18]

The *Schulchan Aruch*, by Rabbi Joseph Caro, was also
criticized by Rabbi Solomon Luria. He censured him for
following Alfasi, Maimonides and Rabbi Ascher in his decisions
of the halakot and ignoring Rashi, Rabbenu Tam and the
Franco-German sages. Luria stated that Rabbi Joseph
Caro based his halakic decisions on wrong readings and hence
built a foundation on errors. [19]

The codifiers of the Code in Israel should avoid the errors
made by Maimonides and Caro. A novella should be appended
in order to make the Code elastic, not static. The codifier must
also take cognizance of the reasons and causes for the enactment of the halakot by the sages.

Justice Silberg dealt with *Haarama* which he interprets,
"evading the law by means of the law itself." [20] *Haarama* is
applicable when the law is not specific. It is only a loop-hole
to get around the law due to its ambiguity. Rabbi Tarfon
and R. Joshua were the first to use this term. According to
the pentateuchal law one is forbidden to slaughter the dam

הכתוב מלאסור האכילה אלא מפני שאסור הבשול כלומר ואפילו בשלו אסור
ואין צריך לומר אכילתו (מאכלות אסורות פ״ט)·

[18] לית אתון רשאין למיבשלא כל דכן למיכל בשר בחלב תרויהון מערבין

בחדא· Deut. 14. 21.

[19] ולא די בזה למהרי״ קאר ומה שעשה פשרה על אילו שלשה הגדולים
הרי הרי״ף והראש והרמבם היכא שהשוו שנים מהם דאזלין בתרייהו ולא חש
לכל הגדולים האחרים כאלו מסורה הקבלה בידו מימות הזקנים ועוד אחרת
לא היו לפניו ספרים מוגהים והעתיקם בטעות כאשר ימצאו בדפוס ולפעמים
בנה יסוד על הטעות ההוא (הקדמה חולין)·

[20] מכוונת כלפי החוק עצמו בחינת "יכה יוסי את יוסי" מערימים על
החוק באמצעות החוק גופו· P. 26.

and its young on the same day. [21] If a dam and its young fall
into a pit on a holiday Rabbi Eleazar maintained that one
animal could be taken out of the pit and slaughtered while
the other animal should remain in the pit but be supplied
with provisions. According to the halakah the Jews were
allowed to work on a holiday only for their sustenance. Thus
if the dam and its young fell into the pit only one animal
could be taken out for slaughtering. Rabbi Joshua held that
in order to release both of the animals from the pit a Jew
may mentally designate one animal for slaughter and take
it out of the pit. Then he may change his mind and decide to
slaughter the other animal. Thus he acquires the right to
take the other animal from the pit and now that they are
both out he may slaughter either one. [22]

Justice Silberg is of the opinion that *Haarama* was a basis
for the sages to introduce *takkanot* [23] The *takkanot* permitted
things which had been previously prohibited. He believes
these to be a sequence of the *Haarama*. He cites the well
known *takkanah* of Prosbol. [24] According to the Pentateuch,
every seventh year was called the sabbatical year, in which,
"every creditor shall release that which he had lent unto
his neighbor; he shall not exact it of his neighbor and of his
brother because God's release had been proclaimed." Hillel
introduced Prosbol, by which the sabbatical year does not

---

[21] Lev. 23. 28.

[22] אותו ואת בנו שנפלו לבור ר׳ אליעזר אומר מעלה את הראשון על
מנת לשחטו ושוחטו והשני עושה לו פרנסה במקומו כדי שלא ימות ר׳ יהושע
אומר מעלה את הראשון על מנת לשחטו ואינו שוחטו וחוזר ומעלה השני רצה
זה שוחט רצה זה שוחט. Bezah 37. Tosefta ibid. 3. 2.
Cf. also Yer. Yeb. 4. 12.

[23] לכשנעיין בדבר נראה כי בכמה מו התקנות הבאות להתיר כבלי איסור
קודם יש הרבה מיסוד ההערמה. P. 40.

[24] P. 41. ואפתח בתקנה המפורסמת ביותר היא תקנת פרוזבל.

359

release the debt and the creditor has the right to demand his
loan. The text of the Prosbol is as follows: "I declare before
you, judges in the place, that I shall collect my debt that I
may have outstanding with . . . whenever I desire." [25] This
declaration the creditor deposited with the court. The word
Prosbol has the connotation προσβολη before the court. There
is a statement in the Mishne that if a creditor deposits the
promissory notes of the debtor the sabbatical year does not
apply to such a loan and the creditor has the right to collect
his debts. [26] If there was such a law, what was Hillel's *takkanah*
of Prosbol? If it is the same, what was the purpose of Hillel's
takkanah? If it is not the same then what is the difference
and why did Hillel introduce the Prosbol? The rabbis of the
middle ages were divided on this point. Some maintained that
Hillel's *takkanah* of Prosbol did not differ from the halakot
given in the Mishne, where it is stated that if the creditor
deposited his promissory notes with the court, the law of the
sabbatical year does not apply to his loan. Others held that
Hillel's *takkanah* of Prosbol did differ from the halakot
stated in the Mishne. [27]

In my article, "Prosbol", [28] I pointed out that Hillel's
takkanah of Prosbol was a modification and later development
of the halakot stated in the Mishne. The law stated in the
Mishne refers only to a loan for which the debtor gave a
promissory note to the creditor. However if a loan was transacted in the presence of witnesses or without witnesses it was
to be forfeited if not paid before the sabbatical year. On the
basis of the previous halakot Hillel introduced the Prosbol,

[25] זו גופו של פרוזבל אני מוסר לכם איש פלוני ופלוני הדיינים שבמקום

פלוני שכל חוב שיש לי שאגבנו כל זמן שארצה· Mishne Sheb. 10. 2.

[26] Ibid.   והמוסר שטרותיו לבית דין אין משמטין·

[27] וכ״ת כיון דמדאורייתא במסירת שטרות סגיא למה הוצרך לתקן פרוזבל·
R. Nissim, (on Alfasi), Git. 4.

[28] *JQR* 1947, pp. 341-362.

i.e., if the creditor has no promissory note from the debtor the creditor writes a note in which he states that a certain person owes him so much money which he will collect whenever he desires and he then deposits it with the court. Such a loan is not forfeited since the law of the sabbatical year is not applicable to it. Thus Hillel's *takkanah* of Prosbol is a development of the halakot recorded in the Mishne. This halakah was instituted at the time of John Hyrcanus I. Hillel introduced the *takkanah* of Prosbol at the time of Herod.

The takkanah of Prosbol has no relation to *Haarama*. *Haarama* is a matter of individuals. When the law is ambiguous an individual had the right to use a loop hole to circumvent it. A *takkanah* was introduced by the sages who sought support for it in the Pentateuch. With regard to the sabbatical year in relation to a loan the Pentateuch states ואת אחיך שמט ידך, what is in your hand. However if the promissory note was deposited with the court the loan was in the hands of the court. This may be designated as a legal fiction but not *Haarama*. There is a vast difference between *Haarama* and takkanah.

Justice Silberg states that Samuel sharply criticized the takkanah of Prosbal, terming it "arrogant." [29] Silberg is well fortified in his statement by passages in the Talmud. However I have pointed out elsewhere that Samuel did not critcize the takkanah of Prosbol. The Prosbol was written before a court of two persons. [30] Samuel was of the opinion that a decision of a court of two persons while it was valid was an arrogant act of the court. Thus the Prosbol, which was transacted before a court of two, according to Samuel was an act of arrogance. [31] Samuel was not against the takka-

---

[29] ואם היה מי שקרא תגר חריף על תקנה זו־האמורא שמואל קרא לה בשם "חוצפה"׃ P. 43.

[30] לבי תרי נמי בית דין קרו להו אמר רב נחמן מנא אמינא להדתנן מוסרני לפניכם פלוני ופלוני הדיינים׃ Git. 32.

[31] Sanh. 5. אמר שמואל שנים שדנו דיניהם דין אלא שנקרא בית דין חצוף׃

nah of Prosbal; he could not be even if he wanted to. As an Amora he could not dispute and make void a takkanah introduced by Hillel. What Samuel criticized was the procedure of the Prosbol which was deposited before a court of two. According to him it should have been deposited before a court of three. To the statement of Samuel the Talmud adds that Rab Nachman remarked that he would confirm the Prosbol. The sages in the Talmud had difficulty in explaining the words of Rab Nachman. [32] However, in my opinion, the words of Rab Nachman are clear. He maintained that a court of two persons is bona fide and said that he tried monetary cases alone. [33] Thus, according to him, the Prosbol which was deposited before a court of two was bona fide. It seems to me that this passage in the Talmud is not amoraic but saboraic, a later edition.

Supporting himself on the Talmud, Justice Silberg said that Hillel introduced the Prosbol on the principle *hefker bet din hefker*, [34] i.e., that the court had the right to renounce property of an individual, to make it *res nulius*. Hillel did not base his takkanah of Prosbol on the principle of *hefker bet din hefker*. As was noted before it was based on the Pentateuch. As a matter of fact the concept of *hefker bet din hefker* came into being after the destruction of the Temple when the Sanhedrin had the religious and civil authority over the people. During the Second Commonwealth the Court had no right to renounce the property of individuals, the civil authorities would not tolerate it. John Hyrcanus I, Janeus Alexander, Queen Salome, John Hyrcanus II, Aristobolus, Herod and the Roman procurators would not allow the Court to exercise such a right. It was in their jurisdiction.

It has been suggested that Samuel was against Hillel's

---

[32] See Git. 36. רב נחמן אמר אקיימנה׃

[33] Sanh. 5. אמר רב נחמן כגון אנא דן דיני ממונות ביחידי׃

[34] P. 43. ואם לשם הצדקתה גייס חרעיון של ״הפקר בית דין הפקר״׃

takkanah of Prosbol as, being a Babylonian where commerce was not yet developed and there were no loan transactions and hence the takkanah of Prosbol was not needed. This assumption betrays lack of comprehension of talmudic law. According to the Mishne if the debtor gave the creditor security for the loan the sabbatical year was not applicable and the loan could be collected at any time although the security did not have the value of the loan. [35] Samuel was of the opinion that if a person gave a loan and the debtor gave a needle as security, which did not have even a fractional value of the loan, the law of the sabbatical year was not applicable and the creditor could collect the loan at any time. [36] Thus it is clear that even in Babylonia there were loan transactions. Furthermore we may deduce that Samuel was not against Hillel's takkanah as he held that if a person gave a loan of, let us say, one thousand dollars and the debtor gave a security something of the value of a needle, the law of the sabbatical year was not applicable. [37] This is certainly a legal fiction. It is evident therefore that Samuel did not oppose Hillel's takkanah which was based on a legal fiction.

Justice Silberg rightly said that the phrase שעבוד הגוף does not occur in the Talmud, that this expression is post-talmudic. Originally the creditor had the right to take the debtor or his children into bondage or sell them into slavery. That the creditor had this right is evident from II Kings, "A certain woman of the wives of the sons of the prophets cried to Elisha saying: 'Thy servant, my husband, is dead, and thou knowest that thy servant feared God and the creditor has come to take unto him my two sons for bond men' ". [38] It is evident from

---

[35] המלוה את חבירו על המשכון אף על פי שהחוב מרובה על המשכון אינו משמט. Tosefta Sheb. 8. 5.

[36] חמלוה על המשכון אינן משמטין שמואל אומר אפילו על המחט. Yer. Sheb. 10.

[37] Cf. Shebuot 43.

[38] II Kings 4. 1-7.

her complaint that in ancient times if the debtor did not pay
his debt his creditor had the right to take him into servitude,
or if he died to take his children into bondage.

We learn from Nehemiah that the Judeans complained to
him, "We have borrowed money for the king's tribute upon
our fields and our vineyards. Yet now our flesh is as the flesh
of our brethren, our children as their children; and lo, we
bring into bondage our sons and our daughters to be servants,
and some of our daughters are brought into bondage already;
neither is it in our power to help it; for other men have our
fields and our vineyards." [39] Hence, after the Restoration,
the creditor had the right over the debtor in person as well
in property. The creditor's right over the debtor, even to
kill him, if the debt was unpaid, was abolished in 313 BCE by
the lex Poetelia. [40] Diodorus said that in Egypt, where
Hellenist Egyptian law prevailed, the creditor had the right
to imprison the debtor or sell him into slavery if the debt
was unpaid. [41] In I Maccabees it is stated that among the
privileges granted by Demetrius to Jonathan was that he
recognized the Temple in Jerusalem as an asylum, "Whoever
shall flee to the Temple in Jerusalem, or to any of its precincts,
whether because they owe money to the king or for any other
debt, shall be released with all they possess in my kingdom." [42]
From this it can be deduced that at the time of Demetrius I
according to the law the creditor had the right over the person
of the debtor and his property.

After the Restoration the sages abolished the right of the
creditor over the person of the debtor. If the debtor gave the
creditor a *shtar*, a promissory note for the loan he placed
his property as a hypothec. The creditor had the right to seize
the property of the debtor but he had no right over his
person, he could not take him in bondage nor imprison him.

[39] Neh. 5. 1-5.
[40] Cf. Gaii *Institutionum Iuris Civilis* III.
[41] I. 79.
[42] 10. 43.

This is the reason why the phrase שעבוד הגוף does not occur in the Talmud.

It is stated in the Talmud that Samuel said that when a creditor sold a promissory note and then remitted the debt the remittance was valid. [43] Many have questioned the ethical side of this law. Justice Silberg quotes Rabbenu Nisim who maintained that the creditor has two rights over the debtor, which are,—1—The creditor has the right on the debtor who is obliged to repay the money borrowed; 2.—The creditor has a lien, right on the debtor's property if the debt is not paid on time; he has the right of seizure. [44] With all due respect to the sages of the Middle Ages I must say that Rabbenu Nisim's view is not well grounded.

The halakic decision of Samuel does not violate the law of equity. It is axiomatic that a creditor has the privilege of remitting a debt owed to him. The promissory note takes effect only on the date the debt is due. It is true that the creditor who received a promissory note for an unpaid loan had the right to seize the property of the debtor to the amount of indebtedness and if the debtor had sold his property after the loan was made the creditor has the right to seize the property from the buyer. The promissory note came into force when the debt had not been paid. It had no value before the date given nor had it value if the money was paid on time. Let us say A has advanced a loan to B and B has given a promissory note to A to be paid on a certain date.

[43] Ket. 86. אמר שמואל המוכר שטר חוב לחבירו וחזר ומחלו מחול׃

[44] ״אבל מוכר שטר חוב אף על פי שמכירתו מדאורייתא יכול למחול לפי ששני שעבודים יש לו למלוה על הלוה שעבוד גופו של לוה שהוא מתחייב לפרוע והוא עיקר השעבוד ושעבוד על נכסיו אם הוא לא יפרע מדין ערב וכדאמרינן נכסוהי דבר אינש אינון ערבין ביה ושעבוד הגוף שיש למלוה על הלוה לאו בר מכירה הוא הלכך אינו נמכר אלא שעבוד נכסים בלבד ואף על פי שאינו נמכר־לא פקע אבל כי חזר ומחלו־פקע שעבוד הגוף וממלא פקע שעבוד נכסים שאינו אלא מדין ערב ״׃

A has the privilege of remitting the loan. When A sells the promissory note to C the buyer is aware that a creditor has the privilege of remitting the debt which he has advanced. Thus the buyer purchased the promissory note on the possibility that if the creditor did not remit the debt and the debtor did not pay on time he has the right to seize the property of the debtor to the value of the debt. He really becomes the agent of the creditor. When A remits the debt owed him by B the purchaser of the promissory note could only collect from A the sum which he paid from it. [45]

Justice Silberg deals with the principle of *Breira* and cites seven examples from tannaitic literature. The term *Breira* never occurs in tannaitic literature. The Babylonian Amoraim introduced this principle and injected it into the halakic statements of Rabbis Meir, Jose and Simon. The Amoraim encountered great difficulties since, according to them, Rabbi Jose contradicts himself. In one place he does not hold the principle of *Breira* while in another place he does. To reconcile the conflicting views of Rabbi Jose the Amoraim reversed one of his statements. [46] Similarly, according to them, they held that Rabbi Simon does not follow the principle of *Breira* while in another halakic statement he does. Again, to reconcile Rabbi Simon's conflicting statements the Amoraim reversed the statement which, to them, he seemed to hold. [47] But this method of reversing statements of the Tannaim is an easy way out. It reminds one modern higher criticism of the Bible. As a matter of fact the Palestinian Talmud in explaining controversies between Rabbis Meir, Jose and Simon gave other reasons for their vieuws. [48] The Palestinian Amoraim do not explain their views on the

---

[45] *Cf.* Ket. 86.

[46] Eur. 37. ‏איפוך ··· ואכתי סבר רבי יוסי אין ברירה והתניא‏

[47] Ibid. ‏והא שמעינן לרבי שמעון דלית ליה ברירה קשיא דרבי שמעון‏

‏אדרבי שמעון אלא איפוך·‏

[48] *Cf.* Yer. ibid. 3. 7.

principle of *Breira*. As I have said, the Amoraim only injected the principle of *Breira* into the tannaitic halakot. It is true that the codifier must reckon with the views of the Amoraim. But he must also be aware of the reasons and background of the halakic statements of the Tannaim.

It seems to me that Rabbi Meir's opinion in regard to the tithe (Tosefta Demoi) is not based on the principle of *Breira* but on the principle of אדם מקדיש דבר שלא בא לעולם that one may sanctify an object which is not yet in existence and may not come into being. The controversy among the Tannaim in regard to *Erubin* is not on the principle of *Breira* but on the principle of intention.

I wonder that Justice Silberg has not referred to the principle of intention, which was introduced by Hillel and followed by his school. The principle of intention was revolutionary. It modified many of the pentateuchal laws and had great effect on the development of halakah. Hitherto only a person's act had been recognized in Judaean jurisprudence. Hillel was the first to introduce intention as a legal principle, that act alone is not considered sufficient to be valid. An act is a voluntary movement of the body, but when there is no volition then it is not an act but an accident, or event. If a man, for example, jumps from a bridge, it is an act because it is accompanied by volition. If he falls or is pushed from a bridge it is an accident or event because there is no volition. Similarly if the hand of a person is forcibly guided to affix his signature on a deed it is not considered an act since will was absent. Intention refers only to a future act—the consequence of the first act, to the ultimate purpose, to the end and not to the means. If a person throws a missile in order to break an object, or to injure some one, the throwing of the missile is an act, the injuring is the consequence of the first act. The second act resulted from the will of throwing with the intention of injuring. Thus intention refers only to the consequence of the first act. The idea of intention was applied not only to ritual laws but also to civil laws and to what is

15

known in modern jurisprudence as criminal laws. For example, if a person threw a stone at some one intending only to strike the person's leg but not intending to kill him, but the stone struck his heart instead causing his death. The school of Hillel, which followed the principle of intention, did not consider such a person guilty of capital punishment since the killing was not premeditaded. [49]

According to the old halakah a woman may be acquired in one of three ways. [50] She may be acquired by money but the act of giving money to the woman does not make her his wife. The man had to give her the money with the intention of marriage. Consequently a minor or imbecile who does act but has not the power of intention cannot marry. [51] Their act in regard to marriage is void.

Hillel's principle of intention aroused great opposition among the conservatives. Shammai strongly opposed this innovation. In the Talmud it is related that once when Hillel brought up the principle of intention Shammai and his followers, who were in the majority, rejected it. Hillel on that day sat before Shammai bowed as a pupil before his teacher. Later, however, intention became a principle in tannaitic jurisprudence. [52]

This essay is not a review of Justice Silberg's book although I hope some day to do so. My purpose was to demonstrate

[49] Cf. S. Zeitlin, "Is a Revival of a Sanhedrin in Israel Necessary for Modification of the Halaka?" *JQR*, 1952, pp. 356-57.

[50] Cf. Mishne Kid. 1. 1.

[51] See Tosefta Yeb. 11. 10.

[52] In my article "Intention as a Legal Principle" published in the *Journal of Jewish Lore and Philosophy*, 1919 I explained that the controversy between the School of Shammai and that of Hillel, recorded in the first Mishne of Beza regarding an egg laid on a holiday was based on the principle of intention. Some of my senior colleagues have criticized me for this assumption since it is contrary to the amoraic interpretation. Ten years later, however, one of them wrote that this controversy was based on intention and claimed that it was his great discovery, making no mention of my article published ten years previously.

the need for a codifier to be aware of the history and background of the law. In his book he reveals profound knowledge of the Babylonian Talmud and the vast rabbinic literature, and in his interpretations demonstrates keen insight and brilliance of mind. But in dealing with the laws he follows the dogmatic method without taking cognizance of the historical reasons for their enactments. To follow the dogmatic method would be placing a strait jacket on the people. To repeat, the laws must be in consonance with life, *they are for the people—not the people for the laws.* Even some of the rabbis of the Middle Ages recognized this principle. To cite only one example;—according to the Talmud wine of the non-Jews, which was not known to be used for libations to the idols, was forbidden not only for drinking but also for the deriving of any benefit therefrom, i.e., to sell it. [53] Maimonides, in his code *Mishne Torah*, followed the Talmud and stated that it is forbidden for a Jew to derive any benefit from wine handled by a non-Jew. [54] On the other hand, Rashi, who lived in Champagne, famous for its wine and where the Jews employed non-Jews in raising grapes and making wine, interpreted the halakah in the Talmud [55] so as to make it possible for the Jews not only to sell the wine but also to drink it. [56] This is a clear indication that in interpreting the halakah the welfare of the people must be considered.

During the Second Commonwealth the sages introduced institutions and laws which are not recorded in the Penta-

---

[53] See Ab. Zarah 31 אילו דברים של גוים אסורין ואיסורין איסור הנאה היין : סתם יינם אסור בהנאה.

[54] וכל יין שיגע בו הגוי הרי זה אסור בהנייה (מאכלות) אסורות.

[55] See Tos. ibid. 57. פירוש רשב״ם והרי״בן בשם רש״י שכתב בתשובת הגאונים כי בזמן הזה אין איסור הנאה במגע נכרי ביין.

[56] *Mordecai ad loc* ... פסקו דגוים בזמן הזה כתינוק בן יומו... אביך רש״י Cf. also Tos. Ab Zarah 57. דתינוק בן יומו אין עושה יין נסך ליאסר אף בשתיה.

teuch.—the laws of possession, partnership, agency,
testamentary succession, etc. Many principles devising the
interpretation of laws were brought forth by them. They were
great jurists. After the destruction of the Temple the Tannaim
continued the process of development of law. The laws were
the product of Judaea. From the third century on a great
center of the Jews flourished in Babylonia. The sages there,
called Amoraim, introduced many laws based on the interpretation of the tannaitic halakot. In Eretz Israel the sages
continued to interpret the tannaitic halakot but in many
instances they disagreed with the Babylonian authorities.
This was due to the different geographic, historical and
social conditions prevailing in these two different countries.

It is true the Geonim maintained that the Babylonian
Talmud, rather the Gamara, was authoritative and where
there was a discrepancy between these two Talmuds the law
had to follow the Babylonian Talmud. [57] The Geonim, who
were Babylonians, continued to study and interpret the
Babylonian Talmud ignoring the Palestinian Talmud. However there is no reason for the rabbis and judges in Israel, or
for that matter anywhere, to hold that the Babylonian
Talmud takes precedence over the Palestinian Talmud. In
codifying the laws one must take cognizance of the halakic
decisions. Justice Silberg, in appealing for a code in Israel,
makes over three hundred references to the Babylonian
Talmud (a few to the Mishne) while he makes only ten
references to the Palestinian Talmud. In other words he
ignores the Palestinian Talmud as a factor in the codification
of the law. In my opinion many of the halakot in the Palestinian Talmud should take precedence over the halakot in
the Babylonian Talmud.

[57] ומלתא דפסיקא בתלמוד דילנא לא מסכינן בה על תלמודא דבני ארץ
ישראל, (האי גאון : תשובות הגאונים ; שמחה אסף); דעל גמרא דילן סמכינן
דבתראי אינון, (אלפסי עירובין י׳).

In concluding his book, Justice Silberg sets forth the
question:—Is there indeed a need for a new code since there
already exist comprehensive codes:—Maimonides, *Tur* and
the *Shulchan Aruch*? [58] There can be no question that the
need for a new code is great since a chaotic state exists in
Israel in regard to religious and civil laws. The author rightly
points out that the judges in Israel utilize different laws in
their decisions,—English, Jewish, French and Ottoman.
However we do not agree with him that the codes of Maimonides and *Tur* and *Schulchan Aruch* are comprehensive.
Even in their times great rabbinic authorities challenged the
decisions. As a matter of fact some of the laws given in their
codes cannot be accepted to-day. A modern civilized society
like Israel cannot blindly follow their decisions. As was
pointed out before the codifier must be aware of the historical
and social causes which brought about the enactment of the
laws. I shall reiterate what I said in my reviews on Silberg's
Personal Life in Israel [59] and Judge Schereschewsky's *Family
Life in Israel.* [60] According to Justice Silberg, if two brothers
have testified that A married a woman in their presence,
the marriage would be void since the witnesses were blood
relations. Judge Schereschewsk followed the same view
when he said that the presence of the two witnesses is
not for testimony but is an integral part of the marriage
procedure; if they are blood relations of one or the other of
the couple the marriage is to be held void. It is true that this
is the halakic decision of the *Shulchan Aruch* but, as I have
pointed out, according to the Tannaim the necessity for
witnesses was not to validate or legalize the marriage but to
serve as proof against those who later might deny the marriage.
This law was introduced in order to prevent the husband or

[58] הישנו צורך בעריכת ספר חוקים חדש לאור הקודיפיקציות המקיפות

של הרמב״ם הטור והשולחן ערוך?

[59] *JQR* October 1958.
[60] *JQR* April 1961.

the wife who might for some reason claim that they were not married which could lead to serious consequences. In criminal cases and in civil transactions two witnesses are required who must be without criminal records and who are not related to the principals. In the case of marriage, however, the necessity for two witnesses was to prevent the denial by either party to the marriage. Thus if the witnesses are related to the bride or to the groom there is no reason to disqualify them, rendering the marriage void, and in the case of children making them illegitimate. This is one of the many instances where a codifier must be aware of the causes for the enactment of laws. The law of the later rabbinic authorities maintained that if a marriage was transacted in the presence of two witnesses who were blood relations to one or the other of the parties such a marriage should be considered void. With all humility I may say that their decision is void since this is contrary to the views of the Tannaim.

Justice Silberg propounded another question;—Is there a possibility in our day to codify the laws? This, I believe, can be done but for it all the intellectual strength must be mobilized. The group who will work on the codification must consist of great talmudic and rabbinic scholars, historians and jurists.

The question may arise,—will such a code be accepted by the people in Israel? Would not such a code arouse great opposition from the ultra orthodox? It undoubtedly would do so; this is to be expected. The sages during the Second Commonwealth were also confronted with great opposition from the Sadducees. Even among the Pharisees the conservative group opposed the school of Hillel's interpretations of the pentateuchal laws. At the Conclave in 65 C.E. some of the Hillelites were killed by the opposing group of the Shammaites. [61] Later, however, the views of the Hillelites were accepted because they followed the spirit of the law

[61] *Cf.* Yer. Shab. 1.

and not the letter of the law. Their views were in consonance
with life. The acceptance of a modern code in Israel could
be readily solved, i.e., by the State. If the civil authorities
should sanction such a code prepared by religious authorities
it would become the law of the State and would be enforced.
The question may arise whether this code would be accepted
by the Jews of the Diaspora where they are now divided
religious groups. We may say a *priori* that it will not be
accepted by the entire Jewry of the Diaspora. The ultra
orthodox would certainly oppose such a code. However if the
codification of the halakot would be in the spirit that they
are made for man, in order to promote their progress, and in
the spirit of the sages of the Second Commonwealth, who
strove to bring the halakot into consonance with life, such
a code would have great influence on the entire Jewry as
did the Mishne.

In my article "Is a Revival of a Sanhedrin in Israel Necessary for Modification of the Halakot?" (*JQR*, 1952) I pointed
out the need for a corpus of halakot based on historical
development. Just as the Roman law became the basis of
western European law so should the corpus of the Pharisaic
halaka of the Second Commonwealth become the basis for
the code of the Third Commonwealth. We do not imply
that the vast rabbinic literature should be ignored. On the
contrary it must be studied carefully and the halakot principles which were introduced by the great rabbis of the Middle
Ages must be seriously considered. As we said before, the
code must be supplied with novella. Can the religious and
civil leaders in Israel meet this historical challenge? Only
the future can disclose.

IS A REVIVAL OF A SANHEDRIN IN ISRAEL NECESSARY FOR MODIFICATION OF THE HALAKA?

I

WHEN the Jews returned from Babylon to Judaea after the Restoration, their religious as well as communal leadership was in the hands of the High Priests who continued to rule them according to the laws of the Pentateuch. We have a right to assume that the customs which came into vogue during the long period of the First Temple were also regarded as holy by the High Priests who ruled over the Jews with the assistance of the Gerousia, the Assembly, but that they disregarded the need of the people for new laws and resisted attempts to modify the Pentateuchal laws. There was, however, another group of Jews who strove to harmonize the law with the new political conditions. They sought to amend and interpret the biblical laws in accordance with the life of the new community. This group was called *Perushim* — Pharisees — Separatists by those who subscribed to the High Priestly idea that nothing in the law could be changed or modified. They were charged with having separated themselves from the Jews and with not yielding obedience to all the laws of the Bible. During the time the High Priestly family ruled over the Jews, it adopted the honorary name of the first High Priest of the Temple during the time of Solomon, Zadok, and called themselves *Zadokites*, Sadducees.[1]

[1] See S. Zeitlin, הצדוקים והפרושים.

339

Thus, the Pharisees were the opposition group to the ruling Sadducees. We do not know how well they succeeded in modifying the Jewish laws, since, from the time of the Restoration to the time of the Hasmonean period, the name of no scholar is mentioned in tannaitic literature, for the entire power was in the hands of the High Priests, or Sadducees, and the Gerousia. Occasionally some of the Assemblies struck out independently, for they had other matters to handle besides the political and social life of the Jews. The Talmud, in fact, ascribes some religious enactments to the Great Assembly, but we do not know to which of the Great Assemblies.[2] There were many Great Assemblies during the Second Commonwealth.[3]

A revolutionary change took place in the development of Judaism with the successful revolt of the Hasmoneans. The High Priests of the family of Zadok were overthrown because of the apostasy of Joshua-Jason and Onias-Menelaus, who were responsible for the suffering of the Jews under Antiochus. A priest not of the family of Zadok was elected. His very election was revolutionary. According to the Bible, God had made a covenant with Phineas, progenitor of Zadok, that the office of the High Priest would remain with his descendants perpetually,[4] and accordingly the office descended from father to son, century after century. They ruled over the people by the authority of the Pentateuch and did not need their consent. There was supposedly something divine about the order of succession. The office of High Priest now was given to a priest of another family. It is true that in the document recording the election of Simon, the High Priesthood was given to him until "a

---

[2] *Idem*, "The Origin of the Synagogue," American Academy for Jewish Research, 1931.

[3] *Ibid*.

[4] Num. 25.13.

true prophet should arise,"[5] but this clause was inserted merely to legalize his election.

Simon was elected High Priest and Governor of Judaea, but he was shorn of religious power over the Jews. The High Priest hitherto had been the vicar of God and had full religious power over the Jews. By the election of Simon, the theocracy, which was the form of government in Judaea from the time of the Restoration, was abolished and a Commonwealth was established. The religious power now no longer rested in the hands of the High Priest. A *Bet Din*, Sanhedrin, was established to deal with the religious problems.[6] The Pharisees who had been in the minority before the Hasmonean period, and had been regarded by the High Priest, the vicar of God, as heretics because they believed in a liberal interpretation of the law, now became the majority power because of their great assistance to the Hasmoneans in their revolt against Hellenization. The Pharisees held the power in the Sanhedrin in all religious matters throughout the entire period of the Second Jewish Commonwealth, with the exception of the last days of the rule of John Hyrcanus who broke with them, and in the time of his son, Alexander Janneus.[6a] Except for this short period they dominated the Jewish religion and molded it. The Sadducees consisting of the wealthy people, became the minority group, while the Pharisees were the leaders of the masses. In the eyes of the Pharisees the name Sadducees became one of reproach, and they were looked upon as heretics, as a group who did not follow the interpretation of the law which the Pharisees called the Tradition of the Elders. The name Sadducees has been synonymous with heresy in Jewish literature since.

[5] I Mac. 14.41.

[6] See S. Zeitlin, "The Political Synedrion and the Religious Sanhedrin," *JQR* 1945.

[6a] Also in the time of Aristobulus.

The establishment of the Sanhedrin, בית דין, was itself an
innovation in Jewish history. In the period of the Judges
the latter ruled the people and judged them, because they
were responsible for the victory of Israel over its enemies,
and hence they became its leaders. In the later period
the kings ruled the people and settled their personal
quarrels.[7] The author of II Samuel relates that when
Absalom plotted the overthrow of the throne of his father,
David, he used to arise early to meet any man who "had
a suit which should come to the king for judgment," and
that he used to say to the people, "O, that I were made
judge in the land, that every man who hath any suit or
cause might come unto me, and I would do him justice."[8]
Solomon, after ascending the throne of his father, prayed
to God that among other things God should grant him
"an understanding heart to judge."[9] To show, in fact,
that God had granted him "a heart to judge," the Bible
relates the well-known story of the quarrel between the
two harlots, as to who was the mother of the child each
claimed. The kings who ruled after Solomon were judges,
and also appointed judges who were responsible to them.
In ancient times it was the custom in the states where
monarchy ruled for the kings to be the judges.[10]

After the Restoration, as was previously stated, the
High Priests were the rulers and the judges of the Jews,
since, according to the Pentateuch, the right to judge
was given to the priests.[11] The Persian king gave authority
to Ezra to appoint judges "who may judge all the people
who are beyond the river," and gave him the right to
punish those who transgressed the laws of God and the

---

[7] *Ibid.*   [8] II Sam. 15.2–4.

[9] I Kings 3.9, לב שמע לשפוט.

[10] Comp. Aristotle, *Politics*, III, 9 (1285b).

[11] Deut. 17.8–12; 33.10, יורו משפטיך ליעקב ותורתך לישראל. Comp. also
Ezek. 44.23–4, ואת עמי יורו . . . ועל ריב המה יעמדו למשפט במשפטי ישפטהו.

laws of the king, by confiscation of goods, by imprisonment, and by death.[12] This authority was also conferred by the subsequent kings of Persia, and later by the Ptolemaic and Seleucidan king upon the High Priest.

With the establishment of a free state, the institution of the Sanhedrin came into being, having a few subsidiary branches. The membership of the body was seventy-one,[12a] but the trial court which tried capital cases consisted of twenty-three members. We find it stated that the Sanhedrin already had existed in the time of David,[13] but these statements are of aggadic character and have no historical significance.

II

The Pharisees, being the dominating group, now strove to realize their idea that religion must be brought into consonance with life, and even sought to amend the Pentateuchal laws if new conditions so warranted; in other words, they tried to make Judaism a living religion, and they interpreted the biblical laws accordingly.

In the Pentateuch the terms מותר, אסור and טרפה, כשר are not found, and anything which was prohibited was signified by the word טמא defiled. Anything that was defiled was taboo which the people were afraid to touch. I shall give a few instances in which the Pharisees amended the

[12] Ezra 7.25–6, מני שפטין ודיינין די להון דאנין לכל עמא.

[12a] It was a legislative body whose function was to interpret the biblical law and fix the halaka. The Sanhedrin of seventy-one never tried any cases which involved capital punishment. However, in cases which involved a trial of the head of the State or the High Priest, for an offense against the State or the Temple, the Sanhedrin of seventy-one could be established as a trial court. This was merely the constitutional right of the Sanhedrin, which had never been applied.

[13] Ber. 3b–4a, בניהו בן יהוידע זה סנהדרין, ונמלכין בסנהדרין; Shab. 56a, שהיה לך לדונו בסנהדרין ולא דנתו . . . The term *Bet Din* is not found in the Bible.

laws of the Pentateuch so as not to make them a burden upon the people, in order that the Jews should be able to observe them.[14]

According to the Pentateuch, "if water be put upon the seed, and aught of their carcasses fall thereon, it is unclean unto you."[15] Since Judaea had to import grain from Egypt where fields were irrigated, that is, if the inhabitants put water on the seed, such a seed was susceptible to uncleanliness, and thus grain could not be imported from there into Judaea. Indeed, one of the conservatives of the Pharisee group, Joshua ben Perahiah, declared that the grain imported from Egypt was unclean,[16] but the Pharisees interpreted the word seed to refer only to that detached from the ground.[17] Thus, if the water had been poured on the seed attached to the ground, the seed does not become susceptible and unclean; therefore, grain could be imported from Egypt.

According to the Pentateuch, if a person was affected by bodily impurity, i. e., experienced a *noctis pollutio*, he had to leave the city and was considered unclean until the sun set and until after he had bathed.[18] That this law was in vogue among the Jews can be deduced from the story told in I Sam. When David did not appear at the table of Saul, his father-in-law, the king did not harbor any resentment against David because he believed he had

[14] The following halakot are presented in this essay to show how the sages amended the laws of the Pentateuch. I dealt with these halakot at length and more thoroughly in the numerous articles which I wrote during the past thirty years on the history and development of the halakot. I shall hereafter refer to these articles. Many scholars have dealt with these halakot but their studies are not historical.

[15] Lev. 11.38, ‏וכי יתן מים על זרע ונפל מנבלתם עליו טמא הוא לכם‎.

[16] See Tosefta Maksh. 3.4, ‏יהושע בן פרחיה אומר חטים הבאות מאלכסנדריא‎ (ἀντολίον‎=‏אנטליא‎) ‏טמא מפני אנטליא שלהן‎ a water-wheel with which the Egyptians irrigated their fields from the Nile.

[17] See Sifra Shemini, comp. S. Zeitlin, "Takkanat Ezra" *JQR* 1917.

[18] Deut. 23.11-2.

contracted a minor uncleanliness, *noctis pollutio.*[19] During
the Second Commonwealth, however, the law that a man
who contracted a minor uncleanliness would have to leave
his family until nightfall and then would have to bathe
to be considered pure was reinterpreted by the Pharisees.
They held the word מחנה to mean מחנה שכינה[20] i. e., the
sanctuary; hence, a person so affected would be deprived
only of the privilege of entering the sanctuary. They also
interpreted the biblical law that he is unclean until sunset
to refer only to eating *terumah* but not to ordinary food;[21]
thus, this law of uncleanliness was made not to apply to
Israelites at all. A few years before the destruction of the
Second Temple the sages·for some reason declared that a
Jew is always in a status of uncleanliness, and that if he
touched *terumah* with his hands, the *terumah* was defiled.
Hence, according to the old law, if a Jew was considered
unclean he was required to go through the ceremony of
being immersed in water. To make this law easier for
the Jews to observe, the sages introduced a new law that
washing the hands was sufficient, and thus arose the
well known institution of washing the hands before meals.[22]
The Talmud ascribes this institution to King Solomon,[23]
but it is clear from the Talmud that the institution of
washing the hands before meals was introduced not long
before the time of Rabbi Eleazar ben Aroch.[24] Washing

---

[19] I Sam. 20.26, כי אמר מקרה הוא בלתי טהור הוא כי לא טהור.

[20] ויצא אל מחוץ למחנה זה מחנה לויה, לא יבא אל תוך המחנה זה מחנה שכינה.

[21] See Tosefta Parah 3.6, מעשר נאכל בטבול יום; Sifra Shemini, מטמא
עד הערב... טהור לחולין מבעוד יום ולתרומה משתחשך; מה ישראל שאינם אוכלים
בתרומה בטעורבי שמש הרי הן אוכלים במעשר טבולי יום (Emor), see more
S. Zeitlin, "Takkanot Ezra" *JQR* 1917.

[22] *Idem, HUCA* I, pp. 369–71.

[23] Shab. 19b, אמר ר' יהודה אמר שמואל בשעה שתיקן שלמה עירובין ונטילת
ידים.

[24] Ḥul. 106a וידיו לא שטף במים אמר ר' אלעזר בן ערך מכאן סמכו חכמים
לנטילת ידים מן התורה.

the hands previous to the meal was considered a מצוה.
Some sages in the Talmud asked מאי מצוה. One answer is
that it was a command to follow the utterances of the
sages. Another sage said the command was to follow the
utterances of Rabbi Eleazar ben Aroch.[25] They did not say
the command was to follow the words of Solomon. These
sages who were quoted in the Talmud did not know that
the institution of washing the hands was ascribed to King
Solomon. It can be readily seen from these two examples
how the sages were interested in harmonizing religion with
life.

The laws of טומאה וטהרה impurity and purity had a
prominent place in the Pentateuch. Almost the entire book
of Leviticus deals with these laws. According to the Pentateuch almost anything can defile a person — a carcass, or
noctis pollutio. It would have been impossible for a Jew,
during the Second Commonwealth, to observe strictly the
laws of impurity and purity. The Pharisees therefore
reinterpreted the biblical laws of impurity and purity, but
did so in the spirit of the Pentateuch and made it possible
for a Jew to observe the law.

The methods of liberally interpreting the Pentateuchal
laws so as to render it possible for the Jews to observe
them, and at the same time to make religion a living force
among the people, were applied to many precepts of the
Torah.

The laws of the Sabbath, for example, were very strict,
according to the book of Exodus. "You shall sit each of
you in his place. Let no man go out of his place on the

---

[25] מאי מצוה? מצוה לשמוע דברי חכמים . . . מצוה לשמוע דברי ר' אלעזר בן ערך.
Some sages were averse to the alleviation of the *takkana* of washing
the hands, among them was R. Eleazar ben Hanoch, and he was
excommunicated for not accepting of this *takkana*, see M. Eduy. 5.6;
Yer. M. K. 3; B. Ber. 19a, את מי נדו את ר' אלעזר בן חנוך שפקפק
[בנטילת ידים] (בטהרת ידים).

seventh day."[26] According to this literal meaning the Jews had no right to leave their places (houses) on the Sabbath; indeed, the Septuagint in translating the word תחתיו has "his house."[27] This would mean that the Jews had no right to go out of their houses on the Sabbath, but four cubits distant from their home. This sort of confinement on the Sabbath was oppressive. They were actually confined in their homes or nearby for the entire Sabbath day.

The modification of the laws of the Sabbath was made gradually. First the word מקום was interpreted to mean "city," and it was held that a Jew might walk on the Sabbath two thousand cubits in any direction within the city;[28] later the law was further modified to allow a Jew to walk two thousand cubits beyond the city limits.[29] Still later this privilege was enlarged.

In order to make the Sabbath still more enjoyable and to make it possible for the Jews to observe it comfortably, the sages introduced the law of *Erub* which was to the effect that if a Jew before the Sabbath indicated a desire to rest on the Sabbath at a place two thousand cubits beyond the limits of the city, and had deposited food at that point, he had the right to traverse on the Sabbath two thousand cubits from that place, i. e., the depository. Hence, if he deposited some food two thousand cubits beyond the limits of the city on Friday, he had a right to walk four thousand cubits on the Sabbath.[30] In the days when the donkey was used for transportation, four thousand cubits was a great distance. Similarly, the sages amended the law in regard to carrying something on the

[26] Ex. 16.29.   [27] ὄικους ὑμῶν.

[28] See Er. 4.2. Tosefta *ibid.* 7.5, נאמר כן מקום . . . אף מקום שנאמר כאן התקין רבן נמליאל הזקן שיהו מהלכין אלפיים אמה לכל רוח R. H. 23b, אלפיים אמה;

[29] Which is called תחום שבת.

[30] See Er. 31b. See more about the institution of *Erubin* S. Zeitlin, *JQR* 1951, pp. 351–61.

Sabbath day. According to the old halaka, the carrying
of any object from one location to another was prohibited.
Again, to make the Sabbath more enjoyable, the sages
introduced עירובי חצרות i. e., that the dwellers in a court
should contribute their share of the ingredients of a dish
to be placed in one of the houses. Thus, all the families
living in the court were considered partners in all the houses
in it. In other words, the houses became common to all;
therefore, the carrying of objects on the Sabbath from one
house to another was permitted to all the occupants.[31]

The same spirit of liberal modification of biblical law
which made religion applicable to life, while at the same
time it permitted the religion to remain a dominating
force in the new state, caused the sages to modify other
biblical laws. The fiftieth year according to the Pentateuch,
is called the jubilee year.[32] It is a holy year, and all the
properties which had been sold before that year had to be
returned to their previous owners;[33] however, with the
changing of the calendar from a solar to a lunar-solar,
the jubilee year disappeared from the Jewish calendar.[34]
The abolishment of the jubilee year was brought about
by clinging to the literal meaning of the words said in
the Bible לכל יושביה "unto all the inhabitants thereof."
Since many of the ten tribes did not return to Judaea
after the Restoration, the laws of the jubilee were not
applicable; there was no totality of inhabitants.[35]

Every seventh year according to the Pentateuch, was
called a sabbatical year in which "every creditor shall
release that which he lent unto his neighbor; he shall not

---

[31] See *ibid.*   [32] Lev. 25.8–11.

[33] *Ibid.* 14–16.

[34] Comp. S. Zeitlin, *The History of the Second Jewish Commonwealth
Prolegomena*, pp. 71–3.

[35] Comp. Ar. 32b, בכלו יובלות ... בזמן שכל יושביה עליה ולא בזמן שנלו
מקצתן.

exact it of his neighbor and of his brother because God's release had been proclaimed."[36]

To observe the sabbatical year as commanded in the Pentateuch would discourage many Jews from lending money to needy ones, lest the debt be not paid before the sabbatical year, since in the sabbatical year the debt would be cancelled and the money would be lost. To encourage commerce which was very highly developed during the Second Commonwealth the sages amended the law so that if the creditor deposited the promisory notes which he received from his debtor, in the court before the approach of the sabbatical year, he could collect his money at any future time, regardless of the sabbatical year.[37]

To encourage business transactions further, Hillel introduced Prosbol προσβουλη.[38] This was an application before the court in which the creditor stated that any debt which was owing to him might be collected at any time the loan would be called, and in such a case the law of the sabbatical year did not affect the repayment of the loan.[39]

Rabbi went further in maintaining that the laws of the sabbatical year in regard to the land[40] are rabbinical and not Pentateuchal. He compared the laws of the sabbatical year to the laws of the jubilee year, and maintained that when the laws of the jubilee year are applicable to the land, then the laws of the sabbatical year also become applicable. When the laws of the jubilee no longer are applicable, then the laws of the sabbatical year are also not so, and hence are now rabbinical and not Pentateuchal.[41] Rabbi was

[36] Deut. 15.1–3.
[37] Comp. Sheb. 10.2, והמוסר שטרותיו לבית דין אינן משמטין.
[38] Ibid.
[39] See S. Zeitlin, "Prosbol: A Study in Tannaitic Jurisprudence" JQR 1947.
[40] Ex. 23.11, ובשנה השביעית תשה; Lev. 25.1–7, והשביעית תשמטנה ונטשתה; שדך לא תזרע וכרמך לא תזמר ... שבהון יהיה לארץ.
[41] See Yer. Git. 4.3, וזה דבר השמיטה שמוט רבי אומר שני שמיטין שמיטה ויובל.

even considering the abolishment of the sabbatical year altogether[42] since it constituted a hardship upon the farmers in his time and said it was only a rabbinical injunction. He was prevented from doing so by his collegue Phinehas ben Jair who was well known for his piety; it was said in the Talmud that even his ass refused to eat untithed corn.[43] As was said before, in order for a creditor to be able to collect his debt regardless of the sabbatical year, he had to deposit his promisory notes in the court, the promisory note itself was also a new institution established by the sages after the Restoration. There is no mention in the Bible of any written document in connection with debts. According to the biblical law, a debtor was bound over to his creditor if he did not pay him the debt. The creditor had the right, if the loan were not paid, to take the debtor and his children into bondage.[44] The creditor had the right over the debtor, or what is called in Roman law *obligatio in personam*.[45] The sages abolished *obligatio in personam*. They introduced *Shetar*, which the debtor gave to the

בשעה שהיובל נוהג השמיטה נוהגת מדברי תורה פסקו היובלות נוהגת שמיטה מדבריהן
איסתי פסקו היובלות לכל יושביה בזמן שיושבין עליה ולא בזמן שגלו מתוכה . . .
נמצאת אומר כיון שגלו שבט ראובן . . . בטלו היובלות. Comp. also B. Git. 36a,
M. K. 2b, משום חורש וזריעה וחרישה בשביעית מי שרי אמר אביי בשביעית בזמן
הזה ורבי היא דתניא רבי אומר וזה דבר השמיטה בשתי שמיטות הכתוב מדבר . . .
See also Tosefat Git. 36a, בזמן שאתה משמט . . . פירש בקונטרס דהשמטת קרקע
א׳ל ההוא. See also Yer. Sheb. 9.6, לא נהגא בבית שני כדאמרינן בירושלמי . . .
נברא חשיד על שטיתו ואת אמר אפקין חלתה אמר ליה חלתה מדברי תורה שביעית
מדרבן גמליאל וחבריו.

[42] See Yer. Dem. 1.1; Tan. 3.1, רבי בעי משרי שמיטתא סלק ר׳ פנחס בן
יאיר לנביה אמר ליה מה עיבוריא עבידין אמר ליה עולשין יפות מה עיבוריא עבידין
אמר ליה עולשין יפות וידע רבי דלית הוא מסכמה עימיה.

[43] *Ibid.;* Hul. 7a.

[44] II Kings 4.1, עבדך אישי מת . . . והנושה בא לקחת את שני ילדי לו לעבדים,
comp. also Neh. 5.4–5, יש אשר אומרים לוינו כסף . . . והנה אנחנו כבשים את
בנינו ואת בנתינו לעבדים.

[45] According to the Roman law, the creditor had the right to kill the debtor if he did not fulfill his *obligatio ex contractu*, this creditor's right over the debtor was abolished in 313 B. C. E. by the *Lex Poctelia.*

creditor, by which he placed his property in mortgage. In this manner the creditor was deprived of the right over the person of the debtor. The creditor had only an *obligatio in rem*. He had the right to seize the property of the debtor,[46] if he did not pay the debt, but he did not have the right to take him or his children in bondage.

The same method of interpretation of Pentateuchal laws also was applied to the laws of injury. The Pentateuchal law is an eye for an eye, and a tooth for a tooth;[47] that is, if a man injured his fellow-man and caused him to lose an eye or a tooth, the law of the Pentateuch gave him the right to demand satisfaction, even to taking out the eye of the man who caused the loss of his eye; however, he had the right to absolve the man who caused him the injury.[48] Injury as well as theft was considered a *private delict*.[49] The State had no right to interfere in private wrongs, or to punish the offender. It was a case between the man who inflicted the injury and the one who suffered thereby. *Talio* was extreme satisfaction which the injured man might demand; however, he might obtain satisfaction by money, and he was the sole judge as to what remedy he should pursue. The sages, however, made it obligatory for the plaintiff to demand money. He could not demand

---

[46] M. B. B. 10, ‏המלוה את חבירו בשטר גובה מנכסים משועבדים‎.

[47] Ex. 21.24.

[48] Comp. also Josephus, *Ant.* 4.8, 35. "He that maimeth any one, let him undergo the like himself and be deprived of the same member of which he deprived the other, unless he that is maimed will accept of money instead of it; for the law makes the sufferer the judge of the value what he hath suffered and permits him to estimate it, unless he will be more severe." A similar conception was held in ancient Rome. *Si membrum rupsit, ni cum eo pacit talio esto*, (The Twelve Tables) that is, if the injured man did not get any satisfaction he might apply to *talio*.

[49] *A private delict* gives rise to an obligation; the law intends that delinquents shall be punished by becoming liable to a personal action by the injured party, the object of such action being either to recover damages or a penalty ‏קנס‎, or both.

extreme *talio*.[50] Rabbi Eliezer opposed such innovation,[51] but the law was not rendered according to his opinion.

The same spirit to amend the law is to be found in all branches of Jewish law, ritual as well as civil.

According to the biblical law a father had a right to give his daughter into marriage, regardless of her age, and the groom had to pay money to the father for this transaction. In other words, a father had the right to sell his daughter, and the money he received from the groom was called *mohar*.[52]

According to an old halaka, a woman may be acquired in marriage in one of three ways. בכסף by money which the groom pays to the father of the girl, or by a שטר *shetar*; through a document by which a father gives away his daughter as a gift, by a bill of sale or a deed of gift; or by ביאה *usus*.[53] The husband had the right to divorce his wife on a mere caprice. There is no law in the Bible to protect her economically, after a divorce or the death of her husband. The sages introduced *ketubah*, a writ in which the groom writes that his wife shall have a lien on all his property in the event he divorces her, or after his death.[54]

---

[50] B. K. 83b. עין תחת עין ממון.

[51] *Ibid.* 84a תניא ר' אליעזר אומר עין תחת עין ממש.

[52] Jacob paid Laban in menial labor to marry his daughters. Similarly David paid King Saul for his daughter Michal two hundred foreskins of the Philistines. The money the groom paid the father for the girl is termed *Mohar*. Shechem offered any amount of *Mohar* to Jacob for his daughter Dinah. According to the biblical law, anyone who seduces a virgin had to pay a fine to the father, an amount equal to the *mohar* for virgins. כסף ישקל כמהר הבתולות; ונתן ... לאבי הנער חמשים כסף. In the Elephantine Papyri a marriage document is recorded (dated about 441 B. C. E.), which reads in parts as follows: "She is my wife and I her husband, from this day forever. I have given you *Mohar* for your daughter, Miphtahia, the sum of five shekels."

[53] Kid. 1.1, האשה נקנית בשלש דרכים ... בכסף בשטר ובביאה.

[54] Comp. Yer. Ket. 8.11; *ibid.* 82b Tosefta *ibid* 12.1, כותב לה כל נכסיי דאית לי אחראין וערבאין לכסף כתובתיך. See more S. Zeitlin, "The Origin of the Ketubah" *JQR* 1933.

The minimum sum of money which had to be paid to the wife in event of divorce or death was two hundred zuzim, if she was a virgin when he married her, or one hundred zuzim if she had been a widow.[55] The old law that a woman may be acquired in marriage by money which the groom paid to the father, or by the *shetar* which the father gave to the groom, was automatically annulled. In modern times the groom gives a ring to the bride, which may be a symbol of a payment of money to her. But this custom of the marriage ring is very old, and was observed by the early Romans,[56] and it was adopted from them by the Jews and Christians alike. The introduction of the *ketubah* was for the purpose of raising the status of the woman both economically and socially.

The sages were progressive in their interpretation of the biblical laws, always with the view of the advancement of society. The progressiveness of the sages is exemplified in all the halakot. The following case will illustrate this. The estate of a deceased person, according to the Pentateuch, is inherited by his sons; where there are no sons, it passes to his daughters, and where there are no daughters, it passes to the nearest kin.[57] It must always remain in the family of the tribe. The idea of testament is not found in the Pentateuch for the simple reason that the property of a deceased person cannot be transferred to a stranger. The sages, however, introduced a new theory of inheritance, so that a person could write a testament whereby after his death part of his property could go to whomsoever he designated, even to a total stranger of the family. A man could give away by testament a part of his property so

[55] לבתולה מאתים ולאלמנה מנה.

[56] See Pliny, *Natural History* 33.1, *etiam nunc sponsae anulus ferreus mittitur, isque sine gemma.* Comp. also Tertullian, *Apolog.* 6. *digito quem sponsus oppignerasset pronubo anulo.*

[57] Num. 27.8–11.

that it should pass, even ten years after his death when
so designated in his testament, and the authorities had to
carry out his provision. This law completely reversed the
Pentateuchal law of inheritance, wherein man was considered mortal and property permanent; since a person has
no right to transfer his property it always had to remain
in the family. According to the tannaitic jurisprudence
man is immortal after death, but the title to property was
limitable by time. With this view on the tannaitic conception of inheritance we may throw light on a controversy
between the Pharisees and Sadducees in regard to inheritance which hitherto had not been readily explained.[58] If
a person, "A", had a son and a daughter, and the son
died during the lifetime of the father and he, the son, had
no male issue, but only a daughter, and then "A" died,
the granddaughter according to the Pharisees inherited all
the property of "A", while the Sadducees maintained that
the property should be divided between the daughter
and the granddaughter. The Pharisees always were lenient,
and their decisions usually were logical, but here the logic
was with the Sadducees. The truth of the matter is that
the Pharisees were consistent in their logical interpretation
of the laws, and their decision in this case was also rendered
according to their liberal principles. According to the
Pentateuch, where there are sons the daughters do not
share the inheritance. The Pharisees injected the new idea
in the matter of inheritance, namely, that a person may
write a testament and bequeath his property to whomsoever
he pleased. If "A" had desired that his daughter should
inherit his property, he could have written a testament

---

[58] Tosefta Yad. 2.20; b. B. B. 115b, אומרים [צדוקים] קובלני (ביהותיים) אומרין
עליכם פרושים מה את בת בני הבא מכח בני שבא מכחי הרי יורשתני בתי הבאה מכחי
אינו דין שתרשתני; כל האומר תירש בת עם בת הבן אפילו נשיא שבישראל אין שומעין
לו שאינן אלא מעשה צדוקים.

bequeathing part of his property to her, since he knew that according to the Pentateuch she was not entitled to inherit his property. As he did not write a testament in favor of his daughter, this meant that he did not wish her to get a part of his property. It was a principle among the Pharisees that the wish of a deceased must be honored. The Sadducees, on the other hand, followed the Pentateuch that a daughter does not inherit when there is a son left, but does so where there is no son. In the preceding case there was no son surviving after the father's death, only a daughter and a grandaughter, and, hence, according to the Sadducees the property was to be divided equally.

The sages introduced new laws to meet the demands of time, in other branches of society, these were the conception of partnership, that more than one person may have rights and title to the same property, and the idea of agency, that a person may transfer his right to another man to act for him, neither of which is found in the Pentateuch. The sages developed new principles very highly with great keenness of insight. There is no mention of possession and title to property in the Pentateuch. The sages divided property into the following categories, private property נכסי יחיד, property which belonged to many נכסי רבים, communal property which belonged to the State, which they called נכסי עולי בבל,[59] and property which belonged to no one, *res nullius* הפקר. The acquisition of property, as well as the right to relinquish it[60] was scientifically developed by the sages, a conception which is not found in the Pentateuch. Similarly, the principles of *jus in rem*

---

[59] See Ned. 5.5, ואיזו דבר של עולי בבל כנון הר הבית והעזרות שבאמצע הדרך; Tosefta Oh. 18.3, חזקת דרכים של עולי בבל.

[60] יאוש, comp. also the controversy between R. Meir and R. Jose on the matter of *Res derelictae*. ר' מאיר . . . כיון שאדם מפקיר דבר מרשותו הפקרו הפקר . . . דר' יוסי די אמר אין הפקר יוצא מתחת . בעלים אלא ב:כיה (Yer. Pea 6).

and *in personam* were expounded to the highest degree of legal science.

The progressiveness of the laws enacted during the Second Commonwealth is exemplified in all the halakot. The principles therein were revolutionary modifications of the Pentateuch. This is shown in the conception of intention which was first introduced by the School of Hillel, and had a great effect on the development of the halaka, and at the same time modified the Pentateuchal laws.[61] Only a person's act had been recognized by the Pentateuch. The idea of intention is not found there. An act takes place when a voluntary movement of the body is made, but when no such movement is made, the result is an accident or event. If a man, for example, jumps·from a bridge, it is an act because it is accompanied by volition. If he falls or is pushed from a bridge, it is an accident or event because there is no volition. Similarly, if the hand of a person is forcibly guided into writing a signature, this is not considered an act since will was absent. Intention refers only to a future act — the consequence of the first act; in other words, to the ultimate purpose, to the end and not to the means. If a person throws a missile in order to break an object, or to injure someone, the breaking and the injuring are the consequence of the act of throwing. The first act resulted from the will of throwing, and that was the means to the end of injuring. Intention refers only to the end, to the consequence of the first act and not to the means.

Work on the Sabbath is prohibited by the Pentateuch. Picking fruit from a tree was considered work and hence prohibited on the Sabbath. According to the new theories the intention of the person had to be considered, and action

[61] See S. Zeitlin, "Studies in Tannaitic Jurisprudence, Intention as a Legal Principle" *Journal of Jewish Lore and Philosophy*.

without intention could not be legally regarded an act. Hence, if a person intended to pick a particular fruit on the Sabbath, but owing to a mistake he picked another fruit, then he had to be considered absolved[62] because he did not accomplish his original intention.

The idea of intention was applied not only to ritual laws but also to civil laws, and to what is known in modern jurisprudence as criminal laws. For example, if a person threw a stone at someone intending only to strike the person's leg and not intending to kill him, but the stone struck his heart instead and caused his death, he was absolved by some sages from capital punishment since his intention had been not to kill but only to injure.[63] The death was not premeditated.

The sages of the Second Commonwealth advanced many new legal principles. They were indeed great jurists. Although the Pentateuch was the basis of the Jewish law and was the constitution of the people, they did not hesitate to interpret and amend the Pentateuchal laws in order to bring them into consonance with life. Their legal principles represented the ideas of justice as developed in a great civilization. The tannaitic conception of law can be compared with that of Roman jurists such as Ateius Capito, Masurius Sabinus, Antistius Labeo, and Julius Proculus. In some respects it was superior and more progressive. While in their opinion the laws were divine they were, however, for the benefit of mankind.

From the Talmud where the tannaitic and amoraic laws are interwoven we can hardly appreciate the principles of

---

[62] Tosefta Kerit. 2.14, נתכוין ללקט תאינים וליקט ענבים . . . ר' אליעזר מתעיב ר' אליעזר מתעיב מלאכה שאינה צריכה לגופיה. According to R. Simon חטאה ור' יהושע פוטר פטור.

[63] M. Sanh. 9.4, נתכוין להרוג את הבהמה והרג את האדם . . . פטור . . . נתכוון פטור להכוהו על מתניו ולא היה בו כדי להמיתו על מתניו והלכה לו על לבו והיה בו כדי להמיתו על לבו ומת פטור.

the sages of the Second Commonwealth, because we can not see the forest on account of the trees. Unfortunately, there was no serious attempt made to give a history of the development of the law of the tannaitic period.

III

The sages who held that Jewish law was not stringent but elastic, and that the Pentateuchal laws could be interpreted and amended did not have easy sailing. As mentioned before, the Sadducees opposed them; and at the end of the Second Jewish Commonwealth they became an insignificant group, looked upon as heretics; they had no further influence on the Jewish people. There also was great opposition to the liberalism and progressiveness of the School of Hillel. Even among the Pharisees were some who opposed the changes; they belonged to the School of Shammai. Some of them followed the Penta-teuchal laws. For instance, Rabbi Eliezer said that he never voiced an opinion on a law unless he had heard it from his teachers.[64] He had great influence because of his great learning and standing in the community. Rabban Gamaliel, his brother-in-law, who was the head of the Sanhedrin, excommunicated him in order to minimize his influence.[65] Indeed, the halaka was decided according to the opinion of the School of Hillel which was progressive, and not according to the School of Shammai. There were others who opposed the liberal Pharisees and called them legalists. This opposition came from the Apocalyptists and the disciples of Jesus. Jesus, as well as the Apocalyptists made his appeal on the ground of ethics alone, and sought to destroy evil by preaching and invoking the conscience of mankind, and threatened the evildoers with punishment in a future world. The Pharisees as leaders of the people felt they had to enact laws to prevent the people from

[64] שלא אמר דבר שלא שמע מרבותיו, שמותי.   [65] B. M. 59b; Ber. 19a.

doing evil, and sought to punish the evildoers in this world. Their laws, however, were based on equity and morals. Society must be ruled by laws, was the opinion of the Pharisees.

While the halakot during the Second Commonwealth generally were progressive, this, however, cannot be said of the halakot which came into being after the destruction of the Temple, particularly after the Hadrianic period. The Jews then lost their political independence. They were persecuted by the Romans, and later by the Christians when Christianity became the dominating religion in Rome. Judaism was only a tolerated religion in the Roman Empire. It became a necessity for the sages to collect all the halakot and codify them in one corpus. This was done under the leadership of Rabbi Judah at the beginning of the third century. He collected all the halakot which were again revaluated in accordance with the conditions of his time. This collection was called the Mishna which had the connotations — "study," and "second," i. e., second to the Pentateuch. Many halakot which were in vogue during the Second Commonwealth were not applicable during the time of Rabbi Judah and hence were not included in the Mishna. For example before the Hadrianic period women were not segregated from men in the synagogue; they were among the seven persons called on the Sabbath to the Torah. This halaka is not included in the Mishna.[65a]

The Amoraim interpreted the Mishna in a similar manner in which the Tannaim interpreted the Scriptures and this process was continued by following generations. The amoraic laws are not as progressive as the tannaitic since the Jews had no political state, and were scattered among other states and religions. The aim of the Amoraim was to save Jews and Judaism, and hence they made laws that

[65a] הכל עולים למניין שבעה . . . אפילו אשה (T. M. 4). See S. Zeitlin, *JQR*, 1948, pp. 305–8.

tended to segregate the Jews from the pagan world. Unquestionably great halakot and new principles were developed by the Amoraim, although they had not the great liberality of the Tannaim. In the early days after the tannaitic period there were two centers of Judaism, a declining one in Palestine, and a growing one in Babylon. There are two Talmuds, the Palestinian and the Babylonian. In many halakot the Palestinian is in disagreement with the Babylonian. This is readily understandable as they reflect the views of the Jews who were living two different modes of life. The Babylonian collection of the halakot was edited at the end of the fifth or beginning of the sixth century and was called Gemara, which has the connotation "study" and "final." It is made up chiefly of the Babylonian halakot in the form of discussion and codified laws. The Palestinian collection was never properly edited. It ends abruptly since the academies of learning were closed after the Nicene council.[66] The Gemara, unlike the Mishna, is the product of the Jews of Babylonia, while the Mishna was the product of Palestinian Jewry. The Babylonian Gemara, owing to the Babylonian Geonim who followed the Amoraim, became the authoritative halakot. Where there is a discrepancy in the halakot between the Palestinian and the Babylonian Talmud the law of the latter prevails.[67]

IV

After the destruction of the Temple the Jewish people, like the Christians, became a religious group. Judaism became a religion, just as did Christianity. There could not have been a question of going back to the source of

[66] 325 C. E.

[67] Comp. ומלתא דפסיקא בתלמוד דילנא ,תשובות הגאונים, מאת שמחה אסף לא סמכינן בה על תלמודא דבני ארץ ישראל (האי נאון); דעל נמרא דילן סמכינן דבתראי אינון, (אלפסי ערובין י').

the halakot, and the Jews were dominated by the rabbis. Even in the darkest period of the Middle Ages, when Judaism was a religion merely tolerated by the Christians and Moslems, Jews had their own religious autonomy. The halakot became the canon law, a religious law by which the Jews were guided. The Jews lived in their ghettos separated from the Christian world. Even in those countries where the Christians did not erect walls to confine the Jews within certain areas, they segregated themselves and lived their own life. The laws which were enacted by the rabbis during the Middle Ages were made more stringent so as to make the Jews conscious of their identity as Jews, and in order to perpetuate Judaism in the midst of Christianity. It is true that the rabbis from time to time lessened the burden of the halakot against the social and economic environment in which the Jews found themselves. To mention only one instance, the Talmud not only prohibited Jews from drinking wine handled or made by non-Jews, but even to derive any benefit from it, i. e., to sell it.[68] Rashi, who lived in Champagne which is famous for its wine and where Jews engaged non-Jews in raising grapes and making wine, interpreted the halakot of the Talmud so as to make it possible for the Jews not only to sell the wine, but also to drink it.[69]

After the French Revolution the Jews were granted

---

[68] Comp. Ab. Zarah 31, אילו דברים של נוים אסורין ואיסורן איסור הנאה יינן נדולים עושין; (שנתנסך לעבודה זרה היין; יין אסור (See however Rashi ... יין נסך (57b) חד אסור אפילו בהנאה (58a).

[69] See Tos. Ab. Zarah 57b, פירוש רשב׳ם והרמב׳ן בשם רש׳י שכתב בתשובות ; comp. Mordecai ad loc. הנאונים כי בזמן הזה אין אסור הנאה במגע (נכרי) גוי ביין אביך רש׳י . . . פסקו דנוים בזמן הזה כתינוק בן יומו . . . דתינוק בן יומו אין עושה . . . אית ליה לשמואל דתינוק בן יומו .See also Tos יין נסך ליאסר אף בשתיה אינו עושה יין נסך ומותר אף בשתיה . . . שפסקו הלכה כשמואל הואיל וסבר ר׳ יהושע בן לוי כותיה והלכה כריב׳ל לנבי ר׳ יוחנן וכ׳ש לנבי רב ושמואל Comp. however. וכל יין שינע בו הנוי הרי זה אסור, XI, הלכות מאכלות אסורות ,Maimonides שיין ישראל שנגע בו הנוי דין כסתם יינן שהוא אסור בהנייה ,Maimonides lived in Egypt where the Jews were not engaged in making wine.

citizenship in most of the countries of western Europe. Automatically their religious autonomy disappeared. They became a part of the population of the countries in which they lived. A movement arose in western Europe, particularly in Germany, under the name of Reformist or, as it is now called, Liberal Judaism. Instead of adjusting the halaka to life Reform Judaism sought to invalidate the Jewish law. The Orthodox Jews in America follow all the halakot which came into existence during the Middle Ages; they have an offshoot who call themselves Neo-Orthodox. Their philosophy and conception of the halakot are not clearly defined. There is another movement which calls itself the Conservative, whose followers assume that they subscribe to historical Judaism. Which historical Judaism they follow, they have never defined. Is it the historical Judaism of Babylonia, of Palestine, or Russia-Poland, or Germany?[70] Again their philosophy of the halaka was never clearly determined.

V

The State of Israel was founded in 1948, almost nineteen centuries after Rome had captured Jerusalem and the Second Commonwealth had become a page in history. We cannot yet realize the revolutionary effect the new State of Israel may have on the entire Jewry and even the entire world.

It is axiomatic that the Jews who live in countries outside of Israel are not politically bound to the State of Israel. They are citizens of the countries in which they live. They share in the growth and development of their respective countries and are involved in their crises. They shed their blood in the time of danger to defend their country. The culture and civilization of the various

[70] Is it the historical Judaism of Zechariah Frankel, Maimonides, Rashi, Saadia, or Hillel?

countries in which the Jews live are an integral part of their life. They cannot and do not owe dual allegiance. They have only one political and economic allegiance — to the countries wherein they live. To say that Jews in America are in *Galuth* is historically wrong. On the other hand, it is axiomatic that Jews all the world over are religiously bound to each other. They have one religion. Judaism, like Christianity, is a universal religion which anyone is welcome to accept regardless of race, and we know that even many pagans have accepted Judaism. During the Second Commonwealth Judaism was a missionary religion; however, unlike Christianity Judaism was originated and was molded in Judaea, and represents the genius of one people. Although many races have accepted Judaism the fact remains that Judaism is the religion of the Jewish people, since the proselytes were a very small minority, and when Christianity became the dominating religion the Jews were prohibited under pain of death to proselytize.

Christianity arose in the hills of Judaea. Its founder was a Jew; the apostles were Jews; the first Christian Church was in Judaea. According to Eusebius, the church historian, the first fifteen bishops were Jews.[11] But Christianity, unlike Judaism, extended itself to many races outside of the Jewish race and became the religion of the Gentiles. People of different nationalities and races accepted the new religion, many by persuasion, more by force. Thus, Christianity as a religion is not a religion of one people, since it has been embraced by many races.

Since Judaism is a religion of one people the Jews over the entire world have a common historical heritage and a common language, the Hebrew language. It became known as the sacred tongue after destruction of the Second Commonwealth. It is true that the Jews during the long dispersion adopted other tongues, in the Arabic period —

[11] *The Church History*, X, 5

Judaeo-Arabic; in the Spanish period — Ladino; in eastern
Europe — Yiddish which was brought from Germany either
by exiles or immigrants from this country. All these
languages had only a passing vogue and were spoken only
by the Jews who lived in a particular country or were
descendants of residents in such a country, while Hebrew
remained the perpetual language, the language of prayers.
Although in modern days in some synagogues the prayers
are in the language of the respective country, still many of
the prayers remain in Hebrew.

The Judaism of today is the creation of the ancient
prophets of Israel and the Pharisees of the land of Judaea.
Judaea always was the holy land for all the Jews. Jerusalem
was the religious metropolis during the Second Commonwealth and has remained so throughout all the ages. The
spiritual leaders in Jerusalem guided the Jews throughout
the world. Christianity, unlike Judaism, the cradle of
which was Judaea, never considered Judaea of importance
in connection with its religion. Judaea was not a holy
land for the Christians. Only the places of Jesus' birth and
burial were *loca sancta*. Rome, where Peter and Paul were
killed, became the center and symbol of Christianity.
James Bryce characterized this fact when he said, "To be
a Roman was to be a Christian, and this idea soon passed
into the converse. To be a Christian was to be a Roman."[72]

While the Jews of the world looked to Judaea for spiritual
guidance, the spiritual leaders could not enforce their ideas
of religion upon world Jewry. Judaism, unlike Catholicism,
is not a theocracy. It is not ruled by a vicar who can
dominate the people religiously. Theocracy was abolished
with the successful revolt of the Hasmoneans, and a
nomocracy was established by which there can be no human
representative of God. There is no hierarchy or hereditary

[72] *The Holy Roman Empire*, p. 13.

office in a nomocracy. The law is to be interpreted by those who are well versed in it.[73] Nor is Judaism like Protestantism. When Christians revolted in the sixteenth century against Rome, one of the most widely circulated ideas was *cujus regio ejus religio*. The Jews on the other hand have no national religions in the different states. The principles of Judaism are adhered to by the Jews over the entire world.

In a democracy, as in our country, the United States of America, religion is separated from the state. It is for the best interest of both state and religion when they are kept separate. Religion must be left to the conscience of the individual. The state has no right to force obedience upon the individual to the precepts of religion. Judaism, however, unlike Christianity, is greatly interwoven with the people. For almost two thousand years Jews lived in the various countries, from the time of the destruction of the Second Commonwealth down to the time of the French Revolution, and in Poland and Russia from the Middle Ages down to the time of the Russian Revolution during the First World War. They were always dominated by religion. It is indeed difficult to separate Judaism from the Israeli. Only with patience, wisdom, and foresight, in the course of time, will the leaders of Israel be able to accomplish this difficult task.

On the other hand, if Israel should become an ordinary, democratic industrial state it will be a great tragedy for Jewry and humanity as a whole. *An ordinary Levantine state will have no effect upon Judaism.* Jewry, as well as the civilized world, has a right to expect from Israel a continuation of the Second Commonwealth. Judaism during this period molded and shaped the civilization of the world, especially through Christianity which is an outgrowth of the Judaism of the Second Commonwealth.

[73] It was well expressed by the sages, "The Torah is not in heaven."

The Jews of the world have a right to look to Israel as a beacon for the development of Judaism.

It is with great regret that I have to state that some rabbis in Israel still have the psychology and mentality developed among their fellow-Jews of the cities of Poland and Roumania, whence they themselves came. They still seek to preserve the Judaism and the religious practices which were in vogue in eastern Europe without recognizing the fact that these religious laws were once enacted as a safeguard for Judaism to survive in the ghettos, and some were introduced as a prevention from assimilation with other peoples. These laws have outlived their purpose in the free State of Israel. There is no need for segregation.

There not only is a wide gulf, but a feeling of hostility between the religious group, who are the minority of the population and who want to enforce the Judaism of eastern Europe, and the young generation of the land. When I was in Jerusalem last summer I became aware of the extreme hostility existing between the two groups. I was there at the time when the bomb was allegedly planned to be thrown on the Knesset. (The entire affair was handled poorly.) The religious people complained to me that there was more freedom of religion in New York than in Jerusalem and that they were persecuted because of their religious observance, while some young people complained that the religious group did not belong to the State of Israel, but rather to the ghettos of eastern Europe. Because of the forcing of this type of Judaism on the people, many have become not only irreligious, but anti-religious. Present day Judaism is indeed in a chaotic state in Israel, and can anticipate little respect from young cultured people in a democratic state. For example, the public buses are not permitted to run on the Sabbath, but private cars are permitted to be used freely; however, in a few sections of the city (where the orthodox are segregated) the streets are barricaded against such cars; but on the street of Ben Yehudah, from the corner of Jaffa Road to the corner of King George, a great number of automobiles are parked for the purpose of taking passengers. The price of a ride of course is greater than the fare on the public bus. The wealthy who have private cars drive on the Sabbath without interference. The man of limited but comfortable means takes a ride on the Sabbath in one of the cars parked on Ben Yehudah Street. These cars usually are filled to seating capacity and some passengers are required to stand. The poor man who cannot afford to pay for a ride on the Sabbath in one of these cars is compelled, usually against his will, strictly to observe the Sabbath.

The present year, 5712 A. M., 1951–1952, happens to be a sabbatical year. According to the Pentateuchal law, no work may be done in the fields during the entire year. The State of Israel is still a poor country, and every bushel of wheat or grain must be utilized to help sustain the population, and therefore the government cannot afford to permit fields to lie uncultivated for one year. Furthermore, the farmers are mostly members of the Mapai, Mapam. Most of them are irreligious, and some of them are even anti-religious, and they would work in the fields regardless of the injunction of the Pentateuch. Therefore, by a strange arrangement a representative of the state, and a Rabbi (Assistant Secretary of Education) sold all the cultivated land to a poor Arab for an exorbitant price. Thus the land of Israel legally belongs to a non-Jew, and there is now no prohibition against working by Jews in the fields during the sabbatical year. Next year the Israeli will redeem the land from the Arab. I believe this is a mockery of the religious law. It is not legal fiction and such a process certainly cannot gain respect among the young people. It is true that before the Passover Jews sell the leavened bread to non-Jews for an exorbitant price, and after the festival get the leaven back. It is a fictitious sale.[73a] In this case, each individual sells his own leavened bread.[74] In the case of the sabbatical year however, the state itself sold the land to an Arab. It is indeed a mockery of religious law.

If the religious leaders of Israel had the courage and foresight of their predecessors the sages of the Second Commonwealth,[75] they would have interpreted the laws of the sabbatical year as given in the Pentateuch not applicable today. They could find support for this by the statement of Rabbi, the codifier of the Mishna, who maintained that the laws of the sabbatical year in his days were rabbinical and not Pentateuchal.[76] Furthermore,

---

[73a] See Tosefta, Pes. 7.24; Yer. *ibid.*, 2.2.

[74] In the foregoing pages we dealt with the עירובין i. e., that according to the old halaka the carrying of any object on the Sabbath into the property of another was prohibited; however, the sages introduced עירובי חצרות that the dwellers in the court should contribute their share of the ingredients of a dish to be placed in one of the houses in the court, by this fiction all the families living in the court were considered partners in all the houses in the court. In other words, the houses became common to all; therefore, the carrying of objects from one house to another on the Sabbath was permitted to all of the inhabitants. However, if a pagan lived in the court in the midst of the Jews, his presence acts as a deterrent to his neighbors from carrying an object on the Sabbath in the court, and *Erub* could not function. In order to make possible the carrying on the Sabbath, the property of the pagan had to be rented from him, ובנכרי עד שישכור. This renting of the property may be a fiction, but the entire עירובין is a legal fiction and can not be on a par with the law of the Sabbatical year; furthermore, in the case of the *Erub* an individual had to rent a property from a pagan.

[75] When Judaism became a universal religion and was no longer an ethnic one, the leaders were eager to make converts to judaism among the pagans. According to the Pentateuch an Ammonite and a Moabite can never join the Jewish community, לא יבא עמוני ומואבי בקהל ד'...עד עולם. The sages interpreted this passage to refer to the male and not to the female, עמוני ולא עמונית, מואבי ולא מואבית. This prohibition was further amended by the statement that since the time of Sennacherib, king of Assyria there were no longer any pure Ammonites or Moabites. ... בקהל בא יהודה גר עמוני לפניהן ... מה אני לבא בקהל בו ביום (Yad. 4) כבר עלה סנחריב מלך אשור ובלבל את כל האמות ... והיתרוהו לבא בקהל S. Zeitlin, "Judaism as a Religion," *JQR* 1944.

[76] See note 41.

they could find support in his statement given in the
Palestinian Talmud that he wanted to proclaim that the
laws of the sabbatical year are no longer applicable at
all.[77] In other words, Jews are allowed to work in the
fields of Israel in a sabbatical year. The religious leaders
in Israel could have found refuge in the statement of Rabbi,
for according to the Talmud the law is always decided
according to Rabbi's opinion.[78]

Rabbi himself used discretion in deciding the law. When
Rabbi Meir had a controversy with his colleagues on a
point of law, the law was decided against Meir's point of
view;[79] however, when Rabbi thought that the law as
interpreted by Rabbi Meir should be followed, he recorded
Rabbi Meir's opinion in the Mishna either as anonymous
or in the name of the sages,[80] i. e., he made Rabbi Meir's
opinion a majority opinion which hence must be followed.
Some of the Israeli religious leaders might say that such
a radical decision about the sabbatical year would arouse
controversies. There is an axiom in the Talmud that the
laws which are Pentateuchal must be discussed first and
then be decided. The laws which are rabbinical were first
to be decided and then discussed.[81] Hence our religious
leaders in Israel should first have decided the law and let
the discussion follow. In our days the laws of the sabbatical
year are only rabbinical. The legal fiction enacted by the
rabbis was rejected anyhow by the ultra orthodox.

If the religious leaders of Israel had foresight and were
interested in making Judaism a living religion and exert an
influence on all the Jews outside of Israel, they should
follow the principles of the sages of the Second Common-

[77] See note 42.   [78] הלכה כרבי מחבירו, Pes. 27a, Eru. 46.
[79] See Eur. 46b, 13b, שאין בדורו של ר' מאיר כמותו ומפני מה לא קבעו . . .
הלכה כמותו.
[80] See Hul. 85a ראה רבי דבריו של ר' מאיר . . . ושנאו בלשון חכמים.   Comp.
also Yer. Yeb. 4.11.
[81] See Eur. 67b, בדאורייתא מותבינן תיובתא והדר עבדינן מעשה בדרבנן עבדינן
מעשה והדר מותבינן תיובתא.

wealth. They interpreted the biblical passages and modified
the laws during that period, in order to make religion
applicable to life.

VI

There is a rabbinical axiom מעשה אבות סימן לבנים, which
may be rendered: "The deeds of the ancestors provide a
sign-post for the coming generation." The spiritual leaders
of Israel likewise should strive to make the religious laws
applicable to life by interpreting the tannaitic laws which
are a product of Judaea.

Some may be apprehensive that the modification of the
laws through new interpretation by the tannaitic halaka
will arouse great opposition from the ultra orthodox. It
undoubtedly will do so; this is to be expected. The sages
during the Second Commonwealth were also confronted
with great opposition from the Sadducees. Even among
the Pharisees, the conservative group opposed Hillel's
interpretation of the Pentateuchal laws. At one conclave,
we are told, some of the Hillelites were killed because of
their views by the opposing group of Shammaites.[82] There
will be opposition not only from the ultra orthodox, but
from the left groups who will urge that the halaka was not
modified sufficiently.

Indeed, the question may arise as to how far the halaka
should be modified. What is the limit? No one can answer
this question. I am certain no one told Hillel and his
colleagues how far they should go in modifying the halaka.
Spiritual leaders, however, should know how far the halaka
can be amended in accordance with the demands of their
time.

[82] Comp. Yer. Shab. 1. הנא ר' יהושע אונייא תלמידי בית שמאי עמדו לה
מלמטה והיו הורגין בתלמידי בית הלל תני ששה מהן עלו והשאר עמדו עליהן בחרבות
וברמחים. Comp. also b, ibid. 17, נעצו הרב בבית המדרש אמר הנכנס יכנס
והיוצא אל יצא ואותו היום היה הלל כפוף ויושב לפני שמאי כאחד מן התלמידים והיה
קשה לישראל כיום שנעשה בו העגל.

History clearly demonstrates that the sages of the Second Commonwealth were responsible for the perpetuation of Judaism as a living religion, and that Judaism's influence has been felt upon the entire civilized world.

Some may maintain that the rabbis have no authority for modifying the law by interpreting the tannaitic halakot, because they have no *Semicha*, and there is no longer a Sanhedrin. These contentions are historically wrong. *Semicha* never ceased in Israel; and, there never was *Semicha* in Babylonia.[83] The reason there was no *Semicha* in Babylonia was due to the fact that the patriarchs of Palestine purposely denied it the privilege of *Semicha* in order to hold it dependent upon the territory of Palestine.[84] The spiritual leaders of Babylonia in order to make certain that their decisions would not be reversed for error, or that an objection should not be raised by a litigant to a decision of the Court, had to receive authorization from the Exilarch.[85] The term *Semicha* is not found in the Palestinian Talmud after the time of Rabbi, and was replaced by the term מנוי "appointment." This is due to the fact that beginning with the time of Rabbi, only the patriarchs had the authority to give authorization, and his appointment meant authorization.[86] The term מנוי is synonymous with סמיכה.[87] *Semicha* was in vogue after Rabbi was dead and continued not only in Palestine, but also in western Europe,[88] where most of the Jews had come

---

[83] San. 14a, אמר ר' יהושע בן לוי אין סמיכה בחוץ לארץ סומכין בארץ ונסמכין בחוצה לארץ מאי?. Comp. Rashi, אם הסומך עומד בארץ והנסמך עומד בבבל. See also note 87.

[84] See *ibid.* 5a.

[85] *Ibid.* אמר רב האי מאן דבעי למידן דינא ואי טעה מיבעיי למיפטרה לישקל רשותא מבי ריש גלותא. See more S. Zeitlin, *Religious and Secular Leadership*, 1943, pp. 105–113.

[86] Yer. Sanh. 1.2, אמרו בית דין שמינה שלא לדעת הנשיא אין מינויו מינוי ונשיא שמינה שלא לדעת בית דין מינויו חזרו והתקינו שלא יהו בית דין ממנין אלא מדעת הנשיא ושלא יהא הנשיא ממנה אלא מדעת בית דין.

[87] *Ibid.* תמן (in Babylonia) קריי למנוייה כמיכתא.

[88] See Yer. Bik. 3.3, יהודה בן טיטוס הוה ברומי ומנוניה ע'ם דיחזור.

from to Palestine, while Babylonia had no *Semicha*. Neither did the Jews of Spain have *Semicha* since the bulk of Spanish Jewry migrated to Spain after the year 711 when the Berbers crossed the Strait of Gibraltar and conquered Spain. Indeed, the communal life of the Jews in western Europe was fashioned as it had been in Palestine,[89] while the communal life in Spain, being of Babylonian origin, was fashioned as it had been in Babylonia. Indeed, the spiritual leaders in Spain never bore the title "rabbi."[90]

Semicha continued among the Jews of western Europe. Isaac bar Sheshet inquired in one of his responsa as to the meaning of *Semicha* which was practiced in France and Germany, whereby the rabbis received it and in turn transmitted it to their disciples.[91] Isaac bar Sheshet, being s Spanish Jew, did not know that the *Semicha* was practiced throughout the ages.

Even Isaac Abrabanel tells us that when he settled in Italy he was amazed at the custom of *Semicha* practiced by the German Jews who had come to Italy and called themselves rabbis. He thought that the German Jews were imitating the Christians who conferred a diploma upon a person to show that he was a doctor.[92] Isaac Abrabanel, being a Spaniard, was unaware of the custom of *Semicha* which the German Jews had and which was a continuation of the practice in Palestine. The well-known controversy between Rabbi Levi ben Habib with Rabbi Jacob

---

[89] See S. Zeitlin, *op. cit.* pp. 25–46.

[90] *Ibid.* pp. 46–57; see note 92.

[91] Ribash, 271, מה זו סטיכה שנהגו בצרפת ואשכנז שהרבנים נסמכים והם סומכים אחרים.

[92] וסתם חבר הוא חכם . . . כי אלו השמות שראוי שיקראו בין חכמי ישראל בגלות
לא רב ולא רבן שהם השמות המסונים לסמוכים לפי שאין כמיכה בחוץ־לארץ . . .
וכן היה בכל ספרד בהיות אנשי הגולה שמה על תלם לא היה ביניהם כמיכה לשום
אדם. האמנם אחרי בואי באיטאליאה מצאתי שנתפשט המנהג אלו לאלו וראיתי התחלתו
בין האשכנזים כלם סומכים ונסמכים ורבנים לא ידעתי מאין בא להם ההתרה זה אם
לא שקנאו מדרכי הגוים העושים דקטורי ויעשו גם הם (נחלת אבות, על פרקי אבות
ed. Venice, p. 191).

Berab was about the renewal of *Semicha* in Palestine. Much has been written on this controversy; however, whatever might have been the underlying reasons for it, it seems to me that these two rabbis were Spanish Jews and did not know that one does not need to renew the *Semicha*.[93] *Semicha* never ceased. It is clear that the rabbis do possess *Semicha*. They have authorization the same as the sages of olden times.

Rabbi Maimon, the ex-Minister of Religion of Israel, raised the question of the revival of the Sanhedrin. Many rabbis opposed his view, namely, that such a revival was against rabbinical law.[94] Since the Sanhedrin as an institution came into being when the Second Jewish Commonwealth was established, naturally there had been no such institution before the Hasmonean period.[95] The institution of Sanhedrin continued to exist after the fall of the State of Judaea. From a cryptic document of the middle of the fourth century, mentioned in the Talmud, we see it was clear that this institution was still in existence, although the members had to assemble in secret because the Roman government, which was now Christian, had forbidden them to assemble for any religious function and to intercalate the years. "A couple had arrived from Rakkath (Tiberias); they were

[93] Maimonides being a Spaniard likewise did not know that *Semicha* was in vogue among the Franco-German Jewry and thought about the revival of *Semicha,* נראין לי הדברים שאם הסכימו כל החכמים שבארץ ישראל למנות דיינים ולסמוך אותם הרי אלו סמוכים . . . (משנה תורה ה' סנהדרין ד'). Maimonides' entire outlook was that of the Spanish and Babylonian Jews. M. T. Sanh. 4.13, 6, 9, וכל דיין הראוי לדון שנתן לו ראש גלות רשות לדון יש לו רשות לדון בכל העולם . . . אם אמר המלוה נלך למקום פלוני שבארץ פלונית לפלוני ופלוני הגדול ונדון לפניו בדין זה שכופין את הלוה והולך עמו וכן מעשים בכל יום בספרד. On the other hand Rabenu Tam being a Frenchman followed the established methods of conducting legal proceedings in vogue in Palestine: בזמן הזה שאין נשיא בישראל נראה דנדול הדור הוה בית הגדול . . . אחרי מתיא בן חרש לרומי הרי אפילו ברומי נקרא בית דין יפה . . . המזמין חבירו לדון ע"כ ידון כאן ואין יכול לדחותו ולומר נלך לבית הועד או לבית דין הגדול (מרדכי סנהדרין 709).

[94] חידוש הסנהדרין במדינתנו המחודשת.   [95] See above p. 343.

captured by an eagle (Rome) while in possession of articles
made in Luz such as purple. Yet through divine mercy
and by their own merits they were released. Further, the
offspring of Nahshon (scion of the family of David) wished
to establish a Nazib (a month); but the Edomite (Romans)
would not permit it. The members of the Sanhedrin,
however, met and established a Nazib in the month in
which Aaron, the priest, died (the month of Ab)."[96] Hence
the Sanhedrin continued to exist for three centuries after
destruction of the Second Temple, but was abolished by
the Roman government; therefore the institution of the
Sanhedrin can be reestablished without waiting for the
Messiah. There is no law in the Talmud which prohibits
the reestablishment of the Sanhedrin. But one thing must
be emphasized, the Sanhedrin cannot have religious
authority over the world Jewry, only a moral influence.
The Sanhedrin had no religious authority over Jews outside
of Judaea during the Second Commonwealth. The Jews of
the other countries willingly, however, followed the halakic
decisions of the Sanhedrin. The Jews of the Diaspora were
dependent on the Sanhedrin in the fixation of the exact
date of the new moon and the festivals. This authority
originally was vested in the Sanhedrin, and later the
patriarch, the head of the Sanhedrin, had authority over
the fixation of the new months. In the middle of the fourth
century the Jewish calendar wherein the days of the new
moon and festivals were specified, was fixed, and the Jews
no longer were dependent upon any scholarly group
(Sanhedrin) or any individual rabbi. Therefore, fears are
groundless that the establishment of the Sanhedrin will lead
to its domination over the religious life of the Jews of the

---

[96] Sanh. 12a, שלחו ליה לרבא זוג בא מרקת ותפשו נשר ובידם הנעשה בלוז
ומאי ניהו תכלת בזכות הרחמים ובזכותם יצאו בשלום ועמוסי יריכי נחשון בקשו לקבוע
נציב אחד ולא הניחו אדומי [רומי] הלו אבל בעלי אסופות נאספו וקבעו לו נציב אחד
בירח שמת בו אהרון הכהן Comp. Yer. Sanh. 10.1, סנהדרין אלא אסופות אין.

world. It is merely a question for the people of Israel to decide.[96a] The spiritual leaders of Israel must decide for themselves. The interpretation and modification of the tannaitic halaka do not require a full Sanhedrin. A group of rabbinical scholars who have *Semicha* have the right to interpret the halaka.[97].

What is most disturbing is that we do not have a corpus of the tannaitic halaka and the Jewish institutions. It is true that Rabbi accumulated the tannaitic halakot in the one collection which he called the Mishna, meaning second, i. e., to the Pentateuch, but numerous halakot are found outside of the Mishna in the Tosefta and Baraitot which can be utilized for a full comprehension of the halakot which came into being during the Second Commonwealth and before the Hadrianic period. Again, in the Mishna Rabbi codified all the laws which he believed the Jews should follow, and many of these laws were a direct reversal of the ones which were in vogue in the time of the Second Commonwealth. Since the Hadrianic persecutions many laws had to be enacted to meet the needs of the Jewish people. These laws no longer were as progressive as they were at the time of the Second Commonwealth. The spiritual leaders had to erect a fence around the laws in order to perpetuate Judaism, and under the law many such fences were erected.

The crying need is for a corpus of the halakot based on historical development which hitherto has not been done. The Talmud was studied throughout the ages in the academies and in the Yeshivot without regard to its historical development. In modern times when scholarly methods

---

[96a] דבר הקמת הסנהדרין נוגע אך ורק למדינת ישראל (הרב סימון ידיעות משרד הדתות, ניסן תשי"א).

[97] Comp. also Ab. Zara 19b, ועצומים כל הרוניה זה תלמיד שהגיע להוראה אפילו מה שתלמיד ותיק עתיד להורות Comp. also Yer. Ḥag. 1.8, ואינו מורה לפני רבו כבר נאמר למשה בסיני.

have been applied to the study of the Talmud, they have been applied mainly to textual criticism which is indeed very important for the texts of the Talmud, but the history and development of the halakot have been neglected. Even the books which we have today on the halakot, such as Rabbi Isaac Herzog's, *The Main Institution of Jewish Law*, are indeed compendiums of Jewish law. They are dogmatic presentations, not historical. A. Gulak's, *The Principles of the Hebrew Law*[98] likewise is a dogmatic presentation of the Jewish law.

It is fortunate that the Jewish Agency had the foresight to prepare men in the fields of economics and politics so that when the State of Israel was organized a government of men of great ability and political acumen was formed and was able to send out ambassadors who are a credit to their country. It is with great regret that we record that the leaders of the Hebrew University, which was founded in the year 1925 during the Mandate, lacked the foresight to prepare men in the halakot of the Second Commonwealth, so that if an independent Jewish State were to be established there would be scholars to prepare a corpus of the halakot of the Second Commonwealth as a basis for the interpretation and modification of the halakot which is sorely needed in the Third Commonwealth.[99]

To produce such a corpus of the tannaitic halaka and the Jewish institutions of the Second Commonwealth, we need not only Talmudists, but men with legal and historical minds and financial resources. Just as the Roman law became the basis of western European law, so should the corpus of the tannaitic halaka of the Second Commonwealth become the basis for the development of the halaka of the Third Commonwealth. Can the Jews meet this historical challenge? Only the future can disclose.

[98] ‏יסודי המשפט העברי סדר דיני ממונות בישראל עפ״י מקורות התלמוד והפוסקים‏.
[99] And still neglect this important area for Israel.

LES « DIX-HUIT MESURES »

Les « dix-huit mesures » nous intéressent tant en elles-mêmes que dans leurs rapports avec l'histoire. C'est un fait unique dans les annales juives qu'un tel débat ou plutôt un tel coup de force, qui a coûté la vie à des hommes. Le Talmud de Jérusalem rapporte que « les disciples de l'école de Schammaï se tenaient en bas et tuaient leurs condisciples de l'école de Hillel ». R. Josué, qui était un Hillélite et qui a peut-être assisté à cette séance mémorable, assure qu' « en ce jour on a nivelé la mesure »[1], ce qu'il explique par cette comparaison : si, quand la mesure est pleine, on veut y ajouter encore, on finit par en faire sortir ce qui y était[2]. De plus, il est relaté que dans la discussion sur l'aptitude à l'impureté des raisins destinés au pressoir (הבוצר לגת), qui, d'après le Talmud, fait partie des dix-huit mesures, « on ficha une épée dans la salle de l'académie, en disant : entre qui veut, personne ne sortira », et « cette journée fut aussi critique pour Israël que celle du veau d'or »[3]. Quant au caractère de ces mesures, l'époque à laquelle les docteurs se sont assemblés pour les décréter prouve qu'elles n'étaient pas exclusivement d'ordre religieux.

Nous nous proposons, dans cette étude, de reconstituer la liste des dix-huit mesures, d'examiner contre qui elles étaient dirigées et de préciser la date à laquelle elles ont été arrêtées.

I. — RECONSTITUTION DES « DIX-HUIT MESURES ».

La Mischna[4] parle d'une manière générale de dix-huit mesures qui furent prises à un certain moment : « Voici quelques-unes des règles qui furent formulées dans la demeure de Hanania·b. Hizkia b. Garon, lorsque les docteurs allèrent lui rendre visite ; on vota alors et les Schammaïtes l'emportèrent sur les Hillélites : dix-huit mesures furent décrétées en ce jour. » Mais la Mischna ne nous dit pas quelles sont ces dix-huit mesures.

---

1. j. *Sabbat*, i, 4.
2. *Ibid.*; T. *Sabbat*, i, 17.
3. *Sabbat*, 17 a.
4. *Sabbat*, i, 4 ; cf. Tossefta, i, 16.

Le Talmud de Jérusalem [1] cite une baraïta d'après laquelle il y eut, outre les dix-huit mesures arrêtées par la majorité schammaïte contre la minorité hillélite, dix-huit autres sur lesquelles l'accord se fit, c'est-à-dire qui furent adoptées sans discussion, et dix-huit encore qui firent l'objet de discussions. Cette baraïta cite même quelques-unes des mesures décrétées à la majorité. Le Talmud babli [2] sait aussi qu'il y a eu plus de dix-huit mesures décrétées. R. Yehouda dit au nom de Samuel : « Dix-huit mesures ont été décrétées et dix-huit discutées. — Mais, objecte-t-on, une baraïta dit que sur dix-huit on s'est mis d'accord ?... » L'amora babylonien connaissait donc la baraïta qui, aux dix-huit mesures décrétées par les Schammaïtes malgré les Hillélites, en ajoute dix-huit acceptées par les uns et les autres.

Mais quelles sont les dix-huit mesures décrétées ? Le Talmud de Babylone s'est heurté à cette question sans pouvoir y répondre d'une manière satisfaisante, parce que les rabbins babyloniens ne connaissaient plus les raisons qui avaient motivé ces mesures ; ils se sont embarrassés de toutes sortes de difficultés et, après bien des discussions, ils ne sont arrivés qu'à grand'peine au bout de leur compte. En voici le catalogue [3]. D'abord, les neuf cas dans lesquels la *terouma* est rendue, par le contact, impropre à la consommation (M. *Zabin*, v, 12) : 1° celui qui mange un aliment impur au premier degré ; 2° celui qui mange un aliment impur au second degré ; 3° celui qui boit des liquides impurs ; 4° celui qui se plonge la tête et la majeure partie du corps dans des eaux puisées ; 5° un homme pur dont la tête et la majeure partie du corps ont été arrosées avec trois *log* d'eau puisée ; 6° le livre ; 7° les mains ; 8° celui qui n'a plus qu'à prendre le jour même un bain de purification ; 9° les aliments et les objets rendus impurs par des liquides. — Puis viennent les cas suivants : 10° un objet placé sous un tuyau (*Mikvaot*, iv, 1) ; 11° tous les objets meubles communiquent l'impureté à une épaisseur d'aiguillon (*Oholot*, xvi, 1) ; 12° quand on vendange pour le pressoir (voir plus loin). Font encore partie, d'après le Babli, des dix-huit mesures : 13° le pain des païens ; 14° leur huile ; 15° leur vin ; 16° leurs filles, et aussi 17° la règle que celui que le sabbat surprend en route remet sa bourse à un païen (*Sabbat*, xxiv, 1) ; enfin, d'après certains amoras, 18° l'assimilation des produits de *terouma* à la *terouma* [1].

1. j. *Sabbat*, i, 7 (3 c, l. 36).
2. *Sabbat*, 15 a.
3. *Ibid.*, 13 b et s.

— Cette énumération montre assez que les amoras babyloniens ne
connaissaient déjà plus le détail des dix-huit mesures et qu'ils se
sont efforcés de réunir à grand renfort d'ingéniosité les différents
cas pour obtenir le chiffre dix-huit.

Revenons maintenant au Yerouschalmi pour voir quelles sont,
d'après lui, les dix-huit mesures. D'après une baraïta, dix-huit
mesures ont été décrétées, dix-huit ont été adoptées d'un plein
accord et dix-huit ont été discutées. Voici celles qui ont été
décrétées (c'est-à-dire imposées par la majorité schammaïte) : 1° le
pain des païens, 2° leur fromage, 3° leur huile, 4° leurs filles,
5° שכבת זרען, 6° מימי רגליהן, 7° הלכות בעל קרי et 8° règles sur les
pays païens. A ces huit cas s'ajoutent les neuf de la mischna de
Zabin. D'après les rabbins de Césarée, les mesures imposées à la
majorité des voix sont seulement au nombre de sept (pour celles
de la baraïta)[2], tandis que les autres sont : 8° celui que le sabbat
surprend en route doit remettre sa bourse à un païen ; 9° cas
analogue : le זב ne doit pas manger avec la זבה pour ne pas
être entraîné au péché ; 10° tous les objets meubles communiquent l'impureté à une épaisseur d'aiguillon ; 11° vendanger dans
un vignoble où l'on a trouvé un tombeau (*Ahilot,* XVIII, 1)[3] ;
12° placer des objets sous un tuyau ; 13°-18° dans six cas douteux
on doit brûler la *terouma* (*Tohorot,* IV, 5). D'après R. Yosé b. R.
Aboun, la règle des produits de *terouma* entre aussi en ligne de
compte. — Les mesures qui ont été décrétées sont les précédentes
(c.-à-d. celles de la première baraïta[4]) ; les autres sont de celles
qui sont énumérées par R. Simon b. Yohaï dans une baraïta : en
ce jour on a décrété sur le pain des païens, leur fromage, leur
vin, leur vinaigre, leur sauce[5], leur saumure, leur marinade, leurs
bouillies, leurs salaisons, leurs mets partagés, écrasés, émiettés,
leur langue, leur témoignage, leurs offrandes, leurs fils, leurs
filles, leurs prémices. — On voit que le Yerouschalmi présente
aussi de la confusion au sujet des dix-huit mesures. C'est à nous
maintenant de préciser ces mesures, de déterminer celles qui ont

---

1. C'est-à-dire que si l'on a semé de la *terouma,* le produit de la récolte est également de la *terouma* et soumis aux mêmes règles de pureté.

2. Les huit cas se réduisent à sept, car שכבת זרע et מי רגלים ne font qu'un ici;
v. T. *Mikvaot,* VI, 7 : שכבת זרע של גוי... טהורה... חוץ ממימי רגלים שבה;
T. *Zabin,* v, 2 : אי אפשר לש"ז שלא במימי רגלים.

3. Cf. Büchler, *Revue,* LXIV, 34-5.

4. Le texte a « les dix précédentes », mais je crois que le mot עשרה a été intro-
duit par erreur, car le nombre dix est étranger à tout le contexte. Cf. Halévi, *Dorot
Harischonim,* I, III, p. 600, n. 29.

5. Je traduis ce mot et les suivants par des à-peu-près.

été imposées par une majorité et celles sur lesquelles on s'était mis d'accord [1].

Une seule baraïta énumère formellement des mesures décrétées et elle ne fait elle-même l'objet d'aucune discussion. Nous pouvons, d'autre part, accepter, avec le Yerouschalmi, de chercher les « autres » mesures parmi celles que R. Simon b. Yohaï assure avoir été décrétées en ce jour. Ce rabbin, disciple de R. Akiba, n'est pas de beaucoup postérieur à la destruction du Temple ; il a pu connaître personnellement R. Josué [2], contemporain du Temple, membre du corps des lévites-chantres [3] et qui a sans doute dû assister à la fameuse séance. L'une des mesures énumérées par R. Simon b. Yohaï, l'interdiction d'accepter les offrandes des païens, se rapporte à un épisode connu par Josèphe [4] : Éléazar, fils de Hanania, s'étant mis à la tête des zélateurs, fit abolir le sacrifice qu'on offrait quotidiennement pour l'empereur. Cet Éléazar était aussi un schammaïte. C'est lui qui déduisait des mots : « rappelle-toi le jour du sabbat » qu'il faut se le rappeler dès le premier jour de la semaine [5] ; or, c'était, non seulement l'opinion, mais la pratique de Schammaï, qui réservait pour le sabbat tout ce qu'il trouvait de bon, et, fidèle au maître, l'école de Schammaï professait que, dès le premier jour de la semaine, on doit penser au prochain sabbat [6]. — Le Talmud nous apprend aussi qu'on refusa d'offrir le sacrifice pour la prospérité de l'empereur et que R. Zacharia b. אבקולוס, prêtre et schammaïte, y acquiesça [7], complaisance qui causa la destruction du Sanctuaire [8] ; ce rabbin est identifié par Krochmal et Jost à Zacharia b. Phalekos ou, comme ils lisent, Amphikalos, un des principaux prêtres zélateurs [9].

Mais si le Yerouschalmi reproduit une baraïta anonyme et celle de R. Simon b. Yohaï, il ne nous donne ni le compte, ni la somme des dix-huit mesures, ni celles qu'il faut choisir dans la liste de R. Simon. Or, beaucoup de points énumérés par celui-ci figurent

---

1. Celles qui ont été débattues sans qu'on ait abouti à se mettre d'accord doivent être cherchées parmi les nombreuses divergences qui séparaient les deux écoles.
2. *Berachot*, 28 a (mais v. Frankel, *Darké*, 168, n. 6).
3. *Arachin*, 11 b.
4. *Guerre*, II, xvii, 2.
5. *Mechilta*, 69 a, Friedmann.
6. *Béça*, 16 a. V. Jawitz, V, ch. vii, p. 149, et Graetz, III[5], Note 26, p. 810.
7. *Guittin*, 56 a.
8. *Ibid.*; T. *Sabbat*, xvi, 7.
9. *Guerre juive*, IV, iv, 1. V. Krochmal, *More*, ch. xi (p. 140, éd. Berlin) ; Jost, *Geschichte*, II, 98.

aussi dans la baraïta : le pain, le fromage, les filles. Le nombre des cas énumérés par R. Simon est précisément de dix-huit; mais en y regardant de près, on s'aperçoit que ce total est factice : il en est qui ne font qu'un avec d'autres, comme שחיקה, חילקה et טיסני, חומץ מורייס et כבוש, שלוק et מליח; c'est aussi l'opinion du Talmud[1]. Le Yerouschalmi a donc raison de choisir les cas restants parmi ceux de R. Simon, car ceux-ci ne forment pas les dix-huit. R. Simon ne prétend pas donner la liste complète des dix-huit interdictions; il en retient celles qui se rapportent aux païens et qui l'intéressaient pour son temps.

En écartant les doubles, nous trouvons chez R. Simon b. Yohaï neuf cas en tout, qui s'ajoutent aux sept de la baraïta. Il reste à en trouver deux pour parfaire la somme de dix-huit. Je crois que nous pouvons compter parmi les dix-huit mesures décrétées de force par les Schammaïtes le cas de הבוצר לגת, cité dans le Babli et qui se confond avec celui de הבוצר בית הפרס, cité par le Yerouschalmi : dans les deux cas, la discussion porte sur le point de savoir si les raisins sont rendus susceptibles d'impureté par le liquide qui en sort. Le Babli[2] ajoute que cette discussion avait déjà eu lieu entre Schammaï et Hillel eux-mêmes; « on ficha une épée dans la salle de l'académie en disant : entre qui veut, personne ne sortira; en ce jour Hillel fut abaissé devant Schammaï et ce fut une journée funeste pour Israël comme celle du veau d'or... Quand Schammaï et Hillel décrétèrent la mesure, elle ne fut pas acceptée; quand leurs disciples la décrétèrent, elle fut acceptée ». Assurément, il y a là bien de la confusion; la discussion entre les deux docteurs est confondue avec le débat sur les dix-huit mesures. Mais quoi qu'il en soit, le cas de הבוצר לגת ne peut pas être de ceux sur lesquels les deux écoles se sont accordées sans discussion; il faut donc le compter parmi ceux qui ont été décrétés, c'est-à-dire qui ont été votés par une majorité de Schammaïtes contre une minorité de Hillélites. — Il faut, pour la même raison, faire entrer dans le compte des dix-huit mesures le cas de המניח כלים תחת הצנור. qui est mentionné dans les deux Talmuds et dont la Tossefta[3] dit formellement qu'on alla aux voix à ce sujet et que les Schammaïtes l'emportèrent sur les Hillélites.

1. V. *Ab. zara*, 29 *b* et s.
2. *Sabbat*, 17 *a*.
3. T. *Sabbat*, I, 19.

Nous pouvons donc établir comme suit la liste des dix-huit mesures :

1. פת.	10. כבוש, שלוק, מלוח.
2. גבינה.	11. חילקה ,שחיקה, טיסני.
3. שמן.	12. לשון.
4. בנות:	13. עדות.
5. שכבת זרע ומימי רגלים.	14. בנים.
6. בעל קרי.	15. מחנות.
7. ארץ העמים.	16. בכורים.
8. יין.	17. הבוצר לגת.
9. חומץ ,ציר, מורייס.	18. המניח כלים תחת הצינור.

C'est seulement après avoir reconstitué le détail des dix-huit mesures que nous pouvons essayer d'en déterminer le caractère en recherchant contre qui elles ont été prises.

II. — LES QUINZE MESURES ANTI-ROMAINES.

Presque toutes ces mesures sont dirigées contre les païens, c'est-à-dire contre les Romains ; c'est ce que Graetz a bien vu. Les unes se rapportent à la prohibition des aliments des païens (n°s 1, 2, 3, 8, 9, 10, 11), les autres tendent à empêcher les relations sociales avec eux (n°s 4 et 14, 5, peut-être 8, 12, 13). Quelques-unes ont une signification politique précise : ce sont celles qui interdisent les sacrifices pour le salut de l'empereur (n°s 15-16). Toutes ont pour but d'établir une séparation tranchée entre Juifs et Romains.

L'une d'elles, le n° 7, qui met l'interdit sur les pays païens, a la même-tendance. Elle avait déjà été décrétée antérieurement, et dans le même but. Le Talmud rapporte que l'impureté des pays païens avait été proclamée sous Yosé b. Yoézer , et voici, à mon avis, comment cette mesure peut s'expliquer. A l'époque des Hasmonéens, beaucoup de Judéens avaient rallié les héros de l'indépendance nationale et les soutenaient dans leur lutte contre la tyrannie gréco-syrienne. Mais beaucoup de Hassidim aussi quittèrent la Palestine pour aller vivre conformément à la religion en Égypte ou dans d'autres pays[2]. C'est alors que Yosé b. Yoézer, « le hassid de la prêtrise »[3], prononça l'interdit sur les pays étrangers

---

1. *Sabbat*, 15 *a*. L'interdiction de la langue grecque n'était pas non plus nouvelle (*B. K.*, 82 *b*).

2. I Maccabées, i. 38.

3. *Haguiga*, ii. 7 : חסיד שבכהנה.

pour arrêter l'émigration hors de la Terre Sainte. C'était prendre
les Hassidim par leur faible : ils voulaient quitter la Palestine pour
servir Dieu en paix, mais comment servir Dieu sur une terre
impure? Il y avait là de quoi les arrêter.

Les mêmes circonstances expliquent une autre disposition légis-
lative de cette époque. Dans la lutte contre les Grecs comme plus
tard dans celle contre les Romains, beaucoup de chefs judéens
étaient contre les hostilités; de nombreux notables et des Hassidim se rallièrent au grand-prêtre Alcime[1]. C'est peut-être de ce
parti piétiste et pacifique qu'est sortie la règle, certainement
ancienne : « l'épée est comme le cadavre »[2], c'est-à-dire quiconque touche une épée qui a donné la mort a un homme est
impur comme s'il avait tué lui-même. C'était empêcher les Hasmonéens de lutter contre les Grecs, car le Pentateuque défend
seulement au prêtre de toucher un mort[3], et voici que l'épée était
assimilée au mort et communiquait directement l'impureté tout
comme un cadavre ! Yosé b. Yoézer, qui était partisan de la lutte
contre l'hellénisme et qui, d'après le Midrasch, mourut martyr à
cette époque[4], s'éleva contre cette interprétation. Il enseigna :
« Quiconque touche un mort est impur[5] », c'est-à-dire est impur
celui-là seulement qui touche à un mort, mais non celui qui
touche une épée. On s'explique maintenant que Yosé, pour avoir
enseigné cette opinion, fut appelé « celui qui permet ». Le Talmud
observe avec une apparence de raison qu'il aurait fallu plutôt
l'appeler « celui qui défend ». Mais en réalité, quelle était donc la
portée de son enseignement? Déjà le Pentateuque avait déclaré
impur celui qui touche un mort (Nombres, xix, 11). Mais c'est que
R. Yosé se montrait large et coulant en n'allant pas plus loin et en
refusant d'assimiler l'épée au cadavre, comme le faisaient certains
Hassidim[6].

Revenons maintenant à l'époque romaine et assurons-nous que
les mêmes mobiles ont pu déterminer les mêmes mesures. A
cette époque, beaucoup de Pharisiens et d'Esséniens, tout en étant
opposés à Rome, refusaient d'entrer en lutte contre l'empire et
aimaient mieux quitter le pays pour pratiquer leur religion en
toute tranquillité. C'était le moment de renouveler l'interdiction

---

1. I Maccabées, vii, 12 et s.
2. חרב הרי הוא כחלל (Pes., 14 b et pass. parall).
3. Lévitique, xxi, 1.
4. Gen. r., lxv.
5. דיקריב במיתא מסאב (Aboda zara, 37 b).
6. Voir Katzenellenbogen, Pharisiens et Sadducéens (en russe).

contre les pays païens pour empêcher l'émigration et la fuite, et
les zélateurs devaient tenir particulièrement à retenir tous les
Juifs, à concentrer contre l'ennemi toutes les forces du pays. La
mesure était on ne peut plus opportune, ou pour mieux dire elle
s'imposait.

III. — LES TROIS MESURES SUR LA PURETÉ.

Il nous reste à expliquer trois mesures qui se rapportent aux
lois de pureté (nos 6, 17 et 18). Elles n'ont aucun rapport avec les
mesures anti-romaines. Il faut leur chercher d'autres raisons.

1° הלכות בעל קרי. D'après le Pentateuque, l'homme qui a eu une
pollution nocturne doit quitter « le camp » israélite [1]. C'était un
usage ancien : Saül excuse une absence de David en se disant qu'il
lui est arrivé « un accident » qui l'a rendu impur [2]. Une telle pratique n'était possible que dans une petite société aux mœurs
patriarcales. Aussi trouvons-nous dans le Talmud qu'Ezra « a
institué le bain de purification pour le *baal kéri* » [3], c'est-à-dire
que ce bain suffisait. Dans le même ordre d'idées, on déclara, par
voie d'interprétation, que le « camp » qu'il devait quitter était celui
de la Schechina, c'est-à-dire le Temple, et celui des Lévites, c'est-
à-dire la Azara, mais non celui d'Israël, c'est-à-dire Jérusalem [4].
On alla plus loin : on permit dans ce cas les bains païens hors de
Palestine, même remplis d'eau puisée [5]. Enfin, on en vint à supprimer le bain de purification lui-même [6]. Ainsi s'explique cette
baraïta à l'air mystérieux [7] : ת"ר בעל קרי שנתנו עליו תשעה קבין מים
טהור. נחום איש גם זו זו לחשה לר' עקיבא, ור' עקיבא לחשה לבן עזאי, ובן
עזאי יצא ושנאה לתלמידיו בשוק... Si Nahum a « murmuré » cette
règle à l'oreille d'Akiba, c'est qu'elle était contraire à la mesure
décrétée par les Schammaïtes [8].

2° הבוצר לגת. Ce cas, qui avait déjà divisé Hillel et Schammaï en
personne, sans que Schammaï eût réussi à imposer son opinion à
Hillel, est d'une nature particulière. Hillel, ce grand réformateur,
à qui l'on doit la réforme du *prozbol* et celle de « la maison d'ha-

---

1. Deutér., xxiii, 11.
2. I Samuel, xx, 26.
3. B. K., 82 b.
4. Pesahim, 68 a ; Sifré, Deutér., 255.
5. Mikvaot, viii, 1.
6. Berachot, 22 a.
7. Ibid.
8. V. Katzenellenbogen, op. cit.

bitation dans une ville » [1], voulait en introduire une autre dans
les lois de pureté, et voici en quoi elle consistait. D'après le Pentateuque, si une chose impure tombe sur une graine, celle-ci
reste pure ; mais si la graine a reçu de l'eau, elle est devenue
apte à l'impureté, et si une chose impure tombe alors sur la
graine, celle-ci est impure [2]. Hillel voulut introduire ici le point
de vue subjectif : la graine ne devient apte à l'impureté que si
on a versé de l'eau intentionnellement, c'est-à-dire en y trouvant son intérêt. Contre cette réforme Schammaï s'éleva avec
force, et c'est là-dessus que porte sa discussion avec Hillel.
D'après lui, les raisins deviennent aptes à l'impureté, car on n'a pas
à tenir compte de l'intention de celui qui les traite. D'après Hillel,
au contraire, les raisins ne deviennent pas aptes à l'impureté, car
le liquide est sorti des raisins sans qu'on l'ait voulu, sans qu'on en
ait eu besoin. Et nous comprenons alors la réplique de Schammaï :
« Si tu me pousses à bout, je décréterai l'impureté contre la cueillette des olives aussi » ; en d'autres termes : si tu veux introduire
le point de vue subjectif dans les questions de pureté et d'impureté,
en sorte qu'une chose ne deviendrait apte à l'impureté que si un
liquide a été répandu intentionnellement sur elle, eh bien ! j'éten-
drai la menace d'impureté même à la cueillette des olives, c'est-à-
dire même au cas où le liquide serait tombé contre le désir et
l'intérêt de l'intéressé.

Là-dessus, le Talmud ajoute : « La défense fut édictée, mais elle
ne fut pas acceptée ; plus tard elle fut reprise par les disciples [3]. »
L'opinion ancienne s'est peut-être conservée dans la première
mischna de *Machschirin*, qui représente encore le point de vue
subjectif [4]. Plus tard les Schammaïtes attaquèrent cette thèse « à
coup d'épées et de lances » et firent prévaloir la leur [5].

3° המניח כלים תחת הצינור. « Si on pose des vases sous un tuyau

---

1. Voici l'économie de cette dernière réforme. D'après le Pentateuque, si un homme
s'est vu obligé de vendre une maison d'habitation dans une ville entourée de murs,
il a la faculté, pendant un an, de reprendre sa maison en remboursant le prix d'achat
(Lévit., xxv, 29-30). Or, certains acheteurs se cachaient le jour où ce terme expirait
pour échapper aux vendeurs qui voulaient exercer leur droit de reprise. Hillel institua
alors que le vendeur n'aurait pas besoin de se mettre à la recherche de l'acheteur,
qu'il lui suffirait de déposer l'argent au tribunal (*Arachin*, 31 b), moyennant quoi il
rentrerait en possession de sa maison.

2. Lévitique, xi, 37-38.

3. *Sabbat*, 17 a.

4. *Machschir*., 1, 1 : כל משקה שתחלתו לרצון אע"פ שאין סופו לרצון או
שכופו לרצון אע"פ שאין תחלתו לרצון הרי זה בכי יותן.

5. Voir l'ouvrage cité de M. Katzenellenbogen.

pour recevoir les eaux de pluie, le *mikvé* devient *impur* soit qu'on
ait posé les vases, soit qu'on les ait seulement oubliés, d'après
l'opinion de l'école de Schammaï ; d'après l'opinion de l'école de
Hillel, le *mikvé* reste pur si on a oublié les vases[1]. » Le motif de
cette mesure est le même que celui de la précédente. Les Hillélites
voulaient introduire le point de vue subjectif dans les règles du
mikvé, une des institutions les plus anciennes. D'après eux, on
doit tenir compte de la volonté de l'homme en pareille matière :
s'il a placé là les vases volontairement et sciemment, il rend
impur le *mikvé* comme si c'étaient des eaux puisées ; mais il n'en
est plus de même s'il y a eu simple oubli de sa part et qu'il n'a
pas eu l'intention de poser les vases en cet endroit. Les Schammaïtes, par contre, ne se préoccupent pas de l'intention de l'intéressé : qu'il ait posé un vase sous un tuyau ou qu'il l'ait oublié
à cette place, le *mikvé* est rendu impur.

IV. — LES MESURES ANTI-SADDUCÉENNES.

Après avoir examiné les dix-huit mesures décrétées, en d'autres
termes imposées par une majorité de Schammaïtes, voyons celles
qui ont été prises d'accord par les deux écoles et qui sont également au nombre de dix-huit.

Ces mesures sont les mêmes d'après le Yerouschalmi et d'après
le Babli, et sur les questions qu'elles concernent, nous ne trouvons
dans le Talmud aucune controverse entre Schammaïtes et Hillélites. En voici la liste :

D'abord, les cinq cas dans lesquels la *terouma* devient impropre
à la consommation :

1. ‫האוכל אוכל ראשון והאוכל אוכל שני‬.

2. ‫השותה משקין טמאים‬.

3. ‫הבא ראשו ורבו במים שאובין‬.

4. ‫טהור שנפל על ראשו ורבו ג' לוג מים שאובין‬.

5. ‫האוכלים והכלים שנטמאו במשקין‬.

Puis les six cas dans lesquels, à cause du doute, la *terouma*
doit être brûlée[2] :

6. ‫ספק בית הפרס‬.

1. *Mikvaot*, IV. 1 (*Sabbat*, 16 b).
2. D'après le Babli, certains comptaient ces cas comme faisant partie des mesures
prises à Ouscha (après la guerre de Bar-Kochba). Mais je crois que, pour des faits
d'histoire palestinienne, on doit plutôt s'en rapporter au Yerouschalmi. Il est d'ailleurs loisible d'admettre que ces mesures ont été *renouvelées* à Ouscha.

7. ‏ספק עפר הבא מארץ העמים.

8. ‏ספק בגר עם הארץ.

9. ‏ספק כלים הנמצאים.

10. ‏ספק רוקין.

11. ‏ספק מי רגלי אדם.

Enfin, les cas suivants :

12. ‏כל המטלטלין מביאין את הטומאה בעובי המרדע.

13. ‏גדולי תרומה תרומה.

14. ‏ידים.

15. ‏טבול יום.

16. ‏ספר.

17. ‏לא יאכל הזב עם הזבה.

18. ‏מי שהחשיך בדרך נותן כיסו לעכו״ם.

Ce qui frappe immédiatement, c'est que presque toutes ces mesures portent sur les lois de pureté. Il faut leur chercher d'autres mobiles et d'autres tendances que les mesures anti-romaines. Elles étaient dirigées, non contre l'ennemi du dehors, mais contre celui de l'intérieur : contre les prêtres sadducéens. Le pontificat était devenu une charge vénale [1]. Les grands-prêtres, nommés par les rois ou par les procurateurs [2], opprimaient le peuple et arrachaient par la force les redevances sacerdotales ; quiconque leur résistait était frappé et brutalisé [3]. Les satiriques du temps dénonçaient avec une âpre verve les abus des grandes familles pontificales, où sévissaient le népotisme et la violence , qui se combattaient d'ailleurs mutuellement à cause de leurs con-voitises, ce qui faisait dire de ces prêtres qu' « ils se tuaient les uns les autres à coups de sortilèges » [5].

Outrés de ces excès de leurs adversaires, les docteurs prirent différentes dispositions pour enlever aux prêtres le bénéfice de certaines redevances [6]. Ils allèrent encore plus loin : ils voulurent rendre en quelque sorte impossible l'usage de la *terouma* ; ils décrétèrent tant d'interdictions que presque toute chose rendait la *terouma* impure : et la *terouma* impure devait être brûlée. Tel est le but poursuivi par beaucoup de ces mesures arrêtées d'un com-mun accord par Schammaïtes et Hillélites : ils déclaraient impur

---

1. *Yebamot*, 61 a.
2. Josèphe, *Antiquités*, XX, *passim*.
3. *Pesahim*, 57 a ; T. *Menahot*, XIII, 21.
4. *Ibid*.
5. j. *Yoma*, I (38 c, 1. 46).
6. *Pesahim*, *l. c.* ; T. *Menahot*, *l. c.*

ce qu'ils voulaient défendre [1], et les prêtres ne pouvaient pas le recevoir. C'est ce que nous comprendrons mieux en considérant d'un peu près quelques-unes des mesures en question.

11. « Celui qui mange un aliment impur au premier degré ou un aliment impur au second degré ne devient impur qu'au second degré » : donc il rend impure la *terouma*, mais non les *houllin*. En principe, celui qui mange un aliment impur du premier degré devrait devenir impur au premier degré et rendre impurs même les *houllin* [2]. La mesure prise avait donc pour résultat de sacrifier la *terouma* des prêtres en sauvant les *houllin* des laïques.

12. « Tous les objets meubles communiquent l'impureté à une épaisseur d'un aiguillon. » Cette mesure rendait la *terouma* autant dire impossible. En effet, tout prêtre qui portait un objet quelconque communiquait l'impureté à la *terouma*, même sans savoir s'il avait « fait abri », suivant l'expression technique (האהיל), sur un cadavre. R. Tarfon, qui était un prêtre, mais qui vivait longtemps après, s'éleva encore contre cette mesure, jurant qu'elle était fausse [3].

14. La mesure relative aux « mains » ne saurait être, à mon avis, celle de l'ablution des mains en vue de la consommation de la *terouma*, comme le Babli l'assure, car cette mesure est beaucoup plus ancienne [4]. Bien mieux, on connaissait même déjà l'ablution des mains pour *houllin* : on en attribuait l'institution à Salomon [5], et R. Éléazar b. Arach, contemporain du Temple [6], n'en parle nullement comme d'une mesure nouvelle [7]. Il faut donc chercher dans un autre sens.

Après chacune des fêtes de pèlerinage, on purifiait la Azara, c'est-à-dire qu'on plongeait dans l'eau tous les vases du Temple [8]. Ce qui n'empêchait pas les prêtres de dire aux pèlerins : « Prenez garde de ne pas toucher aux vases, car nous ne pouvons pas les plonger dans un bain de purification. » [9] Le Talmud sait encore

---

1. On ne se servait pas encore des termes מותר אסור et אסור.

2. To *horot*, ii, 2.

3. Oho *l*, xvi, 1 : אקפח את בני שזו הלכה מקופחת ששמע השומע וטעה : שהדאכר עובר והמרדע על כתפו והאהיל צדו על הקבר וטמאוהו.

4. V. Krochmal, *Moré*, ch. xiii.

5. *Sabbat*, 14 b : אמר ר' יהודה אמר שמואל בשעה שתקן שלמה עירובין ונטילת ידים...

6. Il mourut avant la naissance de R. Akiba (T. *Nedarim*, vi, 5).

7. *Houllin*, 106 a : וידיו לא שטף במים א"ר אלעזר בן ערך מכאן סמכו חכמים לנט"י מן התורה.

8. *Haguiga*, iii, 7.

9. *Ibid.*

T. LXVIII, N° 135   3

qu'on n'immergeait pas l'autel d'or et le candélabre, évidemment
parce qu'un israélite ne pouvait pas les toucher. Mais les Pharisiens entendaient ne faire aucune distinction entre les prêtres et
le peuple ; ils demandaient aux Sadducéens de plonger dans l'eau,
après la fête, tous les objets du sanctuaire touchés par les prêtres,
comme ils faisaient pour ceux de la Azara, touchés par les laïques.
Une fois, rapporte le Talmud [1], on purifia le candélabre (lorsque
les Pharisiens eurent le dessus). « Voyez ! dirent les Sadducéens,
les Pharisiens purifient le disque du soleil ! » Les Pharisiens
s'étaient livrés à une manifestation : ils avaient voulu montrer que
le candélabre, bien qu'il ne puisse être touché que par les prêtres,
doit être immergé après la fête : c'est qu'ils mettaient les prêtres
sur le même pied que les laïques et non parce qu'ils se montraient
plus sévères en matière de pureté et de purification [2].

15. Le Talmud défalque le cas du *teboul-yom* comme étant d'origine biblique [3]. Mais c'est que les Amoraïm, ne connaissant plus
les mobiles qui avaient inspiré les « dix-huit mesures », confon-
dent ce cas avec celui de la Bible. En réalité, ce n'est pas la même
chose. D'après le Pentateuque, un homme impur doit, à l'expiration de ses jours d'impureté, non seulement prendre un bain, mais
encore attendre le coucher du soleil [4]. Les Pharisiens prétendaient
que cette règle ne s'applique pas aux laïques [5], mais seulement
aux prêtres [6], et ce fut la disposition qu'ils décrétèrent avec les
« dix-huit mesures ». La preuve en est que R. Josué qualifie cette
disposition de chose nouvelle [7].

16. Le cas du « livre » est dirigé contre les Sadducéens en général. Ceux-ci avaient, vers la fin de l'époque du second Temple,
secoué leur torpeur et essayaient de recouvrer leur pouvoir sur le
peuple par l'intermédiaire des prêtres. Les Pharisiens se virent
obligés d'enlever les armes aux mains de leurs adversaires en
édictant que le « livre » rend impure la *terouma* : c'était assez pour
empêcher les prêtres de se servir de l'Écriture, car ils étaient
obligés de se soumettre dans la pratique aux Pharisiens [8]. On ne

---

1. j. *Haguiga*, iii, 8.
2. V. Katzenellenbogen, *ouvrage cité*.
3. *Sabbat*, 14 *b* : סמי מכאן טבול יום.
4. Lévitique, xv, 5 et s. ; Deutér., xxiii, 12.
5. *Sifra*, 22 : מה ישראל שאינם אוכלים בתרומה במעורבי שמש הרי הן אוכלים במעשר טבולי יום. Cf. *Teboul-Yom*, ii, 2.
6. *Zebahim*, ii, 1 ; T. *Zebahim*, xii, 15 ; *Zebahim*, 98 *b*.
7. T. *Teboul-Yom*, ii, 14.
8. *Yoma*, 19 *b* ; T. *Yoma*, i, 18 ; *Nidda*, 33 *b*.

lut donc pas dans les exemplaires de l'Écriture[1] ; « on défendit de lire les livres de l'Écriture le jour du sabbat, pour ne pas empêcher l'étude[2] » : le peuple étant libre le sabbat, les Pharisiens voulaient qu'il se rendît dans leurs écoles pour entendre la loi orale et non qu'il lût l'Écriture[3]. Cette mesure frappa en plein cœur les Sadducéens, qui s'évertuèrent à la battre en brèche dans leurs controverses avec R. Yohanan b. Zaccaï[4].

17 et 18. Ces deux points manifestent, entre les Schammaïtes et les Hillélites, un accord sur un principe qui, ailleurs, les divise. D'après l'école de Schammaï, on ne doit pas en général établir une « haie » dans le but de préserver un homme d'une faute grave. Ainsi, quoique la chair d'oiseau ne puisse pas être mangée avec du fromage, on peut servir les deux plats à la même table[5], sans se laisser arrêter par la crainte qu'on les mange : c'est à l'homme à faire attention. D'après les Hillélites, on ne doit « ni manger, ni servir » les deux en même temps, car on craint que l'homme les mange s'ils lui sont servis, et on doit faire une « haie » pour lui épargner la possibilité d'une faute. Toutefois, en matière de *arayot*, les Schammaïtes accordent à leurs contradicteurs qu'il faut faire une « haie » et que « le זב ne doit pas manger avec sa femme זבה, afin qu'ils ne soient pas entraînés au péché ». De même, pour le sabbat, « si quelqu'un est surpris en route par le sabbat, il doit remettre sa bourse à un non-juif », car si on ne lui laisse pas cette faculté, il en viendra — l'homme tient tant à son argent ! — à profaner le sabbat.

V. — L'ÉPOQUE DES « DIX-HUIT MESURES ».

En se fondant sur certains indices, on a soutenu que les « dix-huit mesures » étaient de beaucoup antérieures à la destruction du second Temple. Ainsi, on a fait valoir que, d'après l'Évangile de Jean, xviii, 28, les Juifs qui vont trouver Ponce-Pilate ne pénètrent pas dans sa demeure pour ne pas devenir impurs et pouvoir manger la pâque le même soir, et on en a conclu que les mesures anti-païennes existaient déjà du temps de Ponce-Pilate (27-37).

---

1. T. *Sabbat*, xiii, 1 : ...אפ"ר שאמרו אין קורין בכה"ק.
2. j. *Schabbat*, 15 b.
3. Cf. *ibid.* : רשב"ר אומר העוסק במקרא מדה שאינה מדה.
4. *Yadayim*, iv, 6 : אומרים צדוקים קובלים אנו עליכם פרושים שאתם אומרים כתבי הקדש מטמאין את הידים.
5. *Houllin*, viii. 1.

Mais l'on ne saurait faire fond sur le quatrième Évangile, qui a une faible valeur historique et où les « figures » dominent les faits. D'une manière générale, on fera bien de ne pas oublier que les Évangiles ont été composés à la fin du premier siècle et au commencement du second et que ces auteurs chrétiens, qui vivaient parmi les Juifs et connaissaient leurs usages, étaient moins forts sur la chronologie et pouvaient croire anciennes des pratiques relativement récentes.

On a allégué, d'autre part, un épisode rapporté par Josèphe : lorsque le procurateur Félix (52-60) envoya un certain nombre de prêtres à Rome, ils ne se nourrirent que de figues et de noix. Mais ce fait ne prouve rien : ces prêtres ne se conformaient pas aux « dix-huit mesures »; ils étaient scrupuleusement sévères en matière de pureté rituelle. C'est ainsi que des « hassidim » observaient également ces lois de pureté et s'abstenaient de manger chez des païens, que les « habérim » évitaient de manger chez les « am-haareç ». L'auteur du Livre de Daniel présente déjà sous cet aspect son héros et ses trois compagnons, et l'auteur de Judith fait emporter à son héroïne de l'huile et du pain, lorsqu'elle se rend auprès d'Holopherne.

Weiss place l'adoption des dix-huit mesures sous le règne d'Agrippa Ier (mort en 44) ou aux environs [1]. Je crois qu'il faut s'en tenir à l'époque proposée par Graetz, mais avec une petite modification. Graetz admet comme date l'année 67, après la défaite du gouverneur de Syrie, Cestius Gallus, et il corrige, dans la mischna de Sabbat, I, 4, Hanania b. Hizkia en Éléazar b. Hanania [2]. Je préfère remonter un peu plus haut, à l'époque du dernier procurateur, Gessius Florus, plus exactement après le massacre que ce procurateur déchaîna à Jérusalem (66) et avant la mise à mort de Hanania; il est donc inutile de corriger la Mischna. La fameuse réunion aurait ainsi eu lieu dans la demeure de Hanania, partisan de la paix avec les Romains. Mais ce fut son fils Éléazar qui l'emporta et qui, comme nous le savons par Josèphe, fit supprimer le sacrifice pour l'empereur et déchaîna ainsi la guerre fatale.

---

1. *Dor*, I, 187.
2. *Geschichte*, III⁵, 810.

Les Principes des Controverses Halachiques entre les écoles de Schammaï et de Hillel

Étude sur la Jurisprudence Tannaïtique

L'étude des principes qui sont à la base des controverses entre les écoles de Hillel et de Schammaï est indispensable, non seulement à l'intelligence de ces controverses, mais encore à celle de la jurisprudence tannaïtique. Les controverses entre Schammaïtes et Hillélites dépassent la centaine et les controverses halachiques entre les Tannaïm tels que Rabbi Eliézer et Rabbi Josué, ou Rabbi Juda et Rabbi Yosé, peuvent être classées parmi les controverses des écoles de Schammaï et de Hillel.

Dans de précédentes études sur la Halacha, j'ai montré que les controverses halachiques entre les Schammaïtes et les Hillélites sont surtout fondées sur quatre principes [1]. Le premier principe sur lequel les écoles de Schammaï et de Hillel se trouvèrent divisées fut la question de la *Semicha :* les Hillélites estimaient que les rabbins avaient le droit d'interpréter et d'amender la Halacha au moyen de fictions légales et d'interprétations. Les Schammaïtes étaient d'un avis opposé et soutenaient que les rabbins n'avaient pas le droit d'ajouter quoi que ce soit à la Loi transmise par la tradition [2]. En second lieu, les Hillélites intro-

---

1. *The Semikah Controversy between the Zugoth*, J. Q. R., 1917.
2. Voir *ibid.* ; le Dᵣ Ginzberg, dans un très ingénieux article, מקימה של ההלכה ישראל, ירושה"א, הרב"א, maintient que la controverse de la Semicha entre les Zougot aussi bien que les controverses entre les écoles de Schammaï et de Hillel roule sur la question de savoir si quelqu'un peut poser ses mains sur l'offrande de paix apportée un jour de fête. La théorie du Dᵣ Ginzberg n'est pas recevable ; nous avons montré dans ledit article que *seules* les écoles de

duisirent une méthode d'interprétation de la Halacha conforme
à l'esprit de la Loi, tandis que les Schammaïtes étaient d'avis
qu'il fallait respecter la lettre de la Loi [1]. En troisième lieu, les
Hillélites voulaient dresser « une haie autour de la Loi » סִיג
לְתּוֹרה : partout où l'on pouvait craindre que la loi biblique ou
une ancienne Halacha fût transgressée, il fallait prendre des
mesures préventives. Mais les Schammaïtes soutenaient que la
Loi stricte devait prévaloir en toutes circonstances : יקוב הדין
את ההר. Un exemple pourra illustrer ce point : suivant l'école
de Schammaï, on peut placer une volaille sur une table où il y
a du fromage, mais il n'est pas permis de la manger, tandis que
les Hillélites disaient qu'il ne fallait pas placer la volaille sur la
même table [2] que le fromage, parce que, bien que la Loi défendît
de manger les deux ensemble, s'ils se trouvaient réunis sur la
même table, on pourrait oublier la défense et les manger en
même temps. Au contraire, les Schammaïtes permettaient de
faire voisiner fromage et volaille sur la même table, car si la Loi
défend de les manger ensemble, elle ne défend pas de les placer
l'un près de l'autre, et il n'est pas nécessaire de prendre des
mesures préventives, car on doit savoir ce qui est défendu et ce
qui est permis.

Schammaï et de Hillel étaient divisées sur la question ci-dessus, tandis que
la controverse de la Semicha entre les Zougot ainsi qu'entre Schammaï et
Hillel roulait sur la question de savoir si nous pouvons nous fier aux rabbins
dans leur interprétation de la Bible, lorsqu'ils en déduisaient de nouvelles
Halachot. Que la controverse sur la Semicha entre Schammaï et Hillel et la
controverse sur la Semicha entre les Zougot ne sont pas les mêmes, c'est ce
qui résulte de la *Tosefta Hag.*, II, 8-10 ביניהם לא נחלקו אלא על הסביכה, הבשה זות
אמר ....דין בית אבות ושנים נשיאים היו לסביך שלא שאמרו הראשונים מזונות שלשה הן
הסמיכה איזו ......ושלשה עשרים של דין בבית אלא בישראל מחלוקת היו לא בתחילה יסו ר'
כביאין אומרים וב"ה ....ביו"ט סובכין אין אומרים ב"ש הלל, ובית שבאי בית עליה שנחלקי
עליהן וסובכין ועולות שלבים.

Le fait que la *Tosefta* demande: « Sur quelle Semicha étaient divisées les
écoles de Hillel et de Schammaï » et non pas sur quelle Semicha les Zougot étaient divisés, montre clairement que l'on ne considérait pas les deux
controverses comme identiques.

1. M. *Git.*, IX, 10: דבר בה כצא כ"אא אשתי את אדם ינרש לא אומרים שבאי בית
דבר. ערות בה כצא כי שנא' הכשילו הקדיהה אפילו אומרים וב"ה דבר ערות בה כצא כי שנא' ערוה
L'école de Schammaï qui pensait qu'il fallait considérer la lettre de la loi
interprète les mots דבר ערות littéralement: *adultère*, tandis que l'école de
Hillel, qui estimait qu'il fallait interpréter les nouvelles Halachot conformément à l'esprit de la loi, dit qu'un homme peut répudier sa femme הקדיהה אפילו
את תבשילו. Comparez également *The Semikah Controversy*.

2. *Edouy.*, V, 2. לא איברים וב"ה ב"ש דברי נאכל ואינו השלחן על הנבינה עב עולה הצוף
נאכל. ולא עולה.

Le quatrième principe concerne l'*intention*. L'école de Hillel ne reconnaît pas seulement à l'intent'on un rôle dans la Loi mais elle y insiste. On doit prendre en considération, non seulement l'acte humain en lui-même, mais encore son intention. L'école de Schammaï n'accordait d'importance légale qu'à l'acte et ne tenait pas compte de l'intention. Cette différence de point de vue affectait tous les compartiments de la loi juive : rituel, civil et criminel [1].

J'ai déjà traité ce point que Schammaï et Hillel étaient divisés sur la question de l'intention, facteur légal de la Loi juive, dans un article intitulé *Les Dix-huit Mesures*, écrit alors que j'étais encore étudiant à l'Ecole Rabbinique de France et publié plus tard dans cette *Revue*, t. LVIII. Cette idée a été développée plus complètement dans un autre article, *The Semikah Controversy between the Zugoth*, dans la *J.Q.R.*, en 1917. J'ai été le premier à présenter l'idée de l' « intention » comme principe légal de la jurisprudence tannaïtique, dans un article intitulé *Intention as a Legal Principle*, dans le *Journal of Jewish Lore and Philosophy*, 1919, où je mettais en évidence que la controverse entre les écoles de Schammaï et Hillel dans la Mischna *Bèça*, I, est fondée sur le principe de l'intention [2].

Suivant la Tora, la nourriture du Sabbat et des fêtes doit être préparée la veille. Les Schammaïtes, pour qui l'intention n'est pas essentielle, estimaient que tout ce qui se trouve préparé, même sans l'intention de l'utiliser un jour de Sabbat ou de fête, peut être mangé ces jours-là. Les Hillélites au contraire, qui demandent que dans chaque acte on retrouve l'intention de son auteur, estimaient que toute nourriture préparée pour le Sabbat ou pour un jour de fête, sans que la personne qui la prépare ait eu l'intention d'en user ces jours là, ne doit pas être mangée le Sabbat ou les fêtes. Ainsi l'œuf pondu un jour de fête est naturellement préparé la veille : l'école de Schammaï estime qu'on peut le manger un jour de fête. L'école de Hillel l'interdit : car bien qu'il y ait eu préparation, il a manqué l'intention d'en user le jour de fête. Le Dr. Blau ne partage pas mon interprétation de la première Mischna de *Bèça* et dit : « Why should

1. Voir Zeitlin, *Intention as a Legal Principle in Journal of Jewish Lore and Philosophy*, 1919.

2. בֵּיצָה שֶׁנּוֹלְדָה בְּיוֹ״ט בֵּ״ש אוֹמְרִים תֵּאָכֵל וּבֵית הֵלֵל אֵיבְרִים לֹא הֵאָכֵל.

he not have had the intention to eat the egg? Indeed, from the controversy itself it appears that such an intention had existed, and it is even more evident from the controversies concerning Sabbath and holidays, the first and second day of the festival, etc., on the first leaves of the above named tractate. The poor Palestinian peasant, who is chiefly concerned here, searched for the egg on the eve of the festival and found none, nevertheless he looked again on the holiday and really found one, and on this the controversy turns. Accordingly an intention to eat it was not lacking » [1]. Il semble que le Dr. Blau n'ait pas compris le principe de l'intention tel que je l'ai exposé dans mon article *Intention as Legal Principle*. L'intention n'est pas simplement le désir d'obtenir une chose déterminée, mais vise essentiellement la conséquence d'un acte, c'est-à-dire le but que l'on veut atteindre grâce à cet acte, et cette conséquence doit être préméditée et désirée. Pour mieux comprendre ce principe, un exemple de la Halacha tannaïtique suffira. Suivant la loi biblique, toute graine trempée dans l'eau est בכי יותן [2]. Suivant les Tannaim, le trempage de la graine dans l'eau doit être voulu et désiré, et par conséquent, si quelqu'un met sa récolte dans l'eau pour la préserver des voleurs, elle n'est pas considérée comme מוכשר לקבל טומאה, [3] car la conséquence de l'acte qui consiste à mettre la récolte dans l'eau, c'est-à-dire le trempage, n'était pas voulu et certainement pas désiré. En conséquence, les Hillélites qui tenaient l'intention pour importante, soutenaient que l'œuf pondu un jour de fête ne doit pas être mangé ce jour-là, faute d'avoir été préparé par la personne avec le désir

---

1. Blau, *Asmakta or Intention*, J. Q. R., 1931. Blau dit que: "For the realization of his idea of intention he (Dr. Zeitlin) is compelled to declare R. Judah, one of the prominent pupils of R. Akiba, who ultimately dislodged the school of Shammai, as a Shammaite". A mon avis la conception de Blau au sujet des écoles de Hillel et de Shammaï est erronée. Il traite apparemment les écoles d'après les hommes et croit par conséquent que R. Juda, le disciple de R. Akiba, doit être Shammaïte, alors qu'à la vérité les écoles différaient sur les questions de principe et non pas d'après des personnalités. Il apparaît donc qu'un disciple n'épouse pas nécessairement les théories de son maître. Comp. אין רבי אלא ב"ש ב"ה יהודה.

Une réponse complète aux arguments de Blau sur l'Asmakta sera donnée dans une de mes prochaines études.

2. Lév., xi, 38.

3. *Machsch.*, 1, 6 המונח פירייהו בעי בבות הנוא איש בבי יותן.

d'en user au jour de fête et parce qu'il n'y avait pas eu acte de la part de cette personne.

On retrouve ce même principe de l'intention dans la controverse entre les écoles de Schammaï et de Hillel, dans la Mischna suivante du traité *Bèça* : השוחט היה ועוף ביום טוב ב"ש אומרים יחפור בדקר ויכסה וב"ה אומרים לא ישחוט אלא אם כן היה לו עפר מוכן מבעוד יום ומודים שאם שחט שיחפר בדקר ויכסה שאפר כירה מוכן הוא.

Suivant la loi biblique, si quelqu'un tue une bête (que l'on a le droit de manger) ou une volaille, le sang doit être recouvert de poussière [1]. L'école de Schammaï estimait que si quelqu'un tuait la bête ou la volaille un jour de fête, il pouvait prendre de la cendre avec sa bêche et en couvrir le sang. Les Hillélites étaient d'avis qu'on ne devait pas tuer de bête ou de volaille à moins d'avoir préparé de la poussière pour couvrir le sang, car les cendres n'avaient pas été préparées en vue de ce but particulier. Toutefois, ils accordaient aux Schammaïtes que s'il arrivait qu'une bête fût abattue un jour de fête sans qu'il ait été préparé de poussière pour couvrir le sang, on pouvait le couvrir avec des cendres, car les cendres du foyer sont préparées par la nature, c'est-à-dire qu'elles sont la conséquence naturelle de la combustion du bois [2].

1. Lév., XVII, 13.
2. Dans le Talmud de Babylone, les Amoraïm trouvent quelque difficulté a expliquer cette Mischna et changent la leçon ואפר כירה מוכן היא שאפר כירה en mais, comme nous l'avons expliqué, la controverse entre les écoles de Hillel et de Schammaï reposant sur la question de l'intention, le changement est superflu. De plus, la Mischna de *Édouyot* contient également l'expression שאפר. Même si l'on accepte la leçon des Amoraim, ma théorie est renforcée par la Mischna. Dans le même article, בכיבוי של ההבלה, M. Ginzberg soutient que la discussion entre les écoles de Schammaï et de Hillel est due à leur condition sociale. Les Schammaïtes appartenaient à la classe aisée et les Hillélites à la classe pauvre :

...... גם היא נובעת מתוך סערתם השונה של שני הכתים, אכילת חיה זעיף היא דבר רגיל לעשירים אבל לא לעניים, ואם פעמים יקרה שגם העני יבין בכעמים כאלה לבבוד יו"ט, בידאי שחתבינו לזה קודם יו"ט. ולכך אמרי ב"ה שלא ישחוט אלא אם כן היה לו עפר מוכן מבעוד יום, שהרי ידע מקודם שוזנע ולזה שצריך לעפר אבל העשירים בכעמים ובאכלית כאלה הם אצלם כן חדברים הרגילים ואינב עשוים עליהם חכנות בשבילם קודם יו"ט, ואם אתה אוכר עליהם שהשיה היה ועוף ביו"ט בשאין להם עפר כן חמובן אתה נוטל בהם גם האפשרית להתענג ביו"ט!

Bien que cette théorie soit très ingénieuse, elle est inacceptable. D'après la Mischna, nous voyons clairement que la controverse entre les écoles de Schammaï et de Hillel repose sur la question de הכנה et c'est ce que dit la Mischna : שאפר כירה מוכן הוא.

Les controverses halachiques entre les écoles de Hillel et de Schammaï étaient surtout fondées sur les principes ci-dessus énumérés. La vie juive se développa de plus en plus durant le second Temple et de nouvelles lois furent rédigées pour répondre aux besoins de la structure économique et sociale. Ces nouvelles Halachot furent fondées à nouveau sur des principes divers sur lesquels les écoles de Schammaï et de Hillel n'étaient pas d'accord. Je voudrais mettre en évidence, dans ce court essai, un des points de ces controverses, relatif à l'acquisition de la propriété.

La propriété se divise en les catégories suivantes :

La propriété privée, *res privatae* [1] : le propriétaire de l'objet a sur lui tous les droits, et tout autre que lui n'a aucune espèce de droit sur cette propriété.

La propriété qui appartient à Dieu, *res sacrae* [2], telle que l'autel dans le Temple, etc.

La propriété publique, *res publicae*, qui appartient à de nombreuses personnes : ainsi une maison de prières, un établissement de bains, un jardin dans la cité [3]. Aucun habitant de la ville n'a de droit de propriété sur ces objets, mais les citoyens d'autres villes peuvent se voir interdire l'usage des bains, de la maison de prières, etc.

La propriété qui appartient à la nation entière : *res communes omnium*, c'est-à-dire la propriété dont chacun a l'usage, mais qui ne peut jamais être acquise exclusivement par une seule personne : tel un puits sur la route, par exemple [4]. N'importe qui peut en utiliser l'eau sans avoir le droit de l'acquérir exclusivement. L'Azara du Temple est un autre exemple du même cas. Tout le monde peut l'utiliser, mais personne ne la possède exclusivement et ne peut empêcher quelqu'un d'autre de s'en servir.

La propriété qui n'est à personne, *res nullius*, telle que les bêtes sauvages dans la forêt. Quiconque prend possession d'une telle propriété en devient le propriétaire.

---

1. נכסי יחיד.
2. הקדש.
3. *Ned.* 7, 5. יאימר דבר של אימה העיר בני הרחוב והבריחין יבית הכנסת.
4. Res communes omnium. Le Talmud l'appelle של כולי בבל, יאימר דבר של, *Ned., ibid.* זולי בבל בנין החבית והבור שבאמצע הדרך.

Res nullius ne s'applique pas nécessairement à des choses n'ayant jamais eu de propriétaire, mais aussi à des objets à la propriété desquels le possesseur a renoncé sans la transférer à un autre, *res pro de relicto habitae*. A cette dernière catégorie appartiennent tous les objets perdus dans des lieux publics sans caractéristiques particulières permettant l'identification. Quiconque trouve un tel objet en devient le propriétaire, car on suppose que le propriétaire antécédent a abandonné ses droits sur cet objet. Dans ce cas, un tel objet est à l'état de *res nullius* et, par conséquent, la personne qui le trouve acquiert le titre de propriétaire du dit objet [1].

Toutefois, si une personne renonce à ses droits de propriété, en stipulant expressément que certaines personnes ne pourront acquérir cette propriété, un tel objet est considéré, suivant Rabbi Méir (un Schammaïte) comme *res nullius*, car au moment où les droits sont abandonnés, l'objet devient הֶפְקֵר. Au contraire, Rabbi Yosé (un Hillélite) ne considère pas un tel objet comme *res nullius*. En abandonnant ses droits, le propriétaire ne perd ni son titre, ni la responsabilité de l'objet. C'est seulement lors de l'acquisition de la propriété par une autre personne que le précédent propriétaire perd la propriété [2]. Les Hillélites estimaient qu'un objet ne peut être *res nullius* que lorsque n'importe qui peut en prendre possession.

1. Comp. M. et Tos. *B. M.* Ch., 1-2.
2. Jer. *Pêa*, 19 *b*. על דעתיה דר' מאיר די אבר כיון שאדם בבקי' דבר מרשותי' הבקירו

הבקר על דעתיה דר' יסי די אבר אין הבקר יצא מרחת ידי הבעלים אלא בזכיה.

Il est intéressant de noter que, si un homme divorce, disant à son épouse : « Tu es libre d'épouser n'importe quel homme, avec une seule exception », Rabbi Eliézer soutient que, dans ce cas, le divorce est valide. Les sages, par contre, étaient d'avis que le divorce n'est pas valide. המגרש את אשתו ואמר

לה הרי את מותרת לכל אדם אלא לאיש כלוני ר' אליוזר כתיר וחכמים אוסרים.

R. Eliézer, qui était Schammaïte, était d'avis que lorsqu'une personne renonce à ses droits sur une propriété, cette propriété ne lui appartient plus, et que par conséquent si un mari renonce à ses droits sur son épouse, celle-ci est divorcée. Les Sages (Hillélites) étaient d'avis que si une personne renonce à ses droits sur un objet, cet objet ne pouvant être acquis reste comme *res nullius*, et le propriétaire ne perd pas son titre à la propriété, ceci en raison du fait qu'il existe une restriction : une personne ne pouvant acquérir cet objet. Donc, d'après les Hillélites, la femme n'était pas divorcée à moins que le mari n'ait renoncé à tous ses droits, sans restriction. Les Amoraïm dans le Talmud de Jérusalem et dans celui de Babylone ont trouvé quelque difficulté à cette Mischna et ils ont essayé de l'expliquer de diverses manières. Comp. également M. *Pêa*, VI, 1.

Il est intéressant de remarquer que la même différence d'opinion qui existait entre les écoles de Hillel et les écoles de Schammaï relativement à la *res nullius*, se retrouve dans la jurisprudence romaine, entre Proculos, de l'école progressiste, et Sabinus, de l'école conservatrice. Proculos soutenait que le seul fait de renoncer à ses droits ne faisait pas déchoir le possesseur de son titre. C'est seulement lors de l'acquisition du bien par un nouveau propriétaire que le précédent perd ses droits. Au contraire, Sabinus soutenait que si un propriétaire renonce à ses droits, le bien cesse de lui appartenir et devient *res nullius* : « Pro derelicto a domino habitam si sciamus, possumus adiquirere, sed Proculos, non desinere eam rem domini esse, nisi ab alio possessa fuerit. Sabinus desinere quidem omittentis esse, non fiere autem alterius, nisi possessa fuerit » [1].

La différence d'opinion sur la *res nullius* entre les Schammaïtes et les Hillélites se reflète dans la Mischna *Pèa*. Suivant la loi biblique, si le propriétaire d'un champ a oub'ié une gerbe, il ne peut revenir la ramasser, elle appartient aux pauvres. Il n'est pas permis aux riches de la ramasser. L'école de Schammaï soutient que ces gerbes appartiennent à la catégorie *res nullius*, car elles sont identiques à des objets perdus, puisque הפקר לעניים הפקר, et le pauvre n'a pas seulement le droit d'en user lui-même, il peut encore les ramasser avec l'intention de les donner à un autre pauvre. Mais les Hillélites soutenaient que si un propriétaire renonce à ses droits en stipulant que certains ne pourront les acquérir, le bien en question ne devient pas *res nullus*, mais *res commun's omnium* : הפקר לעניים אינו הפקר mais אף שיופקר לעשירים אף. Par conséquent, la gerbe oubliée par son propriétaire sur le champ n'appartient qu'aux pauvres, alors que le riche n'en peut user, et ne doit pas être considérée comme *res nullius*, mais bien comme *res communes omnium*. Les pauvres peuvent en user, mais ne doivent pas la donner à d'autres pauvres. C'est une propriété commune [2].

De ce point de vue nous comprenons pleinement les controverses entre les écoles de Schammaï et de Hillel dans la Mischna de *Pèa*, dans laquelle le traité *Edouyot* classe ces controverses

1. Comp. également Zuckermandel, *Tosefta, Mischna und Baraita* II, p. 13.
2. M. *Pèa*, VI, 1.

comme מקולי בית שמאי ומחומרי בית הלל, les Halachot dans lesquelles les Schammaïtes étaient plus accommodants, tandis que les Hillélites étaient plus stricts. Si toutes les gerbes d'un champ étaient d'un *kab*, sauf une de quatre *kabbim*, au cas où cette dernière aurait été oubliée, l'école de Schammaï déclare qu'elle n'est pas שכחה et que le propriétaire peut revenir la chercher, tandis que les Hillélites la considèrent comme שכחה et maintiennent qu'elle appartient aux pauvres [1]. Les Schammaïtes considèrent שכחה comme *res nullius* de même qu'un objet perdu, et, conformément à leur point de vue, la gerbe qui se distingue de toutes les autres gerbes du champ et qui possède une marque d'identification, appartient au propriétaire du champ, de même que tout objet perdu par quelqu'un et possédant une marque d'identification : celui qui le trouve ne peut en réclamer la propriété et doit le rendre à son possesseur [2]. Mais les Hillélites, qui ne considéraient pas שכחה comme *res nullius* et pensaient que l'on ne pouvait établir de comparaison avec un bien égaré, tenaient qu'il s'agissait de *res communes omnium* et disaient que, dans le cas où toutes les gerbes d'un champ seraient d'un *kab*, sauf une de quatre *kabbim*, cette dernière se trouvant oubliée par le propriétaire est considérée comme שכחה et appartient aux pauvres.

On retrouve le même principe dans les autres controverses des écoles de Schammaï et de Hillel. Une gerbe se trouve près d'un mur de pierres ou près d'une meule, et le propriétaire a oublié cette gerbe particulière [3]. Les Schammaïtes disent qu'elle n'est pas שכחה et que le propriétaire peut revenir la prendre, de même qu'une personne perdant un objet près d'un mur : celui qui le trouve ne peut se l'approprier [4]. Les Hillélites, qui soutenaient que שכחה ne doit pas être considéré comme *res nullius*,

---

1. *Ibid. Edouy.*, IV, 3 כל עומרי השדה של קב קב ואחד של א־בעה קבין ושכחו בית שמאי אומרים אינו שכחה ובית הלל אומרים שכחה.

2. M. *B. M.*, II בצא אחר הנפה אי אחר הנד־ ...... אילו מציאת שלו ואילו חייב להכריז ...... אף השמלה היתה בכלל כל אלה, למה יצאת בה שמלה ביוחדת שיש בה סמנים. ...... אף כל דבר שיש סבנים ויש לו תובעים חייב להכריז.

3. M. *Péa*, VI, 2 ; *Edouy.*, IV, 4. ...... העומר שהוא סמוך לגפה ...... ושכחו בית שמאי אומרים אינו שכחה ובית הלל אומרים שכחה.

4. B. *M.*, 11, 3. מצא אחר הגפה או אחר הנדר ...... הרי יה לא ינע בהן. Comp. également *Tos.*, *ibid.*, III, 2 ; *ibid.*, 19 b. אמר ר' אילעא' שאלתי את ר' יהושע באילו עומרין חלוקין ב"ש וב"ה אמר לו כתירה הזאת בעומר הסמוך לגפה ...... ושכחו ב"ש

estimaient qu'une gerbe oubliée près d'un mur par son propriétaire appartient aux pauvres.

Ainsi la controverse entre Schammaïtes et Hillélites relativement à ce qui est classé ב"ה ומחומרי ב"ש מקולי est, en réalité, la
conséquence logique de leurs points de vue relativement à *res
nullius* [1]. J'ai montré ailleurs que, dans les Halachot de הכנה,
les Schammaïtes étaient accommodants לקולא, tandis que les
Hillélites étaient stricts להומרא; au contraire, dans les Halachot
מוקצא les positions sont renversées, en conséquence de leurs
points de vue sur הכנה et sur מוקצא [2].

Je crois qu'en nous rappelant que Schammaïtes et Hillélites
n'étaient pas du même avis touchant *res nullius*, nous pourrons
expliquer la controverse entre Rabbi Eliézer et les sages, relativement à *Pèa*, controverse dans laquelle les derniers tamuldistes
ont trouvé beaucoup de difficultés. Si quelqu'un (un pauvre),
qui a ramassé *pèa* (le propriétaire d'un champ doit laisser aux
pauvres le grain oublié dans un coin) dit : « Je l'ai ramassé pour
un pauvre », Rabbi Eliézer dit qu'il a acquis ce *pèa* pour un
certain pauvre, auquel il appartient alors. Les sages disent que
cela n'appartient à aucun pauvre en particulier, mais que tout
pauvre peut l'avoir [3]. Eliézer (Schammaïte) était d'avis que *pèa*,
comme שכחה, est *res nullius* et que n'importe qui peut en devenir
possesseur avec l'intention de le donner à un autre pauvre, de
même que מציאה, un objet perdu. Les docteurs (Hillélites), qui
soutenaient que *pèa*, tout comme *schikha*, n'est pas *res nullius*,
mais bien *res communes omnium*, estimaient que cela n'était la
propriété de personne, mais bien celle de chaque pauvre. Celui
qui ramasse *pèa* ne doit pas le donner au pauvre pour qui il l'a
ramassé, car *pèa* n'est pas *res nullius*, et il ne peut en consé-

---

איפרים שכחה וב"ה אופרים אינו שכחה, וכשבאתי אצל ר' אליעזר אכר לא נחלקו ב"ש וב"ה
כי הניפר הספיך דנפה...... שהוא שכחה ועל מה נחלקו שנטלו ונתנו בצר הנפה......ושכחו
שבית שבאי איפרים אינן שכחה בפני שזכה בו, ובית הלל אומרים שכחה.

1. Le Dr. Ginzberg estime (dans le même article) que la controverse entre
les Schammaïtes et les Hillélites reposait sur l'intention. Je crois toutefois
que ce point n'est pas impliqué par le texte de la Mischna, d'où nous avons
le droit d'inférer que la controverse roulait sur la question de *Hefker*, *res
nullius*.

2. Voir S. Zeitlin, *Intention as a Legal Principle*, *Journal of Jewish Lore
and Philosophy*, p. 307.

8. M. *Pèa*, IV, 9 זכה אומר ר' אליעזר עני זו לאיש פלוני הרי זה יאבר את הבאה זו רבש
רדבים איפרים יתנה לעני שנבצא ראשון.

Cf. toutefois *B.M.*, 9 b.

quence en faire sa propriété particulière. Il n'a que le droit d'en user, et par conséquent le premier pauvre qui survient peut s'en emparer.

Dans le présent article, de même que dans les précédents sur l'*Intention* et sur l'*Asmachta*, j'ai essayé de montrer que les controverses entre les écoles de Schammaï et de Hillel sont fondées sur des principes légaux bien définis. Quelques savants ont traité de la Halacha, mais sans se placer à un point de vue historique et critique. Dans leurs travaux, on n'essaye pas de différencier la Halacha tannaïtique de la Halacha amoraïque. La Halacha tannaïtique entra en vigueur à une période où les Juifs vivaient leur propre vie, dans leur propre pays, et sous leur propre juridiction, tandis que la Halacha amoraïque s'est développée sous des conditions différentes, dans la Diaspora.

Je pense que l'étude de la jurisprudence tannaïtique et de son développement n'est pas seulement pour nous un problème académique ; c'est également un problème vital pour les jeunes colonies de Palestine. La Halacha des Tannaïm fut une création de ce pays, et l'Université Hébraïque du Mont Scopus serait l'institution désignée pour entreprendre un traité de la jurisprudence tannaïtique, établi suivant les règles de la critique historique.

הפקר ויאוש

מחקר משפטי עפ"י הספרות התנאית

מאת

שניאור זלמן צייטלין

1 ה פ ק ר

המשפט התלמודי מחלק את הנכסים לאלה הסוגים: א) נכסי יחיד (Res Privatae) נכסים שהם קנין אדם פרטי ושאין לשום אדם אחר זכות עליהם; ב) נכסי גבוה (Res Sacrae) דברים שהם שייכים לבית המקדש[1]; ג) נכסי רבים (Res Publicae) נכסים שבעלים רבים עליהם, כגון בית הכנסת, ובית המרחץ, וכדומה, שכל בני הכנסת יכולים ליהנות מכל תשמישי קדושה שבו, אבל אינם יכולים להוציא ממנו לצורך עצמם למכרם או לתתם במתנה, וכן בית המרחץ שייך לכל בני העיר ליהנות ממנו אבל אין רשות לשום איש מבני העיר לעשותו קנין פרטי[2]; ד) נכסי צבור (Res omnium communes) נכסים השייכים לכל בני המדינה כגון הבאר באמצע הדרך והעזרה אשר כל האנשים שבמדינה יכולים ליהנות מהן אבל אסור להם לתפוס אותן ברשותו כקנין פרטי. התלמוד מכנה את הסוג הזה "דבר של עולי בבל"[3]; ה) נכסי הפקר (Res nullius) דברים שאין להם בעלים, למשל: חיתו יער, דגי הים, שאין שום בעלות עליהם, כל המחזיק בהם הרי הוא זוכה בהם ונעשים לנכסי יחיד.

באופן זה כל כל דבר שבהפקר יכל להיהפך לנכסי יחיד, וכן כל נכסי יחיד יכולים להיהפך לדבר שבהפקר, דהיינו אם בעל הנכסים הפרטים מפקיר את נכסיו,

---

1 או נכסי הקדש, כלים שנשתמש בהן גבוה, תוספתא מעילה, נ; לשום הקדש, שם.

2 מעילה, פ' ד'; נדרים, פ' ה'. ואיזהו דבר של אותה העיר כגון הרחבה המרחץ ובית הכנסת.

3 נדרים, שם, ואיזהו דבר של עולי בבל כגון הר הבית והעזרות והבור שבאמצע הדרך; חזקת דרכים של עולי בבל, (תוספתא אהלות, י"ח נ'); השווה, ביצה, ל"ט, ושל עולי בבל כרגלי הממלא ... סר סבר בירא דהפקרא הוא ומר סבר בירא דשותפי. לפי רב ששת "דבר של עולי בבל" נחשב לדבר של הפקר, הדעה זו היא לפי ב"ש. (עי' למטה בדבר המחלוקת בין ב"ש ובין ב"ה בדבר פאה.) אבל המסקנה של התלמוד היא, "דכולי עלמא בירא דהפקרא היא", וה לפי דעת בית שמאי ולא בית הלל, כי בנכסי עולי בבל יש איזו צד הגבלה. עי' נ"כ הערה 24.

שסה

438

זאת אומרת שאין בעלות על אותם הנכסים שהיו לפני זה קנין פרטי, כל הקודם ומחזיק באלו הנכסים זוכה בהם ונעשים נכסים שלו, נכסי יחיד, אחרי שבעל הנכסים הוציא אותם מרשותו והפקירם בפועל, מה שנקרא בחוקי הרומאים Res Derelictae. הרוצה לעשות את נכסיו הפקר צריך להפקיר אותם בלי הגבלה, למשל אם אמר אני מפקיר את נכסי לכל מלבד לפלוני ואלמוני, לפי דעת בית הלל הנכסים הללו אינם הפקר כי אם נכסי רבים, אולם לפי בית שמאי הם נכסי הפקר אפילו אם הגדיר את ההפקר.

לפי חוקי הרומאים אין נכסי יחיד נעשים נכסי הפקר אלא אם בעל הנכסים ביטל את זכותו על נכסיו והוציא אותם מרשותו, אבל אצל היהודים נכסי יחיד יכולים להיעשות לנכסי הפקר בלי רצון הבעלים, כגון שמיטה, על פי גזרת הכתוב.

שכחה ופאה

לפי התורה אם בעל השדה שכח עומר בשדה אינו יכול לשוב ולקחתו, והעומר הזה שייך לעניים. העשיר אינו יכול לזכות "בשכחה" כי היא דוקא לעניים. הילכך השכחה לפי התורה מוגבלת בתכנה. לפי בית שמאי האומרים כי "ההפקר" יכול להיות מוגבל, הרי שכחתו בתורת הפקר. "הפקר לעניים הפקר", אבל לפי דברי בית הלל שהפקר המוגבל אינו הפקר, כי אם נכסי רבים, "הפקר לעניים אינו הפקר עד שיפקיר אף לעשירים כשמיטה"[4].

לפי השקפה זו נוכל לבאר את המשנה בפאה, ביתר בירור: "העומר שהוא סמוך לגפה ולגדיש וכלים ושכחו, בית שמאי אומרים אינו שכחה ובית הלל אומרים שכחה"[5]. לפי בית שמאי העומר ששכחו הרי זה הפקר, לכן אם הוא שכח אותו בשדה הרי זה "שכחה". אבל אם שכח את העומר אצל גפה וכו' דהיינו אצל דבר מסוים אינו שכחה, כמו אם איזו איש מצא אבידה אצל הגפה או הגדר אינו אבידה, "הרי זה לא יגע בהן"[6]. אבל לפי דברי בית הלל שדבר המופקר צריך להיות בלי הגבלה, לכן העומר הנשכח בשדה אינו הפקר, מפני שהוא מוגבל רק לעניים ולא לעשירים. "העומר שהוא סמוך לגפה ושכחו" דהיינו אצל דבר מסוים הרי זה שכחה לפי דברי בית הלל, מפני ששכחה אינה בגדר הפקר לפי דבריהם, אלא בגדר נכסי רבים מצד ההגבלה שבה.

בענין המחלוקת של המשנה בפאה "העומר שהוא סמוך לגפה וכו', התוספתא והירושלמי מוסיפים: "אמר ר' אילעאי שאלתי את ר' יהושע באילו עומרין חלוקין בית שמאי ובית הלל אמר לו התורה הזאת על העומר הסמוך לגפה ולגדיש ולבקר

---

4 בית שמאי אומרים הפקר לעניים הפקר ובית הלל אומרים אינו הפקר עד שיפקור אף לעשירים כשמיטה, פאה, ו', א'. לפי דברי בית שמאי יש כי אם ד' סוגים, א) נכסי יחיד, ב) נכסי גבוה, ג) נכסי רבים, ד) נכסי הפקר, נכסי צבור הם ג'כ נחשבים כמו נכסי הפקר.

5 שם, פ' ו'.

6 ב'מ, ב', מצא אחר הגפה...הרי זה לא יגע בהן.

ולכלים ושכחו (וב"ש אומרים אינו שכחה ובית הלל אומרים שכחה)[7] כשבאתי
שאלתי אצל ר' אליעזר אמר לי (לא נחלקו בית שמאי ובית הלל על העומר
שהוא סמוך לגפה... ושכחו שהוא שכחה)[8] מודים באילו שאין שכחה, על מה
נחלקו על העומר שהחזיקו (שנטלו) בו להוליכו לעיר ונתנו בצד הגפה (ושכחו)
שב"ש אומרים אינו שכחה מפני שזכה בו וב"ה אומרים שכחה, וכשבאתי והרצתי
את הדברים לפני ר' אלעזר בן עזריה אמר לי התורה (הברית) הן הן הדברים
שנאמרו למשה בסיני (בחורב)[9]. לפי דברי התוספתא ר' אליעזר אמר "לא נחלקו
בית שמאי ובית הלל על העומר... שאין שכחה" אבל הגרסא הנכונה היא "הוא
שכחה" וכן היא בירושלמי[10].

לפי ב"ש אם בעל הבית נטל את העומר להוליכו לעיר ושכחו אצל הגפה אינו
שכחה מפני שזכה בו. המלה "זכה בו" לכאורה משמע דבר שזוכה בו מעכשיו
ושלא היה שייך לו קודם לכן. אבל בעל הבית שהחזיק את העומר הרי החזיק
את שלו (כלומר חפצו), ואין שייך לומר בזה "זכה בו". אולם נוכל לפרש כך:
כי כל העומרים שבשדה הרי בכוח הם נכללים בכלל שכחה, כי כל אחד ואחד
מהם יכול להיות "שכחה" כל זמן שהוא בשדה דהיינו אם בעל הבית שכח, והעומר
ששכח יצא מרשותו, לכן אם בעל הבית נטל עומר אחד בשדה על מנת להוליכו
לעיר, באופן זה לא יכל לבוא יותר בכלל שכחה ונעשה לשלו – זכה בו. וזה מה
שב"ש אומרים לפי דברי ר' אליעזר אם בעה"ב שכח עומר כזה אצל הגפה אינו
שכחה, כי שכח אצל דבר מסויים. אבל לפי דברי ב"ה אם שכח עומר כזה אצל
הגפה הרי זה שכחה. כי שכחה ופאה אין להן דין הפקר ובעה"ב לא זכה בו,
ולעומר כזה אין דין אבידה ולכן בכל מקום שבעה"ב ששכח את העומר הרי זה
שכחה.

אפילו שר' אלעזר בן עזריה הסכים לדברי ר' אליעזר שהמחלוקת שבין ב"ש
ובין ב"ה היא לא על העומר שנשכח אצל גפה וגדיש, שהרי בזה גם בית שמאי
מודים שהוא שכחה, אלא על מה נחלקו – על עומר שהחזיקו בעל הבית, ור'
אלעזר בן עזריה עוד הוסיף ואמר: התורה אלו הדברים שנאמרו למשה בסיני –
בכל זאת רבי, כשסדר את המשנה ראה את דברי ר' יהושע ולא דברי ר' אליעזר,
וסתם את המשנה כדברי ר' יהושע, כי המחלוקת היא בין ב"ש ובין ב"ה בעומר
שסמוך לגפה ושכחו. אבל בעומר שהחזיקו הבעה"ב להוליכו לעיר ושכחו, בזה
מודים בית הלל לבית שמאי שאינו שכחה[11]. מפני שבשעה שבעה"ב החזיק באותו

7 יר' פאה, ו'.

8 שם.

9 שם. ר' אלעאי היה תלמידו של ר' אליעזר, מנחות, י"ח.

10 הגר"א נ"כ גורס בתוספתא במקום אינו שכחה, שכחה. עי' תוספות ראשונים, ע' ל"ו,
מאת שאול ליברמן.

11 העומר שהחזיק בו להוליכו אל העיר ושכחו, מודים שאינו שכחה, פאה, ו', ב'. "מודים
שאינו שכחה" דהיינו מודים ב"ה לב"ש אם הבעה"ב נטל את העומר להוליכו לעיר ושכחו אצל
הגפה שאינו שכחה כי שכח דבר משלו. השווה מקומה של ההלכה בחכמת ישראל, מאת ר' לוי

עומר כדי להוליכו לעיר הרי הוא שלו ויצא, מתורת שכחה שכן אם שכחו אצל
דבר מסויים, יש לו דין אבידה, ולכן אינו שכחה.

לפי התוספתא וכן בירושלמי אם הבעה"ב החזיק את העומר להוליכו לעיר
ונתנו על גב חברו ושכח את שניהם התחתון שכחה והעליון אינו שכחה, ר' שמעון
אומר שניהם אינם שכחה, התחתון מפני שהוא מכוסה והעליון מפני שזכה בו[12]. ולכן
לדברי ר' שמעון העליון אינו שכחה מפני שבעה"ב זכה בו, וזה הוא הטעם שב"ש
נותנים אליבא דר' אליעזר להעומר ששכח בעה"ב אצל הגפה כשאינו שכחה מפני
שזכה בו.

באחד ממאמרי הראיתי כי ר' שמעון החזיק בשיטת בית הלל[13]: "אין לנו אלא
ב"ש כר' יהודה וב"ה כר' שמעון"[14] ומכאן הרי נוכל להוכיח כי ר' שמעון החזיק
בדעת בית שמאי. התוספתא זו מובאה בתלמוד בבלי סוטה, מ"ה, "עומר שהחזיק
בו להוליכו לעיר והניחו על גב חבירו ושכחו התחתון שכחה והעליון אינו שכחה.
ר' שמעון בן יהודה אומר משום ר' שמעון שניהם אינם שכחה, התחתון מפני שהוא
טמון והעליון מפני שהוא צף". שהגרסא העיקרית היתה "צף" ולא "זכה" מוכח
מהשקלא וטריא שבגמרא[15]. והמלים "זכה בו" בהתוספתא והירושלמי תקנו במקום
המלה "צף" עפ"י מסקנת התלמוד בבלי: ... "עד כאן לא פליגי אלא בתחתון
אבל בעליון דברי הכל לא הוי שכחה, שאני התם כיון דאחזיק בי זכה ביה". לכן
נוכל לומר כי טעמו של ר' שמעון שסובר "העליון אינו שכחה" לא מפני שבעה"ב
"זכה בו" אלא מפני שהוא "צף", שהתורה אמרה "ושכחת עומר בשדה", בשדה ולא
כשהוא צף.

מן התוספתא אנחנו לומדים כי לפי התנא קמא העומר התחתון שכחה, אבל לפי
ר' שמעון התחתון אינו שכחה מפני שהוא מכוסה. באופן שטחי נוכל לומר כי הטעם
שר' שמעון שסובר "העומר התחתון אינו שכחה מפני שמכוסה", הוא כי לשכחה יש דין
הפקר, וזה נגד דעת בית הלל, כמו אם איזה איש איש מצא דבר-אבידה שהיא מכוסה
אינה נקראת אבידה[16]. אבל באמת ר' שמעון סובר כי שכחה אין לה דין הפקר,
ומדוע "התחתון" אינו שכחה? "מפני שזוכר את העליון". וכן ר' יונה מפרש את
המשנה "או שחפוהו בקש אינה שכחה, חוזכר את הקשים"[17].

נינצבורג, ע' 32. ע' ג'כ מאמרי "Les Principes des Controverses Halachiques entre
les êcoles de Schammai et de Hillel," REJ. 1932, pp. 73-83.
[12] תוספתא, שם, נ' נ; ירושלמי, שם, ו' ג.
Studies in Tannaitic Jurisprudence, Intention as a Legal Principle, [13]
Journal of Jewish Lore and Philosophy, Vol. 1, 1910.
[14] שבת קמ'נ א', ומקבילים.
[15] ושכחת עומר בשדה פרט לטמון ... אמר ר'א פרט לשצפו עומרים לתוך שדה
חבירו ... חא שמע עומר שהחזיקו בו להוליכו לעיר ... והעליון טפני שהוא צף ... והא טפני
שהוא צף קאמר איםא טפני שהוא כצף ... וטין בטינו הוי צף.
[16] מצא כלי באשפה אם מכוסה לא ינע בו, ב'מ, ב'.
[17] ירוש' פאה, ו', נ'.

לפי שיטתי, נוכל לבאר את המשנה בפאה, פ"ד: "מי שליקט פאה ואמר הרי
זה לפלוני [עני] ר' אליעזר אומר זכה לו, וחכמים אומרים יתננה לעני הנמצא ראשון".
פאה היא מוגבלת לעניים, ובכן לפי בית שמאי שאינם מקפידים על הגבלה, יש
לפאה דין הפקר, ומי שהחזיק בה הרי היא שלו ונעשית נכסי יחיד והוא יכול לעשות
בה כל מה שלבו חפץ ויתן אותה לכל מי שירצה, ולכן לפי דעת ר' אליעזר שהיה
שמותי (מבית שמאי)[18] אם עני ליקט את הפאה יכול ליתן אותה לעני אחר.[19]
אבל לדברי חכמים היינו בית הלל, שלדעתם פאה אינה בסוג נכסי הפקר כי אם
בסוג נכסי רבים, אם עני ליקט את הפאה ליתן אותה לעני אחר הרי הוא יכול
ליתן לאיזו עני שהוא, כי פאה אינה הפקר ואינה נעשית לשלו.

לפי הגמרא בב"מ ט', המחלוקת בין ר' אליעזר וחכמים איננה בין עני לעני,
כלומר אם עני ליקט את הפאה בעד עני אחר, בזה החכמים נ"כ מודים כי הוא
צריך ליתן לאותו העני שבעבדו ליקט, המחלוקת היא לפי דברי הגמרא בעשיר
שליקט בעד עני.[20] אבל לפענ"ד המחלוקת העיקרית בין ר' אליעזר וחכמים היא
בין עני לעני ולא בין עשיר לעני. גם מן השקלא וטריא בגמרא יש להוכיח כי
המחלוקת היא בין עני לעני. "אמר ליה ר"נ לעולא ולימא מר מעני לעני מחלוקת
דהא מצייא הכל עניים אצלה ותנן היה רוכב על גבי בהמה וראה את המציאה
ואמר לחבירו תנה לי נטלה ואמר אני זכיתי בה זכה בה, אי אמרת בשלמא מעני
לעני מחלוקת מתניתין מני רבנן היא, אלא אם אמרת בעשיר ועני מחלוקת אבל
מעני לעני דברי הכל זכה לו הא מני לא רבנן ולא ר' אליעזר, א"ל מתני' דאמר
תחילה". כדי לומר כי המשנה היא לפי דעת החכמים מסיק עולא ואומר "מתניתן
דאמר תחלה". "שרישא דמתניתין היא "בתחילה" הוא מוכיח מסיפא "אם משתנה
לו אמר אני זכיתי בה תחילה לא אמר כלום, תחילה למה לו פשיטא אע"ג
דלא אמר תחילה תחילה קאמר. אלא לאו הא קמ"ל רישא דאמר תחילה"[21] אבל
המלה "תחילה" איננה ברישא.

מדברי הירושלמי[22] מוכח כי הדעה שהמחלוקת בין ר' אליעזר וחכמים בין
עשיר לעני, אבל בין עני לעני הכל מודים שזכה, איננה אלא לפי דעת ר' יהושע
בן לוי שאמר "בבעל הבית עשיר נחלקו אבל בבעל הבית עני מאחר שהוא ראוי
ליטול זכה".[23] לכן לפי המאן דאמר שרק הראוי ליתן זכה אבל לא הראוי

18 ור' ליעזר לאו שמותי הוא, ירושלמי תרומות, ה, ד, עי' נ"כ תוספות, נדה, ז; רש"י
שבת, ק"ל.

19 השווה ביצה, ה', כרם רבעי היה לו לר' אליעזר במזרח לוד בצד כפר טבי ובקש
להפקירו לעניים.

20 אמר עולא א"ר יהושע בן לוי מחלוקת מעשיר לעני דר' אליעזר סבר מינו ... ורבנן
סברי חד מנו אסרינן תרי מינו לא אסרינן, אבל מעני לעני דברי הכל זכה לו.

21 שם, י'.

22 פאה, ד', ה.

23 "ר' יהושע בן לוי אמר בבעל הבית עשיר נחלקו אבל בבעל הבית עני מאחר שהוא
ראוי ליטול זכה. אמר ר' זעירא ר"א ור' יוחנן ורי"ל שלשתם אמרו דבר אחד ... ר' יוחנן

ליטול, המחלוקת בין ר' אליעזר וחכמים תהיה נ"כ בין עני לעני. לפי ר' אליעזר,
העני שליקט היה ראוי ליטול, לכן אם ליקט את הפאה בעד עני אחר זכה לו; אבל
לפי החכמים שרק הראוי ליתן זכה אבל לא הראוי ליטול, העני הזה שליקט היה
רק ראוי ליטול, לכן אם ליקט את הפאה בעד עני אחר, לא זכה העני בעד מי
שליקט ויכול ליתן לאיזה עני שירצה.

כפי הנראה היא היא המחלוקת בין האמוראים הראשונים בדבר מציאה.
לפי דברי ר' יוחנן ,המגביה מציאה לחבירו קנה חבירו' הטעם הוא שהוא סובר
כמו ר' יהושע בן לוי כי הראוי ליטול זכה.²⁴ אולם לפי ריש לקיש שרק הראוי
ליתן זכה אבל לא הראוי ליטול ,אין אדם זוכה לחבירו במציאה'.

אמר אדם זוכה לחבירו במציאה וריש לקיש אמר אין אדם זוכה לחבירו במציאה. ר' רדיפה
אמר איתפלגון ר' יונה ור' יוסי חד אמר הראוי ליטול זכה וחרנא אמר הראוי ליתן זכה. מאן
דמר הראוי ליטול זכה כ"ש הראוי ליתן. ומאן דמר הראוי ליתן אבל ליטול לא, מתניתא פליגא על
מ"ד הראוי ליטול זכה... והא מתניתא פליגי על מ"ד הראוי ליתן זכה דתנינן תמן עישור שאני
עתיד למוד נתון נתון שעקיבה (א) בן יוסף כדי שיזכה בו לעניים... ור"ע ראוי ליטול היה (הוא)
פתר לה קודם שהעשיר, ואפי' תומר משהעשיר תופחת כשהיה פרנס ויד הפרנס כיד העני,
מילתיה דר' יהושע בן לוי אמרה הראוי ליטול זכה דאמר ריב"ל בבעל הבית עשיר נחלקו
אבל בבעל הבית עני מאחר שהוא ראוי ליטול זכה". (השוה מעשר שני, ה, ה' ד').

לפי הירושלמי המחלוקת בין ר' אליעזר וחכמים אינה מטעם ה.מגו' כמו שמפרש התלמוד
בבלי (ב"מ, ט') דר' אליעזר סבר מינו דאי בעי מפקר נכסיה והוי עני השתא נמי חזי
ליה ומינו דכי לנפשיה זכי נמי לחבריה, ורבנן סברי חד מינו אמרינן תרי מינו לא אמרינן
(ב"מ, ט'). כפי הנראה מגיטין י"א, המחלוקת בין ר' אליעזר וחכמים היא בעיקרין של ,התופס
לבעל חוב במקום שחב לאחרים'.

²⁴ בעלי התוספות (גיטין י"א, ב') ראו סתירה בדברי ר' יוחנן, האומר במקום אחד
שהמגביה מציאה לחבירו קנה חבירו, ובמקום אחר שהתופס לבעל חוב במקום שחב לחבירו
לא קנה (ב"מ, י', ר' נ"כ ח'). לפי דעת בעלי התוספות הא בהא תליא, כדאמר רב נחמן ורב
חסדא דאמרו תרווייהו המגביה מציאה לחבירו לא קנה חבירו מאי טעמא הוי תופס לבעל חוב
במקום שחב לחבירו, והתופס לבעל חוב במקום שחב לחבירו לא קנה חבירו (שם). אבל באמת
אין שום סתירה בדברי ר' יוחנן. כפי שאמרנו סובר ר' יוחנן שהראוי ליטול זכה לכן הסנביה
מציאה לחבירו קנה חבירו, והאיש שהגביה זכה בה ונעשית שלו ויכול ליתן לחבירו
ואין פה .במקום שחב לחבירו'. רב נחמן ורב חסדא כפי הנראה סוברים כי רק הראוי ליתן
זכה ולא הראוי ליטול, לכן המגביה מציאה לחבירו לא קנה, כי ,המגביה' היה ראוי ליטול
אבל לא ליתן, והוי במקום שחב לאחרים. לפי דברינו אין אנו צריכים להתירוצים של בעלי
התוספות (עי' שם). בביצה, ל"ט, מביא התלמוד מחלוקת אחת בין רב נחמן ובין רב ששת:
אחמר מילא ונתן לחבירו רב נחמן אמר כרגלי מי שנתמלאו לו ורב ששת אמר כרגלי המסלא...
כולי עלמא בירא דהפקרא היא אלא הכא במגביה מציאה לחבירו נקמא חבירון קא מפליני
מר סבר קנה ומר סבר לא קנה' רש"י (שם) שינה את הגירסא המגביה מציאה לחבירו קנה
חבירו ל.המגביה מציאה להבירו', ולא גרס .קנה חברו'. לפי דעת רש"י אם נגרוס .קנה חבירו'
תהיה קשיא מציאה דרב נחמן אדרב נחמן. פה (בביצה) רב נחמן סובר המגביה מציאה לחבירו קנה
חבירו, ובב"מ אומר רב נחמן לא קנה חבירו (עי' רש"י). ר"ת סובר כי יש לקיים את הגרסא
.קנה חבירו' ולא תהיה סתירה בדברי רב נחמן. לפי דעת ר"ת ,מר סבר קנה' היינו רב ששת,
,ומר סבר לא קנה' היינו רב נחמן, ובכן אין סתירה בדברי רב נחמן. עי' נ"כ המאור הקטן
ביצה שם; הענות הראב"ד; וחדושי הרשב"א.

443

לפי דברינו המחלוקת בין ב"ש ובין ב"ה בענין הפקר היא כך. לפי ב"ש אם
הפקיר איזו חפץ אפילו בהגבלה, דהיינו אם הוציא אנשים שלא יוכלו לזכות, הרי
זה הפקר לכל אדם חוץ מאלו האנשים, אבל לפי דעת בית הלל שהפקר מוכרח
להיות בלי הגבלה לכן אם אדם הפקיר איזה דבר והתנה מלבד לאחדים שלא
יוכלו לזכות אין דין הפקר חל על החפץ. לפי השטה הזאת נוכל לבאר פלוגתא
אחת בין ר' אליעזר והחכמים בנוגע לגט: .המגרש את אשתו ואמר לה הרי את
מותרת לכל אדם אלא לאיש פלוני ר' אליעזר מתיר וחכמים אוסרים"25 ר' אליעזר
שהיה שמתו סובר אם הבעל מגרש את אשתו שהיתה קנינו ונותן לה גט שיחרור
לעשות אותה בת חורין, להתיר אותה לכל בני חוץ לאיזה איש, הרי זה דומה
לאדם שמפקיר איזה דבר מקנינו בהגבלה ולפי דברי ב"ש הרי זה הפקר. לכן
לפי דעת ר' אליעזר האשה הגם שנתגרשה בהגבלה הרי היא מותרת לכל בני אדם
מלבד להאיש ההוא המותנה. אבל לפי דברי ב"ה כמו שהפקר מוכרח להיות בלי
הגבלה כך גירושין צריכין להיות בלי הגבלה. לכן המגרש את אשתו ואמר לה
חוץ מאיש פלוני אינה מגורשת לדברי החכמים (ב"ה).

ע ב ד

ע"פ חוקי הרומאים אם האדון הפקיר את עבדו העבד נעשה הפקר ודין Res
nullius לו. אבל אינו משוחרר. מצבו לא נשתנה, והוא נשאר עבד, וכל הקודם
בו לזכות זכה ונעשה עבדו26. אבל במשפט התלמודי אנו מוצאים חלוקי דעות
בין האמוראים הראשונים. לפי דעת שמואל המפקיר את עבדו יצא לחירות, מפני
שבעל העבד ביטל את בעלותו על העבד, וממילא יצא לחירות ואינו צריך לגט
שיחרור27. כפי הנראה מסוגית התלמוד סבר רב שהגם שהעבד יצא לחירות אם
אדונו הפקירו, בכל זאת .צריך גט שיחרור"28. דעת ר' יוחנן בנוגע למצבו של
העבד אינה ברורה. לפי הבבלי דעת ר' יוחנן היא המפקיר את עבדו הוא נעשה
לבן חורין אבל צריך לגט שיחרור29 אבל לפי הירושלמי כפי הנראה אמוראי
נינהו, יש מחלוקת בדבר, אם ר' יוחנן סבירא ליה אם העבד שבעליו הפקירו צריך
לגט שיחרור אם לאו. .ר' אבהו בשם ר' יוחנן אמר המפקיר את עבדו אינו רשאי
לשעבדו ואינו רשאי לכתוב לו גט שיחרור,30 אמר ליה ר' זעירא כל עמא אמרין
דהוא צריך ואת אומר אינו צריך".31

---

23 משנה גיטין, ט', א; עי' נ"כ דברי הגמרא שם. דתניא א"ר יוסי בר' יהודה לא נחלקו
ר' אליעזר וחכמים על המגרש את אשתו ואמר לה הרי את מותרת לכל אדם חוץ מפלוני שאינה
מגורשת... עי' נ"כ תוספתא שם ירושלמי שם.
26 Rudolph Sohm, *The Institutes of Roman Law*, p. 173.
27 אמר שמואל המפקיר את עבדו יצא לחירות ואינו צריך גט שיחרור, גיטין, ל"ח, ומקבילים.
28 ר' חייא בר אבין אמר רב אחד זה ואחד זה יצא לחירות וצריך גט שיחרור. שם.
29 והאמר עולא אמר ר' יוחנן המפקיר עבדו יצא לחירות וצריך גט שיחרור. שם, לט.
30 ירושלמי, גיטין, ד'.   31 שם. ע' הערה 33.

בבבלי מביא עולא דעת ר' יוחנן. המפקיר את עבדו יצא לחירות וצריך גט
שיחרור". המאמר של עולא בשם ר' יוחנן הוא בשינוי ממה שר' אבהו אומר בשם
ר' יוחנן בירושלמי, אך אפשר לומר כי אמוראי נינהו אליבא דר' יוחנן, שניהם
מסרו אותה ההלכה של ר' יוחנן רק בשני לשונם[32]. אולם קצת קשה, כי אם נרד
לעומקו של דבר נראה כי יש מעין סתירה בין דברי עולא בשם ר' יוחנן ובין דברי
ר' אבהו בשם ר' יוחנן. לפי ר' אבהו סבר אם האדון הפקיר את עבדו
אינו רשאי להשתעבד בו, משמע שהוא אינו בן חורין אך האדון אינו רשאי
להשתעבד בו מפני שהפקירו ואינו עבדו עוד. אבל אינו רשאי ליתן לו גט שיחרור
מפני שהפקירו ואין לו עליו רשות. ולדברי עולא בשם ר' יוחנן, העבד נעשה בן
חורין אם הפקירו האדון אך צריך ליתן לו גט שיחרור.

אלמלא דמסתפינא הייתי אומר כי ר' אבהו ועולא נחלקו בדעת ר' יוחנן, לפי
עולא דעת ר' יוחנן היא כי המפקיר את עבדו יצא לחירות וצריך גט שיחרור,
אבל לפי ר' אבהו, דעת ר' יוחנן היא כי המפקיר את עבדו אינו יוצא לחירות
והוא נעשה עבד שאין לו בעלים, דהיינו–הפקר. והיות שהאדון הוציא אותו
מרשותו, אינו רשאי ליתן לו גט שיחרור מפני שפקעה זכותו של אדונו עליו[33].

<hr>

[32] אמוראי נינהו אליבא דר' יוחנן, ב"מ, ל"ח; יבמות, ט"ז, וסקבילים.

[33] אבל יש איזה קושיא בדברי הירושלמי. כ"ע אמרין דהוא צריך ואת אומר אינו צריך.
אבל הרשב"א בחידושיו (גיטין) מביא את הירושלמי בנוסחא אחרת: ר' אייל בשם ר' יהושע בן
לוי רבו המתיאש מעבדו אינו רשאי לשעבדו וצריך (לכתוב) לו גט שיחרור, שמע ר' יוחנן
ואמר יפה לימדנו ר' יושע בן לוי... ר' אייל בשם ר' יהודה בר' המתיאש מעבדו אינו רשאי
לשעבדו ואינו צריך לכתוב לו גט שיחרור. אמר ליה ר' זעירא כל עמא אמרין דהוא צריך
ותימר אינו צריך. לפי הנוסחא שיש לנו בירושלמי, ר' זעירא אומר. כל עמא אמרין דהוא
צריך" בתשובה לדברי ר' אבהו בשם ר' יוחנן שאמר המפקיר את עבדו אינו רשאי לשעבדו
ואינו רשאי לכתוב לו גט שיחרור. אבל לפי נוסחת הירושלמי שהרשב"א מביא, ר' זעירא אמר
כל עמא צריך" לר' אייל בשם ר' יהודה בר' המתיאש מעבדו וכו'.

שהגירסא הנכונה היא כמו שמביא הרשב"א מוכח מהשקלא והטריא בירושלמי, ר' אילא
בשם ריש לקיש כמאן דאמר אינו צריך... ברם כמאן דאמר צריך לכתוב לו גט שחרור
והיוצא משום יאוש ... ועוד הביטוי ... כל עמא אמרין דהוא צריך" יכול להיות טופנה רק נגד
ר' אייל בשם ר' יהודה שאמר המתיאש מעבדו אינו רשאי לשעבדו ואינו צריך לכתוב לו גט
שיחרור. כי באמת הן ר' יהושע בן לוי והן ר' יוחנן סוברים כי המתיאש צריך ליתן לו גט שיחרור,
אבל אי אפשר שביטוי זה יבוא בניגוד לדברי ר' אבהו בשם ר יוחנן. המפקיר את עבדו ...
אינו רשאי לכתוב לו גט שיחרור. כל עמא אמרין דהוא צריך כי אין מן דאמר בכל הירושלמי
הסובר שהמפקיר את עבדו צריך לכתוב לו גט שיחרור.

לפי דעתי, דברי ר' זעירא שאמר כל עמא אמרין דהוא צריך" אינם מופנים לר' אבהו
שאמר בשם ר' יוחנן המפקיר את עבדו, אך לדברי ר' אילו שאמר בשם ר' יהודה המתיאש
מעבדו, כמו שמביא הרשב"א בחידושיו.

הרשב"א לא הביא את כל דברי הירושלמי כי אם מה שהיה צורך לו לענינו. לפי דעתי
הירושלמי מביא שני מאמרים מר' יוחנן: א) שמעון בר בא בשם ר' יוחנן עבד שברח מן השבויין
אצל רבו אין רבו רשאי לשעבדו וצריך לכתוב לו גט שיחרור; ב) ר' אבהו בשם ר' יוחנן
המפקיר את עבדו אינו רשאי לשעבדו ואינו רשאי לכתוב לו גט שיחרור. בדבר עבד שברח,
ר' יוחנן סובר שרבו הראשון ז־נו רשאי לשעבדו, וכדי לעשות אותו בן חורין צריך לכתוב לו

ודעת ר' יוחנן מתאימה לחוקי הרומאים שאם האדון מפקיר את עבדו אין הלה
נעשה בן חורין והוא עבד אך במעמד הפקר Res nullius.

לכן לפי הסברתי ג' דעות הן בהפקר של עבד. לפי דעת שמואל, המפקיר
את עבדו יצא לחירות ואינו צריך לגט שיחרור, מפני שבעת שאדונו הפקירו הוא
נעשה בן חורין. לפי דעת רב העבד יצא לחירות אבל זקוק הוא לגט שיחרור.
לפי ר' אבהו ר' יוחנן סבר כי העבד לא יצא לחירות כשהפקירו האדון ואין רשות
להאדון ליתן לו גט שיחרור. דעת ר' יוחנן היא אליבא דר' שמעון בן גמליאל
שלפי דעתו אם עבד נשבה ואדונו כבר התיאש ממנו ואיש אחר פדה אותו, הן
לשם בן חורין והן לשם עבד רבו השני ישתעבד בו.[34] מפני שאף שאדונו הראשון
נתייאש ממנו ופקעה זכותו עליו, עוד עבד הוא, ורבו השני יכול להשתמש בו. לפי
עולא דעת ר' יוחנן היא כי המפקיר את עבדו נעשה בן חורין אך צריך ליתן לו
גט שיחרור, והיא היא דעת רב.[35]

דברי שמואל הם פשוטים הם. אם האדון הפקיר את עבדו הרי הוא בן חורין
ואינו צריך לגט שיחרור. וגם דברי ר' יוחנן (אליבא דר' אבהו) הם ברורים.
המפקיר את עבדו בטל את זכותו עליו ולכן אינו רשאי ליתן לו גט שיחרור והוא
נשאר במעמד של עבדות. אבל רב שאמר המפקיר את עבדו יצא לחירות וצריך
גט שיחרור דבריו צריכים הסברה, אם האדון הפקיר את עבדו בכן פקעה זכותו
עליו, ואיך הוא יכול ליתן לו גט שיחרור?[36] (כן דעת ר' יוחנן אליבא דעולא
צריכה בירור).

כפי הנראה המחלוקת שבין רב ושמואל היא מיוסדה על המחלוקת דר' מאיר
ור' יוסי בהפרינציפ של הפקר. כפי שידוע, לבעל הנכסים יש זכות על הנכסים
אבל יש לו נ"כ אחריות, למשל אם שורו וחמורו הזיקו חייב באחריותם. לפי ר'
מאיר בעת שבעל הנכסים הפקיר את נכסיו יצאו מרשותו, ונעשו הפקר, ופקעה
זכותו עליהם ופטור מאחריותם.[37] ר' יוסי סובר אין הפקרו נעשה הפקר אלא
בזכיה.[38] דהיינו כל זמן שאדם אחר לא זכה בנכסים עוד אחריותם עליו. לכן

<hr>

גט שיחרור. כי המתיאש מעבדו צריך לכתוב לו גט שיחרור. אבל אם הפקיר את עבדו אינו
רשאי לכתוב לו גט שיחרור, מפני שפקעה זכותו מעליו. עבד כזה לפי דעת ר' יוחנן אין לו
תקנה. וכן משמע נ"כ מדברי אמימר, "המפקיר את עבדו אותו העבד אין לו תקנה" (גיטין, מ').
34 עבד ונשבה ופדאהו . . . רשב"ג אומר בין כך ובין כך ישתעבד. משנה גיטין, ד'. השווה
ספר הזכות, שם (ישתעבד ארבו ראשון). ראה הערה 60.
35 כי סליק ר' חייא בר יוסף אמר להאי שמעתא דרב קסי דרבי יוחנן א"ל אמר רב
הכי והוא לא אמר הכי והאמר עולא א"ר יוחנן המפקיר את עבדו וכו', הכי קאמר ליה אמר
רב כוותיה . . . גיטין, ל"ט. עי' לעווין, אוצר הגאונים, גיטין, 75. ראה למטה ע' שע"ח [וי"ד].
36 לפי דעת רש"י (שם, ל"ח) וכותב לו גט להחירו בבת ישראל. עי' תוספות שם, ד"ה
המפקיר עבדו.
37 "דר' מאיר די אמר כיון שאדם מפקיר דבר מרשותו הפקרו הפקר". ירושלמי, פאה, ו'.
38 "דר' יוסי די אמר אין הפקר יוצא מתחת ידי בעלים אלא בזכיה אין הפקרו הפקר".
ירושלמי, שם; עי' נ"כ בבלי נדרים, מ"ג.

בנוגע להמאסר שטובא בהתלמוד בבלי "מיתיבי (כדתניא) המפקיר את כרמו ולשחר

דעת שמואל היא כר' מאיר – כיון שהפקירו הפקר ונעשה בן
חורין ואינו צריך לגט שיחרור. דעת רב היא כר' יוסי שאין הפקר יוצא מתחת
ידי הבעלים אלא בזכיה. לכן להאדון יש אחריות עליו ולא פקעה זכותו עליו, לפי
זה יש לו רשות ליתן לו שטר שיחרור[39].

לפי דעת ר' יוסי „אין הפקר יוצא מתחת ידי הבעלים אלא בזכיה" לכן אם
אחד הדיר הנאה מחבירו והיו שניהם בדרך ואין לחבירו מה לאכל, אם המדיר
הפקיר את שלו, חבירו לא יכול לאכל מזה[40], מפני שלא יצא מרשות המדיר ואינו
הפקר. אבל לפי התנא קמא דהיינו ר' מאיר „הלה נוטל ואוכל"[41] שלפי דעת ר'
מאיר כיון שאדם מפקיר יצא דבר מרשותו ונעשה הפקר, לכן חבירו יכול ליטול
לאכל מפני שלא שייך עוד להמדיר.

II יאוש

לפי חוקי הרומאים נכסי יחיד יוכלו להיעשות הפקר, אם בעל הנכסים הוציא
בפועל את הנכסים ובכוונה להפקירם – רק אז הם הפקר, אבל אם הוציא אותם
בפועל דהיינו השליך את הנכסים אך בלי כוונה לעשותם הפקר אינם הפקר[42].
למשל: אם בעל הספינה הטיל אל הים כמה חפצים מן הספינה כדי להקל את
כובד הספינה מפני סערת הים – החפצים האלה אינם הפקר, מפני שבעל החפצים
לא חשב לעשותם הפקר[43]. אבל במשפט התלמודי נכסי יחיד לא רק שיכולים

עמד (והשכים בבקר) ובצרו חייב בפרט ובעוללות ובשכחה ובפאה ופטור מן המעשר' (נדרים,
מ"ד, וטקבילים) אבאר במאמרי הפקר ויאוש במשפט התלמודי.

[39] השווה למטה בענין יאוש. ראה חדושי הריטב"א על גיטין, פרק ד'.

[40] המודר הנאה מחבירו ואין לו מה יאכל... היו מהלכין בדרך ואין לו מה יאכל נותן
לאחרים לשום מתנה והלה מותר בה, אם אין עמהם אחר מניח על הסלע או על הגדר ואומר
הרי הן מופקרים לכל מי שיחפוץ והלה נוטל ואוכל ור' יוסי אוסר (משנה נדרים, ד').

[41] השווה ירושלמי, שם, תנא ר' מאיר אומר כיון שאדם מפקיר יצא דבר מרשותו, ר' יוסי
אומר...; בבלי, שם, מ"ג, אמר ר' יוחנן מ"ט דר' יוסי קסבר הפקר כמתנה מה מתנה עד
דאתיא מרשות נותן לרשות מקבל אף הפקר עד דאתי לרשות זוכה.

ד"ר יחיאל מיכל גוטמן במאמרו „נכסי הפקר ונכסי מדבר" בקובץ „זאת ליהודה" סבר
כי טעמיה של ר' יוסי האוסר: לפי שבברור הדבר, שאין הפקר זה הפקר ממש, ואין שם על
צד האמת רק איש אחד שיכול לזכות בו, והרי הוא כנותנו מתנה לאיש הזה ולא מפקיר ממש".
גוטמן לא הבין כנראה את הסוגיא של הפקר; ולא ירד לעמקו של העקרון של המחלוקת בין
ר' מאיר ובין ר' יוסי בנוגע להפקר.

Qua ratione verius esse videtur, si rem pro derelicto a domino habitam [42]
occupaverit quis, statim eum dominum effici. Pro derelicto autem habetur, quod
dominus ea mente abjecerit, ut id rerum suarum esse nollet, ideoque statim domi-
nus esse desinit. (Institutionum Justiniani lib. II.)

Alia causa est earum rerum, quae in tempestate maris, levandae navis [43]
causa, ejiciuntur; hac enim dominorum permanent, quia palam est eas non eo
animo ejici quod quis eas habere non vult, sed quo magis cum ipsa navi maris

להיעשות נכסי הפקר כשבעליהם מוציאים אותם מתחת ידיהם ומפקירים אותם
אלא גם אם איזה חפץ נגנב, גמל או נאבד והבעלים מתייאשים ממנו, החפץ הזה
יצא מתחת הבעלים ונעשה הפקר. ולכן אם אבד לאיש איזה חפץ ברשות הרבים
המוצא אותו הרי זה שלו, מפני שהבעלים נתייאשו ממנו. אולם אם חפץ שיש בו
סימן נאבד או היה מוטל אצל דבר מסוים כמו אצל הגפה והגדיש והבעלים לא
נתייאשו ממנו, המוצא חפץ כזה הרי אינו שלו ושייך עוד להבעלים, מפני שלא
נתייאשו וחייב להכריז. וכן הגנב או הגזלן צריך להחזיר רק את דמי הגנבה או
הגזלה אבל לא את החפץ בעצמו שגנבו מפני שהבעלים נתייאשו ונעשה ע"י כך
כמו הפקר והגנב או הגזלן קנה אותו.

כפי שאמרנו לעיל חוקי הרומאים נכסי יחיד יכולים להיעשות הפקר
רק אם בעל הנכסים הוציא בפועל את הנכסים דהיינו res derelictae, אבל לא
על ידי יאוש. לפי דעת התנאים נכסי יחיד יכולים להיעשות הפקר הן
ע"י derelictio והן ע"י יאוש. ע"י derelictio מובן. כי כמו שבעל הנכסים
יכול למכור את נכסיו או ליתנם במתנה כך הוא יכול להפקירם. אבל הדעה,
כי ע"י יאוש יוכלו נכסי יחיד להיעשות כמו הפקר, בנויה על התורה. עפ"י גזרת
הכתוב אם בעל השדה שכח עומר בשדה זכותו פקעה מהעומר. (והמחלוקת בין בית
שמאי ובין בית הלל היא אם העומר הוא בכלל הפקר או בכלל נכסי רבים,
אליבא דכולי עלמא בעל השדה אם שכח את העומר בטלה זכותו עליו.) על
הפרינציפ הזה בנויים כל דיני יאוש בספרות התנאית.

עפ"י התורה יכול אדם להפסיד זכותו אף שלא ברצונו, כלומר שלא הפקיר
את נכסיו. לכן לפי דעת התנאים, אם אבד איזה דבר או יצא דבר מרשותו ע"י
אחרים, כגון ע"י גנבה או גזלה או ע"י סבות שונות כמו שטפו נהר[44] יצא מרשותו
אם התייאש, והאיש שגנב או גזל או מצא את האבידה הרי זה שלו. והיות שאדם
יכול להפסיד את זכותו אפילו שלא ברצונו, לכן הגדירו התנאים את דיני יאוש ואמרו
כל דבר שיש בו סימן או שאבד אצל דבר מסויים אין זו אבידה, כלומר לא פקעה
כוחו של הבעל עליו[45].

periculum effugiat. Qua de causa, si quis eas fluctibus expulsas, vel etiam in
ipso mari nactus, lucrandi animo abstulerit, furtam committit; nec longe dis-
cedere videntur ab his quae de rheda currente non intelligentibus dominis cadunt.
Ibid.

[44] שטף נהר עצים ואבנים וקורות מזה ונתן לזה אם נתייאשו הבעלים הרי אלו שלו,
תוספתא, ב"ק, פ"י, המציל מן הנהר ... אם נתייאשו הבעלים הרי אלו שלו, משנה, ב"ק,
פ"י. אבל ע' ירושלמי ב"מ פ"ב מניין ליאוש בעלין מן התורה ... אשר האבד ממנו; השווה נ"כ
ב"ק ס"ו אמר רבה רבה יאוש ... לא ידעינין אי דאורייתא אי דרבנן. ע"ז אדון במ"א.

[45] האמוראים האחרונים עוד הגדירו ביותר את דיני היאוש בנוגע לחפץ שיצא מיד בעליו
שלא ברצונו. עי' ב"ק ס"ו-ח'. בדבר יאוש כדי קני או לא קני, ראה תוספות ב"ק ס"ז ד"ה אמר
ע:לא; וד"ה הוא דאמר כצנועין (דף ס"ח); גיטין, נ"ה ד"ה מאי טעמא יאוש כדי לא קני; ע'
נ"כ שו"ת הרשב"א תתקס"ח.

בנוגע לדעת ר' יוחנן ור"ש בן לקיש ומחלוקות אמוראי בבל בדבר יאוש, אדון במקום אחר

על פי ההלכה הישנה כל דבר שיש לו שם כלי מקבל טומאה, אבל לא החפץ
שאין עליו שם כלי, אולם אם בעל החפץ חושב להשתמש בחומר הכלי כמו כלי,
למשל העור, אם בעל העור חושב לכסות בו חמורו או פרדו הרי זה נקרא כלי
ומקבל טומאה. אולם אם בדעתו לעשות מהעור נעלים או אוכף הרי אינו עדיין
כלי ואינו מקבל טומאה. ״עורות של בעל הבית מחשבה מטמאתן ושל עבדן אין
מחשבה מטמאתן, של גנב מחשבה מטמאתן ושל גזלן אין מחשבה מטמאתן, ר'
שמעון אומר חילוף הדברים של גזלן מחשבה מטמאתן ושל גנב אין מחשבה מטמאתן
מפני שלא נתייאשו הבעלים״[46]. ממשנה זו מוכח כי הגנב (או הגזלן לפי ר' שמעון)
קונה את החפץ שגנבו ונעשה שלו ולכן מחשבתו מטמאתו. הגנב או הגזלן קונה את
החפץ מפני שבעל החפץ נתייאש ממנו ונעשה הפקר.

ההבדל בין אם האיש הוציא את החפץ מרשותו ברצונו ובין שנתייאש הימנו הוא
בזה: אם ברצונו הוא יכול להפקיר נכסי דניידא או נכסי דלא ניידא, אבל אם
נתייאש הוא יכול להתייאש אך רק מנכסי דניידא, דהיינו אם אבד לו איזה דבר
או נגנב או נגזל ממנו. אבל מנכסי דלא ניידא לא יוכל להתייאש, לכן לפי דעת
החכמים קרקע אינה נגזלת. לפי זה הנחל שדה לא יוכל לקנותו ביאוש כי השדה
אינו יוצא מרשות הבעלים ביאוש, ואם גזל שדה. ״ושטפה נהר אומר לו הרי שלך
לפניך״[47] מפני הטעם שקרקע אינה נגזלת ומעולם לא יצא השדה מרשות הבעלים
וכן נסתפחה השדה של הבעלים, זאת היא הדעה הכללית, אבל ר' אליעזר סובר
כי קרקע ג״כ נגזלת ולכן אם גזל שדה ושטפו נהר חייב הגזלן להעמיד להבעלים
שדה מעלייא[48], מפני שקנה את השדה שגזל ונעשה שלו, ושדהו נשטף ולא של
הבעלים. שקרקע אינה נגזלת מוכח מדברי הגמרא בסוכה: ״אמר להו רב הונא
להנהו אוונכרי כי בניתי אסא מכותים (גוים) לא תגוזו אתון אלא למזה אינהו ויהבו
לכו מאי טעמא סתם כותים (גוים) גזלני ארעתא נינהו וקרקע אינה נגזלת״[49] וכן
נראה מדברי התלמוד ב״ב. ראובן שגזל שדה משמעון ומכרו ללוי ואתא יהודה
וקא מערער על שדה זה דשביד לוי דשלו הוא, לא ליזל שמעון שממנו נגזל השדה
לאסהוד ללוי, מפני שהוא נוגע בדבר שקרקע אינה נגזלת והשדה עוד שייך לשמעון
ולכן לא יכול להעיד לטובת לוי[50].

[46] כלים, כ״ו, ח׳. השוה נ״כ ספרא פ׳ מצורע.

[47] ב״ק פרק י׳ משנה ה׳. השוה נ״כ Gaii, Inst. II, 71, Quod si flumen partem
aliquam ex tuo praedio detraxerit et ad meum praedium attulerit, haec pars
tua manet;

Quod si vis fluminis partem aliquam ex tuo praedio detraxerit, et vicini
praedio attulerit, palam est eam tuam permanere. Inst. Just.

[48] הנחל שדה מחברו... אם מחמת הגזלן חייב להעמיד לו שדה אחר, מסנה ב״ק, פ״י;
ת״ר הנחל שדה מחברו ושטפה נהר חייב להעמיד לו שדה אחר דברי ר' אליעזר, וחכמים
אומרים אומר לו הרי שלך לפניך שם, קי״ז. אמר ר' יוחנן והלא אמרו אין קרקע נגזלת
ולמה אמרו חייב להעמיד לו שדה קנס קנסוהו, ירושלמי, ב״ק, פ״י.

[49] ראה תוספות, סוכה, ל׳, ע״ב.

[50] ראה רשב״ם ב״ב, ס״ד, ע״א.

הטעם שקרקע אינה נגזלת הוא מפני שאי אפשר לזח ממקומה[51]. לפי זה
נוכל להבין את הדעה המובאה בירושלמי הגם שקרקע אינה נגזלת ומעולם לא
יצאה מרשות הבעלים בכל זאת יש יאוש לקרקע. לפי טעם זה, שקרקע אינה נגזלת
הוא מפני החוק הטבעי שאינה יכולה לזח ממקומה כלומר דלא ניידא, עבדים הגם
שהוקשו לקרקעות לית מאן דפליג שיש להם יאוש, מפני שהם ניידי[52]. ובדבר
זה מלה יש מחלוקת בדבר. ״מל עבדים והזקינו״ לפי תנא קמא צריך הגזלן לשלם
להנגזל בעד העבדים ״כשעת הגזלה״ מפני שהגזלן קנה את העבדים וברשותו
הזקינו. אבל לפי דעת ר׳ מאיר יוכל הגזלן להשיב להנגזל את העבדים[53] שמעולם
לא קנה את העבדים ולא יצאו מרשות הנגזל, וכשם שאין גזלה לקרקע כך אין
גזלה לעבדים. לפי התלמודים הלכה כדברי האומר אין גזלה לעבדים[54].

בדיני יאוש, לית מאן דפליג אם האדון נתייאש מעבדו, יצא העבד מרשותו
ואין רבו רשאי לשעבדו, אבל אינו נעשה בן חורין בלי גט שיחרור, ונשאר במצב עבדות
״ואין לו תקנה אלא בשטר״[55]. לכן אם העבד ברח והאדון התייאש ממנו הוא יצא
מרשות האדון ואינו רשאי לשעבדו, וצריך ליתן לו גט שיחרור. ״מתיה דרבה בר
זוטרא ערקת אתייאש מינה אתא שאל לר׳ חנניה ולר׳ יהושע בן לוי אמר אינו רשאי
לשעבדה מהו ליכתב לה גט שיחרור, אמר ליה אם כתבת יאות את עבד[56]. וכן
אם העבד נשבה וברח ובא אצל רבו אין רבו רשאי לשעבדו, וכדי לעשותו בן
חורין צריך רבו לכתוב לו גט שיחרור.

הדעה הזאת, מובאה בירושלמי בשם ר׳ יוחנן: ״שמעון בר בא בשם ר׳ יוחנן
עבד שברח מן השבויין אצל רבו אין רבו רשאי לשעבדו וצריך לכתוב לו גט
שיחרור״[57]. הטעם הוא שבעת שנשבה העבד נתייאש האדון ממנו ובכן יצא מרשותו
והוא אינו עבדו עוד, לכן רבו אין רשאי לשעבדו, אבל כדי לעשותו בן חורין
ולהפטר מאחריותו צריך רבו לכתוב לו גט שיחרור. בתלמוד בבלי מובאים דברי
ר׳ יוחנן בשנוי. ״אמר רב שמן בר אבא א״ר יוחנן עבד שברח מבית האסורים
יצא לחירות ולא עוד שכופין את רבו וכותב לו גט שיחרור״. כאן אי אפשר לומר
כי אמוראי נינהו אליבא דר׳ יוחנן, כי האמורא שמביא דברי ר׳ יוחנן בירושלמי
הוא הוא שמביא דברי ר׳ יוחנן בבבלי. אך אפשר לומר כי שתי הלכות שונות הן

---

[51] השווה תוספות, ב״מ, ס״א ע״א, ד״ה אלא לאו דגזל.

[52] עי׳ הערה 55.

[53] מל בהמה והזקינה עבדים והזקינו משלם כשעת הגזלה, ר׳ מאיר אומר בעבדים אומר
לו הרי שלך לפניך. משנה ב״ק, פ״ט. השווה נ״כ תוספתא ב״ק פ״י.

[54] אמר רב חנינא בר אבדימי אמר רב הלכה כר׳ מאיר. שם, צ״ו, ע״ב, ראה שם צ״ה,
סדאפיך רב ותני... וחכמים אוסרים בעבדים אומר לו הרי שלך לפניך. עי׳ נ״כ ירושלמי.
שם, אמר אביי דשמואל בר׳ אמי בשם יהודה הלכה כר׳ מאיר.

[55] ...דאמר ר׳ יהושע בן לוי אסרו לפני רבי נתייאשתי מפלוני עבדי מהו אמר להן
אומר אני אין לו אין לו תקנה אלא בשטר... אמר ליה בפירוש שמיע לי, אמר מר אמר להן אומר
אני אין לו תקנה אלא בשטר (גיטין, ל״ט).

[56] ירושלמי, גיטין פ״ד.

[57] שם.

ונמסרו האחת בבבלי והאחת בירושלמי. אולם אם נעיין היטב בהלכות אלו, נראה
שהן סותרות זו את זו. עפ"י הירושלמי שמעון בר בא אמר בשם ר' יוחנן אם עבד
ברח מן השבויין ובא אצל רבו אין רבו רשאי לשעבדו מפני שנתיאש ממנו ופקעה
זכותו מעליו, הוא אינו עובדו עוד, אך לעשותו בן חורין אדונו צריך ליתן לו גט
שיחרור. דעת ר' יוחנן מתאימה איפוא לדעת ר' שמעון בן גמליאל דמתניתן שעבד
שנשבה ואיש אחר פדה אותו אפילו לשום בן חורין רבו השני יוכל להשתעבד בו.58
על פי הבבלי רב שמן (שמעון) בר אבא אמר בשם ר' יוחנן אם עבד ברח מבית
האסורים יצא לחירות, מפני שנתיאש ממנו הוא נעשה בן חורין. והיות שלא הפקירו
אלא נתיאש ממנו כופין אותו ונותן לו גט שיחרור. דעה זו של ר' יוחנן כפי שמסרה
רב שמן תהיה נגד דעת ר' שמעון בן גמליאל59. וכן השאלה לפנינו היא, איך
נתהוותה הסתירה הזאת? הרי אי אפשר לומר כי ר' יוחנן בעצמו סותר את דבריו.

נראה לי כי כי דעותיהם של האמוראים האלה שמביאים את דברי ר' יוחנן בשני
נובעות משיטות שונות של הבבלי והירושלמי בדבר מעמד העבד שהפקירו אדוניו.
כפי שאמרתי לעיל אמוראי בבל, דהיינו שמואל ורב, סוברים שאם האדון הפקיר
את עבדו הוא נעשה בן חורין, והחילוק ביניהם הוא אם העבד צריך לגט שיחרור
או לאו, ולכן המתיאש מעבדו נ"כ יצא לחירות אלא שצריך הוא לגט שיחרור.
חכמי דמערבא סברו כמו חכמי הרומאים שאם האדון הפקיר את עבדו הוא נעשה
הפקר אבל לא בן חורין, ולכן אם התיאש מעבדו פקעה זכותו על עבדו ולכן
אינו יכול לשעבדו, וכדי לעשות אותו לבן חורין צריך לכתוב לו גט שיחרור. לכן
דעת ר' יוחנן שמובאה בבבלי היא לפי שיטת התלמוד בבלי. ודעת ר' יוחנן
המובאה בירושלמי היא לפי שיטת הירושלמי המתאימה לחוקי הרומאים בעניני
הפקר בנוגע לעבדים.

בתלמוד בבלי גם כן מובאת סתירה בדברי ר' יוחנן. אמנם סתירה זו איננה
נמצאת בין דברי ר' יוחנן כפי שנמסרו בירושלמי ובין דבריו המובאים בבבלי.
הקושיא בדברי ר' יוחנן היא שלפי ר' שמעון בן גמליאל "בין כך ובין כך ישתעבד"
ור' יוחנן סבר "כל מקום ששנה ר' שמעון בן גמליאל במשנתנו הלכה כמותו חוץ
מערב וצידן וראיה אחרונה" והוא בעצמו אמר (לפי הבבלי) "עבד שברח מבית
האסורים יצא לחירות" ובכן יש סתירה. התלמוד מתרץ איפוא את הקושיא בדברי
ר' יוחנן, שר' שמעון בן גמליאל אמר "בין כך ובין כך ישתעבד" משום טעמיה
דחזקיה. דאמר חזקיה "מפני מה אמרו בין כך ובין כך ישתעבד שלא יהא כל
אחד ואחד הולך ומפיל עצמו לנייסות ומפקיע את עצמו מיד רבו" כלומר: רשב"ן

58 עבד שנשבה ופדאהו לשם עבד ישתעבד לשם בן חורין לא ישתעבד, ר' שמעון בן
גמליאל אומר בין כך ובין כך ישתעבד. עי' למעלה הערה 34.

59 אמר רבן שמן בר אבא א"ר יוחנן עבד שברח מבית האסורים יצא לחירות ולא עוד
שכופין את רבו וכותב לו גט שיחרור הנן ר' שמעון בן גמליאל אומר בין כך ובין כך ישתעבד
ואמר רבה בר בר חנה א"ר יוחנן כל מקום ששנה רבי שמעון בן גמליאל במשנתנו הלכה כמותו
חוץ מערב וצידן וראיה אחרונה, בשלמא לאביי מוקי לה להאי לפני יאוש והאי שאחר יאוש
אלא לרבא דאמר לאהר יאוש קשיא דר' יוחנן אדרבי יוחנן (גיטין, ל"ח).

ג"כ סובר דהעבד *ענובה* ואיש אחר פדו אינו רשאי לישתעבד בו, אבל מפני מה
אמר בין כך ובין כך ישתעבד בו, שלא ילך העבד ויפיל עצמו לנייסות ומפקיע
עצמו מיד רבו, אבל עבד שברח מבית האסורים שאני, ובזה בטלה הסתירה בדברי
ר' יוחנן. „עבד שברח מבית האסורים יצא לחירות" ובין ר' יוחנן שאמר „כל מקום
ששנה רשב"ג במשנתנו הלכה כמותו".

לפע"ד התירוץ הזה דחוק: ראשית, לפי הירושלמי חזקיה מברר ונותן טעם
לדברי התנא קמא. „עבד *שנשבה* ופדאוהו לשם עבד ישתעבד, לשם בן חורין לא
ישתעבד". ועל זה אמר ר' אבהו בשם חזקיה: „בריך היה שאפילו לשם עבד לא
ישתעבד, ולמה אמרו ישתעבד? שלא יהא העבד מבריח את עצמו מן שבויין".
ושנית: לפי התוספתא „עבד *שנשבה* ופדאוהו אם לשם עבד ישתעבד ורבו נותן את
דמיו, אם לשם חירות לא ישתעבד ואין רבו נותן דמיו. רשב"ג אומר בין כך ובין
כך ישתעבד ורבו נותן דמיו". מן התוספתא משמע שאם איזה עבד *נשבה* ואיש אחר
פדו, אם האיש פדה אותו לשם עבד יוכל להשתעבד בו, אבל לרבו הראשון יש
הרשות להחזיר להאיש את דמי הפדיון ולשחררהו. אמר ר' זעירא *מתניתא* אמרה
כן רבו נותן דמיו ומשחררו, ירושלמי) אבל אם העבד נפדה לשם חרות „לא
ישתעבד" ורבו הראשון אינו צריך להשיב את דמי הפדיון. לפי דברי ר' שמעון
בן גמליאל אין נפקא מינה אם האיש פדה אותו לשם עבד או לשם בן חורין, הוא
יכול להשתעבד בו *ועודנו בעבדותו עומד*. אבל לרבו הראשון יש הרשות להחזיר
להאיש את דמי פדיונו ולשחררהו. רשב"ג נותן טעם לדבריו: „בין כך ובין כך
ישתעבד" ולרבו הראשון הרשות להחזיר להאיש את דמי פדיונו ולשחררהו. למה
יפדה אותו?[60] הטעם, „כשם שישראל מצווין לפדות את בני חורין, כך הן מצווין

60 לפי שיטתנו „בין כך ובין כך ישתעבד" היינו לרבו השני. רבנו אלפסי, רש"י, ר"ת
והרשב"א מפרשים „בין כך ובין כך ישתעבד" לרבו הראשון. הרשב"א בחידושיו על גיטין אומר
„ויש מי שפירש ישתעבד לרבו השני... ובתוספתא מפרשים לשם עבד ישתעבד לרבו שני, לשם
בן חורין ישתעבד לרבו ראשון. וגם זה אינו אחוור לפי מה שכתבתי. אבל רש"י ז"ל פירש דבין
כך ובין כך ישתעבד ישתעבד לרבו ראשון (לפי חזקיה דף ל"ז ע' ב') וכ"כ נכון ומחוור. וגם
ר"ת הניה בספרים בין כך ובין כך ישתעבד לרבו ראשון וכ"נ לי מן התוספתא, דתנינא בתוס'
דמכילתין עבד *שנשבה* ופדאוהו אם לשם עבד ישתעבד ורבו נותן את דמיו וכ' רשב"ג אומר בין
כך ובין כך ישתעבד ורבו נותן את דמיו".

הנם שכל אלו נדולי הראשונים שמזהם אנו שותים מפרשים „שבין כך ובין כך ישתעבד"
לרבו ראשון, לפע"ד הדעה, „מי שפירש ישתעבד לרבו שני" היא היא הנכונה.

הרשב"א מביא ראיה לדבריו מן התוספתא, אבל כמדומה לי שמתוספתא זו נוכל להוכיח
ש„בין כך ובין כך ישתעבד" משמע דוקא לרבו שני ולא לרבו הראשון. רשב"ג מנמק את דבריו
מדוע אמר בין כך ובין כך ישתעבד? מפני שישראל מצווין לפדות את העבדים. משמעותם
של דברי רשב"ג יכולה להיות רק לרבו השני ולא לרבו הראשון. כן הבין ר' זעירא את דברי
התוספתא „מתניתא אמרה כן רבו נותן את דמיו ומשחררו". משמע שרבו הראשון נותן דמי פדיונו
לרבו השני ומשחררו.

לפי דעתי הטעם שרבנו אלפסי, רש"י, ר"ת ורשב"א והריטב"א מפרשים דברי רשב"ג ישתעבד
לרבו הראשון נובע מדעת מדעת אמוראי בבל הכובדים מדוע אמר רשב"ג בין כך ובין כך ישתעבד לא
מפני שהוא עבד אחרי כאיש אחר פדו, אלא מפני הטעם שלא יוציא את עצמו מבעלות אדונו ע"י

לפרות את העבדים". מן התוספתא מוכח כי טעמיה של רשב"ג אינו כפי שאמר
חזקיה. לפי חזקיה העבד שנשבה הוא יוצא לחירות, ולמה אמרו ישתעבד? כדי
למנוע את העבדים מלמסור את עצמם לנייסות ולהעשות שבי כדי לצאת לחירות.
אבל לפי דברי רשב"ג המובאים בתוספתא שנשבה העבד שנפדה נשאר בעבדותו
ולא נעשה בן חורין.

הסתירה בדברי ר' יוחנן כפי שהיא מובאת בהבבלי נובעת באמת משיטת
אמוראי בבלי שאם הארון נתייאש מעבדו הוא יוצא לחירות. לפי דעתם ר' יוחנן
סובר עבד שברח מבית האסורים יצא לחירות, לכן ראו סתירה במה שאמר הלכה
כרשב"ג בכל מקום ששנה במשנתו,[61] ודחקו לבאר כי רשב"ג סובר נ"כ כי העבד
שברח ואדונו נתייאש הימנו נעשה בן חורין, ולמה אמר ,בין כך ובין כך ישתעבד"?
כדי שלא ליתן לעבד הזדמנות להפקיע את עצמו מן עבדות ע"י בריחה לנייסות
ולהעשות שבי.

לפי שיטתנו זו אנו יכולים לבאר את השנוי בבבלי ובירושלמי בדברי ר' יוחנן
בנוגע למצב העבד לאחר שהפקירו רבו.[62] דעתם של חכמי בבל היתה שאם
הארון הפקיר את עבדו הוא נעשה בן חורין. לכן עולא הבבלי[63] מביא דעת ר'
יוחנן שהמפקיר את עבדו יצא לחירות. חכמי א"י סברו כי העבד נעשה הפקר
ואינו יצא לחירות, לכן ר' אבהו הא"י מביא דברי ר' יוחנן שהמפקיר את עבדו
אינו יצא לחירות אך נעשה הפקר. לפי זה השינוי שנמצא בבבלי ובירושלמי בדבר
ר' יוחנן אינו בא מפני שאמוראי נינהו אליבא דר' יוחנן, אלא מתוך השקפות שונות
של התלמוד בבלי והתלמוד דבי מערבא בנוגע למעמד העבד אם רבו הפקירו.

במסה זו נסיתי לברר את העקרון של הפקר ויאוש במשפט של התנאים
(והאמוראים הראשונים) ולא דנתי בדבר הפקר ויאוש במשפט התלמודי. מנקודת
השקפה היסטורית והתפתחות המשפט זקוקים אנו להבדיל בין התנאים והאמוראים
ונ"כ בין ארץ ישראל לבבל ולא לערבבם. כי הערבוב מביא לידי טשטוש
התהומים. יכולים אנו לדבר ע"ד המשפט התלמודי רק מתוך ההשקפה ההיסטורית
ולא הרוגמטית. הדרך הרוגמתית היא לימוד ההלכה הפסוקה בלי שים לב למי
שהורה, השופט או הדין צריך לפסוק את הדין לפי ההלכה שנתקבלה.

בריחה לנייסות, ולכן לפי זה הטעם, ,בין כך ובין כך ישתעבד" יוכל להיות מוסבים אך ורק
לגבי רבו הראשון. אבל לפי שהוכחנו, כי טעמיה של רשב"ג הוא שאע"פ שאיש אחר פדה את
העבד מן השבויין לאחר שבעליו נתייאשו ממנו בכל זאת עודנו עבד, דברי רשב"ג שאמר ,בין
כך ובין כך ישתעבד" מכוונים דוקא לרבו השני. דעת ר' יהושע בן לוי ,המתיאש מעבדו אינו
רשאי לשעבדו וצריך לכתוב לו גט שיחרור" מתאימה איפוא לדעת ר' שמעון בן גמליאל.
61 הסתירה הא אליבא דרבא דאמר לאחר יאוש אבל אביי מוקי לה להאי לפני יאוש
והאי לאחר יאוש.
62 ראה למעלה ע' שע"ב נח].
63 עולא נולד בארץ ישראל והיה תלמידו של ר' יוחנן. אח"כ ירד לבבל וגר שם ומת בבבל.
,נח עולא לתמן ואמרה בשם ר' יוחנן ,ירושלמי דמאי. א', ד'). ,עולא דהוה סליק לא"י נח
נפשיה בחוץ לארץ" (כתובות, ק', א'). ,עולא נחותא הוה א'דמך תמן" (ירושלמי. ט', ד').

TABLE OF CONTENTS
VOLUME I

TABLE OF CONTENTS
VOLUME II

TABLE OF CONTENTS
VOLUME III